HARCOURT SCHOOL PUBLISHERS

STORY
town

Oh, the doors you will open!

Harcourt School Publishers

StoryTown is the new PreK–6 reading/language arts program from **Harcourt School Publishers.** With surprises around every corner and adventure just down the street, you'll find *StoryTown* is a great place to read.

Welcome to *StoryTown!*

StoryTown is filled with a variety of literature—nonfiction that supports reading include news articles, biographies, research, and more. Fiction stories include wonderful narratives, poems, plays, and fantasy. ***StoryTown*** also:

- offers materials tailored to each students' reading level.
- provides teachers with materials that deliver differentiated instruction.
- helps teachers plan effectively, and manage their entire classroom.

Harcourt School Publishers

StoryTown—a great place to read!

Beginning readers feel right at home with

StoryTown's **Kindergarten program.**

5 Teacher Editions

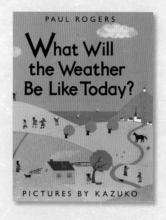
20 Big Books

20 Little Books

45 Pre-decodable and Decodable Books

30 On-Level Readers

30 Below-Level Readers

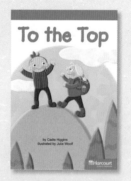
30 Advanced Readers

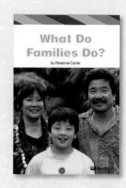
30 ELL Readers

Library Books Collection (20 titles)

15 Trade Books in Challenge Resource Kits

Read-Aloud Anthology

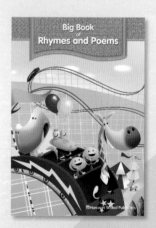
Big Book of Rhymes and Poems

The *StoryTown* **Kindergarten program** also includes:

- Professional Development Book
- Teacher Resource Book
- Big Book Audiotext CDs
- Leveled Readers Teacher Guides
- Leveled Readers Benchmark Assessment
- Photo Cards
- Sound/Spelling Cards
- Phonics Practice Book and Teacher Edition
- Practice Book Collection (10 titles)
- Word Builder and Word Builder Cards
- High-Frequency Word Cards
- Alphabet Cards

- Music CD
- Sounds of Letters CD
- Letter/Sound Rhymes Chart
- Tactile Letter Cards
- Write-on/Wipe-off Board
- Story Retelling Cards
- Instructional Routine Cards
- Kindergarten Assessments
- Magnetic Letters

Great instruction for *StoryTown's* smallest residents, too!

The *StoryTown* **Pre-Kindergarten Program** includes:

- Teacher Edition
- Teacher Resource Book
- Picture/Picture Word Cards
- Magnetic Letters
- Big Alphabet Cards
- Center Activity Cards
- Alphabet Masters
- School Friends Puppets

- Stories and More
- Nursery Rhymes Anthology
- Big Book of Rhymes and Songs
- Big Book Collection
- Lap Book Collection
- Music CD
- Oral Language Development Cards

StoryTown offers students a collection of tools for reading.

StoryTown Student Editions
Grades 1–6

StoryTown's motivating **Student Editions** include the perfect mix of nonfiction and narrative selections. Students develop robust vocabularies in *StoryTown* based on carefully selected words for instruction. Student-friendly explanations and meaningful learning activities get students involved in thinking about, using, and noticing new words in school and all around town.

The **StoryTown Library Books Collection** (Grades 1–6) includes twelve trade books per grade to engage students through easy, average, and challenging books.

Grade 6 shown

Students can visit **StoryTown** whenever they want with the **StoryTown Student eBook** (Grades 1–6). The **Student eBook** provides an interactive way for students to engage with text. A state-of-the-art interface presents **StoryTown** literature, instructional audio, interactive story maps, and activities.

StoryTown delivers differentiated instruction.

Leveled Readers (Grades K–6) with individual Teacher Guides for each title

StoryTown residents can find 120 different titles at each grade level for On-Level, Below-Level, Advanced, and ELL Readers. Each reader aligns to weekly skills, reinforcing high frequency words, vocabulary, phonics, and comprehension.

30 On-Level Readers

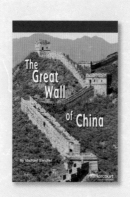
30 Below-Level Readers

30 Advanced Readers

30 ELL Readers

The ***StoryTown Leveled Reader System*** (Grades K–6) includes a single copy of 120 leveled readers and individual 8-page guided reading lessons for each title. In addition, the system includes 4 spiral charts with activities for each title organized around the On-Level, Below-Level, Advanced, and English Language Learner Collections. Benchmark Assessments are available for each grade.

The ***Harcourt Leveled Readers Online*** database provides access to 840 new *StoryTown* leveled readers that can be assigned to students in school, at home, anywhere!

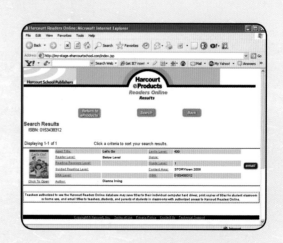

In **StoryTown,** leveled practice reinforces what students are learning.

- **StoryTown Practice Books** provide on-level activities to strengthen reading and language skills.
- **StoryTown's Extra Support Copying Masters** provide reproducible pages that parallel **Practice Book** activities—accommodating the below-level readers.
- The **Challenge Copying Masters,** for above-level readers, provide leveled practice for the advanced student, mirroring the skills found in the **Practice Book.**

Teacher Resource Books include useful instructional materials such as blackline versions of Readers' Theater selections and copying masters for patterns, manipulatives, and graphic organizers.

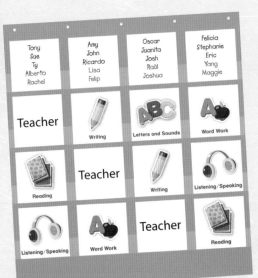

Literacy Center Kit (Grades K–6) strengthens skills taught each week in the critical areas of reading. Kit components include:

- Literacy Center Activity Cards on table top easels
- Literacy Center Pocket Chart
- Literacy Center Pocket Chart Icon Cards

StoryTown supports all levels of readers

StoryTown includes scaffolded materials to help every student.

The **Strategic Intervention Resource Kit** (Grades K–6) is designed for students who need extra support. Teachers can preteach and reteach the same comprehension and vocabulary skills that are taught each week in the core program. The kit includes a **Strategic Intervention Interactive Reader, Teacher Guide, Teacher Resource Book, Practice Book and Teacher's Guide,** and **Audiotext CD.** Each grade-level kit includes additional components, such as the **Sounds of Letters CD, Alphabet Masters, Builder Cards, Phoneme Phone**...and more!

The **Challenge Resource Kit** (Grades K–6) stimulates students with motivating trade books that serve as the springboard for author studies, genre studies, and critical thinking. Each grade-level kit includes a **Teacher Guide, Challenge Student Activities,** and **Challenge Book Packs.**

The **ELL Extra Support Kit** (Grades K–6) provides additional support to ELL students and helps teachers preteach and reteach the core skills, strategies, and vocabulary. A **Teacher Guide, Student Handbook,** and **Copying Masters** are included.

PLUS **StoryTown** has an **Intensive Intervention Program** for students who are reading below grade level. The **Primary** Program (Grades K–3) includes **Teacher Guides, Student Practice Books,** and additional components, such as the **Magnetic Letters, Reading Rods®,** and **Photo Cards**. The **Intermediate** Program (Grades 4–6) includes **Teacher Guides** and **Practice Masters,** each focusing on the essential elements of reading—phonemic awareness, phonics, vocabulary, fluency, and text comprehension.

StoryTown isn't only for students.

StoryTown teacher materials provide teachers with the opportunity to focus their attention on what is important—their students!

StoryTown Teacher Editions
Grades 1–6

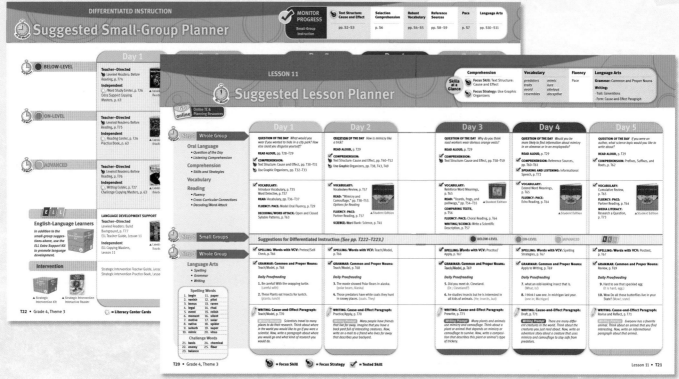

Grade 4

Teachers will benefit from *StoryTown's* well-organized instructional planners. Planners help organize daily lessons and differentiate instruction.

StoryTown is connected!

State-of-the-art technology makes the experience effortless by packing all the tools and resources in the right places.

The *StoryTown Online Teacher Edition and Planning Resources* is the perfect solution for the busy teacher. It can be accessed from anywhere there is an Internet connection. It organizes the instructional path and provides support resources including *Spelling, Phonics, and Grammar Practice Books*, plus *Leveled Readers*.

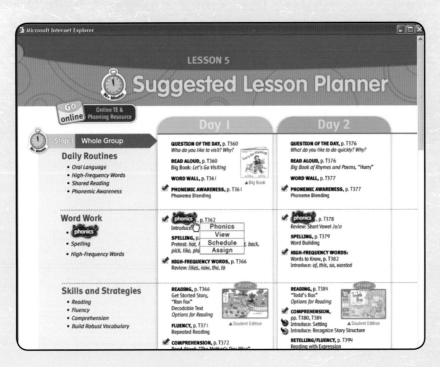

Professional Development videos are part of the *Online TE and Planning Resources,* and are available online through podcasting, making them accessible and a great way to learn on the go!

Teachers who do not have Internet access can use the *StoryTown One-Stop Planner CD-ROM*. Included on the CD-ROM are:

- *Teacher Edition* pages with a calendar planner
- Point-of-use instructional support resources that will print, view, and schedule instruction
- Differentiated instruction using *Leveled Readers*

StoryTown makes classroom planning easier and faster for teachers!

StoryTown offers additional resources for success.

The **Writer's Companion Student Edition** (Grades 1–6) and **Teacher Edition** (Grades K–6) deepen students' understanding of the elements and traits of effective writing. These components explicitly demonstrate how students can incorporate those elements and traits into their own writing.

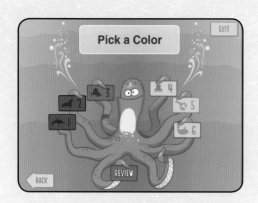

In the **Splash into Phonics** (Grades K–3) CD-ROM, games and activities are submerged in scenic ocean destinations and provide the background for reinforcing phonics.

In the **Comprehension Expedition** (Grades 3–6) CD-ROM, Special Agent Bird takes readers on exciting expeditions through swamps, forests, mountains, and beyond. Their journey provides practice and reinforcement of comprehension skills taught and tested in **StoryTown.**

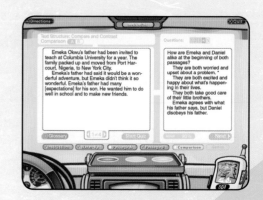

StoryTown equips teachers with a variety of tools to evaluate students, maximizing their learning potential. **Assessment options include:**

Monitor Progress (Grades K–6)

Daily Monitor Progress notes, which inform instruction, are provided in the *Teacher Edition.*

Weekly Lesson Tests Copying Masters and *Teacher Editions* (Grades 1–6) monitor student comprehension of the literature selections and the skills taught. Test sections include:

- Selection Comprehension, including open-ended questions
- Focus Skill
- Robust Vocabulary
- Grammar

- Research Skill or Vocabulary Skill
- High-Frequency Words (Grades 1 & 2)
- Decoding/Phonics (Grades 1–3)
- Fluency ("Fresh Reads")

Additional Assessment Options (Grades 1–6):

- Theme Tests and Teacher Edition
- Benchmark Assessments and Teacher Edition
- Diagnostic Assessments
- Online Assessment

Additional Resources Available (Grades 1–6):

- Grammar Practice Book and Teacher Edition (TE)
- Spelling Practice Book and TE
- Phonics Practice Book and TE
- Test Prep System
- Questioning the Author Comprehension Guide
- Story Retelling Cards (Grades K–2)

- Reading Transparencies
- Language Arts Transparencies
- Fluency Builders
- Instructional Routine Cards
- Read-Aloud Anthology (Grades K–3)
- Sound/Spelling Cards (Grades 1, 2)
- Photo Cards (Grade 1)
- Audiotext CDs

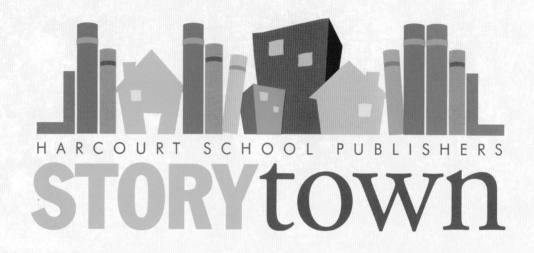

HARCOURT SCHOOL PUBLISHERS
STORYtown

That was just a peek...**StoryTown** has so much more—For additional information, **call 1-800-225-5425**

www.harcourtschool.com

Harcourt
SCHOOL PUBLISHERS

Harcourt and the Harcourt Logo are trademarks of Harcourt, Inc. registered in the United States of America and/or other jurisdictions. Copyright © by Harcourt, Inc. All rights reserved. Printed in USA. 9997-85665-1

HARCOURT SCHOOL PUBLISHERS
STORYtown

Twists and Turns

TEACHER EDITION

Senior Authors

Isabel L. Beck • Roger C. Farr • Dorothy S. Strickland

Authors

Alma Flor Ada • Roxanne F. Hudson • Margaret G. McKeown
Robin C. Scarcella • Julie A. Washington

Consultants

F. Isabel Campoy • Tyrone C. Howard • David A. Monti

Harcourt
SCHOOL PUBLISHERS

www.harcourtschool.com

ISBN 10 0-15-353689-6
ISBN 13 978-0-15-353689-2

1 2 3 4 5 6 7 8 9 10   030   17 16 15 14 13 12 11 10 09 08 07

Program Authors

SENIOR AUTHORS

Isabel L. Beck
Professor of Education and Senior Scientist at the Learning Research and Development Center,
University of Pittsburgh

RESEARCH CONTRIBUTIONS:
Reading Comprehension, Vocabulary, Beginning Reading, Phonics

Roger C. Farr
Chancellor's Professor Emeritus of Education and Former Director for the Center for Innovation in Assessment,
Indiana University, Bloomington

RESEARCH CONTRIBUTIONS:
Instructional Assessment, Reading Strategies, Reading in the Content Areas

Dorothy S. Strickland
Samuel DeWitt Proctor Professor of Education and The State of New Jersey Professor of Reading,
Rutgers University, The State University of New Jersey

RESEARCH CONTRIBUTIONS:
Early Literacy, Elementary Reading/ Language Arts, Writing, Intervention

AUTHORS

Alma Flor Ada
Professor Emerita,
University of San Francisco

RESEARCH CONTRIBUTIONS:
Literacy, Biliteracy, Multicultural Children's Literature, Home-School Interaction, First and Second Language Acquisition

Roxanne F. Hudson
Assistant Professor, Area of Special Education
University of Washington

RESEARCH CONTRIBUTIONS:
Reading Fluency, Learning Disabilities, Interventions

Margaret G. McKeown
Senior Scientist at the Learning Research and Development Center,
University of Pittsburgh

RESEARCH CONTRIBUTIONS:
Vocabulary, Reading Comprehension

Robin C. Scarcella
Professor, Director of Academic English and ESL,
University of California, Irvine

RESEARCH CONTRIBUTIONS:
English as a Second Language

Julie A. Washington
Professor, College of Letters and Sciences,
University of Wisconsin

RESEARCH CONTRIBUTIONS:
Understanding of Cultural Dialect with an emphasis on Language Assessment, Specific Language Impairment and Academic Performance; Early Childhood Language and Early Literacy of African American Children

CONSULTANTS

F. Isabel Campoy
President, Transformative Educational Services

RESEARCH CONTRIBUTIONS:
English as a Second Language, Applied Linguistics, Writing in the Curriculum, Family Involvement

David A. Monti
Professor Emeritus Department of Reading and Language Arts,
Central Connecticut State University

RESEARCH CONTRIBUTIONS:
Reading Comprehension, Alternative Assessments, Flexible Grouping

Tyrone C. Howard
Associate Professor Urban Schooling,
University of California, Los Angeles

RESEARCH CONTRIBUTIONS:
Multicultural Education, The Social and Political Context of Schools, Urban Education

Theme 3: As We Grow

Lesson 11

SOCIAL STUDIES

Theme Writing   **Reading-Writing Connection** T100
Student Writing Model: Friendly Letter

Lesson 12

SOCIAL STUDIES

Reference Materials

Additional Resources

Data-Driven Instruction

 ASSESS

Use assessments to track student progress.

  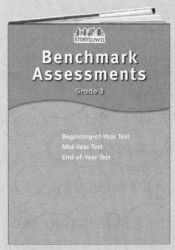

▲ **Weekly Lesson Tests (grades 1–6)**

▲ **Theme Tests**

▲ **Benchmark Assessments**
- Beginning-of-Year
- Mid-Year
- End-of-Year

 StoryTown Online Assessment

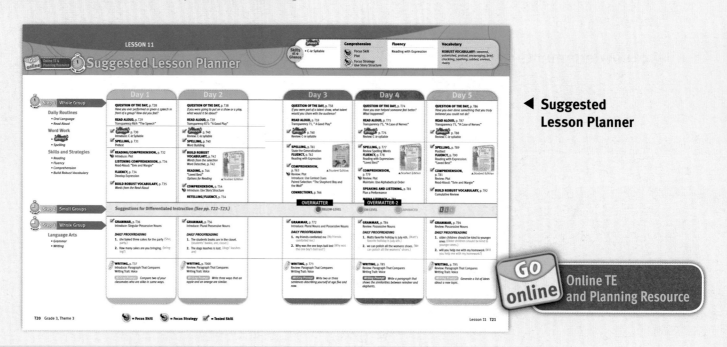 **TEACH**

Provide instruction in key areas of reading.

◄ **Suggested Lesson Planner**

Online TE and Planning Resource

③ DIFFERENTIATE INSTRUCTION

Use daily Monitor Progress notes to inform instruction.

✓ MONITOR PROGRESS

Partner Reading

IF students need more support in fluency-building and in using appropriate pace,	THEN have them echo-read with you, paying close attention to punctuation marks to direct their pace.

Small-Group Instruction, p. S4:
- ● BELOW-LEVEL: Reteach
- ● ON-LEVEL: Reinforce
- ● ADVANCED: Extend

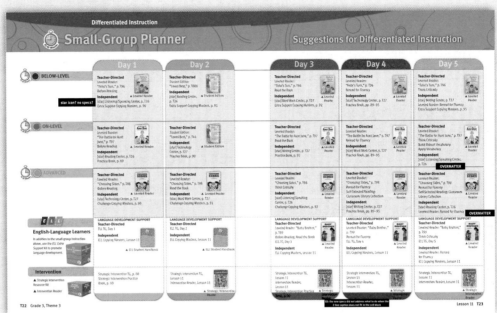

▲ Suggested Small-Group Planner

④ ASSESS, REMEDIATE, AND EXTEND

Use assessment results to remediate instruction.

INTENSIVE INTERVENTION PROGRAM

▲ Strategic Intervention Resource Kit

▲ Challenge Resource Kit

- • Phonics
- • Comprehension
- • Vocabulary
- • Fluency

Overview of a Theme

- **Explicit Systematic Instruction**

- **Spiral Review of Key Skills**

- **Abundant Practice and Application**

- **Point-of-Use Progress-Monitoring**

- **Support for *Leveled Readers***

- **Digital Support for Teachers and Students**

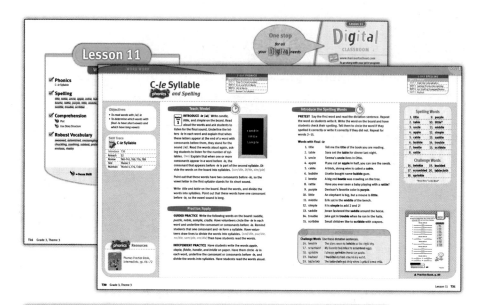

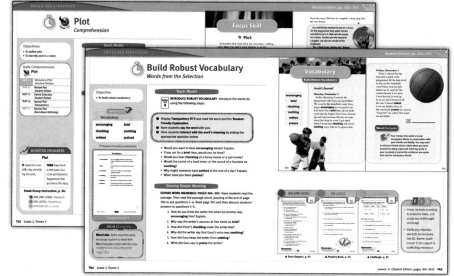

- **Review Skills and Strategies**

- **Build and Review Vocabulary**

- **Celebrate with Readers' Theater**

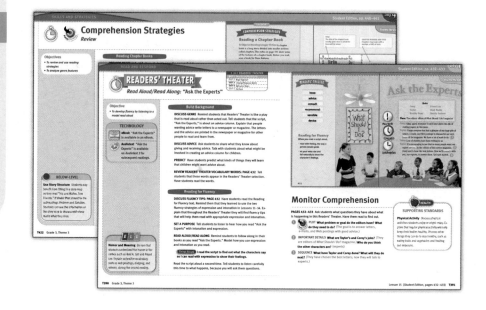

READING-WRITING CONNECTION

- **Reading - Writing Connection in *Student Edition***

- **Instruction in *Teacher Edition***

- **Focus on the Six Traits of Good Writing:**
  - Organization
  - Ideas
  - Sentence Fluency
  - Word Choice
  - Voice
  - Conventions

- **Develop a Variety of Writing Strategies**

- **Develop <u>One</u> Major Form Through the Writing Process:**
  - Personal Narrative
  - Response to Literature
  - Friendly Letter
  - Story
  - Explanatory Essay
  - Research Report

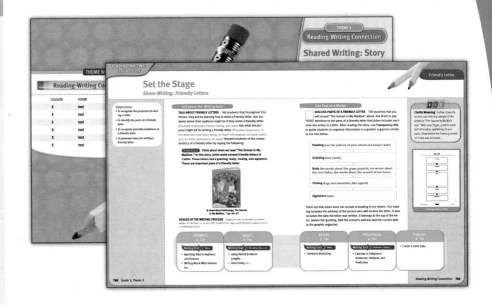

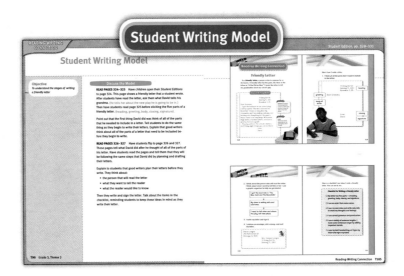

Student Writing Model

Overview of a Lesson

- **Lesson Resources**

- **Suggested Lesson Planner**

- **Suggested Small-Group Planner**

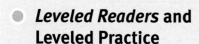

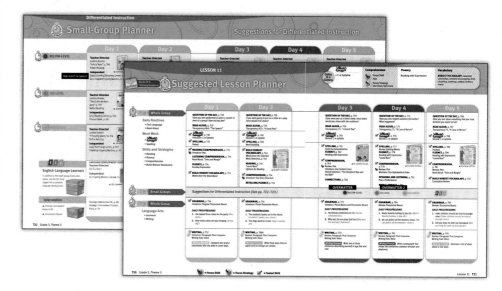

- *Leveled Readers* and **Leveled Practice**

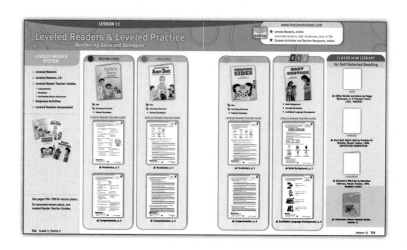

ROUTINES

- Oral Language
- Read Aloud

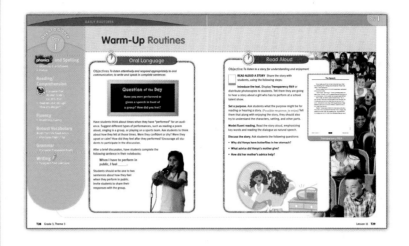

PHONICS/SPELLING

- Connect Letter and Sound
- Decode Longer Words
- Spelling Pretest and Posttest
- Introduce and Review Structural Elements

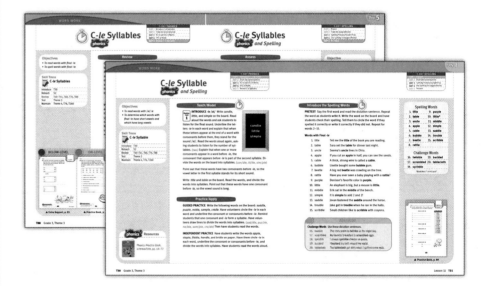

Overview of a Lesson (continued)

READING

- **Main Selections**

- **Paired Selections**

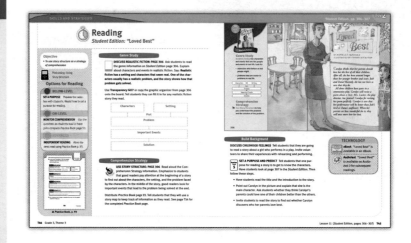

FLUENCY

- **Explicit Instruction in Rate, Accuracy, and Prosody**

- **Repeated Readings**

- **Readers' Theater**

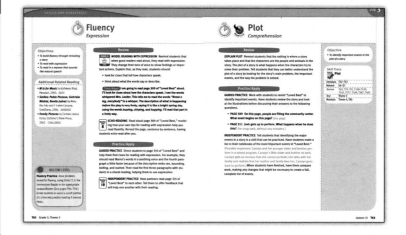

COMPREHENSION

- **Focus Skills**

- **Focus Strategies**

- **Listening Comprehension**

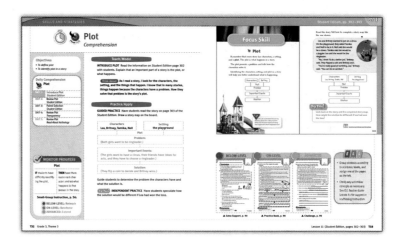

ROBUST VOCABULARY

- **Robust Vocabulary**
  - Tier-Two Words

- **Instructional Routines**

- **Student-Friendly Explanations**

LANGUAGE ARTS

- **Grammar and Writing**

- **Speaking and Listening**

- **Media Literacy**

LEVELED READERS

- **Reinforce Skills and Strategies**

- **Review Vocabulary**

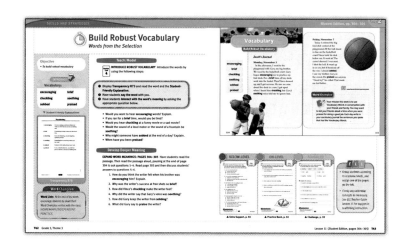

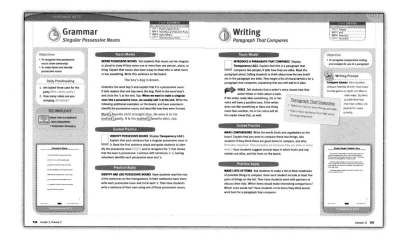

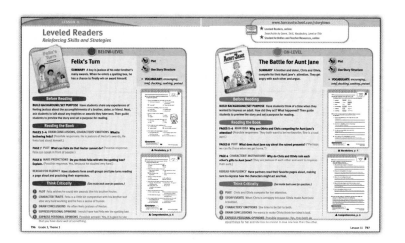

Introducing the Book

Discuss the Book's Organization

Have students turn to each of the following features in the *Student Edition*. Briefly discuss how each part helps readers use the book and understand the literature.

- **Contents** Shows titles, authors, and page numbers.

- **Comprehension Strategies** Describes tools readers can use to read well.

- **Theme Overview** Lists literature, skills, and strategies in that theme.

- **Lesson Overview** Lists literature, focus skill, and focus strategy in that lesson.

- **Focus Skill** Provides instruction in skills related to the literature.

- **Vocabulary** Builds robust vocabulary words from the selection.

- **Genre Study** Describes the characteristics of the selection's genre.

- **Focus Strategy** Tells how to use strategies during reading.

- **Paired Selection** Presents literature connected to the main selection.

- **Connections** Provides questions and activities related to both selections.

- **Reading-Writing Connection** Connects the literature to a good model of student writing.

- **Glossary** Provides student-friendly explanations for robust vocabulary words from each selection.

- **Index of Titles and Authors** Shows titles and authors of literature in alphabetical order.

Introduce Comprehension Strategies

Read with students pages 10–11. Tell them that these pages introduce the strategies they will use as they read their *Student Edition*.

Monitor Comprehension

PERSONAL READING PORTFOLIO   Have each student begin a personal reading portfolio. Students can use the "My Reading Log" page on *Teacher Resource Book* page 64 to record how they self-select books, the strategies they use before and during reading, and how long they read outside of class each day.

STRATEGY BOOKMARK   Have students make a bookmark from a sheet of heavy paper and write the comprehension strategies on it. Tell students that as they read, they should use the bookmark to remind them of the strategies they can use.

RESPONSE NOTEBOOK   Ask students to keep a notebook to record their responses to selections and to monitor their progress as readers.

- They may use a spiral-bound notebook or sheets of paper stapled together.

- They should create sections to write about which strategies work best for them and to develop their own plans for reading different kinds of selections.

- They should also set aside a section of the notebook for a vocabulary journal, where they will list new or interesting words they come across in their reading.

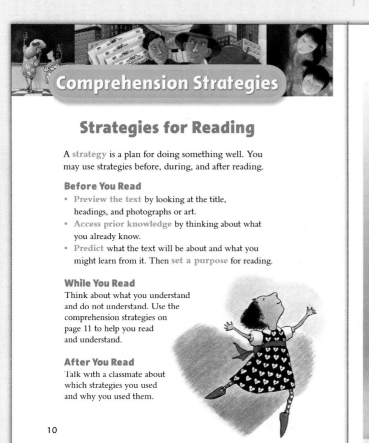

Comprehension Strategies

Strategies for Reading

A strategy is a plan for doing something well. You may use strategies before, during, and after reading.

Before You Read
- Preview the text by looking at the title, headings, and photographs or art.
- Access prior knowledge by thinking about what you already know.
- Predict what the text will be about and what you might learn from it. Then set a purpose for reading.

While You Read
Think about what you understand and do not understand. Use the comprehension strategies on page 11 to help you read and understand.

After You Read
Talk with a classmate about which strategies you used and why you used them.

10

Strategies to Use During Reading

- **Use Story Structure** Keep track of the characters, setting, and plot events to help you understand a story.
- **Summarize** Pause as you read to think about the most important ideas in the text.
- **Ask and Answer Questions** Ask yourself and others questions about what you read. Answer questions your teacher asks to better understand.
- **Use Graphic Organizers** Use charts and diagrams to help you read.
- **Monitor Comprehension** When you do not understand what you read, use one of these fix-up strategies.

  - Reread
  - Read Ahead
  - Adjust Reading Rate
  - Self-Correct

11

As We Grow

Theme Resources

 STUDENT EDITION LITERATURE

Lesson 11

PAIRED SELECTIONS

"Loved Best,"
pp. 306–323
REALISTIC FICTION

"The Shepherd Boy and the Wolf,"
pp. 324–325
FABLE

Lesson 14

PAIRED SELECTIONS

"One Small Place in a Tree,"
pp. 408–425
EXPOSITORY NONFICTION

"Be a Birdwatcher,"
pp. 426–427
EXPOSITORY NONFICTION

Lesson 12

PAIRED SELECTIONS

"A Pen Pal for Max,"
pp. 338–359
REALISTIC FICTION

"Postcards from Around the Globe,"
pp. 360–361
POSTCARDS

Lesson 15   Theme Review

READERS' THEATER

"Ask the Experts,"
pp. 432–439
ADVICE COLUMN

Lesson 13

PAIRED SELECTIONS

"A Tree Is Growing,"
pp. 370–395
EXPOSITORY NONFICTION

"Ancient Trees Survive in California's Mountains,"
pp. 396–399
NEWS FEATURE

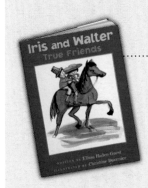

COMPREHENSION STRATEGIES

"Iris and Walter: True Friends,"
pp. 440–445
REALISTIC FICTION

 Literature selections are available on Audiotext 3.

THEME 5 CLASSROOM LIBRARY

For Self-Selected Reading

▲ **Day Light, Night Light**
by Franklyn M. Branley

Discusses sources and uses of light energy and well as properties of light.

▲ **Donavan's Word Jar**
by Monalisa DeGross

Donavan's collection of interesting words helps him solve problems for others.

▲ **Classroom Library Teacher Guide**

ADDITIONAL RESOURCES

▲ **Writer's Companion**

▲ **Grammar Practice Book**

▲ **Spelling Practice Book**

▲ **Literacy Center Kit**

▲ **Read Aloud Anthology**

▲ **Reading Transparencies**

▲ **Language Arts Transparencies**

▲ **Fluency Builders**

▲ **Picture Card Collection**

PROFESSIONAL DEVELOPMENT

- **Professional Development Book**
- **Go online** **Online Professional Development**
- **Videos for Podcasting**

Leveled Resources

● BELOW-LEVEL

-  Focus Skills
- Focus Strategies
- Robust Vocabulary

● ON-LEVEL

- Focus Skills
- Focus Strategies
- Robust Vocabulary

● ADVANCED

- Focus Skills
- Focus Strategies
- Robust Vocabulary

E L L

- Build Background
- Concept Vocabulary
- Scaffolded Language Development

Leveled Reader System

- **Leveled Readers**
- **Leveled Readers CD**
- **Leveled Reader Teacher Guides**
  - Vocabulary
  - Comprehension
  - Oral Reading Fluency Assessment
- **Response Activities Flip Charts**
- **Leveled Readers Assessment**

TECHNOLOGY

GO online www.harcourtschool.com/storytown

✔ Leveled Readers, *Online Database* Searchable by Genre, Skill, Vocabulary, Level, or Title

✔ Student Activities and Teacher Resources, *online*

Teaching suggestions for the Leveled Readers can be found on pp. T96–T99, T194–T197, T282–T285, T366-T39, T438–T441

Strategic Intervention Resource Kit,
Lessons 11–15

Strategic Interactive Intervention
Reader: *Climbing Higher*

- "Proud of You"
- "Her Pal Max"
- "Plants"
- "What Is Inside?"
- "Did You Know?"

Also available:

- Strategic Intervention Teacher Guide
- Game Boards
- Strategic Intervention Practice Book
- Skill Cards

 Intervention Strategic Interactive Reader e-Book

 ## ELL Extra Support Kit,
Lessons 11–15

- ELL Teacher Guide
- ELL Readers
- ELL Practice Book

Challenge Resource Kit,
Theme 3

- Challenge Book Pack
- Challenge Student Activities
- Teacher Guide

Leveled Practice

 BELOW-LEVEL
Extra Support Copying Masters

 ON-LEVEL
Practice Book

 ADVANCED
Challenge Copying Masters

English-Language Learners
Copying Masters

INTENSIVE INTERVENTION PROGRAM

GRADES K–3 Sets of intervention material providing targeted instruction in:

- Phonics
- Comprehension
- Vocabulary
- Fluency

Digital Classroom
to go along with your Print Program

 online www.harcourtschool.com/storytown

FOR THE TEACHER

Prepare

GO online **Professional Development**

in the Online TE

📱 **Videos for Podcasting**

PROFESSIONAL DEVELOPMENT

Plan & Organize

GO online **Online TE & Planning Resource***

Teach

GO online **Transparencies**

access from the Online TE

Assess

GO online **Online Assessment***

with Student Tracking System and Prescriptions

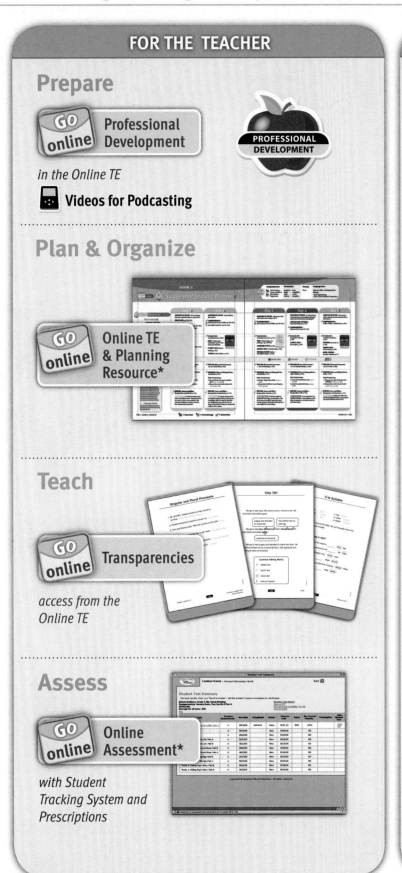

FOR THE STUDENT

Read

GO online **Student ebook***

GO online **Strategic Intervention Interactive Reader**

GO online **Leveled Readers**

● BELOW-LEVEL
● ON-LEVEL
● ADVANCED

E L L

Practice & Apply

💿 **Splash into Phonics** CD-ROM

💿 **Comprehension Expedition** CD-ROM

 * Also available on CD-ROM

Monitor Progress
to inform instruction for Theme 3

Plan Ahead

 ## MONITOR PROGRESS

Looking Back to Theme 2

IF performance was	THEN, in addition to core instruction, use these resources:
● **BELOW-LEVEL** **Reteach**	• Below-Level Leveled Readers • Leveled Reader System • Extra Support Copying Masters • Strategic Intervention Resource Kit • Intensive Intervention Program
● **ON-LEVEL** **Reinforce**	• On-Level Leveled Readers • Leveled Reader System • Practice Book
● **ADVANCED** **Extend**	• Advanced-Leveled Readers • Leveled Reader System • Challenge Copying Masters • Challenge Resource Kit

 ## ONLINE ASSESSMENT

✔ Prescriptions for Reteaching

✔ Weekly Lesson Tests

✔ Theme Test

✔ Student Profile System to track student growth

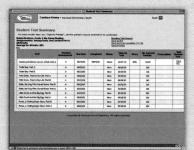

 www.harcourtschool.com/storytown

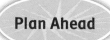 ## THEME 3 TESTED SKILLS

Domain	Skills
PHONICS/SPELLING	• C-*le* Syllable • Consonant Digraphs: /n/*kn*, *gn*; /r/*wr*; /f/*gh* • Consonants: /s/*c*; /j/*g*, *dge* • V/CV and VC/V Syllable Patterns
COMPREHENSION	• Comprehension of Grade-level Text 🌀 Plot 🌀 Author's Purpose
VOCABULARY	• Robust Vocabulary • Use Context Clues
FLUENCY	• Oral Reading Fluency 📱 Podcasting: Assessing Fluency
GRAMMAR	• Possessive Nouns • Singular and Plural Pronouns • Subject and Object Pronouns • Pronoun-Antecedent Agreement
WRITING FORMS	• Paragraph That Compares • Realistic Story • Explanation • Cause and Effect Paragraph • Friendly Letter
WRITING TRAITS	• Voice • Sentence Fluency
RESEARCH/STUDY SKILLS	• Use Graphic Aids

Theme at a Glance

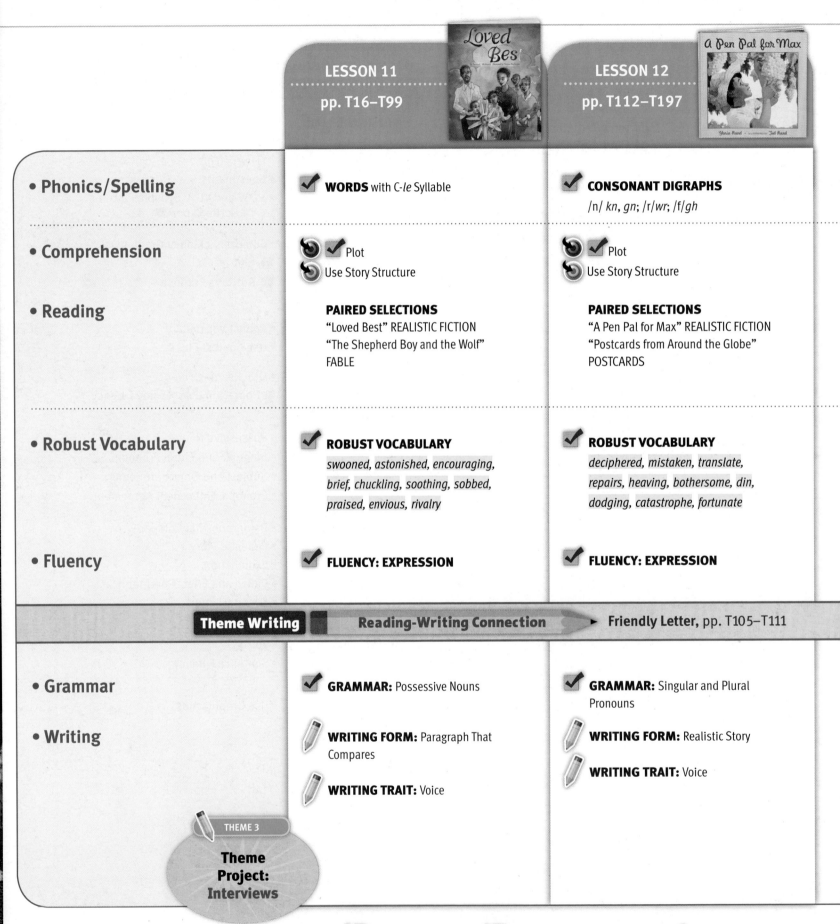

	LESSON 11 pp. T16–T99	**LESSON 12** pp. T112–T197
• **Phonics/Spelling**	✔ **WORDS** with C-*le* Syllable	✔ **CONSONANT DIGRAPHS** /n/ *kn, gn*; /r/*wr*; /f/*gh*
• **Comprehension** • **Reading**	✔ Plot Use Story Structure **PAIRED SELECTIONS** "Loved Best" REALISTIC FICTION "The Shepherd Boy and the Wolf" FABLE	✔ Plot Use Story Structure **PAIRED SELECTIONS** "A Pen Pal for Max" REALISTIC FICTION "Postcards from Around the Globe" POSTCARDS
• **Robust Vocabulary** • **Fluency**	✔ **ROBUST VOCABULARY** *swooned, astonished, encouraging,* *brief, chuckling, soothing, sobbed,* *praised, envious, rivalry* ✔ **FLUENCY: EXPRESSION**	✔ **ROBUST VOCABULARY** *deciphered, mistaken, translate,* *repairs, heaving, bothersome, din,* *dodging, catastrophe, fortunate* ✔ **FLUENCY: EXPRESSION**

Theme Writing ▮ **Reading-Writing Connection** ➤ **Friendly Letter**, pp. T105–T111

• **Grammar** • **Writing**	✔ **GRAMMAR:** Possessive Nouns ✏ **WRITING FORM:** Paragraph That Compares ✏ **WRITING TRAIT:** Voice	✔ **GRAMMAR:** Singular and Plural Pronouns ✏ **WRITING FORM:** Realistic Story ✏ **WRITING TRAIT:** Voice

THEME 3

Theme Project: Interviews

 = Focus Skill    = Focus Strategy   ✔ = Tested Skill

LESSON 13 pp. T198–T285	LESSON 14 pp. T286–T369	Theme Review LESSON 15 pp. T370–T441

LESSON 13 pp. T198–T285

 CONSONANTS /s/c; /j/g, dge

 Author's Purpose
 Ask Questions

PAIRED SELECTIONS
"A Tree Is Growing" EXPOSITORY NONFICTION
"Ancient Trees Survive" NEWS FEATURE

 ROBUST VOCABULARY
tugged, paused, columns, absorb, protects, rustling, dissolve, particles, scavenger, self-sufficient

 FLUENCY: INTONATION

LESSON 14 pp. T286–T369

V/CV AND VC/V SYLLABLE PATTERNS

Author's Purpose
Ask Questions

PAIRED SELECTIONS
"One Small Place in a Tree" EXPOSITORY NONFICTION
"Be a Birdwatcher" EXPOSITORY NONFICTION

ROBUST VOCABULARY
sprout, damp, suppose, roost, spears, strikes, glimpse, maze, transformation, harmony

FLUENCY: INTONATION

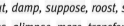

LESSON 15 pp. T370–T441

 **READERS' THEATER**

"Ask the Experts"

• **Build Fluency**

• **Review and Build Vocabulary**

 COMPREHENSION STRATEGIES

"Iris and Walter: True Friends"

REVIEW FOCUS STRATEGIES
 Use Story Structure
Ask Questions

 Writing Traits ➤ Voice, Sentence Fluency

 GRAMMAR: Subject and Object Pronouns

 WRITING FORM: Explanation

 WRITING TRAIT: Sentence Fluency

GRAMMAR: Pronoun-Antecedent Agreement

 WRITING FORM: Cause-and-Effect Paragraph

 WRITING TRAIT: Sentence Fluency

ADDITIONAL REVIEW

 Focus Skills

• Plot
• Author's Purpose

 and Spelling

Grammar

 Writing: Revise and Publish

Planning for Reading Success

Tested Skill	Teach/Model	✓ Monitor Progress	Additional Support
COMPREHENSION Plot	Lesson 11, pp. T32–T33	Lesson 11, p. T32	Small-Group Instruction pp. S6–S7, S18–S19
Author's Purpose	Lesson 13, p. T215	Lesson 13, p. T249	Small-Group Instruction pp. S30–S31, S42–S43
ROBUST VOCABULARY	Lessons 11–15, Build Robust Vocabulary, pp. T35, T42–T43, T55, T131, T138–T139, T153, T217, T224–T225, T241, T305, T312–T313, T325, T388, T395, T405	Lessons 11–15, pp. T93, T191, T279, T363	Small-Group Instruction pp. S10–S11, S22–S23, S34–S35, S46–S47
USE CONTEXT CLUES	Lesson 11, pp. T70–T71	Lesson 11, p. T70	Small-Group Instruction pp. S8–S9
USE GRAPHIC AIDS	Lesson 13, pp. T250–T251	Lesson 13, p. T250	Small-Group Instruction pp. S32–S33
DIBELS FLUENCY • Expression • Intonation	Lesson 11, p. T54 Lesson 13, p. T240	Lesson 11, p. T78 Lesson 13, p. T264	Small-Group Instruction pp. S4–S5 Small-Group Instruction pp. S28–S29
WRITING CONVENTIONS Grammar	Lessons 11–14, pp. T36, T56, T72, T132, T154, T170, T218, T242, T258, T306, T326, T342	Lessons 11–14, pp. T94, T192, T280, T364	Small-Group Instruction pp. S12–S13, S24–S25, S36–S37, S48–S49
WRITING	Lesson 11, p. T36 Reading-Writing Connection, pp. T100–T111 Lesson 12, p. T133 Lesson 13, p. T219 Lesson 14, p. T307	Scoring Rubric, p. T95 Scoring Rubric, p. T109 Scoring Rubric, p. T193 Scoring Rubric, p. T281 Scoring Rubric, p. T365	Small-Group Instruction, pp. S12–S13, S24–S25, S36–S37, S48–S49

= Focus Skill

Review	Assess
Lesson 11, pp. T63, T79, T91 Lesson 12, pp. T122–T129, T161, T177, T 189	Weekly Lesson Tests 11, 12 Theme 3 Test
Lesson 13, pp. T249, T265, T277 Lesson 14, pp. T302–T303, T333, T349,T361	Weekly Lesson Tests 13, 14 Theme 3 Test
Lessons 11–14, Cumulative Review, pp. T92–T93, T190–T191, T278–T279, T362–T363	Weekly Lesson Tests 11-15 Theme 3 Test
Lesson 12, pp. T168–T169	Weekly Lesson Tests 11, 12
Lesson 14, pp. T334–T335	Weekly Lesson Tests 13, 14
Lesson 12, pp. T152 Lesson 14, pp. T324	Oral Reading Fluency Tests
Lesson 15, pp. T396, T406, T416, T428, T436	Weekly Lesson Tests 11–14 Theme 3 Test
Lesson 15, pp. T397, T407, T417, T429, T437	Theme 3 Test

INTEGRATED TEST PREP

In the *Teacher Edition*

• Rubrics, p. R7

• Daily Writing Prompts, pp. T20–T21, T116–T117, T202–T203, T290–T291, T374–T375

• Writing on Demand, pp. T110–T111

• Short Response, pp. T52, T150, T322

• Extended Response, p. T239

TEST PREP SYSTEM

• Teach/Model Transparencies

• Practice Workbook: Reading and Writing

TEST PREP MINUTES

For early finishers, at the beginning of class, or at any time:

• **USE GRAPHIC AIDS Look for graphic aids that are in your classroom. Make sketches of the graphic aids. Then write a sentence for each that tells how it is used.** (The map of the building on the classroom door helps us escape if there is a fire.)

• **WRITING/PLOT Imagine that your class is getting a new classroom pet. Write notes about some important events that would happen.** (The students would be excited. They would have to care for the pet.)

• **ROBUST VOCABULARY Draw a setting where there would be a din. Be sure to include many things that would make noise.**

• **WRITING Write an encouraging note to a friend or family member. Be sure to write things that will make the other person feel good.**

Theme Project
Interviews of School Staff Members

Objectives
- *To write questions, conduct interviews, and organize information in the form of an oral and visual presentation*

Materials
- computer with presentation software
- pencil
- paper
- poster board
- crayons or markers

Getting Started

Tell students that they will be conducting interviews to find out more about the people who work at their school and how these people help others grow through learning.

Explain that in an interview one person asks questions and another person answers them. Students will present the information from their interview in a multimedia slide show or a poster presentation.

Along the Way

1. **Brainstorm**   Lead students to name staff members that they would like to interview, such as the principal, librarian, or PE teacher. Assign students to groups and have each group select a person to interview. Have students begin to think of questions.

2. **Plan**   Remind students to ask questions about how the interviewed person helps students grow through learning. List the following interview tips:
   - Begin questions with *How* and *Why* to encourage specific answers.
   - Think of many questions, and then choose only the best questions to ask.
   - Avoid asking personal questions.

3. **Interview**   Help students arrange a time for the interviews, remind students to record the questions and the answers, and instruct students to organize the answers in a logical way that addresses the main idea.

4. **Publish**   Have students organize their information in multimedia slide shows or on posters. Students should make their presentations visually appealing. Provide a variety of art supplies.

LISTENING AND SPEAKING

Working in groups offers students opportunities to develop their listening and speaking skills. As they work on their projects, guide them to do the following:

- **Listen attentively by making eye contact and facing the speaker as other group members share ideas.**
- **Respond appropriately and politely to questions, comments, and observations made by others.**
- **Speak clearly using appropriate rate, volume, and pitch.**

SUGGESTIONS FOR INQUIRY

The theme project can be extended in a variety of ways to help students learn more about the world around them. Help students formulate questions about others in their communities, such as

- **Which jobs in our community involve helping living things grow in some way?**
- **In what ways are reading and writing skills used in these jobs?**

Invite students to research answers to these questions using various resources, including interviews. After they complete their research, invite them to present to the class what they learned.

Practice Before students interview staff members, have them practice reading their interview questions aloud.

BELOW-LEVEL

Formulating Questions If students are unsure of what questions to include in their interviews, have them think of what information they would like to know about the person's job. Then, with the students, think of questions they could ask that would elicit the information they are looking for.

What I Want to Know	What Question I Could Ask
It looks like fun to be the PE teacher. Would that be a good job for me?	What do you like best about your job?

School-Home Connection

Include highlights of the students' interviews in your class newsletter. Not only will the students be proud of seeing their work published, but the parents will have an opportunity to get to know the staff members better.

Build Theme Connections

As We Grow

Relate To Personal Experience

BUILD BACKGROUND Ask students to discuss some of the ways they learn about the world around them. For example, students can learn about other people by asking them questions and spending time with them. They learn about their community by attending events, visiting public places, and watching what people do. Students can learn about their country by reading, traveling, and talking with people who have been to faraway places. Use the poem to help students talk about their experiences.

The More I Will Know

My parents, my family,
My friends at home,
Help me to learn
All that I know.

My teachers, my books,
What I do at school,
Help me to learn
Things that are new.

All that I see,
The places I go,
Help me learn
The things that I know.

As I get older,
The more that I grow,
The more I experience,
The more I will know.

—DIANE MILNE

Talk About the Theme

DISCUSS THEME Have students read the theme title and discuss the illustration. Ask what the theme title "As We Grow" means. Ask students how they have grown since the beginning of the school year.

DISCUSS THEME AND STORIES Have students look through the stories in the theme. Ask students to discuss what the title and the illustrations tell them about the stories and what the characters will learn. Ask students what they might learn by reading the selections in the theme.

Talk About Fine Art

DISCUSS FINE ART Have students look at the photo of the artwork. Tell students that the title of this piece names the type of art and that the artist is unknown. Ask students to tell what they see in the art and what it makes them think about. Ask how the art relates to the theme, "As We Grow." Ask what they think the artist was thinking about as the piece was created.

Lesson 11

WEEK AT A GLANCE

☑ **Phonics**
C–*le* Syllable

☑ **Spelling**
title, table, uncle, apple, cable, bubble, beetle, rattle, purple, little, middle, simple, saddle, trouble, scribble

☑ **Comprehension**
🔘 Plot
🔘 Use Story Structure

☑ **Robust Vocabulary**
swooned, astonished, encouraging, brief, chuckling, soothing, sobbed, praised, envious, rivalry

Reading
"Loved Best" by Patricia C. McKissack
REALISTIC FICTION
"The Shepherd Boy and the Wolf" retold by Doris Orgel FABLE

☑ **Fluency**
Expression

☑ **Grammar**
Possessive Nouns

☑ **Writing**
Form: Paragraph that Compares
Trait: Voice

Speaking/Listening
Plan a Performance

Media Literacy
Review Posters

☑ **Weekly Lesson Test**

🔘 = Focus Skill   🔘 = Focus Strategy   ☑ = Tested Skill

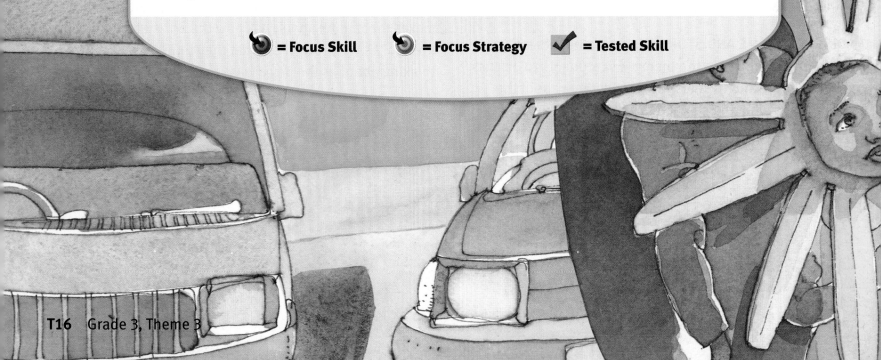

One stop *for all your* **Digital** *needs*

Digital
CLASSROOM

 www.harcourtschool.com/storytown
To go along with your print program

FOR THE TEACHER

Prepare
 Professional Development

in the Online TE

 Videos for Podcasting

Plan & Organize
 Online TE & Planning Resource*

Teach
 Transparencies

access from the Online TE

Assess
 Online Assessment*

with Student Tracking System and Prescriptions

FOR THE STUDENT

Read
 Student eBook*

 Strategic Intervention Interactive Reader

 Leveled Readers

Practice & Apply
 Splash into Phonics CD-ROM

 Comprehension Expedition CD-ROM

 Also available on CD-ROM

Literature Resources

Go online eBook STUDENT EDITION

By Patricia C. McKissack   illustrated by Yvonne Buchanan

Genre: Realistic Fiction

RETOLD BY DORIS ORGEL AND
ILLUSTRATED BY DAVID SCOTT MEIER

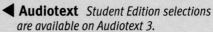

Genre: Fable

◀ **Audiotext** *Student Edition selections are available on Audiotext 3.*

Accelerated Reader™ ◀ *Practice Quizzes for the Selection*

THEME CONNECTION: AS WE GROW
Comparing Realistic Fiction and a Fable

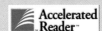

Paired Selections

SOCIAL STUDIES **Loved Best, pp. 306–323**
SUMMARY Patricia C. McKissack tells the story of a young girl who tries to prove that her parents love her the best.

LANGUAGE ARTS **The Shepherd Boy and the Wolf, pp. 324–325**
SUMMARY Doris Orgel retells Aesop's fable of the shepherd boy who learns the importance of speaking the truth.

Support for Differentiated Instruction

LEVELED READERS

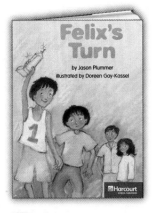

Felix's Turn
by Jason Plummer
illustrated by Doreen Gay-Kassel

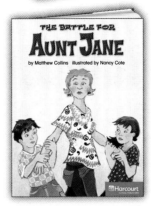

THE BATTLE FOR Aunt Jane
by Matthew Collins   illustrated by Nancy Cote

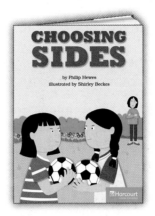

CHOOSING SIDES
by Philip Hewes
illustrated by Shirley Beckes

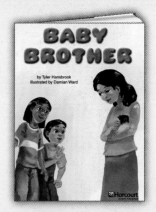

BABY BROTHER
by Tyler Hansbrook
illustrated by Damian Ward

● **BELOW-LEVEL**   ● **ON-LEVEL**   ○ **ADVANCED**   **E L L**

LEVELED PRACTICE

◀ **Strategic Intervention Resource Kit, Lesson 11**

◀ **Strategic Intervention Interactive Reader, Lesson 11**
Strategic Intervention Interactive Reader Online

◀ **ELL Extra Support Kit, Lesson 11**

◀ **Challenge Resource Kit, Lesson 11**

● **BELOW-LEVEL**
Extra Support Copying Masters, pp. 90–92, 94–95

● **ON-LEVEL**
Practice Book, pp. 89–95

○ **ADVANCED**
Challenge Copying Masters, pp. 90–92, 94–95

ELL Copying Masters, Lesson 11

ADDITIONAL RESOURCES

bear

- Spelling Practice Book, pp. 35–37
- Grammar Practice Book, pp. 37–40
- Reading Transparencies R69–R76
- Language Arts Transparencies LA21–LA22
- Test Prep System
◀ Literacy Center Kit, Cards 51–55
- Writer's Companion
◀ Fluency Builders
◀ Picture Card Collection
- Read-Aloud Anthology

ASSESSMENT

✔ **Monitor Progress**

✔ **Weekly Lesson Test, Lesson 11**
- Comprehension
- Phonics and Spelling
- Focus Skill
- Robust Vocabulary
- Grammar
- Use Context Clues

www.harcourtschool.com/storytown

GO online
- Online Assessment
- *Also available on CD-ROM— ExamView®*

Suggested Lesson Planner

90+ Minutes

GO online — Online TE & Planning Resources

Step 1 — Whole Group
20-60 Minutes

Daily Routines
- *Oral Language*
- *Read Aloud*

Word Work
-  phonics
- *Spelling*

Skills and Strategies
- *Reading*
- *Fluency*
- *Comprehension*
- *Build Robust Vocabulary*

Day 1

QUESTION OF THE DAY, p. T28
Have you ever performed or given a speech in front of a group? How did you feel?

READ ALOUD, p. T29
Transparency R69: "The Speech"

✔  phonics p. T30
Introduce: C-*le* Syllable

✔ **SPELLING,** p. T31
Pretest

✔ **READING/COMPREHENSION,** p. T32
🔵 Introduce: Plot

LISTENING COMPREHENSION, p. T34
Read-Aloud: "Evie and Margie"

FLUENCY, p. T34
Develop Expression

✔ **BUILD ROBUST VOCABULARY,** p. T35
Words from the Read-Aloud

Day 2

QUESTION OF THE DAY, p. T38
If you were going to put on a show or a play, what would it be about?

READ ALOUD, p. T39
Transparency R71: "A Good Play"

✔  phonics p. T40
Review: C-*le* syllable

✔ **SPELLING,** p. T40
Word Building

✔ **BUILD ROBUST VOCABULARY,** p. T42
Words from the selection
Word Detective, p. T42

▲ Student Edition

READING, p. T44
"Loved Best" *Options for Reading*

✔ **COMPREHENSION,** p. T54
🔵 Introduce: Use Story Structure

RETELLING/FLUENCY, p. T54
Expression

✔ **BUILD ROBUST VOCABULARY,** p. T68
Words About the Selection

Step 2 — Small Groups
45-60 Minutes

Step 3 — Whole Group
45 Minutes

Language Arts
- *Grammar*
- *Writing*

Suggestions for Differentiated Instruction *(See pp. T22–T23.)*

✔ **GRAMMAR,** p. T36
Introduce: Singular Possessive Nouns

DAILY PROOFREADING
1. she baked three cakes for the party (She; party.)
2. How many cakes are you bringing. (bringing?)

WRITING, p. T37
Introduce: Paragraph That Compares
Writing Trait: Voice

Writing Prompt *Compare two of your classmates who are alike in some ways.*

✔ **GRAMMAR,** p. T56
Introduce: Plural Possessive Nouns

DAILY PROOFREADING
1. The students books are in the closet. (students' books; are; closet.)
2. The dogs leashes is lost. (dogs' leashes are)

WRITING, p. T57
Review: Paragraph That Compares
Writing Trait: Voice

Writing Prompt *Write three ways that an apple and an orange are similar.*

 = Focus Skill  = Focus Strategy ✔ = Tested Skill

Skills at a Glance

 phonics
• C-*le* Syllable

Comprehension

Focus Skill
Plot

Focus Strategy
Use Story Structure

Fluency
Reading with Expression

Vocabulary

ROBUST VOCABULARY: swooned, astonished, encouraging, brief, chuckling, soothing, sobbed, praised, envious, rivalry

Day 3

QUESTION OF THE DAY, p. T58
If you were part of a talent show, what talent would you share with the audience?

READ ALOUD, p. T59
Transparency 71, " A Good Play"

 p. T60
Review: C-*le* syllable

✔ **SPELLING,** p. T61
State the Generalization
FLUENCY, p. T62
Reading with Expression

✔ **COMPREHENSION,**
p. T63
Review: Plot
Introduce: Use Context Clues
Paired Selection: "The Shepherd Boy and the Wolf"

▲ Student Edition

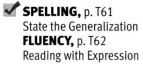

CONNECTIONS, p. T66

✔ **BUILD ROBUST VOCABULARY,** p. T68
Review

Day 4

QUESTION OF THE DAY, p. T74
Have you ever helped someone feel better? What happened?

READ ALOUD, p. T75
Transparency 75, "A Case of Nerves"

 p. T76
Review: C-*le* syllable

✔ **SPELLING,** p. T77
Review Spelling Words
FLUENCY, p. T78
Reading with Expression: "Loved Best"

✔ **COMPREHENSION,**
p. T79
Review: Plot
Maintain: Use Alphabetical Order

▲ Student Edition

SPEAKING AND LISTENING, p. T81
Plan a Performance

MEDIA LITERACY, p. T81
Review Posters

✔ **BUILD ROBUST VOCABULARY,** p. T82
Review

Day 5

QUESTION OF THE DAY, p. T86
Have you ever done something that you truly believed you could not do?

READ ALOUD, p. T87
Transparency 75, "A Case of Nerves"

 p. T88
Review: C-*le* syllable

✔ **SPELLING,** p. T89
Posttest
FLUENCY, p. T90
Reading with Expression: "Loved Best"

✔ **COMPREHENSION,**
p. T91
Review: Plot
Read-Aloud: "Evie and Margie"

▲ Student Edition

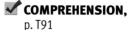

✔ **BUILD ROBUST VOCABULARY,** p. T92
Cumulative Review

 BELOW-LEVEL　 ON-LEVEL　 ADVANCED　

✔ **GRAMMAR,** p. T72
Introduce: Plural Nouns and Possessive Nouns

DAILY PROOFREADING

1. my friends comforted me (My friends comforted me.)
2. Why was the one boys ball lost (Why was the one boy's ball lost?)

✔ **GRAMMAR,** p. T84
Review: Possessive Nouns

DAILY PROOFREADING

1. Matts favorite holiday is july 4th. (Matt's favorite holiday is July 4th.)
2. we can polish all the womens shoes. (We can polish all the womens' shoes.)

✔ **GRAMMAR,** p. T94
Review: Possessive Nouns

DAILY PROOFREADING

1. older children should be kind to younger ones (Older children should be kind to younger ones.)
2. will you help me with my homework (Will you help me with my homework?)

 WRITING, p. T73
Review: Paragraph That Compares
Writing Trait: Voice

Writing Prompt *Write two or three sentences describing yourself at age five and now.*

WRITING, p. T85
Review: Paragraph That Compares
Writing Trait: Voice

Writing Prompt *Write a paragraph that shows the similarities between reindeer and elephants.*

 WRITING, p. T95
Review: Paragraph That Compares
Writing Trait: Voice

Writing Prompt *Generate a list of ideas about a new topic.*

Suggested Small-Group Planner

45–60 Minutes

	Day 1	**Day 2**

BELOW-LEVEL
15-20 Minutes

Day 1

Teacher-Directed
Leveled Reader:
"Felix's Turn," p. T96
Before Reading

Independent
 Listening/Speaking Center, p. T26
Extra Support Copying Masters, p. 90

▲ Leveled Reader

Day 2

Teacher-Directed
Student Edition:
"Loved Best," p. T44

Independent
⭐ Reading Center, p. T26
Extra Support Copying Masters, p. 91

▲ Student Edition

ON-LEVEL
15-20 Minutes

Day 1

Teacher-Directed
Leveled Reader:
"The Battle for Aunt Jane,"
p. T97
Before Reading

Independent
 ⭐ Reading Center, p. T26
Practice Book, p. 89

▲ Leveled Reader

Day 2

Teacher-Directed
Student Edition:
"Loved Best," p. T44

Independent
⭐ Technology
Center, p. T27
Practice Book, p. 90

▲ Student Edition

ADVANCED
15-20 Minutes

Day 1

Teacher-Directed
Leveled Reader:
"Choosing Sides," p. T98
Before Reading

Independent
 ⭐ Technology Center, p. T27
Challenge Copying Masters, p. 90

▲ Leveled Reader

Day 2

Teacher-Directed
Leveled Reader:
"Choosing Sides," p. T98
Read the Book

Independent
⭐ Word Work Center, p. T27
Challenge Copying Masters, p. 91

▲ Leveled Reader

English-Language Learners

In addition to the small-group instruction
above, use the *ELL Extra
Support Kit* to promote
language development.

LANGUAGE DEVELOPMENT SUPPORT
Teacher–Directed
ELL TG, Day 1

Independent
ELL Copying Masters,
Lesson 11

▲ ELL Student
Handbook

LANGUAGE DEVELOPMENT SUPPORT
Teacher–Directed
ELL TG, Day 2

Independent
ELL Copying Masters,
Lesson 11

▲ ELL Student
Handbook

Intervention

▲ Strategic Intervention   ▲ Intervention Reader
Resource Kit

Strategic Intervention TG, Lesson 11
Strategic Intervention Practice Book,
Lesson 11

Strategic Intervention TG,
Lesson 11
Intervention Reader,
Lesson 11

▲ Intervention
Reader

	Comprehension	phonics	**Vocabulary**	**Fluency**	**Robust Vocabulary**	**Language Arts** ✓ LANGUAGE ARTS CHECKPOINT
MONITOR PROGRESS Small-Group Instruction	Plot pp. S6–S7	C-*le* Syllable pp. S2–S3	Use Context Clues pp. S8–S9	Reading with Expression pp. S4–S5	*swooned, astonished, encouraging, brief, chuckling, soothing, sobbed, praised, envious, rivalry* pp. S10–S11	Grammar: Possessive Nouns Writing: Paragraph That Compares pp. S12–S13

Day 3

Teacher-Directed
Leveled Reader:
"Felix's Turn," p. T96
Read the Book

Independent
⭐ Word Work Center, p. T27
Extra Support Copying Masters, p. 92

▲ Leveled Reader

Teacher-Directed
Leveled Reader:
"The Battle for Aunt Jane," p. T97
Read the Book

Independent
⭐ Writing Center, p. T27
Practice Book, p. 92

▲ Leveled Reader

Teacher-Directed
Leveled Reader:
"Choosing Sides," p. T98
Think Critically

Independent
⭐ Listening/Speaking Center, p. T26
Challenge Copying Masters, p. 92

▲ Leveled Reader

LANGUAGE DEVELOPMENT SUPPORT
Teacher–Directed
Leveled Reader: "Baby Brother," p. T99
Before Reading; Read the Book
ELL TG, Day 3

Independent
ELL Copying Masters, Lesson 11

▲ Leveled Reader

Strategic Intervention TG,
Lesson 11
Intervention Reader, Lesson 11
Strategic Intervention
Practice Book, Lesson 11

▲ Intervention Reader

Day 4

Teacher-Directed
Leveled Reader:
"Felix's Turn," p. T96
Reread for Fluency

Independent
⭐ Technology Center, p. T27
Practice Book, pp. 89–95

▲ Leveled Reader

Teacher-Directed
Leveled Reader:
"The Battle for Aunt Jane," p. T97
Reread for Fluency

Independent
⭐ Word Work Center, p. T27
Practice Book, pp. 89–95

▲ Leveled Reader

Teacher-Directed
Leveled Reader:
"Choosing Sides," p. T98
Reread for Fluency
Self-Selected Reading:
Classroom Library Collection

Independent
⭐ Writing Center, p. T27
Practice Book, pp. 89–95

▲ Leveled Reader

LANGUAGE DEVELOPMENT SUPPORT
Teacher–Directed
Leveled Reader: "Baby Brother," p. T99
Reread for Fluency
ELL TG, Day 4

Independent
ELL Copying Masters, Lesson 11

▲ Leveled Reader

Strategic Intervention TG,
Lesson 11
Intervention Reader,
Lesson 11

▲ Intervention Reader

Day 5

Teacher-Directed
Leveled Reader:
"Felix's Turn," p. T96
Think Critically

Independent
⭐ Writing Center, p. T27
Leveled Reader: Reread for Fluency
Extra Support Copying Masters, p. 95

▲ Leveled Reader

Teacher-Directed
Leveled Reader:
"The Battle for Aunt Jane," p. T97
Think Critically
Build Robust Vocabulary:
Apply Vocabulary

Independent
⭐ Listening/Speaking Center, p. T26
Leveled Reader: Reread for Fluency
Practice Book, p. 95

▲ Leveled Reader

Teacher-Directed
Leveled Reader:
"Choosing Sides," p. T98
Reread for Fluency
Self-Selected Reading: Classroom Library Collection

Independent
⭐ Reading Center, p. T26
Leveled Reader: Reread for Fluency
Challenge Copying Masters, p. 95

▲ Leveled Reader

LANGUAGE DEVELOPMENT SUPPORT
Teacher–Directed
Leveled Reader: "Baby Brother," p. T99
Think Critically
ELL TG, Day 5

Independent
Leveled Reader: Reread for Fluency
ELL Copying Masters, Lesson 11

▲ Leveled Reader

Strategic Intervention TG,
Lesson 11
Intervention Reader, Lesson 11

▲ Intervention Reader

Leveled Readers & Leveled Practice
Reinforcing Skills and Strategies

LEVELED READER SYSTEM

- **Leveled Readers**
- **Leveled Readers, CD**
- **Leveled Reader Teacher Guides**
  - *Comprehension*
  - *Vocabulary*
  - *Oral Reading Fluency Assessment*
- **Response Activities**
- **Leveled Readers Assessment**

See pages T96–T99 for lesson plans.

For extended lesson plans, see *Leveled Reader Teacher Guides.*

BELOW-LEVEL

- **Text Structure: Cause and Effect**
- **Use Graphic Organizers**
- Selection Vocabulary

LEVELED READER TEACHER GUIDE

▲ Vocabulary, p. 5

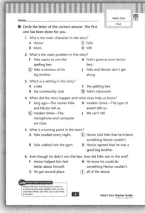

▲ Comprehension, p. 6

ON-LEVEL

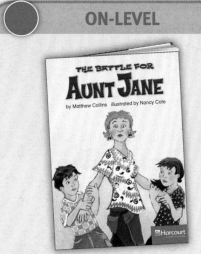

- **Text Structure: Cause and Effect**
- **Use Graphic Organizers**
- Selection Vocabulary

LEVELED READER TEACHER GUIDE

▲ Vocabulary, p. 5

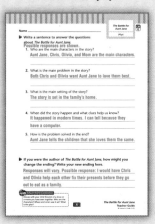

▲ Comprehension, p. 6

ADVANCED

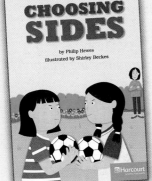

CHOOSING SIDES
by Philip Hewes
illustrated by Shirley Beckes

🌀 **Text Structure: Cause and Effect**

🌀 **Use Graphic Organizers**

● **Selection Vocabulary**

LEVELED READER TEACHER GUIDE

▲ **Vocabulary, p. 5**

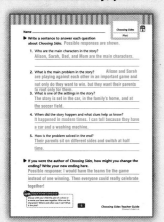

▲ **Comprehension, p. 6**

ELL

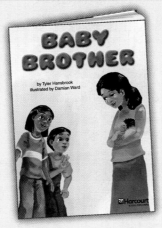

BABY BROTHER
by Tyler Hansbrook
illustrated by Damian Ward

🌀 **Text Structure: Cause and Effect**

🌀 **Use Graphic Organizers**

● **Selection Vocabulary**

LEVELED READER TEACHER GUIDE

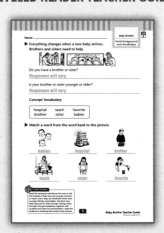

▲ **Build Background, p. 5**

▲ **Scaffold Language Development, p. 6**

CLASSROOM LIBRARY

Self-Selected Reading

EASY

▲ *Officer Buckle and Gloria* by Peggy Rathmann, G. P. Putnam's Sons, 1995. FANTASY

AVERAGE

▲ *Day Light, Night Light* by Franklyn M. Branley, Harper Collins, 1975. EXPOSITORY NONFICTION

CHALLENGE

▲ *Donavan's Word Jar* by Monalisa DeGross, Harper Trophy, 1994. REALISTIC FICTION

▲ **Classroom Library Teacher Guide, Lesson 11**

Literacy Centers

Management Support

While you provide direct instruction to individuals or small groups, other students can work on literacy center activities.

▲ Literacy Centers Pocket Chart

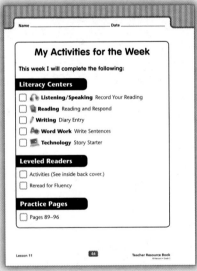

My Activities for the Week

This week I will complete the following:

Literacy Centers

- [ ] Listening/Speaking Record Your Reading
- [ ] Reading Reading and Respond
- [ ] Writing Diary Entry
- [ ] Word Work Write Sentences
- [ ] Technology Story Starter

Leveled Readers

- [ ] Activities (See inside back cover.)
- [ ] Reread for Fluency

Practice Pages

- [ ] Pages 89–96

▲ Teacher Resource Book, p. 44

Homework for the Week

TEACHER RESOURCE BOOK, PAGE 14

The Homework Copying Master provides activities to complete for each day of the week.

LISTENING/SPEAKING

Record Your Reading

Objective
To read familiar texts fluently

Record Your Reading

MATERIALS
- cassette recorder
- blank cassette
- Student Edition
- Reading Log or paper
- pencil

1. Choose a page with text from "Loved Best," and record yourself reading it.

2. Listen to your recording. Be sure to follow along in the book as you listen.

3. Think about what you could do to improve your reading.

4. Read and record again if you have time.

5. Use your Reading Log to keep track of what you read.

Grade 3 Lesson 11

⭐ **Literacy Center Kit • Card 51**

READING

Read and Respond

Objective
To organize information in a story map

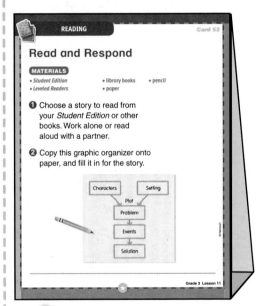

Read and Respond

MATERIALS
- Student Edition
- Leveled Readers
- library books
- paper
- pencil

1. Choose a story to read from your *Student Edition* or other books. Work alone or read aloud with a partner.

2. Copy this graphic organizer onto paper, and fill it in for the story.

Grade 3 Lesson 11

⭐ **Literacy Center Kit • Card 52**

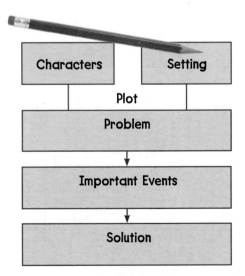

WRITING

Diary Entry

Objective
To write a diary entry from a character's point of view

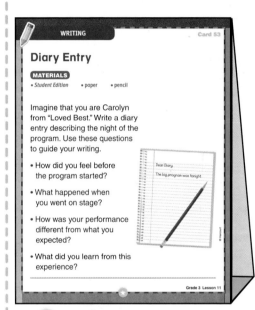

WRITING — Card 53

Diary Entry

MATERIALS
• *Student Edition* • paper • pencil

Imagine that you are Carolyn from "Loved Best." Write a diary entry describing the night of the program. Use these questions to guide your writing.

• How did you feel before the program started?

• What happened when you went on stage?

• How was your performance different from what you expected?

• What did you learn from this experience?

Grade 3 Lesson 11

⭐ **Literacy Center Kit • Card 53**

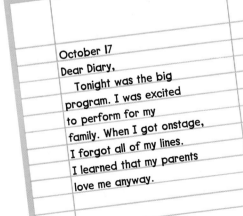

October 17
Dear Diary,
    Tonight was the big program. I was excited to perform for my family. When I got onstage, I forgot all of my lines. I learned that my parents love me anyway.

WORD WORK

Write Sentences

Objective
To write sentences using Vocabulary Words

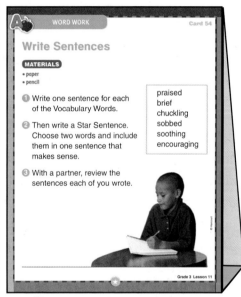

WORD WORK — Card 54

Write Sentences

MATERIALS
• paper
• pencil

❶ Write one sentence for each of the Vocabulary Words.

❷ Then write a Star Sentence. Choose two words and include them in one sentence that makes sense.

❸ With a partner, review the sentences each of you wrote.

praised
brief
chuckling
sobbed
soothing
encouraging

Grade 3 Lesson 11

⭐ **Literacy Center Kit • Card 54**

The cool breeze felt soothing for a brief moment.

TECHNOLOGY

Story Starter

Objective
To use a computer to type a story starter

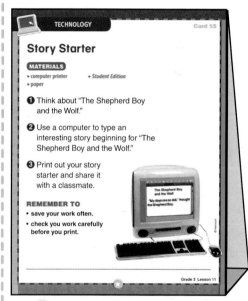

TECHNOLOGY — Card 55

Story Starter

MATERIALS
• computer printer • *Student Edition*
• paper

❶ Think about "The Shepherd Boy and the Wolf."

❷ Use a computer to type an interesting story beginning for "The Shepherd Boy and the Wolf."

❸ Print out your story starter and share it with a classmate.

REMEMBER TO
• save your work often.
• check you work carefully before you print.

Grade 3 Lesson 11

⭐ **Literacy Center Kit • Card 55**

The Shepherd Boy and the Wolf

"Wolf! Wolf!" cried the bored shepherd boy.

Day at a Glance

Day 1

 **and Spelling**
- Introduce: C-*le* Syllables
- Pretest

Reading/ Comprehension

 Introduce: Plot
Student Edition, pp. 302–303
- *Read-Aloud Anthology*: "Evie and Margie"

Fluency
- Model Oral Fluency

Robust Vocabulary
Words from the Read-Aloud
- Introduce: *tragic, limp*

Grammar
- Introduce: Possessive Nouns

Writing
- Paragraph That Compares

Warm-Up Routines

Oral Language

Objectives *To listen attentively and respond appropriately to oral communication; to write and speak in complete sentences*

Question of the Day

Have you ever performed or given a speech in front of a group? How did you feel?

Have students think about times when they have "performed" for an audience. Suggest different types of performances, such as reading a poem aloud, singing in a group, or playing on a sports team. Ask students to think about how they felt at those times. Were they confident or shy? Were they upset or calm? How did they feel after they performed? Encourage all students to participate in the discussion.

After a brief discussion, have students complete the following sentence in their notebooks:

> **When I have to perform in public, I feel _____.**

Students should write one to two sentences about how they feel when they perform in public. Invite students to share their responses with the group.

Read Aloud

Objective *To listen to a story for understanding and enjoyment*

READ ALOUD A STORY Share the story with students, using the following steps:

Introduce the text. Display **Transparency R69** or distribute photocopies to students. Tell them they are going to hear a story about a girl who has to perform at a school talent show.

Set a purpose. Ask students what the purpose might be for reading or hearing a story. (Possible response: to enjoy) Tell them that along with enjoying the story, they should also try to understand the characters, setting, and other parts.

Model fluent reading. Read the story aloud, emphasizing key words and reading the dialogue as natural speech.

Discuss the story. Ask students the following questions:

- **Why did Vonya have butterflies in her stomach?**
- **What advice did Vonya's mother give?**
- **How did her mother's advice help?**

The Speech

Vonya woke up with her stomach doing flip flops. It felt like something was fluttering around inside her! "Mom!" she called. "I don't feel good."

Vonya's mother came to the bed, leaned down, and asked what was the matter.

"I don't know," said the girl. "I woke up thinking about the talent show. It's today, and I'm going to have to sing in front of a hundred people. All of a sudden my stomach feels AWFUL!"

With a smile, her mother patted Vonya's hand. "You're just nervous. Those are only butterflies in your stomach. It's a feeling some people have when they are nervous. Don't worry. Just practice your song while you get dressed. Keep practicing whenever you have a chance, even if it's only in your head. You'll be fine."

"Really?" Vonya asked. Before her feet were on the floor, the words of the song formed in her mind. Then, singing, she walked out of her room. She would be fine. The noise from her singing was sure to make those little butterflies go away!

Grade 3, Lesson 11   Ra   Warm-Up: Day 1

Transparency R69

C-*le* Syllable
 phonics *and Spelling*

5-DAY PHONICS	
DAY 1	Introduce C-*le* Syllable
DAY 2	State the Generalization
DAY 3	VC-*le* and VCC-*le* Words
DAY 4	VVC-*le* Words
DAY 5	Review C-*le* Syllables

Objectives

- *To read words with /əl/ le*
- *To determine which words with final -le have short vowels and which have long vowels*

Skill Trace

Tested ✔ **C-*le* Syllable**

Introduce	T30
Reteach	S2
Review	T40–T41, T60, T76, T88, T384
Test	Theme 3
Maintain	Theme 4, T76, T260

 phonics Resources

Phonics Practice Book, Intermediate, pp. 66–72

Teach/Model

Routine Card 1 **INTRODUCE -*le* /əl/** Write *candle, little,* and *simple* on the board. Read aloud the words and ask students to listen for the final sound. Underline the letters -*le* in each word and explain that when these letters appear at the end of a word with consonants before them, they stand for the sound /əl/. Read the words aloud again, asking students to listen for the number of syllables. (two) Explain that when one or more consonants appear in a word before -*le*, the consonant that appears before -*le* is part of the second syllable. Divide the words on the board into syllables. (*can/dle, lit/tle, sim/ple*)

candle
little
simple

Point out that these words have two consonants before -*le,* so the vowel in the first syllable stands for its short sound.

Write *title* and *table* on the board. Read the words, and divide the words into syllables. Point out that these words have one consonant before -*le,* so the vowel sound is long.

Practice/Apply

GUIDED PRACTICE Write the following words on the board: *saddle, puzzle, noble, sample, cradle.* Have volunteers circle the -*le* in each word and underline the consonant or consonants before -*le*. Remind students that one consonant and -*le* form a syllable. Have volunteers draw lines to divide the words into syllables. (*sad/dle, puz/zle, no/ble, sam/ple, cra/dle*) Then have students read the words.

INDEPENDENT PRACTICE Have students write the words *apple, staple, fiddle, handle,* and *bridle* on paper. Have them circle -*le* in each word, underline the consonant or consonants before -*le,* and divide the words into syllables. Have students read the words aloud.

5-DAY SPELLING

DAY 1 Pretest
DAY 2 State the Generalization
DAY 3 Spelling Practice/Handwriting
DAY 4 Use Spelling Strategies/Review
DAY 5 Posttest

Introduce the Spelling Words

PRETEST Say the first word and read the dictation sentence. Repeat the word as students write it. Write the word on the board and have students check their spelling. Tell them to circle the word if they spelled it correctly or write it correctly if they did not. Repeat for words 2–15.

Words with Final -le

1. title — Tell me the **title** of the book you are reading.
2. table — Sara set the **table** for dinner last night.
3. uncle — Seema's **uncle** lives in Ohio.
4. apple — If you cut an **apple** in half, you can see the seeds.
5. cable — A thick, strong wire is called a **cable**.
6. bubble — Lisette bought some **bubble** gum.
7. beetle — A big red **beetle** was crawling on the tree.
8. rattle — Have you ever seen a baby playing with a **rattle**?
9. purple — Denison's favorite color is **purple**.
10. little — An elephant is big, but a mouse is **little**.
11. middle — Erik sat in the **middle** of the bench.
12. simple — It is **simple** to add 2 and 2!
13. saddle — Jovan fastened the **saddle** around the horse.
14. trouble — Jake got in **trouble** when he ran in the halls.
15. scribble — Small children like to **scribble** with crayons.

ADVANCED

Challenge Words Use these dictation sentences.
16. twinkle — The stars seem to **twinkle** in the night sky.
17. scrambled — My favorite breakfast is **scrambled** eggs.
18. sprinkle — I always **sprinkle** cheese on pasta.
19. buckled — I **buckled** my belt around my waist.
20. tablecloth — The **tablecloth** got dirty when I spilled some milk.

Spelling Words

1. title
2. table
3. uncle
4. apple
5. cable
6. bubble
7. beetle
8. rattle
9. purple
10. little*
11. middle
12. simple
13. saddle
14. trouble
15. scribble

Challenge Words

16. twinkle
17. scrambled
18. sprinkle
19. buckled
20. tablecloth

*Word from "Loved Best"

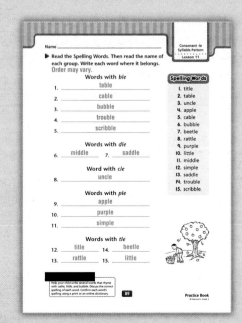

▲ Practice Book, p. 89

Plot
Comprehension

Objectives
- *To define plot*
- *To identify plot in a story*

Daily Comprehension

Plot

DAY 1:	Introduce Plot *Student Edition*
DAY 2:	Review Plot *Student Edition*
DAY 3:	Paired Selection *Student Edition*
DAY 4:	Review Plot *Transparency*
DAY 5:	Review Plot *Read-Aloud Anthology*

 MONITOR PROGRESS

Plot

IF students have difficulty identifying the plot,	**THEN** have them name each character and tell what happens to that person in the story.

Small-Group Instruction, p. S6:

- **BELOW-LEVEL:** Reteach
- **ON-LEVEL:** Reinforce
- **ADVANCED:** Extend

Teach/Model

INTRODUCE PLOT Read the information on *Student Edition* page 302 with students. Explain that an important part of a story is the plot, or what happens.

Think Aloud As I read a story, I look for the characters, the setting, and the things that happen. I know that in many stories, things happen because the characters have a problem. How they solve that problem is the story's plot.

Practice/Apply

GUIDED PRACTICE Have students read the story on page 303 of the *Student Edition*. Draw a story map on the board.

Characters Lea, Britney, Tamika, Nell	Setting the playground

Plot

Problem:
(Both girls want to be ringleader.)

Important Events:
(The girls want to have a circus, their friends have ideas for acts, and they have to choose a ringleader.)

Solution:
(They flip a coin to decide and Britney wins.)

Guide students to determine the problem the characters have and what the solution is.

Try This! **INDEPENDENT PRACTICE** Have students speculate how the solution would be different if Lea had won the toss.

Focus Skill

🐾 Plot

Remember that every story has characters, a setting, and a **plot.** The plot is what happens in a story.

The plot presents a problem and tells how the characters solve it.

Identifying the characters, setting, and plot in a story will help you better understand what is happening.

```
┌────────────┬──────────┐
│ Characters │ Setting  │
└──────┬─────┴─────┬────┘
       │   Plot    │
    ┌──┴───────────┴──┐
    │     Problem     │
    └────────┬────────┘
    ┌────────┴────────┐
    │ Important Events│
    └────────┬────────┘
    ┌────────┴────────┐
    │    Solution     │
    └─────────────────┘
```

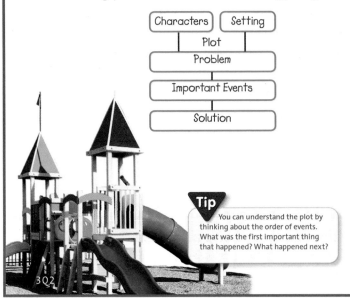

Tip
You can understand the plot by thinking about the order of events. What was the first important thing that happened? What happened next?

302

Read the story. Tell how to complete a story map like the one shown.

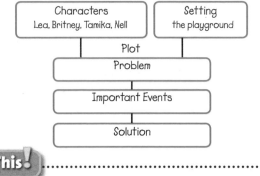

Lea and Britney wanted to put on a circus. On the playground, they asked Tamika and Nell to be in it. Nell said she would be a clown. Tamika said she would be a juggler. Lea said she would be the ringleader.

"No, I think I'd do a better job," Britney said. They flipped a coin and Britney won.

"You're really good at tumbling, Lea," Britney said. "You can be an acrobat."

```
┌────────────────────────┬──────────────────┐
│      Characters        │     Setting       │
│ Lea, Britney, Tamika,  │  the playground   │
│        Nell            │                   │
└───────────┬────────────┴────────┬──────────┘
            │        Plot         │
     ┌──────┴─────────────────────┴──┐
     │          Problem              │
     └───────────────┬───────────────┘
     ┌───────────────┴───────────────┐
     │      Important Events         │
     └───────────────┬───────────────┘
     ┌───────────────┴───────────────┐
     │          Solution             │
     └───────────────────────────────┘
```

Try This!

Look back at the story and the completed story map. How might the solution be different if Lea had won the toss?

GO online www.harcourtschool.com/storytown

303

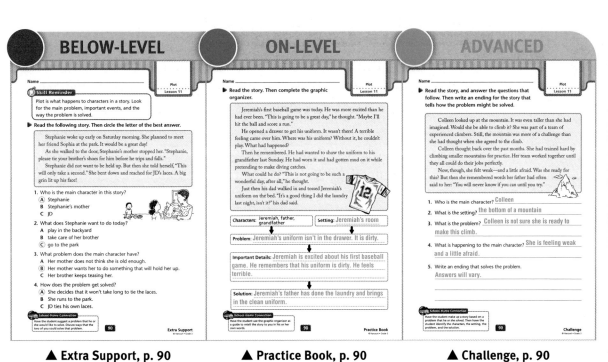

▲ Extra Support, p. 90   ▲ Practice Book, p. 90   ▲ Challenge, p. 90

ELL

• Group students according to academic levels, and assign one of the pages on the left.

• Clarify any unfamiliar concepts as necessary. See *ELL Teacher Guide* Lesson 11 for support in scaffolding instruction.

Listening Comprehension
Read Aloud

Objectives

- *To recognize the elements of realistic fiction*
- *To set a purpose for listening*
- *To identify plot events in a story*

Build Fluency

Focus: Expression Tell students that good readers do not read every word in the same way. Good readers use the expression of their voice to show feelings and to tell what is important.

"RESEARCH SAYS"

Fluency Instruction "Based on acknowledged reading theory, fluency instruction holds promise for improving reading for all students in the 'real world' of classrooms."

—Rasinski, Padek, et al. (1994), p. 164

Stories from Other Lands Tell students to think about stories they know from their own language and to share one with the class. Have them provide a rough translation of the story, explaining its meaning to the class.

Before Reading

CONNECT TO PRIOR KNOWLEDGE Ask students if they have ever been in a play or performance. Have volunteers discuss what the experience was like. Did they have to try out for a part? Did they get the part they wanted? Were there problems they had to overcome?

▲ **Read-Aloud Anthology, "Evie and Margie," p. 38**

Routine Card 2 **GENRE STUDY: REALISTIC FICTION** Remind students that realistic fiction tells a story that could happen in real life. Point out that in most realistic fiction, there is a problem that the characters face. Model setting a purpose for listening:

Think Aloud When a story is realistic fiction, I know I will listen to find out how the characters solve a problem.

REVIEW: PLOT Point out that realistic fiction stories have a plot: the main character has a problem, and a series of events leads to a solution. Read aloud "Evie and Margie," telling students to listen for the characters' problem and for what happens because of it.

After Reading

RESPOND Have students discuss what makes "Evie and Margie" realistic fiction. Be sure they mention the characters who behave and talk like real people, the realistic settings of their homes and school, and the real-life problem of the girls both wanting to play Cinderella. Ask students what they think of the ending, or solution to the problem. Is it something that would happen in real life? Do they like the solution?

Build Robust Vocabulary
Words from the Read-Aloud

Teach/Model

Routine Card 3

INTRODUCE ROBUST VOCABULARY Use *Routine Card 3* to introduce the words.

❶ Put the word in **selection context.**

❷ Display Transparency R70 and have students read the word and the **Student-Friendly Explanation.**

❸ Have students **say the word** with you.

❹ Use the word in other contexts, and have students **interact with the word's meaning.**

❺ Remove the transparency. Say the Student-Friendly Explanation again, and ask students to **name the word** that goes with it.

❶ **Selection Context:** Margie **swooned** and fell down on the floor weeping.

❹ **Interact with Word Meaning:** Would you swoon when you heard terrible news, or when you went for a walk?

❶ **Selection Context:** Everyone was **astonished** by Margie's free-flowing tears.

❹ **Interact with Word Meaning:** When would you be astonished: when you see an elephant on TV or when there is an elephant in the schoolyard?

Practice/Apply

GUIDED PRACTICE Ask students the following:

• When might a person *swoon*?

• Have you ever been *astonished* by anything? Describe what it was and what happened.

Objective

• *To develop robust vocabulary through discussing a literature selection*

Tested

INTRODUCE ✓

Vocabulary: Lesson 11

swooned

astonished

▼ **Student-Friendly Explanations**

Vocabulary

1. **swooned** If you had a terrible shock or surprise that made you faint or fall, you might have swooned.

2. **astonished** When you are amazed and surprised by something, you are astonished.

3. **envious** If you feel envious, you want something that someone else has.

4. **rivalry** People who have a rivalry are competing against each other for something.

Grade 3, Lesson 11   Rb   Vocabulary

Transparency R70

Total Physical Response Have volunteers show how they would *swoon* from terrible news. Then have others act *astonished* when they hear different news.

Grammar
Singular Possessive Nouns

5-DAY GRAMMAR

DAY 1 Singular Possessive Nouns
DAY 2 Plural Possessive Nouns
DAY 3 Plural Nouns and Possessive Nouns
DAY 4 Apply to Writing
DAY 5 Possessive Nouns Review

Objectives

- *To recognize that possessive nouns show ownership*
- *To understand and identify possessive nouns*

Daily Proofreading

1. she baked three cake for the party (She; cakes; party.)
2. How many cakes are you bringing. (bringing?)

TECHNOLOGY

www.harcourtschool.com/ storytown
Grammar Glossary

Possessive Nouns

1. The dog's ball rolled underneath the bushes.
dog's

2. We went to our cousin's basketball game.
cousin's

3. Josiah left his grandma's house on Tuesday.
grandma's

4. To get to the playground, walk past Eli's house.
Eli's

5. When the girl's package came, she was happy.
girl's

6. The zookeeper washed the elephant's trunk.
elephant's

7. I thought that character's actions were strange.
character's

8. My aunt's painting is beautiful.
aunt's

Grade 3, Lesson 11   LA9   Grammar: Possessive Nouns

Transparency LA21

Teach/Model

DEFINE POSSESSIVE NOUNS Tell students that nouns can be singular or plural to show if they name one or more than one person, place, or thing. Explain that nouns also have a way to show who or what owns or has something. Write this sentence on the board:

The boy's dog is brown.

Underline the word *boy's* and explain that it is a possessive noun. It tells readers that one boy owns the dog. Point to the word *boy's* and circle the *'s* at the end. Say: **When we want to make a singular noun into a possessive noun, we usually add *'s* at the end.** Write the following additional examples on the board, and have volunteers identify the possessive nouns and describe how they were formed.

Mark's favorite shirt is bright blue. He wore it to his brother's party. It is his mother's favorite shirt, too.

Guided Practice

IDENTIFY POSSESSIVE NOUNS Display **Transparency LA21**. Explain that each sentence has a singular possessive noun in it. Read the first sentence aloud and guide students to identify the possessive noun (dog's) and to recognize the *'s* that shows that the noun is possessive. Continue with sentences 2–5, having volunteers identify each possessive noun and *'s*.

Practice/Apply

IDENTIFY AND USE POSSESSIVE NOUNS Have students read the rest of the sentences on the transparency. In their notebooks have them write each possessive noun and circle each *'s*. Then have students write a sentence of their own using one of those possessive nouns.

5-DAY WRITING	
DAY 1	Introduce
DAY 2	Prewrite
DAY 3	Draft
DAY 4	Revise/Edit
DAY 5	Revise/Edit

Writing
Paragraph That Compares

Teach/Model

INTRODUCE A PARAGRAPH THAT COMPARES Display **Transparency LA22.** Explain that this is a paragraph that compares two people; it tells how they are alike. Read the paragraph aloud, telling students to think about how the two brothers in the paragraph are alike. Then begin a list of characteristics for a paragraph that compares, explaining that you will add to it later.

WRITING TRAIT **VOICE** Tell students that a writer's voice shows how that writer thinks or feels about a topic. If the writer really likes something, his or her voice will have a positive tone. If the writer does not like something or likes one thing more than another, his or her voice will let the reader know that, as well.

Paragraph That Compares
• Tells how two or more things are alike
• Has a topic sentence that tells what is being compared

Guided Practice

MAKE COMPARISONS Write the words *fruits* and *vegetables* on the board. Explain that you want to compare these two things. Ask students if they think these are good items to compare, and why. (Possible response: They probably are because they are alike in many ways.) Have students suggest several ways in which fruits and vegetables are alike, and list them on the board.

Practice/Apply

MAKE LISTS OF ITEMS Ask students to make a list in their notebooks of possible things to compare. Have each student include at least five pairs of things on the list. Then have students work with partners to discuss their lists. Which items would make interesting comparisons? Which ones would not? Have students circle items they think would work best for a paragraph that compares.

Objective

• *To recognize comparative writing and analyze its use in a paragraph*

Writing Prompt

Compare Games Have students compare how two of their classmates' favorite games or sports are alike in some ways. Students should check that they have written any possessive nouns correctly.

Student Model: Realistic Story

Amy had never written a letter on paper. She always sent e-mail or instant messages instead. She even sent thank-you notes for birthday presents and invitations for parties by e-mail. "I don't like to write letters," she said stubbornly. "It takes too long!"

So the day a letter came for her, she was very surprised. She could not imagine whom it was from. Everyone she knew was on her e-mail buddy list. Amy looked at the envelope. The postmark said Anchorage, Alaska.

"I don't know anyone in Alaska!" Amy said to her mother. "Who could be sending this to me?"

Grade 3, Lesson 12   **LAb**   Writing: Realistic Story

Transparency LA22

Day at a Glance
Day 2

 **and Spelling**
- Review: C-*le* Syllables

Robust Vocabulary
Words from the Selection
- Introduce: *encouraging, brief, chuckling, soothing, sobbed, praised*

Comprehension
 Use Story Structure
 Plot

Reading
- "Loved Best," *Student Edition,* pp. 306–323

Fluency
- Expression

Robust Vocabulary
Words About the Selection
- Introduce: *envious, rivalry*

Grammar
- Review: Possessive Nouns

Writing
- Paragraph That Compares

Warm-Up Routines

 Oral Language

Objectives *To listen attentively and respond appropriately to oral communication; to write and speak in complete sentences*

Question of the Day

If you were going to put on a show or play, what would it be about?

Discuss with students how shows and plays come in all different varieties. There are funny plays and musical shows, plays that are similar to realistic fiction, and shows that have dancing, like a ballet. Ask students what kinds of shows or plays they have seen.

Then ask students to answer the following writing prompt in their notebooks:

If I were going to put on a _____, it would be about _____.

Have them add a sentence or two about why they chose that topic. Invite volunteers to share what they wrote.

Read Aloud

Objectives *To listen to a poem for understanding and enjoyment; to respond to a poem through discussion*

READ ALOUD A POEM Using the following steps, share the poem with students:

Introduce the text. Display **Transparency R71** or distribute photocopies to the students. Tell them they are going to listen to the poem "A Good Play," by Robert Louis Stevenson.

Set a purpose. Ask students what the purpose might be for reading a poem about children playing. (for enjoyment)

Model fluent reading. Read the poem aloud. Pause after each line and emphasize punctuation and the rhyming of words.

Discuss the poem. Ask students the following questions:

- **How did the children build their ship?** (on the stairs, with chairs and pillows)

- **Which words in the poem rhyme?** (stairs/chairs, pillows/billows, nails/pails, take/cake, etc.)

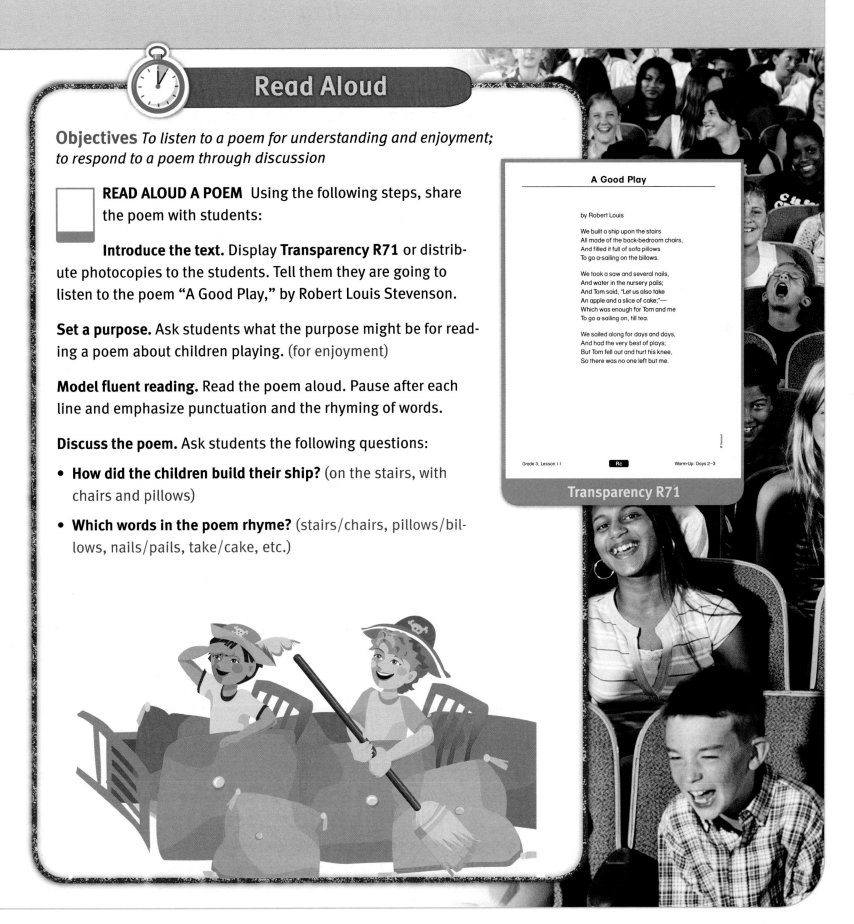

A Good Play

by Robert Louis

We built a ship upon the stairs
All made of the back-bedroom chairs,
And filled it full of sofa pillows
To go a-sailing on the billows.

We took a saw and several nails,
And water in the nursery pails;
And Tom said, "Let us also take
An apple and a slice of cake;"—
Which was enough for Tom and me
To go a-sailing on, till tea.

We sailed along for days and days,
And had the very best of plays;
But Tom fell out and hurt his knee,
So there was no one left but me.

Grade 3, Lesson 11   Rc   Warm-Up: Days 2–3

Transparency R71

C-*le* Syllable
phonics *and Spelling*

Objectives

- *To read words with the letter pattern VCC-*le
- *To divide -*le *words into syllables*

Skill Trace

 Tested C-*le* Syllable

Introduce	T30
Reteach	S2
Review	T40–T41, T60, T76, T88, T384
Test	Theme 3
Maintain	Theme 4, T76, T260

Spelling Words

1.	title	9.	purple
2.	table	10.	little*
3.	uncle	11.	middle
4.	apple	12.	simple
5.	cable	13.	saddle
6.	bubble	14.	trouble
7.	beetle	15.	scribble
8.	rattle		

Challenge Words

16.	twinkle	19.	buckled
17.	scrambled	20.	tablecloth
18.	sprinkle		

*Word from "Loved Best"

Short Vowels + Final -*le*

STATE THE GENERALIZATION Display **Transparency R72** and have students look at the words in Part A. Ask what is similar about the words. (They all end with -*le*; they all have one or two consonants before the -*le*.)

Remind students that -*le* and the consonant that comes before it form a syllable. Point to words 1–3 and ask students where each word is divided into syllables. (between the consonants) Point out that when a word has two consonants before -*le*, the vowel sound in the first syllable is short. Have students read the words. Call attention to words 4–6 and ask where these words are divided into syllables. (after the first vowel) Point out that when a word has one consonant before -*le*, the vowel sound in the first syllable is long. Have students read the words.

Have students read silently the sentences in Part A. Then have volunteers read them aloud.

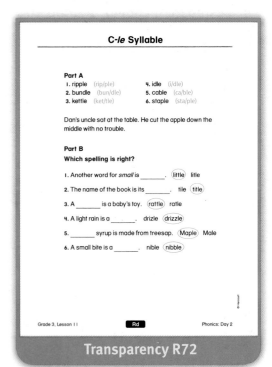

C-*le* Syllable

Part A
1. ripple (rip/ple)   4. idle (i/dle)
2. bundle (bun/dle)   5. cable (ca/ble)
3. kettle (ket/tle)   6. staple (sta/ple)

Dan's uncle sat at the table. He cut the apple down the middle with no trouble.

Part B
Which spelling is right?
1. Another word for *small* is _____.   (little) litle
2. The name of the book is its _____.   tile (title)
3. A _____ is a baby's toy.   (rattle) ratle
4. A light rain is a _____.   drizle (drizzle)
5. _____ syrup is made from treesap.   (Maple) Male
6. A small bite is a _____.   nible (nibble)

Grade 3, Lesson 11   **Rd**   Phonics: Day 2

Transparency R72

BELOW-LEVEL

Build Words Write the syllables *cat* and *tle* on the board. Remind students to pronounce -*tle* as /təl/. Have students read both syllables and then blend them to form *cattle*. Repeat with *simple*.

ADVANCED

Make a List Have students search classroom books to find words that include the letter pattern VCC-*le*. Ask them to list the words they find in their notebook. Encourage them to add to the list as they find new words.

5-DAY PHONICS/SPELLING

DAY 1	Pretest
DAY 2	State the Generalization
DAY 3	Spelling Practice/Review
DAY 4	Use Spelling Strategies/Review
DAY 5	Posttest

USE THE GENERALIZATION Call students' attention to Part B on **Transparency R72.** Read aloud the first sentence. Then point to the two word choices. Remind students that a consonant and -*le* form the final syllable, and the presence of two consonants before -*le* usually means the vowel sound in the first syllable is short.

Then ask a volunteer to read the two words. Establish that *little* is the correct spelling, and write the word to complete the sentence. Work with students to complete the second sentence, pointing out that *tile* has the CVC*e* pattern and does not have two syllables. Have students choose the correct spelling of the word to complete each of the remaining sentences.

 WRITE Dictate several spelling words for students to write in their notebooks.

✓ MONITOR PROGRESS

Phonics: C-*le* Syllable

| **IF** students spell double-consonant words with only one consonant, | **THEN** have them write *little* on one side of an index card and *table* on the other. Ask them to circle *tt* and write *Short Vowel*. On the other side, have them circle *b* and write *Long Vowel*. |

Small-Group Instruction, p. S2:

● **BELOW-LEVEL:** Reteach
● **ON-LEVEL:** Reinforce
● **ADVANCED:** Extend

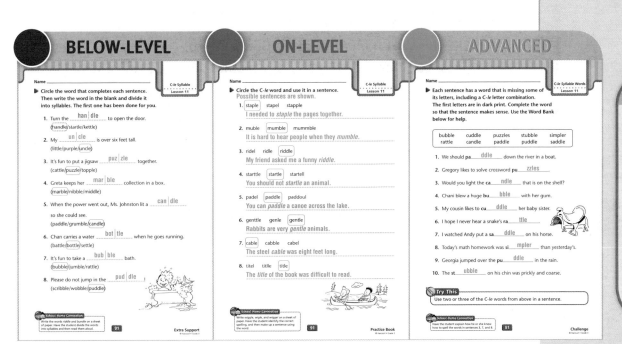

▲ Extra Support, p. 91   ▲ Practice Book, p. 91   ▲ Challenge, p. 91

E L L

- Group students according to academic levels, and assign one of the pages on the left.
- Clarify any unfamiliar concepts as necessary. See *ELL Teacher Guide* Lesson 11 for support in scaffolding instruction.

Build Robust Vocabulary
Words from the Selection

Objective

- *To build robust vocabulary*

INTRODUCE **Tested** ✓

Vocabulary: Lesson 11

encouraging	brief
chuckling	soothing
sobbed	praised

▼ **Student-Friendly Explanations**

Vocabulary

1. **encouraging**	An encouraging word from a friend can make you feel that you can do something well.
2. **brief**	If something is brief, it does not take much time.
3. **chuckling**	If you are chuckling, you are laughing quietly to yourself.
4. **soothing**	Something that is soothing makes you feel calm.
5. **sobbed**	Someone who sobbed cried very hard.
6. **praised**	If you praised someone, you told that person that he or she did something well.

Grade 3, Lesson 11   **Re**   Vocabulary: from the Selection

Transparency R73

Word Champion

Word Lists At the end of the week, encourage students to share their Word Champion entries with the class.

HOMEWORK/INDEPENDENT PRACTICE

Teach/Model

Routine Card 4

INTRODUCE ROBUST VOCABULARY Introduce the words by using the following steps:

❶ Display **Transparency R73** and read the word and the **Student-Friendly Explanation.**
❷ Have students **say the word** with you.
❸ Have students **interact with the word's meaning** by asking the appropriate question below.

- Would you want to hear **encouraging** words? Explain.
- If you ran for a **brief** time, would you be tired?
- Would you hear **chuckling** at a funny movie or a sad movie?
- Would the sound of a loud motor or the sound of a fountain be **soothing**?
- Why might someone have **sobbed** at the end of a day? Explain.
- When have you been **praised**?

Develop Deeper Meaning

EXPAND WORD MEANINGS: PAGES 304–305 Have students read the passage. Then read the passage aloud, pausing at the end of page 304 to ask questions 1–4. Read page 305 and then discuss students' answers to questions 5–6.

1. How do you think the writer felt when his brother was **encouraging** him? Explain.
2. Why was the writer's success at free shots so **brief**?
3. How did Vince's **chuckling** make the writer feel?
4. Why did the writer say that Gary's voice was **soothing**?
5. How did Gary keep the writer from **sobbing**?
6. What did Gary say to **praise** the writer?

Vocabulary

Build Robust Vocabulary

encouraging

brief

chuckling

soothing

sobbed

praised

Jacob's Journal

Monday, November 3

In the afternoon, I went to the playground with Gary, my big brother. We raced to the basketball court. Gary began **encouraging** me to practice my foul shots. For a **brief** time, all my shots went into the basket. Then Vince showed up, and I got nervous. He saw me miss about five shots in a row. I got upset when I heard him **chuckling**, but Gary's **soothing** voice told me to ignore him.

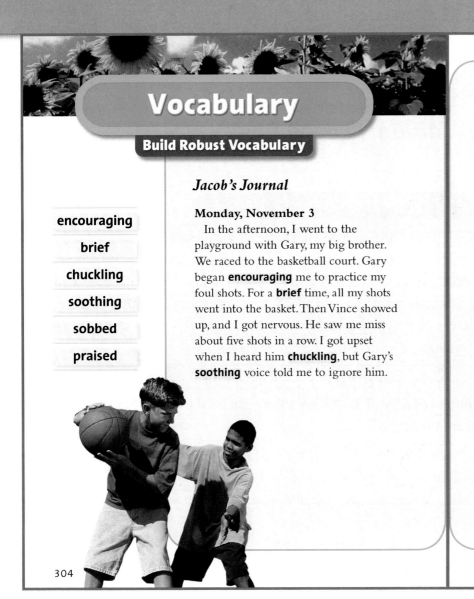

Friday, November 7

Today I entered the big foul-shot contest at the playground. All the kids stood in line on the basketball court. Vince took his shot before me. It went in! The crowd cheered. I was next. I shot the ball. It went up in an arc, but it bounced off the rim. I almost **sobbed**. I saw my brother, Gary, in the crowd. He **praised** me anyway. "Great try!" he called. That made me feel better.

 www.harcourtschool.com/storytown

Word Champion

Your mission this week is to use Vocabulary Words in conversation with your friends and family. You may want to tell your friends about a time when you were praised for doing a good job. Each day write in your vocabulary journal the sentences you spoke that had the Vocabulary Words.

304

305

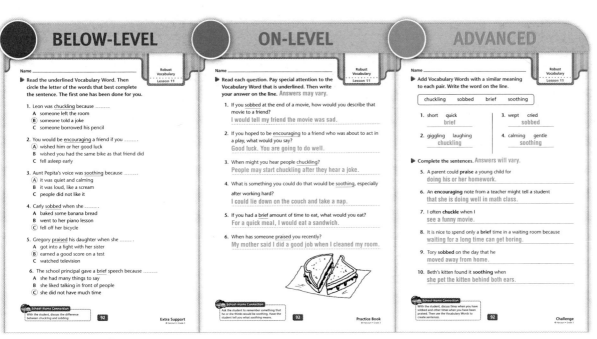

BELOW-LEVEL

▲ Extra Support, p. 92

ON-LEVEL

▲ Practice Book, p. 92

ADVANCED

▲ Challenge, p. 92

- Group students according to academic levels, and assign one of the pages on the left.

- Clarify any unfamiliar concepts as necessary. See *ELL Teacher Guide* Lesson 11 for support in scaffolding instruction.

Reading
Student Edition: "Loved Best"

Objective

- *To use story structure as a strategy of comprehension*

 Podcasting: Use Story Structure

Options for Reading

 BELOW-LEVEL

SET A PURPOSE Preview the selection with students. Model how to set a purpose for reading.

 ON-LEVEL

MONITOR COMPREHENSION Use the questions as students read, or have pairs complete *Practice Book* page 93.

 ADVANCED

INDEPENDENT READING Have students read, using *Practice Book* p. 93.

▲ Practice Book, p. 93

Genre Study

DISCUSS REALISTIC FICTION: PAGE 306 Ask students to read the genre information on *Student Edition* page 306. Explain about characters and events in realistic fiction. Say: **Realistic fiction has a setting and characters that seem real. One of the characters usually has a realistic problem, and the story shows how that problem gets solved.**

Use **Transparency GO7** or copy the graphic organizer from page 306 onto the board. Tell students they can fill it in for any realistic fiction story they read.

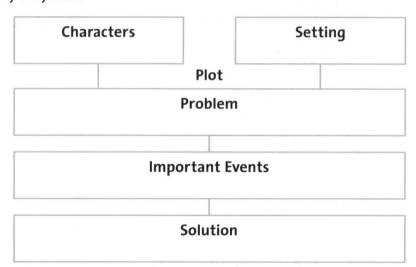

Comprehension Strategy

USE STORY STRUCTURE: PAGE 306 Read aloud the Comprehension Strategy information. Emphasize to students that good readers pay attention at the beginning of a story to find out about the characters, the setting, and the problem faced by the characters. In the middle of the story, good readers look for important events that lead to the problem being solved at the end.

Distribute *Practice Book* page 93. Tell students that they will use a story map to keep track of information as they read. See page T54 for the completed *Practice Book* page.

Genre Study

Realistic fiction has characters and events that are like people and events in real life. Look for

- characters who behave as real people might.
- problems that are similar to problems in real life.

Characters | Setting
Plot
Problem
Important Events
Solution

Comprehension Strategy

Use Story Structure to help you understand the problem and the solution of the problem.

306

Loved Best

BY PATRICIA C. McKISSACK
ILLUSTRATED BY YVONNE BUCHANAN

Carolyn thinks that her parents should love her the best of all their children. After all, she has been around longer than her younger brother and sister, Josh and Dana! Recently, she has not been so sure that they do.

All three children have parts in a community play. Carolyn will recite a poem about a river. Mrs. Lasiter, the play director, has praised Carolyn for reciting her poem perfectly. Carolyn is sure that her performance will be better than Josh's bird or Dana's sunflower. When her parents see how wonderful she is, they will once more love her best.

307

Build Background

DISCUSS CHILDHOOD FEELINGS Tell students that they are going to read a story about a girl who performs in a play. Invite volunteers to share their experiences with rehearsing and performing.

Routine Card 5

SET A PURPOSE AND PREDICT Tell students that one purpose for reading a story is to get to know the characters. Have students look at page 307 in the *Student Edition*. Then follow these steps.

- Have students read the title and the introduction to the story.

- Point out Carolyn in the picture and explain that she is the main character. Ask students whether they think Carolyn's parents could love one of their children better than the others.

- Invite students to read the story to find out whether Carolyn discovers who her parents love best.

TECHNOLOGY

 eBook "Loved Best" is available in an eBook.

 Audiotext "Loved Best" is available on *Audiotext 3* for subsequent readings.

On the evening of the program, everybody began arriving at the community center. The room was fully decorated like a bright spring day. Bees were buzzing, birds were chirping, and rabbits were hopping about. Then it was show time. "Break a leg, everybody," whispered Mrs. Lasiter nervously. ①

The audience sang the "Star-Spangled Banner" way off-key. Somebody else gave a welcome. And the play began. ②

308   309

Monitor Comprehension

PAGES 308–309 Direct students' attention to the illustration on pages 308–309. Ask what is happening. Point out that this looks like a school play or program of some kind.

① **UNDERSTAND FIGURATIVE LANGUAGE What do you think Mrs. Lasiter means when she says, "Break a leg, everybody"?** (Possible response: "Break a leg" is an expression that actors use. It encourages people to do well. Mrs. Lasiter means for everyone to do well.)

② **IMPORTANT DETAILS How would you know that a special event is about to take place?** (Possible response: The audience sings the "Star-Spangled Banner." Someone gives a welcome to the crowd.)

Apply
Comprehension Strategies

Use Story Structure As students read, help them think about the story's beginning, middle, and ending.

Think Aloud Right away, I notice that the setting of the story is in the community center. From reading the introduction, I know that Carolyn is the main character. She will be the person with the problem, so I will look to see what she does and says.

The first scene up was performed by Dana's age group. The sunflower garden. **①**

Dana and all ten of the little three- through five-year-old sunflowers followed the six-year-old sun across the sky. White fluffy clouds hung from the ceiling, and a carpet of green grass covered the floor.

Carolyn looked from behind the big sheet that served as a curtain. Mama was smiling as she watched little Dana lean toward the sun just as a real flower does.

Daddy was busy taking video, never missing a minute of it. Granddaddy was enjoying himself too. He was snapping pictures, one after the other. *She is cute,* thought Carolyn. *But wait until it's my turn. I'm going to blow them all away.*

When it was Josh's turn Carolyn could see Mama holding her breath, especially when it was time for Josh to sing. He was so good. Not one mistake. Daddy got so involved with listening, he almost forgot to start the camera. In fact **②** Grandmama took over the video so Daddy could concentrate on Josh's performance.

At the end Josh stepped forward and took a bow. Everybody cheered and applauded. Carolyn applauded and yelled out a big, "Yo, bro!" Josh heard her and grinned. He'd never looked happier. **③**

Wait till I do my thing, though, thought Carolyn.

310   311

Monitor Comprehension

PAGES 310–311 Have students look at the illustration to see if Carolyn is performing. Then have them read to find out how the play begins.

① **SEQUENCE How does the play begin?** (Dana performs as part of the sunflower garden.)

② **CAUSE/EFFECT Why does Daddy almost forget to videotape Josh?** (Possible response: Josh's singing is so good that Daddy is distracted.)

③ **CHARACTERS' EMOTIONS How does Carolyn feel about Dana's and Josh's performances?** (She likes them.) **How does she think hers will compare? How do you know?** (Possible response: She thinks her performance will be better. She thinks, "Wait till I do my thing" and "I'm going to blow them all away.")

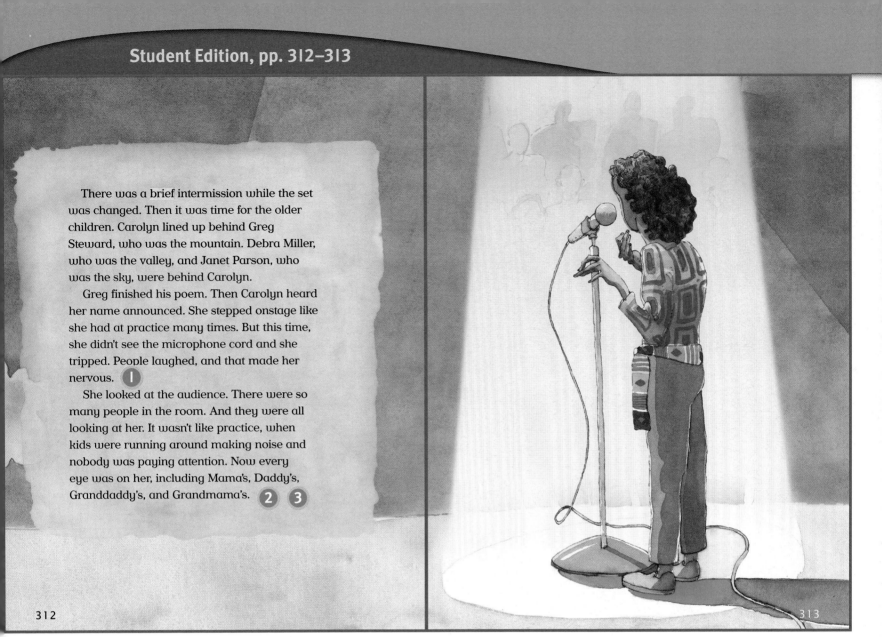

There was a brief intermission while the set was changed. Then it was time for the older children. Carolyn lined up behind Greg Steward, who was the mountain. Debra Miller, who was the valley, and Janet Parson, who was the sky, were behind Carolyn.

Greg finished his poem. Then Carolyn heard her name announced. She stepped onstage like she had at practice many times. But this time, she didn't see the microphone cord and she tripped. People laughed, and that made her nervous. ❶

She looked at the audience. There were so many people in the room. And they were all looking at her. It wasn't like practice, when kids were running around making noise and nobody was paying attention. Now every eye was on her, including Mama's, Daddy's, Granddaddy's, and Grandmama's. ❷ ❸

312

313

Monitor Comprehension

PAGES 312–313 Before reading, have students look at the picture on page 313. Ask how they would feel standing in front of a lot of people. Have students read to find out how Carolyn feels.

❶ **IMPORTANT DETAILS What happens when Carolyn first walks onstage? What problem does that cause?** (She trips over the microphone cord and gets nervous.)

❷ **IDENTIFY WITH CHARACTERS How does Carolyn feel when she is onstage?** (Possible response: She realizes everyone is looking at her. She is nervous. She is not sure she will do a good job.)

❸ **MAKE PREDICTIONS What do you think will happen?** (Possible response: She will freeze; or, she will do fine.)

E L L

Perform It Act out what happens to Carolyn when she is onstage. Invite students to act out what a person might do if he or she were nervous. (For example, shuffling feet, hands shaking)

> Carolyn searched for the first words of the poem, but she couldn't remember them.
>
> "I am the river," Mrs. Lasiter whispered from offstage. Everybody heard her and they laughed again.
>
> "I . . . am . . . the river," said Carolyn. The microphone squeaked and she jumped. More laughter.
>
> Where were the words? Her memory was like a blank sheet of paper. Nothing. ①
>
> How many times had she said that dumb poem? She wanted the earth to open up and swallow her whole. "I can't remember. . . ." She sobbed. ②
>
> Then someone began to applaud. She had seen that done for little kids who messed up. This wasn't supposed to happen—not to her. ③
>
> Feeling humiliated and not knowing what to do, she ran. Bounding offstage, she bolted for the side door and rushed into the parking lot.
>
> Strong arms caught her just as she collapsed beside the family car. "Carolyn." It was Mama who held her tightly. Mama's voice was as soothing as a warm breeze. "You're going to be fine, daughter. Just fine."

314   315

Monitor Comprehension

PAGES 314–315 Have students read to find out what happens next.

① **CONFIRM PREDICTIONS What happens to Carolyn onstage?** (Possible response: She cannot remember her poem.)

② **UNDERSTAND FIGURATIVE LANGUAGE What does the author mean when she says Carolyn wants "the earth to open up and swallow her whole"?** (Possible response: Carolyn wants to disappear from this bad situation as quickly as possible.)

③ **Focus Skill PLOT What is Carolyn's problem?** (She cannot remember the poem.) **What else do you think Carolyn is worried about?** (Possible response: She is worried whether her parents really love her, now that she has messed up.)

Use Multiple Strategies

Use Prior Knowledge Explain to students that what they already know from reading and from their own experiences can help them understand the way characters behave in a story. Ask students what they would do if they were in a situation that made them nervous.

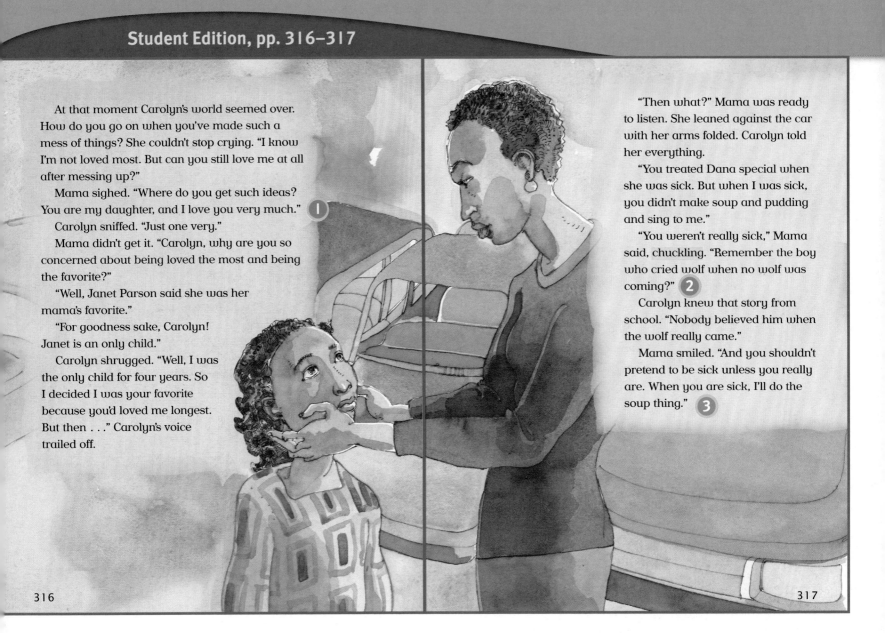

At that moment Carolyn's world seemed over. How do you go on when you've made such a mess of things? She couldn't stop crying. "I know I'm not loved most. But can you still love me at all after messing up?"

Mama sighed. "Where do you get such ideas? You are my daughter, and I love you very much." ①

Carolyn sniffed. "Just one very."

Mama didn't get it. "Carolyn, why are you so concerned about being loved the most and being the favorite?"

"Well, Janet Parson said she was her mama's favorite."

"For goodness sake, Carolyn! Janet is an only child."

Carolyn shrugged. "Well, I was the only child for four years. So I decided I was your favorite because you'd loved me longest. But then . . ." Carolyn's voice trailed off.

"Then what?" Mama was ready to listen. She leaned against the car with her arms folded. Carolyn told her everything.

"You treated Dana special when she was sick. But when I was sick, you didn't make soup and pudding and sing to me."

"You weren't really sick," Mama said, chuckling. "Remember the boy who cried wolf when no wolf was coming?" ②

Carolyn knew that story from school. "Nobody believed him when the wolf really came."

Mama smiled. "And you shouldn't pretend to be sick unless you really are. When you are sick, I'll do the soup thing." ③

316   317

Monitor Comprehension

PAGES 316–317 Have students read to see how Carolyn and her mother will discuss the problem.

① **IMPORTANT DETAILS What does Carolyn's mother say to make her feel better?** (Possible response: Carolyn's mother tells her that she loves her.)

② **CHARACTERS' MOTIVATION Why hadn't Carolyn's mother made soup and pudding for her?** (Carolyn was only pretending to be sick.)

③ **MAKE PREDICTIONS How do you think Carolyn's problem will be solved?** (Possible response: Carolyn will come to understand that her mother loves all her children the same and will be able to go back and recite her poem.)

Apply
Comprehension Strategies

Use Story Structure Ask students to think again about the beginning, middle, and ending of the story. Mention that this seems to be the middle of the story, since we are learning more about Carolyn's problem—whether she is loved best. Ask students to think about what kind of solution might occur in the end.

"Okay." Carolyn agreed she was wrong. "But," she continued, "you put Josh's paper on the refrigerator and fixed him a cake for getting the singing part. But you didn't put my paper up there."

Mama didn't hesitate. "You've had your fair share of papers on the refrigerator. Josh is so shy. Things don't come easy for him like they do for you. So when I saw him trying new things and getting a perfect paper, I thought he needed extra attention." ❶

Mama handed Carolyn tissues. Carolyn blew her nose on one and dried her eyes with the other. "I'm sorry," she said.

Mama looked Carolyn in the eye. "I could never love one of my children *more* than the other. But all three of you are loved the *best* I know how." ❷

Suddenly a sunflower and a bird appeared around the side of the car.

"Don't cry, Carolyn," said Dana. "It will be okay."

"Come on Carolyn. Don't give up. You wouldn't let me give up," said Josh. "You're our big sister, the only one we have." ❸

318

319

Monitor Comprehension

PAGES 318–319 Ask students to think about a time that a parent did something that, at first, they did not understand. Then have them read on to find out Carolyn's mother's explanation.

❶ **CAUSE AND EFFECT What was Mama's reason for putting Josh's paper on the refrigerator?** (He was shy, so he needed extra attention when he did well.)

❷  **PLOT Is Carolyn's problem solved? How do you know?** (Possible response: Yes. She knows that her parents love her, and she is ready to overcome her fear of performing.)

❸ **DRAW CONCLUSIONS How do Dana and Josh feel about Carolyn? How do you know?** (Possible responses: They love her; they admire her; they come to find her and tell her not to give up.)

HEALTH

SUPPORTING STANDARDS

Helping Others Discuss with students how the members of Carolyn's family helped her overcome her fear. Discuss what they might have said if they were Carolyn's friend. Present situations such as a friend moving away, a friend suggesting a dangerous activity, or a friend losing a pet, and work with students to prepare thoughtful dialogue.

Just then Dad found them. And behind him were Grandmama and Granddaddy.

"Carolyn," Daddy said, "do you think, maybe, you might want to try doing your poem again? Mrs. Lasiter said you could go on after the sky."

Carolyn thought about it. Mama gave her an encouraging nod. "You know who's loved best?" Carolyn said.

"No. Who?" the family asked.

"You are all loved best," said Carolyn, winking at Mama. Then she went back inside with her scarves flowing like a river.

320

Think Critically

1. What is the problem in "Loved Best," and how is it solved? PLOT

2. How does Carolyn feel after she sobs onstage? CHARACTERS' EMOTIONS

3. If you were Carolyn, would you have tried to say the poem again? Explain. EXPRESS PERSONAL OPINIONS

4. How can you tell that the author thinks Carolyn is wrong to pretend she is sick? DRAW CONCLUSIONS

5. WRITE Write about a time when you did something brave. SHORT RESPONSE

321

Think Critically

Respond to the Literature

1. Problem: Carolyn wants to be loved the most. When she forgets the poem, she thinks her family won't love her. Solution: Her family says they love her, and Carolyn goes back to say the poem. **PLOT**

2. She feels embarrassed. **CHARACTERS' EMOTIONS**

3. Possible response: Yes, because I would've felt worse if I hadn't tried to say the poem again. **EXPRESS PERSONAL OPINIONS**

4. Possible response: The mother tells Carolyn that she shouldn't act sick unless she really is. Carolyn agrees. **DRAW CONCLUSIONS**

5. WRITE Possible response: I read a story, which I had written, in front of the whole school. My brother helped me practice. **WRITING RESPONSE/RELATE TO PERSONAL EXPERIENCE**

ANALYZE AUTHOR'S PURPOSE

Author's Purpose Remind students that authors have a purpose, or reason, for writing. After students have finished reading "Loved Best," ask:

Why did the author write "Loved Best"?

- to tell readers how to put on a play
- to persuade readers that they should practice before reciting a poem
- to entertain readers with a story about Carolyn and her problems

Meet the Author
Patricia C. McKissack

Before Patricia McKissack became a writer, she was a listener. On hot summer evenings her family would sit on the porch and recite poems and tell stories. When she was older she realized that those stories helped her become a writer.

When Patricia McKissack grew up, she became a teacher. It was then that she realized there were not many books about African Americans. So she decided to write one. She thought that she would then go back to teaching or do something else. More than twenty years later, Patricia McKissack is still writing!

Meet the Illustrator
Yvonne Buchanan

Yvonne Buchanan grew up in New York City. Once her mother bought her a pad of colored construction paper. That was the start of her career as an illustrator.

Yvonne Buchanan thinks that it's important for illustrators to know about other things besides art. She has won awards for illustrating children's books, but she has also recently begun to write for children. She enjoys storytelling and hopes to do more in the future.

GO online www.harcourtschool.com/storytown

322

323

Meet the Author and the Illustrator

PAGES 322–323 Patricia McKissack learned about storytelling from her family. Stories continue to be a family affair for her; she and her husband, Fred, have written more than a hundred books together. All of her books deal with African Americans.

As a child, Yvonne Buchanan had to wash off her walls, on which she had drawn a cartoon character. Now no one would ask her to remove her art. She has illustrated numerous children's books, written and published six children's books, and is in demand as a political illustrator.

Ask students to read pages 322–323 for more information about the author and the illustrator.

Check Comprehension
Retelling

Objectives

- *To practice retelling a story*
- *To read with expression*

RETELLING RUBRIC

4	Uses details to clearly retell the story
3	Uses some details to retell the story
2	Retells the story with some inaccuracies
1	Is unable to retell the story

Professional Development

Podcasting: Auditory Modeling

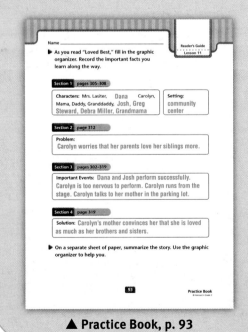

▲ Practice Book, p. 93

Retell

DIBELS
Oral
Reading
Fluency
ORF

Focus Skill

PLOT Remind students that the plot is made up of the events, or things that happen, in a story. Keeping track of what is happening and when it happens can help a reader understand the story better. The plot includes the main character's problem and the solution. Ask students to name Carolyn's main problem in the story "Loved Best." (Carolyn believes her parents love her siblings more than her.)

Routine Card 6

WRITE A SUMMARY Guide students to refer to the graphic organizer on *Practice Book* page 93 to write a short summary of the story, including all the important events.

Fluency
Expression

Teach/Model

DIBELS
Oral
Reading
Fluency
ORF

READING WITH EXPRESSION Explain that good readers show feeling and mood, or expression, as they read, matching what the writer has the characters say or think. For example, when a character is scared, a good reader will make his or her voice go higher. Readers can make their voices fierce for anger or squeaky and fast to show excitement.

Read page 311 of "Loved Best" aloud, emphasizing expression. Have students track the print as you read. Discuss how reading with expression makes the story more interesting.

Practice/Apply

Routine Card 9

PARTNER-READ Have partners read page 311 aloud, alternating paragraphs. When they have finished, have partners switch parts and read page 311 again.

Build Robust Vocabulary
Words About the Selection

Teach/Model

Routine Card 3 | **INTRODUCE THE WORDS** Use *Routine Card 3* to introduce the words.

❶ Put the word in **selection context**.
❷ Display **Transparency 70** and read the word and the **Student-Friendly Explanation**.
❸ Have students **say the word** with you.
❹ Use the word in other contexts, and have students **interact with the word's meaning**.
❺ Remove the transparency. Say the Student-Friendly Explanation again, and ask students to **name the word** that goes with it.

❶ **Selection Context:** Carolyn felt **envious** of the way her parents treated her brother and sister.

❹ **Interact with Word Meaning:** Would you be envious of a friend's toy that you also had or a toy that you didn't have?

❶ **Selection Context:** Carolyn feels a **rivalry** with her brother and sister because she thinks she is competing against them for her parents' love.

❹ **Interact with Word Meaning:** Would there be a rivalry between players on the same team or on two different teams?

Practice/Apply

GUIDED PRACTICE Ask students to do the following:

• List things that might make you envious of someone else. How are the things on the list alike and how are they different?

• Work with a partner to think of examples of rivalry. Then brainstorm words, such as *competitive*, to describe a rivalry.

Objective

• *To develop robust vocabulary through discussing a literature selection*

 Tested

INTRODUCE ✓

Vocabulary: Lesson 11

envious

rivalry

▼ **Student-Friendly Explanations**

Vocabulary

1. **swooned** If you had a terrible shock or surprise that made you faint or fall, you might have swooned.

2. **astonished** When you are amazed and surprised by something, you are astonished.

3. **envious** If you feel envious, you want something that someone else has.

4. **rivalry** People who have a rivalry are competing against each other for something.

Grade 3, Lesson 11   Rb   Vocabulary

Transparency R70

Grammar
Plural Possessive Nouns

5-DAY GRAMMAR	
DAY 1	Singular Possessive Nouns
DAY 2	**Plural Possessive Nouns**
DAY 3	Plural Nouns and Possessive Nouns
DAY 4	Apply to Writing
DAY 5	Possessive Nouns Review

Objectives

- *To identify plural possessive nouns*
- *To use plural possessive nouns correctly*

Daily Proofreading

1. The students books are in the closet (students'; closet.)
2. The dogs leashes is lost. (dogs'; are)

▲ Grammar Practice Book, p. 37

Teach/Model

DISCUSS PLURAL POSSESSIVE NOUNS Remind students that *plural* means "more than one" and that a plural noun names more than one person, place, or thing. Say: **Most plural nouns end in *s*. If I want to show that one of these plural nouns owns or has something, I just add an apostrophe (') after the final *s*.** Then write the following incorrect sentence on the board:

The students desks are in a row.

Explain that the word *students* is a plural noun and that the students have the desks. Add the apostrophe (') and read the sentence aloud.

Guided Practice

CORRECT PLURAL POSSESSIVE NOUNS Write the following incorrect sentences on the board.

The boys poems were good ones.
The girls performances were wonderful.

Read aloud the first sentence, pointing out that the word *boys* should be made possessive because the poems belong to the boys. Guide students to determine where the apostrophe should be, and write it after the final *s*. Read aloud the second sentence and guide students to determine how to make the word *girls* possessive. (girls')

Practice/Apply

WRITE PLURAL POSSESSIVES Write the following words on the board.

mothers	friends
tigers	teachers

On a separate sheet of paper, have students write each word and then make it possessive. (mothers', friends', tigers', teachers') Then have them write sentences using each word. Have pairs share their sentences to be sure that their plural possessive forms are correct.

5-DAY WRITING

DAY 1	Introduce
DAY 2	Prewrite
DAY 3	Draft
DAY 4	Revise/Edit
DAY 5	Revise/Edit

Writing
Paragraph That Compares

Prewrite

 REVIEW COMPARISONS Display **Transparency LA22**. Remind students of the characteristics of a paragraph that compares. Point out the signal words *alike*, *both*, and *same*. Add that characteristic to the list.

FIND AND CHOOSE A TOPIC Direct students to the lists they made of possible things to compare. Tell them to choose a pair of things that have lots of similarities, because things that are alike in many ways make a good topic for a paragraph that compares.

> ### Paragraph That Compares
> - Has a topic sentence that tells what is being compared.
> - Tells how two or more things are alike.
> - Uses signal words such as *both, alike,* and *same.*

MODEL PREWRITING Tell students that you will compare fruits and vegetables. Write *Fruits* and *Vegetables* as column headings, and add traits of each. As you write a trait in the Fruits column, ask aloud, **Is that trait also true of vegetables?**

Fruits	Vegetables
good to eat	good to eat
grow on trees and plants	grow on plants
good for you	good for you
colorful	colorful

WRITING TRAIT ▶ **VOICE** Guide students to think about words that express how they think or feel about the topic they have chosen.

Practice/Apply

PREWRITING A PARAGRAPH THAT COMPARES Have students write the names of the two items they will compare as column headings. Then have them list the traits or qualities of each. Tell them to keep their lists for use on Day 3.

Objective

- *To choose a topic and generate ideas for a paragraph that compares*

 ## Writing Prompt

List to Compare Have students write three ways that an apple and an orange are alike.

E L L

Prewriting Have students share with a partner their lists of traits and then discuss their ideas.

Day at a Glance
Day 3

phonics **and Spelling**
- Review: C-*le* Syllables
- Spelling Practice

Fluency
- Expression
- "Loved Best," *Student Edition,* pp. 309, 315

Comprehension

Review: Plot

Reading
- "The Shepherd Boy and the Wolf," *Student Edition,* pp. 324–325

Read!

Robust Vocabulary
- Review: *swooned, astonished, encouraging, brief, chuckling, soothing, sobbed, praised, envious, rivalry*
- Introduce: Use Context Clues

Grammar
- Plural Nouns and Possessive Nouns

Writing
- Paragraph That Compares

Warm-Up Routines

Oral Language

Objectives *To listen attentively and respond appropriately to oral communication; to write and speak in complete sentences*

Question of the Day
If you were part of a talent show, what talent would you share with the audience?

Remind students that everyone has some special talent that can be shared with others—drawing, singing, playing a sport, and so on.

Have students discuss ways in which people might share their talents, such as in a talent show, at an art show, or with a video or audio recording. Then have students write at least two sentences in their notebooks in response to the following prompts:

My talent is _____.
I would like to share my talent by _____.

When they have finished, have students share their writing with the class.

Read Aloud

Objectives *To read poetry fluently; to listen to a poem*

REVIEW THE POEM Display **Transparency R71**, or distribute photocopies to the students. Tell them you are going to reread the poem "A Good Play."

Set a purpose. Ask students what the purpose might be for reading a poem again. (Possible responses: to enjoy it again, to listen for rhymes and rhythm) Tell students to listen and follow along as you read the poem aloud, noting when you pause.

Model fluent reading. Read the poem aloud. Do not emphasize the rhyming words at the end of lines. Instead, move smoothly through the lines, pausing only to follow the punctuation.

Choral-read. Tell students to follow along as you read the poem aloud. Remind them to listen carefully for pronunciation and pauses. Then ask the class to do a choral reading of the poem. Begin by having students read with you a few times. Then have them repeat it several times until their final reading is in unison and sounds like your modeling.

A Good Play

by Robert Louis

We built a ship upon the stairs
All made of the back-bedroom chairs,
And filled it full of sofa pillows
To go a-sailing on the billows.

We took a saw and several nails,
And water in the nursery pails;
And Tom said, "Let us also take
An apple and a slice of cake;"—
Which was enough for Tom and me
To go a-sailing on, till tea.

We sailed along for days and days,
And had the very best of plays;
But Tom fell out and hurt his knee,
So there was no one left but me.

Grade 3, Lesson 11 — Rc — Warm-Up: Days 2–3

Transparency R71

C-*le* Syllable

phonics

5-DAY PHONICS	
DAY 1	Introduce C-*le* Syllable
DAY 2	State the Generalization
DAY 3	VC-*le* and VCC-*le* Words
DAY 4	VVC-*le* Words
DAY 5	Review C-*le* Syllables

Objectives

- *To read words with long vowels and final* -le
- *To sort* -le *words according to whether they have short or long vowels*

Skill Trace

Tested ✓ **C-*le* Syllables**

Introduce	T30
Reteach	S2
Review	**T40–T41, T60, T76, T88, T384**
Test	Theme 3
Maintain	Theme 4, T76, T260

C-*le* Syllable

maple	topple	grumble	idle	riddle
cable	cuddle	pickle	staple	able

Long Vowels	Short Vowels
(ma/ple)	(top/ple)
(i/dle)	(grum/ble)
(ca/ble)	(rid/dle)
(sta/ple)	(cud/dle)
(a/ble)	(pic/kle)

Grade 3, Lesson 11   **R7**   Phonics: Day 3

Transparency R74

Teach/Model

SHORT VOWEL + FINAL -*le* Write the words *middle* and *uncle* on the board. Ask students how many consonants appear in each word before -*le*. (two) Ask students what sound -*le* stands for in these words. (/əl/) Remind students that -*le* forms a syllable with the consonant that comes before it. Have students divide the words into syllables. (mid/dle, un/cle) Point out that the words have a short vowel sound in the first syllable. Then pronounce the two syllables of each word before blending to pronounce the word. Have students repeat.

LONG VOWEL + FINAL -*le* Write the words *cradle* and *title* on the board. Ask students how many consonants appear before -*le*. (one) Ask students what sound -*le* stands for in these words. (/əl/) Remind students that -*le* forms a syllable with the consonant that comes before it. Have students divide the words into syllables. (cra/dle, ti/tle) Point out that the words have a long vowel sound in the first syllable. Then pronounce the two syllables of each word before blending to pronounce the word. Have students repeat.

Guided Practice

IDENTIFY LONG VOWEL C-*le* AND SHORT VOWEL C-*le* WORDS Display **Transparency R74.** Point to the word *maple*. Help students establish that the word ends with a single consonant followed by -*le*. Ask how it is divided into syllables. (ma/ple) Ask what vowel sound should be pronounced in the first syllable. (long *a* sound; /ā/) Write *maple* in the chart under the heading *Long Vowels* and draw a line to divide it into syllables. Repeat with *topple*, pointing out the two consonants before -*le* and the short vowel sound in the first syllable.

Practice/Apply

INDEPENDENT PRACTICE Have students copy the chart and sort the remaining words on **Transparency R74.** Have them write each word in the *Short Vowels* or *Long Vowels* column and mark the syllable division.

C-le Words

phonics *and Spelling*

5-DAY SPELLING
DAY 1 Pretest
DAY 2 State the Generalization
DAY 3 Spelling Practice/Handwriting
DAY 4 Use Spelling Strategies/Review
DAY 5 Posttest

Review Spelling Words

DOUBLE CONSONANTS Call students' attention to the words on **Transparency R74.** Point out that *topple, riddle,* and *cuddle* include double consonant letters, while other short vowel words have two different consonant letters. Explain that words with double consonant letters are harder to spell because only one consonant sound is heard. Tell students to remember that words with a short vowel sound in the first syllable and *-le* need two consonant letters before *-le*.

WRITE Explain that writing offers valuable spelling practice. Ask students to write riddles in which they use at least five spelling words. Encourage them to use the chart to check the spelling of these words.

Handwriting

ORGANIZATION Remind students that they need to stay on the lines as they write. They should not slope their writing up or down. Be sure students hold their papers still and at an angle that allows them to write on the lines easily.

ADVANCED

Make a Word Search Distribute graph paper. Have students use a 10 x 10 grid to construct a word search with as many spelling words as possible. Direct students to write their words either left to right or top to bottom and to fill the remaining boxes with miscellaneous letters. Have students trade with a partner to solve each other's puzzles.

Spelling Words

1. **title**	9. **purple**
2. **table**	10. **little***
3. **uncle**	11. **middle**
4. **apple**	12. **simple**
5. **cable**	13. **saddle**
6. **bubble**	14. **trouble**
7. **beetle**	15. **scribble**
8. **rattle**	

Challenge Words

16. **twinkle**	19. **buckled**
17. **scrambled**	20. **tablecloth**
18. **sprinkle**	

*Word from "Loved Best"

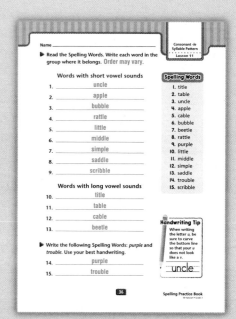

▲ Spelling Practice Book, p. 36

Fluency
Expression

Objectives

- *To build fluency through rereading a story*
- *To read with expression*
- *To read in a manner that sounds like natural speech*

Additional Related Reading

- *M Is for Music* by Kathleen Krull. Harcourt, 2003. **EASY**
- *Smiles: Pablo Picasso, Gabriela Mistral, Benito Juárez* by Alma Flor Ada and F. Isabel Campoy. Santillana, 2000. **AVERAGE**
- *Family Pictures* by Carmen Lomas Garza. Children's Book Press, 2005. **CHALLENGE**

BELOW-LEVEL

Fluency Practice Have students reread for fluency, using Story 11 in the *Strategic Intervention Interactive Reader* or the appropriate *Leveled Reader.* (See pages T96–T99.) Guide students to select a small portion of a story and practice reading it several times.

Review

DIBELS Oral Reading Fluency **ORF** **MODEL READING WITH EXPRESSION** Remind students that when good readers read aloud, they read with expression. They change their tone of voice to show feelings or important actions. Explain that, as they read, students should

- look for clues that tell how characters speak.
- think about what the words say or describe.

Think Aloud **I am going to read page 309 of "Loved Best" aloud. I'll look for clues about how the characters speak. I see the words** *whispered Mrs. Lasiter.* **This tells me to read the words** *"Break a leg, everybody"* **in a whisper. The description of what is happening** *before* **the play is very lively, saying it is like a bright spring day, using the words** *buzzing, chirping,* **and** *hopping.* **I'll read that part in a lively way.**

Routine Card **8** **ECHO-READING** Read aloud page 309 of "Loved Best," modeling how your own tips for reading with expression help you read fluently. Reread the page, sentence by sentence, having students echo-read after you.

Practice/Apply

GUIDED PRACTICE Direct students to page 315 of "Loved Best" and help them find clues for reading with expression. For example, they should read Mama's words in a soothing voice and the fourth paragraph a little faster because of the descriptive verbs *ran, bounding, bolting,* and *rushed.* Then read the first three paragraphs with students in a choral reading, helping them to use expression.

Routine Card **10** **INDEPENDENT PRACTICE** Have partners read page 315 of "Loved Best" to each other. Tell them to offer feedback that will help one another with their reading.

Plot
Comprehension

Review

EXPLAIN PLOT Remind students that the setting is where a story takes place and that the characters are the people and animals in the story. The plot of a story is what happens when the characters try to solve their problem. Tell students that they can better understand the plot of a story by looking for the story's main problem, the important events, and the way the problem is solved.

Practice/Apply

GUIDED PRACTICE Work with students to revisit "Loved Best" to identify important events. Have students review the story and look at the illustrations before discussing their answers to the following questions.

• **PAGE 309 On this page, people are filling the community center. What event begins on this page?** (the play)

• **PAGE 311 Josh gets up to perform. What happens when he does this?** (He sings well, without any mistakes.)

INDEPENDENT PRACTICE Tell students that identifying the major events in a story is a skill that can be practiced. Have students make a list in their notebooks of the most important events in "Loved Best." (Possible responses: Carolyn and her younger sister and brother perform in a school program; Carolyn's little sister and brother do well; Carolyn gets so nervous that she cannot perform; she talks with her family and realizes that her mother and family love her; Carolyn goes back to perform.) When students have finished, have them compare work, making any changes that might be necessary to create a full, complete list of events.

Objective

• *To identify important events in the plot of a story*

Skill Trace

 Plot

Introduce	T32–T33
Reteach	S6
Review	T63, T79, T91, T128–T129, T161, T177, T189, T387, T402
Test	Theme 3
Maintain	Theme 4, T80

Reading
Student Edition: Paired Selection

Objectives

- *To understand the distinguishing features of literary texts*
- *To understand the theme and purpose of a fable*

Genre Study

DISCUSS FABLES Tell students that "The Shepherd Boy and the Wolf" is a fable. Tell them that fables are stories that teach lessons about life. The author wants to send a message through the story.

NARRATIVE ELEMENTS Mention that fables contain the following:

- animal or human characters

- a setting in a faraway place or a long-ago time

- a plot that includes a lesson about life

USE PRIOR KNOWLEDGE/SET A PURPOSE Have students read aloud the title "The Shepherd Boy and the Wolf." Guide students to use prior knowledge and set a purpose for reading. Ask students what they think the purpose for reading a fable might be. (Possible responses: for enjoyment, to learn a lesson about life.) Have students read "The Shepherd Boy and the Wolf."

Respond to the Fable

MONITOR COMPREHENSION After students read, ask:

- **CHARACTERS' MOTIVATIONS** Why does the boy call "wolf" the first two times? (Possible response: He wants some excitement; he is bored.)

- **SEQUENCE** What happens after the boy calls "wolf" the first two times? (All the villagers come running to him.)

- **GENRE** What lesson does the author want to teach with the fable? (Possible response: Do not ask for help when you do not need it, or you will not get it when you really do.)

Writing Prompt

Reflection Have students write two sentences about how they could apply the lesson of "The Shepherd Boy and the Wolf" to their own lives.

Social Studies

Fable

The Shepherd Boy and the Wolf

RETOLD BY DORIS ORGEL
ILLUSTRATED BY DAVID SCOTT MEIER

"All the sheep ever do is say 'baa' and munch grass," thought the shepherd boy. He wished something would happen.

"I know: I'll invent some excitement." He cupped his hands to his mouth and shouted: "Help, a wolf is near!"

The villagers came running. "Where's the wolf?" they asked.

The shepherd boy laughed and said, "Fooled you!"

Another day, for fun, he cried, "Wolf! Wolf!" again. The villagers came running — and were fooled again.

One day a wolf really did appear, hungrily eyeing the sheep. "Help! WOLF!" the shepherd boy yelled, terrified. "This time it's really true!"

But nobody believed him.

Well, *you* know what happened: The wolf killed many sheep that day and had himself a mutton feast. The shepherd boy was sorry and never cried "wolf" again.

324   325

LITERARY ANALYSIS

Fables Explain to students that when they are thinking about fables, they should ask themselves:

- Who are the characters? Are they like me or someone I know?

- What is the setting? How does the setting affect what happens?

- What lesson does the fable teach? What can I learn?

Have students work in pairs to answer these questions for "The Shepherd Boy and the Wolf."

E L L

Global Fables Encourage students to share fables from their own cultures. When possible, have the class look for similarities between those fables and other familiar fables.

Connections

Objectives

- *To make connections between texts*
- *To make connections between texts and personal experiences*
- *To respond to text through writing*

Comparing Texts

1. Possible responses: Carolyn tries to get her mother's attention by pretending she is sick. The shepherd tries to get attention by pretending a wolf is near. **TEXT TO TEXT**

2. Possible response: They are loving to Carolyn and help her to be brave enough to say the poem again. **TEXT TO SELF**

3. Possible response: The setting is a community center. It seems like community centers I've been to before, with a big room and a parking lot outside. **TEXT TO WORLD**

Connections

Comparing Texts

1. How is Carolyn's behavior in "Loved Best" similar to the behavior of the shepherd boy in "The Shepherd Boy and the Wolf"?

2. What did you like about Carolyn's parents?

3. In what ways does the setting in "Loved Best" seem like a place you could visit in real life?

Vocabulary Review

Danny sobbed for a brief moment.

Word Pairs

Work with a partner. Write each Vocabulary Word on a card. Place the cards face down. Take turns flipping over two cards and writing a sentence that uses both words. Read your sentences to your partner and decide whether the Vocabulary Words are used correctly.

- encouraging
- brief
- chuckling
- soothing
- sobbed
- praised

326

Fluency Practice

Partner Reading

Choose your favorite section from "Loved Best." Take turns with a partner reading your sections aloud. Read each character's words as if a real person were speaking. Give feedback after each reading.

Writing

Write a New Scene

Write what you think happens next in "Loved Best." Use the same characters and setting, but think of new events to help you plan the next scene.

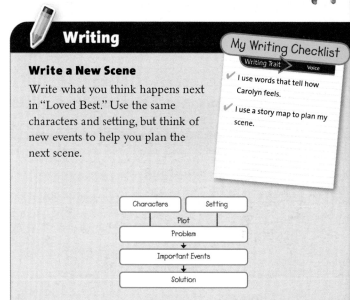

My Writing Checklist

Writing Trait — Voice

✓ I use words that tell how Carolyn feels.

✓ I use a story map to plan my scene.

Characters	Setting

Plot

Problem
↓
Important Events
↓
Solution

327

VOCABULARY

Tell students that their sentences can be silly or serious. When partners have written several sentences, have them compare their sentences to those of another pair.

FLUENCY

Partner Reading Explain that in order to show feeling when reading aloud, people show expression with their voices. Remind students to use tone of voice to emphasize important words. Ask pairs to alternate reading the paragraphs on pages 306–307 of "Loved Best." Encourage them to give their partners feedback that will help them read with expression.

WRITING

 Write a New Scene Have students use their notebooks to draw and complete a story map. Tell them to refer to the organizer as they plan and write their new scene.

PORTFOLIO OPPORTUNITY

Students may wish to place their new scenes in their portfolios.

Build Robust Vocabulary

Objectives

- *To review robust vocabulary*
- *To demonstrate knowledge of word meaning*

 REVIEW | Tested ✓

Vocabulary: Lesson 11

swooned	soothing
astonished	sobbed
encouraging	praised
brief	envious
chuckling	rivalry

Review Robust Vocabulary

USE VOCABULARY IN DIFFERENT CONTEXTS Remind students of the meanings of the Vocabulary Words introduced on Days 1 and 2. Then provide students with the following examples and questions. Encourage them to discuss each word in a new context.

swooned

- **What might a person look like as he or she swooned?** Have students pretend to swoon.
- **What might cause a person to swoon?**

astonished

- **Give examples of situations in which a person might be astonished.**
- **How would you look if you were astonished?**

envious

- **Would you feel envious if a friend got into trouble? Why or why not?**
- **When might someone feel envious?**

rivalry

- **Do you know of two sports teams that have a big rivalry with each other? Who are they and why is there a rivalry?**

praised

- **What might you do so you would be praised in school?**
- **For what would you like to be praised?**

brief

- If your teacher asked you to write a brief story, would it be long or short? Why?

- How could you make a long story brief?

chuckling

- What kind of mood would people be in if they were chuckling? Explain.

- What kind of story might make you chuckle?

sobbed

- If your best friend sobbed, what would you do to help?

soothing

- When would you want to hear a soothing voice?

- What other sounds are soothing?

encouraging

- How could you be encouraging to someone who lost a race?

- When have encouraging words been helpful to you?

▼ Student-Friendly Explanations

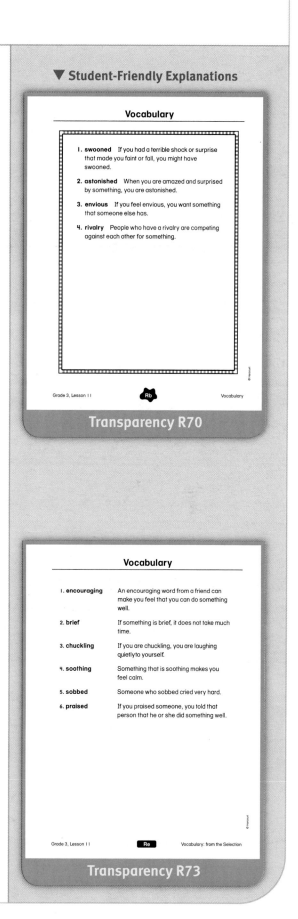

Vocabulary

1. **swooned**   If you had a terrible shock or surprise that made you faint or fall, you might have swooned.

2. **astonished**   When you are amazed and surprised by something, you are astonished.

3. **envious**   If you feel envious, you want something that someone else has.

4. **rivalry**   People who have a rivalry are competing against each other for something.

Grade 3, Lesson 11   Rb   Vocabulary

Transparency R70

Vocabulary

1. **encouraging**   An encouraging word from a friend can make you feel that you can do something well.

2. **brief**   If something is brief, it does not take much time.

3. **chuckling**   If you are chuckling, you are laughing quietly to yourself.

4. **soothing**   Something that is soothing makes you feel calm.

5. **sobbed**   Someone who sobbed cried very hard.

6. **praised**   If you praised someone, you told that person that he or she did something well.

Grade 3, Lesson 11   Re   Vocabulary: from the Selection

Transparency R73

Use Context Clues
Comprehension

Objectives

- *To define context clues*
- *To use context clues and synonyms to find meanings for unknown words*

Skill Trace

 Use Context Clues

Introduce	T70–T71
Reteach	S8
Review	T178, T403, T413
Test	Theme 3
Maintain	Theme 4, T264

 MONITOR PROGRESS

Use Context Clues

IF students have trouble identifying synonyms,	**THEN** have them use a thesaurus to find synonyms for easy words.

Small-Group Instruction, p. S8:

● **BELOW-LEVEL:** Reteach
● **ON-LEVEL:** Reinforce
● **ADVANCED:** Extend

Teach/Model

INTRODUCE CONTEXT CLUES Tell students that one way to learn what a new word means is to look at the words around it. These other words can give clues about the word's meaning. These are called context clues.

Explain that if students come to a word they do not know, they can look for nearby words that they know. Read aloud the following sentence as an example: "Jermaine *dashed* to the finish line. He was out of breath when he reached the end." Point out to students that the second part of the sentence gives clues to the meaning of *dashed*. (ran hard)

Guided Practice

USE CONTEXT CLUES Write the following sentence from "Loved Best" on the board and underline the word *bolted*.

> **Bounding offstage, she <u>bolted</u> for the side door and rushed into the parking lot.**

Read the sentence aloud. Guide students through the following questions to find the meaning of the word *bolted*.

1. **What is happening in this sentence?** (Carolyn is running off the stage and outside to the parking lot.)
2. **What word in the sentence probably has a meaning similar to the word *bolted*?** (rushed)
3. **If you replace the word *bolted* with the word *rushed*, does the sentence seem to have the same meaning?** (yes)

Explain that the context clues in the sentence helped you figure out that the word *bolted* means about the same as *rushed*.

Practice/Apply

USE CONTEXT CLUES Have students practice using context clues. Write the following sentences on the board:

When the first frog <u>leaped</u>, the other frogs jumped, too. The huge puddle held an <u>enormous</u> amount of water.

Have students find the word in the sentence that is a synonym of the underlined word. (leaped/jumped; enormous/huge)

Remind students that these synonyms help them understand the meanings of the underlined words.

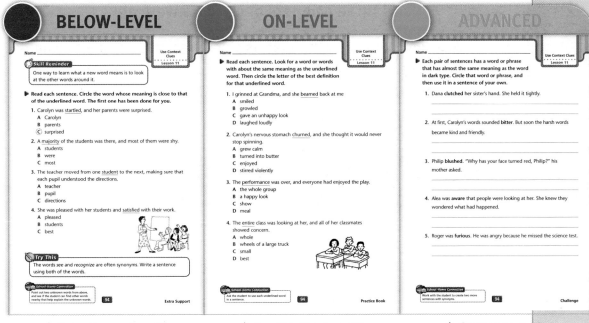

▲ **Extra Support, p. 94**   ▲ **Practice Book, p. 94**   ▲ **Challenge, p. 94**

ELL

- Group students according to academic levels and assign one of the pages on the left.

- Clarify any unfamiliar concepts as necessary. See *ELL Teacher Guide*, Lesson 11, for support in scaffolding instruction.

Grammar
Plural Nouns and Possessive Nouns

5-DAY GRAMMAR

DAY 1	Singular Possessive Nouns
DAY 2	Plural Possessive Nouns
DAY 3	**Plural Nouns and Possessive Nouns**
DAY 4	Apply to Writing
DAY 5	Possessive Nouns Review

Objectives

- *To identify plural nouns and plural possessive nouns*
- *To use plural possessive nouns correctly*

Daily Proofreading

1. my friend's comforted me (My friends; me.)
2. Where was that boys ball found. (boy's; found?)

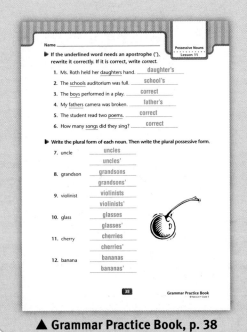

▲ Grammar Practice Book, p. 38

Teach/Model

DISCUSS PLURAL POSSESSIVE NOUNS Remind students that *plural* means "more than one." Then write the following sentence on the board:

The singer's songs were beautiful.

Tell students that this sentence refers to several songs, so an *s* has been added at the end of the word *song*. Remind students that the word *singer* is a singular noun. Circle the apostrophe in *singer's* and explain that the *'s* at the end of the word lets us know that the word is a singular possessive noun. Say: **Suppose I wanted to talk about the songs of more than one singer. I would write it this way:**

The singers' songs were beautiful.

Explain that when a noun is plural and already has an *s* at the end, you simply add an apostrophe.

Guided Practice

CORRECT PLURAL POSSESSIVE NOUNS Write the following sentence on the board:

All three campers backpacks were alike.

Explain that the noun *campers* is plural. Read the sentence aloud, guiding students to see that the noun *campers* needs to be possessive because the backpacks belong to three campers. On the board, help a volunteer add an apostrophe (') to make *campers'*.

Practice/Apply

WRITE PLURAL POSSESSIVES Read the following sentence aloud: **Her cousins' dogs are very cute.** Then have students write two sentences in their notebooks, one with a singular possessive noun and the other with a plural possessive noun. Have pairs check each other's work to make sure the plurals are spelled correctly.

5-DAY WRITING	
DAY 1	Introduce
DAY 2	Prewrite
DAY 3	**Draft**
DAY 4	Revise/Edit
DAY 5	Revise/Edit

Writing
Paragraph That Compares

Draft a Paragraph

INTRODUCE NEW CHARACTERISTICS Explain that a paragraph that compares should have key details about the things being compared. For example, a paragraph comparing fruits and vegetables would mention that both have colorful skins or peels, and that they are both healthful foods.

Paragraph That Compares

- Tells how two or more things are alike
- Has a topic sentence that tells what is being compared
- Uses signal words such as *both, alike,* and *same*
- Gives details of the things being compared

DRAFT A PARAGRAPH THAT COMPARES Have students use their lists from Day 2 to help them draft a paragraph that compares.

WRITING TRAIT **VOICE** As students write their drafts, remind them that they can let their feelings and ideas show in their writing by using words that express likes and dislikes.

CONFER WITH STUDENTS Support students as they write. As the class works, check in with individual students and offer encouragement for what they are doing well. Make constructive suggestions for improving an aspect of their writing, as needed. For example, point out places where they should make the comparison clearer.

Objectives

- *To recognize and understand paragraphs that compare*
- *To draft a paragraph that compares*

Writing Prompt

Comparison Have students write two or three sentences describing themselves at age five and now.

▲ Writer's Companion, Lesson 11

ADVANCED

Expand It Encourage students to write a paragraph comparing themselves and a friend or family member.

Day at a Glance

Day 4

 phonics and Spelling
- Review: VC-*le* Syllables

Fluency
- Expression
- "Loved Best," *Student Edition*, pp. 306, 314–315

Comprehension

Focus Skill
- Review: Plot
- Maintain: Use Alphabetical Order

Speaking/Listening/ Media Literacy
- Presentation of Posters
- Create a Poster

Robust Vocabulary
- Review: *swooned, astonished, encouraging, brief, chuckling, soothing, sobbed, praised, envious, rivalry*

Grammar
- Review: Possessive Nouns

Writing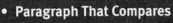
- Paragraph That Compares

Warm-Up Routines

 ## Oral Language

Objectives *To listen attentively and respond appropriately to oral communication; to write and speak in complete sentences*

> ### Question of the Day
>
> **Have you ever helped someone feel better? What happened?**

Talk with students about times when they have helped people who were upset or feeling bad about something. How did they know what was wrong? What did they do to help?

Tell students to suppose that a friend is very nervous about being in a show, performance, or sports contest. What might they do to help that friend feel better? Give students time to share their ideas before asking them to answer the following prompt in their notebooks:

> **If someone is feeling nervous,**
>
> **I can help by _____.**

Students should write 1 to 2 sentences about how they could help someone who is nervous. Invite volunteers to share their responses.

Read Aloud

Objectives *To listen to fiction for understanding and enjoyment; to emphasize fluency in reading*

READ ALOUD A STORY Display **Transparency R75** or distribute photocopies to students. Tell them they are going to hear the story "The Speech."

Set a purpose. Ask students what the purpose might be for reading a story that is similar to another story they have read. (Possible responses: to see how different characters deal with similar situations; for enjoyment)

Model fluent reading. Read the story aloud, pausing slightly at the ends of sentences and using appropriate voice inflection for the dialogue.

Discuss the story. Ask:

• **What is the story problem?**

• **In the story, how might Willie's mom have said "I'm not sure I can go through with it"? What emotion should you try to show in your voice?**

• **How does Willie try to help his mother?**

A Case of Nerves

Willie watched as his mother moved about the kitchen in a hurry. He could tell she was upset. She was so nervous she could not sit still or smile. When Willie asked what was wrong, she said, "I have to give a speech at work today. I haven't felt this nervous since my third grade play! I'm not sure I can go through with it."

Poor Mom, thought Willie. "Is your speech important?" he asked.

"Yes," she said. "That's why I'm so nervous. I'm supposed to be showing people how to use our new computer system. There will be real problems if people can't use it."

Willie thought about her words. "I remember when I had to recite a poem last year," he said. "I was so sure I was going to fall right off the stage. I was so scared I would forget the words that I could hardly walk. But you told me that all I had to do was to just think of one word at a time. I did fine. You will, too, Mom. Just take it one word at a time."

Willie watched his mother's face as a big smile grew. "You're absolutely right."

Grade 3, Lesson 11   **Rg**   Warm-Up: Days 4–5

Transparency R75

C-*le* Syllable
phonics

5-DAY PHONICS	
DAY 1	Introduce C-*le* Syllable
DAY 2	State the Generalization
DAY 3	VC-*le* and VCC-*le* Words
DAY 4	**VVC-*le* Words**
DAY 5	Review C-*le* Syllables

Objective

- *To read words with a vowel pair and final* -le

Skill Trace

Tested C-*le* Syllable

Introduce	T30
Reteach	S2
Review	T40–T41, T60, T76, T88, T384
Test	Theme 3
Maintain	Theme 4, T76, T260

C -*le* Syllable

Part A

beetle	needle	trouble
noodle	beagle	double

Part B

A <u>needle</u> can be very sharp. (nee/dle)

Sam took his <u>poodle</u> for a walk. (poo/dle)

This building has a tall <u>steeple</u>. (stee/ple)

We saw an <u>eagle</u> overhead. (ea/gle)

Grade 3, Lesson 11   Rh   Phonics: Day 4

Transparency R76

Review

READ WORDS WITH FINAL -*le* On the board, write the sentence *My uncle put the saddle and the bridle in the stable.* Have students locate the words that end with -*le* and tell how to divide them into syllables. (*un/cle, sad/dle, bri/dle, sta/ble*) Ask them which of these words have long vowel sounds and which have short vowel sounds. (long: *bridle, stable*; short: *uncle, saddle*)

un cle
sad dle
bri dle
sta ble

-*le* WORDS WITH TWO VOWELS
Display **Transparency R76.** Point to the word *beetle*. Ask where words with a vowel and a single consonant before -*le* are divided into syllables. (between the vowel and the consonant -*le*) Divide the word. Ask what vowel sound students expect in the first syllable. (long) Pronounce each syllable, and then blend the sounds to read *beetle*. Repeat with *needle*. Call students' attention to *trouble*, and point out that the letters *ou* in *trouble* stand for /u/.

Practice/Apply

GUIDED PRACTICE Point to *noodle, beagle,* and *double* on **Transparency R76.** Have students copy them in their notebooks. Then guide students to underline the vowel pairs and divide each word into syllables. Then have students read the words aloud.

INDEPENDENT PRACTICE Call attention to the sentences in Part B. Have students write the underlined words, circle the vowel pairs, and divide the word into syllables. Have students read the sentences aloud.

C-*le* Syllables
phonics *and Spelling*

5-DAY SPELLING

DAY 1	Pretest
DAY 2	State the Generalization
DAY 3	Spelling Practice/Handwriting
DAY 4	**Use Spelling Strategies/Review**
DAY 5	Posttest

Use Spelling Strategies

USE C-*le* PATTERNS Remind students that when they hear a two-syllable word ending with /əl/, they know the word most likely ends with -*le*. If they hear a long vowel sound in the first syllable, the word is spelled with one consonant letter before -*le*. Say *table* and write it on the board. Remind students that in some words that have a long vowel sound in the first syllable, the vowel sound is spelled with two vowel letters. Say *beetle* and write it on the board.

Remind students that if they hear a short vowel sound in the first syllable, they know the word most likely has two consonants before -*le*. Say *simple* and write it on the board. Point out that sometimes the two consonants are doubles and they will hear only one sound, but the short vowel sound will remind them to spell the word with two consonant letters. Say *scribble* and write it on the board.

APPLY TO WRITING Have students look through their own unedited writing for words ending in -*le*. Ask them to make sure that the word is spelled according to the rules they have learned. Ask them to fix any mistakes and check their respellings with a dictionary.

Objective

- *To use letter patterns with -le to spell and write words*

Spelling Words

1.	**title**	9.	**purple**
2.	**table**	10.	**little***
3.	**uncle**	11.	**middle**
4.	**apple**	12.	**simple**
5.	**cable**	13.	**saddle**
6.	**bubble**	14.	**trouble**
7.	**beetle**	15.	**scribble**
8.	**rattle**		

Challenge Words

16.	**twinkle**	19.	**buckled**
17.	**scrambled**	20.	**tablecloth**
18.	**sprinkle**		

*Word from "Loved Best"

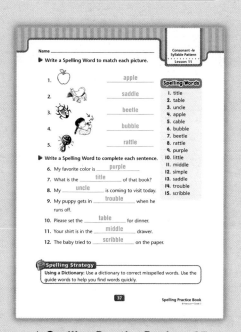

▲ Spelling Practice Book, p. 37

ADVANCED

Write a Story Have students write a story that uses as many words with final -*le* as possible. Permit students to use different forms of these words, such as *eagles* or *sizzled*. Remind them that the stories must make sense. Then have them check with a partner or a dictionary if they are not sure they have spelled each word correctly. Encourage students to share their stories.

eagles   sizzled

Fluency
Expression

Objectives

- *To build fluency by rereading a story*
- *To read with expression*
- *To read in a manner that sounds like natural speech*

 ### BELOW-LEVEL

Fluency Practice Before they read as part of a group, have students work in pairs to practice reading with expression. Have partners give each other tips on how to read with more expression.

 ### MONITOR PROGRESS

Fluency

IF students have trouble reading with expression,	**THEN** have them read aloud very softly, then loudly, in a high voice and a low voice.

Small-Group Instruction, p. S4:

- **BELOW-LEVEL:** Reteach
- **ON-LEVEL:** Reinforce
- **ADVANCED:** Extend

Review

DIBELS Oral Reading Fluency ORF

MODEL READING WITH EXPRESSION Remind students that, as they read, good readers vary the sound of their voices to show expression. Explain that, depending on what is happening in the selection, there are several things that readers can change in order to show expression. Discuss the following items:

▲ Student Edition, pp. 306–323

- tone of voice (soft, angry, firm, and so on)
- reading speed (slow, quick, and so on)
- volume (soft, loud, and so on)
- pitch (high voice, medium voice, or low voice)

Think Aloud As I read pages 318–319 of "Loved Best," I am going to change my voice so that the sound of the reading makes sense with what is going on in the story. I am going to read quietly when a character is speaking quietly. I will sound stern when someone is saying something that is serious. I will speed up my voice when something exciting is happening, and I will slow it down for parts that are quiet and slow.

MATCH THE TEXT Model a fluent reading of pages 318–319 from "Loved Best," having students track the print as you read. Then ask volunteers to read the pages, each one reading two or three sentences.

Practice/Apply

REPEATED READING Organize students into small groups, assigning the members of each group paragraphs on pages 318–319 of "Loved Best" to read. Have students read their assigned paragraphs several times, making sure that they change tone of voice, speed, volume, and pitch to match the text. Then have group members read the passage together.

Plot
Comprehension

Review

EXPLAIN PLOT Ask students to explain what the plot of a story is. (the events that take place, including the problem and the solution to the problem) Remind students that good readers pay attention to the problems and the events that lead to a solution of those problems.

Practice/Apply

GUIDED PRACTICE Display **Transparency R69.** Have students reread the passage to determine the plot of the story. Ask:

- **What is the problem in the story?** (Vonya is nervous about singing in front of an audience.)

- **What are the important events in the story?** (Vonya wakes up feeling nervous, she talks with her mother about it, and her mother gives her some advice.)

- **How is the problem solved in the story?** (Vonya practices, which calms her and makes her feel less nervous and more confident.)

INDEPENDENT PRACTICE Have students reread the introduction of "Loved Best" on page 307. Ask what problem Carolyn has. (She wants her parents to love her best.) Ask what Carolyn thinks will fix this problem. (Her parents will see how wonderful she is in the play and will love her best.) Ask what the solution is to the problem. (Carolyn's parents love Carolyn, her brother, and her sister equally. They cannot love one of them more.)

Objectives
- *To review the features of plot*
- *To identify plot in a selection*

Skill Trace
 Plot

Introduce	T32–T33
Reteach	S6
Review	T63, T79, T91, T128–T129, T161, T177, T189, T387, T402
Test	Theme 3
Maintain	Theme 4, T80

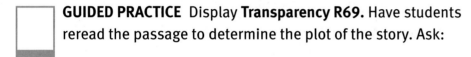

The Speech

Vonya woke up with her stomach doing flip flops. It felt like something was fluttering around inside her! "Mom!" she called. "I don't feel good."

Vonya's mother came to the bed, leaned down, and asked what was the matter.

"I don't know," said the girl. "I woke up thinking about the talent show. It's today, and I'm going to have to sing in front of a hundred people. All of a sudden my stomach feels AWFUL!"

With a smile, her mother patted Vonya's hand. "You're just nervous. Those are only butterflies in your stomach. It's a feeling some people have when they are nervous. Don't worry. Just practice your song while you get dressed. Keep practicing whenever you have a chance, even if it's only in your head. You'll be fine."

"Really?" Vonya asked. Before her feet were on the floor, the words of the song formed in her mind. Then, singing, she walked out of her room. She would be fine. The noise from her singing was sure to make those little butterflies go away!

Grade 3, Lesson 11   Ro   Warm-Up: Day 1

Transparency R69

Use Alphabetical Order

Objective

• *To use alphabetical order to organize words*

Skill Trace

 Tested **Use Alphabetical Order**

Introduce	Theme 1, T66–T67
Reteach	Theme 1, S8, S20
Review	Theme 1, T162–T163
Test	Theme 1
Maintain	Theme 3, T80

Reinforce the Skill

REVIEW ALPHABETICAL ORDER Remind students that information is often arranged in the order of the letters of the alphabet, from A to Z. Review how to look for a word in a dictionary or a topic in an encyclopedia.

Tell students that organizing words in alphabetical order is called *alphabetizing*. When alphabetizing a group of words, students should look at the first letter of each word and think about the order of the alphabet. If more than one word begins with the same letter, they should look at the second letter, third letter, or more, all the way through the word.

Think Aloud As I compare two or more words that start with the same letter or letters, I look for the first letter in each word that is different. Then I check the alphabet in my head and decide which letter comes first.

Practice/Apply

GUIDED PRACTICE Write the following words on the board:

pencil   peel   peak

Guide students to find the first letter that is different in each word. Have them circle those letters. (the third; *n, e, a*) Then ask volunteers to name the words in aphabetical order. (peak, peel, pencil)

INDEPENDENT PRACTICE Write these words on the board:

whose   whine   what   when

Have students copy the words in their notebooks. Then ask them to circle the first letter that is different in each word before writing the words in alphabetical order.

Speaking and Listening
Presentation of Posters

Speaking

PLAN A PERFORMANCE Remind students of the play performance in which Carolyn and her brother and sister took part. Invite students to work in small groups to brainstorm ideas for a class performance. Then have individuals create a poster for the class show.

DELIVER A PRESENTATION Have students display and tell about their posters. Encourage them to speak naturally, as if they were talking with their friends.

ORGANIZING CONTENT

- Make notes of two or three important points you want to share.

- Plan an introduction and a concluding sentence.

Before students make their presentations, share the **speaking strategies** at the right. After students make their presentations, encourage audience members to ask questions.

Listening

PAY ATTENTION Share the **listening strategies** with students. Then have them listen carefully to the presentations. Invite them to use the strategies to find clues to how the speaker feels about things he or she is comparing.

Invite volunteers to state facts heard in the presentation and identify the speaker's opinions. Remind students that listeners often can tell how speakers feel by how they present facts and information.

See rubrics for Speaking and Listening on page R5.

Media Literacy

REVIEW POSTERS Display posters or advertisements for various local events. Call attention to the essential parts—date, time, and location of each event. Then discuss with students how the people who made the announcement made the event appealing.

Objectives

- *To deliver a presentation*
- *To pay attention to the speaker*
- *To know personal listening preferences*

SPEAKING STRATEGIES

- Use your voice to share your opinion.
- Speak loudly to be heard across the room.
- Speak as if you are talking to a friend.
- Look at the audience.
- Use your face and hands to show how you feel.

LISTENING STRATEGIES

- Pay attention throughout the presentation.
- Listen for the speaker's tone of voice.
- Watch the speaker's movements and facial expressions.

Build Robust Vocabulary

Objectives

- *To review robust vocabulary*
- *To demonstrate knowledge of word meaning*

REVIEW | Tested ✓

Vocabulary: Lesson 11

swooned	soothing
astonished	sobbed
encouraging	praised
brief	envious
chuckling	rivalry

Extend Word Meanings

USE VOCABULARY IN DIFFERENT CONTEXTS Remind students of the meanings of the Vocabulary Words. Then discuss the words with students in a new context.

swooned/astonished Have students place their hands over their open mouth if they hear about something that would leave them astonished and swooning. Have them pretend to yawn if they would not be astonished.

winning a prize	**a surprise party for you**
seeing a talking dog	**feeding ducks**

envious Tell students that if the situation you name would make them envious, they should nod their heads *yes*. If it would not, have them shake their heads *no*.

someone else's getting the largest piece of pizza

your best friend getting a newer, better scooter

you getting a pizza all to yourself

you and your family going on a picnic

rivalry Tell students to say *rivalry* when they hear something that sounds like a rivalry.

each brother thinking he's the best ballplayer

you going grocery-shopping

two teams competing once a year

your best friend liking your shirt

praised/encouraging Tell students that if the situation you name would be a good time for encouraging praise, they should clap once. If it is not, they should do nothing.

almost scoring a goal	**falling while in a race**
doing something naughty	**spelling all the words right**

Word Relationships

ANTONYMS Remind students that antonyms are words with opposite meanings. Write the Vocabulary Words on the board, and have students write them. Have students suggest antonyms for as many of the Vocabulary Words as possible.

praised (scolded)

rivalry (friendship)

sobbed (laughed)

brief (long)

soothing (irritating)

encouraging (discouraging)

chuckling (crying)

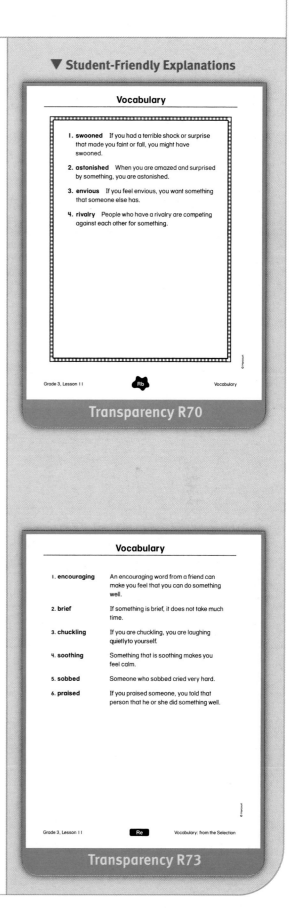

▼ **Student-Friendly Explanations**

Vocabulary

1. **swooned** If you had a terrible shock or surprise that made you faint or fall, you might have swooned.

2. **astonished** When you are amazed and surprised by something, you are astonished.

3. **envious** If you feel envious, you want something that someone else has.

4. **rivalry** People who have a rivalry are competing against each other for something.

Grade 3, Lesson 11   Rb   Vocabulary

Transparency R70

Vocabulary

1. **encouraging** An encouraging word from a friend can make you feel that you can do something well.

2. **brief** If something is brief, it does not take much time.

3. **chuckling** If you are chuckling, you are laughing quietly to yourself.

4. **soothing** Something that is soothing makes you feel calm.

5. **sobbed** Someone who sobbed cried very hard.

6. **praised** If you praised someone, you told that person that he or she did something well.

Grade 3, Lesson 11   Re   Vocabulary: from the Selection

Transparency R73

Grammar
Possessive Nouns

5-DAY GRAMMAR

DAY 1	Singular Possessive Nouns
DAY 2	Plural Possessive Nouns
DAY 3	Plural Nouns and Possessive Nouns
DAY 4	**Apply to Writing**
DAY 5	Possessive Nouns Review

Objectives

- *To use singular possessive nouns correctly in writing*
- *To use plural possessive nouns correctly in writing*

Daily Proofreading

1. Matts favorite holiday is july 4th. (Matt's; July)
2. we can polish all the girls shoes. (We; girl's)

▲ **Grammar Practice Book, p. 39**

Review

DISCUSS SINGULAR AND PLURAL POSSESSIVE NOUNS Review that a possessive noun shows ownership. Remind students that a singular noun names one person, place, thing, or animal. A plural noun names more than one. Tell students that there are two primary rules for writing singular and plural possessive nouns:

- To make a singular noun possessive, add an apostrophe (') and the letter *s* ('s).

- For plural nouns that end in *s*, make them possessive by adding just an apostrophe (') after the *s*.

Practice/Apply

GUIDED PRACTICE Write the following words on the board:

dog

baseball player

Next to the first word, write *dog's,* explaining that this is the singular possessive form. Then have a volunteer write the word *dogs',* guiding students to understand that this is the plural possessive form of the word. Guide students to do the same thing with *baseball player.* (baseball player's; baseball players')

INDEPENDENT PRACTICE Ask students to think of several items from home. Have students write two sentences describing those objects, using at least one singular possessive noun (Possible response: sister's doll) and one plural possessive noun (Possible response: cats' food). Have students share their sentences with a partner.

5-DAY WRITING	
DAY 1	Introduce
DAY 2	Prewrite
DAY 3	Draft
DAY 4	**Revise/Edit**
DAY 5	Revise/Edit

Writing
Paragraph That Compares

Write a Paragraph

WRITE Have students continue writing a paragraph that compares. Explain that they will be able to revise their writing during today's lesson. Tell students that, as they revise, they should make sure they have included details that help show how the things are alike. Explain that their paragraph should conclude with a sentence that sums up the comparison in an interesting way. Tell them to work on that final sentence as they revise their work.

> ## Paragraph That Compares
>
> - Has a topic sentence that tells what is being compared.
> - Tells how two or more things are alike.
> - Uses signal words such as *both, alike,* and *same* to show similarities.
> - Gives details of the things being compared.
> - Sums up the main idea at the end.

VOICE Remind students that they can use positive and negative words to make their own voice clear in the paragraph.

REVISE Have students read their drafts to a partner. Explain that partners should check that they can understand which two things are being compared and what makes them similar. The checklist can help students make sure their paragraphs have all the correct elements.

Give students time to finish their paragraph and revise it. When students are done, have them look carefully for singular possessive and plural possessive nouns and make sure that they have been used correctly. Tell students to keep their writing to revise further and edit on Day 5.

Objectives

- *To revise a paragraph that compares*
- *To reveal voice in writing*

Writing Prompt

Comparison Write a paragraph that shows the similarities between reindeer and elephants.

BELOW-LEVEL

Revising Aloud If students have trouble identifying editing changes that need to be made, encourage them to read the paragraph aloud, very slowly, tracking each word with a pencil.

Day at a Glance

Day 5

 **phonics** and Spelling

- Review: C-*le* Syllables
- Posttest: Words with C-*le* Syllables

Fluency

- Expression
- "Loved Best," *Student Edition*, pp. 306–323

 Read!

Comprehension

 Focus Skill • Review: Plot

- *Read-Aloud Anthology*, "Evie and Margie"

Robust Vocabulary

- Cumulative Review

Grammar

- Review: Possessive Nouns

Writing

- Paragraph That Compares

Warm-Up Routines

Oral Language

Objectives *To listen attentively and respond appropriately to oral communication; to write and speak in complete sentences*

Question of the Day

What have you done that, at first, you thought you couldn't do?

Ask students if they ever accomplished something they had thought was impossible, such as playing a musical instrument, doing something in sports, or playing a certain kind of game. Give students time to share experiences. Then ask: **How were you able to do this?** If necessary, remind students that practice and help from others often can lead people to succeed at difficult things. Encourage students to share examples.

When several ideas have been shared, ask students to use their notebooks to write two or three sentences in response to the following writing prompt:

I really surprised myself by _____.

Invite volunteers to present their ideas.

Read Aloud

Objectives *To read fluently; to read fiction for understanding and enjoyment*

Use the following steps to share the passage with students:

REVIEW THE STORY Display **Transparency R75** or distribute photocopies to students. Tell them that you are going to reread the story about Willie and his mother.

Set a purpose. Ask students what the purpose might be for reading or listening to a story again. (to enjoy; to understand details better) Tell students they will be listening and following along in order to enjoy the story. Then they will read with a partner to practice reading fluently.

Model fluent reading. Read the story aloud, using expression.

Partner reading. In pairs, have one student reread the story while the other follows along and provides assistance and feedback about fluency. Then have partners switch and repeat the reading.

A Case of Nerves

Willie watched as his mother moved about the kitchen in a hurry. He could tell she was upset. She was so nervous she could not sit still or smile. When Willie asked what was wrong, she said, "I have to give a speech at work today. I haven't felt this nervous since my third grade play! I'm not sure I can go through with it."

Poor Mom, thought Willie. "Is your speech important?" he asked.

"Yes," she said. "That's why I'm so nervous. I'm supposed to be showing people how to use our new computer system. There will be real problems if people can't use it."

Willie thought about her words. "I remember when I had to recite a poem last year," he said. "I was sure I was going to fall right off the stage. I was so scared I would forget the words that I could hardly walk. But you told me that all I had to do was to just think of one word at a time. I did fine. You will, too, Mom. Just take it one word at a time."

Willie watched his mother's face as a big smile grew. "You're absolutely right."

Grade 3, Lesson 11 | Rg | Warm-Up: Days 4–5

Transparency R75

C-*le* Syllables

phonics

5-DAY PHONICS	
DAY 1	Introduce C-*le* Syllables
DAY 2	State the Generalization
DAY 3	VC-*le* and VCC-*le* Words
DAY 4	VVC-*le* Words
DAY 5	Review C-*le* Syllable

Objectives

- *To read words with final* -le
- *To spell words with final* -le

Skill Trace

 Tested C-*le* Syllables

Introduce	T30
Reteach	S2
Review	T40–T41, T60, T76, T88, T384
Test	Theme 3
Maintain	Theme 4, T76, T260

Review

C-*le* PATTERN Write the words *pebble, tumble,* and *gentle* on the board. Ask students what sound -*le* stands for in these words. (/əl/) Review that the words are divided into syllables so that a consonant and -*le* form the final syllable. Have volunteers come to the board to divide the words into syllables. (peb/ble, tum/ble, gen/tle) Remind students that when there are two consonants before the letters -*le*, the vowel sound in the first syllable is short. Then have students read the words aloud.

peb ble   tum ble   gen tle

Write the words *noble, staple, bugle,* and *eagle* on the board. Have volunteers come to the board to divide the words into syllables. (no/ble, sta/ple, bu/gle, ea/gle) Remind students that when there is one consonant before -*le*, the vowel sound in the first syllable is long. Then have students read the words aloud.

no/ble
sta/ple
bu/gle
ea/gle

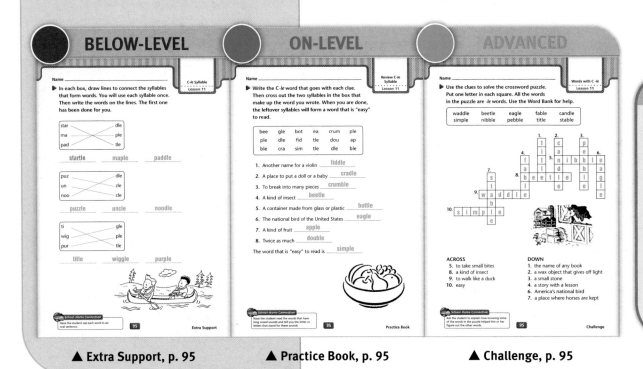

BELOW-LEVEL   **ON-LEVEL**   **ADVANCED**

▲ **Extra Support, p. 95**   ▲ **Practice Book, p. 95**   ▲ **Challenge, p. 95**

E L L

- Group students according to academic levels, and assign one of the pages on the left.

- Clarify any unfamiliar concepts as necessary. See *ELL Teacher Guide* Lesson 11 for support in scaffolding instruction.

 # C-*le* Syllables
phonics *and Spelling*

5-DAY SPELLING
DAY 1	Pretest
DAY 2	State the Generalization
DAY 3	Spelling Practice/Handwriting
DAY 4	Use Spelling Strategies/Review
DAY 5	Posttest

Assess

POSTTEST To assess students' progress in spelling, use the dictation sentences from Day 1.

Words with Final -*le*

1. title — Tell me the **title** of the book you are reading.
2. table — Sara set the **table** for dinner last night.
3. uncle — Seema's **uncle** lives in Ohio.
4. apple — You can see the seeds if you cut an **apple** in half.
5. cable — A thick, strong wire is called a **cable**.
6. bubble — Inés bought some **bubble** gum.
7. beetle — There was a big red **beetle** on the tree.
8. rattle — Have you ever seen a baby playing with a **rattle**?
9. purple — Denison's favorite color is **purple**.
10. little — An elephant is big, but a mouse is **little**.
11. middle — Erik sat in the **middle** of the bench.
12. simple — It is **simple** to add 2 and 2!
13. saddle — Jovan fastened the **saddle** around the horse.
14. trouble — Jake got in **trouble** when he ran in the halls.
15. scribble — Small children like to **scribble** with crayons.

✏️ **WRITING APPLICATION** Instruct students to write a paragraph using eight spelling words of their choosing.

Objective
• *To spell words with final* le

Spelling Words
1.	**title**	9.	**purple**
2.	**table**	10.	**little***
3.	**uncle**	11.	**middle**
4.	**apple**	12.	**simple**
5.	**cable**	13.	**saddle**
6.	**bubble**	14.	**trouble**
7.	**beetle**	15.	**scribble**
8.	**rattle**		

Challenge Words
16.	**twinkle**	19.	**buckled**
17.	**scrambled**	20.	**tablecloth**
18.	**sprinkle**		

*Word from "Loved Best"

ADVANCED

Challenge Words Use these dictation sentences.
16. twinkle — The stars seem to **twinkle** in the night sky.
17. scrambled — My favorite breakfast is **scrambled** eggs.
18. sprinkle — I always **sprinkle** cheese on top of pasta.
19. buckled — I **buckled** my belt around my waist.
20. tablecloth — The **tablecloth** got dirty when I spilled food.

Fluency
Expression

Objectives

- *To read fluently with expression*
- *To speak to or perform for an audience*

ASSESSMENT

Monitoring Progress Periodically, take a timed sample of students' oral reading and measure the number of words read correctly per minute. Students should be accurately reading approximately 92 words per minute in the middle of Grade 3.

Fluency Support Materials

 Fluency Builders, Grade 3, Lesson 11

 Audiotext *Student Edition* selections are available on *Audiotext 3*.

 **Strategic Intervention Teacher Guide, Lesson 11**

Readers' Theater

 DIBELS Oral Reading Fluency **ORF**

PERFORM "LOVED BEST" To help students improve their fluency, have them perform "Loved Best" as Readers' Theater. Use the following steps:

▲ Student Edition, pp. 306–323

- Discuss how the characters might act and sound in different parts of the story.

- Discuss the parts of the story without dialogue, and explain that readers can still use expression to reinforce what is happening in the text.

- Read "Loved Best" aloud, modeling fluent and expressive reading as students follow along.

- Put students in groups and have each group member choose a character or one part of the narration. Students reading minor characters might want to double up on parts. Have individuals practice rereading their parts before practicing in a group.

- Listen to the groups read. Provide feedback and support.

- Invite groups to read the story to their classmates. Remind them to focus on reading with expression.

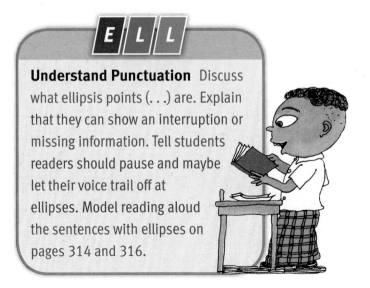

ELL

Understand Punctuation Discuss what ellipsis points (. . .) are. Explain that they can show an interruption or missing information. Tell students readers should pause and maybe let their voice trail off at ellipses. Model reading aloud the sentences with ellipses on pages 314 and 316.

Plot
Comprehension

Review

REVIEW THE SKILL Ask students what the plot of a story is. (the events that happen; usually includes a problem and its solution)

USE PRIOR KNOWLEDGE/SET A PURPOSE Tell students to listen for the problem and solution as you reread "Evie and Margie." Guide students to use prior knowledge and set a purpose for listening.

▲ Read-Aloud Anthology, "Evie and Margie," p. 38

Practice/Apply

GUIDED PRACTICE Monitor listening comprehension as you read, using the following questions:

- **What is the main problem in the story?** (Evie and Margie both want to be Cinderella in the play.)

- **How is the problem solved?** (Evie gets to perform as an understudy, and Margie gets to do another performance.)

INDEPENDENT PRACTICE Create a graphic organizer for students to map the plot of the story. Have students fill it in.

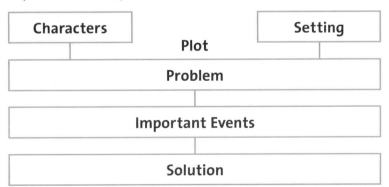

Objectives

- *To review plot*
- *To represent plot with a graphic organizer*

Skill Trace

 Plot

Introduce	T32–T33
Reteach	S6
Review	T63, T79, T91, T128–T129, T161, T177, T189, T387, T402
Test	Theme 3
Maintain	Theme 4, T80

E L L

Act It Out To help students understand what happens and why, give them the chance to act out the story in small groups. Remind students that the main events make up the story's plot.

Build Robust Vocabulary

Objective
• *To review robust vocabulary*

REVIEW **Tested** ✓

Vocabulary

Lesson 10	Lesson 11
inviting	swooned
amusing	astonished
investigate	encouraging
expert	brief
laboratory	chuckling
various	soothing
suspect	sobbed
confess	praised
perplexed	envious
inquisitive	rivalry

Cumulative Review

MAKE WORD WEBS Guide students to complete word webs to enhance their understanding of *swooned, sobbed,* and *envious.* Draw a word web on the board with *swooned* in the center oval. Have students suggest situations in which someone might have swooned. Write their responses in the word web. You might want to offer a suggestion to get them started.

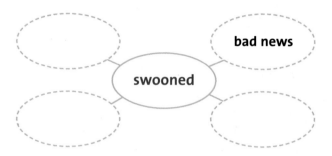

Have students create their own webs for *sobbed.* After they write *sobbed* in the center, ask students to think of reasons someone might have sobbed. Then, in the surrounding ovals, have them write the reasons. Continue in the same manner with *envious.* Ask students to make word webs that show different reasons someone might feel envious.

REVIEW VOCABULARY Discuss students' answers to these questions.

1. Would it be unusual if someone began **chuckling** when you said something **amusing**? Why or why not?

2. Why would you be **astonished** if you learned that someone was **inviting** five hundred people to your birthday party?

3. When might a scientist be **praised** for work done in a **laboratory**?

4. If a friend of yours **swooned**, would you be **inquisitive** about what happened?

5. If you heard a strange noise outside, would you **investigate** it, or would you ignore it after a **brief** moment or two? Explain.

6. If two people argued all the time, would you **suspect** that there was a **rivalry** between them? Why or why not?

7. What **encouraging** news might an **expert** in science want to hear?

8. Would you be **perplexed** if someone in your family **sobbed** again and again? Why or why not?

✓ MONITOR PROGRESS

Build Robust Vocabulary

IF students have difficulty understanding the vocabulary words,	**THEN** have them look the words up in a dictionary and copy the definitions.

Small-Group Instruction, p. S10:

● **BELOW-LEVEL:** Reteach

● **ON-LEVEL:** Reinforce

● **ADVANCED:** Extend

Grammar
Possessive Noun Review

5-DAY GRAMMAR

DAY 1	Singular Possessive Nouns
DAY 2	Plural Possessive Nouns
DAY 3	Plural Nouns and Possessive Nouns
DAY 4	Apply to Writing
DAY 5	Possessive Nouns Review

Objectives

- *To recognize singular and plural possessive nouns*
- *To use singular and plural possessive nouns correctly*

Daily Proofreading

1. older children should be kind to younger one's. (Older; ones)
2. will you help me with my homework. (Will; homework?)

✔ LANGUAGE ARTS CHECKPOINT

If students have difficulty with the concepts, see pages S12–S13 to reteach.

▲ Grammar Practice Book, p. 40

Review

REVIEW SINGULAR AND PLURAL POSSESSIVE NOUNS Review the rules for singular and plural possessive nouns:

- To make a singular possessive noun, add an apostrophe (') and the letter *s* ('s) at the end of a singular noun.

- For plural nouns that end in *s,* add an apostrophe (') at the end of the plural noun to make a possessive noun.

Practice/Apply

GUIDED PRACTICE Write the following phrases on the board and point to the first one:

my uncle house

my uncles house

Guide students in adding an apostrophe (') and an *s* to the word *uncle* in the first phrase to show a singular possessive noun. (uncle's) Then elicit that an apostrophe is needed in the second phrase to make *uncles* a plural possessive noun. (uncles')

INDEPENDENT PRACTICE On the board, write the following sentences:

The frogs lives were in danger.

The dancers leg was broken.

Have students rewrite the sentences, correcting the possessive form by adding apostrophes where appropriate. (frogs'; dancer's)

5-DAY WRITING	
DAY 1	Introduce
DAY 2	Prewrite
DAY 3	Draft
DAY 4	Revise/Edit
DAY 5	Revise/Edit

Writing
Paragraph That Compares

Revise/Edit

PRACTICE EDITING Encourage students to use editing marks as they revise their writing.

Editor's Marks	
∧	Add
⅄	Take out
⌿	Change
⌄	Add a period
⊙	Capitalize

Share

REVISE AND SHARE PARAGRAPHS Have pairs or small groups read each other's work. Tell students to use the characteristics of paragraphs that compare as a checklist. Have students also review for correct use of possessive nouns. Then have students revise their paragraphs. Tell them to keep their writing in their work portfolios.

Objective

- *To revise and reflect on a paragraph that compares*

Writing Prompt

Self-Selected Writing Have students generate a list of ideas about a new topic of their choice for writing.

WEEKLY LESSON TEST

▲ Weekly Lesson Tests, Lesson 11

- Selection Comprehension
- and Spelling
- Focus Skill
- Use Context Clues
- Robust Vocabulary
- Grammar
- Fluency Passage **FRESH READS**

 For prescriptions, see p. A2. Also available electronically on StoryTown Online Assessment and ExamView.

SCORING RUBRIC

	6	5	4	3	2	1
FOCUS	Completely focused, purposeful.	Focused on topic and purpose.	Generally focused on topic and purpose.	Somewhat focused on topic and purpose.	Related to topic but does not maintain focus.	Lacks focus and purpose.
ORGANIZATION	Ideas progress logically; paper conveys sense of completeness.	Organization mostly clear, paper gives sense of completeness.	Organization mostly clear, but some lapses occur; may seem unfinished.	Some sense of organization; seems unfinished.	Little sense of organization.	Little or no sense of organization.
SUPPORT	Strong, specific details; clear, exact language; freshness of expression.	Strong, specific details; clear, exact language.	Adequate support and word choice.	Limited supporting details; limited word choice.	Few supporting details; limited word choice.	Little development, limited or unclear word choice.
CONVENTIONS	Varied sentences; few, if any, errors.	Varied sentences; few errors.	Some sentence variety; few errors.	Simple sentence structures; some errors.	Simple sentence structures; many errors.	Unclear sentence structures; many errors.

REPRODUCIBLE STUDENT RUBRICS for specific writing purposes and presentations are available on pages R5–R8.

Leveled Readers
Reinforcing Skills and Strategies

Felix's Turn

by Jason Plummer
illustrated by Doreen Gay-Kassel

Genre: Realistic Fiction

BELOW-LEVEL

Felix's Turn

SUMMARY A boy is jealous of his older brother's many awards. When he enters a spelling bee, he has a chance to finally win an award himself.

 Plot

 Use Story Structure

- **ROBUST VOCABULARY:**
encouraging, brief, chuckling, soothing, sobbed, praised

Before Reading

BUILD BACKGROUND/SET PURPOSE Have students share any experiences of feeling jealous about the accomplishments of a brother, sister, or friend. Next, ask students to talk about any trophies or awards they have won. Then guide students to preview the story and set a purpose for reading.

Reading the Book

PAGES 3–4 DRAW CONCLUSIONS, CHARACTERS' EMOTIONS What is bothering Felix? (Possible response: He is jealous of Hector's awards.)

PAGE 7 PLOT What can Felix do that Hector cannot do? (Possible response: Felix can speak in front of people.)

PAGE 8 MAKE PREDICTIONS Do you think Felix will win the spelling bee? Explain. (Possible response: Yes, because he studied very hard.)

REREAD FOR FLUENCY Have students form small groups and take turns reading a page aloud and practicing their expression.

Think Critically *(See inside back cover for questions.)*

1 **PLOT** Felix wishes he could win awards like his brother Hector.

2 **CHARACTER TRAITS** Felix is a little bit competitive with his brother but also very hard working and he has a sense of humor.

3 **DRAW CONCLUSIONS** He often feels jealous of Hector.

4 **EXPRESS PERSONAL OPINIONS** I would have had Felix win the spelling bee.

5 **EXPRESS PERSONAL OPINIONS** Accept reasonable responses.

LEVELED READER TEACHER GUIDE

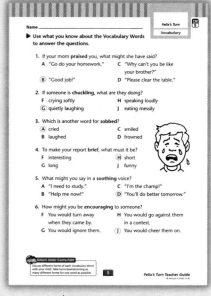

▲ Vocabulary, p. 5

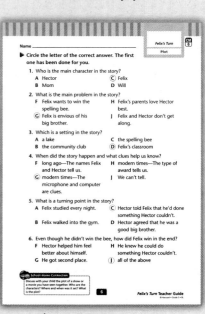

▲ Comprehension, p. 6

Genre: Realistic Fiction

ON-LEVEL

The Battle for Aunt Jane

SUMMARY A brother and sister, Chris and Olivia, compete for their Aunt Jane's attention. They get angry with each other and argue.

 Plot

 Use Story Structure

• **ROBUST VOCABULARY:**
encouraging, brief, chuckling, soothing, sobbed, praised

Before Reading

BUILD BACKGROUND/SET PURPOSE Have students think of a time when they wanted to impress an adult. How did they act? What happened? Then guide students to preview the story and set a purpose for reading.

Reading the Book

PAGES 5–6 MAIN IDEA Why are Olivia and Chris competing for Aunt Jane's attention? (They both want to be her favorite; she is a cool aunt.)

PAGE 7 CHARACTERS' MOTIVATIONS Why do Chris and Olivia ruin each other's gifts to Aunt Jane? (They are jealous and want to impress their aunt.)

PAGE 8 PLOT What does Aunt Jane say about the ruined presents? ("Perhaps we can fix these when we get home.")

REREAD FOR FLUENCY Have partners read their favorite pages aloud, making sure to express how the characters might act and feel.

Think Critically *(See inside back cover for questions.)*

1. **PLOT** Chris and Olivia compete for her attention.

2. **STORY EVENTS** when Chris is unhappy because Olivia made Aunt Jane breakfast.

3. **CHARACTERS' EMOTIONS** She tries to be fair to both.

4. **DRAW CONCLUSIONS** He wants to make Olivia think her idea is bad.

5. **EXPRESS PERSONAL OPINIONS** Possible response: Yes, they both do good things for her and she has no reason to love one less than the other.

LEVELED READER TEACHER GUIDE

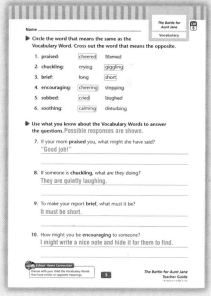

▲ Vocabulary, p. 5

▲ Comprehension, p. 6

Leveled Readers
Reinforcing Skills and Strategies

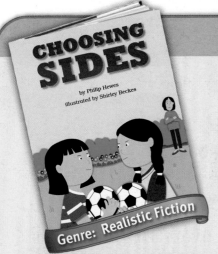

 **ADVANCED**

Choosing Sides

SUMMARY Two sisters discover that their soccer teams will play each other in the championship game. The younger sister wants their mom to root for her.

 Plot

 Use Story Structure

- **ROBUST VOCABULARY:** *encouraging, brief, chuckling, soothing, sobbed, praised*

LEVELED READER TEACHER GUIDE

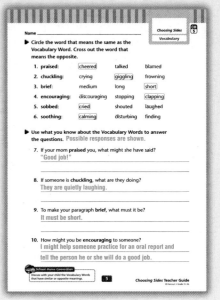

▲ Vocabulary, p. 5

Before Reading

BUILD BACKGROUND/SET PURPOSE Have students talk about what it is like to compete against a brother, sister, or friend. Then guide students to preview the story and set a purpose for reading.

Reading the Book

PAGE 5 PLOT What is the problem between Alison and Sarah? (Possible response: They are very competitive and both want to win.) **How can they both be winners?** (Possible response: by playing their best)

PAGE 8 MAKE JUDGMENTS Are Alison and Sarah like brothers or sisters you know? How? (Possible response: Yes, brothers and sisters argue but also love each other.)

REREAD FOR FLUENCY Have partners take turns reading pages aloud, changing their voice to add expression and to show what is happening in the story.

Think Critically   *(See inside back cover for questions.)*

1. **PLOT** The girls realize they will be playing against each other.

2. **IMPORTANT DETAILS** Sarah's team

3. **CHARACTERS' TRAITS** Possible response: She's very competitive and likes to win.

4. **DRAW CONCLUSIONS** Possible response: Yes, the story mentions that they usually play together, and they both seem to feel bad about fighting.

5. **EXPRESS PERSONAL OPINIONS** Possible response: Yes, I do. Sarah has already won and seems confident enough.

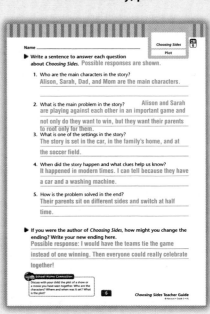

▲ Comprehension, p. 6

www.harcourtschool.com/storytown

★ Leveled Readers, online:
Searchable by Genre, Skill, Vocabulary, Level, or Title
★ Student Activities and Teacher Resources, online

E L L

Genre: Realistic Fiction

Baby Brother

SUMMARY A brother and sister wait for their new baby brother to come home from the hospital. The sister expects that everything will change and she will not get any attention.

- Build Background
- Concept Vocabulary
- Scaffolded Language Development

Before Reading

BUILD BACKGROUND/SET PURPOSE Have students discuss how the arrival of a new baby brother or sister would change their lives. What would they have to do differently? What new responsibilities would they have? How would it be fun? Then guide students to preview the story and set a purpose for reading.

Reading the Book

PAGES 3–4 DRAW CONCLUSIONS Why do you think Elena is so unhappy about the new baby? (Possible response: She is worried a new baby will get all the attention.)

PAGES 10–11 MAKE COMPARISONS How are Elena's and Victor's feelings about the baby different? (Possible response: Elena does not want to lose the attention of her parents by having another brother. Victor is excited to be a big brother.)

REREAD FOR FLUENCY Have partners search for parts in which the characters are speaking. Students should read what they say and decide if the character is happy or angry. Then they should practice reading so that they sound like a happy or angry person.

Scaffolded Language Development

(See inside back cover for teacher-led activity.)

Provide additional examples and explanation as needed.

LEVELED READER TEACHER GUIDE

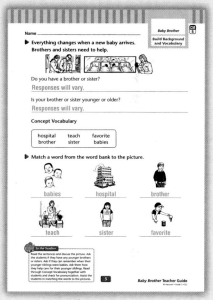

▲ Build Background, p. 5

▲ Scaffolded Language Development, p. 6

THEME WRITING OVERVIEW

Reading-Writing Connection ➤ Friendly Letter

LESSON	FORM	TRAIT
11	Paragraph that Compares	Voice
12	Realistic Story	Voice
13	Explanation	Sentence Fluency
14	Cause and Effect	Sentence Fluency
15	Student Choice: Revise and Publish	Voice and Sentence Fluency

Reading-Writing Connection

Friendly Letter

Focus on

Voice and Sentence Fluency

Students will

- Use a literature model to generate ideas

- Select a topic

- Plan and draft a friendly letter

- Revise the letter for voice by adding interesting words and phrases

- Revise the letter by elaborating and enhancing sentence fluency

- Publish a final version of the friendly letter

Set the Stage
Friendly Letter

Objectives

- *To recognize the purposes for writing a letter*
- *To identify the parts of a friendly letter*
- *To recognize possible audiences of a friendly letter*
- *To generate ideas for writing a friendly letter*

Introduce the Writing Form

TALK ABOUT FRIENDLY LETTERS Tell students that throughout this theme, they will be learning how to write a friendly letter. Ask students whom their audience might be if they wrote a friendly letter. (Possible responses: friend, family member, pen pal) Ask what the purpose might be for writing a friendly letter. (Possible responses: to tell what you have been doing; to share information; to thank someone; to invite someone to an event) Remind students of the characteristics of a friendly letter by saying the following:

Think Aloud Think about when we read "The Sunset in My Mailbox." In this story, Julien wrote several friendly letters to Caitlin. These letters had a greeting, body, closing, and signature. These are important parts of a friendly letter.

▲ Read-Aloud Anthology, "The Sunset in My Mailbox," pp. 44–47

STAGES OF THE WRITING PROCESS Adjust the pacing to meet students' needs. Guide them back and forth between the stages until the final product meets established criteria.

PREWRITE, p. T106	DRAFT, p. T107
Writing Trait ▸ Voice	**Writing Trait ▸ Sentence Fluency**
• Writing About What Interests You • Matching Voice to Audience and Purpose	• Sentence Variety (Length) • Avoid *I, I, I*

Use Text as a Model

DISCUSS PARTS OF A FRIENDLY LETTER Tell students that you will reread the letters in "The Sunset in My Mailbox" aloud. Ask them to pay attention to the parts of a letter that Julien includes each time she writes to Caitlin and to note where you add the information (shown as red annotations below) to the graphic organizer.

Heading

Greeting Dear Caitlin,

Body She wrote about the juice bar, cornflakes, and sunsets

Closing Hugs and smoochies, Bon appétit

Signature Julien

Point out that Julien does not include a heading in her letters. Tell students that the heading includes the address of the person writing the letter and the date the letter was written. Add your school's address and the current date to the heading in the graphic organizer. Then have students open their Student Editions to page 356, from "A Pen Pal for Max," read the letter, and point out its parts.

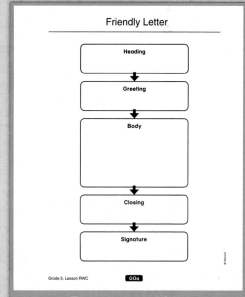

E L L

Clarify Meaning Gather students so they can look at a sample of the letters on Student Edition page 356 and from "The Sunset in My Mailbox." With your finger, point to each part of a letter, explaining its purpose. Show where the heading would be if one were included.

Friendly Letter

Heading

Greeting

Body

Closing

Signature

Grade 3, Lesson RWC   GOa

Transparency LA23

REVISE, p. T108

Writing Trait > **Sentence Fluency**

• Sentence Stretching

PROOFREAD, p. T108

Writing Trait > **Conventions**

• Commas in Compound Sentences, Subjects, and Predicates

PUBLISH, p. T109

Writing Trait > **Presentation**

• Make a Clean Copy

Student Writing Model

Objective

To understand the stages of writing a friendly letter

Discuss the Model

READ PAGES 328–329 Have children open their *Student Editions* to page 328. This page shows a friendly letter that a student wrote "Loved Best" and "A Pen Pal for Max." After students have read the letter, ask them what David tells his grandma. (He tells her about the new play he is going to be in.) Then have students read page 329 before briefly reviewing the five parts of a friendly letter. (heading, greeting, body, closing, signature). Point out the return address in the heading and the date below it. Also point out the commas used in each part.

Note that the first thing David did was to recall the parts that he needed to include in a letter. Tell students to do the same thing as they begin to write their letters.

READ PAGES 330–331 Have students turn to pages 330 and 331. These pages tell what David did after he thought of all of the parts of his letter. Have students read the pages, and tell them that they will be following the same steps that David did by planning and drafting their letters.

Explain to students that good writers plan their letters before they write. They think about:

- their audience and purpose for writing
- what they want to tell the reader
- what the reader would like to know

Encourage students to use a graphic organizer when they need to brainstorm ideas for writing.

Then tell students that good writers write a draft of the letter, review it, and sign it if everything is correct. Talk about the items in the checklist, reminding students to keep these ideas in mind as they write their letter.

Reading-Writing Connection

Friendly Letter

In a **friendly letter,** a person writes to someone he or she knows. A friendly letter has five parts, like those in the letters in "A Pen Pal for Max." I wrote this letter to tell my grandmother about my school's play.

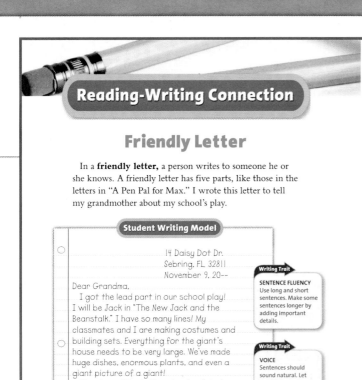

Student Writing Model

14 Daisy Dot Dr.
Sebring, FL 32811
November 9, 20--

Dear Grandma,
    I got the lead part in our school play! I will be Jack in "The New Jack and the Beanstalk." I have so many lines! My classmates and I are making costumes and building sets. Everything for the giant's house needs to be very large. We've made huge dishes, enormous plants, and even a giant picture of a giant!
    The play will be in the school cafeteria next Friday night. I hope you can be there!
                        Love,
                        David

Writing Trait

SENTENCE FLUENCY
Use long and short sentences. Make some sentences longer by adding important details.

Writing Trait

VOICE
Sentences should sound natural. Let your feelings show through.

328

Here's how I write a letter.

1. I think of all the parts that I need to include in the letter.

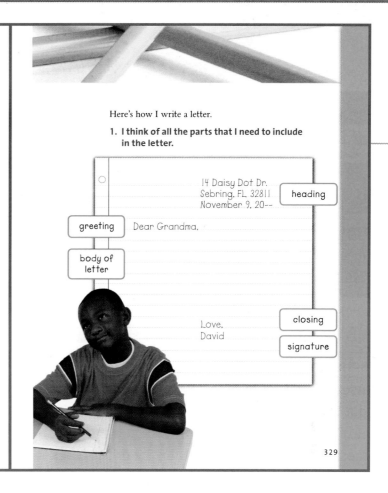

14 Daisy Dot Dr.
Sebring, FL 32811
November 9, 20--   **heading**

greeting   Dear Grandma,

body of letter

                        Love,   **closing**
                        David

                                         signature

329

2. I think about the person who will read the letter. I think about what I want to tell him or her. I use a graphic organizer to help me get started.

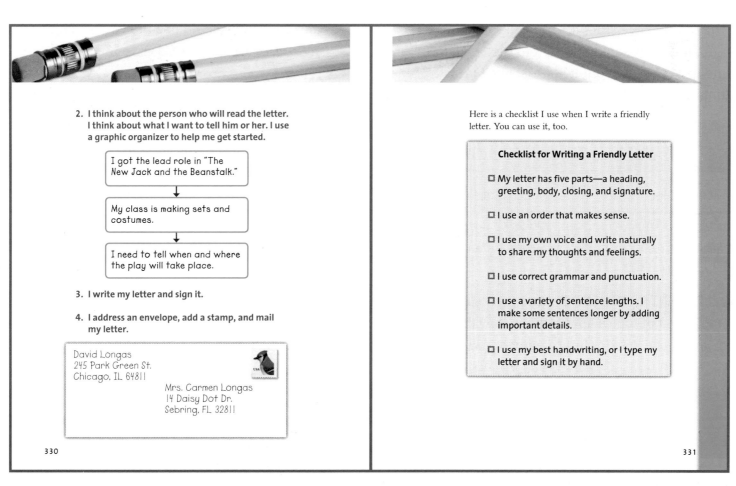

I got the lead role in "The New Jack and the Beanstalk."

↓

My class is making sets and costumes.

↓

I need to tell when and where the play will take place.

3. I write my letter and sign it.

4. I address an envelope, add a stamp, and mail my letter.

David Longas
245 Park Green St.
Chicago, IL 64811

        Mrs. Carmen Longas
        14 Daisy Dot Dr.
        Sebring, FL 32811

330

Here is a checklist I use when I write a friendly letter. You can use it, too.

Checklist for Writing a Friendly Letter

☐ My letter has five parts—a heading, greeting, body, closing, and signature.

☐ I use an order that makes sense.

☐ I use my own voice and write naturally to share my thoughts and feelings.

☐ I use correct grammar and punctuation.

☐ I use a variety of sentence lengths. I make some sentences longer by adding important details.

☐ I use my best handwriting, or I type my letter and sign it by hand.

331

Prewrite

WRITING ABOUT WHAT INTERESTS YOU
Writing Trait > Voice

Objective
To learn how to use appropriate voice when writing about familiar events and experiences

Teach/Model

DISCUSS VOICE Explain to students that in "The Sunset in My Mailbox," Julien's letters were always about things important to her. A good writer's personality, or voice, shows when that person writes about something important or something he or she cares about. The writing becomes more interesting.

Apply to Writing

GUIDED PRACTICE Draw a chart like the one below on the board. Have students think of topics at home and at school that are important to them and that they would like to write about in letters. Elicit ideas from volunteers and write the ideas on the board.

School	Home
school play	soccer game
talent show	new pet
field trip	birthday party

INDEPENDANT PRACTICE Have students brainstorm their own list of topics about things they care about and save those lists for future reference when writing.

MATCHING VOICE TO AUDIENCE AND PURPOSE
Writing Trait > Voice

Objective
To learn how to use appropriate voice that considers the audience and purpose

Teach/Model

CONSIDER AUDIENCE AND PURPOSE Have students think about to whom they are going to write their letter. Good writers use their voice to make the reader feel as if the writer is talking directly to them. When they choose a topic, good writers always think about what their audience will be interested in.

Think Aloud **I am thinking about writing a letter to my mother. She might like to know about me and how I'm doing. I feel comfortable talking to her on the phone and would use the same kind of voice in my writing to her.**

Apply to Writing

GUIDED PRACTICE List the following audience and purpose on the board. Guide students to consider how the voice might differ in each case. Write their responses.

Audience	Purpose	Voice
Principal	to tell about winning an award	I am proud to write that we won.
Best friend		This is so cool! We won. We won!

INDEPENDENT PRACTICE Have students choose a topic, an audience, and a purpose for writing a letter. Then have them write a couple of sentences, considering their voice. Confer with students on their language.

Draft

SENTENCE VARIETY (LENGTH)
Writing Trait > Sentence Fluency

Objective
To use varied sentence length

Teach/Model

VARYING SENTENCE LENGTH Explain that good writers vary the length of their sentences to make their writing more interesting and less choppy. They use a combination of long and short sentences to create changing rhythms. One way to vary sentence length is to write compound sentences. Explain that these are two sentences joined together with words such as *and, but,* or *yet.* Explain that using different sentence lengths will make the writing sound more natural.

Apply to Writing

GUIDED PRACTICE Write the following senteces on the board.

> **Uncle Jeff went hiking. He climbed Mount Ryan. He later climbed Green Mountain. He climbed Strawberry Hill later.**

Guide students by asking them how they might write using varied sentence length in the last two sentences. Record their responses.

> **He later climbed Mount Ryan and Strawberry Hill.**

INDEPENDENT PRACTICE Have students begin drafting their letters, considering sentence variety as they write. Confer with students as they draft.

AVOIDING *I, I, I*
Writing Trait > Sentence Fluency

Objective
To avoid choppiness in writing

Teach/Model

AVOIDING CHOPPY WRITING Read the following sentences to the class: *I went to the store. I went with my mom. I needed new shoes. I got sneakers.* Ask what the sentences have in common. (All begin with "I.") Explain that good writers avoid using *I* too many times in their writing. Then read the following: *I needed new shoes, so my mom took me to the store. She bought me new sneakers.* Explain that both sets of sentences tell the same information, but the second only uses the word *I* once.

Apply to Writing

GUIDED PRACTICE Have students continue drafting their friendly letters. Encourage them to circle the word *I* each time it appears in their draft. Explain that since they are writing to someone they know, they are writing about things that they have been doing, and they are likely to have used the word *I* several times.

INDEPENDENT PRACTICE Have students continue drafting but consider starting sentences in a variety of ways as they write. Confer with students as they draft, but remind them that they can revise later.

Revise/Proofread

SENTENCE STRETCHING
Writing Trait > Sentence Fluency

Objective
To use effective sentence variety by including descriptive language

Teach/Model

EFFECTIVE DESCRIPTION Read aloud the first paragraph from *Read-Aloud Anthology* page 46 of "The Sunset in My Mailbox." Discuss the vivid language used to describe the cereal. Tell students that descriptive language helps readers almost see the images described. Explain that the writing is also interesting because the writer used both short and long sentences. Use **Transparency LA24** to demonstrate using editing marks to revise for this effect.

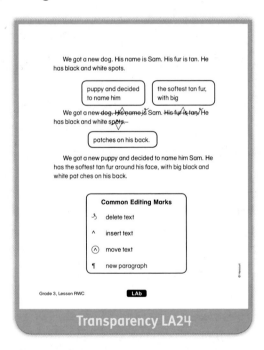

Transparency LA24

Apply to Writing

PRACTICE/APPLY Have students revise their drafts for effective descriptive language.

COMMAS IN COMPOUND SENTENCES, SUBJECTS, AND PREDICATES
Writing Trait > Conventions

Objective
To use commas in elaborated sentences

Review

COMMA USAGE Guide students to remember that in a friendly letter, commas are used in the date, greeting, and closing. Remind students also that when two sentences are joined together in a compound sentence, a comma is placed at the end of the first sentence.

Tell students that good writers proofread their writing to make sure they have used correct punctuation. Ask a volunteer to offer an example of a compound sentence from his or her draft. Write the sentence on the board, demonstrating correct placement of the comma. Have students review their letter to make sure they have correctly used commas in their writing.

Apply to Writing

PRACTICE/APPLY Have students proofread their drafts, make corrections, and share their corrections with a partner. Remind students to check for correct ending punctuation, as well as correct comma usage. Circulate as students proofread and offer guidance as needed.

Evaluate/Publish

PUBLISHING
Writing Trait > Presentation

Objective
To publish a friendly letter

Make a Clean Copy

SHARE LETTERS   In preparation for publishing their friendly letters, organize students into groups to share each other's writing. Students should read their letters to each other to locate needed corrections before creating a clean copy. Encourage students to mail their final letters or share them by reading them aloud to a partner.

 TECHNOLOGY

CREATE STATIONERY Show students how to change the look of a letter typed on the computer. Display different fonts and show how to create a border and insert clip art. Encourage students to type their letters and select a border that matches the theme of the letter.

 PORTFOLIO OPPORTUNITY

Invite students to keep a copy of their friendly letter in their portfolios to revisit in the future.

✔ ASSESSMENT

OBSERVATION CHECKLIST   Have students work in small groups using the checklist to self-assess their writing. Students can discuss how they met certain points and help each other if they have problems with others. Discuss how these points support the traits of writing and appear in rubrics.

- ☐ The letter has a heading, greeting, body, closing, and signature.
- ☐ The order of the information makes sense.
- ☐ The writer uses his or her own voice, sharing thoughts and feelings and writing about things that matter to him or her.
- ☐ Correct grammar and punctuation are used.
- ☐ A variety of sentence lengths are used.
- ☐ The letter is neatly written or typed, then signed.

Note: A 4-point rubric appears on page R8.

SCORING RUBRIC

	6	5	4	3	2	1
FOCUS	Completely focused, purposeful.	Focused on topic and purpose.	Generally focused on topic and purpose.	Somewhat focused on topic and purpose.	Related to topic but does not maintain focus.	Lacks focus and purpose.
ORGANIZATION	Ideas progress logically; paper conveys sense of completeness.	Organization mostly clear, paper gives sense of completeness.	Organization mostly clear, but some lapses occur; may seem unfinished.	Some sense of organization; seems unfinished.	Little sense of organization.	Little or no sense of organization.
SUPPORT	Strong, specific details; clear, exact language; freshness of expression.	Strong, specific details; clear, exact language.	Adequate support and word choice.	Limited supporting details; limited word choice.	Few supporting details; limited word choice.	Little development, limited or unclear word choice.
CONVENTIONS	Varied sentences; few, if any, errors.	Varied sentences; few errors.	Some sentence variety; few errors.	Simple sentence structures; some errors.	Simple sentence structures; many errors.	Unclear sentence structures; many errors.

REPRODUCIBLE STUDENT RUBRICS for specific writing purposes and presentations are available on pages R5–R8.

Reading-Writing Connection   T109

Writing on Demand

PREPARATION

Objectives

- *To write in response to a narrative prompt*
- *To organize ideas using graphic organizers*
- *To revise and proofread for grammar, punctuation, capitalization, and spelling*

Prepare to Write

DISCUSS TIMED WRITING   Tell students that in this theme they have written a friendly letter in which they tell about an experience. On a writing test, however, they may have as little as 45 minutes to write about an experience. Explain that a timed test will usually give students a general idea of what to write about through a prompt.

ANALYZE THE PROMPT   Write the following prompt on the board or make multiple copies for students. Then have students read the prompt. Explain that the topic of the prompt is a memorable school experience.

Everyone remembers special moments from school.

Think about a special school experience you have had.

Now write a story about what happened during that special school experience.

The prompt limits the topic to *a school experience*. An experience outside of school would not belong in this narrative. Point out that the prompt asks students to *think and write* about a memorable school experience. They should rehearse ideas as a strategy for writing about this prompt.

DISCUSS ORGANIZATION   Tell students that to do well on a timed writing test such as this one, they must remember the features of good narrative writing.

- The narrative is told in logical order.
- Facts and details support the main ideas.
- Exact, vivid words bring details to life.

DISCUSS BUDGETING TIME   Remind students that the test allows 45 minutes to write an essay. Recommend that they budget their time as follows:

Budgeting Time	
Prewrite	10 minutes
Draft	25 minutes
Revise & Proofread	10 minutes

Explain that some students will need more or less time for each step. Ask them to think about how much time they will need to complete each step.

Write the Narrative

RESPOND TO A PROMPT Write the following prompt on the board and have students begin writing. Tell them to use two pencils with different colors, beginning with the regular lead color.

> *Everyone has visited a special place that he or she will always remember.*
>
> *Think about a special place you have visited that you will always remember.*
>
> *Now write a story about a special place you have visited that you will always remember.*

TIMED-WRITING STRATEGY Let students know when the first 20 minutes have passed. At the end of 45 minutes, ask students to finish writing the essay in the other color pencil. After finishing, they can see how much more time they needed and strategize about what they can do in the future to finish on time.

DISCUSS TIMED WRITING Ask students to discuss their experiences during the timed writing assignment. Ask questions such as the following:

- Were you able to finish on time? Why or why not?
- Does your writing include all the things mentioned in the prompt? Why or why not?
- In what ways was your prewriting helpful as you wrote your draft?
- What changes did you make in your topic sentence or your details as you revised your composition?

EVALUATE Display the rubric on page R7 and discuss what is necessary for receiving a 6. Provide copies of the rubric for students and have them work independently or in pairs to evaluate their papers.

Note: A 4-point rubric appears on page R8.

	SCORING RUBRIC					
	6	**5**	**4**	**3**	**2**	**1**
FOCUS	Completely focused, purposeful.	Focused on topic and purpose.	Generally focused on topic and purpose.	Somewhat focused on topic and purpose.	Related to topic but does not maintain focus.	Lacks focus and purpose.
ORGANIZATION	Ideas progress logically; paper conveys sense of completeness.	Organization mostly clear, paper gives sense of completeness.	Organization mostly clear, but some lapses occur; may seem unfinished.	Some sense of organization; seems unfinished.	Little sense of organization.	Little or no sense of organization.
SUPPORT	Strong, specific details; clear, exact language; freshness of expression.	Strong, specific details; clear, exact language.	Adequate support and word choice.	Limited supporting details; limited word choice.	Few supporting details; limited word choice.	Little development, limited or unclear word choice.
CONVENTIONS	Varied sentences; few, if any, errors.	Varied sentences; few errors.	Some sentence variety; few errors.	Simple sentence structures; some errors.	Simple sentence structures; many errors.	Unclear sentence structures; many errors.

REPRODUCIBLE STUDENT RUBRICS for specific writing purposes and presentations are available on pages R5–R8.

PORTFOLIO OPPORTUNITY Students may keep their compositions in portfolios and compare them with earlier narrative writing to assess their progress.

Lesson 12

WEEK AT A GLANCE

✔ Phonics
Consonant Digraphs /n/*kn, gn;* /r/*wr;* /f/*gh*

✔ Spelling
gnat, knew, sign, knob, gnaw, write, knees, wrinkle, kneel, wrist, cough, known, rough, wrench, knight

✔ Comprehension
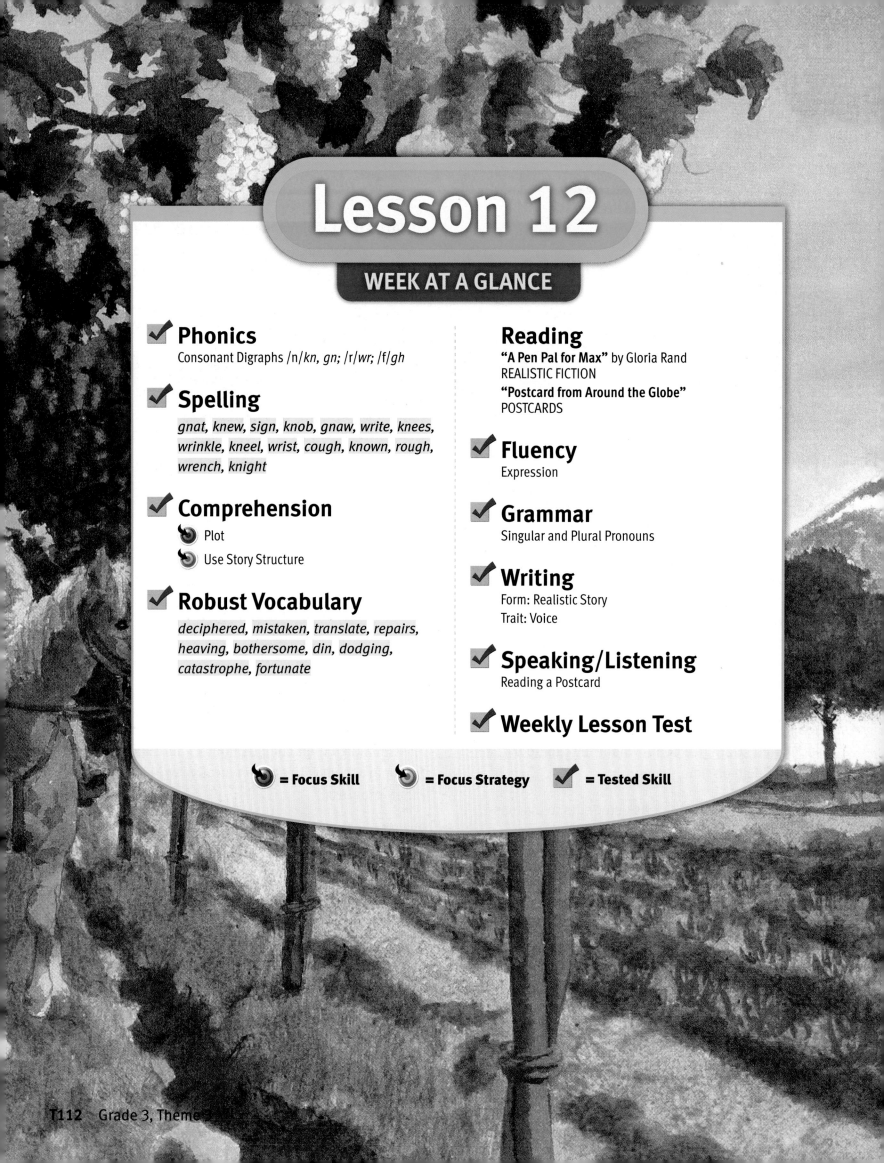 Plot

Use Story Structure

✔ Robust Vocabulary
deciphered, mistaken, translate, repairs, heaving, bothersome, din, dodging, catastrophe, fortunate

Reading
"A Pen Pal for Max" by Gloria Rand
REALISTIC FICTION
"Postcard from Around the Globe"
POSTCARDS

✔ Fluency
Expression

✔ Grammar
Singular and Plural Pronouns

✔ Writing
Form: Realistic Story
Trait: Voice

✔ Speaking/Listening
Reading a Postcard

✔ Weekly Lesson Test

= Focus Skill   = Focus Strategy   ✔ = Tested Skill

One stop
for all
your **Digital** *needs*

Digital
CLASSROOM

 www.harcourtschool.com/storytown
To go along with your print program

FOR THE TEACHER

Prepare    Professional Development

in the Online TE

 Videos for Podcasting

Plan & Organize   Online TE & Planning Resource*

Teach    Transparencies

access from the Online TE

Assess   Online Assessment*

with Student Tracking System and Prescriptions

FOR THE STUDENT

Read    Student eBook*

 Strategic Intervention Interactive Reader

 Leveled Readers

Practice & Apply   Splash into Phonics CD-ROM

 Comprehension Expedition CD-ROM

 Also available on CD-ROM

GO online | eBook **STUDENT EDITION**

STUDENT EDITION

A Pen Pal for Max

Gloria Rand · ILLUSTRATED BY Ted Rand

Genre: Realistic Fiction

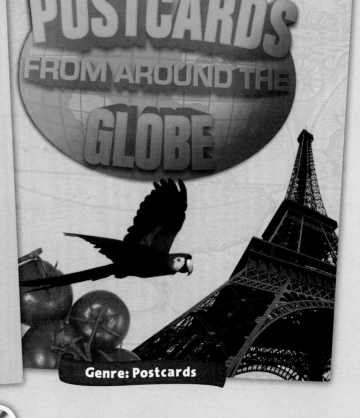

POSTCARDS FROM AROUND THE GLOBE

Genre: Postcards

◀ **Audiotext** *Student Edition selections are available on Audiotext 3.*

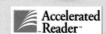
Accelerated Reader ◀ *Practice Quizzes for the Selection*

THEME CONNECTION: As We Grow
Comparing Realistic Fiction and Postcards

....

Paired Selections

SOCIAL STUDIES **A Pen Pal for Max, pp. 338–359**
SUMMARY Max's idea to send a letter to the United States in a box of grapes results in a long-distance friend.

SOCIAL STUDIES **Postcards from Around the Globe, pp. 360–361**
SUMMARY A collection of postcards shows how friends keep in touch and learn about other countries.

Support for Differentiated Instruction

LEVELED READERS

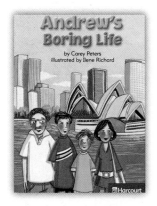

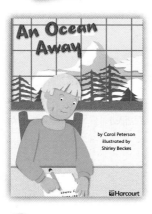

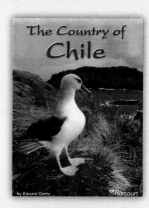

● **BELOW-LEVEL**　　● **ON-LEVEL**　　● **ADVANCED**　　**E L L**

LEVELED PRACTICE

◀ **Strategic Intervention Resource Kit, Lesson 12**

◀ **Strategic Intervention Interactive Reader, Lesson 12**
Strategic Intervention Interactive Reader Online

◀ **ELL Extra Support Kit, Lesson 12**

◀ **Challenge Resource Kit, Lesson 12**

● **BELOW-LEVEL**
Extra Support Copying Masters, pp. 98–100, 102–103

● **ON-LEVEL**
Practice Book, pp. 97–103

● **ADVANCED LEVEL**
Challenge Copying Masters, pp. 98–100, 102–103

E L L

ELL Copying Masters, Lesson 12

ADDITIONAL RESOURCES

bed

- Spelling Practice Book, pp. 38–40
- Grammar Practice Book, pp. 41–44
- Reading Transparencies R77–R84
- Language Arts Transparencies LA25–LA26
- Test Prep System
◀ Literacy Center Kit, Cards 56–60
- Writer's Companion
◀ Fluency Builders
◀ Picture Card Collection
- Read-Aloud Anthology

✓ ASSESSMENT

✔ **Monitor Progress**

✔ **Weekly Lesson Test, Lesson 12**
- Comprehension
- Phonics and Spelling
- Focus Skill
- Robust Vocabulary
- Grammar
- Use Context Clues

www.harcourtschool.com/storytown

- Online Assessment
- *Also available on CD-ROM— ExamView®*

ePlanner* **90+ Minutes** # Suggested Lesson Planner

	Day 1	Day 2

Step 1 Whole Group

Daily Routines
- *Oral Language*
- *Read Aloud*

Word Work
- phonics
- *Spelling*

Skills and Strategies
- *Reading*
- *Fluency*
- *Comprehension*
- *Build Robust Vocabulary*

Day 1

QUESTION OF THE DAY, p. T124
What would you tell a new friend about yourself?

READ ALOUD, p. T125
Transparency R77: "Ben's First Day"

 phonics p. T126
Introduce: Consonant Digraphs

SPELLING, p. T127
Pretest

READING/COMPREHENSION, p. T128
Introduce: Plot

LISTENING COMPREHENSION, p. T130
Read-Aloud: "The Sunset in My Mailbox"

FLUENCY, p. T130
Develop Expression

BUILD ROBUST VOCABULARY, p. T131
Words from the Read-Aloud

Day 2

QUESTION OF THE DAY, p. T134
How do you "talk" with friends?

READ ALOUD, p. T135
Transparency R79: "The Letter"

 phonics p. T136
Review: Consonant Digraphs

SPELLING, p. T137
Word Building

BUILD ROBUST VOCABULARY, p. T138
Words from the selection
Word Detective, p. T139

READING, p. T140
"A Pen Pal for Max"
Options for Reading

▲Student Edition

COMPREHENSION, p. T152
Introduce: Use Story Structure

RETELLING/FLUENCY, p. T152
Reading with Expression

BUILD ROBUST VOCABULARY, p. T166
Words About the Selection

 ### Step 2 Small Groups

 ### Step 3 Whole Group

Suggestions for Differentiated Instruction (*See pp. T118–T119.*)

Language Arts
- *Grammar*
- *Writing*

GRAMMAR, p. T132
Introduce: Define Pronoun

DAILY PROOFREADING
1. her wrote to Amira cousin (Amira wrote to her cousin.)
2. hours drove for six They (They drove for six hours.)

 WRITING, p. T133
Realistic Story
Writing Trait: Voice

Writing Prompt Write two sentences on a topic of your choice. Give each sentence a different voice by using different words and expressing different feelings.

GRAMMAR, p. T154
Introduce: Discuss Singular Pronouns

DAILY PROOFREADING
1. The sandwich was so good that Billy ate them all. (ate it all.)
2. Nora's friend visited it. (visited her.)

 WRITING, p. T155
Realistic Story
Writing Trait: Voice

Writing Prompt Write five words that would describe the main character in your story.

 = Focus Skill  = Focus Strategy  = Tested Skill

Skills at a Glance

phonics	Comprehension	Fluency	Vocabulary
• Consonant Digraphs	**Focus Skill** Plot **Focus Strategy** Use Story Structure	Reading with Expression	**ROBUST VOCABULARY:** *deciphered, mistaken, translate, repairs, heaving, bothersome, din, dodging, catastrophe, fortunate*

Day 3

QUESTION OF THE DAY, p. T156
What is a postcard? How is it like a letter?

READ ALOUD, p. T157
Transparency R79: "The Letter"

 p. T158
Review: Consonant digraphs

✓ **SPELLING,** p. T159
State the Generalization

✓ **FLUENCY,** p. T160
Reading with Expression

✓ **COMPREHENSION,** p. T161
Review: Plot
Introduce: Use Context Clues
Paired Selection: "Postcards from Around the Globe"
▲ Student Edition

CONNECTIONS, p. T164

✓ **BUILD ROBUST VOCABULARY,** p. T166
Review

Day 4

QUESTION OF THE DAY, p. T172
Why would you choose to write to someone instead of calling him or her on the telephone?

READ ALOUD, p. T173
Transparency R83: "Grandma's Party"

 p. T174
Review: Consonant digraphs

✓ **SPELLING,** p. T175
Review Spelling Words

✓ **FLUENCY,** p. T176
Reading with Expression: "A Pen Pal for Max"

✓ **COMPREHENSION,** p. T177
Review: Plot
Maintain: Synonyms and Antonyms
▲ Student Edition

SPEAKING AND LISTENING, p. T179
Reading a Postcard

✓ **BUILD ROBUST VOCABULARY,** p. T180
Review

Day 5

QUESTION OF THE DAY, p. T184
What events do you like to have your friends tell you about?

READ ALOUD, p. T185
Transparency R83: "Grandma's Party"

 p. T186
Review: Consonant digraphs

✓ **SPELLING,** p. T189
Posttest

✓ **FLUENCY,** p. T188
Reading with Expression: "A Pen Pal for Max"

✓ **COMPREHENSION,** p. T189
Review: Plot
Read-Aloud: "The Sunset in My Mailbox"
▲ Student Edition

✓ **BUILD ROBUST VOCABULARY,** p. T190
Cumulative Review

 BELOW-LEVEL ON-LEVEL ADVANCED E L L

✓ **GRAMMAR,** p. T170
Introduce: Plural Pronouns

DAILY PROOFREADING

1. I saw Mr. and Mrs. Wells and waved at it. (at them.)
2. Keely and I invited Sue to walk with me. (with us.)

 WRITING, p. T171
Realistic Story
Writing Trait: Voice

Writing Prompt *Jot down the main problem your character faces and the solution to the problem.*

✓ **GRAMMAR,** p. T182
Review: Singular and Plural Pronouns

DAILY PROOFREADING

1. Jim waved to Max, who waved back at them. (at him.)
2. Ms. Jenkins repeated the question he had asked. (she had asked.)

 WRITING, p. T183
Realistic Story
Writing Trait: Voice

Writing Prompt *Write a brief summary of your partner's story. Exchange summaries so you can see if your story is clear.*

✓ **GRAMMAR,** p. T192
Review: Singular and Plural Pronouns

DAILY PROOFREADING

1. We asked Mari to come with him. (with us.)
2. The dogs barked, but then it wagged their tails. (they wagged)

WRITING, p. T193
Realistic Story
Writing Trait: Voice

Writing Prompt *Have students generate a list of ideas about a new topic of their choice for writing.*

Suggested Small-Group Planner

45–60 Minutes

15-20 Minutes
BELOW-LEVEL

15-20 Minutes
ON-LEVEL

15-20 Minutes
ADVANCED

	Day 1	Day 2
BELOW-LEVEL	**Teacher-Directed** Leveled Reader: "Andrew's Boring Life," p. T194 Before Reading **Independent** ⭐ Listening/Speaking Center, p. T122 Extra Support Copying Masters, p. 98 ▲ Leveled Reader	**Teacher-Directed** Student Edition: "A Pen Pal for Max," p. T140 **Independent** ⭐ Reading Center, p. T122 Extra Support Copying Masters, p. 99 ▲ Student Edition
ON-LEVEL	**Teacher-Directed** Leveled Reader: "An Ocean Away," p. T195 Before Reading **Independent** ⭐ Reading Center, p. T122 Practice Book, p. 89 ▲ Leveled Reader	**Teacher-Directed** Student Edition: "A Pen Pal for Max," p. T140 **Independent** ⭐ Technology Center, p. T123 Practice Book, p. 90 ▲ Student Edition
ADVANCED	**Teacher-Directed** Leveled Reader: "Trading Places," p. T196 Before Reading **Independent** ⭐ Technology Center, p. T123 Challenge Copying Masters, p. 98 ▲ Leveled Reader	**Teacher-Directed** Leveled Reader: "Trading Places," p. T196 Read the Book **Independent** ⭐ Word Work Center, p. T123 Challenge Copying Masters, p. 99 ▲ Leveled Reader

ELL

English-Language Learners

In addition to the small-group instruction above, use the ELL Extra Support Kit to promote language development.

LANGUAGE DEVELOPMENT SUPPORT
Teacher-Directed
ELL TG, Day 1

Independent
ELL Copying Masters, Lesson 12
 ▲ ELL Student Handbook

LANGUAGE DEVELOPMENT SUPPORT
Teacher-Directed
ELL TG, Day 2

Independent
ELL Copying Masters, Lesson 12
 ▲ ELL Student Handbook

Intervention

▲ Strategic Intervention Resource Kit   ▲ Intervention Reader

Strategic Intervention TG, Lesson 12
Strategic Intervention Practice Book, Lesson 12

Strategic Intervention TG, Lesson 12
Intervention Reader, Lesson 12
 ▲ Intervention Reader

MONITOR PROGRESS

Small-Group Instruction

Comprehension	 phonics	Vocabulary	Fluency	Robust Vocabulary	Language Arts
Plot	Consonant Digraphs /n/kn, gn; /r/wr; /f/gh	Use Context Clues	Reading with Expression	deciphered, mistaken, translate, repairs, heaving, bothersome, din, dodging, catastrophe, fortunate	✔ LANGUAGE ARTS CHECKPOINT Grammar: Singular and Plural Nouns Writing: Realistic Story
pp. S18–S19	pp. S14–S15	pp. S20–S21	pp. S16–S17	pp. S22–S23	pp. S24–S25

Day 3

Teacher-Directed
Leveled Reader: "Andrew's Boring Life," p. T194
Read the Book
Independent
⭐ Word Work Center, p. T123
Extra Support Copying Masters, p. 100

 ▲ Leveled Reader

Teacher-Directed
Leveled Reader: "An Ocean Away," p. T195
Read the Book
Independent
⭐ Writing Center, p. T123
Practice Book, p. 99

 ▲ Leveled Reader

Teacher-Directed
Leveled Reader: "Trading Places," p. T196
Think Critically
Independent
⭐ Listening/Speaking Center, p. T122
Challenge Copying Masters, p. 100

 ▲ Leveled Reader

Teacher-Directed
Leveled Reader: "The Country of Chile," p. T197
Before Reading; Read the Book
ELL TG, Day 3
Independent
ELL Copying Masters, Lesson 12

 ▲ Leveled Reader

Strategic Intervention TG, Lesson 12
Intervention Reader, Lesson 12
Strategic Intervention Practice Book, Lesson 12

 ▲ Intervention Reader

Day 4

Teacher-Directed
Leveled Reader: "Andrew's Boring Life," p. T194
Reread for Fluency
Independent
⭐ Technology Center, p. T123
Practice Book, pp. 97–103

 ▲ Leveled Reader

Teacher-Directed
Leveled Reader: "An Ocean Away," p. T195
Reread for Fluency
Independent
⭐ Word Work Center, p. T123
Practice Book, pp. 97–103

 ▲ Leveled Reader

Teacher-Directed
Leveled Reader: "Trading Places," p. T196
Reread for Fluency
Self-Selected Reading: Classroom Library Collection
Independent
⭐ Writing Center, p. T123
Practice Book, pp. 97–103

▲ Leveled Reader

Teacher-Directed
Leveled Reader: "The Country of Chile," p. T197
Reread for Fluency
ELL TG, Day 4
Independent
ELL Copying Masters, Lesson 12

 ▲ Leveled Reader

Strategic Intervention TG, Lesson 12
Intervention Reader, Lesson 12

 ▲ Intervention Reader

Day 5

Teacher-Directed
Leveled Reader: "Andrew's Boring Life," p. T194
Think Critically
Independent
⭐ Writing Center, p. T123
Leveled Reader: Reread for Fluency
Extra Support Copying Masters, p. 103

▲ Leveled Reader

Teacher-Directed
Leveled Reader: "An Ocean Away," p. T195
Think Critically
Independent
⭐ Listening/Speaking Center, p. T122
Leveled Reader: Reread for Fluency
Practice Book, p. 103

 ▲ Leveled Reader

Teacher-Directed
Leveled Reader: "Trading Places," p. T196
Reread for Fluency
Self-Selected Reading: Classroom Library Collection
Independent
⭐ Reading Center, p. 122
Leveled Reader: Reread for Fluency
Challenge Copying Masters, p. 102

▲ Leveled Reader

Teacher-Directed
Leveled Reader: "The Country of Chile," p. T197
Think Critically
ELL TG, Day 5
Independent
Leveled Reader: Reread for Fluency
ELL Copying Masters, Lesson 12

 ▲ Leveled Reader

Strategic Intervention TG, Lesson 12
Intervention Reader, Lesson 12

 ▲ Intervention Reader

Leveled Readers & Leveled Practice
Reinforcing Skills and Strategies

LEVELED READER SYSTEM

- **Leveled Readers**
- **Leveled Readers, CD**
- **Leveled Reader Teacher Guides**
  - *Comprehension*
  - *Vocabulary*
  - *Oral Reading Fluency Assessment*
- **Response Activities**
- **Leveled Readers Assessment**

See pages T194–T197 for lesson plans.

For extended lesson plans, see *Leveled Reader Teacher Guides*.

BELOW-LEVEL

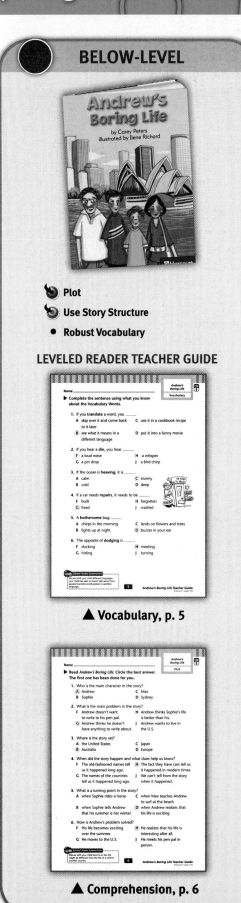

🌀 Plot
🌀 Use Story Structure
● Robust Vocabulary

LEVELED READER TEACHER GUIDE

▲ Vocabulary, p. 5

▲ Comprehension, p. 6

ON-LEVEL

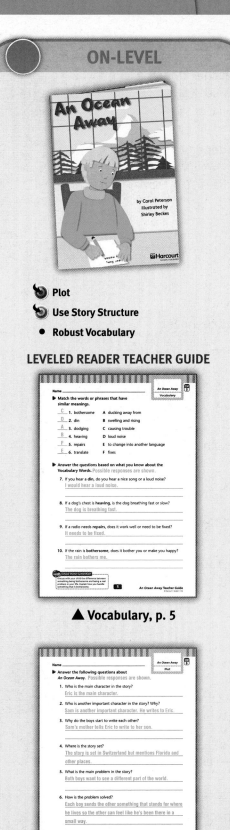

🌀 Plot
🌀 Use Story Structure
● Robust Vocabulary

LEVELED READER TEACHER GUIDE

▲ Vocabulary, p. 5

▲ Comprehension, p. 6

ADVANCED

TRADING PLACES
by Sam Silver
illustrated by Barbara Vagnozzi

- Plot
- Use Story Structure
- Robust Vocabulary

LEVELED READER TEACHER GUIDE

▲ **Vocabulary, p. 5**

▲ **Comprehension, p. 6**

ELL

The Country of Chile
by Edward Cantu

- Build Background
- Concept Vocabulary
- Scaffolded Language Development

LEVELED READER TEACHER GUIDE

▲ **Build Background, p. 5**

▲ **Scaffolded Language Development, p. 6**

CLASSROOM LIBRARY

Self-Selected Reading

EASY

▲ *Officer Buckle and Gloria* by Peggy Rathmann, G. P. Putnam's Sons, 1995. FANTASY

AVERAGE

▲ *Day Light, Night Light* by Franklyn M. Branley, Harper Collins, 1998. EXPOSITORY NONFICTION

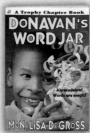

CHALLENGE

▲ *Donavan's Word Jar* by Monalisa DeGross, Harper Trophy, 1994. REALISTIC FICTION

▲ **Classroom Library Teacher Guide, Lesson 13**

Lesson 12 **T121**

Management Support

While you provide direct instruction to individuals or small groups, other students can work on literacy center activities.

▲ **Literacy Centers Pocket Chart**

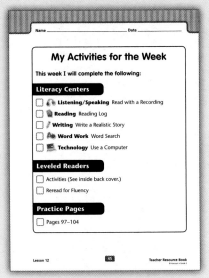

My Activities for the Week

This week I will complete the following:

Literacy Centers

☐ **Listening/Speaking** Read with a Recording
☐ **Reading** Reading Log
☐ **Writing** Write a Realistic Story
☐ **Word Work** Word Search
☐ **Technology** Use a Computer

Leveled Readers

☐ Activities (See inside back cover.)
☐ Reread for Fluency

Practice Pages

☐ Pages 97–104

▲ **Teacher Resource Book, p. 45**

Homework for the Week

TEACHER RESOURCE BOOK, PAGE 15

The Homework Copying Master provides activities to complete for each day of the week.

LISTENING/SPEAKING

Read with a Recording

Objective
To read familiar text with fluency

LISTENING/SPEAKING   Card 56

Read with a Recording

MATERIALS
- CD/cassette player
- *Student Edition*
- *Audiotext 3*
- Reading Log or paper
- pencil

❶ With a partner, listen to "A Pen Pal for Max" on the *Audiotext*.

❷ Follow along in the book, and read aloud with the recording.

❸ Use your Reading Log to keep tracl of what you read.

A Pen Pal for Max

Grade 3 Lesson 12

⭐ **Literacy Center Kit • Card 56**

READING

Reading Log

Objective
To select and read books independently

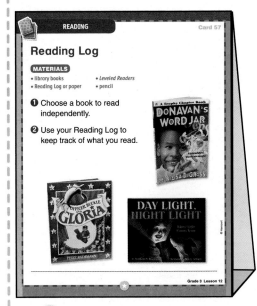

READING   Card 57

Reading Log

MATERIALS
- library books
- *Leveled Readers*
- Reading Log or paper
- pencil

❶ Choose a book to read independently.

❷ Use your Reading Log to keep track of what you read.

DONAVAN'S WORD JAR

OFFICER BUCKLE GLORIA

DAY LIGHT, NIGHT LIGHT

Grade 3 Lesson 12

⭐ **Literacy Center Kit • Card 57**

www.harcourtschool.com/storytown

GO online

★ Additional Literacy Center Activities
★ Resources for Parents and Teachers

Differentiated
for Your Needs

 WRITING

Plan a Story

Objective
To plan a realistic story

 WORD WORK

Word Search

Objective
To categorize words using a graphic organizer

TECHNOLOGY

Use a Computer

Objective
To make a list using the computer

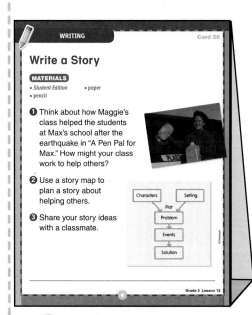

Literacy Center Kit • Card 58

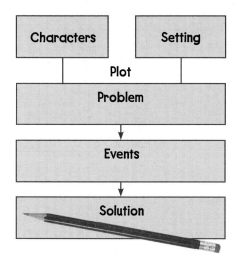

Literacy Center Kit • Card 59

words with *kn*	words with *gn*	words with *wr*
know	gnat	write
knock	gnaw	wrong
knead		wring

Literacy Center Kit • Card 60

Places to Visit
1. Hawaii
2. Colorado
3. New York
4. Puerto Rico

Day at a Glance

Day 1

 **phonics and Spelling**

- Introduce: Digraphs *kn*, *gn*, *wr*, and *gh*
- Pretest

Reading/ Comprehension

 Review: Plot
Student Edition, pp. 334–335

- *Read-Aloud Anthology:* "The Sunset in My Mailbox"

Fluency

- Model Oral Fluency

Robust Vocabulary

Words from the Read-Aloud
- Introduce: *deciphered, mistaken*

Grammar

- Introduce: Pronouns

Writing

- Realistic Story

Warm-Up Routines

 Oral Language

Objectives *To listen attentively and respond appropriately to oral communication; to record ideas and reflections*

Question of the Day

**What would you tell
a new friend about yourself?**

Lead the class in a discussion of new friendships. Tell students that one of the fastest ways to make a new friend is to learn you are alike in some ways. Brainstorm with students what things about themselves they might share with a new friend. Some possibilities include birth dates, favorite foods, after-school activities, and other interests.

After brainstorming, ask students to pick one thing that they would like to share with someone they have never met. Then have them complete the following writing prompt in their notebooks:

> **An important thing to know
> about me is _____ .**

Have students add one to two sentences about why this information is important to know. Invite volunteers to share their responses. Encourage listeners to ask questions.

Read Aloud

Objective *To listen for understanding and enjoyment*

READ ALOUD A REALISTIC STORY Using these steps, read aloud "Ben's New School":

Introduce the text. Display **Transparency R77** or distribute photocopies to students. Explain that you are going to read a realistic story about how Ben makes new friends.

Set a purpose. Ask students why they might read or listen to a story. (for enjoyment; to learn about certain events or certain kinds of people) Remind students that a realistic story has characters and events that could be real. Tell them that, as they listen, they should think about the plot.

Model fluent reading. Read the story aloud, expressively.

Discuss the story. Ask students the following questions:

• **What happens at the beginning of the story?**

• **What happens by the end of the story?**

Ben's New School

Ben spent his first day at his new school feeling lonely and afraid. He did not know anyone and this school went through sixth grade. At his old school, the third-graders had been the oldest students. Nobody talked to him.

The next day, Ben went to gym class. His classmates all talked to one another and left him out. Mr. Smith quieted the class and said, "Today we have a special treat. Ms. Ramos is going to show us about archery. Who has tried archery?"

Ben's grandfather was a keen archer and he had been teaching Ben about archery since Ben could remember. Ben quickly raised his hand. Mr. Smith called on Ben to assist Ms. Ramos.

Ben helped set up the target and checked that the arrows and bow were in place. Then Ms. Ramos sent twelve arrows into the target. Next, she let Ben try. Ben hit the target, too. Other students also tried, but none of them could hit the target.

After class, all the students wanted to know how Ben had learned archery. Some of them said they wanted to learn. One boy, Chan, rode the same bus as Ben, so they sat together and talked about archery all the way home. He invited Ben to his house so he could learn more.

Grade 3, Lesson 12   **R8**   Warm-Up: Day 1

Transparency R77

Consonant Digraphs *kn, gn, wr, gh* and Spelling

5-DAY PHONICS	
DAY 1	Introduce Digraphs *kn, gn, wr, gh*
DAY 2	Words with /n/ *kn, gn*
DAY 3	Words with /r/ *wr*
DAY 4	Words with /f/ *gh*
DAY 5	Review *kn, gn, wr, gh*

Objectives

- *To read words with silent letters*
- *To explore words with the letter combinations* kn, gn, wr, *and* gh

Skill Trace

Tested **Digraphs /n/*kn, gn;* /r/*wr;* /f/*gh***

Introduce	Grade 2
Reintroduce	T126
Reteach	S14
Review	T136–T137, T158, T174, T186, T400–T401
Test	Theme 3
Maintain	Theme 4, T344

"RESEARCH SAYS"

Decoding Instruction "Children receiving direct code instruction improved in word reading at a faster rate and had higher word recognition skills than those receiving implicit code instruction."

–Foorman et al. (1998), p. 37

 **Resources**

Phonics Practice Book, Intermediate, pp. 73–75

Teach/Model

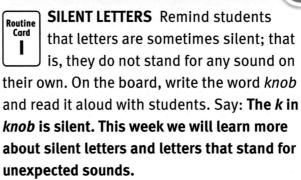

Routine Card 1 **SILENT LETTERS** Remind students that letters are sometimes silent; that is, they do not stand for any sound on their own. On the board, write the word *knob* and read it aloud with students. Say: **The *k* in *knob* is silent. This week we will learn more about silent letters and letters that stand for unexpected sounds.**

INTRODUCE *kn, gn*, AND *wr* Circle the letter pair *kn* in *knob* and cross out the *k*. Remind students that the initial *k* in this word is silent and that the letter pair *kn* is pronounced /n/. Continue with *gnat/gn* (/n/) and *wrist/wr* (/r/). Mention that the first consonant is silent in all three of these letter combinations.

INTRODUCE *gh* Write *gh* on the board. Explain that *gh* is a common letter pair in English, and that it can stand for different sounds. Tell students that one of these sounds is /f/ and that /f/*gh* usually is found at the end of a word or syllable. On the board, add the letters *rou* before *gh* to form the word *rough*. Point out that the *ou* in this word stands for the sound /u/. Then help students say the word parts /r/-/u/-/f/ before blending them to read the word *rough*.

Practice/Apply

GUIDED PRACTICE On the board, write *knee, gnaw, write,* and *tough*. Guide students to identify the consonant pair in each word and the sound it stands for. (*kn* and *gn* /n/; *wr* /r/; *gh* /f/) Ask volunteers to read the words aloud. Remind students that some of the letters in these pairs are silent and that *gh*, in *tough*, stands for the sound /f/.

INDEPENDENT PRACTICE On the board, write *wrench, gnome, knit,* and *enough*. Have students write the words and circle the consonant pairs *kn, gn, wr,* and *gh*. (*wrench/wr, gnome/gn, knit/kn, enough/gh*) Then have students write the letter that stands for the sound they hear in that consonant pair. (r, n, n, f)

5-DAY SPELLING

DAY 1	Pretest
DAY 2	Spelling Instruction/Practice
DAY 3	Spelling Practice/Handwriting
DAY 4	Use Spelling Strategies/Review
DAY 5	Posttest

Introduce the Spelling Words

PRETEST Say the first word and read the dictation sentence. Repeat the word as students write it. Write the word on the board and have students check their spelling. Tell them to circle the word if they spelled it correctly or write it correctly if they did not. Repeat with words 2–15.

Words with Digraphs *kn, gn, wr, gh*:

1. gnat   A tiny **gnat** bit me.
2. knew   No one **knew** LaShonda's middle name.
3. sign   The **sign** says, "No Parking."
4. knob   Turn the **knob** to make the radio louder.
5. gnaw   Beavers **gnaw** on wood.
6. write   Marianna likes to **write** poetry.
7. knees   Calvin fell and hurt his **knees**.
8. wrinkle   Alma ironed the **wrinkle** from her skirt.
9. kneel   Would you rather stand, sit, or **kneel**?
10. wrist   Your **wrist** connects your hand and arm.
11. cough   Please cover your mouth when you **cough**.
12. known   I have **known** Danny for three years.
13. rough   Sandpaper is very **rough**.
14. wrench   Please hand me the **wrench**.
15. knight   The brave **knight** rescued the princess.

ADVANCED

Challenge Words Use these dictation sentences.

16. knitting   My grandmother is **knitting** a pair of socks.
17. laughter   **Laughter** is good medicine.
18. wring   Don't forget to **wring** the towel.
19. unknown   The answer to that question is **unknown**.
20. playwright   The **playwright** explained the setting of her story.

Spelling Words

1.	gnat	9.	kneel
2.	knew	10.	wrist
3.	sign	11.	cough
4.	knob	12.	known
5.	gnaw	13.	rough
6.	write*	14.	wrench
7.	knees	15.	knight
8.	wrinkle		

Challenge Words

16.	knitting	19.	unknown
17.	laughter	20.	playwright
18.	wring		

*Word from "A Pen Pal for Max"

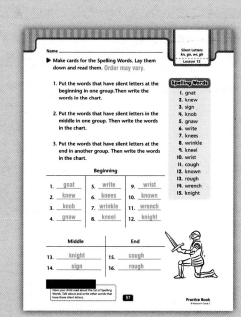

▲ Practice Book, p. 97

Lesson 12   **T127**

Plot
Comprehension

Objectives
- *To define plot*
- *To identify the plot in a story*

Daily Comprehension

 Plot

DAY 1:	Introduce Plot *Student Edition*
DAY 2:	Review Plot *Student Edition*
DAY 3:	Paired Selection *Student Edition*
DAY 4:	Review Plot *Transparency*
DAY 5:	Review Plot *Read-Aloud Anthology*

✔ MONITOR PROGRESS

Plot

IF students have trouble recognizing the plot of a story,	**THEN** have them tell the events from a favorite movie or television show. Explain that these events are the plot.

Small-Group Instruction, p. S18:

- ● **BELOW-LEVEL:** Reteach
- ● **ON-LEVEL:** Reinforce
- ● **ADVANCED:** Extend

Teach/Model

REVIEW PLOT Have students read *Student Edition* page 334. Remind them that all stories have a beginning, a middle, and an ending. Model how to identify the problem and solution.

Think Aloud As I read the beginning, I ask myself, "What is the character's problem or goal?" When I think I know what the problem is, I continue reading to find important events. I know that the important events usually lead to the solution of the problem.

Practice/Apply

GUIDED PRACTICE Have students read the passage on *Student Edition* page 335. Draw the graphic organizer on the board. Guide students to find the characters, setting, and problem in the story.

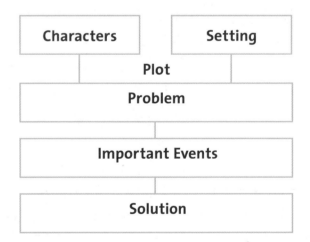

 **INDEPENDENT PRACTICE** Have students reread the story and identify who helped Emma solve her problem. (her father)

E L L

Try This Ask volunteers to retell the story. Have students refer to the text to get the correct order. Remind them that what they talked about was the plot.

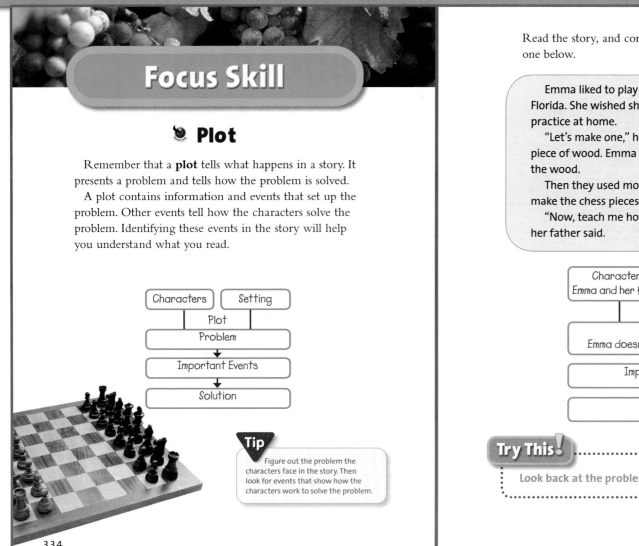

Focus Skill

🌟 Plot

Remember that a **plot** tells what happens in a story. It presents a problem and tells how the problem is solved.

A plot contains information and events that set up the problem. Other events tell how the characters solve the problem. Identifying these events in the story will help you understand what you read.

```
┌────────────┐ ┌─────────┐
│ Characters │ │ Setting │
└────────────┘ └─────────┘
         Plot
┌──────────────────────────┐
│        Problem           │
└──────────────────────────┘
             ↓
┌──────────────────────────┐
│     Important Events     │
└──────────────────────────┘
             ↓
┌──────────────────────────┐
│        Solution          │
└──────────────────────────┘
```

Tip

Figure out the problem the characters face in the story. Then look for events that show how the characters work to solve the problem.

334

Read the story, and complete a story map like the one below.

Emma liked to play chess at her school in Orlando, Florida. She wished she could have a chessboard to practice at home.

"Let's make one," her father said. He cut a square piece of wood. Emma painted the chessboard on the wood.

Then they used modeling clay to make the chess pieces.

"Now, teach me how to play!" her father said.

```
┌──────────────────────┐ ┌──────────────────┐
│ Characters:          │ │ Setting:         │
│ Emma and her father  │ │ Orlando, Florida │
└──────────────────────┘ └──────────────────┘
            Plot
┌──────────────────────────────────────────┐
│ Problem:                                   │
│ Emma doesn't have a chessboard.            │
└──────────────────────────────────────────┘
┌──────────────────────────────────────────┐
│ Important Events:                          │
└──────────────────────────────────────────┘
┌──────────────────────────────────────────┐
│ Solution:                                  │
└──────────────────────────────────────────┘
```

Try This!

Look back at the problem. Who helps Emma solve it?

GO online www.harcourtschool.com/storytown

335

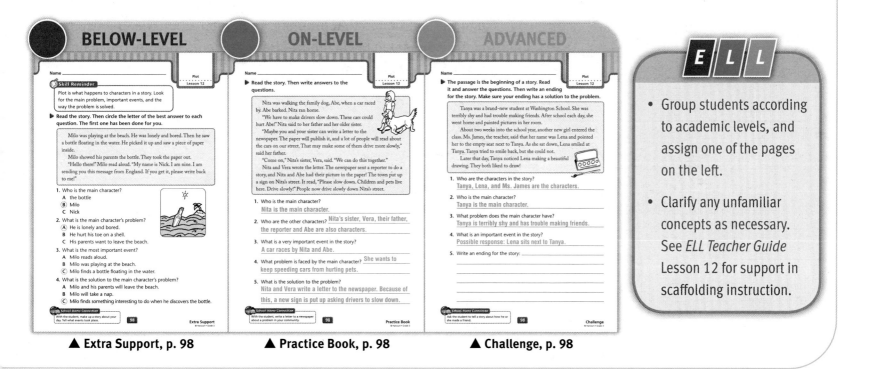

▲ Extra Support, p. 98   ▲ Practice Book, p. 98   ▲ Challenge, p. 98

ELL

- Group students according to academic levels, and assign one of the pages on the left.

- Clarify any unfamiliar concepts as necessary. See *ELL Teacher Guide* Lesson 12 for support in scaffolding instruction.

 Listening Comprehension
Read Aloud

Objectives

- *To set a purpose for listening*
- *To understand characteristics of realistic fiction*
- *To identify the plot in a story*

Build Fluency

Focus: Expression Tell students that good readers read aloud with expression. Using expression, such as changing your tone of voice, can help listeners understand and appreciate what happens in a story.

Before Reading

CONNECT TO PRIOR KNOWLEDGE Explain that you will read a story about a pen pal who receives some unusual gifts. Ask students if they have ever received a strange gift. Have volunteers describe their experiences.

▲ Read-Aloud Anthology, "The Sunset in My Mailbox," p. 44

Routine Card 2 **GENRE STUDY: REALISTIC FICTION** Explain that a realistic story has characters and events that are like people and events in real life.

Think Aloud When I read a realistic fiction story, I look for the setting to be a place that is or could be real. I expect that the characters will say and do things that I, or people I know, might say and do. I know that the problem in the story will be one a real person might have.

Tell students that when they listen to or read realistic fiction, their purpose should be to enjoy the story.

 REVIEW: PLOT Remind students that the plot is the events in a story. Explain that a plot has a beginning, a middle, and an ending. It tells about the problem that the characters face and the solution to that problem. Then read aloud the first two pages of "The Sunset in My Mailbox." Have students identify the main character and her problem.

Have students listen to identify more important events as you read the rest of the story aloud.

After Reading

RESPOND Ask students how they know this story is realistic fiction. (Possible response: Caitlin could be a real person; the setting is like a real house; a person could have a pen pal that sends strange things.) Ask students if they think Caitlin looks forward to getting more letters from Julien. Why? (Yes, because she never knows what she is going to find.)

Build Robust Vocabulary
Words from the Read-Aloud

Teach/Model

Routine Card 3

INTRODUCE ROBUST VOCABULARY Use *Routine Card 3* to introduce the words.

❶ Put the word in **selection context**.
❷ Display Transparency R78 and read the word and the **Student-Friendly Explanation**.
❸ Have students **say the word** with you.
❹ Use the word in other contexts, and have students **interact with the word's meaning**.
❺ Remove the transparency. Say the Student-Friendly Explanation again and ask students to **name the word** that goes with it.

❶ **Selection Context:** Even though the grape fruitbar had melted on it, Caitlin **deciphered** Julien's letter.
❹ **Interact with Word Meaning:** What is more likely to need to be deciphered, a printed letter or a handwritten letter?

❶ **Selection Context:** Caitlin thought Julien must be **mistaken**, because no one could put a sunset in an envelope.
❹ **Interact with Word Meaning:** What would cause you more problems, to be mistaken about the date of a test or to be mistaken about one problem in your homework?

Practice/Apply

GUIDED PRACTICE Ask students the following:

• What kinds of codes have you *deciphered*? How were these codes *deciphered*?

• Have you ever been *mistaken* about an important date?

Objective
• *To develop robust vocabulary by discussing literature*

Tested

INTRODUCE ✔

Vocabulary: Lesson 12

deciphered   mistaken

▼ **Student-Friendly Explanations**

Vocabulary

1. **deciphered** If you have figured out a message that is difficult to understand or that is written in code, then you have deciphered it.

2. **mistaken** If you are wrong about something, you are mistaken.

3. **catastrophe** A catastrophe is something really terrible that has happened.

4. **fortunate** If you are fortunate, you are very lucky.

Grade 3, Lesson 12   Rb   Vocabulary

Transparency R78

Make Connections Tell students that they **decipher** words when they read and understand English. When they make an error, they are **mistaken**.

Grammar
Pronouns

5-DAY GRAMMAR

DAY 1	Define Pronouns
DAY 2	Singular Pronouns
DAY 3	Plural Pronouns
DAY 4	Apply Pronouns to Writing
DAY 5	Singular and Plural Pronouns Review

Objectives

- *To recognize that pronouns replace nouns*
- *To identify pronouns*

Daily Proofreading

1. Amira writed to she cousin.
   (wrote; her cousin)
2. They drov for six hour.
   (drove; hours)

TECHNOLOGY

 www.harcourtschool.com/
storytown
Grammar Glossary

Singular and Plural Pronouns

1. Mr. and Mrs. Valdez hurried so they would be on time. they; Mr. and Mrs. Valdez

2. Charlie wished he could hit a home run. he; Charlie

3. Tom and Gianna said, "We had a picnic at the park." we; Tom and Gianna

4. Lisa's friends waited for her to join them. her, them; Lisa, Lisa's friends

5. I asked Sam to go with me to the store. I, me; the speaker

6. Marcus wrote a letter and mailed it. it; letter

Grade 3, Lesson 12   LA6   Grammar: Singular and Plural Pronouns

Transparency LA25

Teach/Model

DEFINE PRONOUNS Explain to students that a *pronoun* is a word that takes the place of a noun. Writers use pronouns to keep from using the same noun over and over again. Write these common pronouns on the board and ask volunteers to read them aloud.

I	you	we	he
she	it	they	me
him	her	them	

Next, write the following sentence from "A Sunset in My Mailbox" on the board and review it as a class.

One week she even sent a snowball.

Point out that the word *she* is a pronoun. It takes the place of the word *Julien*.

Guided Practice

IDENTIFY PRONOUNS Display **Transparency LA25**. Read aloud the first sentence and guide a volunteer to identify the pronoun. (they) Then guide another volunteer to identify the word or words *they* takes the place of (Mr. and Mrs. Valdez) Work on items 2–3 together.

Practice/Apply

IDENTIFY PRONOUNS AND THE NOUNS THEY REPLACE Have students copy sentences 4–6 onto paper. Then ask them to underline each pronoun and to draw an arrow to the noun it replaces.

5-DAY WRITING	
DAY 1	Introduce
DAY 2	Prewrite
DAY 3	Draft
DAY 4	Draft
DAY 5	Revise/Edit

Writing
Realistic Story

Teach/Model

INTRODUCE A REALISTIC STORY Display **Transparency LA26**. Mention that this is a good example of the beginning of a realistic story. Read aloud the story on the transparency. Then together develop a list of the characteristics of a realistic story. Leave the list in place so you can add more characteristics on Days 2–4.

A Realistic Story

- Includes characters and settings that could be real
- Includes events that could happen

WRITING TRAIT **VOICE** Point out to students that the topic of a story, the writer's feeling about the topic, and the words and phrases that he or she uses all create a unique voice, or a special style of writing. Explain that when a writer's voice is clear, his or her personality and beliefs come through to the reader.

Guided Practice

IDENTIFY VOICE Point out that the author's use of the words *never* and *always* in the first two sentences helps tell the reader how the author feels about letters and e-mail. Read the rest of the paragraph. Discuss how the author could change the last two sentences to change the voice.

Practice/Apply

PRACTICE WITH VOICE Have students write a sentence about each of the following topics: the ocean, a bear, winter. Have partners compare their sentences and discuss how their ideas, words, and feelings are different.

Objectives

- *To recognize realistic writing*
- *To recognize and use appropriate voice*

Writing Prompt

Sentences Have students write two sentences on a topic of their choice. Encourage them to give each sentence a different voice by using words to express different feelings.

Student Model: Realistic Story

Amy had never written a letter on paper. She always sent e-mail or instant messages instead. She even sent thank-you notes for birthday presents and invitations for parties by e-mail. "I don't like to write letters," she said stubbornly. "It takes too long!"

So the day a letter came for her, she was very surprised. She could not imagine whom it was from. Everyone she knew was on her e-mail buddy list. Amy looked at the envelope. The postmark said Anchorage, Alaska.

"I don't know anyone in Alaska!" Amy said to her mother. "Who could be sending this to me?"

Grade 3, Lesson 12   **LAb**   Writing: Realistic Story

Transparency LA26

Day at a Glance

Day 2

 **and Spelling**
- Words with *kn, gn*

Robust Vocabulary

Words from the Selection
- Introduce: *translate, repairs, heaving, bothersome, din, dodging*

Comprehension

 Use Story Structure

 Review: Plot

Reading

- "A Pen Pal for Max," *Student Edition*, pp. 338–354

Fluency

- Expression

Robust Vocabulary

Words About the Selection
- Introduce: *catastrophe, fortunate*

Grammar

- Singular Pronouns

Writing

- Realistic Story

Warm-Up Routines

Oral Language

Objectives *To listen attentively and respond appropriately to oral communication; to write and speak in complete sentences*

Question of the Day

How do you "talk" with friends?

Remind students that "talk" can mean anything from speaking in person to e-mailing to conversing on the telephone. Then ask students how they "talk" with their friends. On the board, make a list of common ways in which students communicate with their friends. (Possible responses may include talking after school, using the telephone, sending e-mails, or writing letters.)

Then ask students to suppose a friend moved away to another town or city. How would they communicate with that person? How would it be different from communicating with friends who are nearby? Encourage students to suggest different ways to communicate across distances. Then have students answer the following in their notebooks:

> **To "talk" with a friend who lives far away, I would _____ because _____.**

Have students write at least one sentence. Then invite volunteers to read their responses aloud.

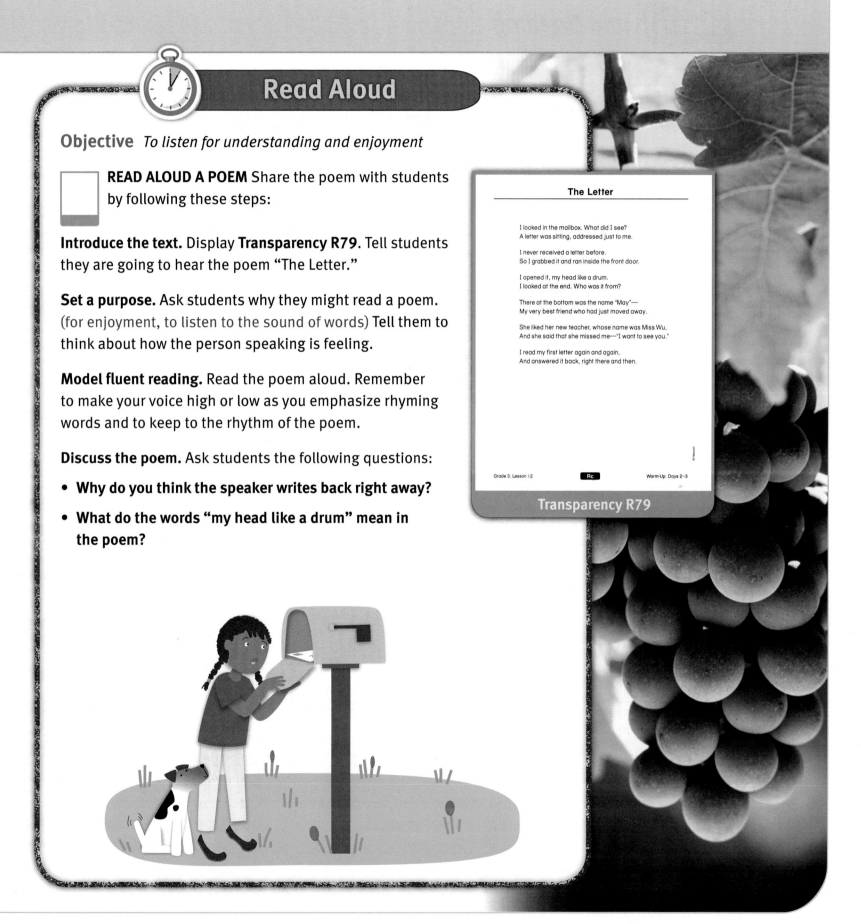

Read Aloud

Objective *To listen for understanding and enjoyment*

READ ALOUD A POEM Share the poem with students by following these steps:

Introduce the text. Display **Transparency R79**. Tell students they are going to hear the poem "The Letter."

Set a purpose. Ask students why they might read a poem. (for enjoyment, to listen to the sound of words) Tell them to think about how the person speaking is feeling.

Model fluent reading. Read the poem aloud. Remember to make your voice high or low as you emphasize rhyming words and to keep to the rhythm of the poem.

Discuss the poem. Ask students the following questions:

• **Why do you think the speaker writes back right away?**

• **What do the words "my head like a drum" mean in the poem?**

The Letter

I looked in the mailbox. What did I see?
A letter was sitting, addressed just to me.

I never received a letter before.
So I grabbed it and ran inside the front door.

I opened it, my head like a drum.
I looked at the end. Who was it from?

There at the bottom was the name "May"—
My very best friend who had just moved away.

She liked her new teacher, whose name was Miss Wu,
And she said that she missed me—"I want to see you."

I read my first letter again and again,
And answered it back, right there and then.

Grade 3, Lesson 12   Rc   Warm-Up: Days 2–3

Transparency R79

Consonant Digraphs *kn, gn, wr, gh*

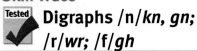 **phonics** *and Spelling*

Objectives

- *To read words with digraphs* kn *and* gn
- *To spell words with digraphs* kn *and* gn

Skill Trace

Tested ☑ **Digraphs /n/ *kn, gn*; /r/ *wr*; /f/ *gh***

Introduce	Grade 2
Reintroduce	T126
Reteach	S14
Review	T136–T137, T158, T174, T186, T400–T401
Test	Theme 3
Maintain	Theme 4, T344

Spelling Words

1. gnat	9. kneel
2. knew	10. wrist
3. sign	11. cough
4. knob	12. known
5. gnaw	13. rough
6. write*	14. wrench
7. knees	15. knight
8. wrinkle	

Challenge Words

16. knitting	19. unknown
17. laughter	20. playwright
18. wring	

*Word from "A Pen Pal for Max"

Teach/Model

REINTRODUCE *kn* AND *gn* Display **Transparency R80**. Direct students to Part A and read aloud the word *knee* (Item 1). Circle the consonant pair *kn* and say /n/, reminding students that the *k* in *kn* is silent and that *kn* is pronounced /n/. Point to *ee* and say /ē/. Have students repeat and then blend sounds together to form the word *knee*. Repeat with Item 2. Then continue with /n/*gn* in Items 3–4.

Call students' attention to Items 5–6. Ask them to identify words with *kn* or *gn*. Underline those letters in the words. Then have students read the words and the sentences aloud.

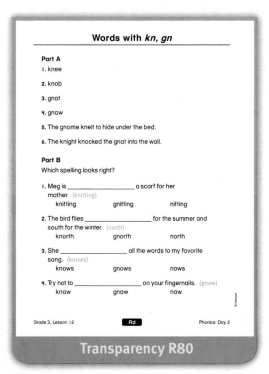

Words with *kn, gn*

Part A
1. knee
2. knob
3. gnat
4. gnaw
5. The gnome knelt to hide under the bed.
6. The knight knocked the gnat into the wall.

Part B
Which spelling looks right?
1. Meg is _____ a scarf for her mother. (knitting)
   knitting   gnitting   nitting
2. The bird flies _____ for the summer and south for the winter. (north)
   knorth   gnorth   north
3. She _____ all the words to my favorite song. (knows)
   knows   gnows   nows
4. Try not to _____ on your fingernails. (gnaw)
   know   gnaw   naw

Grade 3, Lesson 12   Rd   Phonics: Day 2

Transparency R80

BELOW-LEVEL

Cross Out *k* and *g* As a way to remind students that letters are not always pronounced, use **Transparency R80** and have them cross out *k* and *g* in words where they appear before *n*.

ADVANCED

Difficult *-gn* Words Write the words *resign, design, reign,* and *assignment* on the board. Have students use dictionaries to find meanings and pronunciations of these words. Then ask them to read the words aloud and use them in sentences.

5-DAY SPELLING
DAY 1 Pretest
DAY 2 Spelling Instruction/Practice
DAY 3 Spelling Practice/Review
DAY 4 Use Spelling Strategies/Review
DAY 5 Posttest

WORDS WITH *kn, gn, wr, gh* Explain that words with silent letters such as letter pairs *kn* and *gn* can make spelling difficult. Tell students that there are no good ways to tell for sure which words are spelled with *kn*, which words are spelled with *gn*, and which words are spelled with *n*, but most words use *n* to stand for /n/. Explain that most words use *r*, not *wr*, to stand for /r/, and most words use *f*, not *gh*, to stand for /f/. Emphasize that students will need to learn the individual words that use *kn*, *gn*, *wr*, and *gh*.

HOW WORDS LOOK Display **Transparency R80**. Draw students' attention to Part B. Ask them to read the sentences and to look at the three possible spellings of the missing words. Have students decide which spelling seems correct for each word. Remind students that one good spelling strategy is to write the word in different ways and then to see which way looks correct.

WRITE Have students choose three *kn* or *gn* spelling words. Have students use the words to write sentences in their notebooks.

MONITOR PROGRESS

Phonics: Digraphs

IF students confuse homophones such as *knight/ night, gnat/Nat,* and *knew/new,*	**THEN** have them make index cards listing the spellings of both words with a picture or description for each.

Small-Group Instruction, p. S14:

● **BELOW-LEVEL:** Reteach
● **ON-LEVEL:** Reinforce
○ **ADVANCED:** Extend

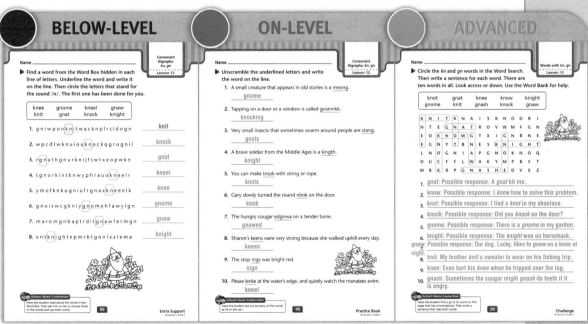

▲ Extra Support, p. 99   ▲ Practice Book, p. 99   ▲ Challenge, p. 99

E L L

• Group students according to academic levels, and assign one of the pages on the left.

• Clarify any unfamiliar concepts as necessary. See *ELL Teacher Guide* Lesson 12 for support in scaffolding instruction.

Build Robust Vocabulary
Words from the Selection

Objectives
- *To build robust vocabulary*

Vocabulary: Lesson 12

translate	bothersome
repairs	din
heaving	dodging

▼ **Student-Friendly Explanations**

Vocabulary

1. **translate** If you translate something, you say or write it in another language.

2. **repairs** When something needs repairs, it needs to be fixed.

3. **heaving** Heaving is throwing something heavy with great effort.

4. **bothersome** When something is bothersome, it bothers you and causes problems.

5. **din** If there is a din, there is so much noise that it is hard to hear anything over it.

6. **dodging** When you are dodging something, you avoid something that is coming toward you.

Grade 3, Lesson 12   Re   Vocabulary: from the Selection

Transparency R81

Word Scribe

Word Lists At the end of the week, encourage students to share their Word Scribe writing with the class.

HOMEWORK/INDEPENDENT PRACTICE

Teach/Model

INTRODUCE ROBUST VOCABULARY Introduce the words using the following steps:

❶ Display **Transparency R81** and read the word and the **Student-Friendly Explanation**.

❷ Have students **say the word** with you.

❸ Have students **interact with the word's meaning** by asking them the appropriate question below.

- If you **translate** a letter, what are you doing to it?
- Why does a car that has been in an accident need **repairs**?
- If the earth begins **heaving**, what might be happening?
- What might a **bothersome** child be doing?
- Is it easy to hear a **din**? Explain.
- How would you move if you were **dodging** a ball?

Develop Deeper Meaning

EXPAND WORD MEANINGS: PAGES 336–337 Have students read the passage. Then read the passage aloud, pausing at the end of page 336 to ask questions 1–2. Read page 337, and then discuss students' answers to questions 3–6.

1. From what language would the guide in Chile **translate**?
2. Why were **repairs** needed in Santiago?
3. Where could you see rocks **heaving** in Chile?
4. Do people in Chile think earthquakes are **bothersome**? Why or why not?
5. Why might earthquakes cause a **din**?
6. What are rock climbers **dodging** when they climb?

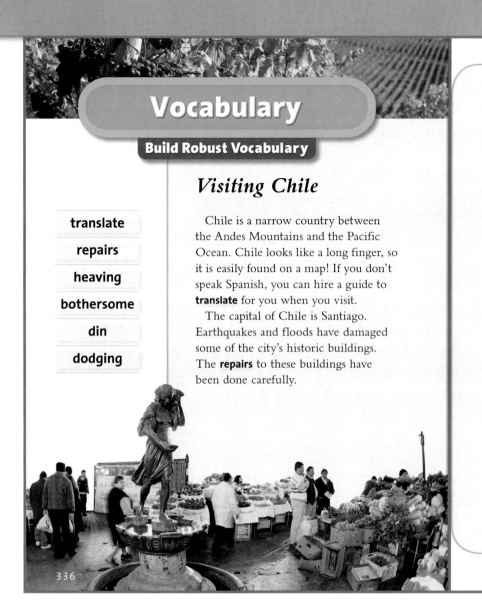

Vocabulary

Build Robust Vocabulary

Visiting Chile

translate

repairs

heaving

bothersome

din

dodging

Chile is a narrow country between the Andes Mountains and the Pacific Ocean. Chile looks like a long finger, so it is easily found on a map! If you don't speak Spanish, you can hire a guide to **translate** for you when you visit.

The capital of Chile is Santiago. Earthquakes and floods have damaged some of the city's historic buildings. The **repairs** to these buildings have been done carefully.

336

If you like adventures, you can climb mountains in Chile. Some mountains in Chile are active volcanoes, still **heaving** rocks and lava when they erupt!

Chile has earthquakes, too. Most are too small to be **bothersome**, but a large one can create quite a **din**. In 1980, the largest earthquake in history was recorded off the coast of Chile. Most of the time, however, Chile is a safe place to visit.

Rock climbers share tales of **dodging** rocks during rockslides.

 www.harcourtschool.com/storytown

Word Scribe

Your mission this week is to use the Vocabulary Words in your writing. For example, write about something you find bothersome. Read what you write to a classmate.

337

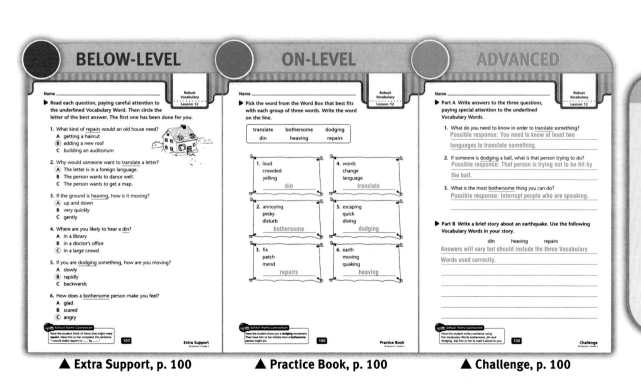

BELOW-LEVEL

▲ Extra Support, p. 100

ON-LEVEL

▲ Practice Book, p. 100

ADVANCED

▲ Challenge, p. 100

E L L

- Group students according to academic levels, and assign one of the pages on the left.

- Clarify any unfamiliar concepts as necessary. See *ELL Teacher Guide* Lesson 12 for support in scaffolding instruction.

Reading
Student Edition: **"A Pen Pal for Max"**

Objective
• *To use story structure to understand plot events*

Podcasting: Use Story Structure

Options for Reading

 BELOW-LEVEL

PREVIEW Model how to preview the selection and set a purpose for reading.

 ON-LEVEL

MONITOR COMPREHENSION Ask the questions as students read, or have pairs complete *Practice Book* page 101.

 ADVANCED

INDEPENDENT READING Have students read, using *Practice Book* p. 101.

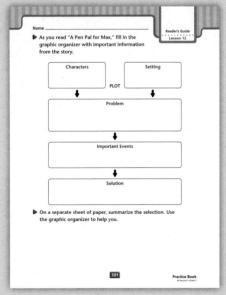

▲ Practice Book, p. 101

Genre Study

DISCUSS REALISTIC FICTION: PAGE 338 Explain that realistic fiction has characters and events that are like people and events in real life. Have students read the genre information about realistic fiction on *Student Edition* page 338. Ask volunteers to name examples of settings and problems that could appear in realistic fiction. Then use **Transparency GO7** or copy the graphic organizer from page 338 onto the board. Tell students that they could fill in the graphic organizer for any realistic fiction story they read.

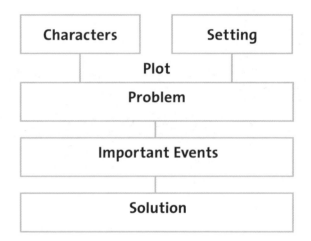

Comprehension Strategy

USE STORY STRUCTURE: PAGE 338 Remind students that stories are organized in a particular way. The beginning introduces the characters, the setting, and sometimes the problem the main character faces. The important events in the middle of the story lead to the solution of the character's problem at the end. Tell students that, while reading "A Pen Pal for Max," they will complete the graphic organizer from *Practice Book* page 101. Explain that the graphic organizer will help them keep track of the plot and the story's most important information as they read. See page T152 for the completed *Practice Book* page.

Realistic Fiction

Genre Study

Realistic fiction has characters and events that are like people and events in real life. Look for

- a setting that could be real.

- problems that characters might face in real life.

Characters	Setting

Plot

Problem

Important Events

Solution

Comprehension Strategy

Use story structure to find clues to the meaning of the story.

338

A Pen Pal for
Max

by Gloria Rand
illustrated by Ted Rand

339

Build Background

DISCUSS CHILE Show students a map of North and South America. Point out Chile on the map as well as the area in which the students live. Then tell them that they are going to read a story about a boy who lives on a fruit farm in Chile. Remind students of the information about Chile on the Vocabulary page.

SET A PURPOSE AND PREDICT Tell students that one purpose for reading realistic fiction is to enjoy the story. Ask them to turn to pages 338–339 in the *Student Edition*. Then follow these steps:

[Routine Card 5]

- Read the title and the author's and illustrator's names to the class.

- If necessary, explain the meaning of the term *pen pal*.

- Identify Max. Ask students to predict what Max does in the story.

- Write students' predictions on the board.

TECHNOLOGY

GO online eBook "A Pen Pal for Max" is available in an eBook.

Audiotext "A Pen Pal for Max" is available on *Audiotext 3* for subsequent readings.

Maximiliano lived in a small house on a huge fruit farm in Chile, South America. The farm belonged to Don Manuel. Max's father worked in the farm's vineyard. That's where grapes were grown to be shipped to markets all over the world. ❶

Max liked living on Don Manuel's farm. He had his own pony there and many friends nearby. ❷

One day Max rode his pony over to the farm's packing house to watch as large wooden bins, each filled with newly harvested grapes, were brought in from the vineyards. He stayed to see the grapes separated in small bunches, wrapped in paper, and put into boxes. These boxes were quickly stacked in waiting trucks for the short ride to a nearby seaport, where they would be loaded onto refrigerated freighters and shipped to many different countries.

"Want to go along for the ride?" the packing house manager jokingly asked Max. "These grapes are about to leave for the United States. Do you have any friends there?" ❸

340

341

Monitor Comprehension

PAGES 340–341 Have students look at the picture. Point out that it shows a vineyard. Ask volunteers what fruit comes from a vineyard. Then have students read the page to find out.

❶ **IMPORTANT DETAILS** **Where is the fruit from Don Manuel's vineyard going?** (to markets all over the world)

❷ **CHARACTER'S EMOTIONS** **How does Max feel about living on the farm?** (He likes it. He has his own pony and friends nearby.)

❸ **MAKE PREDICTIONS** **Do you think Max has friends in the United States? Why or why not?** (Possible response: No, the United States is very far away. He probably knows only people who live nearby.)

Apply
Comprehension Strategies

Focus Strategy

Use Story Structure Help students recognize story elements in the beginning of "A Pen Pal for Max." Have students answer these questions about the story:

• **Who is the main character?** (Max)

• **Where is the setting of the story?** (a huge farm in Chile, South America)

Max had none. And that's when he got the idea that it would be fun to have a friend in a faraway place. Quickly he turned his pony around and headed home. As soon as he got there he secretly wrote this note:

> Hola,
>
> Mi nombre es Maximiliano Farías. Me gustaría ser tu amigo. Por favor, escríbame.
>
> Maximiliano Farías
> Casilla 74
> El Monte, Chile

In English it read: "Hello, my name is Maximiliano Farías. I would like to be your friend. Please write to me." He signed his name and gave his address.

Max tucked the note into his shirt pocket and rode back to the packing house, where grapes were still being brought in and prepared for shipping. When no one was looking, Max slipped the note into a box of grapes.

"Maybe someone will find this," Max said to himself. "Maybe that person will write an answer to me and we can become friends." ② ③

343

Monitor Comprehension

PAGES 342–343 Point out that the letter is written in Spanish. Remind students to do their best to read the words even if they don't understand all of them. Guide them to identify the parts of the letter.

① SEQUENCE What does Max do after talking with the packing house manager? (He writes a letter and slips it into a box of grapes that are going to the U.S.)

② DRAW CONCLUSIONS Why does Max write the letter? (He wants to make a new friend in a faraway place.)

③ IMPORTANT DETAILS Why does Max include his address? (He hopes someone will write back to him. That person will need his address.)

E L L

Letter in Spanish Have students whose first language is Spanish translate Max's letter for others who do not speak Spanish. Students can talk about the meanings of the words and phrases in each language. Point out that the word *escribir* means "to write." It is similar to the English words *inscribe*, *describe*, and *scribble*.

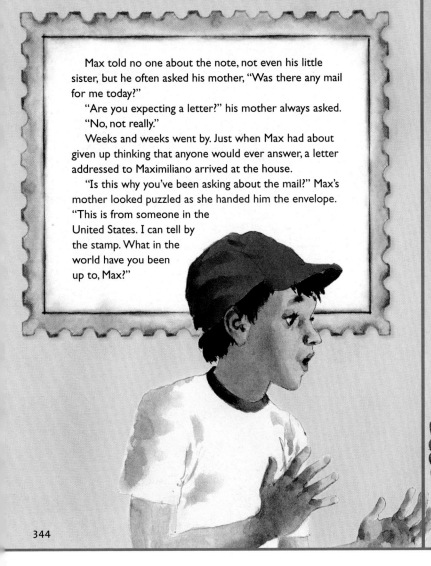

Max told no one about the note, not even his little sister, but he often asked his mother, "Was there any mail for me today?"

"Are you expecting a letter?" his mother always asked.

"No, not really."

Weeks and weeks went by. Just when Max had about given up thinking that anyone would ever answer, a letter addressed to Maximiliano arrived at the house.

"Is this why you've been asking about the mail?" Max's mother looked puzzled as she handed him the envelope. "This is from someone in the United States. I can tell by the stamp. What in the world have you been up to, Max?"

As he ripped open the envelope, Max told his mother about the note he'd put into a box of grapes. Then in a disappointed voice he said, "Oh, no. Look at this. I've gotten a letter I can't read." ②

Max's mother recognized that the letter was written in English, even though she could not read it herself.

"Don Manuel speaks and writes the English language. Maybe if you ask nicely, he'll translate this letter for you." ③

344

345

Monitor Comprehension

PAGES 344–345 Have students look at the illustrations and make predictions about the letter Max might receive.

① **CHARACTERS' EMOTIONS How does Max feel when he gets an answer to his letter? When he gets the letter, what does he do to show this feeling?** (He is excited. He rips open the letter.)

② **PLOT What surprise does Max get when the letter comes?** (He cannot read it.)

③ **PLOT Who can help Max with his problem?** (Don Manuel can translate for Max because he knows English.)

Max hurried down the dusty road to Don Manuel's house. The housekeeper answered his knock on the mansion's impressive front door.

"Come along," she said as she led Max into a grand room where Don Manuel was enjoying a late-afternoon cup of tea.

"Hello, Max. What brings you here?" Don Manuel asked. Max explained about his secret note. **1**

"Well, what an interesting thing to do." Don Manuel smiled. "Hand me the letter and I'll read it to you."

The letter was from a girl named Maggie. She explained that her father was the produce manager at a large grocery store in a big city in the United States. He'd found Max's note as he was opening up boxes of Chilean grapes. **2**

"My father brought your note home and told me to take it to school. He was sure my teacher, Ms. Moore, who is also the school's Spanish teacher, could read it for me. Ms. Moore did, and she thinks you might be about my age. I'm ten years old," Maggie explained. "Are you ten years old, too? Write back." **3**

346

347

Monitor Comprehension

PAGES 346–347 Have students read to find out what the letter says and who it is from.

1 SPECULATE **Why do you think Max kept his letter a secret?** (Possible response: he might have thought other people would think him foolish.)

1 IMPORTANT DETAILS **How does Maggie get Max's letter?** (Her father finds it in the boxes of grapes and brings it home from work.)

3 SPECULATE **Why might Maggie's teacher think that Max is ten years old?** (Possible response: because of his handwriting or the words he uses.)

Use Multiple Strategies

Ask Questions Have students discuss questions they have about the story and their understanding of it. Encourage them to ask "why" questions.

That evening Max wrote to Maggie. Then Maggie wrote back to Max. They became regular pen pals. They wrote to each other often.

They wrote about school, soccer games, and their hobbies. They wrote about what they'd like to be when they grew up. ①

348

They wrote about the weather where they lived and how when it was summer in South America, it was winter in North America. They even wrote about how bothersome little brothers and sisters could be. ②

349

Monitor Comprehension

PAGES 348–349 Have students make predictions about what Max and Maggie might write about. Then have them read to find out about the pen pals.

① **MAKE COMPARISONS** **What do Maggie and Max have in common?** (They are about the same age; they both go to school and play soccer. They also enjoy writing letters.)

② **DRAW CONCLUSIONS** **Why do you think Max and Maggie continue to write to each other?** (They have a lot in common and enjoy learning about each other.)

E L L

Discuss Hobbies Point out the word *soccer* and ask students what the sport is called in their home language. Then explain the word *hobbies*. Elicit from volunteers the things they like to do and point out that these things are called *hobbies*.

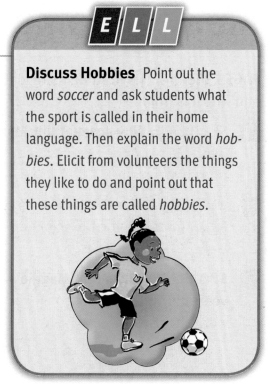

Don Manuel was always glad to translate for Max, and that's what he was doing one day when there was a loud rumbling sound and his big house began to shake. Furniture tumbled, vases and lamps crashed to the floor, tiles fell off the roof, and a cloud of dust rose up around everything. It was a terrible earthquake. **1**

"Come on!" Don Manuel cried out as he grabbed Max's hand. Together they ran out into the garden, dodging falling parts of the old farm mansion.

"Here, hang on to me," Don Manuel yelled over the din of the quake, trying to stay on his feet out in the middle of a large lawn that was heaving up and down. "You'll be fine, just hang on. This shaking is sure to stop soon." **2** **3**

Monitor Comprehension

PAGES 350–351 Have students look at the illustrations and predict what happens to Max and his family.

1 *Focus Skill* **PLOT** **What important event happens?** (Max is caught in an earthquake.)

2 **CHARACTERS' EMOTIONS** **What do you think Max is feeling? Why?** (He must be really scared with parts of the building falling.)

3 **IMPORTANT DETAILS** **How does Don Manuel help Max?** (Possible response: He leads Max out of danger. He talks to him and tells Max that he will be fine.)

SUPPORTING STANDARDS

The earth's surface is constantly changing over time. It is actually made up of pieces, called plates, which can move. Sometimes this movement causes the land to shake. This shaking is known as an earthquake. Earthquakes usually happen very quickly, but they can cause tremendous damage.

In the distance Max could see his pony running down the dirt road toward home. He wanted to run home, too, but Don Manuel said that wasn't a good idea. Debris was still crashing down everywhere. ❶

"Stay right here until the earth quiets down," he told Max. "It won't be long." ②

As soon as the ground seemed to be moving less, Don Manuel said, "It's okay to go on home now. Your mother is probably worried sick. Hurry! Just don't get near any of the farm buildings in case more tiles fall from the roofs!" ③

353

Monitor Comprehension

PAGES 352–353 Say: **Do you think Max and Don Manuel are safe outside?** Have students continue reading to learn what happens to Max.

❶ **MAKE INFERENCES** **Why does Max want to run home, as his pony has?** (He wants to be with his family and make sure they are safe.)

② **IMPORTANT DETAILS** **Why does Don Manuel tell Max to stay until the earth quiets down?** (Possible response: There is a lot of debris falling everywhere. He wants Max to be safe.)

③ **MAKE PREDICTIONS** **Max is going home to his family. How do you think they will be?** (Accept reasonable responses.)

ANALYZE AUTHOR'S PURPOSE

Author's Purpose Remind students that authors have a purpose, or reason, for writing. After students have finished reading "A Pen Pal for Max," ask:
Why did the author write "A Pen Pal for Max"?

• to tell readers how to get a pen pal

• to teach about Chile, grapes, and earthquakes

• to entertain readers with a story about friendship

Max reached his house in record time, just as his father was returning from the vineyards. His mother and sister, who had been at home during the whole horrible earthquake, hugged them both. They were all very happy to be together but still badly frightened by the force of the rumbling earth. **1**

The next day Max learned that his school was closed because it had so many broken windows and large cracks in the walls. It would take weeks for the needed repairs to be made. Since the earth was still trembling and moving now and then, Max was glad to be home. **2**

354

After a while the quake became only a scary memory, and Max went back to school.

"There's a nice surprise waiting for you here, Max," the school principal said as he pointed to a pile of boxes outside Max's classroom door. "These are all addressed to you and your classmates."

355

Monitor Comprehension

PAGES 354–355 Say: **Look at the characters on pp. 354 and 355. How are they feeling in each picture?** Have students read to find out the effects of the earthquake.

1 **CONFIRM PREDICTIONS Were your predictions about Max's family right? Explain.** (Possible response: Yes, they were not hurt but were very scared.)

2 **CAUSE/EFFECT What effect did the earthquake have on Max's life?** (It scared him, damaged his school, and closed his school for a while.)

SOCIAL STUDIES

SUPPORTING STANDARDS

When a natural disaster occurs, many people offer help. Discuss with students ways they could make a difference by helping people in need.

Lesson 12 (*Student Edition*, pages 354–355) **T149**

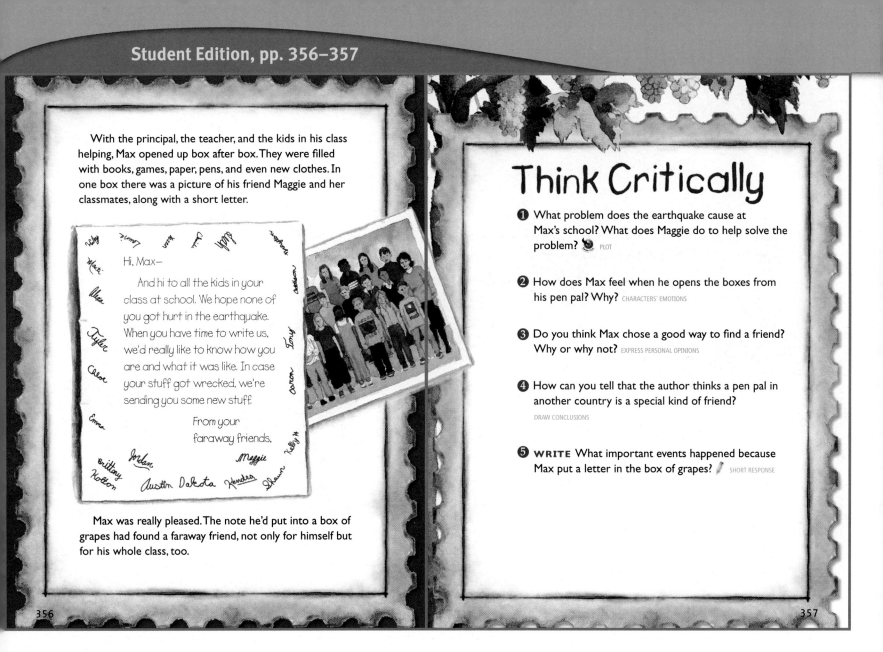

With the principal, the teacher, and the kids in his class helping, Max opened up box after box. They were filled with books, games, paper, pens, and even new clothes. In one box there was a picture of his friend Maggie and her classmates, along with a short letter.

Hi, Max—

And hi to all the kids in your class at school. We hope none of you got hurt in the earthquake. When you have time to write us, we'd really like to know how you are and what it was like. In case your stuff got wrecked, we're sending you some new stuff.

From your faraway friends,

Max was really pleased. The note he'd put into a box of grapes had found a faraway friend, not only for himself but for his whole class, too.

Think Critically

❶ What problem does the earthquake cause at Max's school? What does Maggie do to help solve the problem? PLOT

❷ How does Max feel when he opens the boxes from his pen pal? Why? CHARACTERS' EMOTIONS

❸ Do you think Max chose a good way to find a friend? Why or why not? EXPRESS PERSONAL OPINIONS

❹ How can you tell that the author thinks a pen pal in another country is a special kind of friend? DRAW CONCLUSIONS

❺ WRITE What important events happened because Max put a letter in the box of grapes? SHORT RESPONSE

356

357

Think Critically

Respond to the Literature

❶ It damages Max's school, so the school is closed for a while. Maggie's class sends supplies. **PLOT**

❷ Max is pleased and surprised by the generosity of people he has never met. **CHARACTERS' EMOTIONS**

❸ Possible response: Yes, Max chose a good way to find a friend. When Max wrote the letter, he made a friend who helped him after the earthquake. **EXPRESS PERSONAL OPINIONS**

❹ Possible response: She shows how friends can help each other from far away. **DRAW CONCLUSIONS**

❺ WRITE Possible response: Max became pen pals with Maggie. Max's class received help from Maggie's class. **WRITING RESPONSE/RECOGNIZE PLOT**

ADVANCED

Think Like a Character Tell students to think about Maggie. How does she hear about the earthquake? What does she say to her classmates to get them to help? What adults help her? Have students work with a partner and write the part of the story after the earthquake as though they are Maggie.

Meet the Author
Gloria Rand

Gloria Rand has written many children's books. They have all been illustrated by her husband, Ted Rand. Most of her books are inspired by real events or by people she knows. The author says she enjoys everything about her work. She likes doing research and interviewing people for her stories. Best of all, she likes the children who read her books. She says, "If a young reader lets us know our books are okay, it makes us feel like winners in every way."

358

About the Illustrator
Ted Rand

Ted Rand illustrated all of his wife's books as well as children's books by other authors. He illustrated more than eighty books in all.

Ted Rand did not always illustrate books. In fact, he didn't start illustrating until he was in his sixties! He liked to add a lot of detail in his illustrations. Some people think his pictures are works of art.

GO online www.harcourtschool.com/storytown

359

Meet the Author and the Illustrator

PAGES 358–359 Ask students to read pages 358–359. Tell students that Gloria Rand lives on Mercer Island, off the coast of Washington State, in a house that she and her husband built. When Gloria Rand writes, she reads her words out loud. She does this because she knows that her stories will often be read aloud, and she wants the words to sound right.

Explain that Ted Rand, who died in 2005, grew up on Mercer Island. He worked for many years drawing ads for different products. The Rands liked to travel for their work, writing and illustrating children's books. They wanted to see and get to know the places they would be writing about and illustrating.

Check Comprehension
Retelling

Objectives

- *To practice retelling a story*
- *To read with expression*

RETELLING RUBRIC

4	Uses details to clearly retell the story
3	Uses some details to retell the story
2	Retells the story with some inaccuracies
1	Is unable to retell the story

Professional Development

Podcasting: Auditory Modeling

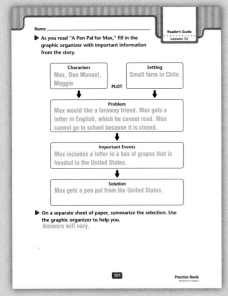

▲ Practice Book, p. 101

Retell

PLOT Remind students that the plot is the series of events, or things that happen, in a story. The beginning introduces the characters, setting, and a bit about the main character's problem. The problem or goal is fully explained in the middle and then solved or reached at the end of the story. Point out that knowing the important events helps readers understand the story. Then ask students to name the most important event in the story. (An earthquake hits Max's village.)

Routine Card 6

WRITE A SUMMARY Have students recall important events from "A Pen Pal for Max." Remind them that a summary contains the main events in a story. Students may refer to the graphic organizer on *Practice Book* page 101 to help them with this. Have students write a brief summary of the selection.

Fluency
Expression

Teach/Model

READING WITH EXPRESSION Tell students that they should always read with expression. This means raising or lowering one's voice to show which character is speaking, characters' feelings, and whether events are exciting. Emphasizing expression, read page 341 from "A Pen Pal for Max." Ask students to follow along and pay attention to the way your voice gets loud or quiet and speeds up or slows down. For example, point out that you use a different tone of voice to show that the packing house manager is speaking.

Practice/Apply

Routine Card 9

PARTNER READING Have students read pages 341–342 with a partner. They should do their best to imitate your reading and to read with expression.

Build Robust Vocabulary
Words About the Selection

Teach/Model

Routine Card 3

INTRODUCE THE WORDS Use *Routine Card 3* to introduce the second two words.

❶ Put the word in **selection context**.
❷ Display Transparency R78 and read the word and the **Student-Friendly Explanation**.
❸ Have students **say the word** with you.
❹ Use the word in other contexts, and have students **interact with the word's meaning**.
❺ Remove the transparency. Say the Student-Friendly Explanation again, and ask students to **name the word** that goes with it.

❶ **Selection Context:** The earthquake was a **catastrophe** for Max's village.
❹ **Interact with Word Meaning:** It was a catastrophe when the town's only supermarket burned to the ground. Which would be a catastrophe: not being able to go out because of rain, or a flood caused by heavy rains?

❶ **Selection Context:** Max was **fortunate** that no one in his family was hurt.
❹ **Interact with Word Meaning:** I felt fortunate when I won the raffle. Would you feel fortunate to lose something, or to find something you lost?

Vocabulary: Lesson 12

catastrophe

fortunate

▼ **Student-Friendly Explanations**

Vocabulary

1. **deciphered** If you have figured out a message that is difficult to understand or that is written in code, then you have deciphered it.

2. **mistaken** If you are wrong about something, you are mistaken.

3. **catastrophe** A catastrophe is something really terrible that has happened.

4. **fortunate** If you are fortunate, you are very lucky.

Grade 3, Lesson 12   **R8**   Vocabulary

Transparency R78

Practice/Apply

GUIDED PRACTICE Ask students to do the following:

• Think of things that could be catastrophes. What could you do to help someone in a catastrophe?

• Think about something that makes you feel fortunate. Talk with a partner. Then, write one or two sentences in your notebooks about feeling fortunate.

E L L

Discuss Real-Life Situations
Point out to students that every country has natural *catastrophes*, such as floods, hurricanes, or droughts. Discuss natural catastrophes in students' home countries.

Grammar
Singular Pronouns

5-DAY GRAMMAR

DAY 1	Define Pronouns
DAY 2	Singular Pronouns
DAY 3	Plural Pronouns
DAY 4	Apply Pronouns to Writing
DAY 5	Singular and Plural Pronouns Review

Objectives
- *To recognize that singular pronouns replace singular nouns*
- *To identify singular pronouns*

Daily Proofreading
1. The sandwhich was so good that Billy ate them all.
   (sandwich; ate it)
2. Nora's friend give her an aple.
   (gave; apple)

▲ Grammar Practice Book, p. 41

Teach/Model

DISCUSS SINGULAR PRONOUNS Remind students that a pronoun is a word that takes the place of a noun. Explain that a singular pronoun replaces a singular noun, or a noun that names one person, place or thing. Then write the following words on the board:

I	you	he	she
me	her	him	it

Read aloud each singular pronoun and point out that these are pronouns students use, hear, and read.

Guided Practice

IDENTIFY SINGULAR PRONOUNS On the board, write these sentences:

Matt threw it away.

He ran to the store.

Read aloud each sentence. Guide students to see that the singular pronoun in the first sentence is *it* and that *it* stands for something that Matt threw away. Ask a volunteer to identify the singular pronoun in the second sentence. (*he*) Then ask what noun the pronoun could replace. (Possible response: the name of a person, such as *Matt*, or a word for a person, such as *boy*.)

Practice/Apply

REWRITE SENTENCES On the board, write these sentences:

Tom ate the pie. (He, it)

Anjali talked to Jane. (She, her)

I asked Nyesha for help. (her)

Have students rewrite the sentences, substituting singular pronouns for the underlined words. Invite volunteers to share their responses.

5-DAY WRITING	
DAY 1	Introduce
DAY 2	Prewrite
DAY 3	Draft
DAY 4	Draft
DAY 5	Revise/Edit

Writing
Realistic Story

Prewrite

DISCUSS PLOT Remind students that the plot of a realistic story is something that could happen in real life.

ANALYZE A LITERATURE MODEL Reread page 350 of "A Pen Pal for Max." The most exciting event in this story is the earthquake, which causes a realistic problem for Max. Add this information to the list of characteristics.

> ### Realistic Story
> - Includes characters and settings that could be real
> - Includes events that could happen
> - Tells about a problem and how it is solved

VOICE Review that a writer's voice is created by the way the author uses words to share ideas and feelings.

MODEL PREWRITING Draw a story map on the board. Work with students to complete it. Help them describe a realistic main character, setting, story problem, and solution.

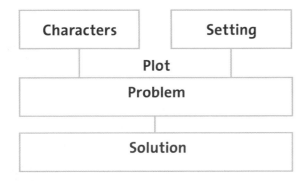

Characters		Setting
	Plot	
	Problem	
	Solution	

Practice/Apply

PREWRITING A REALISTIC STORY Have students complete a story map for a realistic story in their notebooks. Have students save their story maps to use on Days 3–5.

Objectives
- *To recognize realistic writing*
- *To recognize and use appropriate voice*
- *To choose a topic and generate ideas for a realistic story.*

Writing Prompt

Describing Words Have students write down five words or phrases that would describe the main character in their story.

> boy
> student
> Chilean
> 10 years old
> friendly

BELOW-LEVEL

Prewriting Elicit from students an interesting story that happened to them. Then help them transform it into a fictional story so they can see how real life can become fiction.

Day at a Glance
Day 3

 and Spelling

- Words with *wr*

Fluency

- Expression
- "A Pen Pal for Max," *Student Edition*, pp. 338–359

Comprehension

 Review: Plot

Reading

- "Postcards from Around the Globe," *Student Edition*, pp. 360–361

Read!

Robust Vocabulary

- Review: *deciphered, mistaken, translate, repairs, heaving, bothersome, din, dodging, catastrophe, fortunate*
- Review: Use Context Clues

Grammar

- Plural Pronouns

Writing ✏

- Realistic Story

Warm-Up Routines

Oral Language

Objectives *To listen attentively and respond appropriately to oral communication; to record ideas and reflections*

Question of the Day

What is a postcard?

How is it like a letter?

Explain what a postcard is, being sure to mention that it sometimes has a picture and always has less writing space than a letter. Discuss with students the different occasions on which you have sent a postcard, emphasizing that postcards are an excellent way to keep in touch when you have little time or are traveling or visiting. Ask students to suggest traits that postcards and letters share, including information, addresses for the people they are going to, and so on. Encourage all students to actively participate in a discussion about the best times to use a postcard and a letter.

Then direct students to answer the following writing prompt in their notebooks.

How are letters and postcards the same, and how are they different?

Students should write two complete sentences as a response. Invite several volunteers to share with the class.

Read Aloud

Objective *To read poetry fluently*

Share the poem with students using the following steps:

REVIEW THE POEM Display **Transparency R79** or distribute photocopies to students. Tell students you are going to reread the poem "The Letter."

Set a purpose. Ask students what reason they might have for rereading a poem. (to understand it better, to enjoy it again, to appreciate and listen to the rhyme and rhythm) Tell them that they will listen and follow along as you read the poem aloud.

Model fluent reading. Read the poem aloud. Use various expressive techniques, such as raising or lowering your voice, to convey the writer's feelings.

Choral-read. Have students track the poem's text and choral-read with you. Remind them to follow your expression and intonation.

The Letter

I looked in the mailbox. What did I see?
A letter was sitting, addressed just to me.

I never received a letter before.
So I grabbed it and ran inside the front door.

I opened it, my head like a drum.
I looked at the end. Who was it from?

There at the bottom was the name "May"—
My very best friend who had just moved away.

She liked her new teacher, whose name was Miss Wu,
And she said that she missed me—"I want to see you."

I read my first letter again and again,
And answered it back, right there and then.

Grade 3, Lesson 12   Rc   Warm-Up: Days 2–3

Transparency R79

Consonant Digraphs
kn, gn, wr, gh phonics

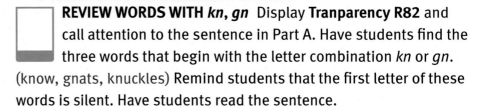

5-DAY PHONICS	
DAY 1	Introduce Digraphs *kn, gn, wr, gh*
DAY 2	Words with /n/ *kn, gn*
DAY 3	Words with /r/ *wr*
DAY 4	Words with /f/ *gh*
DAY 5	Review *kn, gn, wr, gh*

Objectives

- *To read words with digraph* wr
- *To read and follow written directions*

Skill Trace

 Tested **Digraphs /n/kn, gn; /r/wr; /f/gh**

Introduce	Grade 2
Reintroduce	T126
Reteach	S14
Review	T136–T137, T158, T174, T186, T400–T401
Test	Theme 3
Maintain	Theme 4, T344

Words with *kn, gn, wr*

Part A   I know there are gnats buzzing around my knuckles.

Part B   1.   Have you ever seen a person wrapping a box?

2. What does a person wringing out a towel look like?

3. Can we make a wreath out of branches and leaves?

4. Is there a wren peeking out of that bird house?

5. Would you point to your wrist, please?

6. Did you watch that worm wriggling across the ground?

Grade 3, Lesson 12   **Rf**   Phonics: Day 3

Transparency R82

Teach/Model

REVIEW WORDS WITH *kn, gn* Display **Tranparency R82** and call attention to the sentence in Part A. Have students find the three words that begin with the letter combination *kn* or *gn*. (know, gnats, knuckles) Remind students that the first letter of these words is silent. Have students read the sentence.

REINTRODUCE WORDS WITH *wr* Write the word *wrong* on the board. Remind students that the initial consonant *w* is silent and the consonant combination *wr* represents the sound /r/. Have students read the word. Write *kn, gn*, and *wr* on the board. As you point to each combination, have students say the sound associated with it. Repeat several times, mixing up the order in which you point to the pairs.

Practice/Apply

GUIDED PRACTICE Display **Transparency R82** and direct students to the first item in Part B. Have them locate the word that begins with *wr*. (wrapping) Circle the initial *wr* and have students give the sound of the letter combination. (/r/) Then guide students to read the word and the sentence. Repeat with the second sentence.

INDEPENDENT PRACTICE Have students work in pairs to do the remaining sentences on Transparency R82 on their own. Have each member of the pair write two of the sentences on a separate sheet of paper. Then, for each sentence, have one student circle the word that begins with *wr*. Have the other student read the word to his or her partner, using the sound /r/ for the letter combination *wr*. Then have both students read the sentences aloud.

Consonant Digraphs *kn, gn, wr, gh* phonics *and Spelling*

5-DAY SPELLING
DAY 1 Pretest
DAY 2 Spelling Instruction/Practice
DAY 3 Spelling Practice/Handwriting
DAY 4 Use Spelling Strategies/Review
DAY 5 Posttest

Review Spelling Words

WORDS WITH *wr* Write the spelling words *write*, *wrinkle*, *wrist*, and *wrench* on the board. Have students read them aloud. Point out that all four words begin with *wr*. Tell students that *wr* always comes at the beginning of a word or syllable. Cover the words on the board and then read them aloud, one by one. Have students write the words on a separate sheet of paper, and have them check their spellings when they are done.

SPELLINGS OF /r/ AND /n/ Explain that most words that begin with the sound /r/ use the spelling *r*. A few words start with the letter combination *wr*. Tell students that they should use *r* unless they know that a particular word uses *wr*. Remind students that this is true for /n/ as well. Unless they know for sure that a word is spelled with *kn* or *gn*, it is best to spell a word with *n* for the sound /n/.

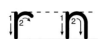 **WRITE** Have students write a short conversation, or dialogue, in which two people use all four of the *wr* spelling words along with at least three other spelling words. Remind students to check their spellings carefully and to use their best handwriting.

Handwriting

LETTER FORMATION Remind students to form the letter *r* carefully. Explain that when the curve of the *r* extends too far, the letter looks like an *n*.

r   n

ADVANCED

Use Spelling Words Have students write a sentence that uses three or more of the spelling words and makes sense.

The playwright told the knight to kneel before the king.

Objective

• *To spell words with* wr
• *To write a dialogue using* wr *words*

Spelling Words

1. gnat	9. kneel
2. knew	10. wrist
3. sign	11. cough
4. knob	12. known
5. gnaw	13. rough
6. write*	14. wrench
7. knees	15. knight
8. wrinkle	

Challenge Words

16. knitting	19. unknown
17. laughter	20. playwright
18. wring	

*Word from "A Pen Pal for Max"

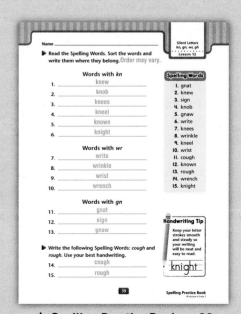

▲ Spelling Practice Book, p. 39

Fluency
Expression

Objectives

- *To read with expression*
- *To use strategies to speak clearly*

Additional Related Reading

- ***Dear Mr. Blueberry***
  by Simon James. Aladdin, 1996.
  EASY
- ***A Letter to Amy***
  by Ezra Jack Keats. Puffin, 1998.
  AVERAGE
- ***Chile: A Question and Answer Book***
  by Kremena Spengler. Capstone, 2005. **CHALLENGE**

BELOW-LEVEL

Fluency Practice Have students reread for fluency, using Story 12 in the *Strategic Intervention Interactive Reader* or the appropriate *Leveled Reader.* (See pages T194–T197.) Guide students to select a small portion of a story and practice reading it several times.

Review

DIBELS Oral Reading Fluency **ORF**

MODEL READING WITH EXPRESSION Remind students that when good readers read aloud, they use expression to show what the characters feel and to identify exciting or scary plot moments. They do this by talking more loudly or softly, more quickly or more slowly. Tell students that as they read, they should

- think about what is happening in the story.

- notice when a character is speaking and think about how he or she is feeling.

Think Aloud **I am going to read aloud part of "A Pen Pal for Max." I will read an exciting part of the story and use expression to help show what is happening. I will think about how the characters feel and use my voice to show their feelings.**

Routine Card 8 **ECHO-READING** Read aloud page 350 of "A Pen Pal for Max." Then read it again, having students echo-read after you. Guide students to recognize the words that Don Manuel speaks on the page and his feelings. For example, tell students to use a loud voice when reading the words *"Come on!" Don Manuel cried out as he grabbed Max's hand.*

Practice/Apply

GUIDED PRACTICE Have partners reread a favorite page from "A Pen Pal for Max." Remind them to think about what the characters are feeling and the mood of that part of the story so they can read with expression. Listen to partners read, giving them feedback and pointers for reading expressively.

Routine Card 7 **INDEPENDENT PRACTICE** Divide students into two groups. Use Routine Card 7 to have students choral-read "A Pen Pal for Max," reading aloud alternating pages of the story. Remind them to use expression while they read.

Plot
Comprehension

Review

EXPLAIN PLOT Remind students that the plot of a story often contains a problem or goal that characters have to solve or reach. Sometimes a story has more than one problem or goal. As they read, students should look for the problems that the characters face.

Practice/Apply

GUIDED PRACTICE Work with students to revisit "A Pen Pal for Max" to look for Max's problems in the story. Ask students the following questions:

- **PAGES 341–342 What goal does Max have at the beginning of the story?** (He would like a faraway friend, or pen pal.)

- **PAGE 345 What problem does he have after this?** (He gets a letter, but it is in English, which he cannot read.)

- **PAGE 354 What greater problem does he face next?** (An earthquake damages his school, so he cannot go to school.)

INDEPENDENT PRACTICE Ask students to think about how the problems are solved. Then have students fill in a two-column chart listing the problems and solutions.

Problems/Goals	Solutions
Max would like a faraway friend.	He puts a note in a box of grapes headed for the U.S.
He gets a letter in English that he cannot read.	Don Manuel translates it for him.
An earthquake damages his school.	Maggie and her classmates send new supplies.

Objectives

- *To identify plot events*
- *To recognize cause-and-effect relationships in literary texts*

Skill Trace

 Plot

Introduce	T32–T33
Reteach	S6
Review	T63, T79, T91, T128–T129, T161, T177, T189, T387, T402
Test	Theme 3
Maintain	Theme 4, T80

Reading
Student Edition: Paired Selection

Objectives

- *To understand the features of postcards*
- *To identify important details of postcards*

Writing Prompt

Write a Message Have students write a brief postcard message from a place they would like to visit. Tell them to describe their place in detail. Have students think about the following questions as they write: What makes this place special? What are you doing there?

Genre Study

DISCUSS POSTCARDS Tell students that "Postcards from Around the Globe" gives examples of writing that you might find or write on a postcard. Postcards are a fun way of communicating with family and friends, either from home or from somewhere else.

TEXT FEATURES Remind students that a postcard is a two-sided card. It usually has a picture on one side and writing space on the other side. The picture often shows an interesting or beautiful place.

Next, tell students that the writing side is divided into two parts. In the space on the left, the sender writes a short message. In the space on the right, the sender writes the name and address of the person who will receive the postcard.

USE PRIOR KNOWLEDGE/SET A PURPOSE Ask students if they have ever received or sent a postcard. Have volunteers describe the picture and message included in their postcards. Read aloud the title "Postcards from Around the Globe." Point out the stamp, address, and written message on each postcard. Then ask what you could learn by reading a postcard from another place in the world. (about another country, about the person who wrote the postcard)

Respond to the Postcards

MONITOR COMPREHENSION As students read the postcards, ask them these questions:

- **IMPORTANT DETAILS Where are the three postcards from?** (California, Costa Rica, and Paris, France)

- **AUTHOR'S PURPOSE Why have the writers sent the postcards?** (to say hello, to give information, to describe an experience)

- **COMPARISON/CONTRAST What topic do the three postcards share?** (They all describe food: tomatoes, bananas, and cheese.)

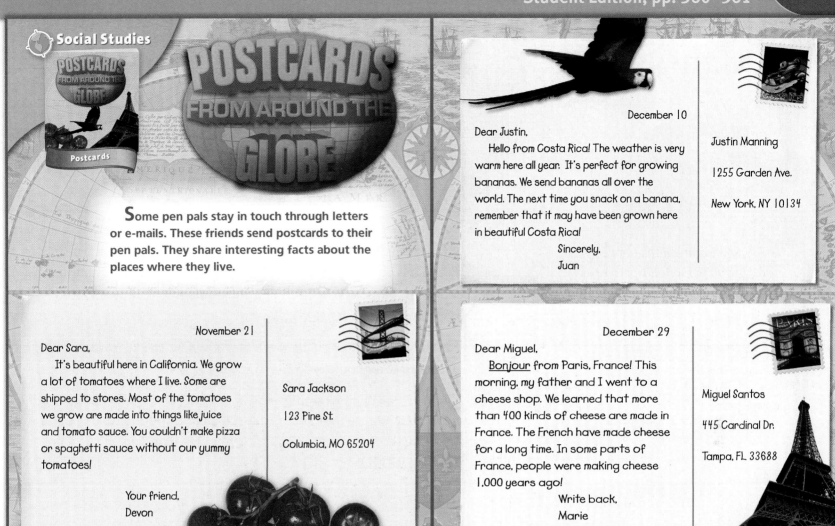

Social Studies

POSTCARDS FROM AROUND THE GLOBE

Some pen pals stay in touch through letters or e-mails. These friends send postcards to their pen pals. They share interesting facts about the places where they live.

November 21

Dear Sara,

It's beautiful here in California. We grow a lot of tomatoes where I live. Some are shipped to stores. Most of the tomatoes we grow are made into things like juice and tomato sauce. You couldn't make pizza or spaghetti sauce without our yummy tomatoes!

Your friend,
Devon

Sara Jackson

123 Pine St.

Columbia, MO 65204

360

December 10

Dear Justin,

Hello from Costa Rica! The weather is very warm here all year. It's perfect for growing bananas. We send bananas all over the world. The next time you snack on a banana, remember that it may have been grown here in beautiful Costa Rica!

Sincerely,
Juan

Justin Manning

1255 Garden Ave.

New York, NY 10134

December 29

Dear Miguel,

Bonjour from Paris, France! This morning, my father and I went to a cheese shop. We learned that more than 400 kinds of cheese are made in France. The French have made cheese for a long time. In some parts of France, people were making cheese 1,000 years ago!

Write back,
Marie

Miguel Santos

445 Cardinal Dr.

Tampa, FL 33688

361

 SOCIAL STUDIES SUPPORTING STANDARDS

LAND AND FOOD Explain to students that people grow different foods, depending on the soil, the growing conditions, and the weather where they live. Rice, for example, grows in places with warm, wet weather. Ask students what kinds of food grow near where they live. Discuss the conditions that make that crop suitable for the area.

 **E L L**

Build Background Use **Picture Cards 49** and **124** to illustrate that vegetables are grown on farms. Use the map to point to areas in the world where these crops are grown. Show **Picture Card 57**. Ask students to speculate where these foods might be grown.

fa... vegetables

Connections

Objectives

- *To make connections between texts*
- *To make connections between texts and personal experiences*
- *To respond to text through writing*

Comparing Texts

1. Possible responses: They are alike because they write to one another; they tell about where they are; one pen pal in each pair lives in the U.S. They are different because they live in different places; Max and Maggie write letters, but these pen pals have written postcards. **TEXT TO TEXT**

2. Possible response: Yes, because I would like to know what it is like to live in another country. **TEXT TO SELF**

3. Possible response: I learned that Chile has earthquakes. I learned from the pictures that some children wear uniforms to school, and they like things that are similar to what we like, such as soccer. **TEXT TO WORLD**

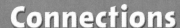

Connections

Comparing Texts

1. How are the pen pals in "A Pen Pal for Max" and "Postcards from Around the Globe" alike? How are they different?

2. Would you like to be pen pals with someone from another country? Explain.

3. What did you learn about Chile that you did not know before?

Vocabulary Review

Rate a Situation

Work with a partner. Read aloud each sentence and point to the spot on the line that shows how you would rate each situation. Discuss your answers.

bothersome ——————————— enjoyable

• You had to make **repairs** to your bicycle.

• The **din** of the construction outside made it difficult to hear your friend.

• You practiced **dodging** during a soccer practice.

| translate |
| repairs |
| heaving |
| bothersome |
| din |
| dodging |

362

Fluency Practice

Partner Reading

Choose a section from "A Pen Pal for Max" that includes characters talking. Meet with a partner. Take turns reading aloud the sections you chose. Remember to read a character's words as a real person would speak.

Writing

Write a Thank-You Note

Write a thank-you note to someone who has helped you. Describe what was done and why you appreciate it. Include the parts of a letter: the date, the greeting, the body, the closing, and the signature.

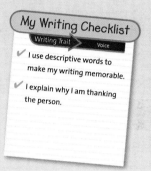

My Writing Checklist

Writing Trait ▶ Voice

✓ I use descriptive words to make my writing memorable.

✓ I explain why I am thanking the person.

363

VOCABULARY

Rate a Situation Instruct pairs of students to consider each situation on p. 362 and then rate each situation. Encourage them to come up with other situations to rate if time allows.

FLUENCY

Partner Reading Tell students to use expression in their voices as they read. Remind them to think about what is happening and make their voices louder or quieter, faster or slower to match the action.

WRITING

 **Write a Thank-You Note** Have students write a thank-you note that uses descriptive language. Have students use their checklists to evaluate their writing.

 PORTFOLIO OPPORTUNITY

Students can place their completed thank-you notes in their portfolios.

Build Robust Vocabulary

Objectives

- *To use vocabulary in different contexts*
- *To demonstate knowledge of word meaning*

INTRODUCE ✓ Tested

Vocabulary: Lesson 12

deciphered	bothersome
mistaken	din
translate	dodging
repairs	catastrophe
heaving	fortunate

Review Robust Vocabulary

USE VOCABULARY IN DIFFERENT CONTEXTS Remind students of the meanings of the Vocabulary Words introduced on Days 1 and 2. Then guide them to discuss each word in a new context.

deciphered

- **Why might you want a note deciphered?**
- **If you deciphered something, would it be harder or easier to read?**

mistaken

- **If you were mistaken about a test answer, what could happen?**
- **How might weather forecasters be mistaken about the weather?**

catastrophe

- **What is an example of a catastrophe caused by nature?**
- **How can people cause a catastrophe?**

fortunate

- **What fortunate thing would you like to have happen to you?**
- **When someone is fortunate, how might he or she act?**

translate

- **Could you translate something that was written in Spanish? Why or why not?**
- **Whom do you know who can speak and translate another language?**

bothersome

- Why might an insect bite be bothersome?
- How might a bothersome pet act?

dodging

- If you were running in a park, what might you have to dodge?
- If rock climbers were dodging rocks, how would they move?

din

- Which would make more of a din, a bird singing or trucks honking their horns?
- How would you describe the din of the crowd at a championship game?

heaving

- If the ground started heaving under you, what would you do?
- What would it look like if you were heaving heavy rocks up from the ground?

repairs

- How might you tell if a car needs repairs?
- What kind of repairs might a home need?

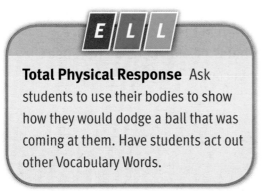

Total Physical Response Ask students to use their bodies to show how they would dodge a ball that was coming at them. Have students act out other Vocabulary Words.

▼ Student-Friendly Explanations

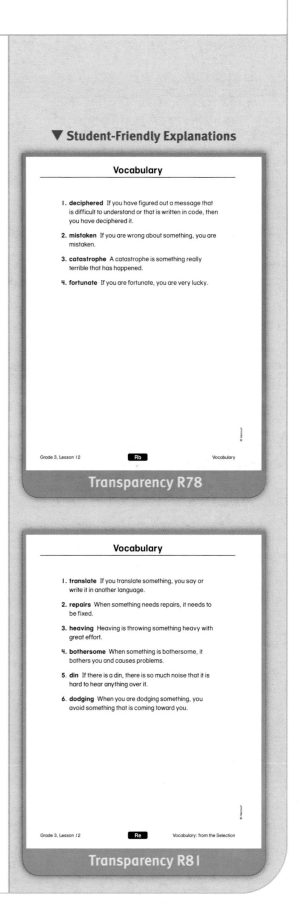

Vocabulary

1. **deciphered** If you have figured out a message that is difficult to understand or that is written in code, then you have deciphered it.

2. **mistaken** If you are wrong about something, you are mistaken.

3. **catastrophe** A catastrophe is something really terrible that has happened.

4. **fortunate** If you are fortunate, you are very lucky.

Grade 3, Lesson 12   Rb   Vocabulary

Transparency R78

Vocabulary

1. **translate** If you translate something, you say or write it in another language.

2. **repairs** When something needs repairs, it needs to be fixed.

3. **heaving** Heaving is throwing something heavy with great effort.

4. **bothersome** When something is bothersome, it bothers you and causes problems.

5. **din** If there is a din, there is so much noise that it is hard to hear anything over it.

6. **dodging** When you are dodging something, you avoid something that is coming toward you.

Grade 3, Lesson 12   Re   Vocabulary: from the Selection

Transparency R81

Use Context Clues
Vocabulary

Objective

- *To use context clues to find the meanings of unknown words*

Skill Trace

 Tested Use Context Clues

Introduce	T70–T71
Reteach	S20
Review	T168–T169
Test	Theme 3
Maintain	Theme 4, T264

✔ MONITOR PROGRESS

Use Context Clues

IF students have trouble identifying context clues,	**THEN** have them underline the words surrounding the unknown word. Students should think about the underlined words to decide if they give meaning to the unknown word.

Small-Group Instruction, p. S20:

- ● **BELOW-LEVEL:** Reteach
- ● **ON-LEVEL:** Reinforce
- ○ **ADVANCED:** Extend

Teach/Model

INTRODUCE CONTEXT CLUES Remind students that they can sometimes figure out the meaning of an unfamiliar word by looking at the words around it. Context clues may include *definitions* (familiar words that define an unfamiliar word) or *descriptions* (details that are clues to an unfamiliar word), which can be used to figure out the meaning of an unknown word. Write the following sentences on the board:

> **Juan opened the <u>missive</u>, a letter from his uncle.**
>
> **The <u>cockatiel</u> flapped its wings and let out a squawk.**

Review the sentences with students. For the first sentence, point out that the word *missive* is followed by a definition, "a letter," that tells readers what the word means.

Think Aloud The other words around cockatiel are "flapped its wings" and "squawked." I ask myself, "What flaps its wings and squawks?" The answer is "a bird." A *cockatiel* must be a kind of bird.

Guided Practice

USE CONTEXT CLUES Write these sentences on the board:

> We sweated in the <u>stifling</u> heat.
>
> A <u>cavern</u> like Mammoth Cave is often home to bats.

Guide students to identify the words that describe or relate to the underlined word in the first sentence. (*sweated, heat*) Then elicit what *stifling* means. ("very hot") Next, ask students to identify the word that defines *cavern* in the second sentence. (*cave*) Guide them to see that "home to bats" is a further clue because they may know that bats often live in caves.

Practice/Apply

USE CONTEXT CLUES Write these sentences on the board:

1. **The capuchin, a black-and-white monkey, is found in Central America.** (a black-and-white monkey)

2. **The room was spare, with only a bed in it.** (nearly empty)

3. **The store sold antique items from long ago.** (old, from long ago)

4. **The flowers had bright hues of red, yellow, and pink.** (colors)

On a separate sheet of paper, have students write the meaning of each underlined word. Then have them tell a partner what clues helped them to define each.

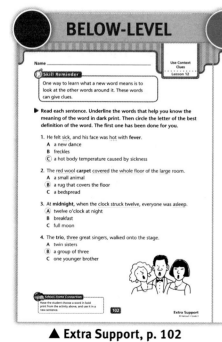

BELOW-LEVEL

Name _____

Use Context Clues
Lesson 12

Skill Reminder

One way to learn what a new word means is to look at the other words around it. These words can give clues.

▶ Read each sentence. Underline the words that help you know the meaning of the word in dark print. Then circle the letter of the best definition of the word. The first one has been done for you.

1. He felt sick, and his face was hot with **fever**.
   A a new dance
   B freckles
   C a hot body temperature caused by sickness

2. The red wool **carpet** covered the whole floor of the large room.
   A a small animal
   B a rug that covers the floor
   C a bedspread

3. At **midnight**, when the clock struck twelve, everyone was asleep.
   A twelve o'clock at night
   B breakfast
   C full moon

4. The **trio**, three great singers, walked onto the stage.
   A twin sisters
   B a group of three
   C one younger brother

School-Home Connection
Have the student choose a word in bold print from the activity above, and use it in a new sentence.

102   Extra Support

▲ **Extra Support, p. 102**

ON-LEVEL

Name _____

Use Context Clues
Lesson 12

▶ Write a definition for each underlined word. Next to the definition, describe the context clues that helped you understand what the word means.

1. Lenny made three attempts to climb the rope before he finally did it.
   Tries; he tried to climb the rope three times before finally climbing it

2. Mr. Robert's red face and loud voice showed that he was furious.
   Very angry; a red face and loud voice usually are signs that someone is very angry

3. The fragile flowers could not live through cold weather.
   Delicate; because the flowers could not live through cold weather, they are not strong.

4. When Angela lost the contest, she was upset and felt dejected.
   Unhappy; if Angela lost, she would be upset and sad

5. Some animals hibernate, or rest and sleep, from late fall to early spring.
   Rest and sleep; the definition "rest and sleep" follows the word hibernate

School-Home Connection
Describe a pebble, a knight, and a blaze, without naming the words, and have the student guess each word.

102   Practice Book

▲ **Practice Book, p. 102**

ADVANCED

Name _____

Use Context Clues
Lesson 12

▶ Read the passage. Then write your own definition for each underlined word.

An earthquake hit the town of Nadina last night. Rescuers came to the town at dawn, just as the sun rose. They helped the victims by treating their wounds. One family was trapped in their house. An oak tree had fallen in front of the only door and the windows were blocked by rubble. Rescuers worked for hours to free them. Finally, they moved the tree and the family could get out. One at a time, each family member emerged from the ruined house into the sunny day. The people watching applauded until their hands hurt.

1. dawn   sunrise
2. victims   people who have been hurt
3. trapped   being stuck in one place
4. emerged   came out
5. applauded   clapped

Try This
Turn your paper over and use three of these words to write your own news article about a natural disaster or catastrophe. Make sure you provide context clues for the words.

102   Challenge

▲ **Challenge, p. 102**

ELL

- Group students according to academic levels, and assign one of the pages on the left.

- Clarify any unfamiliar concepts as necessary. See *ELL Teacher Guide* Lesson 12 for support in scaffolding instruction.

Grammar
Plural Pronouns

5-DAY GRAMMAR	
DAY 1	Define Pronouns
DAY 2	Singular Pronouns
DAY 3	**Plural Pronouns**
DAY 4	Apply Pronouns to Writing
DAY 5	Singular and Plural Pronouns Review

Objectives

- *To recognize that plural pronouns replace plural nouns or compound subjects*
- *To identify plural pronouns*

Daily Proofreading

1. i saw Mr. and Mrs. Wells and waved at it. (I; at them)
2. Keely and I invited Sue to walk wit me. (with us)

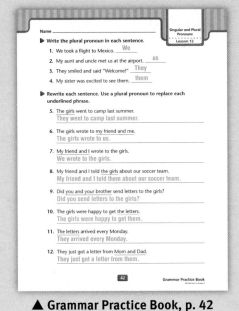

▲ **Grammar Practice Book, p. 42**

Teach/Model

DISCUSS PLURAL PRONOUNS Write these pronouns on the board:

we   us   you   they   them

Tell students that the words on the board are plural pronouns that replace plural nouns (such as *birds*, *friends*) or groups of nouns (such as *Max and Maria*, *students and teachers*). Also, point out that the pronoun *you* can be either singular or plural. Then write the following sentences on the board:

Jane and I went to the movies.

David clapped for the singers.

Read the first sentence aloud. Explain that the plural pronoun *we* can be used in place of the underlined words. Then read aloud the second sentence. Lead students to understand that the plural pronoun *them* can be used in place of the underlined words.

Guided Practice

USE PLURAL PRONOUNS Write the following sentences on the board:

Burt talked to Denny and me. (us)

The teachers had a meeting. (They)

You and Mattie can meet me there. (You)

Work with students to replace the underlined words with plural pronouns.

Practice/Apply

USE PLURAL PRONOUNS Have partners write five sentences, one with each plural pronoun, on a separate sheet of paper. Remind them to check each other's work when they are finished. Then invite volunteers to share their sentences with the class.

5-DAY WRITING
DAY 1 Introduce
DAY 2 Prewrite
DAY 3 Draft
DAY 4 Draft
DAY 5 Revise/Edit

Writing
Realistic Story

Draft a Realistic Story

REVIEW A LITERATURE MODEL Read aloud pages 340–342 of "A Pen Pal for Max" in the *Student Edition*. Point out that the beginning of a realistic story introduces a realistic setting (a huge farm in Chile, South America), a realistic main character (Max), and a problem (Max cannot read the letter he receives). Point out the following as you add the last item to the list of characteristics:

Realistic Story

- Includes characters and settings that could be real

- Includes events that could happen

- Tells about a problem and how it is solved

- Includes a plot with a beginning, a middle, and an ending

 DRAFT A STORY Have students use their completed graphic organizers from Day 2 as they begin to draft their own realistic stories. Remind students about using pronouns, but tell them they can revise their writing for this later.

WRITING TRAIT **VOICE** As students write their stories, remind them to use ideas, words, and feelings that reveal their personal voices.

CONFER WITH STUDENTS Meet with individual students to help them as they write. If students are having trouble with their plots, suggest they expand their graphic organizers to include notes about the important events that happen in the middle and ending of the story.

Objectives

- *To recognize and understand realistic writing*
- *To draft a realistic story*

 Writing Prompt

Problem and Solution Have students jot down the main problem their character faces and the solution to the problem.

▲ Writer's Companion, Lesson 12

 ADVANCED

Alternate Endings Encourage students to write an alternate ending to their story in which the solution or outcome is different.

Day at a Glance

Day 4

phonics and Spelling

- Review Consonant Diagraphs
  kn, gn, wr, gh

Fluency

- Expression
- "A Pen Pal for Max,"
  Student Edition, pp. 338–359

Read!

Comprehension

Focus Skill
  Review: Plot

- Maintain: Synonyms and
  Antonyms

Speaking/Listening

- Reading a Postcard

Robust Vocabulary

- Review: *deciphered, mistaken,*
  translate, repairs, heaving,
  bothersome, din, dodging,
  catastrophe, fortunate

Grammar

- Review: Pronouns

Writing

- Realistic Story

Warm-Up Routines

Oral Language

Objectives *To listen attentively and respond appropriately to oral communication; to write and speak in complete sentences*

Question of the Day

**Why would you choose to write
to someone instead of calling
him or her on the telephone?**

Explain that there are many reasons a person would choose to write to someone instead of calling him or her on the telephone. Point out that a person might think that it is more special to write a letter than to make a quick telephone call. Maybe one person does not have a telephone or lives too far away. Continue to discuss, and ask students to suggest other reasons.

After students have given several suggestions, ask them to respond in their notebooks to the writing prompt:

> **Name two reasons you would
> write to someone instead of calling
> him or her on the telephone.**

Students should write two or three complete sentences. Invite volunteers to share their responses with the class.

Read Aloud

Objective *To read fiction for understanding and enjoyment*

Using the following steps, share the story with students:

READ ALOUD A STORY Display **Transparency R83** or distribute photocopies to students. Say that you are going to read the story "Grandma's Party" aloud.

Set a purpose. Ask students what purpose they might have for reading a story called "Grandma's Party." (for enjoyment, to find out what kind of party it is) Tell them that they should listen and follow along to understand and enjoy the story.

Model fluent reading. Read the story aloud, using expression as you read. Then have students echo-read the story.

Discuss the story. After you have finished reading, ask:

- **Why is Brenda writing a letter instead of telephoning?**
- **What does Brenda describe in her letter?**

Grandma's Party

Brenda sat in the living room. Colored streamers, balloons, glitter, and photographs surrounded her. It was the morning after her grandmother's eightieth birthday party. All she could think of was telling her friend Ernesto about it. She wished she could call him, but he had just moved out of town. So, Brenda decided to write him a letter.

Dear Ernesto,

Grandma's birthday party was awesome! She loved the Big Band music. She said she felt young again. She and grandpa can still boogie-woogie. They even sang for us. They still know all the words! We had a wonderful time. You would have enjoyed it, too.

I hope your new place is great!

Your friend,
Brenda

Brenda smiled. She placed her letter in an envelope. It was ready to be mailed. She knew Ernesto would write back quickly. She couldn't wait. Now, if only her mom or dad, or even her older sister, would just wake up.

Grade 3, Lesson 12   **Rg**   Warm-Up: Days 4–5

Transparency R83

Consonant Digraphs
kn, gn, wr, gh phonics

5-DAY PHONICS

DAY 1	Introduce Digraphs *kn, gn, wr, gh*
DAY 2	Words with *kn, gn*
DAY 3	Words with *wr*
DAY 4	**Words with *gh***
DAY 5	Review *kn, gn, wr, gh*

Objectives

- *To review the digraphs* kn, gn, *and* wr
- *To read words in which* gh *stands for the sound* /f/

Skill Trace

Tested ✓ **Digraphs /n/kn, gn; /r/wr; /f/gh**

Introduce	Grade 2
Reintroduce	T126
Reteach	S14
Review	T136–T137, T158, T174, T186, T400–T401
Test	Theme 3
Maintain	Theme 4, T344

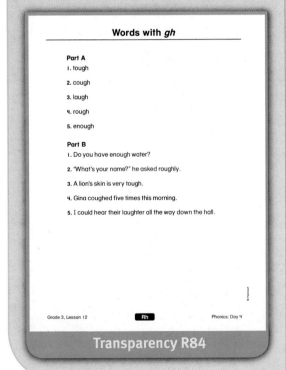

Words with *gh*

Part A
1. tough
2. cough
3. laugh
4. rough
5. enough

Part B
1. Do you have enough water?
2. "What's your name?" he asked roughly.
3. A lion's skin is very tough.
4. Gina coughed five times this morning.
5. I could hear their laughter all the way down the hall.

Grade 3, Lesson 12   Rh   Phonics: Day 4

Transparency R84

Review

REVIEW *kn, gn, wr* On the board, write the sentence *I know I went the wrong way at the stop sign.* Have students identify the words that use the digraphs *kn, gn,* and *wr.* (*know, wrong, sign*) Remind them that digraphs *kn* and *gn* are generally pronounced /n/, and that *wr* is pronounced /r/. Then have students read the words and the entire sentence aloud.

> I know I went the
> wrong way at
> the stop sign.

INTRODUCE /f/*gh* Explain that some words use the letter combination *gh* but that this letter pair seldom stands for /g/ or /h/. Tell students that *gh* can stand for the sound /f/ when it appears at the end of a syllable and after the vowel pairs *ou* or *au*. Write the spelling words *cough, rough,* and *knight* on the board and highlight the *gh* letter pair in each. Remind students that *cough* and *rough* are examples of words in which *gh* stands for /f/, but point out that *gh* does not stand for /f/ in *knight*.

Practice/Apply

GUIDED PRACTICE Display **Transparency R84**. Tell students that all the words in Part A have the letter pair *gh* standing for /f/. Point to *tough*. Circle the final *gh*. Move your finger under the letters and say /t/, /u/, /f/. Have students repeat. Then move your finger more quickly this time and blend the sounds together to say *tough*. Have students say the word. Repeat with Items 2–5. Stress that even though *cough, tough,* and *rough* end with the same four letters, the vowel sounds are different: /u/ in *tough* and *rough*, /o/ in *cough*.

INDEPENDENT PRACTICE Have students read the sentences in Part B. Ask them to identify the words with *gh*, write them, and circle the *gh*. Point out that some of these words do not end with *gh*. Then have students read the words and the sentences aloud.

Consonant Digraphs *kn, gn, wr, gh* phonics *and Spelling*

5-DAY SPELLING
DAY 1 Pretest
DAY 2 Spelling Instruction/Practice
DAY 3 Spelling Practice/Handwriting
DAY 4 Use Spelling Strategies/Review
DAY 5 Posttest

Use Spelling Strategies

WORDS WITH /f/gh Display **Transparency R84**. Call students' attention to the five words in Part A. Explain that these are the five most common words in which *gh* stands for the sound /f/. Tell students that they should use the spelling *f, ff,* or even *ph* instead of *gh* for the sound /f/, except in the cases of these five words and their forms.

USE SPELLING STRATEGIES Remind students that remembering what a word looks like can be a useful spelling strategy, especially for words spelled with *kn, gn, wr,* and *gh*. Write the following two words on the board: *coff, cough*. Challenge students to determine which one is spelled correctly. (cough) Repeat with *gnat/nat; nees/knees; rist/wrist; naw/gnaw; kneel/neel; nown/known; rench/wrench*. (gnat, knees, wrist, gnaw, kneel, known, wrench)

HOMOPHONES Point out that some of the spelling words sound just like other words. Write the following word pairs on the board: *knew/ new, knob/nob, write/right, rough/ruff, knight/night*. Have partners use a dictionary to look up the meanings of one pair of words. Then discuss the meaning of each word. Explain that students will have to remember which meaning they intend when writing to know how to spell the word correctly.

knew/new   knob/nob   write/right
        rough/ruff   knight/night

Objectives

- *To spell words with /f/gh*
- *To identify words in which /f/ is spelled with the letter pair* gh

Spelling Words

1.	gnat	9.	kneel
2.	knew	10.	wrist
3.	sign	11.	cough
4.	knob	12.	known
5.	gnaw	13.	rough
6.	write*	14.	wrench
7.	knees	15.	knight
8.	wrinkle		

Challenge Words

16.	knitting	19.	unknown
17.	laughter	20.	playwright
18.	wring		

Word from "A Pen Pal for Max"

ADVANCED

Word Sort Have students generate words that include the sound /f/. Ask them to sort these words according to the spelling of /f/ in each. Have them make a chart with columns labeled *f, ff, ph,* and *gh* and write words that fit the spelling pattern below each label. Instruct students to consult a dictionary to learn or check spellings. Have them explain their results when they are done.

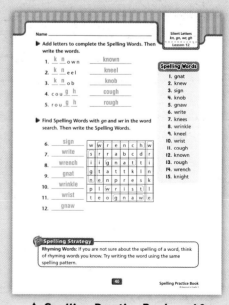

▲ Spelling Practice Book, p. 40

Fluency
Expression

Objectives

- *To build fluency by rereading a story*
- *To read with expression*

BELOW-LEVEL

Fluency Practice Read the words of a character in "A Pen Pal for Max" with expression. Have students echo-read the character's words to improve their use of expression in reading aloud.

MONITOR PROGRESS

Fluency

IF students have trouble identifying when characters are speaking,	**THEN** go over the use of quotation marks with them.

Small-Group Instruction, p. S16:

- ● **BELOW-LEVEL:** Reteach
- ● **ON-LEVEL:** Reinforce
- ● **ADVANCED:** Extend

Review

DIBELS
Oral Reading Fluency
ORF

MODEL READING WITH EXPRESSION Remind students that when they read aloud, they should use expression to show characters' thoughts and feelings and to interpret the events. Tell them that when they read they should:

▲ **Student Edition, pp. 338–359**

- think about what is happening in the story. Is the mood happy? sad? exciting? scary?

- notice when characters are speaking and think about how they are feeling.

Think Aloud **I am going to read part of "A Pen Pal for Max" aloud. I am going to change the tone and expression in my voice when different characters speak and to show how they are feeling. I am also going to pay attention to the mood of the story and change my expression to show the mood.**

Practice/Apply

Routine Card 8

ECHO-READ Model reading page 344 from "A Pen Pal for Max" aloud. Then reread it, having students echo-read. When you have finished, ask students to read each sentence aloud, guiding them to include the appropriate expression in their voices.

 # Plot
Comprehension

Review

EXPLAIN PLOT Ask students to explain what plot is in a story. (the events of the story that tell what happens) Remind them that a plot has a beginning, a middle, and an ending and that it usually tells about a problem and its solution.

Practice/Apply

GUIDED PRACTICE Display **Transparency R77.** Have students read "Ben's New School." Ask students to pay attention to the plot events. Then ask:

- **Who are the characters?** (Ben, Chan)

- **What is the problem in the story?** (Ben is lonely because he does not have a friend at his new school.)

- **How is it solved?** (Ben meets a new friend.)

- **What events take place in the story?** (Possible responses: Ben is lonely and afraid; he is the only student in gym who knows archery; Chan is interested in archery, so they start talking and become friends.)

INDEPENDENT PRACTICE Have students reread page 354 of "A Pen Pal for Max." Ask them the following questions:

- **What important events take place?** (Max is reunited with his family. Max cannot go to school because it is closed.)

- **What problem is introduced on this page?** (Max cannot go to school because it is closed.)

Objective

- *To identify plot events and problem and solution*

Skill Trace

 Plot

Introduce	T32–T33
Reteach	S6
Review	T63, T79, T91, T128–T129, T161, T177, T189, T387, T402
Test	Theme 3
Maintain	Theme 4, T80

Ben's New School

Ben spent his first day at his new school feeling lonely and afraid. He did not know anyone and this school went through sixth grade. At his old school, the third-graders had been the oldest students. Nobody talked to him.

The next day, Ben went to gym class. His classmates all talked to one another and left him out. Mr. Smith quieted the class and said, "Today we have a special treat. Ms. Ramos is going to show us about archery. Who has tried archery?"

Ben's grandfather was a keen archer and he had been teaching Ben about archery since Ben could remember. Ben quickly raised his hand. Mr. Smith called on Ben to assist Ms. Ramos.

Ben helped set up the target and checked that the arrows and bow were in place. Then Ms. Ramos sent twelve arrows into the target. Next, she let Ben try. Ben hit the target, too. Other students also tried, but none of them could hit the target.

After class, all the students wanted to know how Ben had learned archery. Some of them said they wanted to learn. One boy, Chan, rode the same bus as Ben, so they sat together and talked about archery all the way home. He invited Ben to his house so he could learn more.

Grade 3, Lesson 12   Ra   Warm-Up: Day 1

Transparency R77

Synonyms and Antonyms

Objective

- *To use knowledge of synonyms and antonyms to determine the meanings of words*

Skill Trace

Tested **Synonyms and Antonyms**

Introduce	Theme 2, T74–T75
Reteach	Theme 2, S8
Review	Theme 2, T170–T171
Test	Theme 2
Maintain	T178

Reinforce the Skill

REVIEW SYNONYMS AND ANTONYMS Write these sentences on the board: **The plant will not flourish in the sun. It will probably die.**

Think Aloud **When I read the first sentence, I am not sure what *flourish* means. So I read the second sentence for clues. I read that the plant "will probably die." That makes me think that *flourish* is the opposite of *die*.**

Remind students that words that mean the opposite of another word are called *antonyms*, while words that mean nearly the same thing as another word are called *synonyms*. Finding synonyms and antonyms in nearby sentences can help readers figure out the meanings of new words.

Practice/Apply

GUIDED PRACTICE Write these sentences on the board: **The hamlet was on a cliff above the sea. The village was so small, it was not on the map.**

Work with students to determine the meaning of *hamlet*, pointing out that *hamlet* and *village* are synonyms.

INDEPENDENT PRACTICE Write these sentences on the board: **Tony waited for his friend to respond, but he did not answer.**

Anya did not mean to break the vase. She hoped her dad would be able to repair it.

Have students write in their notebooks the underlined word, the synonym or antonym that helped explain its meaning, and whether the two words are synonyms or antonyms. Then they should write two funny sentences with both words.

Speaking and Listening
Reading a Postcard

Speaking

POSTCARDS Invite students to select one of the postcards from "Postcards from Around the Globe" (*Student Edition*, pages 360–361) to present to the class.

> #### ORGANIZING CONTENT
>
> Share the following **organizational tips** with students.
>
> - Note descriptive and sensory details.
>
> - Note parts of the postcard you want to emphasize.
>
> - Use a self-stick note to cover the address and date, since you will not read those parts.

Before students read to a small group or in front of the class, share the **speaking strategies** at the right. Remind students to use the punctuation to tell them when to pause and when to read with excitement.

Listening

RESPONDING Share the **listening strategies** with students. Have them mentally note details to understand the structure of each postcard. At the end of each presentation, ask students the name of the person who wrote the postcard. Then invite volunteers to tell the message of the postcard.

See rubrics for Speaking and Listening on page R5.

Objectives

- *To plan and present dramatic interpretations of experiences with clear diction, pitch, tempo, and tone*
- *To listen attentively to a speaker*

SPEAKING STRATEGIES

- Practice presenting the postcard so that you sound as if you are speaking, not reading.

- Use eye contact and movements to make your presentation more enjoyable.

LISTENING STRATEGIES

- Listen carefully for the name of the person who wrote the postcard.

- Listen for what the writer is saying.

- Look at the speaker.

Build Robust Vocabulary

Objectives

- *To review robust vocabulary*
- *To demonstrate knowledge of word meanings*

Tested

INTRODUCE ✓

Vocabulary: Lesson 12

deciphered	bothersome
mistaken	dodging
translate	din
repairs	catastrophe
heaving	fortunate

Extend Word Meanings

USE VOCABULARY IN DIFFERENT CONTEXTS Remind students of the **Student-Friendly Explanations** of the Vocabulary Words. Then discuss each word with them in a new context.

deciphered Tell students that if an item you name might need to be deciphered, they should raise their hands. If it might not need to be deciphered, they should shake their heads from side to side.

a menu in French	**a neatly typed note**
a stop sign	**a messy, scribbled note**

mistaken Read these math sentences. If the answer is wrong, ask students to say "Mistaken!" If the answer is correct, have students say, "Correct!"

$3 + 4 = 7$	$5 + 3 = 9$
$2 + 3 = 6$	$7 + 7 = 14$

catastrophe/fortunate Tell students to put their hand over their mouths if they think the event you name could be a catastrophe. Have them clap if the event is fortunate.

a volcano erupts near a town

a boy finds his lost dog

school is closed because of stormy weather

bothersome/repairs/din Tell students to raise their hand if the repair you name would cause a bothersome din and to keep their hand down if it would not.

using a jackhammer to dig up a road

repairing a watch

repairing a computer

using a hammer to fix a shelf

Word Relationships

SYNONYMS Remind students that synonyms are words that mean almost the same. Say the following sentences and then say the underlined word. Have students name a Vocabulary Word that is a synonym of and that could replace the underlined word or words.

1. **The hurricane was a real <u>disaster</u>.** (catastrophe)
2. **The <u>lifting</u> of the earth was the most frightening thing in the earthquake.** (heaving)
3. **When they were digging the tunnel, the <u>racket</u> of the machinery was dreadful.** (din)
4. **A buzzing mosquito is <u>annoying</u> in the summer.** (bothersome)
5. **We have <u>figured out</u> the coded message.** (deciphered)
6. **I think you are <u>wrong</u>; I have never been to New York City.** (mistaken)
7. **I do not read Spanish. Can you <u>decipher</u> this for me?** (translate)
8. **Thomas will be able to <u>fix</u> your computer.** (repair)

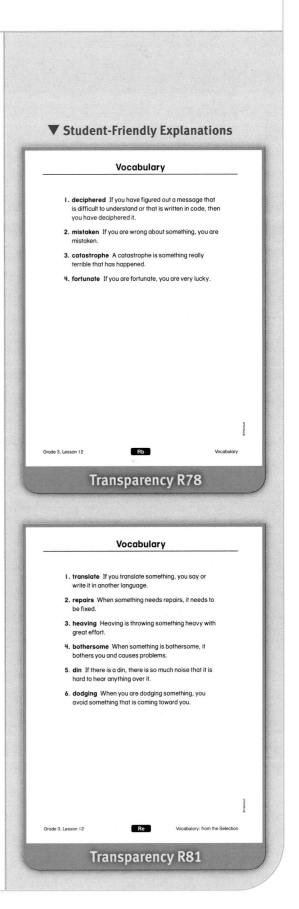

▼ **Student-Friendly Explanations**

Vocabulary

1. **deciphered** If you have figured out a message that is difficult to understand or that is written in code, then you have deciphered it.
2. **mistaken** If you are wrong about something, you are mistaken.
3. **catastrophe** A catastrophe is something really terrible that has happened.
4. **fortunate** If you are fortunate, you are very lucky.

Grade 3, Lesson 12   Rb   Vocabulary

Transparency R78

Vocabulary

1. **translate** If you translate something, you say or write it in another language.
2. **repairs** When something needs repairs, it needs to be fixed.
3. **heaving** Heaving is throwing something heavy with great effort.
4. **bothersome** When something is bothersome, it bothers you and causes problems.
5. **din** If there is a din, there is so much noise that it is hard to hear anything over it.
6. **dodging** When you are dodging something, you avoid something that is coming toward you.

Grade 3, Lesson 12   Re   Vocabulary: from the Selection

Transparency R81

Grammar
Apply to Writing

5-DAY **GRAMMAR**	
DAY 1	Define Pronouns
DAY 2	Singular Pronouns
DAY 3	Plural Pronouns
DAY 4	**Apply Pronouns to Writing**
DAY 5	Singular and Plural Pronouns Review

Objectives

- *To identify singular and plural pronouns*
- *To write sentences with singular and plural pronouns*

Daily Proofreading

1. Jim waved to Max, who waved bak at them. (back at him)
2. Ms. Jenkins repeated the quesstion her had asked. (question she)

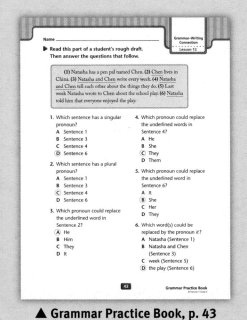

▲ Grammar Practice Book, p. 43

Review

DISCUSS PRONOUNS Review that a *pronoun* is a word that takes the place of a noun. A singular pronoun takes the place of a singular noun. A plural pronoun takes the place of a plural noun or compound subject. Then write the following sentences on the board:

> **She jumped into the swimming pool.**
>
> **We went to the museum.**

Read the sentences aloud. Ask students to identify the singular pronoun in the first sentence and the plural pronoun in the second sentence. (She, We)

Practice/Apply

GUIDED PRACTICE Write the following sentences on the board:

> **Karla ate too much.**
>
> **Silvio talked to Frank and Will.**

Work with students to replace the underlined nouns with singular or plural pronouns. Read aloud the first sentence and point out that *Karla* is a singular noun. Ask students to name a pronoun to replace it. (She) Then help students replace *Frank and Will* with a plural pronoun. (them)

INDEPENDENT PRACTICE Have students write five sentences, using singular and plural pronouns. Tell them to write one sentence for each of the following pronouns: *I*, *you*, *it*, *we*, and *them*. Then have them review their work with a partner. Invite volunteers to share some of their sentences with the class.

Writing
Realistic Story

5-DAY WRITING

DAY 1	Introduce
DAY 2	Prewrite
DAY 3	Draft
DAY 4	**Draft**
DAY 5	Revise/Edit

Draft a Realistic Story

 DRAFT A STORY Tell students that they will continue to work on their stories. Review the characteristics of realistic fiction. Then have students read page 355 of the *Student Edition*. Point out that dialogue, or a conversation between characters, can be an important part of realistic fiction. Add this point to the list of characteristics.

Realistic Story

- Includes characters and settings that could be real
- Includes events that could happen
- Tells about a problem and how it is solved
- Includes a plot with a beginning, a middle, and an ending
- May include dialogue

WRITING TRAIT **VOICE** Remind students that the ideas, words, and feelings they use in their stories should reveal their personal voice.

CONFER WITH STUDENTS Continue to meet with students one-on-one as they write. Encourage them to add dialogue to their stories. If they are having difficulty, ask questions such as "What would you say if you were in this situation?" and "What do you think [character's name] would say now?" Encourage students to use pronouns, where appropriate, to add variety to their dialogue.

Objectives

- *To draft a realistic story*
- *To create a story in which plot events are in order and complete*

 ## Writing Prompt

Summarize Have students read their drafts to a partner. Have them write a brief summary of their partner's story. Students should then exchange summaries so they can see if their story is clear.

Neutral Pronouns Some students may have trouble understanding that the word "it" is gender-neutral. Tell them that in English this pronoun is used to replace nouns that are neither male nor female. Say several sentences that include the word "it."

Day at a Glance

Day 5

 and Spelling
- Review: Digraphs *kn, gn, wr, gh*
- Posttest

Fluency
- Expression
- "A Pen Pal for Max," *Student Edition*, pp. 338–359

 Read!

Comprehension
 Review: Plot

- *Read-Aloud Anthology:* "The Sunset in My Mailbox"

Robust Vocabulary
- Cumulative Review

Grammar
- Review: Singular and Plural Pronouns

Writing ✏
- Realistic Story

Warm-Up Routines

 Oral Language

Objectives *To listen attentively and respond appropriately to oral communication; to write and speak in complete sentences*

Question of the Day

What events do you like to have your friends tell you about?

Ask students if they enjoy hearing about what their friends and relatives have done. Talk with students about what kinds of events interest them, such as celebrations, sporting events, and trips.

Encourage students to describe an event that friends or relatives have told them about. After students have offered several ideas, ask them to respond to the following writing prompt in their notebooks:

Name one event that a friend or relative has told you about. What happened? What made it interesting?

Students should write a few complete sentences. Invite volunteers to share their sentences with the class.

Read Aloud

Objective *To listen to a story for understanding and enjoyment*

REVIEW THE TEXT Display **Transparency R83** or distribute photocopies to students. Tell them that you are going to reread the story "Grandma's Party."

Set a purpose. Ask students what the purpose might be for reading or listening to a story again. (Possible response: for enjoyment, to practice fluency) Tell them that they will listen and follow along to enjoy the story.

Model fluent reading. Read the story aloud. Use expression and an enthusiastic tone when reading Brenda's letter. Then have students echo-read each sentence.

Partner-reading. Have students take turns reading the story aloud while their partners listen and follow along.

Grandma's Party

Brenda sat in the living room. Colored streamers, balloons, glitter, and photographs surrounded her. It was the morning after her grandmother's eightieth birthday party. All she could think of was telling her friend Ernesto about it. She wished she could call him, but he had just moved out of town. So, Brenda decided to write him a letter.

Dear Ernesto,

Grandma's birthday party was awesome! She loved the Big Band music. She said she felt young again. She and grandpa can still boogie-woogie. They even sang for us. They still know all the words! We had a wonderful time. You would have enjoyed it, too.

I hope your new place is great!

Your friend,
Brenda

Brenda smiled. She placed her letter in an envelope. It was ready to be mailed. She knew Ernesto would write back quickly. She couldn't wait. Now, if only her mom or dad, or even her older sister, would just wake up.

Grade 3, Lesson 12   Rg   Warm-Up: Days 4–5

Transparency R83

Consonant Digraphs
kn, gn, wr, gh phonics

5-DAY PHONICS

DAY 1	Introduce Digraphs *kn, gn, wr, gh*
DAY 2	Words with *kn, gn*
DAY 3	Words with *wr*
DAY 4	Words with *gh*
DAY 5	Review Digraphs *kn, gn, wr, gh*

Objective

• *To read words with the digraphs* kn, gn, wr, *and* gh

Skill Trace

Tested **Digraphs /n/kn, gn; /r/wr; /f/gh**

Introduce	Grade 2
Reintroduce	T126
Reteach	S14
Review	T136–T137, T158, T174, T186, T400–T401
Test	Theme 3
Maintain	Theme 4, T344

Review

DIGRAPHS *kn, gn* Write the words *know, knuckle, gnat, sign, knife,* and *gnaw* on the board. Have students find and circle the letter combinations *kn* and *gn* where they appear in each word. Remind students that all of the circled combinations stand for the sound /n/. Have students read the words aloud.

DIGRAPH *wr* Write *wriggle, wrong, wrap, wrestle,* and *wreck* on the board. Circle the letter pair *wr* where it appears, and point out that it comes at the beginning of each word. Ask students what sound *wr* stands for (/r/), and have them read the words aloud.

DIGRAPH /f/*gh* Write *rough, tough, laugh, cough,* and *enough* on the board. Have students tell where the letter pair *gh* appears in each word. (at the end) Establish that *gh* stands for the sound /f/ in each of these words. Have students read the words aloud. Remind them that it is important to know how to read the digraphs *kn, gn, wr,* and *gh* when these letter pairs are present.

BELOW-LEVEL   **ON-LEVEL**   **ADVANCED**

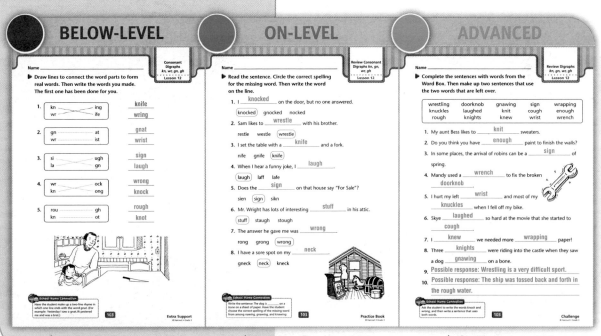

▲ Extra Support, p. 103   ▲ Practice Book, p. 103   ▲ Challenge, p. 103

E L L

• Group students according to academic levels, and assign one of the pages on the left.

• Clarify any unfamiliar concepts as necessary. See *ELL Teacher Guide* Lesson 12 for support in scaffolding instruction.

Consonant Digraphs *kn, gn, wr, gh* *and Spelling*

5-DAY SPELLING

DAY 1	Pretest
DAY 2	Spelling Instruction/Practice
DAY 3	Spelling Practice/Handwriting
DAY 4	Use Spelling Strategies/Review
DAY 5	Posttest

Assess

POSTTEST Assess students' progress. Use the dictation sentences from Day 1.

Words with Consonant Digraphs *kn, gn, wr, gh*

1.	gnat	A tiny **gnat** bit me.
2.	knew	No one **knew** LaShonda's middle name.
3.	sign	This **sign** says, "No Parking."
4.	knob	Turn the **knob** to make the radio louder.
5.	gnaw	Beavers **gnaw** on wood.
6.	write	Marianna likes to **write** poetry.
7.	knees	Calvin fell and hurt his **knees**.
8.	wrinkle	Alma ironed the **wrinkle** from her skirt.
9.	kneel	Would you rather stand, sit, or **kneel**?
10.	wrist	Your **wrist** connects your hand and arm.
11.	cough	Please cover your mouth when you **cough**.
12.	known	I have **known** Danny for three years.
13.	rough	Sandpaper is very **rough**.
14.	wrench	Please hand me the **wrench**.
15.	knight	The brave **knight** rescued the princess.

WRITING APPLICATION Have students choose eight to ten spelling words. Tell them to use these words in a descriptive paragraph about a topic of their choosing. Remind students to double-check the spelling of each of these words.

Objective

• *To spell words with digraphs* kn, gn, wr, *and* gh

Spelling Words

1.	gnat	9.	kneel
2.	knew	10.	wrist
3.	sign	11.	cough
4.	knob	12.	known
5.	gnaw	13.	rough
6.	write*	14.	wrench
7.	knees	15.	knight
8.	wrinkle		

Challenge Words

16.	knitting	19.	unknown
17.	laughter	20.	playwright
18.	wring		

*Word from "A Pen Pal for Max"

ADVANCED

Challenge Words Use these dictation sentences.

16. knitting   My grandmother is **knitting** a pair of socks.
17. laughter   **Laughter** is good medicine.
18. wring   Don't forget to **wring** the towel.
19. unknown   The answer to that question is **unknown**.
20. playwright   The **playwright** explained the setting of her story.

Fluency
Expression

Objective

- *To read fluently with appropriate expression*

ASSESSMENT

Monitoring Progress Periodically, take a timed sample of students' oral reading and measure the number of words read correctly per minute. Students should be accurately reading approximately 92 words per minute in the middle of Grade 3.

Fluency Support Materials

Fluency Builders,
Grade 3, Lesson 12

Audiotext *Student Edition* selections are available on *Audiotext 3.*

Strategic Intervention Teacher Guide,
Lesson 12

Readers' Theater

DIBELS Oral Reading Fluency **ORF**

PERFORM "A PEN PAL FOR MAX" To help students improve their fluency, have them perform "A Pen Pal for Max" as Readers' Theater. Use the following steps:

▲ **Student Edition, pp. 338–359**

- Discuss each character and his or her role in the story. Ask students to think about how each character might act and sound.

- Discuss the changes in mood in the story and how the characters' and narrator's voices can show the mood.

- Read "A Pen Pal for Max" aloud, modeling fluent and expressive reading as students follow along.

- Divide the class into groups and assign each student a part to read. Students can take the parts of Max, Max's mother, Don Manuel, and the narrator.

- Have groups practice reading the story with expression, especially when reading characters' dialogue.

- Listen to each group read. Provide feedback and encouragement. Remind students to focus on reading with expression and smoothness.

BELOW-LEVEL

Review Dialogue Remind students that the parts of the story inside *quotation marks* are dialogue, the words the characters speak. Model reading the dialogue with expression that sets it apart from the rest of the text. Then have students echo-read with you.

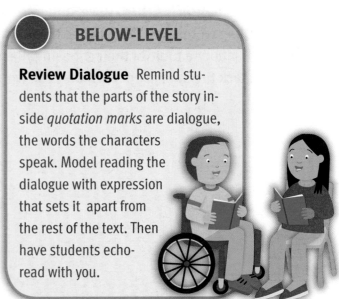

Plot

Comprehension

Review

REVIEW THE SKILL Ask students to tell what plot is. (Possible responses: the events in a story including problem and solution) Point out that some stories, such as "A Pen Pal for Max," have more than one problem and solution.

▲ **Read-Aloud Anthology**
"The Sunset in My Mailbox," p. 44

USE PRIOR KNOWLEDGE/SET A PURPOSE Tell students that they will listen as you reread "The Sunset in My Mailbox." Tell students that the problem in this story isn't stated. Tell them to listen carefully for clues to the problem.

Practice/Apply

GUIDED PRACTICE Display **Transparency GO7** or distribute copies of *Teachers Resource Book* p. 92 to students. Ask students the following questions and fill in the chart with their responses.

- **Who are the characters and what is the setting in this story?** (Caitlin, Julien, Caitlin's mom, the mailman; Caitlin's house)

- **What are the important events in the story?** (Caitlin receives odd gifts from her pen pal. She gets a melted juicebar, cornflakes, and a fingerprint)

- **Think about these events and how they cause a problem for Caitlin. What is Caitlin's problem?** (Caitlin is worried how Julien will send a sunset through the mail.)

INDEPENDENT PRACTICE Tell students to think about how Caitlin's problem is resolved. Have them complete the graphic organizer with a partner.

Objectives

- *To identify plot while listening to a story*
- *To review plot*

Skill Trace

 Tested **Plot**

Introduce	T32–T33
Reteach	S6
Review	T63, T79, T91, T128–T129, T161, T177, T189, T387, T402
Test	Theme 3
Maintain	Theme 4, T80

BELOW-LEVEL

Explain Flashback Point out to students that most of the events in the story are in time order. One paragraph, however, takes place earlier. In it, Caitlin describes things that Julien sent her when they first became pen pals. Stress that this paragraph is out of time order. The author includes it to give more information about Julien.

Build Robust Vocabulary

Objectives

- *To review robust vocabulary*
- *To organize word meanings in order to demonstrate knowledge of word relationships*
- *To clarify understanding of word meanings*

INTRODUCE ✓ **Tested**

Vocabulary

Lesson 11	Lesson 12
swooned	deciphered
astonished	mistaken
encouraging	translate
brief	repairs
chuckling	heaving
soothing	bothersome
sobbed	din
praised	dodging
envious	catastrophe
rivalry	fortunate

Cumulative Review

WORD RELATIONSHIPS Guide students to find a synonym (word with a similar meaning), an antonym (word with the opposite meaning), and an example for the Vocabulary Words *mistaken* and *din*. Create a four-column chart on the board and review it with students.

Word	Synonym	Antonym	Example
1. mistaken	wrong	correct	You are mistaken about school being open on Memorial Day.
2. din	noise	silence	The din in the room made it difficult to hear.

Read aloud the meaning of the word *mistaken*. Explain its synonym, antonym, and example as listed on the board. Repeat for the word *din*.

Then have students create their own four-column charts for the words *catastrophe* and *fortunate* on a separate sheet of paper. Tell them to write synonyms, antonyms, and examples for as many words as possible. Invite volunteers to share their responses with the class.

REVIEW VOCABULARY Discuss students' answers to these questions.

1. If someone's chest was **heaving,** could the person be **chuckling**? Why or why not?

2. Would it be **bothersome** if a baby **sobbed** for hours? Why or why not?

3. If a friend was trying to **translate** a sentence, what **encouraging** thing could you say?

4. Why would you be **praised** for **dodging** the ball in a game of dodgeball?

5. What **soothing** thing could you say to a child who is scared by a **din**?

6. If your car engine stopped working, would you need a **brief** stop for **repairs**? Explain.

 MONITOR PROGRESS

Build Robust Vocabulary

IF students do not demonstrate understanding of the words and have difficulty using them correctly,	**THEN** model using each word in several sentences. Have the students repeat each sentence.

Small-Group Instruction, p. S22:

● **BELOW-LEVEL:** Reteach
● **ON-LEVEL:** Reinforce
● **ADVANCED:** Extend

Grammar
Singular and Plural Pronouns

5-DAY GRAMMAR

DAY 1 Define Pronouns
DAY 2 Singular Pronouns
DAY 3 Plural Pronouns
DAY 4 Apply Pronouns to Writing
DAY 5 Singular and Plural Pronouns Review

Objectives

- *To recognize singular and plural pronouns*
- *To write singular and plural pronouns correctly*

Daily Proofreading

1. we asked Maria to come with him. (We; with us)
2. The dogs barked, but than it wagged their tails. (then; they wagged)

✔ LANGUAGE ARTS CHECKPOINT

If students have difficulty with the concepts, see pages S24–S25 to reteach.

▲ **Practice Book, p. 104**

Review

REVIEW SINGULAR AND PLURAL PRONOUNS Review the rules for using singular and plural pronouns.

- A pronoun is a word that is used in place of a noun.
- A singular pronoun replaces a singular noun.
- A plural pronoun takes the place of a plural noun or a group of nouns.

Practice/Apply

GUIDED PRACTICE Write these sentences on the board:

> **The players ran up and down the field.**
>
> **Ellie kicked the ball hard.**
>
> **Mara passed the ball to Tomás.**

Read aloud the first sentence. Explain that the word *They* can replace *The players* in the first sentence. Then work with volunteers to replace the underlined words in the remaining sentences. (it, him)

INDEPENDENT PRACTICE Write these sentences on the board:

> Lara sang a song for the parents.
>
> The song sounded great.
>
> Everyone clapped for Lara.

Ask students to rewrite the sentences, using singular or plural pronouns in place of the underlined words. Then review and correct their answers as a class. (them, It, her)

Writing
Realistic Story

5-DAY WRITING	
DAY 1	Introduce
DAY 2	Prewrite
DAY 3	Draft
DAY 4	Draft
DAY 5	Revise/Edit

Revise/Edit

REVISE Have students read their draft to a partner. Have partners check for the characteristics of a realistic story. Monitor partners' conversations, and model comments and questions, such as, "I'd like to know a bit more about how the problem was solved" and "Why did he say that?"

Encourage students to use editor's marks as they revise their stories. Remind them to check that they have used singular and plural pronouns correctly.

Editor's Marks	
≡	Capitalize
/	Lowercase
⊙	Add a period

Share

SHARE STORIES After students have revised their stories, have them read their stories to a small group. Tell them to use their checklist or a rubric for reviewing each other's writing. Students should keep their writing in their work portfolios.

Objectives

- *To proofread a realistic story*
- *To share and reflect upon realistic stories*

Writing Prompt

Self-Selected Writing Have students generate a list of ideas about a new topic of their choice for writing.

WEEKLY LESSON TEST

▲ Weekly Lesson Tests, Lesson 12

- Selection Comprehension with Short Response
- and Spelling
- Focus Skill
- Use Context Clues
- Robust Vocabulary
- Grammar
- Fluency Passage **FRESH READS**

GO online For prescriptions, see p. A3. Also available electronically on *StoryTown*—ExamView®.

 Podcasting: Assessing Fluency

NOTE: A 4-point rubric appears on page R8.

SCORING RUBRIC

	6	5	4	3	2	1
FOCUS	Completely focused, purposeful.	Focused on topic and purpose.	Generally focused on topic and purpose.	Somewhat focused on topic and purpose.	Related to topic but does not maintain focus.	Lacks focus and purpose.
ORGANIZATION	Ideas progress logically; paper conveys sense of completeness.	Organization mostly clear, paper gives sense of completeness.	Organization mostly clear, but some lapses occur; may seem unfinished.	Some sense of organization; seems unfinished.	Little sense of organization.	Little or no sense of organization.
SUPPORT	Strong, specific details; clear, exact language; freshness of expression.	Strong, specific details; clear, exact language.	Adequate support and word choice.	Limited supporting details; limited word choice.	Few supporting details; limited word choice.	Little development, limited or unclear word choice.
CONVENTIONS	Varied sentences; few, if any, errors.	Varied sentences; few errors.	Some sentence variety; few errors.	Simple sentence structures; some errors.	Simple sentence structures; many errors.	Unclear sentence structures; many errors.

REPRODUCIBLE STUDENT RUBRICS for specific writing purposes and presentations are available on pages R5–R8.

Leveled Readers
Reinforcing Skills and Strategies

BELOW-LEVEL

Andrew's Boring Life

SUMMARY An Australian boy named Andrew writes to his new American pen pal, Sophie, for a school project. Andrew thinks his life is too boring to write about, but he is wrong.

Genre: Realistic Fiction

 Plot

 Use Story Structure

- **ROBUST VOCABULARY:** *translate, repairs, heaving, bothersome, din, dodging*

Before Reading

BUILD BACKGROUND/SET PURPOSE Ask students if they have ever had a pen pal. Where did their pen pal live? What did they learn about their pen pal's home? Then guide students to preview the story and set a purpose for reading.

Reading the Book

PAGES 3–4 CHARACTERS' EMOTIONS Why isn't Andrew excited to have a pen pal? (Possible response: He thinks his life is too boring to write about.)

 PAGE 8 PLOT At the end of the story, what does Andrew think of his life? (He thinks it is not boring.)

PAGE 9 MAKE PREDICTIONS Do you think Andrew and Sophie will keep writing to each other when the project is over? (Possible response: Yes, they both seem to enjoy it.)

REREAD FOR FLUENCY Have partners read Andrew's and Sophie's letters aloud to each other with expression, paying attention to the exclamations.

Think Critically
(See inside back cover for questions.)

1. **PLOT** at the end of the story

2. **IMPORTANT DETAILS** It's a project with his class and Sophie's class.

3. **CAUSE/EFFECT** Possible response: She lives in a place that is very different from Andrew's home.

4. **IMPORTANT DETAILS** Kangaroos are very fast. In the story, Andrew said he could not catch one.

5. **EXPRESS PERSONAL OPINION** Accept reasonable responses.

LEVELED READER TEACHER GUIDE

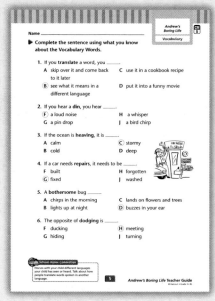

▲ Vocabulary, p. 5

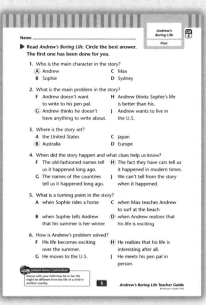

▲ Comprehension, p. 6

www.harcourtschool.com/storytown

★ Leveled Readers, online:
   Searchable by Genre, Skill, Vocabulary, Level, or Title
★ Student Activities and Teacher Resources, online

ON-LEVEL

Genre: Realistic Fiction

An Ocean Away

SUMMARY Eric and Sam become pen pals. Each boy wishes he could visit a place very different from his own home.

 Plot

 Use Story Structure

• **ROBUST VOCABULARY:**
  translate, repairs, heaving, bothersome, din, dodging

Before Reading

BUILD BACKGROUND/SET PURPOSE Have students discuss whether they have ever wanted to live someplace else. What kind of new place would they like to experience? What would they miss about their own home? Then guide students to preview the story and set a purpose for reading it.

Reading the Book

PAGE 8 IMPORTANT DETAILS Does Eric like working in his family's hotel? Explain. (Yes, he likes meeting people from different places.)

PAGE 8 PROBLEM/SOLUTION What can Sam send to Eric to make him feel closer to the ocean? (sand and shells)

PAGE 8 PLOT What are both Eric and Sam going to do some day? (They are both going to get where they want to go.)

REREAD FOR FLUENCY Have partners take turns reading pages aloud with expression, emphasizing the feelings in Sam's and Eric's letters.

Think Critically   *(See inside back cover for questions.)*

1 **PLOT** Possible response: in the letters they write to each other

2 **IMPORTANT DETAILS** They all think it will be too cold.

3 **DRAW CONCLUSIONS** Possible response: He listens to the people at the hotel.

4 **CAUSE/EFFECT** Possible response: Sam says he will never get close to a mountain.

5 **EXPRESS PERSONAL OPINIONS** Accept reasonable responses.

LEVELED READER TEACHER GUIDE

▲ Vocabulary, p. 5

▲ Comprehension, p. 6

Leveled Readers
Reinforcing Skills and Strategies

Genre: Realistic Fiction

ADVANCED

Trading Places

SUMMARY Emma and Ashwin become pen pals after they both move to a new country. They help each other feel happy in their new homes and send reminders of their old homes.

 Plot

 Use Story Structure

- **ROBUST VOCABULARY:** *translate, repairs, heaving, bothersome, din, dodging*

Before Reading

BUILD BACKGROUND/SET PURPOSE Have students discuss what it would be like to move to another country. What would be different? Would anything stay the same? Guide students to preview the story and set a purpose for reading.

Reading the Book

PAGE 5 PLOT Why does Emma's father think she will enjoy writing to Ashwin? (Possible responses: they have a lot in common; both have moved from one country to another.)

PAGE 12 MAKE PREDICTIONS How do you think Ashwin will feel when he sees the pictures Emma sent him? (Possible response: happy to see his old home)

REREAD FOR FLUENCY Have students form small groups and take turns reading pages aloud with expression, giving special attention to the feelings in the letters.

Think Critically   *(See inside back cover for questions.)*

1. **PLOT** Possible response: Emma's dad gives Emma Ashwin's address.

2. **IMPORTANT DETAILS** They each used to live where the other does now.

3. **CHARACTERS' TRAITS** Possible responses: Ashwin and Emma are both homesick but also very curious about their new homes; Emma likes basketball, while Ashwin likes cricket.

4. **DRAW CONCLUSIONS** Possible response: Yes, because people move all the time.

5. **EXPRESS PERSONAL OPINIONS** Accept reasonable responses.

LEVELED READER TEACHER GUIDE

▲ Vocabulary, p. 5

▲ Comprehension, p. 6

E L L

The Country of Chile

Genre: Expository Nonfiction

The Country of Chile

SUMMARY Chile is a country with a wide variety of animals, climates, and natural features.

- **Build Background**
- **Concept Vocabulary**
- **Scaffolded Language Development**

Before Reading

BUILD BACKGROUND/SET PURPOSE Have students discuss what they know about the country of Chile. Where is it located? What is the land like? Are there mountains? Seacoasts? What animals might live there? Then guide students to preview the story and set a purpose for reading.

Reading the Book

PAGE 6 IMPORTANT DETAILS What people lived in Chile first? Who came after them? (Native Americans; people from Spain)

PAGES 8–13 AUTHOR'S PURPOSE What has the author told you about Chile that makes you think it would be an interesting country to visit? (Possible response: It has mountains, lakes, deserts, and geysers; it also has interesting animals, such as penguins.)

REREAD FOR FLUENCY Have students form small groups and take turns reading a page aloud with expression, paying special attention to the exclamations.

Scaffolded Language Development

(See inside back cover for teacher-led activity.)

Provide additional examples and explanation as needed.

LEVELED READER TEACHER GUIDE

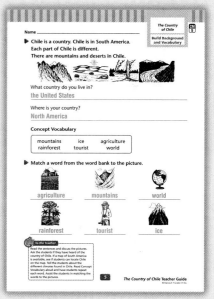

▲ Build Background, p. 5

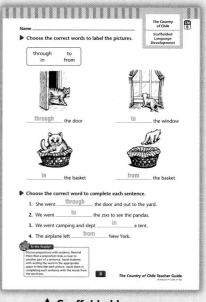

▲ Scaffolded Language Development, p. 6

Lesson 13

WEEK AT A GLANCE

✔️ **Phonics**
Consonants /s/c; /j/g, dge

✔️ **Spelling**
ice, age, rice, edge, stage, giant, range, judge, ledge, police, recent, bridge, office, strange, central

✔️ **Comprehension**
 Author's Purpose
 Ask Questions

✔️ **Robust Vocabulary**
tugged, paused, columns, absorb, protects, rustling, dissolve, particles, scavenger, self-sufficient

Reading
"A Tree Is Growing" by Arthur Dorros
EXPOSITORY NONFICTION
"Ancient Trees Survive" by April Pulley Sayre
NEWS FEATURE

✔️ **Fluency**
Intonation

✔️ **Grammar**
Subject and Object Pronouns

✔️ **Writing**
Form: Explanation
Trait: Sentence Fluency

Speaking/Listening
Explanation

Media Literacy
Viewing Diagrams

✔️ **Weekly Lesson Test**

 = Focus Skill   = Focus Strategy   ✔️ = Tested Skill

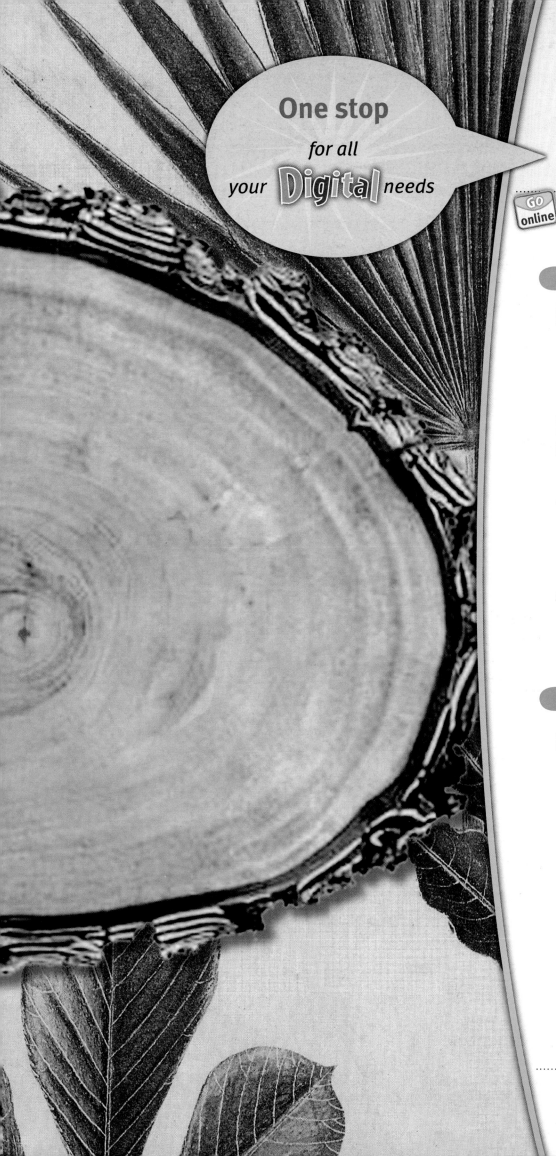

One stop
for all
your **Digital** *needs*

Lesson 13
Digital
CLASSROOM

 www.harcourtschool.com/storytown
To go along with your print program

FOR THE TEACHER

Prepare Professional Development

in the Online TE

 Videos for Podcasting

Plan & Organize  Online TE & Planning Resource*

Teach Transparencies

access from the Online TE

Assess  Online Assessment*

with Student Tracking System and Prescriptions

FOR THE STUDENT

Read Student eBook*

 Strategic Intervention Interactive Reader

 Leveled Readers

Practice & Apply Splash into Phonics CD-ROM

Comprehension Expedition CD-ROM

 *Also available on CD-ROM

Literature Resources

STUDENT
EDITION

GO online · eBook STUDENT EDITION

Genre: Expository Nonfiction

Genre: News Feature

◀ **Audiotext** *Student Edition selections are available on Audiotext 3.*

 Accelerated Reader® ◀ *Practice Quizzes for the Selection*

THEME CONNECTION: As We Grow
Comparing Expository Nonfiction and a News Feature

....

Paired Selections

 SCIENCE **A Tree Is Growing, pp. 370–395**
SUMMARY Arthur Dorros explains the stages in the growth of a tree.

 SCIENCE **Ancient Trees Survive, pp. 396–399**
SUMMARY April Pulley Sayre writes about the world's oldest living trees, the bristlecone pines.

Support for Differentiated Instruction

LEVELED READERS

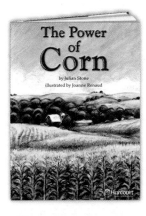

● **BELOW-LEVEL**　　● **ON-LEVEL**　　● **ADVANCED**　　**E L L**

LEVELED PRACTICE

◀ **Strategic Intervention Resource Kit, Lesson 13**

◀ **Strategic Intervention Interactive Reader, Lesson 13**
Strategic Intervention Interactive Reader Online

◀ **ELL Extra Support Kit, Lesson 13**

◀ **Challenge Resource Kit, Lesson 13**

● **BELOW-LEVEL**
Extra Support Copying Masters, pp. 106–108, 110–111

● **ON-LEVEL**
Practice Book, pp. 105–112

● **ADVANCED LEVEL**
Challenge Copying Masters, pp. 106–108, 110–111

E L L

ELL Copying Masters, Lesson 13

ADDITIONAL RESOURCES

- Spelling Practice Book, pp. 41–43
- Grammar Practice Book, pp. 45–48
- Reading Transparencies R85–R92
- Language Arts Transparencies LA27–LA28
- Test Prep System
◀ **Literacy Center Kit, Cards 61–65**
- Writer's Companion
◀ **Fluency Builders**
◀ **Picture Card Collection**
- Read-Aloud Anthology

ASSESSMENT

✔ **Monitor Progress**

✔ **Weekly Lesson Test, Lesson 13**
- Comprehension
- Phonics and Spelling
- Focus Skill
- Robust Vocabulary
- Grammar
- Use Graphic Aids

www.harcourtschool.com/storytown

- Online Assessment
- *Also available on CD-ROM— ExamView®*

ePlanner* **Suggested Lesson Planner**

Day 1

 Step 1 Whole Group

Daily Routines
- *Oral Language*
- *Read Aloud*

Word Work
-  phonics
- *Spelling*

Skills and Strategies
- *Reading*
- *Fluency*
- *Comprehension*
- *Build Robust Vocabulary*

QUESTION OF THE DAY, p. T210
What kinds of living things grow where you live?

READ ALOUD, p. T211
Transparency R85: "Sunflowers"

✔  phonics p. T212
Introduce: Consonants /s/c; /j/g, dge

✔ **SPELLING,** p. T214
Pretest: *ice, age, rice, edge, stage, giant, range, judge, ledge, police, recent, bridge, office, strange, central*

✔ **READING,** Phonics, p. T215
🌀 Introduce: Author's Purpose

LISTENING COMPREHENSION, p. T216
Read-Aloud: "The Money Tree"

FLUENCY, p. T216
Develop Intonation

✔ **BUILD ROBUST VOCABULARY,** p. T217
Words from the Read-Aloud

Day 2

QUESTION OF THE DAY, p. T220
What is your favorite season of the year? Why?

READ ALOUD, p. T221
Transparency R87: "Autumn"

✔  phonics p. T222
Review: Consonants

✔ **SPELLING,** p. T223
Word Building

✔ **BUILD ROBUST VOCABULARY,** p. T224
Words from the selection
Word Detective, p. T224

READING, p. T226
"A Tree Is Growing"
Options for Reading

✔ **COMPREHENSION,** p. T240
🌀 Introduce: Ask Questions

RETELLING/FLUENCY, p. T240
Reading with Intonation

✔ **BUILD ROBUST VOCABULARY,** p. T241
Words About the Selection

▲ Student Edition

 Step 2 Small Groups

 Step 3 Whole Group

Language Arts
- *Grammar*
- *Writing*

Suggestions for Differentiated Instruction *(See pp. T202–T203.)*

✔ **GRAMMAR,** p. T218
Introduce: Subject Pronouns

DAILY PROOFREADING
1. we watched how the tree blue in the wind. (We; blew)
2. The jiant crossed the brigde in three steps. (giant; bridge)

 WRITING, p. T219
Introduce: Explanation
Writing Trait: Sentence Fluency

Writing Prompt *Write a paragraph explaining the purpose of one of the items in the classroom, such as an eraser or ruler.*

✔ **GRAMMAR,** p. T242
Introduce: Object Pronouns

DAILY PROOFREADING
1. Them were late for dinner (They were)
2. mary and me went to the shopping mall. (Mary and I)

 WRITING, p. T243
Review: Explanation
Writing Trait: Sentence Fluency

Writing Prompt *Write three questions and provide answers in explanations.*

 = **Focus Skill**    = **Focus Strategy**    = **Tested Skill**

Skills at a Glance

phonics	Comprehension	Fluency	Vocabulary
• Consonants /s/c; /j/g, dge	**Focus Skill** Author's Purpose **Focus Strategy** Ask Questions	Reading with Intonation	**ROBUST VOCABULARY:** *tugged, paused, columns, absorb, protects, rustling, dissolve, particles, scavenger, self-sufficient*

Day 3

QUESTION OF THE DAY, p. T244
What does your body need in order to stay healthy and keep growing?

READ ALOUD, p. T245
Transparency R90: "Autumn"

 p. T246
Review: Consonants

✔ **SPELLING,** p. T247
State the Generalization
FLUENCY, p. T248
Reading with Intonation

✔ **COMPREHENSION,** p. T249
Review: Author's Purpose
Introduce: Use Graphic Aids
Paired Selection: "Ancient Trees Survive"

CONNECTIONS, p. T254

✔ **BUILD ROBUST VOCABULARY,** p. T256
Review

ANCIENT TREES SURVIVE IN CALIFORNIA'S MOUNTAINS
▲Student Edition

Day 4

QUESTION OF THE DAY, p. T260
Why do people like to spend time outdoors?

READ ALOUD, p. T261
Transparency R91: "Plant It Small, Grow It Tall"

 p. T262
Review: Consonants

✔ **SPELLING,** p. T263
Review Spelling Words
FLUENCY, p. T264
Reading with Intonation

✔ **COMPREHENSION,** p. T265
Review: Author's Purpose
Maintain: Use Reference Sources

SPEAKING AND LISTENING, p. T267
Explanation

MEDIA LITERACY, p. T267
Viewing Diagrams

✔ **BUILD ROBUST VOCABULARY,** p. T268
Review

A Tree Is Growing by Arthur Dorros
▲Student Edition

Day 5

QUESTION OF THE DAY, p. T272
Where do you go to enjoy nature?

READ ALOUD, p. T273
Transparency R91: "Plant It Small, Grow It Tall"

 p. T274
Review: Consonants

✔ **SPELLING,** p. T275
Posttest
FLUENCY, p. T276
Reading with Intonation

✔ **COMPREHENSION,** p. T277
Review: Author's Purpose
Read-Aloud: "The Money Tree"

✔ **BUILD ROBUST VOCABULARY,** p. T278
Cumulative Review

A Tree Is Growing by Arthur Dorros
▲Student Edition

 BELOW-LEVEL   ON-LEVEL   ADVANCED   E L L

✔ **GRAMMAR,** p. T258
Review: Using *I* and *me*

DAILY PROOFREADING

1. We gave she a lemon tree (her; tree.)
2. Were you planning on spending the weekend with we (us?)

✔ **GRAMMAR,** p. T270
Review: Subject and Object Pronouns

DAILY PROOFREADING

1. to get to the mall, us have to pass the stadium. (To; we)
2. Why did them travel by boat (they; boat?)

✔ **GRAMMAR,** p. T280
Review: Subject and Object Pronouns

DAILY PROOFREADING

1. the horse in the meadow belongs to they (The; them.)
2. her and her friend skipped as they watered the flowers (She; flowers.)

 WRITING, p. T259
Review: Explanation
Writing Trait: Sentence Fluency

Writing Prompt *Write about what you find most amazing about trees. Explain why you find it amazing.*

 WRITING, p. T271
Review: Explanation
Writing Trait: Sentence Fluency

Writing Prompt *Write a journal entry using the following sentence starter: "The best way to enjoy nature is by..."*

WRITING, p. T281
Review: Conventions
Writing Trait: Sentence Fluency

Writing Prompt *Write a brief explanation about a topic of your choice.*

Differentiated Instruction

Suggested Small-Group Planner

	Day 1	Day 2
BELOW-LEVEL	**Teacher-Directed** Leveled Reader: "Daffodil Spring," p. T282 Before Reading **Independent** Listening/Speaking Center, p. T208 Extra Support Copying Masters, p. 106 ▲ Leveled Reader	**Teacher-Directed** Student Edition: "A Tree Is Growing," p. T388 **Independent** Reading Center, p. T208 Extra Support Copying Masters, p. 107 ▲ Student Edition
ON-LEVEL	**Teacher-Directed** Leveled Reader: "Wind in the Pines," p. T283 Before Reading **Independent** Reading Center, p. T208 Practice Book, p. 105 ▲ Leveled Reader	**Teacher-Directed** Student Edition: "A Tree Is Growing," p. T388 **Independent** Technology Center, p. T209 Practice Book, p. 106 ▲ Student Edition
ADVANCED	**Teacher-Directed** Leveled Reader: "The Power of Corn," p. T284 Before Reading **Independent** Technology Center, p. T209 Challenge Copying Masters, p. 106 ▲ Leveled Reader	**Teacher-Directed** Leveled Reader: "The Power of Corn," p. T284 Read the Book **Independent** Word Work Center, p. T209 Challenge Copying Masters, p. 107 ▲ Leveled Reader

English-Language Learners

In addition to the small-group instruction above, use the *ELL Extra Support* kit to promote language development.

LANGUAGE DEVELOPMENT SUPPORT
Teacher-Directed
ELL TG, Day 1

Independent
ELL Copying Masters, Lesson 13

▲ ELL Student Handbook

LANGUAGE DEVELOPMENT SUPPORT
Teacher-Directed
ELL TG, Day 2

Independent
ELL Copying Masters, Lesson 13

▲ ELL Student Handbook

Intervention

▲ Strategic Intervention Resource Kit   ▲ Intervention Reader

Strategic Intervention TG, Lesson 13
Strategic Intervention Practice Book, Lesson 13

Strategic Intervention TG, Lesson 13
Intervention Reader, Lesson 13

▲ Strategic Intervention Reader

T204   Grade 3, Theme 3

	Comprehension	phonics	Comprehension	Fluency	Robust Vocabulary	Language Arts
MONITOR PROGRESS	Author's Purpose	Consonants /s/c;/j/g, dge	Use Graphic Aids	Reading with Intonation	*tugged, paused, columns, absorb, protects, rustling, dissolve, particles, scavenger, self-sufficient*	✓ LANGUAGE ARTS CHECKPOINT Grammar: Subject and Object Pronouns Writing: Explanation
Small-Group Instruction	pp. S30–S31	pp. S26–S27	pp. S32–S33	pp. S28–S29	pp. S34–S35	pp. S36–S37

Day 3

Teacher-Directed
Leveled Reader:
"Daffodil Spring," p. T282
Read the Book

Independent
 Word Work Center, p. T209
Extra Support Copying Masters, p. 106

▲ Leveled Reader

Teacher-Directed
Leveled Reader:
"Wind in the Pines," p. T283
Read the Book

Independent
 Writing Center, p. T209
Practice Book, p. 106

▲ Leveled Reader

Teacher-Directed
Leveled Reader:
"The Power of Corn," p. T284
Think Critically

Independent
 Listening/Speaking Center, p. T208
Challenge Copying Masters, p. 108

▲ Leveled Reader

LANGUAGE DEVELOPMENT SUPPORT
Teacher-Directed
Leveled Reader: "Our Backyard," p. T285
Before Reading; Read the Book
ELL TG, Day 3

Independent
ELL Copying Masters, Lesson 13

▲ Leveled Reader

Strategic Intervention TG, Lesson 13
Intervention Reader, Lesson 13
Intervention Practice Book

▲ Intervention Reader

Day 4

Teacher-Directed
Leveled Reader:
"Daffodil Spring," p. T282
Reread for Fluency

Independent
 Technology Center, p. T209
Practice Book, pp. 105–111

▲ Leveled Reader

Teacher-Directed
Leveled Reader:
"Wind in the Pines," p. T283
Reread for Fluency

Independent
 Word Work Center, p. T209
Practice Book, pp. 105–111

▲ Leveled Reader

Teacher-Directed
Leveled Reader:
"The Power of Corn," p. T284
Reread for Fluency
Self-Selected Reading: Classroom Library Collection

Independent
 Writing Center, p. T209
Practice Book, pp. 105–111

▲ Leveled Reader

LANGUAGE DEVELOPMENT SUPPORT
Teacher-Directed
Leveled Reader: "Our Backyard," p. T285
Reread for Fluency
ELL TG, Day 4

Independent
ELL Copying Masters, Lesson 13

▲ Leveled Reader

Strategic Intervention TG, Lesson 13
Intervention Reader, Lesson 13

▲ Intervention Reader

Day 5

Teacher-Directed
Leveled Reader:
"Daffodil Spring," p. T282
Think Critically

Independent
 Writing Center, p. T209
Leveled Reader: Reread for Fluency
Extra Support Copying Masters, p. 111

▲ Leveled Reader

Teacher-Directed
Leveled Reader:
"Wind in the Pines," p. T283
Think Critically

Independent
 Listening/Speaking Center, p. T208
Leveled Reader: Reread for Fluency
Practice Book, p. 95

▲ Leveled Reader

Teacher-Directed
Leveled Reader:
"The Power of Corn," p. T284
Reread for Fluency
Self-Selected Reading: Classroom Library Collection

Independent
 Reading Center, p. T208
Leveled Reader: Reread for Fluency

▲ Leveled Reader

LANGUAGE DEVELOPMENT SUPPORT
Teacher-Directed
Leveled Reader: "Our Backyard," p. T285
Think Critically
ELL TG, Day 5

Independent
Leveled Reader: Reread for Fluency
ELL Copying Masters, Lesson 13

▲ Leveled Reader

Strategic Intervention TG, Lesson 13
Intervention Reader, Lesson 13

▲ Intervention Reader

Leveled Readers & Leveled Practice

Reinforcing Skills and Strategies

LEVELED READER SYSTEM

- **Leveled Readers**
- **Leveled Readers, CD**
- **Leveled Reader Teacher Guides**
  - *Comprehension*
  - *Vocabulary*
  - *Oral Reading Fluency Assessment*
- **Response Activities**
- **Leveled Readers Assessment**

See pages T282–T285 for lesson plans.

For extended lesson plans, see *Leveled Reader Teacher Guides.*

BELOW-LEVEL

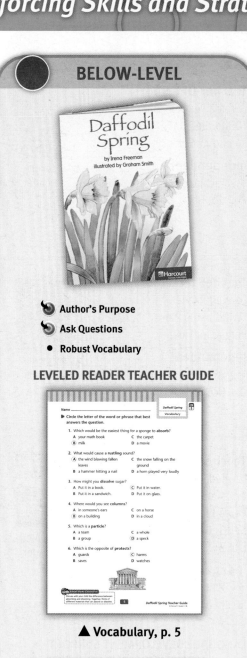

- 🐌 Author's Purpose
- 🐌 Ask Questions
- • Robust Vocabulary

LEVELED READER TEACHER GUIDE

▲ Vocabulary, p. 5

▲ Comprehension, p. 6

ON-LEVEL

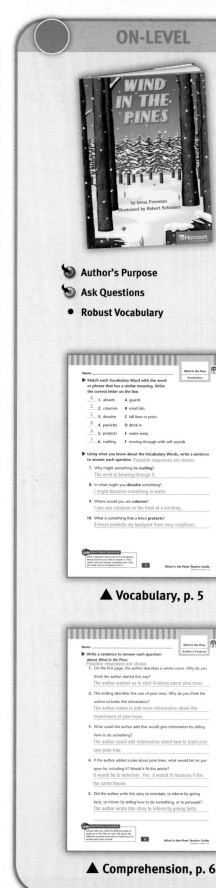

- 🐌 Author's Purpose
- 🐌 Ask Questions
- • Robust Vocabulary

▲ Vocabulary, p. 5

▲ Comprehension, p. 6

ADVANCED

- Author's Purpose
- Ask Questions
- Robust Vocabulary

LEVELED READER TEACHER GUIDE

▲ Vocabulary, p. 5

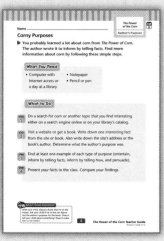

▲ Comprehension, p. 6

E L L

- Build Background
- Concept Vocabulary
- Scaffolded Language Development

LEVELED READER TEACHER GUIDE

▲ Build Background, p. 5

▲ Scaffolded Language Development, p. 6

CLASSROOM LIBRARY

Self-Selected Reading

EASY

▲ *Officer Buckle and Gloria* by Peggy Rathmann, G. P. Putnam's Sons, 1995. FANTASY

AVERAGE

▲ *Day Light, Night Light* by Franklyn M. Branley, Harper Collins, 1998. EXPOSITORY NONFICTION

CHALLENGE

▲ *Donavan's Word Jar* by Monalisa DeGross, Harper Trophy, 1994. REALISTIC FICTION

▲ Classroom Library Teacher Guide, Lesson 13

Literacy Centers

15 Min. each

Management Support

While you provide direct instruction to individuals or small groups, other students can work on literacy center activities.

▲ **Literacy Centers Pocket Chart**

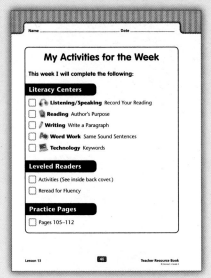

▲ **Teacher Resource Book, p. 46**

Homework for the Week

TEACHER RESOURCE BOOK, PAGE 16
The Homework Copying Master provides activities to complete for each day of the week.

 LISTENING/SPEAKING

Record Your Reading

Objective
To read aloud with proper intonation

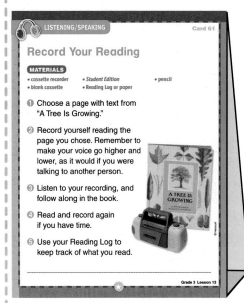

LISTENING/SPEAKING   Card 61

Record Your Reading

MATERIALS
- cassette recorder
- blank cassette
- Student Edition
- Reading Log or paper
- pencil

❶ Choose a page with text from "A Tree Is Growing."

❷ Record yourself reading the page you chose. Remember to make your voice go higher and lower, as it would if you were talking to another person.

❸ Listen to your recording, and follow along in the book.

❹ Read and record again if you have time.

❺ Use your Reading Log to keep track of what you read.

Grade 3 Lesson 13

⭐ **Literacy Center Kit • Card 61**

 READING

Author's Purpose

Objective
To identify author's purpose

READING   Card 62

Author's Purpose

MATERIALS
- Student Edition
- pencil
- paper

❶ Read "The Shepherd Boy and the Wolf" on pages 324–325 of your *Student Edition*.

❷ Write what you think is the author's purpose. Give details from the story that support your idea. Remember that an author may write to entertain, inform, or persuade his or her readers.

Grade 3 Lesson 13

⭐ **Literacy Center Kit • Card 62**

The author's purpose in "The Shepherd Boy and the Wolf" is to teach a lesson. The boy learns not to lie, because people don't believe him after he tells lies.

WRITING

Write a Paragraph

Objective
To write a paragraph with details

WORD WORK

Same-Sound Sentences

Objective
To read words with soft c and soft g

TECHNOLOGY

Keywords

Objective
To use electronic technology to create a list

WRITING   Card 63

Write a Paragraph

MATERIALS
• *Student Edition*   • pencil
• paper

❶ Write a paragraph that explains why trees are important. Use details from "A Tree Is Growing" to support your main idea.

❷ Read your paragraph to a classmate.

Grade 3 Lesson 13

Literacy Center Kit • Card 63

WORD WORK   Card 64

Same-Sound Sentences

MATERIALS
• paper
• pencil

❶ Copy the following words onto your paper:

agent	giraffe	cell
cent	circle	count
cup	gas	gentle
piece	grass	gust
large	ginger	giant

❷ Circle all of the words with soft *c* or soft *g*.

❸ Choose either the soft *c* or soft *g* sound to write a tongue twister. Write a sentence with as many words with that sound as you can.

The gentle giraffe ate ginger.

Grade 3 Lesson 13

Literacy Center Kit • Card 64

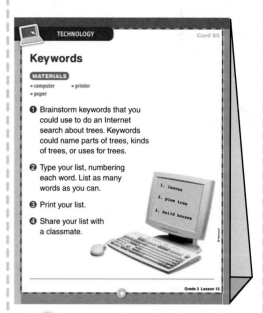

TECHNOLOGY   Card 65

Keywords

MATERIALS
• computer   • printer
• paper

❶ Brainstorm keywords that you could use to do an Internet search about trees. Keywords could name parts of trees, kinds of trees, or uses for trees.

❷ Type your list, numbering each word. List as many words as you can.

❸ Print your list.

❹ Share your list with a classmate.

1. leaves
2. pine tree
3. build houses

Grade 3 Lesson 13

Literacy Center Kit • Card 65

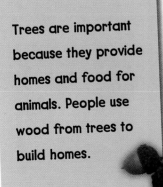

Trees are important because they provide homes and food for animals. People use wood from trees to build homes.

1. trees
2. branches
3. palm tree
4. apple tree

Day at a Glance

Day
1

 **and Spelling**

- Introduce: Consonants /s/*c*; /j/*g*, *dge*
- Pretest

Reading

- Phonics Skill, *Student Edition*, pp. 366–367

Reading/ Comprehension

 Introduce: Author's Purpose

- *Read-Aloud Anthology*: "The Money Tree"

Fluency

- Model Oral Fluency

Robust Vocabulary

Words from the Read-Aloud

- Introduce: *tugged, paused*

Grammar

- Introduce: Subject Pronouns

Writing

- Explanation

Warm-Up Routines

 Oral Language

Objective *To listen and respond informally*

Question of the Day

What kinds of living things grow where you live?

Tell students that, whether they live in the city or in the country, they can always find living things around them. In the city, grass may grow between cracks in the sidewalk. On a farm there may be fields of wheat or corn. In most places there are animals, too. Some are wild, and some are pets. Have students discuss the different kinds of living things that can be found in their area. (trees, plants, pets, wild animals such as squirrels and deer)

After a brief discussion, have students complete the following sentence in their notebooks:

> **Some plants and animals that live in my area are _____.**

Students should write several informative sentences telling what living and growing things are found in the area where they live. Invite students to share their responses with the group.

Read Aloud

Objective *To listen and respond informally to information*

READ ALOUD A SELECTION Share the selection with students, using the following steps:

Introduce the text. Display **Transparency R85** or distribute photocopies to students. Tell students you are going to read a nonfiction selection about sunflowers.

Set a purpose. Ask students what the purpose might be for reading or listening to this nonfiction selection. (to learn or to enjoy) Explain that, while they are enjoying the selection, they should try to understand why the author wrote it.

Model fluent reading. Read the selection aloud, using intonation to make the information more interesting.

Discuss the selection. Ask students the following questions:

• **What do sunflowers need in order to grow strong and tall?**

• **How is a sunflower seed different from a full-grown plant?**

Sunflowers

Have you ever seen a sunflower seed? Actually, you might not know that you saw one because sunflower seeds are very small. Sunflower seeds are no larger than one of your fingernails. When a sunflower is fully grown, though, the plant can be more than six feet tall, and the flower may be larger than a dinner plate!

Once sunflower seeds are planted, it takes about a week for them to sprout. Then the flowers begin to grow. To reach their full size, sunflowers need a lot of sunshine. In fact, they need at least six hours of sunlight each day. Perhaps this is why sunflowers are so tall. They might be trying to reach the sun that they need so much!

Grade 3, Lesson 13 — R85 — Warm-Up: Day 1

Transparency R85

Consonants /s/c; /j/g, dge

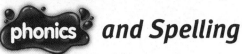 **and Spelling**

5-DAY PHONICS	
DAY 1	Introduce /s/c and /j/g, dge
DAY 2	Words with Final ge and dge
DAY 3	Words with Final ce
DAY 4	Other Words with /s/c and /j/g, dge
DAY 5	Review /s/c and /j/g, dge

Objective

- *To use decoding strategies to clarify pronunciation*

Skill Trace

 Tested **Consonants: /s/c; /j/g, dge**

Introduce	Grade 2
Reintroduce	T212
Reteach	S26
Review	T222–T223, T246, T262, T274, T410
Text	Theme 3
Maintain	Theme 4, T176

BELOW-LEVEL

Try Sounds Write the words on the board on cards. Tell students to try both sounds for *c* and *g* to see which makes a familiar word.

 **Resources**

 **Phonics Practice Book, Intermediate, pp. 79–84**

 Teach/Model

 Routine Card 1 **SOUNDS FOR *c* AND *g*** Write *cap* and *rug* on the board and have students read the words. Circle the *c* in *cap* and ask what sound the *c* stands for in this word. (/k/) Repeat with the *g* in *rug*. (/g/)

INTRODUCE /s/c AND /j/g, dge Have students read *Student Edition* page 366. Explain that *c* usually stands for the sound /k/, but when it is followed by *e* or *i*, it usually stands for /s/. This sound is sometimes called the soft sound of *c*. The letter *g* usually stands for /g/, but when it is followed by *e* or *i*, it stands for /j/. This is called the soft sound of *g*. Write the letters *dge* and the word *edge* on the board. Read the word and explain that the pattern *dge* also stands for /j/.

cap

rug

Phonics Skill

Words with Soft *c* and Soft *g*

The letter *c* can stand for the /s/ sound you hear in *city*. This happens when *c* is followed by *e* or *i*.

The letter *g* can stand for the /j/ sound you hear in *giant*. This often happens when *g* is followed by *e* or *i*.

Read the words in the chart, and listen for the soft sounds of the letters *c* and *g*.

Words with the soft *c* sound as in *city*	Words with the soft *g* sound as in *giant*
cent	gem
ceiling	germ

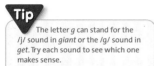

Tip
The letter *g* can stand for the /j/ sound in *giant* or the /g/ sound in *get*. Try each sound to see which one makes sense.

366

Read the story and look at the chart. Tell which words have soft *c* as in *city* or soft *g* as in *giant*.

I had such a strange dream last night! I was walking in circles in a giant forest. I could smell spices like cinnamon and ginger. At the center of the forest, I met a man in a general's outfit. "Are you a citizen of this forest?" he asked.

"Gee, I don't think so," I said.

"Then we'd better get you back to the city," he said gently.

Words with the soft *c* sound as in *city*	Words with the soft *g* sound as in *giant*

Try This!

Look back at the story. Add one sentence to tell more about the dream. Use a word that has soft *c* as in *city* or soft *g* as in *giant*.

 www.harcourtschool.com/storytown

367

Practice/Apply

GUIDED PRACTICE Copy the graphic organizer on page 367 onto the board. Have students read page 367.

Work with students to identify words with /s/*c* and /j/*g* in the first two sentences. (strange, circles, giant) Have students complete the chart.

Try This! **INDEPENDENT PRACTICE** Help students with the Try This! activity by telling them to think of words with /s/*c* and /j/*g* first.

Introduce /s/c and /j/g, dge

phonics and Spelling

5-DAY SPELLING	
DAY 1	Pretest
DAY 2	State the Genreralization
DAY 3	Spelling Practice/Handwriting
DAY 4	Review Spelling Strategies
DAY 5	Posttest

Objective

- *To spell words correctly with orthographic patterns*

Spelling Words

1.	ice	9.	ledge
2.	age	10.	police
3.	rice	11.	recent
4.	edge	12.	bridge
5.	stage	13.	office
6.	giant*	14.	strange
7.	range	15.	central
8.	judge		

Challenge Words

16.	celery	19.	margin
17.	ceiling	20.	imagine
18.	difference		

*Word from "A Tree Is Growing"

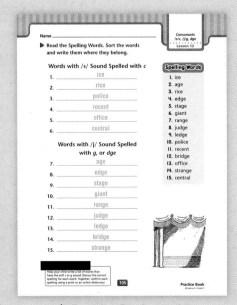

▲ Practice Book, p. 105

Introduce Spelling Words

PRETEST Say the first spelling word and read the dictation sentence. Repeat the word as students write it. Write the word on the board and have students check their spelling. Tell them to circle the word if they spelled it correctly or write it correctly if they did not. Repeat for spelling words 2–15.

Words with /s/c and /j/g

1.	ice	I like to drink water with **ice** in it.
2.	age	I first went to school at the **age** of five.
3.	rice	**Rice** and beans can make a good meal.
4.	edge	Do not stand so close to the **edge** of the cliff!
5.	stage	José enjoys performing on **stage**.
6.	giant	You are a **giant** compared to a newborn baby.
7.	range	The grades **range** from an A to a C.
8.	judge	The **judge** made the driver pay a fine.
9.	ledge	The bird sat on a narrow **ledge** outside my window.
10.	police	The **police** were directing traffic.
11.	recent	I visited my cousin on my most **recent** vacation.
12.	bridge	They are building a new **bridge** across the river.
13.	office	Ms. Harrison works in the principal's **office**.
14.	strange	Last night I heard a **strange** noise.
15.	central	The zoo is in the **central** part of town.

ADVANCED

Challenge Words Use these dictation sentences.

16.	celery	We eat **celery** and carrots after school.
17.	ceiling	My dad can touch the **ceiling**!
18.	difference	One **difference** between the brothers is their height.
19.	margin	Do not write in the **margin** of your paper.
20.	imagine	**Imagine** you are on a sunny beach.

Author's Purpose
Comprehension

Teach/Model

INTRODUCE AUTHOR'S PURPOSE Explain that when authors write stories, articles, or books, they usually write with a purpose in mind. Sometimes, authors have more than one purpose. For example, a fiction writer usually hopes to entertain readers with a good story. However, that writer might also have a message to communicate to readers, such as informing readers about new information or persuading readers to agree with an opinion she or he has.

Think Aloud As I read a fiction story, I pay attention to what characters say or how the author describes the setting. These things give me a clue about what the author is trying to do other than entertain me.

Practice/Apply

Elicit from students a summary of the realistic fiction story "A Pen Pal for Max." Guide them to see that one of the author's purposes is to entertain readers with a good story. Then ask what other purpose the author might have. (Possible responses: to inform people about what life is like in Chile, to convince people to get a pen pal)

Objectives

• *To identify an author's purpose for writing*

Daily Comprehension

Author's Purpose

DAY 1:	Introduce Author's Purpose *Student Edition*
DAY 2:	Review Author's Purpose *Student Edition*
DAY 3:	Paired Selection *Student Edition*
DAY 4:	Review Author's Purpose *Transparency*
DAY 5:	Review Author's Purpose *Read-Aloud Anthology*

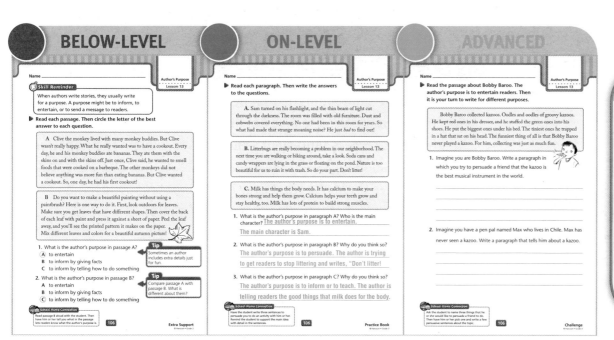

▲ Extra Support, p. 106   ▲ Practice Book, p. 106   ▲ Challenge, p. 106

ELL

• Group students according to academic levels and assign one of the pages on the left.

• Clarify unfamiliar concepts and vocabulary. See *ELL Teacher Guide* Lesson 13 for support in scaffolding instruction.

Listening Comprehension
Read Aloud

Objectives

- *To connect and relate prior experiences*
- *To understand characteristics of fiction*

Build Fluency

Focus: Intonation Tell students that a good reader does not read every word in a sentence the same way. The reader makes his or her voice go up or down depending on what the text says. Explain that reading a question is a good example. The reader's voice goes up at the end of a question.

Use What You Know Ask students what they know about how fast a tree grows. Then invite them to discuss why the tree in "The Money Tree" is unusual.

Before Reading

CONNECT TO PRIOR KNOWLEDGE Tell students they will be listening to a fictional story about a woman who finds a money tree growing in her yard. Have them discuss what life might be like if money suddenly began to grow on trees. Have volunteers share their answers.

▲ Read-Aloud Anthology, "The Money Tree," p. 48

Routine Card 2

GENRE STUDY: FICTION Explain that there are many purposes for listening. Tell students that when they listen to fiction, they should listen to enjoy it.

Think Aloud **As I read the beginning of "The Money Tree," I realize that something strange is happening in Miss McGillicuddy's yard. From this, I get the idea that the events happening are probably not real. A tree takes years to grow big. I think this is a made-up, or fiction, story.**

REVIEW: AUTHOR'S PURPOSE Remind students that authors want to entertain their readers, but they might also want to inform readers about a subject or persuade them about an idea that the authors have.

After Reading

RESPOND Remind students that fiction can be realistic, which is like real life, or fantastic, which is not like real life. Ask students to decide whether this story is fantasy or reality and to explain their answers. (Possible response: Much of it is realistic, but the money tree is a fantasy.) Have them use what they know about realistic fiction and fantasy to think of other examples of both genres.

Build Robust Vocabulary
Words from the Read-Aloud

Teach/Model

Routine Card 3

INTRODUCE ROBUST VOCABULARY Use *Routine Card 3* to introduce the words.

❶ Put the word in **selection context.**
❷ Display **Transparency R86** and read the word and the **Student-Friendly Explanation.**
❸ Have students **say the word** with you.
❹ Use the word in other contexts, and have students **interact with the word's meaning.**
❺ Remove the transparency. Say the Student-Friendly Explanation again, and ask students to **name the word** that goes with it.

❶ **Selection Context:** Miss McGillicuddy **tugged** at her kite to get it out of the tree.
❹ **Interact with Word Meaning:** Would you tug a wagon or a ball?

❶ **Selection Context:** Miss McGillicuddy **paused** for a moment while gardening.
❹ **Interact with Word Meaning:** Would you pause to invite someone to join in your game or to score a goal?

Practice/Apply

GUIDED PRACTICE Ask students to do the following:

• Tell about something you have tugged. Why did you have to tug rather than pull gently?

• Why might someone pause during a game?

Objective

• To use sentence and word context to find meaning of unknown words

INTRODUCE ✔

Vocabulary: Lesson 13

| tugged | paused |

▼ **Student-Friendly Explanations**

Vocabulary

1. **tugged** If you tugged something, you pulled it hard.
2. **paused** If you paused, you stopped what you were doing for a moment.
3. **scavenger** An animal is a scavenger if it collects leftover and unwanted objects.
4. **self-sufficient** If something is self-sufficient, it makes everything it needs.

Grade 3, Lesson 13   Rb   Vocabulary

Transparency R86

E L L

Total Physical Response Act as if you are fishing and trying to pull in a large fish, saying, *I have to tug at the rod to bring in a big fish.* Then jog across the room, stop, and then start again, saying, *I paused during my jogging so I could catch my breath.*

Grammar
Subject Pronouns

5-DAY GRAMMAR	
DAY 1	Subject Pronouns
DAY 2	Object Pronouns
DAY 3	Using *I* and *me*
DAY 4	Apply to Writing
DAY 5	Subject and Object Pronouns Review

Objective

• *To identify subject pronouns*

Daily Proofreading

1. we watched how the tree blue in the wind. (We; blew)
2. The jiant crossed the brigde in three steps. (giant, bridge)

TECHNOLOGY

 Go online www.harcourtschool.com/ storytown
Grammar Glossary

Subject Pronouns

1. Do you know Tami Rodriguez?
2. I read two books last month.
3. We all went to visit her.
4. He disagreed with Cami.
5. They always go to Miami for vacation.
6. "Yes, it is exciting," Matti answered.

Grade 3, Lesson 13   LAa   Grammar: Subject Pronouns

Transparency LA27

Teach/Model

INTRODUCE SUBJECT PRONOUNS Remind students that the subject of a sentence is *who* or *what* performs the action in the sentence. Write the following sentences on the board.

> **Amal and Louie ran to the store.**
> **They ran to the store.**

Explain that *Amal and Louie* is the subject of the first sentence. In the second sentence, those words are replaced by the subject pronoun *They*. Tell students that not all kinds of pronouns can be used as the subject of a sentence. List the following on the board, explaining that these seven pronouns are subject pronouns: *I, you, he, she, it, we,* and *they*. Have a volunteer say a sentence with two or more nouns. Then, have another volunteer replace the subject(s) with a pronoun. Ask the class if the sentence uses the correct pronouns.

Guided Practice

USE SUBJECT PRONOUNS Display **Transparency LA27**. Explain that each sentence has a subject pronoun. Read the first sentence aloud. Then circle the word *you* and point out that *you* is a subject pronoun in this sentence. As a class, work through Items 2 and 3.

Practice/Apply

WRITE WITH PRONOUNS Ask students to write transparency Items 4–6 in their notebooks. Then have them circle the subject pronoun in each sentence. When they are finished, ask them to share their answers.

Writing
Explanation

5-DAY WRITING	
DAY 1	Introduce
DAY 2	Prewrite
DAY 3	Draft
DAY 4	Revise/Edit
DAY 5	Proofread/Share

Teach/Model

INTRODUCE "EXPLANATION" Display **Transparency LA28** and tell students that it is an explanation. Read aloud the paragraph. Discuss the paragraph, having students identify the ideas that support the paragraph topic. Together, begin to list characteristics of an explanation. Keep these characteristics on the board through Day 5.

> **Explanation**
> • Gives facts and details about a topic
> • Explains what or how

WRITING TRAIT **SENTENCE FLUENCY** Point out that the sentences in the explanation flow smoothly. Several sentences use subject pronouns. All the sentences are about the topic of planting a vegetable garden.

Guided Practice

GENERATE FACTS AND DETAILS Draw the graphic organizer on the board. Ask students to name a fact they knew before reading the paragraph and write it in the first column. Model naming something you learned from reading **Transparency LA28** and write it in the second column.

What I Know	What I Learned

Practice/Apply

WRITE FACTS AND DETAILS Have students copy the graphic organizer into their notebooks. Invite small groups to work together to think of more information and details to add to it. Then encourage groups to share their information and details.

Objective

• *To develop supporting ideas with information that relates to the focus*

Writing Prompt

Explaining a Purpose Have students write a paragraph explaining the purpose of one of the items in the classroom, such as an eraser or a ruler.

Student Model: Explanation

It is easy to enjoy fresh vegetables from your own garden. First, you need a plot of ground. Clear the ground of weeds, dig the soil, and then rake it smooth. Choose the vegetables you would like to grow and buy seeds. Plant the seeds in a row and cover them with soil. Then water them gently. Keep the soil moist and hope the sun shines. In a few days, you will see tiny green shoots. Care for your plants by keeping them watered. Pull out some plants so the ones left are not crowded. In a few weeks, you will enjoy fresh vegetables picked from your own garden!

Grade 3, Lesson 13   LAb   Writing: Explanation

Transparency LA28

Day at a Glance

Day 2

phonics and Spelling

- Review: Consonants: /s/c; /j/g, dge

Robust Vocabulary

Words from the Selection

- Introduce: *columns, absorb, protects, rustling, dissolve, particles*

Comprehension

 Ask Questions

 Review: Author's Purpose

Reading

- "A Tree Is Growing," *Student Edition*, pp. 370–395

Read!

Fluency

- Intonation

Robust Vocabulary

Words About the Selection

- Introduce: *scavenger, self-sufficient*

Grammar

- Introduce: Object Pronouns

Writing ✏

- Explanation

Warm-Up Routines

Oral Language

Objectives *To listen attentively and respond informally to oral presentations; to respond to questions with appropriate elaboration*

Question of the Day

What is your favorite season of the year? Why?

Remind students that each season of the year is different and that people often have a favorite season. Perhaps they like a certain kind of weather—hot, cold and snowy, and so on. Perhaps they like a season because it reminds them of a happy experience. Talk with students about their favorite seasons and why they like them.

Encourage as many students as possible to participate in the discussion by asking and answering questions. After several students have had a chance to contribute to the discussion, have all students use complete sentences to respond in their notebooks to the following prompt:

> **My favorite season of the year is _____ because _____.**

Invite volunteers to share their responses with classmates.

Read Aloud

Objective *To listen and respond informally to poems*

READ ALOUD A POEM Share the poem with students using these steps:

Introduce the text. Display **Transparency R87** or distribute photocopies. Tell students they are going to hear the poem "Autumn."

Set a purpose. Ask students to suggest a purpose for reading a poem. (for enjoyment, to learn what someone thinks) Tell students to listen to find out how the poet feels about fall.

Model fluent reading. Read the poem aloud, following the poem's natural pace and rhythm.

Discuss the poem. Ask:

- **What does the poet mean by "And though this tree seems dead today"?**

- **How do you think the poet feels about autumn?**

Autumn

I lie on my back and look up to see
A towering giant way above me.
Drifting down from branches tall,
Bright colored leaves begin to fall.

Very soon the tree is bare,
Cold but swaying in autumn air.
And though this tree seems dead today,
It will bloom again, one fine spring day.

Grade 3, Lesson 13   Rc   Warm-Up: Days 2–3

Transparency R87

Consonants /s/c; /j/g, dge

 and Spelling

Objective

- *To use decoding strategies to clarify pronunciation*

Skill Trace

 Consonants: /s/c; /j/g, dge

Introduce	Grade 2
Reintroduce	T212
Reteach	S26
Review	T222–T223, T246, T262, T274, T410
Test	Theme 3
Maintain	Theme 4, T176

Spelling Words

1. **ice**	9. **ledge**
2. **age**	10. **police**
3. **rice**	11. **recent**
4. **edge**	12. **bridge**
5. **stage**	13. **office**
6. **giant***	14. **strange**
7. **range**	15. **central**
8. **judge**	

Challenge Words

16. **celery**	19. **margin**
17. **ceiling**	20. **imagine**
18. **difference**	

*Word from "A Tree Is Growing"

Review Words in Context

STATE THE GENERALIZATION Display **Transparency R88**. Indicate the words in the first row. Remind students that these words all include the letter pattern *dge*. Say the words. Explain that the pattern *dge* is used when a word has a short vowel followed immediately by the final /j/ sound.

Point to the second row of words. Explain that these words end with the letter pattern *ge*. Say the words. Tell students that when the sound /j/ comes directly after a long vowel or a consonant, the letter combination *ge* is used.

Call students' attention to Part B on the transparency. Help them identify the words in the first sentence with *g*. Then have them identify the word with the soft sound of *g*, and have them tell how they know. (*imagine*; the letter *g* is followed by *i*) Follow the same procedure for each sentence, having students identify the word that has a soft *c* or *g*.

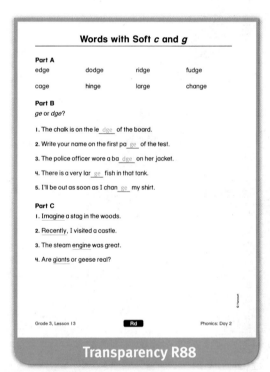

Transparency R88

BELOW-LEVEL

Skywriting Have students "sky-write" the letter combinations *ge* and *dge* while saying the sound /j/. Repeat as necessary to help students associate the letters with the sound.

ADVANCED

Words with Endings Write the words *ranger, judged, badges, strangers, pages,* and *drawbridge* on the board. Have students read each word and write a sentence to go with it.

5-DAY SPELLING	
DAY 1	Pretest
DAY 2	State the Generalization
DAY 3	Spelling Practice/Handwriting
DAY 4	Use Spelling Strategies/Review
DAY 5	Posttest

PRACTICE SPELLING RULES Draw students' attention to the sentences in Part C of **Transparency R88**. Have students read the first sentence. Establish that the missing word is *ledge,* and help students decide whether *ledge* ends with *ge* or *dge,* eliciting that *ledge* ends with *dge.* Have students write *ledge.* Continue with Sentences 2–5.

WRITE Then have students write in their notebooks sentences with the following spelling words: *age, bridge, judge, range, stage, strange,* and *edge.*

MONITOR PROGRESS

Phonics: /j/ge, dge

IF students have difficulty remembering when to use *ge* and when to use *dge* for final /j/,

THEN give students this memory aid: *dge* goes with short vowels because the vowels are too "short" to reach all the way to *ge,* so *d* is added as a bridge.

Small-Group Instruction, p. S26:

● **BELOW-LEVEL:** Reteach
● **ON-LEVEL:** Reinforce
● **ADVANCED:** Extend

BELOW-LEVEL

Consonants: ge and dge
Lesson 13

Name _____

▶ Read each sentence. Circle the correctly spelled word, and write it in the blank. The first one has been done for you.

1. Please open your book to the first ___page___
   (page) padge

2. The police chief wore a shiny ___badge___
   bage (badge)

3. I stood at the ___edge___ of the dock to look at the fish.
   ege (edge)

4. They built a new ___bridge___ across the river.
   brige (bridge)

5. The birds live in a big ___cage___ at the zoo.
   (cage) cadge

6. The ___judge___ wore a long black robe.
   juge (judge)

7. At what ___age___ did you start school?
   adge (age)

8. That was a ___strange___ and scary movie.
   (strange) strandge

107 Extra Support

▲ **Extra Support, p. 107**

ON-LEVEL

Consonants: -ge and -dge
Lesson 13

Name _____

▶ Read the story. Complete the spelling of each word. Use *-ge* or *-dge.*

Last month, I was in a play called "The Lar__ge__ Bird." The play takes place in a town called Bri__dge__ View. In the story, a stran__ge__ oran__ge__ bird flies into town and sits on a le__dge__ at the top of the town hall. The people of the town try to capture the bird and put it in a ca__ge__. But they cannot quite reach the e__dge__ of the roof where the bird is sitting!

I played a girl who is eight years of a__ge__. She tells the people that the bird is never going to bu__dge__ and that they should just leave the bird alone. The people of the town chan__ge__ their minds. They decide to let the bird stay on top of the building. It is a great play!

107 Practice Book

▲ **Practice Book, p. 107**

ADVANCED

Words with Final -ge and -dge
Lesson 13

Name _____

▶ Complete each sentence with a word that ends with the sound /j/ spelled *-ge* or *-dge.* Use the Word Bank for help.

| edge | orange | cage | stage | range |
| strange | change | dodge | charge | bridge |

1. Ms. Willis has to ___change___ planes at the airport in Miami.
2. The lion paced around in the ___cage___.
3. Hank and Chris love to play ___dodge___ ball.
4. My pencil rolled off the ___edge___ of my desk.
5. The singers walked out onto the ___stage___.
6. That store will ___charge___ a dollar for each pad of paper.
7. I crossed a ___bridge___ over the Mississippi River.
8. The teacher thought it was ___strange___ that so many students were absent on Tuesday.
9. The cattle grazed on the ___range___.
10. I ate a juicy ___orange___ for breakfast.

107 Challenge

▲ **Challenge, p. 107**

ELL

- Group students according to academic levels, and assign one of the pages on the left.
- Clarify any unfamiliar concepts as necessary. See *ELL Teacher Guide* Lesson 13 for support in scaffolding instruction.

Build Robust Vocabulary

Words from the Selection

Objective

- *To build robust vocabulary*

INTRODUCE Tested ✓

Vocabulary: Lesson 13

columns	rustling
absorb	dissolve
protects	particles

▼ Student-Friendly Explanations

Vocabulary

1. **columns** A column is a tall, circular structure that holds up part of a building.

2. **absorb** Something absorbs a liquid if it soaks up the liquid.

3. **protects** When you protect something, you keep it safe.

4. **rustling** When light objects are rustling, they are moving and making a soft, crackling sound.

5. **dissolve** When something dissolves, it mixes completely with a liquid.

6. **particles** Tiny pieces of something are called particles.

Grade 3, Lesson 13 · Re · Vocabulary

Transparency R89

Word Detective

Word Lists Have students rearrange the words in their lists so they are in alphabetical order and then compare their lists with a partner.

HOMEWORK/INDEPENDENT PRACTICE

Teach/Model

INTRODUCE ROBUST VOCABULARY Introduce the words using the following steps:

❶ Display **Transparency R89** and read the word and the **Student-Friendly Explanation**.

❷ Have students **say the word** with you.

❸ Have students **interact with the word's meaning** by asking the appropriate question below.

- What do **columns** hold up in a building?

- What will **absorb** spilled milk?

- What kinds of **particles** have you brushed from your clothes?

- Will sugar **dissolve** in water if you stir it?

- What kind of clothing **protects** firefighters?

- What might you hear **rustling** in the fall?

Develop Deeper Meaning

EXPAND WORD MEANINGS: PAGES 368–369 Have students read the passage. Then read the passage aloud, pausing at the end of page 368 to ask questions 1–3 below. Read page 369, and then discuss students' answers to questions 4–5 below.

1. Do the tree trunks look like **columns** rising from the forest floor?

2. Which trees **absorb** the most sun in the rain forest?

3. Do you think the canopy **protects** the animals?

4. What animals besides squirrels might make a **rustling** sound in the trees?

5. Would the **particles** of nutrients **dissolve** if it did not rain? Why or why not?

Vocabulary

Build Robust Vocabulary

Rain Forest Layers

columns

absorb

protects

rustling

dissolve

particles

Rain forests are made of four layers. The top layer is the emergent layer. Here, the trees are very tall. They stand like giant **columns** growing from the forest floor. Their leaves **absorb** the most sun. Animals such as eagles, monkeys, and bats live in this layer.

Next, the leafy canopy layer **protects** many animals. They can find food and water there and also hide from enemies.

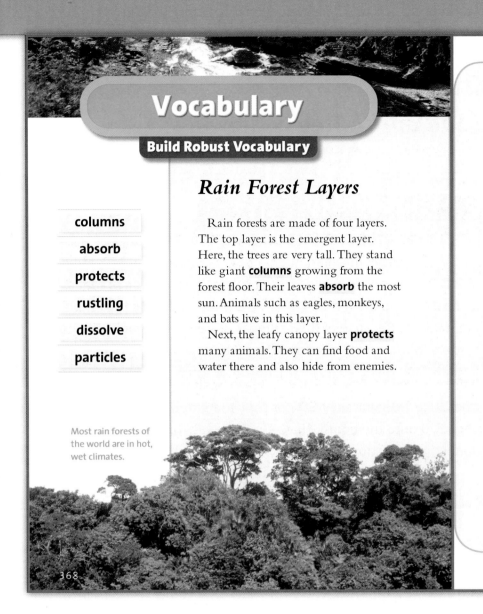

Most rain forests of the world are in hot, wet climates.

It is difficult to see animals in the canopy layer, but the forest is full of their sounds. Monkeys leap from tree to tree, **rustling** the leaves as they search for fruit.

Below the canopy is the understory. Jaguars and leopards lie in wait on thick branches there.

The lowest level is the forest floor. It is difficult for plants to grow there in the dark. The heavy rains often **dissolve** the nutrients in the soil and wash them away. Snakes and insects live on the forest floor.

Earthworms in the forest floor break down soil into **particles**.

 online www.harcourtschool.com/storytown

Word Detective

Your mission this week is to look for the Vocabulary Words in science books or on Internet sites about nature. Each time you read a Vocabulary Word, write it in your vocabulary journal. Don't forget to tell where you found the word.

368

369

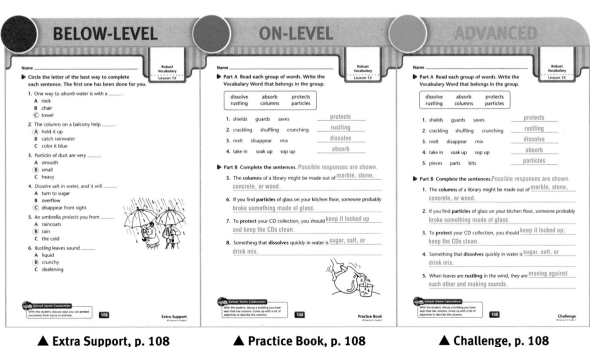

BELOW-LEVEL

▶ Circle the letter of the best way to complete each sentence. The first one has been done for you.

1. One way to *absorb* water is with a _____.
   A rock
   B chair
   C towel

2. The *columns* on a balcony help _____.
   A hold it up
   B catch rainwater
   C color it blue

3. *Particles* of dust are very _____.
   A smooth
   B small
   C heavy

4. *Dissolve* salt in water, and it will _____.
   A turn to sugar
   B overflow
   C disappear from sight

5. An umbrella *protects* you from _____.
   A raincoats
   B rain
   C the cold

6. *Rustling* leaves sound _____.
   A liquid
   B crunchy
   C deafening

▲ Extra Support, p. 108

ON-LEVEL

▶ Part A Read each group of words. Write the Vocabulary Word that belongs in the group.

| dissolve | absorb | protects |
| rustling | columns | particles |

1. shields   guards   saves — protects
2. crackling   shuffling   crunching — rustling
3. melt   disappear   mix — dissolve
4. take in   soak up   sop up — absorb

▶ Part B Complete the sentences. Possible responses are shown.

5. The **columns** of a library might be made out of marble, stone, concrete, or wood.

6. If you find **particles** of glass on your kitchen floor, someone probably broke something made of glass.

7. To **protect** your CD collection, you should keep it locked up and keep the CDs clean.

8. Something that **dissolves** quickly in water is sugar, salt, or drink mix.

▲ Practice Book, p. 108

ADVANCED

▶ Part A Read each group of words. Write the Vocabulary Word that belongs in the group.

| dissolve | absorb | protects |
| rustling | columns | particles |

1. shields   guards   saves — protects
2. crackling   shuffling   crunching — rustling
3. melt   disappear   mix — dissolve
4. take in   soak up   sop up — absorb
5. pieces   parts   bits — particles

▶ Part B Complete the sentences. Possible responses are shown.

1. The **columns** of a library might be made out of marble, stone, concrete, or wood.

2. If you find **particles** of glass on your kitchen floor, someone probably broke something made of glass.

3. To **protect** your CD collection, you should keep it locked up; keep the CDs clean.

4. Something that **dissolves** quickly in water is sugar, salt, or drink mix.

5. When leaves are **rustling** in the wind, they are moving against each other and making sounds.

▲ Challenge, p. 108

E L L

• Group students according to academic levels, and assign one of the pages on the left.

• Clarify any unfamiliar concepts as necessary. See *ELL Teacher Guide* Lesson 13 for support in scaffolding instruction.

Reading
Student Edition: **"A Tree Is Growing"**

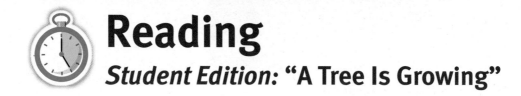

Objectives

- *To understand the distinguishing features of expository nonfiction*
- *To ask questions about the text*

Options for Reading

BELOW-LEVEL

SET A PURPOSE Preview the selection with students. Model how to set a purpose for reading.

ON-LEVEL

MONITOR COMPREHENSION Use the questions as students read, or have partners complete *Practice Book* page 109.

ADVANCED

INDEPENDENT READING Have students read, using *Practice Book* page 109.

▲ **Practice Book, p. 109**

Genre Study

EXPOSITORY NONFICTION: PAGE 370 Ask students to read the genre information on *Student Edition* page 370. Point out that expository nonfiction explains information or ideas. In a piece of expository nonfiction the author's purpose is to explain information. Because of this, authors use a clear organization to help readers follow and understand the text.

Point out that "A Tree Is Growing" is expository nonfiction about trees. Use **Transparency GO4** or copy the graphic organizer from page 370 onto the board. Have students use this chart as they read a nonfiction selection.

What I Know	What I Read	What I Learned

Comprehension Strategies

ASK QUESTIONS: PAGE 370 Read aloud the Comprehension Strategy information on page 370. Point out that good readers **ask questions** as they read. Then they look in the text to find the answers. Discuss some of the questions readers might ask when reading expository nonfiction, such as: What is the author trying to say? How does this happen? Why does it happen? What are the causes and effects of this? Encourage students to write down their questions and then return to them later to see if the text gives the answers.

Distribute Practice Book page 109. Tell students they will use the chart to keep track of information as they read. See page T240 for the completed *Practice Book* page.

Genre Study

Expository nonfiction explains information and ideas. Look for

* illustrations and captions.

* facts and details to help you learn about a topic.

| What I Know | What I Read | What I Learned |

Comprehension Strategy

Ask questions to help you explore important ideas in the selection.

370

A Tree Is Growing

by Arthur Dorros
illustrated by S. D. Schindler

371

Build Background

DISCUSS EXPLORING NATURE Tell students that they are going to read a selection about the life cycle of trees. Discuss what students know about trees. Then have them fill in the first box on *Practice Book* page 109.

Routine Card 5

SET A PURPOSE AND PREDICT Remind students that one purpose for reading is to learn new information. Have them look at page 371. Then follow these steps:

* Read the title and author with students.

* Point out the leaves and tree trunk in the illustration. Ask students to use text features, such as the title and the illustration, to predict specific things the selection might teach.

* List students' predictions on the board.

* Invite students to read the selection to find out more about trees.

TECHNOLOGY

 eBook "A Tree Is Growing" is available in an eBook.

 Audiotext "A Tree Is Growing" is available on *Audiotext 3* for subsequent readings.

A giant tree may look as if it has always been big. But even the biggest tree keeps growing and changing. **1**

In the spring you can see that a tree is growing as you watch buds on the branches unfold into leaves. **2**

Bristlecone pines are the oldest known living trees on earth. Some have been growing for five thousand years— since before the pyramids in Egypt were built. **3**

372   373

Monitor Comprehension

PAGES 372–373 Direct students to begin reading.

1 **DRAW CONCLUSIONS** What is one way that all trees are alike? (All trees keep growing.)

2 **SEQUENCE** What happens after the buds appear? (The buds unfold into leaves.)

3 **MAKE COMPARISONS** How is the bristlecone pine in the picture the same as or different from trees near your home? (Answers will vary.)

Apply
Comprehension Strategies

Ask Questions Ask: What questions do you have after reading these pages?

Think Aloud I see on page 372 that watching leaves can help you know that a tree is growing. But do trunks grow? I have never noticed one getting bigger. How can someone tell how old a tree is? I am going to remember these questions as I keep reading because I might find the answers.

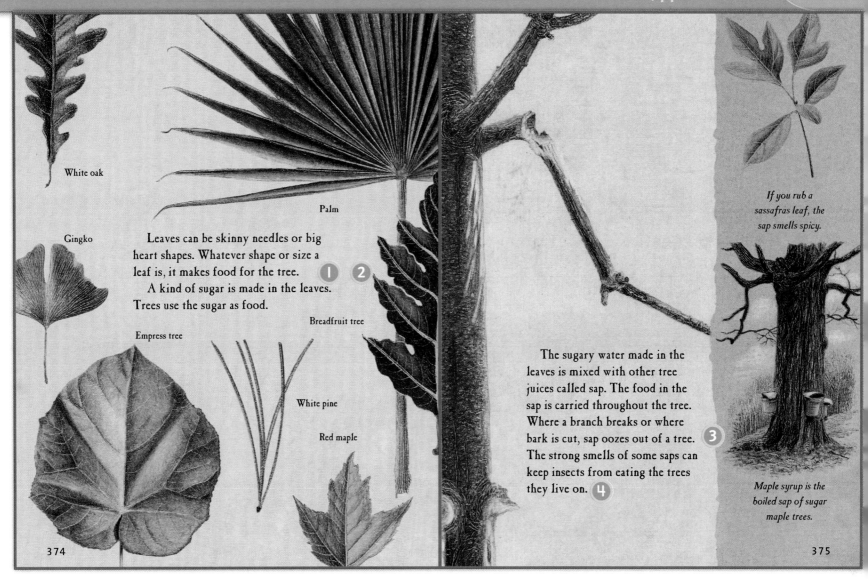

White oak

Palm

Gingko

Leaves can be skinny needles or big heart shapes. Whatever shape or size a leaf is, it makes food for the tree. ① ②
A kind of sugar is made in the leaves. Trees use the sugar as food.

Empress tree

Breadfruit tree

White pine

Red maple

If you rub a sassafras leaf, the sap smells spicy.

The sugary water made in the leaves is mixed with other tree juices called sap. The food in the sap is carried throughout the tree. Where a branch breaks or where bark is cut, sap oozes out of a tree. ③ The strong smells of some saps can keep insects from eating the trees they live on. ④

Maple syrup is the boiled sap of sugar maple trees.

374   375

Monitor Comprehension

PAGES 374–375 Have students read to find out about the leaves of trees.

① **USE GRAPHIC AIDS What information is in the illustrations on page 374?** (Possible responses: that there are many types of tree leaves; what the leaves of particular trees look like)

② **IMPORTANT DETAILS What do all leaves do?** (Possible response: make food for the tree)

③ **CONTEXT CLUES Using the words and images on page 375, what does the word *oozes* mean?** (Possible responses: runs, drips)

④ **IMPORTANT DETAILS What is one thing that sap does?** (Possible responses: carries food throughout the tree; keeps insects from eating the trees)

Moth caterpillar

Baobab trees store water in the trunks. When a baobab tree trunk is swollen with water, it is round and fat. In dry weather, the tree gets water from the trunk. Then the trunk gets thinner.

A tree needs sunlight, air, soil, and water to grow. Water travels through passages in the trunk and branches up to the leaves. The water moves up the trunk as if it is being sucked through a straw.
  Sugary sap made in the leaves travels down other passages in the trunk, taking food to different parts of the tree.

376

Monitor Comprehension

PAGES 376–377 Ask students what they think the two images on the left side of page 376 show. Then have students read to find out if they are correct.

1. **AUTHOR'S PURPOSE Why did the author include the two pictures on the left side of page 376?** (Possible response: to show the changes in the baobab tree when it has a lot of water in its trunk and when it does not)

2. **USE GRAPHIC AIDS What does the diagram on page 377 show?** (Possible response: the way water travels through a tree)

3. **AUTHOR'S CRAFT/IMAGERY To what does the author compare the movement of water in a tree? Why does the author say this?** (Possible response: to water being sucked through a straw; to help readers understand—most people have used a straw)

E L L

Explain Figurative Language
Clarify that authors use imagery to help readers understand what they are saying. Explain that "as if it is being sucked through a straw" means that the nutrients are sucked up rather than down through the tree. Demonstrate it for the students, if necessary.

White oak

A few kinds of trees drop roots from branches into the soil to gather water. Banyan tree roots grow into columns all around the tree.

Growing roots are strong. A root can lift a sidewalk or split a rock as it grows. By splitting the rock, it helps make soil.

The roots of a tree grow into the ground and hold the tree in place. Roots are like pipelines. They absorb water and carry it into the tree.

A tree's roots spread out far underground. They usually grow out a little farther than the tree's branches.

Trees need minerals to grow. Minerals are tiny particles that are found in the soil. Salt is one kind of mineral. Like salt, other minerals dissolve in water. They are mixed in with the water that roots absorb and are carried throughout the tree.

Mushrooms growing among the roots of a tree can help it get minerals. And the mushrooms and plants growing near a tree get water brought by the tree's roots.

Bicolored boletus mushrooms

Earthworms

Beetle grub

378

379

Monitor Comprehension

PAGES 378–379 Ask students to discuss what they know about tree roots. Then have them read to learn more.

1 **CAUSE/EFFECT Why do trees send out so many roots?** (Possible responses: to hold the tree in place; to absorb water)

2 **IMPORTANT DETAILS How do a tree and a mushroom help each other?** (Possible response: Mushrooms help trees get minerals; trees give mushrooms water.)

Use Multiple Strategies

Reread Say: After I read all of page 378, I am a little confused because banyan tree roots don't seem like the ones described on this page. So I reread the section on the top left side of page 378. It tells me that banyan tree roots are very different from the roots of most trees. Banyan roots drop down from branches instead of growing beneath the soil. This helps me understand the difference between these kinds of roots.

Flicker

Bark is the skin of a tree. The outer layer of bark protects the tree. When an oak tree is young, the bark is as smooth as a baby's skin. As the tree grows older, the bark becomes rough and cracked. **1**

380

Polyphemus moth

Looking at the bark of a tree can help you know what kind of tree it is.

The cork used for bulletin boards is the peeled-off outer bark of a cork oak tree. **2**

Honey locust bark has spines to help protect the tree.

381

Monitor Comprehension

PAGES 380–381 As a group, discuss what you already know about bark. Then discuss what you would like to learn. Finally, read to find out more.

1 COMPARE/CONTRAST **How is the bark on a young tree different from that on an old tree?** (Possible response: A young tree has smooth bark; an old tree has rough, cracked bark)

2 IMPORTANT DETAILS **How do people use the bark of a cork tree?** (Possible response: to make bulletin boards)

 SCIENCE

SUPPORTING STANDARDS

Ideal Environment Explain that plants and animals have ideal environments in which they can live and grow. Ask students to name a few plants and animals. Discuss their ideal environment and how they affect the environments where they live.

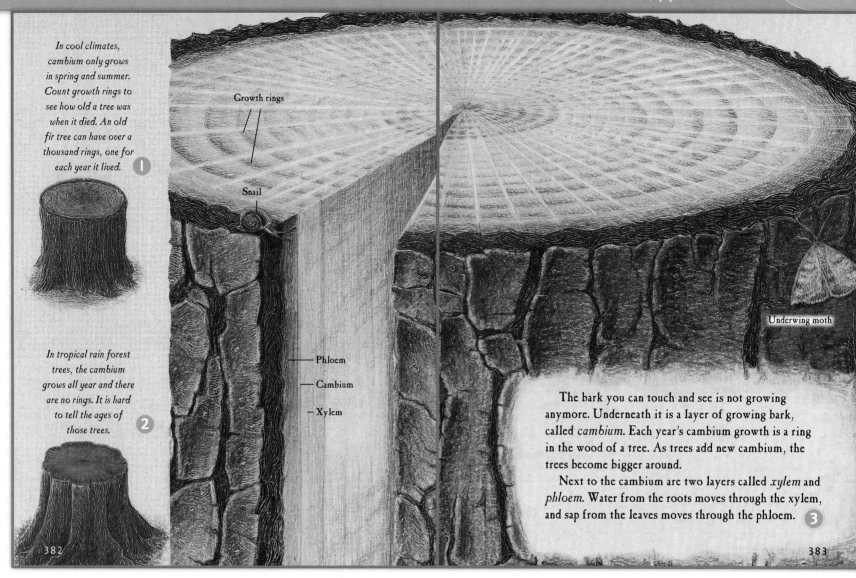

In cool climates, cambium only grows in spring and summer. Count growth rings to see how old a tree was when it died. An old fir tree can have over a thousand rings, one for each year it lived. **1**

In tropical rain forest trees, the cambium grows all year and there are no rings. It is hard to tell the ages of those trees. **2**

Growth rings

Snail

Phloem

Cambium

Xylem

Underwing moth

The bark you can touch and see is not growing anymore. Underneath it is a layer of growing bark, called *cambium*. Each year's cambium growth is a ring in the wood of a tree. As trees add new cambium, the trees become bigger around.

Next to the cambium are two layers called *xylem* and *phloem*. Water from the roots moves through the xylem, and sap from the leaves moves through the phloem. **3**

382

383

Monitor Comprehension

PAGES 382–383 Have students look at the diagrams and predict what these pages are about.

1 **EXPRESS PERSONAL OPINIONS How would you feel if you found a tree that was a thousand years old?** (Possible responses: impressed, interested)

2 **COMPARE/CONTRAST Why is it easier to find the age of a tree in a cold climate than in a tropical one?** (Possible response: Each ring in a cold climate tree represents a year of its life; tropical trees do not have rings.)

3 **IMPORTANT DETAILS What are *xylem* (zī´ləm) and *phloem* (flō´əm)? Why are they important?** (Possible responses: They are part of the trunk and carry water and sap.)

E L L

Find Definitions in Text Work with students to use the context of a passage to look for definitions of words they do not know. For example, page 382 first uses the word *cambium*, but a definition does not occur until page 383, which says "a layer of growing bark." Discuss other ways students can find definitions of words, such as with a dictionary or glossary.

Trees grow bigger around, and they grow taller. As a tree grows, lower branches may fall off, making the trunk look longer. But the branches do not move upward on the trunk. A tree grows taller only at the top, as the tips of the top branches grow upward. **①**

If you find a mark on a tree trunk today, that mark would stay at the same height for as long as the tree lives. **②**

Sequoias are some of the tallest trees in the world—over three hundred feet tall.

10 years   20 years   30 years

Wild turkey

50 years   200 years

384   385

Monitor Comprehension

PAGES 384–385 Before students read the page, ask them to predict where the main "growth" of the tree occurs. Record their answers on the board and then read these pages to find out more.

① **IMPORTANT DETAILS What part of the tree grows taller?** (Possible response: only the top)

② **DRAW CONCLUSIONS If you mark your own height on a tree, where will that same mark be the next year?** (Possible response: in the same spot)

Write Captions Have students select an illustration from the selection and write a caption for it. Encourage students to do research, if necessary, and to use their own knowledge and information from the selection in their writing.

Catkins

Nectar-eating bat

Calabash tree

Purple finch
(male)

Saucer
magnolia

Birds, insects, and even bats are attracted to flowers to drink their sweet juices. When they brush the flowers, the animals get a powder called pollen on them. The animals carry the pollen to other flowers. When the pollen mixes with certain parts of the flowers, seeds grow. Wind also helps pollinate flowers.

In the spring, you can smell tree flowers. Tree flowers are found in many shapes and colors, and have many different smells. Parts of the flowers grow to become seeds. Oak trees have dangling clumps of flowers called catkins that help make acorns, the seeds of an oak tree.

Honey bee

Wild cherry

Purple finch
(female)

386

387

Monitor Comprehension

PAGES 386–387 Ask students to describe any wild birds they have seen. Were they near buildings? In fields or yards? In trees? Talk with students about why birds might be in trees. Record their ideas on the board. Then have students read to find out more.

1 SYNTHESIZE How do birds and insects help make more trees?
(Possible response: They carry pollen from flower to flower, which makes new seeds grow.)

2 CONTEXT CLUES What is an acorn? (the seed of an oak tree)

3 SYNTHESIZE Why do you think tree flowers have many different colors, shapes, and smells? (Possible response: to attract different birds, animals, and insects so they can carry pollen from flower to flower)

Language Discussion Lead students in a discussion of the names for birds in different languages or cultures. If helpful, create a poster with pictures of birds and label them with their names in various languages.

Sugar maple

An oak tree can drop more than fifty thousand acorns in one year. Only a few of them grow into oak trees. Most are eaten, are crushed, rot, or land in a place where they cannot take root.

Acorns can be carried away and dropped or buried by animals to grow in new places. Other kinds of seeds blow in the wind or float on water. ① ②

Sugar maple seed

Acorns

388

Gray squirrel ③

Different kinds of trees make seeds with different coverings. Nuts, cones, and fruits all have seeds inside.

Brazil nut

Mountain pine cone

Cherry

Coconuts are seeds of a palm tree. A coconut can float across the ocean and sprout on a sandy beach.

389

Monitor Comprehension

PAGES 388–389 Have students continue reading to find out about oak trees.

① **IMPORTANT DETAILS What is one way that oak trees can spread to different areas?** (Possible response: Animals can carry acorns to new places.)

② **SPECULATE Would it be good if all acorns turned into trees? Why or why not?** (Possible response: No, because there would be too many trees or too many of one kind of tree.)

③ **AUTHOR'S PURPOSE Why might the author and the illustrator have included information and illustrations of animals?** (Possible responses: to provide more information; to make the selection more entertaining)

Apply
Comprehension Strategies

Focus Strategy **Ask Questions** Say: When I read the first sentence on page 388, I wonder how that fact could be true because there are not that many trees. Is this true? I will keep reading to see if I can find an answer to my question.

Autumn is a great time to collect leaves. Each tree has its own special color.

Tulip poplar

Gingko

Big-tooth aspen

Sweet gum

Pin oak

In cool climates, trees stop growing in autumn. The leaves of many trees stop making sugary food for the tree, and they lose their green color. Then you can see the red, brown, yellow, and orange colors that are also in the leaves.

Pine trees and some other trees have needles or leaves that do not change color in autumn.

Beetles

Spider

Earthworms

Millipede

Mole

When leaves fall to the ground, insects and worms eat them. The chewed and eaten bits of leaves make the soil better for growing trees and other plants.

390   391

Monitor Comprehension

PAGES 390–391 Tell students that another word for the season fall is *autumn*. Have students suggest words they associate with autumn. (Possible responses: leaves, cool weather) Then ask them to read to find out what happens to trees in fall.

1 TEXT FEATURES What does the left column on page 390 show readers? (Possible response: the colors that different leaves turn in autumn)

2 SEQUENCE What happens to trees after the weather turns cool? (Possible response: They stop growing.)

3 SYNTHESIZE Do the leaves of all trees change color in fall? (no) **Why not?** (Possible response: Trees with needles do not change color.)

ANALYZE AUTHOR'S PURPOSE

Author's Purpose Remind students that authors have a purpose, or reason, for writing. After students have finished reading "A Tree Is Growing," ask:

Why did the author write "A Tree Is Growing"?

• to persuade readers to take care of trees

• to entertain readers with a story about animals

• to inform readers about trees

Lesson 13 (*Student Edition*, pages 390–391) **T237**

White oak

Trees rest in the cold of winter, and their branches are bare. They may look as if they are dead. But look closely and you can see small buds that will become leaves and flowers in the spring.

Horse chestnut

In the spring, listen to the wind rustling the leaves.
The trees are growing again.

White oak

392

393

Monitor Comprehension

PAGES 392–393 Before reading, have students think about how the selection began. (with spring) Then make predictions about how the selection will end. Direct them to finish reading the selection.

1 **CONFIRM PREDICTIONS/AUTOR'S** **Did the selection end the way students predicted? Why did the author structure the text this way?** (Possible response: Yes; it finished with spring, to show how the tree grows throughout a year.)

2 **AUTHOR'S VIEWPOINT** **How do you think this author feels about trees? Explain your answer.** (Possible response: The author admires trees; he includes many interesting details.)

3 **EXPRESS PERSONAL OPINIONS** **What did you think of this selection? Explain your answer.** (Accept reasonable responses.)

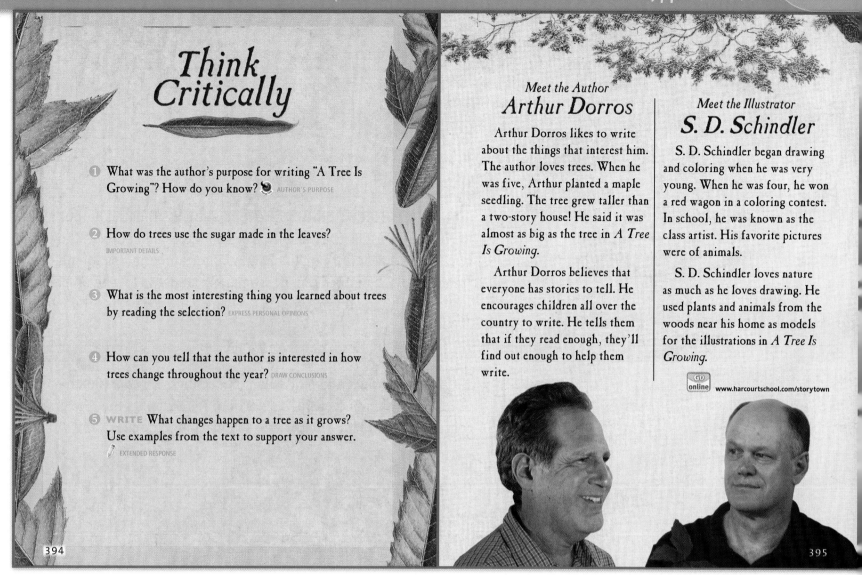

Think Critically

1. What was the author's purpose for writing "A Tree Is Growing"? How do you know? AUTHOR'S PURPOSE

2. How do trees use the sugar made in the leaves? IMPORTANT DETAILS

3. What is the most interesting thing you learned about trees by reading the selection? EXPRESS PERSONAL OPINIONS

4. How can you tell that the author is interested in how trees change throughout the year? DRAW CONCLUSIONS

5. WRITE What changes happen to a tree as it grows? Use examples from the text to support your answer. EXTENDED RESPONSE

Meet the Author
Arthur Dorros

Arthur Dorros likes to write about the things that interest him. The author loves trees. When he was five, Arthur planted a maple seedling. The tree grew taller than a two-story house! He said it was almost as big as the tree in *A Tree Is Growing*.

Arthur Dorros believes that everyone has stories to tell. He encourages children all over the country to write. He tells them that if they read enough, they'll find out enough to help them write.

Meet the Illustrator
S. D. Schindler

S. D. Schindler began drawing and coloring when he was very young. When he was four, he won a red wagon in a coloring contest. In school, he was known as the class artist. His favorite pictures were of animals.

S. D. Schindler loves nature as much as he loves drawing. He used plants and animals from the woods near his home as models for the illustrations in *A Tree Is Growing*.

GO online   www.harcourtschool.com/storytown

Think Critically

Respond to the Literature

1. The author's purpose is to inform the reader. He gives facts about how trees grow. **AUTHOR'S PURPOSE**

2. They use it as food. **IMPORTANT DETAILS**

3. Responses will vary. **EXPRESS PERSONAL OPINIONS**

4. The text structure the author uses is sequenced in the order of the seasons. The author does this so he can explain how the tree changes throughout the year. **DRAW CONCLUSIONS**

5. WRITE Trees grow taller and bigger around. Many trees have flowers in the spring. Oak trees grow and drop acorns. Where winters are cold, many trees lose their leaves until spring. **EXTENDED RESPONSE/SUMMARIZE**

MEET THE AUTHOR & THE ILLUSTRATOR

Page 395 Tell students that Arthur Dorros, the author of "A Tree Is Growing," has written more than twenty books. As a child, Dorros loved science and reading, so it seems natural that he grew up to write scientific books for young people. But not all Dorros's books are nonfiction—he has written many books about animals that have exciting adventures.

Illustrator S. D. Schindler lives in Philadelphia, Pennsylvania, where he draws for many children's books.

RUBRIC For additional support in scoring this item, see the rubrics on p. R7.

Lesson 13 (*Student Edition*, pages 394–395)   **T239**

Check Comprehension
Summarizing

Objectives

- *To summarize a selection*
- *To read with intonation in a manner that sounds like natural speech*

RETELLING RUBRIC

4	Uses details to clearly summarize the selection
3	Uses some details to summarize the selection
2	Summarizes the selection with some inaccuracies
1	Is unable to summarize the selection

Professional Development

Podcasting: Auditory Modeling

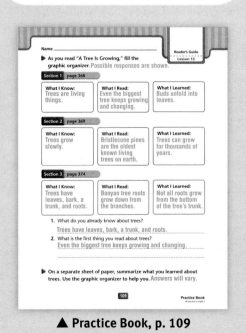

▲ **Practice Book, p. 109**

Summarize

AUTHOR'S PURPOSE Remind students that the author's purpose is the reason he or she writes something. Knowing whether a writer is trying to explain, entertain, or persuade helps readers focus on the main message. Ask students to give one reason why the author wrote "A Tree Is Growing." (Possible response: to inform readers about trees)

Routine Card 6

WRITE A SUMMARY Have students write a summary of "A Tree Is Growing." Remind them that a summary contains the main ideas and details of a selection. Tell students that the graphic organizer on *Practice Book* page 109 may help them.

Fluency
Intonation

Teach/Model

DIBELS
Oral Reading Fluency
ORF

READING WITH INTONATION Explain that good readers speak clearly and change their voices as they read to help listeners understand the text. This is called intonation. Remind students that end marks are an important clue for intonation. For example, at the end of a question, a reader's voice usually goes up, but at the end of a statement, a reader's voice goes down. Explain that in nonfiction most sentences are statements, but intonation is still important.

Have students open to page 374 of "A Tree Is Growing." Read the paragraph aloud, with appropriate intonation, and tell students to note where your voice gets higher and lower.

Practice/Apply

PARTNER READING Have students read aloud page 375 to a partner, using intonation.

Build Robust Vocabulary
Words About the Selection

Objective
• *To develop robust vocabulary through discussion*

INTRODUCE ✓ Tested
Vocabulary: Lesson 13

scavenger   self-sufficient

▼ **Student-Friendly Explanations**

Vocabulary

1. **tugged** If you tugged something, you pulled it hard.
2. **paused** If you paused, you stopped what you were doing for a moment.
3. **scavenger** An animal is a scavenger if it collects leftover and unwanted objects.
4. **self-sufficient** If something is self-sufficient, it makes everything it needs.

Grade 3, Lesson 13   Rb   Vocabulary

Transparency R86

Self-Sufficient Explain to students that some English words have a hyphen. That means they are a combination of two words put together. Have students look up *self* and *sufficient* in a dictionary. Then, have them define the word *self-sufficient*.

Grammar
Object Pronouns

5-DAY GRAMMAR

DAY 1	Subject Pronouns
DAY 2	**Object Pronouns**
DAY 3	Using *I* and *me*
DAY 4	Apply to Writing
DAY 5	Subject and Object Pronouns Review

Objectives

- *To identify pronouns*
- *To use pronouns*

Daily Proofreading

1. Them were late for dinner
   (They; dinner.)
2. mary and me went to the
   shopping mall. (Mary and I
   or We)

Teach/Model

INTRODUCE OBJECT PRONOUNS Remind students that, in a sentence, an object is a noun that is *not* the subject of the sentence. Write the following sentences on the board.

> **The dog chewed the bone.**
>
> **The dog chewed it.**

Explain that *dog* is the subject of the first sentence. *Bone* is the object—the thing that the dog acts upon. Point out that in the second sentence, the word *it* replaces *the bone*. Pronouns that take the place of objects are called object pronouns. They include *me, you, him, her, it, us,* and *them.*

Guided Practice

IDENTIFY CORRECT OBJECT PRONOUNS Write the following sentences on the board:

> **The teachers applauded Mrs. Chan.**
>
> **Shantay planned the party.**

Read the first sentence aloud. Ask students which object pronoun can replace Mrs. *Chan* (*her*), emphasizing that it is important to use object pronouns to replace object nouns in sentences. Repeat with the second sentence, asking whether *party* can be replaced with the word *it*.

Practice/Apply

USE OBJECT PRONOUNS Write the following sentences on the board:

> **Mario called Mia.**
>
> **Mia ran to Mario and his friends.**

Have students rewrite the sentences, replacing the object nouns with the appropriate object pronouns. (Mario called her; Mia ran to them.) Then have them speak their sentences to a partner.

Name _____

Subject and Object Pronouns Lesson 13

▶ Write the pronoun in each sentence. Then label each pronoun as *subject* or *object.*

1. Ms. Edison teaches us about flowers.
   us; object

2. A student asks her how flowers grow.
   her; object

3. Ms. Edison answers him.
   him; object

4. She talks to the class about sunlight.
   She; subject

5. Flowers need it to make food and grow.
   it; object

6. We learn more about flowers.
   We; subject

7. Bees collect pollen from them.
   them; object

8. I write a paper on flowers.
   I; subject

Try This
Find four sentences in a book or magazine that have pronouns. Copy the sentences. Underline the subject pronouns. Circle the object pronouns. Accept reasonable responses.

45   Grammar Practice Book

▲ **Grammar Practice Book, p. 45**

Writing
Explanation

5-DAY WRITING	
DAY 1	Introduction
DAY 2	Prewrite
DAY 3	Draft
DAY 4	Revise/Edit
DAY 5	Revise/Edit

Prewrite

REVIEW EXPLANATION Tell students that an explanation usually begins with a topic sentence that states the main idea. It lets readers know what will be explained. Then add to the list of traits of an explanation:

WRITING TRAIT **SENTENCE FLUENCY**
Point out that as a paragraph develops, its sentences should provide more detail about the topic. To vary the sentences, students should use object pronouns as they elaborate.

MODEL PREWRITING Draw the graphic organizer on the board. Model choosing a topic and then fill in the first column on the chart with some facts and details about the topic.

> ### Explanation
> - Gives facts and details about a topic
> - Explain what or how
> - Starts with a topic sentence

What I Know	What I Learned

Practice/Apply

PREWRITING AN EXPLANATION Tell students to choose an interesting topic that they know something about and could explain to someone else. Have students fill in the first column of the graphic organizer. Then invite them to find additional information in reference sources and to write their findings in the second column. When they have finished, tell students to write a clear topic sentence for their explanations.

Objectives
- *To successfully prewrite*
- *To prepare for writing by mapping ideas*

Writing Prompt

Write Questions Suggest that students write three questions to be answered in their explanations.

E L L

Prewriting Have students name three facts or details that they already know about their topic. If they cannot name three facts, have students find a different topic to write about.

DAILY ROUTINES

Day at a Glance

Day 3

 **and Spelling**

- Review: Consonants /s/c; /j/g, dge

Fluency

- Intonation
- "A Tree Is Growing," *Student Edition*, pp. 370–395

Comprehension

 Author's Purpose

- Introduce: Use Graphic Aids

Reading

- "Ancient Trees Survive" *Student Edition*, pp. 396–399

Robust Vocabulary

- Review: *tugged, paused, columns, absorb, protects, rustling, dissolve, particles, scavenger, self-sufficient*

Grammar

- Introduce: Using *I* and *me*

Writing ✏️

- Explanation

Warm-Up Routines

 Oral Language

Objectives *To respond critically to oral communication; to write sentences about a topic*

Question of the Day

What does your body need in order to stay healthy and keep growing?

Remind students that they have learned some of the things that trees need in order to grow tall and strong. Ask students to list some of the things that human beings (particularly young people) need so that they can stay healthy and grow properly. (food, drink, air, shelter, sleep) Then have students respond in their notebooks to the following prompt:

In order to stay healthy and keep growing, I need _____.

Have students write at least two sentences describing their needs. Invite volunteers to share their responses with classmates.

Read Aloud

Objectives *To listen to poems; to speak with intonation*

REVIEW THE POEM Display **Transparency R87,** or distribute photocopies of it. Tell students that you are going to reread the poem "Autumn."

Set a purpose. Ask students why someone might read or listen to a poem again. (to enjoy it or to practice fluency) Tell them to listen and follow along as you read the poem, paying attention to the way you make your voice lower or higher as you read.

Model fluent reading. Read the poem aloud, choosing appropriate times to make your voice lower and higher.

Partner-read. Tell students to read the poem with a partner. Partners should read together and then take turns reading aloud and listening to each other.

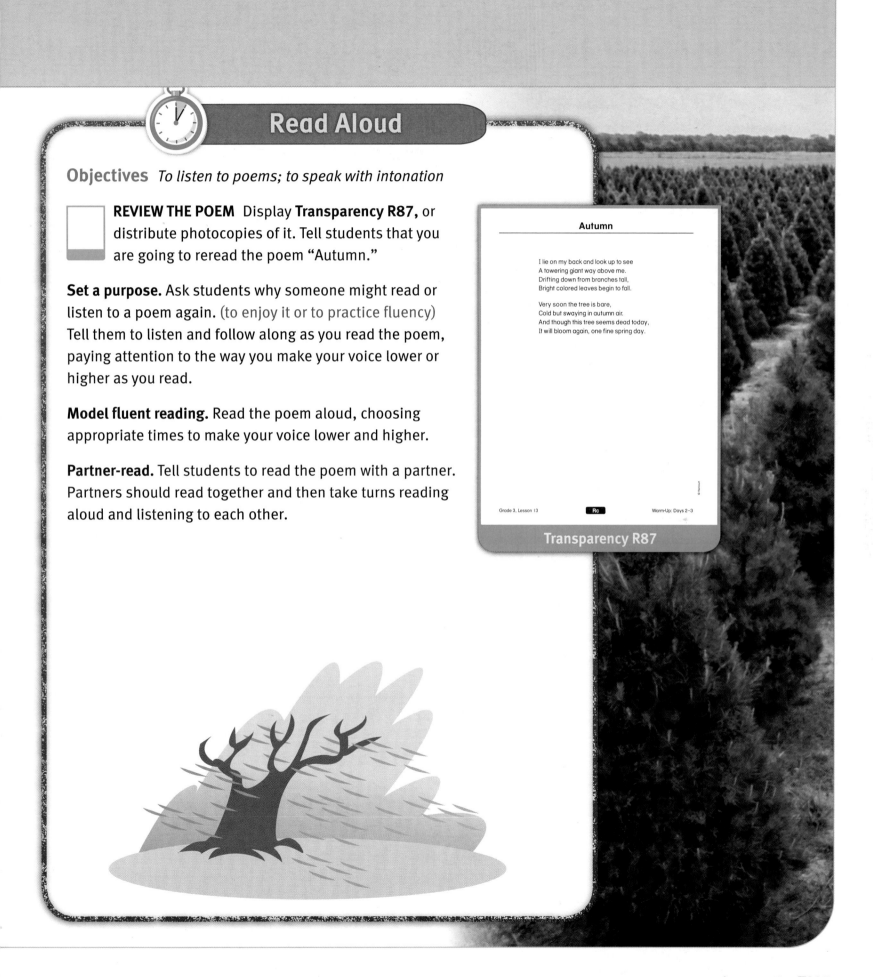

Autumn

I lie on my back and look up to see
A towering giant way above me.
Drifting down from branches tall,
Bright colored leaves begin to fall.

Very soon the tree is bare,
Cold but swaying in autumn air.
And though this tree seems dead today,
It will bloom again, one fine spring day.

Grade 3, Lesson 13   **Rc**   Warm-Up: Days 2–3

Transparency R87

Consonants /s/c; /j/g, dge phonics

5-DAY PHONICS	
DAY 1	Introduce /s/c and /j/g
DAY 2	Words with Final ge and dge
DAY 3	**Words with Final ice, ace, ce**
DAY 4	Other Words with /s/c and /j/g
DAY 5	Review /s/c and /j/g

Objective

• *To use decoding strategies to clarify pronunciation*

Skill Trace

Tested **Consonants: /s/c; /j/g, dge**

Introduce	Grade 2
Reintroduce	T212
Reteach	S26
Review	T222–T223, T246, T262, T274, T410
Test	Theme 3
Maintain	Theme 4, T176

Words with Soft *c* and *g*

Part A

ice	ace	edge	age
dice	face	hedge	cage
lice	lace	ledge	page
mice	mace	wedge	rage
nice	pace	dredge	sage
rice	race	pledge	wage
vice	place	sledge	stage
price	space		
slice	brace		
spice	trace		
twice			

Part B

police	office	refrigerator	imagine
celery	ceiling	margin	difference

Part C

1. The prince ate a bowl of rice. (prince, rice)

2. Do not write in the margin of the page. (margin, page)

3. Take my advice and do not glance away from the road when you ride a bike. (advice, glance)

4. Let's race the sledges. (race, sledges)

Grade 3, Lesson 13   **Rf**   Phonics: Day 3

Transparency R90

Teach/Model

WORDS WITH SOFT *c* and *g* Write the words *ice, ace, edge,* and *age* on the board. Point out that the letters *c* and *g* are followed by the letter *e*. Ask students what sound *c* stands for (/s/) and what sound *g* and *dge* stand for. (/j/) Have volunteers read the words aloud. Then have students divide a page into four columns and copy the words as column heads. Tell them to list as many words as they can using these phonograms. Have volunteers read aloud their lists. Display **Transparency R90** and have volunteers read aloud the words in Part A. Have students compare their lists to the lists on the transparency.

LONGER WORDS WITH SOFT *c* AND SOFT *g* Call attention to the words in Part B on the transparency. Have students note the letter that follows *c* or *g* in each word. Have students read the words.

Practice/Apply

GUIDED PRACTICE Read aloud the first sentence in Part C, identifying the words with *c*. Ask how *c* should be pronounced. (/s/) Continue with item 2, helping students identify the words with /j/g, *dge*.

INDEPENDENT PRACTICE Have students read sentences 3–4. Have them write in their notebooks each word with the sound /s/ or /j/, underlining the letter or letters that stand for the sound.

Consonants /s/c; /j/ge, dge
 and *Spelling*

5-DAY SPELLING	
DAY 1	Pretest
DAY 2	State the Generalization
DAY 3	**Spelling Practice/Handwriting**
DAY 4	Use Spelling Strategies/Review
DAY 5	Posttest

Review Spelling Words

REVIEW THE GENERALIZATION Remind students that the letter *s* usually stands for /s/, but that the letter *c* can stand for that sound when *c* is followed by *i* or *e*. The letter *j* usually stands for /j/, but *g* can stand for the sound when *g* is followed by *i* or *e*. The spelling *dge* can also stand for /j/, usually at the end of a word or syllable. Tell students they will have to remember which words are spelled with *c*, *g*, or *dge*.

✏️ **WRITE** Remind students that they can practice spelling by writing. Have students write the spelling words in their notebooks. Remind them to check their work. Then have them write five sentences that each include two of the words, such as *The police chief went back to his office.* Have students use different words in each sentence. Have students read their sentences aloud to a partner.

Handwriting

LETTER FORMATION Review proper formation of the letter *g* with students. Remind them that the letter must descend far enough so that it cannot be confused with *o* or *a,* and that at the bottom it must "hook" clearly enough to the left so as not to be confused with *q.*

go

ADVANCED

Use Spelling Words Challenge students to use three spelling words in a single sentence that makes sense.

Spelling Words

1.	**ice**	9.	**ledge**
2.	**age**	10.	**police**
3.	**rice**	11.	**recent**
4.	**edge**	12.	**bridge**
5.	**stage**	13.	**office**
6.	**giant***	14.	**strange**
7.	**range**	15.	**central**
8.	**judge**		

Challenge Words

16.	**celery**	19.	**margin**
17.	**ceiling**	20.	**imagine**
18.	**difference**		

*Word from "A Tree Is Growing"

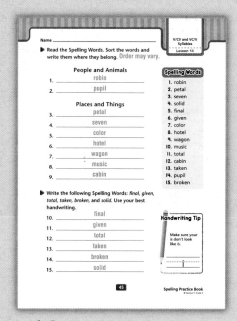

▲ Spelling Practice Book, p. 45

Fluency
Intonation

Objectives

- *To build fluency through rereading a selection*
- *To read with intonation*
- *To read in a manner that sounds like natural speech*

Additional Related Reading

- ***Red Leaf, Yellow Leaf*** by Lois Ehlert. Harcourt, 1998. **EASY**
- ***Under the Sunday Tree*** by Eloise Greenfield. HarperTrophy, 1991. **AVERAGE**
- ***Sky Tree*** by Thomas Locker. HarperTrophy, 2001. **CHALLENGE**

BELOW-LEVEL

Fluency Practice Have students reread for fluency, using Story 13 in the *Strategic Intervention Interactive Reader* or the appropriate *Leveled Readers*. (See pages T282–T285.) Guide students to select a small portion of a story and practice reading it several times.

Review

DIBELS
Oral
Reading
Fluency
ORF

MODEL READING WITH INTONATION Remind students that when good readers read nonfiction aloud, their voice expresses the feeling of the passage. Good readers change the pitch or intonation of their voice, making it go high and low when reading words and phrases that need emphasis. They also use end marks as clues for reading particular words and sentences.

Tell students that as they read nonfiction they should make their voices go up and down, depending on:

- how important words are.
- end marks and other punctuation.

Think Aloud **I'm going to read page 388 in "A Tree Is Growing." I notice that the first sentence tells about fifty thousand acorns. That's a lot of acorns from one tree, so I will emphasize the words *fifty thousand* by raising my voice slightly.**

CHORAL-READING Read aloud page 388 of "A Tree Is Growing" and model fluent reading. Then reread the page, having students read along with you. Remind them to follow your expression and phrasing.

Practice/Apply

GUIDED PRACTICE Direct students to page 388 once again and guide them to identify the places where they should raise or lower their voices. Reread the passage with them, helping students to hear the emphasis in each sentence.

Routine Card 10

INDEPENDENT PRACTICE Have partners reread page 388 and give each other helpful and positive feedback about their reading.

Author's Purpose
Comprehension

Review

EXPLAIN AUTHOR'S PURPOSE Remind students that an author's purpose is the reason he or she writes something. There are several reasons authors write something: to inform, to entertain, or to persuade. Sometimes, a writer might want to entertain readers while also informing them.

To identify the author's purpose, readers need to consider what the main message is and why the author would want to give that message. Say: **In "A Tree Is Growing," the main message is what trees are like and how they grow and change during the year. The author wants to inform readers about trees.** The author also has specific purposes on some pages, such as to explain what bark is or what roots do.

Practice/Apply

GUIDED PRACTICE Discuss the following passages from "A Tree Is Growing," working with students to find details and facts that help identify the author's specific purpose.

- **PAGE 379 FIRST PARAGRAPH** (Possible response: Details and facts such as *roots hold the tree in place*, *roots are like pipelines*, and *roots absorb water and carry it to the tree* show that the author's purpose is to tell what roots are and what they do.)

- **PAGE 380** (Possible response: Details such as *bark is the skin of a tree* and *the outer layer of bark protects the tree* show that the author's purpose is to tell what bark is and what it does.)

INDEPENDENT PRACTICE Have students read page 383. Then have them write the author's purpose and list facts showing how the author achieved his or her purpose. (Possible response: Cambium is a layer of growing bark. The author's purpose is to tell what bark is made of.)

Objectives

- *To recognize author's purpose*
- *To use details from text to support answers*

Skill Trace

 Author's Purpose

Introduce	T215
Reteach	S30
Review	T249, T265, T277, T302–T303, T333, T349, T361, T412, T433
Test	Theme 3
Maintain	Theme 4, T348

Use Graphic Aids
Comprehension

Objectives

- *To identify how graphic aids help with comprehension*
- *To use graphic aids successfully*

Skill Trace

Tested **Use Graphic Aids**

Introduce	T250–T251
Reteach	S32
Review	T334–T335
Test	Theme 3

MONITOR PROGRESS

Use Graphic Aids

IF students have trouble understanding the difference between a graphic aid and a graphic organizer,	**THEN** tell them "An aid helps me understand something, and an organizer helps me *organize* information."

Small-Group Instruction, p. S32:

- **BELOW-LEVEL:** Reteach
- **ON-LEVEL:** Reinforce
- **ADVANCED:** Extend

Teach/Model

INTRODUCE GRAPHIC AIDS Discuss graphic aids with students. Emphasize that there are many kinds of graphic aids—photographs, drawings, maps, charts, graphs, and diagrams. Explain that graphic aids are used in books, magazines, newspapers, and other reading material for several reasons. They help explain ideas, gather and organize information, and even make reading more enjoyable. Guide students as they thumb through the *Student Edition*, helping them identify different graphic aids and their uses. (For example, the chart on page 116 helps readers find out about the parts of a book.)

Guided Practice

USE GRAPHIC AIDS Have students turn to page 382 and look at the graphic aid. Help them understand that this graphic aid is a diagram that shows the parts of a tree trunk. Point out the labels and how they give readers additional information about trees and bark. Guide students to answer the following questions about the diagram.

- **What can you see if you slice through the tree trunk?** (growth rings)

- **Where does cambium appear in the tree trunk?** (between phloem and xylem)

Practice/Apply

USE GRAPHIC AIDS Have students study the information presented in the graphic aid on *Student Edition* pages 384–385 and answer the following questions in their notebooks.

1. **What is spread across these pages?** (a tree at different stages, beginning at 10 years of age and going up to 200 years)

2. **What animal is shown in front of the 30-year-old tree?** (a wild turkey)

3. **At what ages is the tree on page 385?** (50 and 200)

4. **How are the changes shown as the tree gets older?** (The tree gets taller and thicker.)

5. **What doesn't change as the trees get older?** (The marked point that is about as high as the turkey's head doesn't change.)

6. **What does the graphic aid help you understand?** (that the top, not the rest of a tree, grows taller)

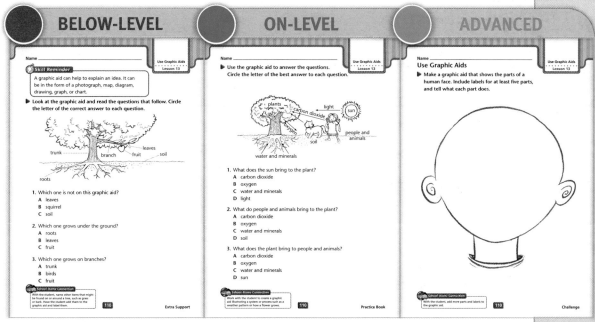

▲ Extra Support, p. 110   ▲ Practice Book, p. 110   ▲ Challenge, p. 110

ELL

- Group students according to academic levels, and assign one of the pages on the left.

- Clarify any unfamiliar concepts as necessary. See *ELL Teacher Guide* Lesson 13 for support in scaffolding instruction.

Science

ANCIENT TREES SURVIVE IN CALIFORNIA'S MOUNTAINS

by April Pulley Sayre

Survivors

The world's oldest trees are the bristlecone pines that grow in California's White Mountains. Some of the trees are more than 4,000 years old. They started to grow at the time of the building of the Egyptian pyramids.

Bristlecones are survivors. Trees need water, soil, sunshine, and warmth; yet these trees live on dry, rocky, cold mountains. They get a lot of sunlight there, but little water, soil, or warmth.

Parts of the oldest trees may look as if they are dead. However, the trees still produce seeds.

Treemont News — Saturday, November 20 D-6

All trees need water to live. Since bristlecone pines live in dry areas, they stay alive by using very little water. They have narrow leaves called needles. Needles don't lose as much water as broad, flat leaves do.

In addition, these pines use very little energy. They are evergreens. This means that they keep their needles in winter. They always look green. However, even evergreens must drop old needles and grow new ones. This happens a few needles at a time, not all at once. White pine trees, for example, keep each needle for about two years. In contrast, bristlecone pines keep each needle for about 30 years! These trees save energy by not making new needles very often.

Some young bristlecone pine cones are a purplish color.

Bristlecone pine trees can remain standing for hundreds of years after they die.

The needles on a bristlecone pine provide energy to the tree.

396

397

![clock icon] # Reading
Student Edition: Paired Selection

Genre Study

DISCUSS NEWS FEATURES Explain that "Ancient Trees Survive" is an example of a news feature. A news feature is nonfiction, tells about current events or interesting topics, and is found in a newspaper.

TEXT FEATURES Tell students that a news feature may include

- a headline with the title of the article
- a first paragraph that tells what the article is about

USE PRIOR KNOWLEDGE/SET A PURPOSE Remind students that one purpose for reading a news feature is to gain information. Then have them read about unusual trees that grow in California.

Objectives

- *To understand the features of a newspaper article*
- *To distinguish between types of nonfiction*

D-7

Bristlecone pine trees can grow to be 60 feet tall.

Some of the bristlecones look dead, but they are still alive. On some, only a small strip of bark and xylem remain alive. Cells in the xylem carry water and soil nutrients up the tree.

It takes only a small strip of xylem to bring water and food to a single branch. That branch makes needles. It forms cones that hold seeds. Such a tree may look half dead, but it can live for thousands of years.

The Oldest Living Bristlecone Pine

The oldest living bristlecone pine is known as "the Methuselah tree." It is at least 4,700 years old. The Methuselah tree lives in the Ancient Bristlecone Pine Forest in California's White Mountains. You can visit the Ancient Bristlecone Pine Forest, but you will not easily find the Methuselah tree. It is not marked. The tree's identity is kept a secret so people will not get too close and harm the tree.

398

Treemont News   Saturday, November 20   D-8

Stories from the Trees

These long-lived trees can help people learn about history. The trees cannot say what happened, but their tree rings hold information. Rainy or snowy years cause wider rings to form. Dry years result in narrow tree rings.

Scientists can drill a small sample from a tree. The sample is the size of a drinking straw. Scientists study the layers that show the rings. This way, they do not have to cut down the tree

to see its rings. By studying tree rings, scientists can learn more about the lives of plants, animals, and people that lived thousands of years ago. The ancient bristlecone pine trees hold stories for people who know how to read them!

399

Respond to the Article

MONITOR COMPREHENSION As students read, ask:

- **DRAW CONCLUSIONS** **Why do you think the author calls the bristlecone trees "survivors"?** (Possible response: because they are able to live where most other trees could not)

- **AUTHOR'S VIEWPOINT** **How do you think the author feels about bristlecone pine trees? How can you tell?** (Possible response: She admires them; she says that the ancient trees have stories to tell.)

- **GENRE** **How can you tell that "Ancient Trees Survive" is a news feature?** (It has a headline. The first paragraph tells what the article will be about.)

List Have students list foods they like to eat. Work with students to identify foods from plants.

Writing Prompt

Write an Advertisement Have students write the text of an advertisement to persuade tourists to visit the bristlecone pine trees of California. Then discuss the differences between the news feature and an advertisement.

 Connections

Comparing Texts

1. Possible response: Like: needs sunlight; has bark; lives long. Different: has needles instead of leaves; can grow with little water, soil, or warmth; is much older than any oak. **TEXT TO TEXT**

2. Possible response: springtime, because many trees have flowers then. **TEXT TO SELF**

3. Possible response: Other plants and animals use parts of the tree as food or as a source of water. **TEXT TO WORLD**

Connections

Comparing Texts

1. How is the bristlecone pine tree in "Ancient Trees Survive in California's Mountains" like the oak tree in "A Tree Is Growing"? How is it different?

2. Now that you know more about trees, what will be your favorite season to look at them? Explain.

3. How does a tree make the world a better place?

Vocabulary Review

A tree's roots absorb particles of water.

Word Sort

Work with a partner. Sort the Vocabulary Words into two categories. Decide whether each word is an *action* or an *object.* Compare your sorted words with your partner's words. Take turns explaining why you put each word where you did. Then choose one word from each category and write a sentence that uses both words.

columns
absorb
protects
rustling
dissolve
particles

Fluency Practice

Repeated Reading

Choose a section from "A Tree Is Growing." Read the passage, letting your voice rise and fall naturally. Use a stopwatch to time your second reading. Repeat until you can read the passage with few or no errors.

Writing

Write a Poem

Write a poem about a tree. Think about what you learned in "A Tree Is Growing" to help you get ideas. Use a graphic organizer to brainstorm interesting words and phrases. Your poem does not have to rhyme, but it should help the reader understand what you like about trees. You might even write your words to form the shape of a tree.

My Writing Checklist
Writing Trait · Sentence Fluency
✓ I use the graphic organizer to plan my poem.
✓ I elaborate on the ideas in my poem.

How trees look	How trees feel	How trees smell

400

401

VOCABULARY

Word Sort Have students discuss their sentences. After two rounds of this activity, encourage partners to work together to use three words in a single sentence.

FLUENCY

Repeated Reading Remind students that fluent readers make their voices lower and higher in a natural way. They pause and have their voices turn down for commas and periods and up for question marks. Ask pairs to alternate reading pages 387–388 of "A Tree Is Growing." Encourage them to give their partners positive feedback on their readings.

WRITING

Write a Poem Remind students that poems create pictures in a reader's mind. Tell students to use information from "A Tree Is Growing" to create images of trees. Have them use these images as they write a poem about trees. Have students use their checklists to evaluate their writing.

📁 PORTFOLIO OPPORTUNITY

Students may choose to place their poems in their portfolios.

Build Robust Vocabulary

Objectives

- *To review robust vocabulary*
- *To demonstrate knowledge of word meaning*

REVIEW **Tested** ✓

Vocabulary: Lesson 13

tugged	rustling
paused	dissolve
columns	particles
absorb	scavenger
protects	self-sufficient

Review Robust Vocabulary

USE VOCABULARY IN DIFFERENT CONTEXTS Remind students of the meanings of the Vocabulary Words. Then guide them to discuss each word in a new context.

tugged

- If you tugged at the branch of a tree, what might happen?

paused

- Why might a teacher pause in the middle of speaking to a class?

scavenger

- What kind of animal do you know of that is a scavenger?

self-sufficient

- In what ways are you self-sufficient?

absorb

- What can a towel absorb?

columns

- If you built a treehouse, would you want columns on the front?

particles

- Imagine that you find particles of crackers on the kitchen floor. What might have happened?

dissolve

- Do you think sugar will dissolve in water?

protects

- How can you protect yourself from sunburn?

rustling

- When would it be pleasant to hear a rustling noise?

▼ **Student-Friendly Explanations**

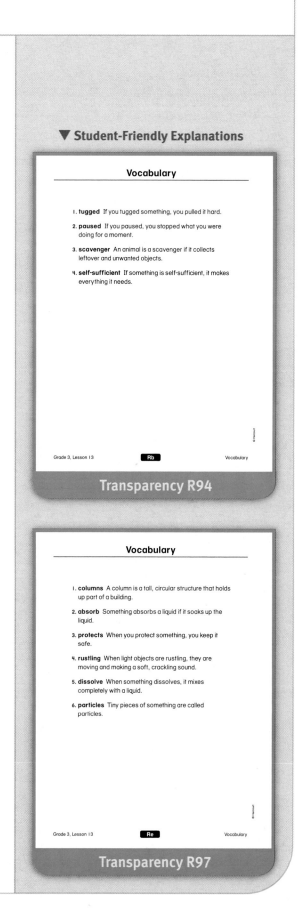

Vocabulary

1. **tugged** If you tugged something, you pulled it hard.
2. **paused** If you paused, you stopped what you were doing for a moment.
3. **scavenger** An animal is a scavenger if it collects leftover and unwanted objects.
4. **self-sufficient** If something is self-sufficient, it makes everything it needs.

Grade 3, Lesson 13 · Rb · Vocabulary

Transparency R94

Vocabulary

1. **columns** A column is a tall, circular structure that holds up part of a building.
2. **absorb** Something absorbs a liquid if it soaks up the liquid.
3. **protects** When you protect something, you keep it safe.
4. **rustling** When light objects are rustling, they are moving and making a soft, crackling sound.
5. **dissolve** When something dissolves, it mixes completely with a liquid.
6. **particles** Tiny pieces of something are called particles.

Grade 3, Lesson 13 · Re · Vocabulary

Transparency R97

Grammar
Using I *and* me

5-DAY GRAMMAR

DAY 1	Subject Pronouns
DAY 2	Object Pronouns
DAY 3	Using *I* and *me*
DAY 4	Apply to Writing
DAY 5	Subject and Object Pronouns Review

Objectives

- *To identify pronouns*
- *To use pronouns*

Daily Proofreading

1. We gave she a lemon tree (gave her; tree.)
2. Were you planning on spending the weekend with we. (with us?)

▲ Grammar Practice Book, p. 46

Teach/Model

INTRODUCE *I* **AND** *ME* Remind students of the pronouns they have learned so far. (*I, me, you, he, him, she, her, it, we, us, they,* and *them*) Write the following sentences on the board:

> **(Your name) wrote a sentence on the board.**
>
> **The class read the sentence back to (Your name).**

Read the first sentence. Then replace your name with *I*. Explain that instead of using your name to talk about yourself as the subject, you usually use the pronoun *I*. Read the second sentence aloud. Then replace your name with *me*. Point out that if you want to refer to yourself as the object, you often use the pronoun *me*.

Guided Practice

USE *I* **AND** *ME* Explain that when you refer to yourself as part of a group, you refer to yourself last. Write the following sentences on the board:

> **My friends and _____ walked home.**
>
> **The teacher called on Jack and _____.**

Read the first sentence aloud. Elicit from students what type and which pronoun goes in the blank. (subject, *I*) Repeat with the next sentence. (object; me)

Practice/Apply

USE *I* **AND** *ME* Have students copy the following sentences in their notebooks and fill in the blanks with *I* or *me*. Then invite volunteers to share their answers.

> **_____ want to plant a tree.** (I)
>
> **Mom said she will help Joe and _____.** (me)
>
> **Joe and _____ will measure it each year.** (I)

Writing
Explanation

5-DAY WRITING
DAY 1 Introduction
DAY 2 Prewrite
DAY 3 Draft
DAY 4 Revise/Edit
DAY 5 Revise/Edit

Draft an Explanation

REVIEW A LITERATURE MODEL Have students open to "A Tree Is Growing," on *Student Edition* page 379. Read the third paragraph aloud. Point out that this paragraph gives a definition of *what* minerals are, how they dissolve in water, and why (so that the roots can absorb them).

Explana-tion

- Gives facts and details about a topic
- Explains what or how
- Starts with a topic sentence
- Answers "What?" "How?" and

DRAFT A PARAGRAPH Have students use their graphic organizers to help them draft their explanations. Remind them to use their topic sentence and to give facts and details about the topic. Explain that a first draft is useful for getting ideas on paper.

SENTENCE FLUENCY As students write their paragraphs, tell them to answer the questions "What?" "How?" and "Why?" to give their readers clear information.

CONFER WITH STUDENTS Meet with individual students, helping them as they write. Encourage students as you provide them with feedback. If they have not explained details, remind them that giving information helps them support their ideas. Model explaining details for them.

Objectives

- *To recognize characteristics of an explanation*
- *To develop supporting ideas with information that relates to the focus*

Writing Prompt

Information Paragraph Have students write what information they find most amazing about trees. Ask them to explain why they find it amazing.

▲ Writer's Companion, Lesson 13

ADVANCED

Elaboration Encourage students to include more details about their topic. Write *What? How?* and *Why?* as the headings in a chart, and show students how to answer each question separately to create details for their writing.

What?	How?	Why?

Day at a Glance
Day 4

 phonics and Spelling
- Review: Consonants /s/c; /j/g, dge

Fluency
- Intonation
- "A Tree Is Growing,"
  Student Edition, pp. 370–395

 **Read!**

Comprehension
- Review: Author's Purpose
- Maintain: Using Reference Sources

Speaking/Listening/ Media Literacy
- Explanation

Robust Vocabulary
- Review: *tugged, paused, columns, absorb, protects, rustling, dissolve, particles, scavenger, self-sufficient*

Grammar
- Apply to Writing

Writing
- Explanation

Warm-Up Routines

Oral Language

Objectives *To respond to speakers; to actively participate in class discussions*

Question of the Day

Why do people like to spend time outdoors?

Help the class brainstorm activities people enjoy doing outdoors. Possible responses include walking, gardening, running, camping, swimming, and climbing. Ask students to think about why people like to spend time outdoors. Ask what attracts people to nature. (Possible responses: the beauty, wind, fresh air, wilderness, animals)

Encourage as many students as possible to participate in the discussion. After a number of students have had a chance to contribute, have them answer the following prompt in their notebooks:

I think people enjoy the outdoors because _____.

Students should write one or two sentences giving the reasons they think people enjoy spending time outdoors. Invite volunteers to share their responses with classmates.

Read Aloud

Objectives *To read fiction for understanding and enjoyment; to read with fluency*

READ ALOUD A STORY Display **Transparency R91** or distribute photocopies to students. Tell them that they are going to hear the story "Plant It Small, Grow It Tall." Ask students if they prefer stories to poems. Give students time to share and explain their preferences and opinions.

Set a purpose. Ask students what the purpose might be for reading a story called "Plant It Small, Grow It Tall." (for enjoyment, to practice reading) Tell students to listen and follow along to enjoy and understand the story.

Model fluent reading. Read the story aloud, raising and lowering your voice at important words and at end marks. Have students echo-read several sentences.

Discuss the story. Talk with students about what happens in the story. Ask:

• How would you summarize this story?

• What do Jerome and Felicity do with the bottle of water?

• What are they looking forward to doing in the future?

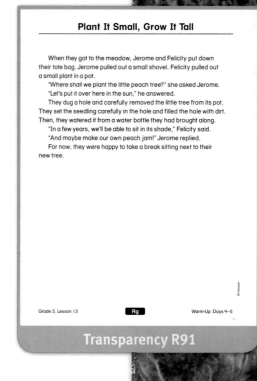

Plant It Small, Grow It Tall

When they got to the meadow, Jerome and Felicity put down their tote bag. Jerome pulled out a small shovel. Felicity pulled out a small plant in a pot.

"Where shall we plant the little peach tree?" she asked Jerome.

"Let's put it over here in the sun," he answered.

They dug a hole and carefully removed the little tree from its pot. They set the seedling carefully in the hole and filled the hole with dirt. Then, they watered it from a water bottle they had brought along.

"In a few years, we'll be able to sit in its shade," Felicity said.

"And maybe make our own peach jam!" Jerome replied.

For now, they were happy to take a break sitting next to their new tree.

Grade 3, Lesson 13   Rg   Warm-Up: Days 4–5

Transparency R91

Consonants /s/c; /j/g, dge

 phonics

5-DAY PHONICS

DAY 1	Introduce /s/c and /j/g
DAY 2	Words with Final ge and dge
DAY 3	Words with Final ace, ice, ce
DAY 4	**Other Words with /s/c and /j/g**
DAY 5	Review /s/c and /j/g

Objectives

- *To read words with /s/c; /j/g, dge*
- *To use decoding strategies to clarify pronunciation*

Skill Trace

Tested ✓ **Consonants: /s/c; /j/g, dge**

Introduce	Grade 2
Reintroduce	T212
Reteach	S26
Review	T222–T223, T246, T262, T274, T410
Test	Theme 3
Maintain	Theme 4, T176

Words with Soft c and g

1. pencil   engine   central   germ
2. citizen   digit   celery   suggest
3. legend   cinder   centimeter   imagine
4. cement   manager   giraffe   cities

Grade 3, Lesson 13   Rh   Phonics: Day 4

Transparency R92

Review

REVIEW FINAL ge, dge, ce Write the words *edge, strange,* and *spruce* on the board. Underline the final *ge, dge,* and *ce*. Have students give the appropriate pronunciation for each of these letter combinations when they appear at the end of a word. (/j/, /j/, /s/) Then have students read the words aloud.

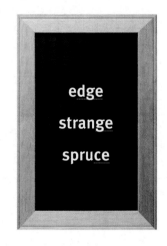

edge

strange

spruce

OTHER WORDS WITH /s/c AND /j/g
Remind students that soft *c* and *g* do not always come at the end of a word. Explain that soft *c* and soft *g* often appear before *i* as well as before *e*. Display **Transparency R92** or distribute photocopies to students. Point to the first word, *pencil*. Have students identify the letter *c* and identify the letter that follows it. (i) Remind students that when *i follows the letter c*, the *c* usually stands for the sound /s/. Break the word into two syllables *pen* and *cil* and help students read the parts. Then have them run the syllables together and read the word *pencil*. Repeat with the other words on the line, guiding students to see that *c* and *g* stand for the sounds /s/ and /j/ in these words.

Practice/Apply

GUIDED PRACTICE Call attention to the word *citizen* on the second line of **Transparency R92**. Help students locate the *c* and identify the vowel that follows it. (i) Ask what sound *c* stands for in this word. (/s/) Help students pronounce the word. Continue with the rest of the line.

INDEPENDENT PRACTICE Have students study the words on Lines 3 and 4 of **Transparency R92**. Ask them to locate the *g* or *c* in each word and the vowel that follows it. Tell them to write *s* after each word in which they hear the sound of /s/ and *j* after each word in which they hear /j/.

Consonants /s/c; /j/g, dge

phonics and Spelling

5-DAY SPELLING

DAY 1	Pretest
DAY 2	State the Generalization
DAY 3	Spelling Practice/Handwriting
DAY 4	**Use Spelling Strategies/Review**
DAY 5	Posttest

Use Spelling Strategies

SPELLING PATTERNS Explain that words that rhyme often belong to the same word families and have the same spelling pattern. Dictate the word *ice* and have students write it in their notebooks. Then say: **The word *ice* rhymes with another spelling word, *rice*. If you can spell *ice*, you can spell *rice*.** Have students write *rice* beneath *ice*. Ask them how the two words are the same and different. (Possible responses: They have the same last three letters, and they each end in *ce*; One has three letters, the other has four.)

Repeat with *edge/ledge, age/stage,* and *range/strange.* Then continue with the following pairs, explaining that, in each pair, one word is a spelling word and the other is not: *judge/fudge, recent/decent,* and *bridge/ridge.*

APPLY TO WRITING Tell students that they can use this rhyming word strategy in their own writing. Have students read through their notebooks or other unedited work. Ask them to find words that they think might be spelled incorrectly and to try to think of a more familiar word that uses the same letter pattern. Encourage students to work together to find potential rhymes for these words, and confirm the spellings in a dictionary before fixing errors.

ADVANCED

Word Sort Have students sort the spelling words into categories. For instance, students might separate the words into **Words with *g*** and **Words with *c*,** or they might group them according to the number of letters in each word. Have students make a chart with labels and include each word in the proper category. If possible, have students sort the words in two different ways, using different categories each time.

Words with *g*	Words with *c*
age	police
edge	rice

Objective

- *To use letter patterns to spell and write words*

Spelling Words

1.	**ice**	9.	**ledge**
2.	**age**	10.	**police**
3.	**rice**	11.	**recent**
4.	**edge**	12.	**bridge**
5.	**stage**	13.	**office**
6.	**giant***	14.	**strange**
7.	**range**	15.	**central**
8.	**judge**		

Challenge Words

16.	**celery**	19.	**margin**
17.	**ceiling**	20.	**imagine**
18.	**difference**		

*Word from "A Pen Pal for Max"

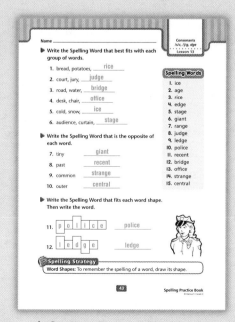

▲ Spelling Practice Book, p. 43

Fluency
Intonation

Objective

- *To use intonation*

BELOW-LEVEL

Fluency Practice Have students identify and record any words they have trouble pronouncing. Ask them to work with a partner and try different pronunciations until they pronounce the word correctly. Then have them return to reading from the text.

 MONITOR PROGRESS

Fluency

IF students have trouble deciding when to make their voices go higher or lower,	THEN offer this guideline: question mark—up; period—down.

Small-Group Instruction, p. S28:

- ● **BELOW-LEVEL:** Reteach
- ● **ON-LEVEL:** Reinforce
- ○ **ADVANCED:** Extend

Review

 DIBELS Oral Reading Fluency **ORF**

MODEL READING WITH INTONATION Remind students that good readers use intonation to emphasize the meaning of the words they read. Tell students that they should sound natural as they read nonfiction by:

▲ *Student Edition*, pp. 370–395

- emphasizing important words.

- looking for end and other punctuation.

[Think Aloud] **I'm going to read page 377 in "A Tree Is Growing." The first sentence tells me what a tree needs to grow. The words *sunlight*, *air*, *soil*, and *water* are important, so I will emphasize them. I also see that there are commas between each of the words in the list, so I will pause slightly between the words.**

MATCH THE TEXT Model fluently reading page 377 from "A Tree Is Growing." Then read it again, having students echo-read. Then ask students to read each sentence aloud several times, guiding them to read with appropriate intonation.

Practice/Apply

Routine Card 7

CHORAL-READING Organize students into groups and assign them alternating paragraphs on pages 379–380. Tell them to read their paragraphs, looking for words to emphasize and punctuation marks. Then have students read their assigned parts along with you. Remind them to use the same intonation, expression, and phrasing as you do.

Author's Purpose
Comprehension

Review

EXPLAIN AUTHOR'S PURPOSE Ask students to explain the reasons authors might write. (Possible responses: to inform, to entertain, to persuade) Explain that if the reader knows the author's purpose, then what he or she reads will be easier to understand.

Practice/Apply

GUIDED PRACTICE Display **Transparency R85** or distribute photocopies to students. Have students reread the passage to identify the author's purpose. Ask:

- **Why do you think the author wrote this selection?** (Possible response: to inform the reader about sunflowers)

- **How can you tell?** (Possible responses: It gives facts; it tells how sunflowers grow.)

INDEPENDENT PRACTICE Have students reread pages 388–389 of "A Tree Is Growing." Ask the following questions, having students write their answers in their notebooks: **Why do you think the author wrote this selection? Why did the author include the drawings of the nuts, cones, and fruit?** (Possible responses: The author wants to explain that trees all have seeds, but their seeds may come in different forms.)

Objective

- *To identify author's purpose*

Skill Trace

Tested ✔ **Author's Purpose**

Introduce	T215
Reteach	S30
Review	T249, T265, T277, T302–T303, T333, T349, T361, T412, T433
Test	Theme 3
Maintain	Theme 4, T348

Sunflowers

Have you ever seen a sunflower seed? Actually, you might not know that you saw one because sunflower seeds are very small. Sunflower seeds are no larger than one of your fingernails. When a sunflower is fully grown, though, the plant can be more than six feet tall, and the flower may be larger than a dinner plate!

Once sunflower seeds are planted, it takes about a week for them to sprout. Then the flowers begin to grow. To reach their full size, sunflowers need a lot of sunshine. In fact, they need at least six hours of sunlight each day. Perhaps this is why sunflowers are so tall. They might be trying to reach the sun that they need so much!

Grade 3, Lesson 13   R9   Warm-Up: Day 1

Transparency R85

Use Reference Sources

Objective

- *To understand which reference source provides particular information*

Skill Trace

 Tested Use Reference Sources

Introduce	Theme 2, T248–249
Reteach	Theme 2, S32
Review	Theme 2, T30–31
Test	Theme 2
Maintain	Theme 3, T266

Reinforce the Skill

REVIEW USING REFERENCE SOURCES Remind students that they already know about a number of reference sources. Write *dictionary*, *encyclopedia*, *thesaurus*, and *atlas* on the board, providing a brief explanation of each. Explain that versions of all these sources can be found on the Internet along with maps, photographs and other information. All these sources can be used when students are working on a research report or essay, or just want to find out about something.

Practice/Apply

GUIDED PRACTICE Guide students to identify the right source to use to find the information described in each question.

- **Where would you find the pronunciation of *ceiling*?** (dictionary)

- **Where would you look to see where Ireland is located?** (a map in an atlas or on the Internet)

- **Where would you look for information about spider monkeys?** (encyclopedia or an Internet site such as a zoo site)

- **Where might you look to see what Mount Rushmore looks like?** (photographs on the Internet or in an encyclopedia article)

INDEPENDENT PRACTICE Ask students to imagine that they have been asked to do the following as part of a report about polar bears:

- You need to find where polar bears live and how far that is from your own home.

- You want a better, more descriptive word to use than *cold*.

- You need to find out exactly what the word *glacier* means.

Ask students to write a paragraph in their notebooks describing how they will find all this information. Ask volunteers to share their work. (Possible response: I would use encyclopedias or go online and look up polar bears. Then I would look at a map in an atlas or online to see where they live. I can use a thesaurus to look up *cold* and a dictionary to look up *glacier*.)

Speaking and Listening
Explanation

Objectives
- *To express thoughts in an organized manner*
- *To understand nonverbal cues used in diagrams*

Speaking

GIVE AN EXPLANATION Invite pairs of students to plan and present their explanations. The may use the explanation from their Writing assignments or create another one.

ORGANIZING CONTENT Share the following **organizational tips** with students:

- Write descriptive notes on index cards so you can refer to them while you are speaking.
- Define any difficult terms you use so that your audience understands what you are trying to say.
- Create a graphic aid like a diagram or chart that shows what you are explaining.

Before students deliver their speeches to a small group or the class, share the **speaking strategies** to the right.

SPEAKING STRATEGIES
- Practice giving your presentation.
- Make sure the graphic aid is big enough so that people can see it.
- Point to each part of your graphic aid as you talk about it.

Listening

RESPONDING Share the **listening strategies** with students. Tell students to think of questions to ask as they listen to speakers. Explain that questions should be about the topic. When a presentation is done, invite listeners to raise their hands to show that they have questions and to ask questions when the speaker calls on them.

See rubrics for Speaking and Listening on page R5.

LISTENING STRATEGIES
- Listen to hear how the speaker explains his or her topic.
- Save questions until the presentation is over.
- Ask questions one at a time and wait for an answer.

Media Literacy

VIEWING DIAGRAMS Point out the diagram on pages 376–377 of the *Student Edition*. Explain that diagrams are detailed pictures that can show a process or something with many parts. Have students discuss the diagrams they used in their presentations. Invite them to compare and contrast their diagrams and explain what each one shows.

Build Robust Vocabulary

Objectives

- *To review robust vocabulary*
- *To demonstrate knowledge of word meaning*

REVIEW Tested ✓

Vocabulary: Lesson 13

tugged	rustling
paused	dissolve
columns	particles
absorb	scavenger
protects	self-sufficient

"RESEARCH SAYS"

Vocabulary Sources "Children recognized the meanings of significantly more words from the story than not from the story, thus indicating that storybook reading was effective for building vocabulary."

–Robbins & Ehri (1994), p. 54

Extend Word Meanings

USE VOCABULARY IN DIFFERENT CONTEXTS Remind students of the meanings and pronunciations of the Vocabulary Words. Then discuss each word in a new context:

tugged Tell students that if one person could move the object you name by tugging it, they should raise their hands. If not, they should shake their heads.

a school bus	a ferry boat
a toy wagon	a weed in a garden

paused Tell students that if they think they were likely to pause while doing the activity you name, wipe one hand across their forehead. If not, they should shake their head for "no."

building a clubhouse	coming in from the rain
opening a birthday present	mowing a lawn

self-sufficient Tell students that if the situation you name is an example of someone or something being self-sufficient, they should draw an "S" in the air. If it is not, have them fold their arms.

a baby bird gets food from its mother

a raccoon collects and eats garbage from a campsite

a person grows and eats vegetables

children play a board game

particles Tell students to clap once if the thing you name would dissolve in water and to do nothing if it could not.

salt	a penny
a paper clip	sugar

Word Relationships

SYNONYMS Ask students what synonyms are. (words with the same or similar meanings) Ask students to suggest synonyms for the Vocabulary Words in the following sentences:

1. The dish towel will **absorb** the spilled milk. (soak up)
2. The **columns** on the porch hold up the roof. (posts)
3. My dog **tugged** on his toy until he broke it. (pulled)
4. There might still be some **particles** of glass on the floor from the broken vase. (fragments, tiny pieces)
5. The shelter **protects** us from the storm. (shields, saves)
6. Riley **paused** in her speech. (stopped)

▼ **Student-Friendly Explanations**

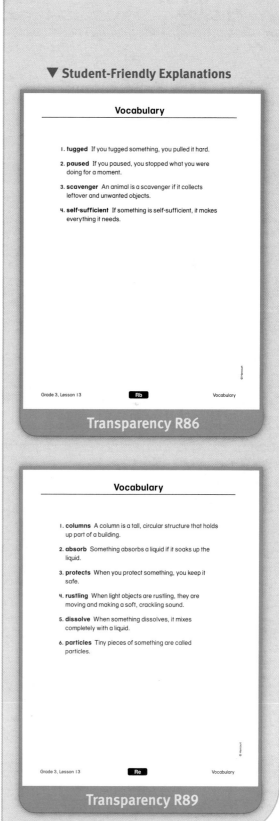

Vocabulary

1. **tugged** If you tugged something, you pulled it hard.
2. **paused** If you paused, you stopped what you were doing for a moment.
3. **scavenger** An animal is a scavenger if it collects leftover and unwanted objects.
4. **self-sufficient** If something is self-sufficient, it makes everything it needs.

Grade 3, Lesson 13   Rb   Vocabulary

Transparency R86

Vocabulary

1. **columns** A column is a tall, circular structure that holds up part of a building.
2. **absorb** Something absorbs a liquid if it soaks up the liquid.
3. **protects** When you protect something, you keep it safe.
4. **rustling** When light objects are rustling, they are moving and making a soft, crackling sound.
5. **dissolve** When something dissolves, it mixes completely with a liquid.
6. **particles** Tiny pieces of something are called particles.

Grade 3, Lesson 13   Re   Vocabulary

Transparency R89

Grammar
Apply to Writing

5-DAY GRAMMAR

DAY 1	Subject Pronouns
DAY 2	Object Pronouns
DAY 3	Using *I* and *me*
DAY 4	**Apply to Writing**
DAY 5	Subject and Object Pronouns Review

Objective

• *To use pronouns in writing*

Daily Proofreading

1. to get to the mall, us have to pass the stadium. (To; we have)
2. Why did them travel by boat (they; boat?)

▲ **Grammar Practice Book, p. 47**

Review

DISCUSS SUBJECT AND OBJECT PRONOUNS Review that pronouns are words that take the place of nouns in a sentence. Remind students that a subject pronoun takes the place of the person, animal, or thing that a sentence is about. An object pronoun takes the place of a person, animal, or thing that receives an action.

• Subject pronouns include: *I, you, he, she, it, we,* and *they*.

• Object pronouns include: *me, you, him, her, it, us,* and *them*.

Practice/Apply

GUIDED PRACTICE Write the following sentences on the board:

Willie and Carolyn watched the play. They enjoyed it.

Read the first sentence aloud and identify *Willie and Carolyn* as the subject and *the play* as the object in the sentence. Ask students which subject pronoun replaces *Willie and Carolyn* in the next sentence. (They) Now ask which pronoun replaces *the play*. (it) Have students suggest other sentences. Have students identify the nouns and name the pronouns that could replace them.

INDEPENDENT PRACTICE Tell students to imagine they work as foresters. Have students write a notebook entry describing the busy day they have had. Ask them to write about both the trees and the people they have worked with. Tell students to circle any subject pronouns and underline any object pronouns in the notebook entry. Have students exchange their writing and check each other's work.

Writing
Explanation

5-DAY WRITING	
DAY 1	Introduce
DAY 2	Prewrite
DAY 3	Draft
DAY 4	**Revise/Edit**
DAY 5	Revise/Edit

Revise a Paragraph

WRITE Have students continue writing their explanations. Explain that they will be able to complete their first drafts and revise their writing during today's lesson. Tell them that their explanations should follow logical order and should end by restating the main idea.

> ### Explanation
> - Gives facts and details about a topic
> - Starts with a topic sentence
> - Answers "What?" "How?" and "Why?"
> - Follows a logical sequence

WRITING TRAIT **SENTENCE FLUENCY**
Remind students that it is important for writers to use different types of sentences in their writing to keep it from sounding choppy.

PRACTICE EDITING To prepare students to edit and proofread, distribute a copy of Editor's Marks (*Teacher Resource Book*, p. 139). Write the following sentence on the board and have them use editor's marks to edit it.

susan gav the small tree to ~~they~~

Editor's Marks	
≡	Capitalize
∧	Insert
/	Lowercase
⊙	Add a period

REVISE Have students read their drafts to partners and work together to make sure their explanations include a clear topic sentence and details that answer questions such as "What?" "How?" and "Why?" Remind them that an important part of revising an explanation is to make sure that all the important details have been included. Tell them to add any details that might be needed. Encourage students to use editor's marks when they revise their paragraphs. Have students save the paragraphs for Day 5.

Objectives

- *To revise an explanation*
- *To use effective sentence variety*
- *To create a paragraph in which the sentences elaborate on the main idea*

Writing Prompt

Sentence Starter Have students write a notebook entry sparked by the following sentence starter: "The best way to enjoy nature is by . . ."

Read Aloud If students have trouble noticing that material is unclear or is missing from their paragraphs, have them read their paragraphs to you. Then read the paragraph back to the student. Discuss areas where there is missing information.

Day at a Glance

Day 5

phonics and Spelling

- Review: Consonants /s/c and /j/g, dge
- Posttest

Fluency

- Intonation
- "A Tree Is Growing," *Student Edition*, pp. 370–395

Read!

Comprehension

Review: Author's Purpose

- Read-Aloud Anthology: "The Money Tree"

Robust Vocabulary

- Cumulative Review

Grammar

- Review: Subject and Object Pronouns

Writing

- Explanation

Warm-Up Routines

Oral Language

Objectives *To respond informally to oral presentations; to prepare for writing*

Question of the Day

Where do you go to enjoy nature?

Help students brainstorm where people go to enjoy the outdoors. On the board, make a list of students' ideas, grouping items in categories that students suggest (for example, Mountains; Beaches; Country; City).

Encourage students to present personal anecdotes or other stories in which people find ways to enjoy nature. After students share several experiences, ask students to use their notebooks to complete the following writing prompt:

> **When I want to enjoy nature,**
> **I go to _____ so I can _____.**

Students should write one or two sentences describing a place they go to enjoy nature and telling what they particularly like to do. Invite several students to share their responses.

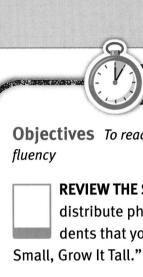

Read Aloud

Objectives *To read fiction for understanding and enjoyment; to read with fluency*

REVIEW THE STORY Display **Transparency R91,** or distribute photocopies of it to students. Tell students that you are going to reread the story "Plant It Small, Grow It Tall."

Set a purpose. Ask students what the purpose might be for rereading this story. (for enjoyment, to practice fluency) Remind students to listen carefully as you read, telling them that they should listen for details and words that will help them recall the main events of the story.

Model fluent reading. Read the story aloud, making your voice go lower and higher at appropriate places.

Partner-read. Have one partner reread the story, while the other follows along and provides help as needed. Then have partners switch and read the story again.

Plant It Small, Grow It Tall

When they got to the meadow, Jerome and Felicity put down their tote bag. Jerome pulled out a small shovel. Felicity pulled out a small plant in a pot.

"Where shall we plant the little peach tree?" she asked Jerome.

"Let's put it over here in the sun," he answered.

They dug a hole and carefully removed the little tree from its pot. They set the seedling carefully in the hole and filled the hole with dirt. Then, they watered it from a water bottle they had brought along.

"In a few years, we'll be able to sit in its shade," Felicity said.

"And maybe make our own peach jam!" Jerome replied.

For now, they were happy to take a break sitting next to their new tree.

Grade 3, Lesson 13 Rg Warm-Up: Days 4–5

Transparency R91

Consonants /s/c; /j/g, dge

phonics

5-DAY PHONICS

DAY 1	Introduce /s/c and /j/g
DAY 2	Words with Final *ge* and *dge*
DAY 3	Words with Final *ce*
DAY 4	Other Words with /s/c and /j/g
DAY 5	Review /s/c and /j/g

Objective

- *To use decoding strategies to clarify pronunciation*

Skill Trace

Tested ✓ **Consonants: /s/c; /j/g, dge**

Introduce	Grade 2
Reintroduce	T212
Reteach	S26
Review	T222–T223, T246, T262, T274, T410
Test	Theme 3
Maintain	Theme 4, T176

Review

WORDS WITH /s/c; /j/g, dge Write the following words on the board:

charge	trace	center	legend	circle
margin	page	lodge	force	badge

Point to each word and have students find the letter *c* or *g* or the spelling pattern *dge*. Ask what letter follows the *c* or *g* and what sound the *c, g,* or *dge* stands for. If necessary, remind students that when *c* is followed by *e* or *i*, it usually stands for its soft sound, /s/. When *g* is followed by *e* or *i*, it usually stands for its soft sound, /j/. The letters *dge* also stand for /j/. Have students read the words aloud.

BELOW-LEVEL　　　**ON-LEVEL**　　　**ADVANCED**

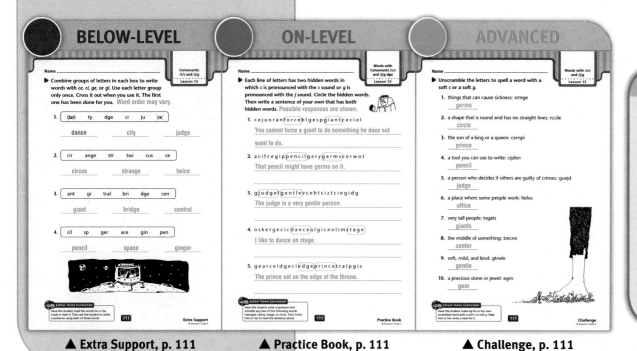

▲ **Extra Support, p. 111**　　　▲ **Practice Book, p. 111**　　　▲ **Challenge, p. 111**

- Group students according to academic levels and assign one of the pages on the left.

- Clarify any unfamiliar concepts as necessary. See *ELL Teacher Guide* Lesson 13 for support in scaffolding instruction.

Consonants: /s/c; /j/g, dge
phonics and Spelling

5-DAY SPELLING
DAY 1 Pretest
DAY 2 State the Generalization
DAY 3 Spelling Practice/Handwriting
DAY 4 Spelling Strategies
DAY 5 Posttest

Assess

POSTTEST Assess students' progress in spelling. Use the dictation sentences from Day 1.

Words with /s/c and /j/g, dge

1. ice   I like to drink water with **ice** in it.
2. age   I first went to school at the **age** of five.
3. rice   **Rice** and beans can make a good meal.
4. edge   Do not stand so close to the **edge** of the cliff!
5. stage   José enjoys performing on **stage**.
6. giant   You are a **giant** compared to a newborn baby.
7. range   The grades **range** from A to C.
8. judge   The **judge** made the driver pay a fine.
9. ledge   The bird sat on a narrow **ledge** outside my window.
10. police   The **police** were directing traffic.
11. recent   I visited my cousin on my most **recent** vacation.
12. bridge   They are building a new **bridge** across the river.
13. office   Ms. Harrison works in the principal's **office**.
14. strange   Last night I heard a **strange** noise.
15. central   The zoo is in the **central** part of town.

✎ WRITING APPLICATION Have students write a paragraph that tells about an adventure they would like to have. Have them include at least six spelling words in their paragraphs.

Objective
- *To spell correctly words with orthographic patterns*

Spelling Words

1.	**ice**	9.	**ledge**
2.	**age**	10.	**police**
3.	**rice**	11.	**recent**
4.	**edge**	12.	**bridge**
5.	**stage**	13.	**office**
6.	**giant***	14.	**strange**
7.	**range**	15.	**central**
8.	**judge**		

Challenge Words

16.	**celery**	19.	**margin**
17.	**ceiling**	20.	**imagine**
18.	**difference**		

*Word from "A Tree Is Growing"

ADVANCED

Challenge If there is time, add the following words.

16. celery   We eat **celery** and carrots after school.
17. ceiling   My dad can touch the **ceiling**!
18. difference   One **difference** between the brothers is their height.
19. margin   Do not write in the **margin** of your paper.
20. imagine   **Imagine** you are on a sunny beach.

Fluency
Intonation

Objective
- *To use strategies to speak clearly*

ASSESSMENT

Monitoring Progress Periodically, take a timed sample of students' oral reading and measure the number of words read correctly per minute. Students should be accurately reading approximately 92 words per minute in the middle of Grade 3.

Fluency Support Materials

Fluency Builders, Grade 3, Lesson 13

Audiotext *Student Edition* selections are available on *Audiotext 3.*

Strategic Intervention Teacher Guide, Lesson 13

Readers' Theater

DIBELS
Oral Reading Fluency
ORF

PERFORM "A TREE IS GROWING" Have students perform "A Tree Is Growing" as Readers' Theater. Use the following procedures:

▲ *Student Edition*, pp. 370–395

- Read aloud the main text of "A Tree Is Growing," modeling fluency and intonation as students follow along.

- Discuss that "A Tree Is Growing" is nonfiction with one or two paragraphs per page. Have students look for sections or words to emphasize.

- Have groups of four or five students read the selection together. Then have them choose different sections, such as the part about bark. Have them read aloud with intonation and expression.

- Listen to groups as they read. Provide feedback and support.

- Invite each group to read the selection to their classmates.

ELL

Main Idea Point out the words in the text that give the main idea on each page. Then ask why the idea is important. Encourage volunteers to point to these words and to use intonation to show meaning. Then read the passage aloud and model fluency.

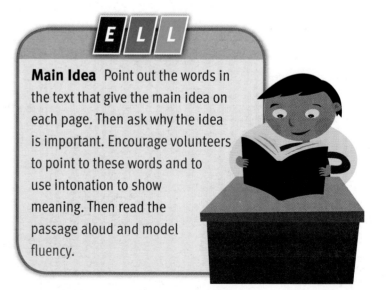

Author's Purpose
Comprehension

▲ **Read-Aloud Anthology,
"The Money Tree," p. 48**

Review

REVIEW THE SKILL Ask students to list some of the reasons an author might write. (to inform, to entertain, to persuade)

USE PRIOR KNOWLEDGE/SET A PURPOSE Tell students they will listen again as you reread "The Money Tree." Guide students to use prior knowledge and set a purpose for listening.

Practice/Apply

GUIDED PRACTICE Use the following questions to monitor students' listening comprehension:

- **How does Miss McGillicuddy solve the problem of the money tree?** (She chops it down.)

- **Why do you think the author never refers to the "leaves" as money?** (Possible response: to show the reader how Miss McGillicuddy thinks)

INDEPENDENT PRACTICE Have students write a paragraph about this author's purpose for writing "The Money Tree." Remind them to use details from the story. Have volunteers share their paragraphs.

Objective
- *To identify author's purpose*

Skill Trace
 Author's Purpose

Tested	
Introduce	T215
Reteach	S30
Review	T249, T265, T277, T302–T303, T333, T361, T412, T433
Test	Theme 3
Maintain	Theme 4, T348

BELOW-LEVEL

Explain Further Tell students that authors can have several reasons for writing a story—for example, they may want to entertain children and teach a lesson at the same time. Have students discuss other reasons authors may have for writing something.

Build Robust Vocabulary

Objective

• *To develop vocabulary through meaningful discussions*

Vocabulary

Lesson 12	Lesson 13
deciphered	tugged
mistaken	paused
translate	columns
repairs	absorb
heaving	protects
bothersome	rustling
din	dissolve
dodging	particles
catastrophe	scavenger
fortunate	self-sufficient

Cumulative Review

MAKE WORD WEBS Guide students to complete word webs to enhance their understanding of *mistaken, scavenger,* and *absorb*. Draw a word web on the board or use **Transparency GO12**. Write *mistaken* in the center oval. Have students share times they were mistaken about something. Write their responses in the empty ovals. You may want to offer a suggestion to help students get started.

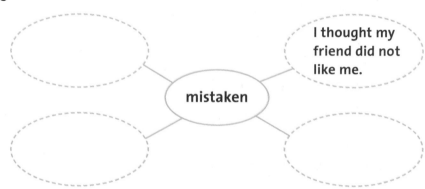

Have students create their own webs for *scavenger*. After students write *scavenger* in the center of their webs, ask them to name different animals that are scavengers. Have them write their responses in the surrounding ovals.

Review Vocabulary

Discuss students' answers to these questions.

1. Would a towel **absorb** salt **particles**?

2. Do you think you would be **fortunate** to be completely **self-sufficient**? Why or why not?

3. When would a **rustling** noise be **bothersome**?

4. Explain why you might **pause** while playing a game that involves **dodging** a ball.

5. Which would be more difficult—**heaving** a large box or **tugging** it across the room? Explain.

6. If **columns** were being built in front of your school, would there be a **din** outside? Explain.

7. What features of a car help **protect** drivers and other people?

8. How is **deciphering** a code like **translating** a language?

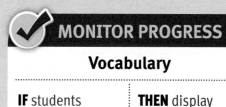

MONITOR PROGRESS

Vocabulary

IF students have forgotten the meanings of words from Lesson 12,	**THEN** display Transparencies R78 and R81 again and have them read the explanation.

Small-Group Instruction, p. S34:

● **BELOW-LEVEL:** Reteach
● **ON-LEVEL:** Reinforce
● **ADVANCED:** Extend

Grammar
Subject and Object Pronouns

5-DAY GRAMMAR

DAY 1 Subject Pronouns
DAY 2 Object Pronouns
DAY 3 Using *I* and *me*
DAY 4 Apply to Writing
DAY 5 Subject and Object Pronouns Review

Objectives

- *To recognize and use subject and object pronouns*
- *To use pronouns in speech*

Daily Proofreading

1. the horse in the meadow belongs to they. (The; them.)
2. her and a freind watered the flowers. (She; friend)

✔ LANGUAGE ARTS CHECKPOINT

If students have difficulty with the concepts, see pages S36–S37 to reteach.

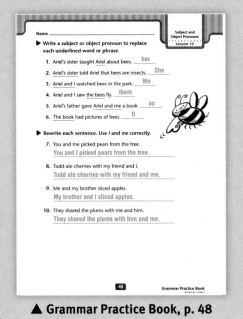

▲ **Grammar Practice Book, p. 48**

Review

REVIEW SUBJECT AND OBJECT PRONOUNS Review and explain the following points:

- A subject pronoun takes the place of the subject of a sentence.
- Subject pronouns include *I, you, he, she, it, we,* and *they.*
- An object pronoun takes the place of a noun that receives an action.
- Object pronouns include *me, you, him, her, it, us,* and *them.*

Practice/Apply

GUIDED PRACTICE Write the following sentence on the board:

The children gave the peach tree to Sally.

Point out the three nouns, and explain that they can all be replaced with pronouns. Point to *the children,* and show that this can be changed to the subject pronoun *They.* Then guide students to replace *the peach tree* and *Sally* with the object pronouns *it* and *her.* (They gave it to her.) Invite volunteers to go to the board and each write a sentence with at least two nouns. Have students identify the nouns. Then have other volunteers rewrite the sentences with the nouns replaced with pronouns.

INDEPENDENT PRACTICE Write the following sentences on the board:

The boy and the girl grinned.
The flower pleased Miss Li.

Ask students to copy the sentences in their notebooks. Then have students underline the nouns and, above them, write the correct pronouns with which to replace them. (The boy and the girl = They; The flower = It; Miss Li = her)

Writing
Explanation

5-DAY WRITING	
DAY 1	Introduce
DAY 2	Prewrite
DAY 3	Draft
DAY 4	Revise/Edit
DAY 5	Revise/Edit

Revise/Edit

REVIEW CONVENTIONS Tell students to check that all their sentences begin with a capital letter and end with an appropriate end mark. Remind them to check that they have used pronouns correctly. If they need to make changes, encouragethem to use editors' marks. Encourage students to make a final check to make sure that they have included all necessary details in the right order. Explain that now is the time to take out, or delete, unnecessary ideas and information.

Share

Have pairs read each other's revised work. Tell students to use the characteristics of an explanation or a rubric as a checklist for reviewing each other's writing. Students should keep their writing in their work portfolios.

Objectives
- *To use punctuation correctly*
- *To correctly use pronouns*

Writing Prompt

Self-Selected Writing Write a brief explanation about a topic of your choice.

WEEKLY LESSON TEST

▲ **Weekly Lesson Tests, Lesson 13**
- Selection Comprehension
- **phonics** and Spelling
- Focus Skill
- Use Graphic Aids
- Robust Vocabulary
- Grammar
- Fluency Passage **FRESH READS**

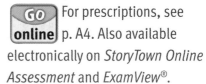 For prescriptions, see p. A4. Also available electronically on *StoryTown Online Assessment* and *ExamView*®.

 Podcasting: Assessing Fluency

NOTE: A 4-point rubric appears on page R8.

SCORING RUBRIC						
	6	**5**	**4**	**3**	**2**	**1**
FOCUS	Completely focused, purposeful.	Focused on topic and purpose.	Generally focused on topic and purpose.	Somewhat focused on topic and purpose.	Related to topic but does not maintain focus.	Lacks focus and purpose.
ORGANIZATION	Ideas progress logically; paper conveys sense of completeness.	Organization mostly clear; paper gives sense of completeness.	Organization mostly clear, but some lapses occur; may seem unfinished.	Some sense of organization; seems unfinished.	Little sense of organization.	Little or no sense of organization.
SUPPORT	Strong, specific details; clear, exact language; freshness of expression.	Strong, specific details; clear, exact language.	Adequate support and word choice.	Limited supporting details; limited word choice	Few supporting details; limited word choice.	Little development; limited or unclear word choice.
CONVENTIONS	Varied sentences; few, if any, errors.	Varied sentences; few errors.	Some sentence variety; few errors.	Simple sentence structures; some errors.	Simple sentence structures; many errors.	Unclear sentence structures; many errors.

REPRODUCIBLE STUDENT RUBRICS for specific writing purposes and presentations are available on pages R5–R8.

Leveled Readers
Reinforcing Skills and Strategies

Genre: Expository Nonfiction

BELOW-LEVEL

Daffodil Spring

SUMMARY Many daffodils grow from bulbs and bulblets. They develop in an interesting way that is different from many of the flowers you may know.

 Author's Purpose

 Ask Questions

• **ROBUST VOCABULARY:** *columns, absorb, protects, rustling, dissolve, particles*

Before Reading

BUILD BACKGROUND/SET PURPOSE Have students discuss what they know about daffodils. What do they look like? When do they bloom? Then guide students to preview the story and set a purpose for reading.

Reading the Book

 PAGE 2 AUTHOR'S PURPOSE What is the most important thing the author wants to tell you? (how daffodils grow)

PAGE 9 SEQUENCE When do gardeners dig up bulbs? Why must they wait until then? (They dig up bulbs in summer; they must wait until the flowers have fallen and the leaves have dried up.)

REREAD FOR FLUENCY Have partners take turns reading a page aloud. Emphasize intonation, or raising or lowering the pitch of your voice as in natural speech.

Think Critically   *(See inside back cover for questions.)*

1 **AUTHOR'S PURPOSE** Possible responses: The book provides information; it does not tell a story; it does not have characters.

2 **UNDERSTAND FIGURATIVE LANGUAGE** Daffodils arrive in the early spring; warmer weather will follow them.

3 **MAKE COMPARISONS** Possible responses: A stem is a tube; a leaf is flat. A stem holds up a plant; a leaf collects sunlight and air for the plant.

4 **IMPORTANT DETAILS** A bulblet is a small part of a bulb itself. It divides at the base of the plant and grows new daffodils without seeds.

5 **AUTHOR'S PURPOSE** Answers will vary.

LEVELED READER TEACHER GUIDE

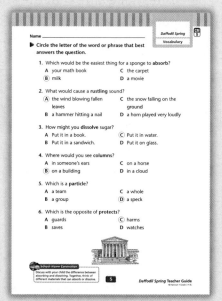

▲ Vocabulary, p. 5

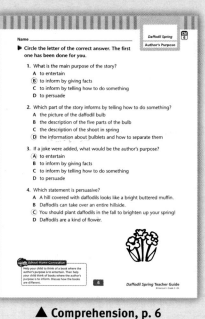

▲ Comprehension, p. 6

GO online

www.harcourtschool.com/storytown

★ Leveled Readers, online:
Searchable by Genre, Skill, Vocabulary, Level, or Title
★ Student Activities and Teacher Resources, online

ON-LEVEL

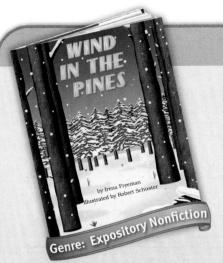

by Irena Freeman
Illustrated by Robert Schuster

Genre: Expository Nonfiction

Wind in the Pines

SUMMARY Pine trees stay a beautiful green all year. Instead of leaves, they have needles, only one fact that sets them apart from other trees.

 Author's Purpose

 Ask Questions

- **ROBUST VOCABULARY:** *columns, absorb, protects, rustling, dissolve, particles*

Before Reading

BUILD BACKGROUND/SET PURPOSE Have students discuss some facts they know about pine trees. Are there any pine trees in the area near the school? What do they look like? Then guide them to preview the story and set a purpose for reading it.

Reading the Book

PAGE 6 COMPARE/CONTRAST How are pine needles different from leaves? (Pine needles do not decay easily.)

PAGE 7 AUTHOR'S PURPOSE What is made from pine trees? (lumber, pine oil, paper, furniture finish)

REREAD FOR FLUENCY Have partners take turns reading a page aloud. Emphasize intonation, encouraging students to change their volume and pitch in order to show expression.

Think Critically
(See inside back cover for questions.)

1. **AUTHOR'S PURPOSE** Possible responses: to provide information about conifers; to compare conifers with other kinds of trees.

2. **IMPORTANT DETAILS** They may not be able to absorb enough food; they may be eaten by rabbits or deer; they may not get enough light to grow.

3. **COMPARE AND CONTRAST** Possible response: They have cones, and other trees have seeds or nuts.

4. **IMPORTANT DETAILS** Possible response: because they are green all year

5. **IMPORTANT DETAILS** animals, insects, disease, and forest fires

LEVELED READER TEACHER GUIDE

▲ Vocabulary, p. 5

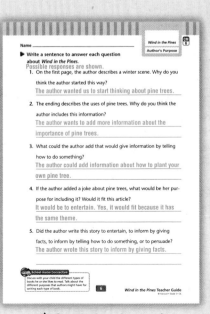

▲ Comprehension, p. 6

Leveled Readers
Reinforcing Skills and Strategies

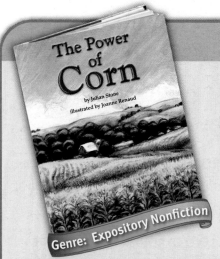

ADVANCED

The Power of Corn

SUMMARY Corn has always been important to America. Even today, we use it in more than 3,000 products.

 Author's Purpose

 Ask Questions

- **ROBUST VOCABULARY:** *columns, absorb, protects, rustling, dissolve, particles*

Before Reading

BUILD BACKGROUND/SET PURPOSE Ask students if they have ever planted or picked vegetables. Have them share their experiences. Then guide students to preview the story and set a purpose for reading.

Reading the Book

PAGE 7 AUTHOR'S PURPOSE **Why do you think this writer wrote about corn?** (Possible response: to inform readers about the history of corn and how important it is to America)

PAGE 11 SPECULATE **Why would a farmer use a combine instead of picking all the corn by hand?** (Combines can pick the corn, strip the husks, and remove the corn from the cob, saving the farmer a lot of work.)

REREAD FOR FLUENCY Have partners take turns reading a page aloud. Tell them to emphasize intonation, raising and lowering their voices naturally.

Think Critically
(See inside back cover for questions.)

1. **AUTHOR'S PURPOSE** Answers may vary, but should relate to informing the reader.

2. **PERSONAL RESPONSE** Answers will vary.

3. **IMPORTANT DETAILS** the kernel

4. **COMPARE AND CONTRAST** Accept reasonable responses.

5. **UNDERSTAND FIGURATIVE LANGUAGE** Both Native Americans and settlers depended on agriculture throughout the country's history (including today), and corn is one of the most important crops.

LEVELED READER TEACHER GUIDE

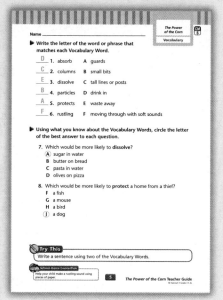

▲ Vocabulary, p. 5

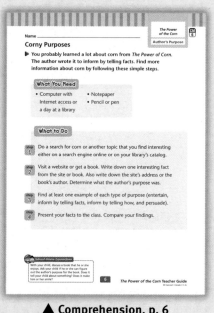

▲ Comprehension, p. 6

E L L

Genre: Realistic Fiction

Our Backyard

SUMMARY A family finds all kinds of exciting things that live and grow in their own backyard.

- **Build Background**
- **Concept Vocabulary**
- **Scaffolded Language Development**

Before Reading

BUILD BACKGROUND/SET PURPOSE Have students discuss the different kinds of animals and plants that might live in their backyard or in a nearby park. Then guide students to preview the story and set a purpose for reading.

Reading the Book

PAGES 6–9 SETTING Where is the garden? (in Abigail's and Ryan's backyard) **What grows in the garden?** (vegetables)

PAGE 14 AUTHOR'S PURPOSE What is the author's purpose? (Possible responses: The author's purpose is to inform readers how the garden vegetables grow. The author tells about the animals and insects that live in a garden.)

REREAD FOR FLUENCY Have students form groups and take turns reading a page aloud, making sure to use dramatic intonation when reading dialogue.

Scaffolded Language Development

(See inside back cover for teacher-led activity.)

Provide additional examples and explanation as needed.

LEVELED READER TEACHER GUIDE

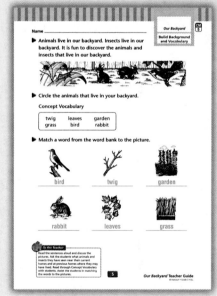

▲ Build Background, p. 5

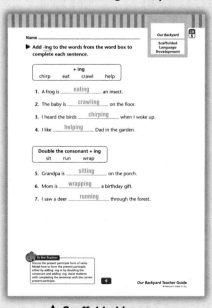

▲ Scaffolded Language
   Development, p. 6

Lesson 14

WEEK AT A GLANCE

✔ **Phonics**
V/CV and VC/V Syllable Patterns

✔ **Spelling**
robin, petal, seven, solid, final, given, color, hotel, wagon, music, total, cabin, taken, pupil, broken

✔ **Comprehension**
 Author's Purpose
 Ask Questions

✔ **Robust Vocabulary**
sprout, damp, suppose, roost, spears, strikes, glimpse, maze, transformation, harmony

Reading
"One Small Place in a Tree" by Barbara Brenner
EXPOSITORY NONFICTION
"Be a Birdwatcher" by Beverly J. Letchworth
EXPOSITORY NONFICTION

✔ **Fluency**
Intonation

✔ **Grammar**
Pronoun-Antecedent Agreement

✔ **Writing**
Form: Cause and Effect
Trait: Sentence Fluency

✔ **Speaking/Listening**
Presentation of Writing

✔ **Weekly Lesson Test**

 = Focus Skill    = Focus Strategy   ✔ = Tested Skill

One stop
for all
your **Digital** *needs*

Digital
CLASSROOM

 www.harcourtschool.com/storytown
To go along with your print program

FOR THE TEACHER

Prepare Professional Development

in the Online TE

 Videos for Podcasting

Plan & Organize  Online TE & Planning Resource*

Teach Transparencies

access from the Online TE

Assess  Online Assessment*

with Student Tracking System and Prescriptions

FOR THE STUDENT

Read Student eBook*

 Strategic Intervention Interactive Reader

 Leveled Readers

Practice & Apply Splash into Phonics CD-ROM

 Comprehension Expedition CD-ROM

*Also available on CD-ROM

Literature Resources

STUDENT EDITION

Go online   eBook STUDENT EDITION

One
Small Place
in a Tree

by
Barbara Brenner

illustrated by
Tom Leonard

Genre: Expository Nonfiction

Be a Birdwatcher

Genre: Expository Nonfiction

◀ **Audiotext** *Student Edition selections are available on Audiotext 3.*

Accelerated Reader   ◀ *Practice Quizzes for the Selection*

THEME CONNECTION: As We Grow
Comparing Expository Nonfiction

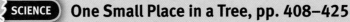

Paired Selections

SCIENCE   **One Small Place in a Tree, pp. 408–425**
SUMMARY Barbara Brenner writes about how a hole in a tree transforms the tree into a home for many creatures.

SCIENCE   **Be a Birdwatcher, pp. 426–427**
SUMMARY Beverly J. Letchworth gives step-by-step instructions on how to go birdwatching.

Support for Differentiated Instruction

LEVELED READERS

● BELOW-LEVEL

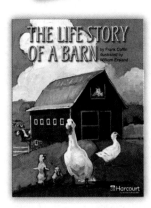 

● ON-LEVEL

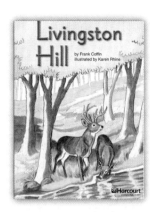 

● ADVANCED

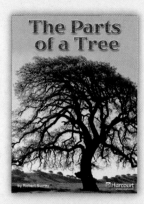

E L L

LEVELED PRACTICE

◀ **Intervention Resource Kit, Lesson 14**

◀ **Strategic Intervention Interactive Reader, Lesson 14**
Strategic Intervention Interactive Reader Online

◀ **ELL Extra Support Kit, Lesson 14**

◀ **Challenge Resource Kit, Lesson 14**

● BELOW-LEVEL
Extra Support Copying Masters, pp. 114–116, 118–119

● ON-LEVEL
Practice Book, pp. 113–119

● ADVANCED LEVEL
Challenge Copying Masters, pp. 114–116, 118–119

E L L
ELL Copying Masters
Lesson 14

ADDITIONAL RESOURCES

- Spelling Practice Book, pp. 44–46
- Grammar Practice Book, pp. 49–52
- Reading Transparencies R93–R100
- Language Arts Transparencies LA29–LA30
- Test Prep System
◀ **Literacy Center Kit, Cards 66–70**
- Writer's Companion
◀ **Fluency Builders**
◀ **Picture Card Collection**
- Read-Aloud Anthology

✓ ASSESSMENT

Monitor Progress

Weekly Lesson Test, Lesson 14
- Comprehension
- Phonics and Spelling
- Focus Skill
- Robust Vocabulary
- Grammar
- Use Graphic Aids

www.harcourtschool.com/storytown

- Online Assessment
- *Also available on CD-ROM—* ExamView®

GO online Online TE & Planning Resources | 90+ Minutes

Suggested Lesson Planner

Day 1

Day 2

 Step 1 Whole Group *(20-60 Minutes)*

Daily Routines
- *Oral Language*
- *Read Aloud*

Word Work
- *phonics*
- *Spelling*

Skills and Strategies
- *Reading*
- *Fluency*
- *Comprehension*
- *Build Robust Vocabulary*

Day 1

QUESTION OF THE DAY, p. T308
Where do animals make their homes?

READ ALOUD, p. T309
Transparency R93: "Full of Life"

✔  *phonics* p. T300
Introduce: V/CV and VC/V Syllable Patterns

✔ **SPELLING,** p. T301
Pretest: *robin, petal, seven, solid, final, given, color, hotel, wagon, music, total, cabin, taken, pupil, broken*

✔ **READING/COMPREHENSION,** p. T302
Introduce: Author's Purpose

LISTENING COMPREHENSION, p. T304
Read-Aloud: "A Log's Life"

FLUENCY, p. T304
Develop Intonation

✔ **BUILD ROBUST VOCABULARY,** p. T305
Words from the Read-Aloud

Day 2

QUESTION OF THE DAY, p. T308
What types of wildlife live near you?

READ ALOUD, p. T309
Transparency R95: "Hey, Bug!"

✔  *phonics* p. T310
Introduce: V/CV and VC/V Syllable Patterns

✔ **SPELLING,** p. T311
Word Building

✔ **BUILD ROBUST VOCABULARY,** p. T312
Words from the Selection
Word Detective, p. T312

READING, p. T314
"One Small Place in a Tree"
Options for Reading

▲Student Edition

✔ **COMPREHENSION,** p. T324
Introduce: Ask Questions

RETELLING/FLUENCY, p. T324
Reading with Intonation

✔ **BUILD ROBUST VOCABULARY,** p. T325
Words About the Selection

 Step 2 Small Groups *(45-60 Minutes)*

 Step 3 Whole Group *(45 Minutes)*

Language Arts
- *Grammar*
- *Writing*

 **Suggestions for Differentiated Instruction (See pp. T292–T293.)**

✔ **GRAMMAR,** p. T306
Introduce: Define *Antecedent*

DAILY PROOFREADING
1. I told he to come over (him; over.)
2. Me and Jan walked there. (Jan and I)

 WRITING, p. T307
Introduce: Cause and Effect
Writing Trait: Sentence Fluency

Writing Prompt *Describe what might cause you to miss the bus.*

✔ **GRAMMAR,** p. T326
Introduce: Agreement in Number

DAILY PROOFREADING
1. The two boys ran to the playground, and he went on the swings (they; swings.)
2. Kayla went on the slide. They had fun. (She)

 WRITING, p. T327
Review: Cause and Effect
Writing Trait: Sentence Fluency

Writing Prompt *Work with a partner to list topics that you could write about in a cause-and-effect paragraph.*

 = Focus Skill  = Focus Strategy  = Tested Skill

phonics
- V/CV and VC/V Syllable Patterns

Comprehension

Focus Skill
Author's Purpose

Focus Strategy
Ask Questions

Fluency
Reading with Intonation

Vocabulary

ROBUST VOCABULARY: *sprout, damp, suppose, roost, spears, strikes, glimpse, maze, transformation, harmony*

Day 3

QUESTION OF THE DAY, p. T328
How do other creatures help humans?

READ ALOUD, p. T329
Transparency R95: "Hey, Bug!"

✔  **phonics** p. T330
Introduce: V/CV and VC/V Syllable Patterns

✔ **SPELLING,** p. T331
State the Generalization
FLUENCY, p. T332
Reading with Intonation

✔ **COMPREHENSION,** p. T333
Review: Author's Purpose ▲Student Edition
Introduce: Use Graphic Aids
Paired Selection: "Be a Birdwatcher"

CONNECTIONS, p. T338

✔ **BUILD ROBUST VOCABULARY,** p. T340
Review

Day 4

QUESTION OF THE DAY, p. T344
What makes a good home for a person? What makes a good home for an animal?

READ ALOUD, p. T345
Transparency R99: "The Perfect Pastime"

✔  **phonics** p. T346
Review: V/CV and VC/V Syllable Patterns

✔ **SPELLING,** p. T347
Review Spelling Words
FLUENCY, p. T348
Reading with Intonation

✔ **COMPREHENSION,** p. T349
Review: Author's Purpose ▲Student Edition
Maintain: Main Idea and Details

SPEAKING AND LISTENING, p. T351
Presentation of Writing

✔ **BUILD ROBUST VOCABULARY,** p. T352
Review

Day 5

QUESTION OF THE DAY, p. T356
In what ways does a forest change over time?

READ ALOUD, p. T357
Transparency R99: "The Perfect Pastime"

✔  **phonics** p. T358
Review: V/CV and VC/V Syllable Patterns

✔ **SPELLING,** p. T359
Posttest
FLUENCY, p. T360
Reading with Intonation

✔ **COMPREHENSION,** p. T361
Review: Author's Purpose ▲Student Edition
Read-Aloud: "A Log's Life"

✔ **BUILD ROBUST VOCABULARY,** p. T362
Cumulative Review

● **BELOW-LEVEL**   ● **ON-LEVEL**   ● **ADVANCED**   E L L

✔ **GRAMMAR,** p. T342
Review: Agreement in Gender

DAILY PROOFREADING

1. Amy asked him, "Mom, can me have my allowance?" (asked her; can I)
2. Jane told Mike her would help with the homework (she; homework.)

 WRITING, p. T343
Review: Cause and Effect
Writing Trait: Sentence Fluency

Writing Prompt *Write your thoughts about the ways in which living things are connected and depend on one another.*

✔ **GRAMMAR,** p. T354
Review: Pronoun-Antecedent Agreement

DAILY PROOFREADING

1. Did Derrick rode him bike to school on Monday (ride his bike; Monday?)
2. my room was a mess so I cleaned her. (My; mess, so I cleaned it.)

 WRITING, p. T355
Review: Cause and Effect
Writing Trait: Sentence Fluency

Writing Prompt *Choose a paragraph from "One Small Place in a Tree" that demonstrates good use of elaboration, and write about how the details are used effectively.*

✔ **GRAMMAR,** p. T364
Review: Pronoun-Antecedent Agreement

DAILY PROOFREADING

1. Tina says her likes to wear green dresses on monday (she; Monday.)
2. latoya and Rima said she enjoyed their bike trip to the lake. (Latoya; they enjoyed)

WRITING, p. T365
Review: Cause and Effect
Writing Trait: Sentence Fluency

Writing Prompt *Make a list of ideas about a new topic for writing. Circle your best idea.*

Suggested Small-Group Planner

45–60 Minutes

	Day 1	Day 2

BELOW-LEVEL
15-20 Minutes

Day 1

Teacher-Directed
Leveled Reader:
"One Hickory Tree in a Forest," p. T366
Before Reading
 ▲ Leveled Reader

Independent
⭐ Listening/Speaking Center, p. T296
Extra Support Copying Masters, p. 114

Day 2

Teacher-Directed
Student Edition:
"One Small Place in a Tree," p. T314
Independent ▲ Student Edition

⭐ Reading Center, p. T296
Extra Support Copying Masters, p. 115

ON-LEVEL
15-20 Minutes

Day 1

Teacher-Directed
Leveled Reader:
"The Life Story of a Barn," p. T367
Before Reading
 ▲ Leveled Reader

Independent
⭐ Reading Center, p. T296
Practice Book, p. 113

Day 2

Teacher-Directed
Student Edition:
"One Small Place in a Tree," p. T314
Independent ▲ Student Edition

⭐ Technology Center, p. T297
Practice Book, p. 114

ADVANCED
15-20 Minutes

Day 1

Teacher-Directed
Leveled Reader:
"Livingston Hill," p. T368
Before Reading
 ▲ Leveled Reader

Independent
⭐ Technology Center, p. T297
Challenge Copying Masters, p. 114

Day 2

Teacher-Directed
Leveled Reader:
"Livingston Hill," p. T368
Read the Book
 ▲ Leveled Reader

Independent
⭐ Word Work Center, p. T297
Challenge Copying Masters, p. 115

English-Language Learners

In addition to the small-group instruction above, use the *ELL Extra Support Kit* to promote language development.

Day 1

LANGUAGE DEVELOPMENT SUPPORT
Teacher-Directed
ELL TG, Day 1

Independent
ELL Copying Masters, Lesson 14

Day 2

LANGUAGE DEVELOPMENT SUPPORT
Teacher-Directed
ELL TG, Day 2

Independent
ELL Copying Masters, Lesson 14

Intervention

▲ Strategic Intervention Resource Kit   ▲ Intervention Reader

Day 1

Strategic Intervention TG, Lesson 14
Strategic Intervention Practice Book, Lesson 14

Day 2

Strategic Intervention TG, Lesson 14
Intervention Reader, Lesson 14

▲ Intervention Reader

| MONITOR PROGRESS Small-Group Instruction | Comprehension Author's Purpose pp. S42–S43 | phonics V/CV and VC/V Syllable Patterns pp. S38–S39 | Comprehension Use Graphic Aids pp. S44–S45 | Fluency Reading with Intonation pp. S40–S41 | Robust Vocabulary sprout, damp, suppose, roost, spears, strikes, glimpse, maze, transformation, harmony pp. S46–S47 | Language Arts ✓ LANGUAGE ARTS CHECKPOINT Grammar: Pronoun-Antecedent Agreement Writing: Cause and Effect pp. S48–S49 |

Day 3

Teacher-Directed
Leveled Reader:
"One Hickory Tree in a Forest,"
p. T366
Read the Book

▲ Leveled Reader

Independent
⭐ Word Work Center, p. T297
Extra Support Copying Masters, p. 116

Teacher-Directed
Leveled Reader:
"The Life Story of a Barn," p. T367
Read the Book

▲ Leveled Reader

Independent
⭐ Writing Center, p. T297
Practice Book, p. 113

Teacher-Directed
Leveled Reader:
"Livingston Hill," p. T368
Think Critically

▲ Leveled Reader

Independent
⭐ Listening/Speaking Center,
p. T296
Challenge Copying Masters, p. 114

LANGUAGE DEVELOPMENT SUPPORT

Teacher-Directed
Leveled Reader:
"The Parts of a Tree," p. T369
Before Reading; Read the Book
ELL TG, Day 3

▲ Leveled Reader

Independent
ELL Copying Masters, Lesson 14

Strategic Intervention TG,
Lesson 14
Intervention Reader, Lesson 14
Strategic Intervention Practice
Book, Lesson 14

▲ Intervention Reader

Day 4

Teacher-Directed
Leveled Reader:
"One Hickory Tree in a Forest,"
p. T366
Reread for Fluency

▲ Leveled Reader

Independent
⭐ Technology Center, p. T297
Practice Book, pp. 113–120

Teacher-Directed
Leveled Reader:
"The Life Story of a Barn," p. T367
Reread for Fluency

▲ Leveled Reader

Independent
⭐ Word Work Center, p. T297
Practice Book, pp. 113–120

Teacher-Directed
Leveled Reader:
"Livingston Hill," p. T368
Reread for Fluency
Self-Selected Reading: Classroom
Library Collection

▲ Leveled Reader

Independent
⭐ Writing Center, p. T297
Practice Book, pp. 113–120

LANGUAGE DEVELOPMENT SUPPORT

Teacher-Directed
Leveled Reader:
"The Parts of a Tree," p. T369
Reread for Fluency
ELL TG, Day 4

▲ Leveled Reader

Independent
ELL Copying Masters, Lesson 14

Strategic Intervention TG,
Lesson 14
Intervention Reader,
Lesson 14

▲ Intervention Reader

Day 5

Teacher-Directed
Leveled Reader:
"One Hickory Tree in a Forest,"
p. T366
Think Critically

▲ Leveled Reader

Independent
⭐ Writing Center, p. T297
Leveled Reader: Reread for Fluency
Extra Support Copying Masters, p. 119

Teacher-Directed
Leveled Reader:
"The Life Story of a Barn," p. T367
Think Critically

▲ Leveled Reader

Independent
⭐ Listening/Speaking Center,
p. T296
Leveled Reader: Reread for Fluency
Practice Book, p. 120

Teacher-Directed
Leveled Reader:
"Livingston Hill," p. T368
Reread for Fluency
Self-Selected Reading: Classroom
Library Collection

▲ Leveled Reader

Independent
⭐ Reading Center, p. T296
Leveled Reader: Reread for Fluency
Challenge Copying Masters, p. 119

LANGUAGE DEVELOPMENT SUPPORT

Teacher-Directed
Leveled Reader:
"The Parts of a Tree," p. T369
Think Critically
ELL TG, Day 5

▲ Leveled Reader

Independent
Leveled Reader: Reread for Fluency
ELL Copying Masters, Lesson 14

Strategic Intervention TG,
Lesson 14
Intervention Reader, Lesson 14

▲ Intervention Reader

Lesson 14 **T293**

Leveled Readers & Leveled Practice
Reinforcing Skills and Strategies

LEVELED READER SYSTEM

- **Leveled Readers**
- **Leveled Readers, CD**
- **Leveled Reader Teacher Guides**
  - *Comprehension*
  - *Vocabulary*
  - *Oral Reading Fluency Assessment*
- **Response Activities**
- **Leveled Readers Assessment**

See pages T366–T369 for lesson plans.

For extended lesson plans, see *Leveled Reader Teacher Guides.*

BELOW-LEVEL

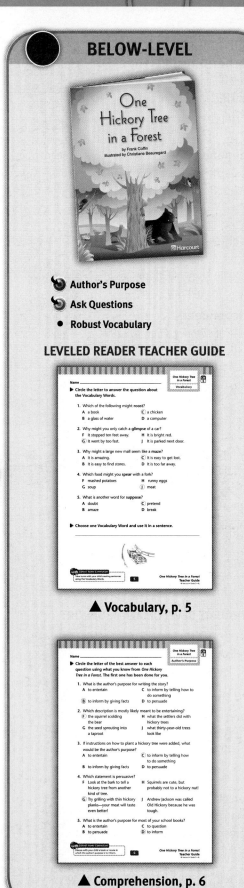

🐾 Author's Purpose

🐾 Ask Questions

● Robust Vocabulary

LEVELED READER TEACHER GUIDE

▲ Vocabulary, p. 5

▲ Comprehension, p. 6

ON-LEVEL

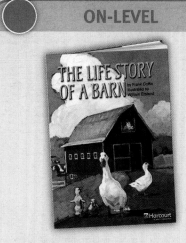

🐾 Author's Purpose

🐾 Ask Questions

● Robust Vocabulary

LEVELED READER TEACHER GUIDE

▲ Vocabulary, p. 5

▲ Comprehension, p. 6

ADVANCED

Livingston Hill by Frank Coffin, illustrated by Karen Rhine

- 🔵 Author's Purpose
- 🔵 Ask Questions
- • Robust Vocabulary

LEVELED READER TEACHER GUIDE

▲ **Vocabulary, p. 5**

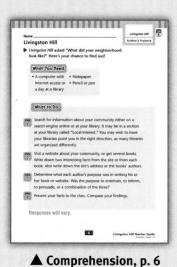

▲ **Comprehension, p. 6**

ELL

The Parts of a Tree by Robert Surrey

- • Build Background
- • Concept Vocabulary
- • Scaffolded Language Development

LEVELED READER TEACHER GUIDE

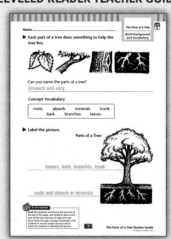

▲ **Build Background, p. 5**

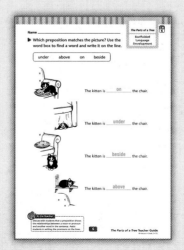

▲ **Scaffolded Language Development, p. 6**

CLASSROOM LIBRARY

Self-Selected Reading

EASY

▲ *Officer Buckle and Gloria* by Peggy Rathmann, G. P. Putnam's Sons, 1995. **FANTASY**

AVERAGE

▲ *Day Light, Night Light* by Franklyn M. Branley, Harper Collins, 1998. **EXPOSITORY NONFICTION**

CHALLENGE

▲ *Donavan's Word Jar* by Monalisa DeGross, Harper Trophy, 1994. **REALISTIC FICTION**

▲ **Classroom Library Teacher Guide, Lesson 14**

Literacy Centers

15 Min. each

Management Support

While you provide direct instruction to individuals or small groups, other students can work on literacy center activities.

▲ **Literacy Centers Pocket Chart**

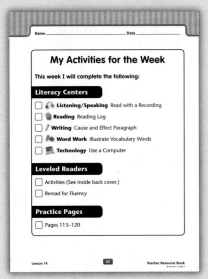

Name _____ Date _____

My Activities for the Week

This week I will complete the following:

Literacy Centers

☐ 🎧 **Listening/Speaking** Read with a Recording
☐ 📖 **Reading** Reading Log
☐ ✏️ **Writing** Cause and Effect Paragraph
☐ 🎨 **Word Work** Illustrate Vocabulary Words
☐ 💻 **Technology** Use a Computer

Leveled Readers

☐ Activities (See inside back cover.)
☐ Reread for Fluency

Practice Pages

☐ Pages 113–120

Lesson 14   47   Teacher Resource Book

▲ **Teacher Resource Book, p. 47**

Homework for the Week

TEACHER RESOURCE BOOK, PAGE 17
The Homework Copying Master provides activities to complete for each day of the week.

🎧 **LISTENING/SPEAKING**

Read with a Recording

Objective
To follow a fluent model to read aloud

🎧 LISTENING/SPEAKING   Card 66

Read with a Recording

MATERIALS
• CD/cassette player
• Audiotext 3
• Student Edition
• Reading Log or paper
• pencil

❶ With a partner, listen to "One Small Place in a Tree" on the *Audiotext*.

❷ Read aloud together with the recording. Follow along in the book.

❸ Use your Reading Log to keep track of what you read.

Grade 3 Lesson 14

⭐ **Literacy Center Kit • Card 66**

📖 **READING**

Reading Log

Objective
To select and read literature independently

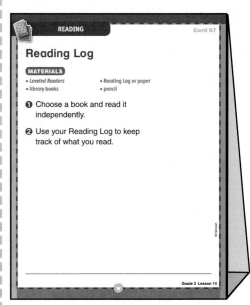

📖 READING   Card 67

Reading Log

MATERIALS
• Leveled Readers
• library books
• Reading Log or paper
• pencil

❶ Choose a book and read it independently.

❷ Use your Reading Log to keep track of what you read.

Grade 3 Lesson 14

⭐ **Literacy Center Kit • Card 67**

WRITING

Cause and Effect Paragraph

Objective
To describe an event using a cause-and-effect structure

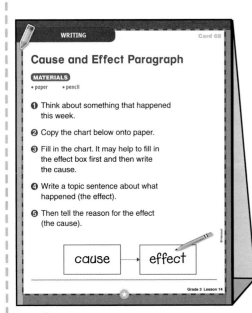

⭐ **Literacy Center Kit • Card 68**

I was tired on Sunday night. I had gone swimming at the beach that day. I ran down the beach with my brother. We didn't get home until late, so I was very tired by the time I crawled into bed.

 WORD WORK

Illustrate Vocabulary Words

Objective
To illustrate understanding of Vocabulary Words

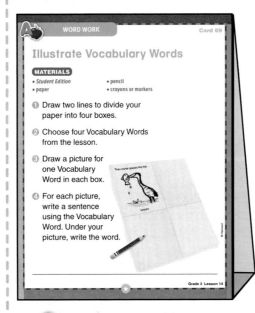

⭐ **Literacy Center Kit • Card 69**

TECHNOLOGY

Use a Computer

Objective
To use electronic technology to type a writing assignment

⭐ **Literacy Center Kit • Card 70**

Day at a Glance

Day 1

 **phonics and Spelling**
- Introduce V/CV and VC/V Syllable Patterns
- Pretest

Reading/Comprehension

 Introduce: Author's Purpose
Student Edition, pp. 404–405

- *Read-Aloud Anthology:* "A Log's Life"

Fluency
- Model Oral Fluency

Robust Vocabulary
Words from the Read-Aloud
- Introduce: *sprout, damp*

Grammar
- Introduce: Pronoun-Antecedent Agreement

Writing
- Cause-and-Effect Paragraph

Warm-Up Routines

 ## Oral Language

Objectives *To listen attentively and respond appropriately to oral communication; to write and speak in complete sentences*

Question of the Day
Where do animals make their homes?

Work with students to brainstorm a list of animals and their homes. Discuss the various kinds of homes animals make or find.

Once students have had time to create and discuss the list, ask them to use their notebooks to respond to the following question:

What creatures live in trees?

Tell students to write several sentences identifying creatures that live in trees. Encourage them to describe both the creatures and their homes.

Invite students to share their responses with the group. Lead a brief discussion to point out creatures that students may not have mentioned, such as insects, lizards or salamanders, and porcupines.

Read Aloud

Objective *To read an article for information and understanding*

READ ALOUD A NONFICTION ARTICLE Use these steps to share the nonfiction selection:

Introduce the text. Display **Transparency R93** or distribute photocopies to students. Explain that you are going to read a nonfiction article called "Full of Life" about dead trees.

Set a purpose. Ask students what the purpose for reading a nonfiction selection might be. (to learn about a subject; for enjoyment; to do research) Tell students to listen to determine what information the author believed was most important to include in this selection.

Model fluent reading. Read the selection aloud; model good intonation by making your voice go higher and lower for emphasis.

Discuss the selection. Ask students the following questions:

- **What information did the author want you to know?**

- **Why do you think the author felt this information was important?**

- **What are some of the animals that depend on snags?**

Full of Life

You might think that an old, dead tree standing in a forest is just an eyesore. Think again. Standing dead trees are called "snags," and snags are important to many kinds of wildlife. Wood ducks, woodpeckers, eagles, and owls build nests in snags. Hawks often use snags as perches. Many small animals such as raccoons, mice, and squirrels also call these hollowed out trees their home.

To us, some of the creatures living in snags are pests. Plenty of ants, beetles, spiders, and earthworms are found in wildlife trees. However, these tiny tenants are an important sources of food for many other species.

Snags may look ready to fall over any minute, but some large trees can stand for more than 150 years after they have died! So, when you see a dead tree, think of the life inside. What may look like an eyesore is actually home-sweet-home to many of our forest friends.

Grade 3, Lesson 14   Ra   Warm-Up: Day 1

Transparency R93

V/CV and VC/V Syllable Patterns *and Spelling*

5-DAY PHONICS	
DAY 1	Introduce V/CV and VC/V Patterns
DAY 2	Words with V/CV Pattern
DAY 3	Words with VC/V Pattern
DAY 4	Identify Vowel Patterns in Words
DAY 5	Review V/CV and VC/V Patterns

Objectives

- *To recognize V/CV and VC/V syllable patterns in words*
- *To use V/CV and VC/V syllable patterns to decode words*

Skill Trace

✓ Tested V/CV and VC/V Syllable Patterns

Introduce	Grade 2
Reintroduce	T300
Reteach	S38
Review	T310–T311, T330, T346, T358, T420
Test	Theme 3

"RESEARCH SAYS"

Decoding "Poor decoding skill leads to little reading and little opportunity to increase one's basic vocabulary and knowledge through reading. . . ."
–Juel (1988), p. 446

 **Resources**

Phonics Practice Book, Intermediate, pp. 85–90

Teach/Model

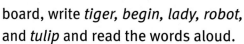

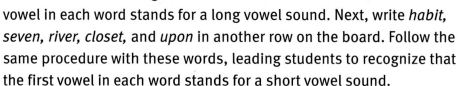

Routine Card 1

REVIEW VOWEL SOUNDS On the board, write *tiger, begin, lady, robot,* and *tulip* and read the words aloud. Guide students to recognize that the first vowel in each word stands for a long vowel sound. Next, write *habit, seven, river, closet,* and *upon* in another row on the board. Follow the same procedure with these words, leading students to recognize that the first vowel in each word stands for a short vowel sound.

INTRODUCE V/CV AND VC/V PATTERNS Remind students that syllables are the "beats" in a word and that each syllable has only one vowel sound. Point out that each word on the board has two vowel sounds and two syllables.

Point to *tiger* and work with students to draw a line after the *i* to form syllables. Then write *V* under each of the vowels and *C* under the consonant between them. Do the same with the word *habit*, separating the syllables after the *b*. Explain that *tiger* and *habit* have a vowel-consonant-vowel pattern that can be helpful in pronouncing words. In *tiger*, the vowel is at the end of the first syllable, and the first vowel has a long vowel sound. In *habit*, the consonant is at the end of the first syllable, and the vowel has a short vowel sound.

Practice/Apply

GUIDED PRACTICE Read the words *begin, lady, seven,* and *river* aloud, working with students to divide the syllables and identify the vowel-consonant-vowel pattern. Then guide students to identify the first vowel sound in each word as either long or short.

INDEPENDENT PRACTICE Have students copy the remaining words into their notebooks. For each word, have them draw a line between the syllables, circle the vowels, and underline the consonant between them. Tell students to write *long* beside each word that has a long first-vowel sound and *short* beside each word that has a short first-vowel sound. Check students' work.

5-DAY SPELLING

DAY 1	Pretest
DAY 2	State the Generalization
DAY 3	Practice Spelling/Handwriting
DAY 4	Use Spelling Strategies/Review
DAY 5	Posttest

Introduce Spelling Words

PRETEST Explain that all of this week's spelling words include the V/CV or VC/V syllable pattern. Say the first word and read the dictation sentence beside it. Repeat the word as students write it. Write the word on the board and have students check their spelling. Direct them to circle the word if they spelled it correctly or write it correctly if they did not. Repeat for words 2–15.

1. robin — A **robin** built a nest in the oak tree.
2. petal — Each **petal** on the daisy is white.
3. seven — Marcus is **seven** years old.
4. solid — Water is a liquid, and ice is a **solid**.
5. final — What is the **final** word on the spelling list?
6. given — Have you **given** your permission slip to me?
7. color — Purple is my favorite **color**.
8. hotel — Emma's family stayed in a **hotel**.
9. wagon — Amar piled leaves in the **wagon**.
10. music — Ming danced to the **music** on the radio.
11. total — We have a **total** of nineteen students in our class.
12. cabin — Mr. Diaz built a **cabin** in the woods.
13. taken — Jada had her picture **taken** on her birthday.
14. pupil — Nick is a **pupil** in Miss Moore's class.
15. broken — My pencil is **broken**.

ADVANCED

Challenge Words Use these dictation sentences.

16. recital — We went to Olivia's ballet **recital**.
17. vanish — The dog seems to **vanish** at bath time.
18. regret — Do you **regret** not going to the game?
19. colony — I wonder how many ants live in that **colony**.
20. visiting — Mario is **visiting** his uncle this weekend.

Spelling Words

1.	**robin**	9.	**wagon**
2.	**petal**	10.	**music**
3.	**seven**	11.	**total**
4.	**solid**	12.	**cabin**
5.	**final**	13.	**taken**
6.	**given**	14.	**pupil**
7.	**color***	15.	**broken**
8.	**hotel**		

Challenge Words

16.	**recital**	19.	**colony***
17.	**vanish**	20.	**visiting**
18.	**regret**		

*Words from "One Small Place in a Tree"

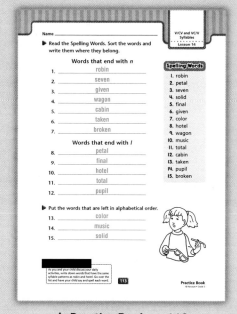

▲ Practice Book, p. 113

Author's Purpose
Comprehension

Objectives

- *To determine the main reason the author wrote the passage*
- *To determine the author's message, underlying theme, and important information in the text*

Daily Comprehension

Author's Purpose

DAY 1:	Introduce Author's Purpose *Student Edition*
DAY 2:	Review Author's Purpose *Student Edition*
DAY 3:	Paired Selection *Student Edition*
DAY 4:	Review Author's Purpose *Transparency*
DAY 5:	Review Author's Purpose *Read-Aloud Anthology*

MONITOR PROGRESS

Author's Purpose

IF students have difficulty recognizing the reason the author wrote a passage,	**THEN** suggest familiar texts, and identify the reason the authors wrote them. Show fairy tales (entertain), newspaper articles (inform), and ads (persuade).

Small-Group Instruction, p. S42:

- ● **BELOW-LEVEL:** Reteach
- ● **ON-LEVEL:** Reinforce
- ○ **ADVANCED:** Extend

Teach/Model

INTRODUCE AUTHOR'S PURPOSE Explain that most authors have a purpose, or reason, for writing. It might be to entertain, to inform, or to persuade the reader. It might even be a combination of these purposes.

Have students read the information on author's purpose on page 404.

Practice/Apply

GUIDED PRACTICE Read aloud the passage on page 405, draw the graphic organizer on the board, and have students copy it. Guide students to complete it.

What I Know	What I Read	Author's Purpose

Try This! **INDEPENDENT PRACTICE** Ask students to speculate what the author's purpose might be for the suggested story. (entertain) Then have them complete an organizer for the suggested story.

ELL

Try This! **Using Pictures** To help students understand the passage, use the picture of a flying squirrel on p. 405. Point out the wing flaps and show how they are attached to the animal's body, as discussed in the passage. Ask which animals actually do fly, and guide students to recognize that birds, bats, and some insects fly. Tell them to think of a paper airplane gliding through the air, and discuss how gliding is different from a bird's flying. Explain that the squirrel glides like the paper plane.

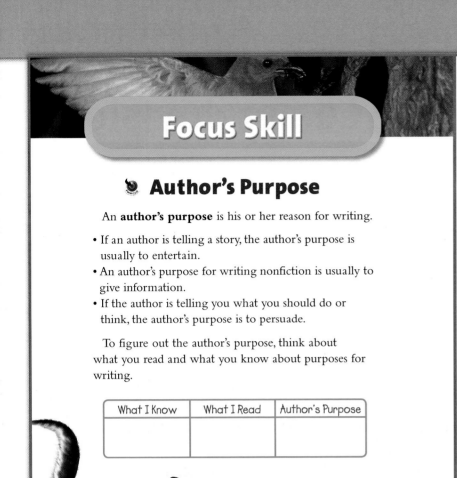

Focus Skill

❧ Author's Purpose

An **author's purpose** is his or her reason for writing.

- If an author is telling a story, the author's purpose is usually to entertain.
- An author's purpose for writing nonfiction is usually to give information.
- If the author is telling you what you should do or think, the author's purpose is to persuade.

To figure out the author's purpose, think about what you read and what you know about purposes for writing.

What I Know	What I Read	Author's Purpose

Tip
An author may also give some information while telling a story. To figure out the author's purpose, identify the main reason the author wrote the passage.

404

Read the passage below. Then use the chart to think about and tell the author's purpose. Tell which clues in the text helped you figure out the author's purpose.

> Flying squirrels do not really fly. They glide or float through the air. The flying squirrel has a flap of skin on each side of its body. The flaps are joined to its front and back legs. When the squirrel wants to glide, it stretches its legs to open the flaps of skin. The flaps are like the wings of a glider. The squirrel steers by moving its front legs. A flying squirrel can glide for more than 100 feet!

What I Know	What I Read	Author's Purpose
Authors give many facts when they write to inform.		

Try This!
What if this author had written a fiction story about a squirrel that flies a plane? What would the author's purpose be then?

 www.harcourtschool.com/storytown

405

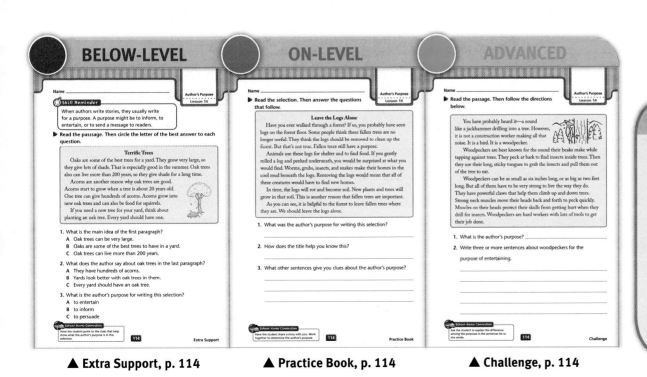

BELOW-LEVEL

Name _____

Skill Reminder
When authors write stories, they usually write for a purpose. A purpose might be to inform, to entertain, or to send a message to readers.

▶ Read the passage. Then circle the letter of the best answer to each question.

Terrific Trees

Oaks are some of the best trees for a yard. They grow very large, so they give lots of shade. That is especially good in the summer. Oak trees also can live more than 200 years, so they give shade for a long time.

Acorns are another reason why oak trees are good. Acorns start to grow when a tree is about 20 years old. One tree can give hundreds of acorns. Acorns grow into new oak trees in about 20 years. Acorns also are food for squirrels.

If you need a new tree for your yard, think about planting an oak tree. Every yard should have one.

1. What is the main idea of the first paragraph?
   A Oak trees can be very large.
   B Oaks are some of the best trees to have in a yard.
   C Oak trees can live more than 200 years.

2. What does the author say about oak trees in the last paragraph?
   A They have hundreds of acorns.
   B Yards look better with oak trees in them.
   C Every yard should have an oak tree.

3. What is the author's purpose for writing this selection?
   A to entertain
   B to inform
   C to persuade

114   Extra Support

▲ **Extra Support, p. 114**

ON-LEVEL

Name _____

▶ Read the selection. Then answer the questions that follow.

Leave the Logs Alone

Have you ever walked through a forest? If so, you probably have seen logs on the forest floor. Some people think these fallen trees are no longer useful. They think the logs should be removed to clean up the forest. But that's not true. Fallen trees still have a purpose.

Animals use these logs for shelter and to find food. If you gently rolled a log and peeked underneath, you would be surprised at what you would find. Worms, grubs, insects, and snakes make their homes in the cool mud beneath the logs. Removing the logs would mean that all of these creatures would have to find new homes.

In time, the logs will rot and become soil. New plants and trees will grow in that soil. This is another reason that fallen trees are important. As you can see, it is helpful to the forest to leave fallen trees where they are. We should leave the logs alone.

1. What was the author's purpose for writing this selection?

2. How does the title help you know this?

3. What other sentences give you clues about the author's purpose?

114   Practice Book

▲ **Practice Book, p. 114**

ADVANCED

Name _____

▶ Read the passage. Then follow the directions below.

You have probably heard it—a sound like a jackhammer drilling into a tree. However, it is not a construction worker making all that noise. It is a bird. It is a woodpecker.

Woodpeckers are best known for the sound their beaks make while tapping against trees. They peck at bark to find insects inside trees. Then they use their long, sticky tongues to grab the insects and pull them out of the tree to eat.

Woodpeckers can be as small as six inches long, or as big as two feet long. But all of them have to be very strong to live the way they do. They have powerful claws that help them climb up and down trees. Strong neck muscles move their heads back and forth to peck quickly. Muscles on their heads protect their skulls from getting hurt when they drill for insects. Woodpeckers are hard workers with lots of tools to get their job done.

1. What is the author's purpose? _____

2. Write three or more sentences about woodpeckers for the purpose of entertaining.

114   Challenge

▲ **Challenge, p. 114**

ELL

- Group students according to academic levels and assign one of the pages on the left.

- Clarify unfamiliar concepts and vocabulary. See *ELL Teacher Guide* Lesson 14 for support in scaffolding instruction.

Listening Comprehension
Read Aloud

Objectives

- *To set a purpose for reading*
- *To understand characteristics of nonfiction*
- *To identify the author's purpose*

Building Fluency

Focus: Intonation Tell students that good readers make their reading voices sound interesting. When they read aloud, they sound as if they are talking or telling a story to someone. Demonstrate this by reading a sentence in a monotone. Then read the same sentence, this time making your voice rise and fall.

Visualization Guide students to make an image in their mind of what the healthy tree looks like before you begin reading. Tell students that as you read, they should change their image to match what they are hearing. Invite students to tell about their images.

Before Reading

CONNECT TO PRIOR KNOWLEDGE Tell students they will be listening to a nonfiction selection about the life of a tree and the animals that depend on the tree. Talk with students about what they know about trees and the creatures that live in and near them.

▲ Read-Aloud Anthology, "A Log's Life," p. 50

Routine Card 2 **GENRE STUDY: NONFICTION** Tell students that when they listen to nonfiction, they should listen for information. Explain that even though nonfiction is written to tell about something, it can also be enjoyable.

> **Think Aloud** **I know that a nonfiction selection is not made up, so I will listen for facts about the topic. I will pay attention to how the selection is organized to help me understand it.**

REVIEW: AUTHOR'S PURPOSE Remind students that an author's purpose usually is to entertain, inform, or persuade and that they should determine the author's purpose as they listen to the selection. Read aloud "A Log's Life."

After Reading

RESPOND Ask students whether they enjoyed listening to "A Log's Life." Mention that the author wrote the selection to inform and to entertain. Ask students how they know that the article is nonfiction.

Build Robust Vocabulary
Words from the Read-Aloud

Teach/Model

Routine Card 3

INTRODUCE ROBUST VOCABULARY Use *Routine Card 3* to introduce the words.

---

❶ Put the word in **selection context**.
❷ Display **Transparency R94** and read the word and the **Student-Friendly Explanation**.
❸ Have students **say the word** with you.
❹ Use the word in other contexts and have students **interact with the word's meaning**.
❺ Remove the transparency. Say the Student-Friendly Explanation again, and ask students to **name the word** that goes with it.

---

❶ **Selection Context:** Toadstools and other fungi such as mildew, molds, and mushrooms **sprout** in these damp places.
❹ **Interact with Word Meaning:** If you planted flower seeds, would you expect them to sprout in a few days or float away in a few days?

❶ **Selection Context:** Toadstools and other fungi sprout in **damp** places.
❹ **Interact with Word Meaning:** Would your swimsuit be damp right after you have been swimming, or a little while later?

Practice/Apply

GUIDED PRACTICE Ask students the following:

- In your kitchen, what would you expect to be dry and what would you expect to be damp?

- How is a sprouting acorn different from an oak tree?

Objective

- *To develop robust vocabulary through discussing a literature selection*

Tested

INTRODUCE ✓
Vocabulary: Lesson 14

sprout

damp

▼ **Student-Friendly Explanations**

Vocabulary	
1. sprout	When something sprouts, it begins to grow.
2. damp	If something is damp, it is a little bit wet.
3. transformation	If someone or something has gone through a transformation, it has been changed.
4. harmony	If two things are living in harmony, they are in agreement, living peacefully.

Grade 3, Lesson 14   R6   Vocabulary

Transparency R94

E L L

Learning Through Examples Draw a seed, a seedling, and a plant to explain how seeds sprout and grow into plants. Use three paper towels to demonstrate wet, dry, and damp.

Grammar
Pronoun-Antecedent Agreement

5-DAY GRAMMAR

DAY 1	Define Antecedent
DAY 2	Agreement in Number
DAY 3	Agreement in Gender
DAY 4	Apply to Writing
DAY 5	Pronoun-Antecedent Agreement Review

Objectives

- *To recognize that antecedents are the words referred to by pronouns*
- *To identify antecedents in sentences*

Daily Proofreading

1. I told he to come over?
   (him; over.)
2. Me and Jan walked there
   (Jan and I; there.)

Pronoun-Antecedent Agreement

1. When the hole has water in it, you can sometimes see a tree frog there.
2. After the grubs become beetles, they eat their way out of the chambers.
3. A bear digs at the tree until it finds insects to eat.
4. Many woodpeckers visit the oak tree to eat, and they have made the hole even bigger.
5. The young boy watched the bluebird until he saw the babies.

Grade 3, Lesson 14   LA9   Grammar: Pronoun-Antecedent Agreement

Transparency LA29

Teach/Model

DEFINE ANTECEDENT Remind students that a pronoun takes the place of a noun. Ask students to suggest several examples of pronouns. (Possible responses: *I, you, he, she, it, they, me, him, her, them*) Write on the board these sentences from "A Log's Life."

The old oak bends and shakes.

It crashes to the forest floor.

Ask students to identify the pronoun. (It) Ask what *It* refers to. (the old oak) Write the word *antecedent* on the board, and explain that an antecedent is the noun that is referred to by the pronoun. Explain that *oak* is the antecedent.

Guided Practice

IDENTIFY ANTECEDENTS Display **Transparency LA29**. Read the first sentence to students and ask them to identify the pronoun. (it) Underline *it*. Then ask them to identify the antecedent. (hole) Circle the antecedent. Continue to guide students through items 2–5.

Practice/Apply

USE ANTECEDENTS As a class, brainstorm pronouns and list them on the board. Instruct students to select four of the pronouns from the board and write sentences using them. Explain that each needs a pronoun and an antecedent that match. For example, the antecedent *Maria* would work well with *she*, but not with *he, it,* or *they*. Allow students to look through the selections in the *Student Edition* to get ideas for their sentences if they need help. Remind students to begin each sentence with a capital letter, capitalize proper nouns, and use correct end punctuation. Have students trade papers with a partner and circle the antecedents in each other's sentences.

Writing
Cause-and-Effect Paragraph

5-DAY WRITING

DAY 1	Introduce
DAY 2	Prewrite
DAY 3	Prewrite
DAY 4	Draft
DAY 5	Revise/Edit

Teach/Model

INTRODUCE CAUSE-AND-EFFECT PARAGRAPH Display **Transparency LA30**. Explain that this is a cause-and-effect paragraph. Read the paragraph aloud. Point out that the first sentence tells the effect and that the second sentence tells the cause, or why something happened. Point out the word *because,* which shows how the cause and effect are related. The other sentences give details about the cause. Work with students to develop a list of characteristics.

> Cause-and-Effect Paragraphs
> - Include the cause or the effect in the first sentence
> - Use key words to show a relationship between the cause and the effect

SENTENCE FLUENCY: ELABORATION Read aloud the third sentence on **Transparency LA30**. Explain that this sentence gives additional information about what happened on Monday and Tuesday. Repeat with the remaining sentences.

Guided Practice

IDENTIFY CAUSE AND EFFECT Write the following on the board:

Paul could watch TV last night because he had done all his homework.

Read the sentence aloud. Then guide students to identify the cause (Paul had done all his homework) and the effect (He could watch TV last night) Have students also note that *Paul* is the antecedent in the sentence.

Practice/Apply

WRITE CAUSE-AND-EFFECT SENTENCES Have students write two cause-and-effect sentences. Have them exchange their sentences with a partner and identify the cause and the effect in each.

Objectives

- *To recognize the components of a cause-and-effect paragraph*
- *To recognize key words that show a relationship between cause and effect*

Writing Prompt

Sentence Have students describe what might cause them to miss the bus.

Student Model: Cause-and-Effect Paragraph

My grade on this week's spelling test was my best ever! Because I studied my spelling words every day, I got an A on my test. On Monday and Tuesday, I wrote each of the words ten times. On Wednesday, I made a word search with the words. On Thursday, I asked my mom to give me a practice test. This showed me that if I study my spelling words every day, then I will do well on Friday's test.

Grade 3, Lesson 14   **LAb**   Writing: Cause-and-Effect Paragraph

Transparency LA30

Day at a Glance

Day 2

 and Spelling

- Review: V/CV and VC/V Syllable Patterns

Robust Vocabulary

Words from the Selection

- Introduce: *suppose, roost, spears, strikes, glimpse, maze*

Comprehension

 Ask Questions

Review: Author's Purpose

Reading

- "One Small Place in a Tree," *Student Edition*, pp. 408–425

Fluency

- Intonation

Robust Vocabulary

Words About the Selection

- Introduce: *transformation, harmony*

Grammar

- Pronoun-Antecedent Agreement

Writing

- Cause-and-Effect Paragraph

Warm-Up Routines

Oral Language

Objectives *To write and speak in complete sentences; to listen and respond to questions with appropriate elaboration*

Question of the Day

What types of wildlife live near you?

Remind students that there are many kinds of wildlife around them—mammals, birds, insects, and so on. Together, brainstorm a list of wild creatures students might encounter in and around school, home, and the community. Invite students to describe any experiences they have had with these creatures. Remind students to listen attentively to the speaker.

Then ask students to respond to the following prompt in their notebooks:

Some types of wildlife that live near me are _____.

Have students write three or four sentences telling about the creatures they encounter regularly. Encourage them to include information about where they see those creatures, what they are like, what they do, and so on.

Invite students to share their responses with the class.

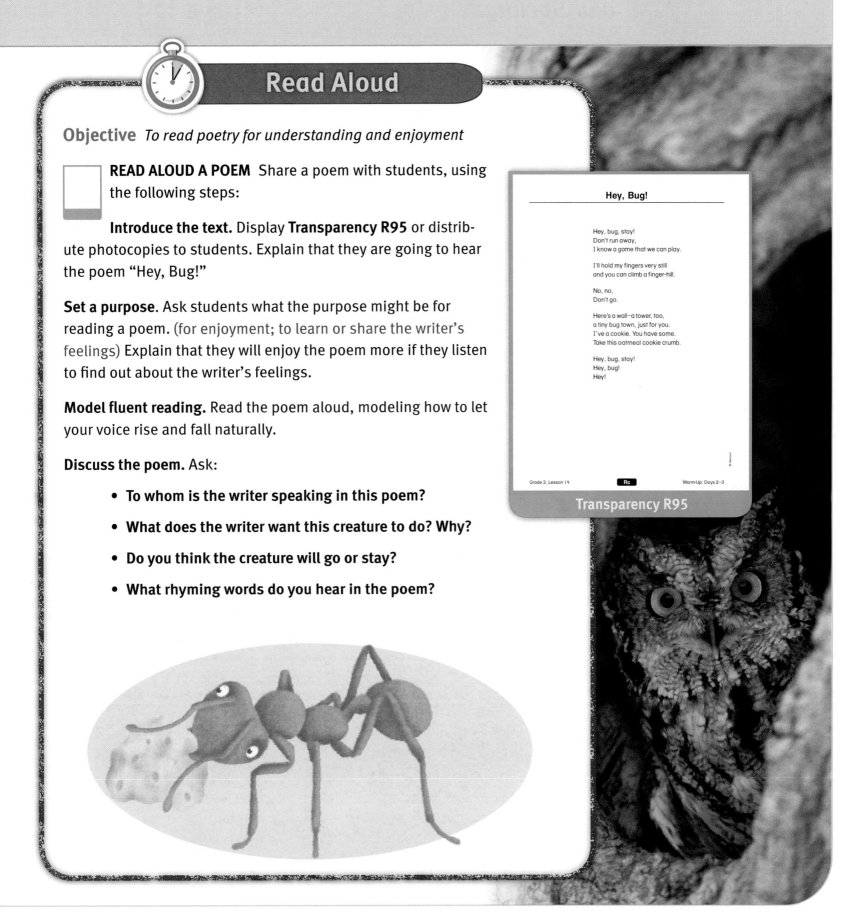

Read Aloud

Objective *To read poetry for understanding and enjoyment*

READ ALOUD A POEM Share a poem with students, using the following steps:

Introduce the text. Display **Transparency R95** or distribute photocopies to students. Explain that they are going to hear the poem "Hey, Bug!"

Set a purpose. Ask students what the purpose might be for reading a poem. (for enjoyment; to learn or share the writer's feelings) Explain that they will enjoy the poem more if they listen to find out about the writer's feelings.

Model fluent reading. Read the poem aloud, modeling how to let your voice rise and fall naturally.

Discuss the poem. Ask:

- **To whom is the writer speaking in this poem?**

- **What does the writer want this creature to do? Why?**

- **Do you think the creature will go or stay?**

- **What rhyming words do you hear in the poem?**

Hey, Bug!

Hey, bug, stay!
Don't run away,
I know a game that we can play.

I'll hold my fingers very still
and you can climb a finger-hill.

No, no,
Don't go.

Here's a wall—a tower, too,
a tiny bug town, just for you.
I've a cookie. You have some.
Take this oatmeal cookie crumb.

Hey, bug, stay!
Hey, bug!
Hey!

Grade 3, Lesson 14   **Rc**   Warm-Up: Days 2–3

Transparency R95

V/CV and VC/V Syllable Patterns
phonics *and Spelling*

Objectives

- *To recognize V/CV and VC/V syllable patterns in words*
- *To use V/CV and VC/V syllable patterns to decode words*

Skill Trace

Tested ✓ **V/CV and VC/V Syllable Patterns**

Introduce	Grade 2
Reintroduce	T300
Reteach	S381
Review	T310–T311, T330, T346, T358, T420
Test	Theme 3

Spelling Words

1.	robin	9.	wagon
2.	petal	10.	music
3.	seven	11.	total
4.	solid	12.	cabin
5.	final	13.	taken
6.	given	14.	pupil
7.	color*	15.	broken
8.	hotel		

Challenge Words

16.	recital	19.	colony*
17.	vanish	20.	visiting
18.	regret		

Words from "One Small Place in a Tree"

V/CV Syllable Patterns

☐ **DISCOVER THE VOWEL SOUND** Display **Transparency R96** or distribute photocopies to students. Remind them that a syllable has only one vowel sound. Work with students to divide the words into syllables, determining whether the syllables are divided before or after the vowel, and labeling the words V/CV or VC/V. Guide students to recognize that in a word where the first vowel has a long sound, the word can be divided after that vowel. In the words where the first vowel has a short sound, the word can be divided after the consonant.

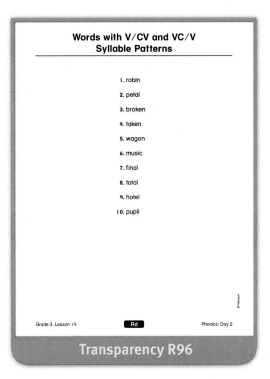

Words with V/CV and VC/V Syllable Patterns

1. robin
2. petal
3. broken
4. taken
5. wagon
6. music
7. final
8. total
9. hotel
10. pupil

Grade 3, Lesson 14   Rd   Phonics: Day 2

Transparency R96

BELOW-LEVEL

Use Visual Clues If students are unsure of whether the words are divided before or after the first vowel, help them write the words and trace the first vowel with a crayon.

ADVANCED

Find Words in Context Have students search their *Student Edition* for words that have the V/CV and VC/V syllable patterns. Direct students to write the words in their notebooks and mark how to divide them into syllables.

5-DAY SPELLING
DAY 1   Pretest
DAY 2   State the Generalization
DAY 3   Spelling Practice/Handwriting
DAY 4   Use Spelling Strategies/Review
DAY 5   Posttest

LONG-VOWEL SORT Have students write the vowel letters as column heads. Tell them to read the first V/CV word *(broken)* on **Transparency R96.** Ask students which long vowel sound is pronounced in the first syllable of the word. (/ō/) Have them write the word under the letter *o*. Instruct students to continue sorting all of the V/CV spelling words by their long vowel sounds. Tell them that one vowel sound will not have any matching words. Have students compare their list with a partner's. (*a-* taken; *e-* [no words]; *i-* final; *o-* hotel, total, broken; *u-* music, pupil)

WRITE Instruct students to write a sentence that includes as many of the long vowel spelling words as possible. Then have students copy the sentence, leaving blanks for the spelling words. Instruct students to trade papers with a partner. Tell students to write their partners' sentences, adding the missing words. Have students check the completed sentences.

MONITOR PROGRESS

V/CV Words

IF students are unsure as to whether a word has a long or a short vowel sound,	THEN instruct students to read the words, using a short vowel sound and then a long vowel sound, and see which sounds right.

Small-Group Instruction, p. S38:

- **BELOW-LEVEL:** Reteach
- **ON-LEVEL:** Reinforce
- **ADVANCED:** Extend

BELOW-LEVEL

Name _____

V/CV and VC/V Syllable Patterns
Lesson 14

▶ Complete each sentence. Choose the correct way to divide the word into syllables. Then write the divided word on the line. The first one has been done for you.

1. My mom's favorite vase was bro|ken _____ (bro/ken, brok/en)

2. What kind of _____ do you like to listen to? (mus/ic, mu/sic)

3. Jessie is _____ in Ms. Chin's class. (pu/pil, pup/il)

4. They stayed in a _____ by the beach. (ho/tel, hot/el)

5. Jamal read the _____ page in his book. (fin/al, fi/nal)

6. What is the _____ cost of the items? (to/tal, tot/al)

7. We have _____ the bus before. (tak/en, ta/ken)

8. Please help me _____ the pages together. (sta/ple, stap/le)

School-Home Connection
Ask the student to tell whether each word has a long or short vowel sound. Then ask him or her to say another word with the same sound.

115   Extra Support

▲ Extra Support, p. 115

ON-LEVEL

Name _____

V/CV and VC/V Syllable Patterns
Lesson 14

▶ Look at each pair of spelling words. Choose the word in each pair that has the V/CV syllable pattern, and write it on the lines. Use the boxed letters to answer the riddle at the bottom of the page.

1. vanish   broken   □
2. total   wagon   □
3. taken   seven   □
4. cabin   music   □
5. final   given   □
6. robin   pupil   □
7. hotel   color   □

Riddle:
Where can you leave your dog when you go to the mall?

Answer:
In the
___ ___ ___ ___ ___ ___ ___
1   2   R 3 4 G 5 O 6 7

School-Home Connection
Read the spelling words on the page to the student. Ask him or her to tell whether each word has a long or short vowel sound.

115   Practice Book

▲ Practice Book, p. 115

ADVANCED

Name _____

V/CV and VC/V Syllable Patterns
Lesson 14

▶ Unscramble each V/CV spelling word from the Word Bank in Part A. Then, in Part B, write a short story that includes all of the words.

| taken | total | final | pupil |
| broken | hotel | music | |

Part A
lippu _____   oelth _____   eboknr _____   netka _____

csmiu _____   attlo _____   lafin _____

Part B
_____
_____
_____
_____
_____
_____
_____

School-Home Connection
Ask the student to read his or her story to you. Then ask the student to point out other words in the story that have long vowel sounds.

115   Challenge

▲ Challenge, p. 115

ELL

- Group students according to academic levels and assign one of the pages on the left.
- Clarify any unfamiliar concepts as necessary. See *ELL Teacher Guide* Lesson 14 for support in scaffolding instruction.

Build Robust Vocabulary
Words from the Selection

Objective
- *To build robust vocabulary*

INTRODUCE ✔ Tested
Vocabulary: Lesson 14

suppose	**strikes**
roost	**glimpse**
spears	**maze**

▼ **Student-Friendly Explanations**

Vocabulary

1. **suppose** When you suppose something, you think that it is happening or that it is going to happen.

2. **roost** A bird will try to roost, or settle, in trees or on branches.

3. **spears** If someone spears something, he or she sticks something sharp through it.

4. **strikes** When something strikes people, it hits them or happens to them.

5. **glimpse** When you get a glimpse of something, you get only a quick peek at it.

6. **maze** If you are in a maze, you are in winding paths that are like a puzzle.

Grade 3, Lesson 14 Re Vocabulary from the Selection

Transparency R97

Word Champion

Sentences At the end of the week, encourage students to share their Word Champion sentences with the class.

HOMEWORK/INDEPENDENT PRACTICE

Introduce Vocabulary

Routine Card 4 **INTRODUCE ROBUST VOCABULARY** Introduce the words, using the following steps:

❶ Display **Transparency R97** and read the word and the **Student-Friendly Explanation**.
❷ Have students **say the word** with you.
❸ Have students **interact with the word's meaning** by asking them the appropriate question below.

- If you caught a **glimpse** of something at the beach, what might it have been?
- What is it like to walk in a **maze**?
- Why might a bird **roost** in a tree?
- What kinds of things might a woodpecker **spear**?
- Have you ever had hail or sleet **strike** you?
- Has there ever been a time when you **supposed** something might happen, and it did? Explain.

Develop Deeper Meaning

EXPAND WORD MEANINGS: PAGES 406–407 Have students read "The Everglades." Then read the passage aloud, pausing at the end of page 406 to ask questions 1–4. Discuss questions 5–6 after reading page 407.

1. What do you **suppose** you would see in the Florida Everglades?
2. Why might the birds **roost** in treetops?
3. How can it be helpful for lightning to **strike** a forest?
4. How would a great blue heron use its beak to **spear** fish?
5. Where would you catch a **glimpse** of a nesting bird?
6. In what ways can a **maze** of roots be helpful to fish?

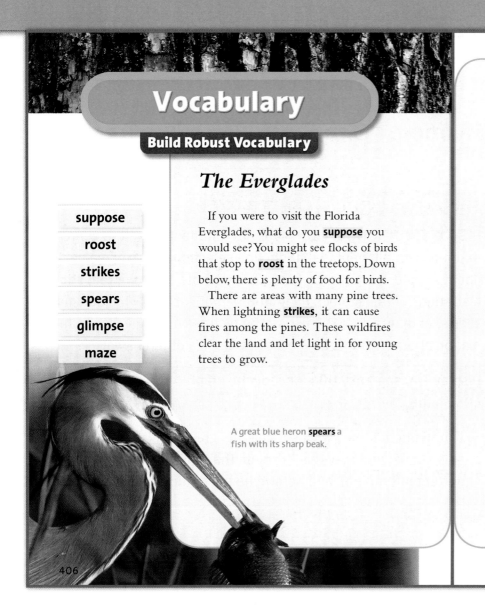

Vocabulary

Build Robust Vocabulary

suppose

roost

strikes

spears

glimpse

maze

The Everglades

If you were to visit the Florida Everglades, what do you **suppose** you would see? You might see flocks of birds that stop to **roost** in the treetops. Down below, there is plenty of food for birds.

There are areas with many pine trees. When lightning **strikes**, it can cause fires among the pines. These wildfires clear the land and let light in for young trees to grow.

A great blue heron **spears** a fish with its sharp beak.

406

Another kind of tree you might see is the mangrove. These strange trees grow in places where fresh river water meets salty ocean water.

You might catch a **glimpse** of birds nesting in the mangroves' branches. Their tangled roots form a **maze**, in which fish can swim and hide.

The roots of a mangrove keep the tree above the salty water.

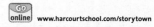
online www.harcourtschool.com/storytown

Word Champion

Your mission this week is to use the Vocabulary Words in conversation with family members or friends. For example, tell a family member about a bird that may roost in your area. Write in your vocabulary journal sentences that use Vocabulary Words.

407

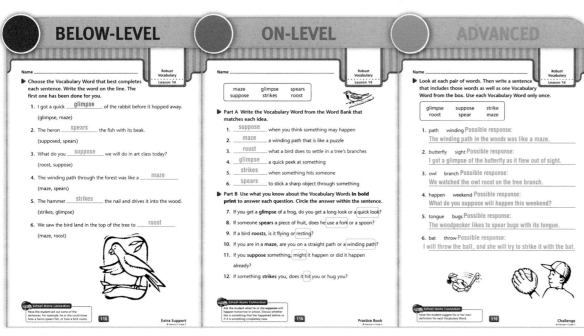

BELOW-LEVEL

Name _____
▶ Choose the Vocabulary Word that best completes each sentence. Write the word on the line. The first one has been done for you.

1. I got a quick _glimpse_ of the rabbit before it hopped away.
   (glimpse, maze)
2. The heron _spears_ the fish with its beak.
   (supposed, spears)
3. What do you _suppose_ we will do in art class today?
   (roost, suppose)
4. The winding path through the forest was like a _maze_.
   (maze, spears)
5. The hammer _strikes_ the nail and drives it into the wood.
   (strikes, glimpse)
6. We saw the bird land in the top of the tree to _roost_.
   (maze, roost)

▲ Extra Support, p. 116

ON-LEVEL

Name _____

| maze | glimpse | spears |
| suppose | strikes | roost |

▶ Part A Write the Vocabulary Word from the Word Bank that matches each idea.

1. _suppose_ when you think something may happen
2. _maze_ a winding path that is like a puzzle
3. _roost_ what a bird does to settle in a tree's branches
4. _glimpse_ a quick peek at something
5. _strikes_ when something hits someone
6. _spears_ to stick a sharp object through something

▶ Part B Use what you know about the Vocabulary Words **in bold print** to answer each question. Circle the answer within the sentence.

7. If you get a glimpse of a frog, do you get a long look or a quick look?
8. If someone spears a piece of fruit, does he use a fork or a spoon?
9. If a bird roosts, is it flying or resting?
10. If you are in a maze, are you on a straight path or a winding path?
11. If you suppose something, might it happen or did it happen already?
12. If something strikes you, does it hit you or hug you?

▲ Practice Book, p. 116

ADVANCED

Name _____
▶ Look at each pair of words. Then write a sentence that includes those words as well as one Vocabulary Word from the box. Use each Vocabulary Word only once.

| glimpse | suppose | strike |
| roost | spear | maze |

1. path winding Possible response:
   The winding path in the woods was like a maze.
2. butterfly sight Possible response:
   I got a glimpse of the butterfly as it flew out of sight.
3. owl branch Possible response:
   We watched the owl roost on the tree branch.
4. happen weekend Possible response:
   What do you suppose will happen this weekend?
5. tongue bugs Possible response:
   The woodpecker likes to spear bugs with its tongue.
6. bat throw Possible response:
   I will throw the ball, and she will try to strike it with the bat.

▲ Challenge, p. 116

ELL

- Group students according to academic levels and assign one of the pages on the left.

- Clarify any unfamiliar concepts as necessary. See *ELL Teacher Guide*, Lesson 14, for support in scaffolding instruction.

Reading

Student Edition: "One Small Place in a Tree"

Objectives

- *To understand nonfiction*
- *To identify author's purpose*

Options for Reading

BELOW-LEVEL

SET A PURPOSE Preview the selection with students. Model how to set a purpose.

ON-LEVEL

GUIDED COMPREHENSION Use the questions as students read, or have pairs complete *Practice Book* page 117.

ADVANCED

INDEPENDENT READING Have students read, using *Practice Book* page 117.

Name _____

▶ As you read "One Small Place in a Tree," fill in the first column of the graphic organizer with what you already know. In the middle column, write the information you read. Fill in the author's purpose after you finish the selection.

What I Know	What I Read	Author's Purpose

1. What is the main reason the author wrote the selection?
   to tell about the ways animals use living and dead trees

2. What is the author's purpose?
   to inform

3. On a separate sheet of paper, summarize the selection. Use the graphic organizer to help you. Answers will vary.

117   Practice Book

▲ **Practice Book, p. 117**

Genre Study

DISCUSS NONFICTION: PAGE 408 Have students read the genre information. Tell them that nonfiction selections contain real facts about a topic. Nonfiction often includes photographs or realistic illustrations of the subject. In addition, nonfiction may include maps, charts, or diagrams. Explain that the pictures often give more information about the topic or show the facts in a different way.

Display **Transparency G04,** or copy the graphic organizer from page 408 on the board.

Tell students that they will be using this graphic organizer to record details about what they read. Explain that this will help them find the important information and determine the author's purpose.

What I Know	What I Read	What I Learned

Comprehension Strategy

ASK QUESTIONS: PAGE 408 Read aloud the comprehension strategy information. Explain that asking questions and looking for answers helps good readers understand what they read. Point out that students can ask themselves the questions, share their questions when partner-reading, or write the questions. Explain that they may have more than one question at a time and that good readers continually think of new questions. Distribute *Practice Book* page 117. Tell students that they will use the chart to keep track of information as they read. See page T324 for the completed *Practice Book* page.

Genre Study

Expository nonfiction explains information and ideas. Look for

- illustrations that support the facts.
- details to help you learn about a topic.

| What I Know | What I Read | What I Learned |

Comprehension Strategy

Ask questions if you are confused about what you are reading.

408

Expository Nonfiction

Award-Winning Author

One Small Place in a Tree

One Small Place in a Tree

by Barbara Brenner

illustrated by Tom Leonard

409

Build Background

DISCUSS LIVING THINGS IN A FOREST Tell students they are going to read about a tree and the ways forest animals depend on it. Invite students to tell about a time they visited or read about a forest. Have them complete the What I Know column on the graphic organizer.

Routine Card 5 **SET A PURPOSE AND PREDICT** Remind students that two purposes for reading a selection are to enjoy and to learn. Have students turn to page 409 in the *Student Edition*. Then follow these steps.

- Read the title and author's name.

- Ask what living things are shown on the page. Have students predict what the small place in the tree might be and why it is important. List predictions on the board.

- Invite students to read to find why the small place in the tree is important.

TECHNOLOGY

 eBook "One Small Place in a Tree" is available in an eBook.

 Audiotext "One Small Place in a Tree" is available on *Audiotext 3* for subsequent readings.

 Podcasting: Ask Questions

A tree hole. One small place in a tree. How does it get there? Who lives inside? ❶ Suppose that you could watch a hole from its beginning. You might see something like this. ❷

410   411

Monitor Comprehension

PAGES 410–411 Direct students to look at the picture and think about the title of the selection. Ask what small place the title might be referring to.

❶ **SPECULATE Look at the hole in the tree. How do you think the hole got there?** (Possible response: animals scratched a hole in the bark, woodpeckers made the hole, animals ate the bark.)

❷ **MAKE PREDICTIONS Why do you think the hole is important?** (Possible response: animals live there.)

Apply
Comprehension Strategies

Ask Questions Explain that good readers ask themselves questions as they read. Tell students to think about what they have read and seen so far. Then ask them to think of a question about the selection.

Focus Strategy

Think Aloud The title of the story is "One Small Place in a Tree." What happens in that small place that is so exciting or important that it deserves an entire article? As I read I'll look for the answer to that question.

Here's one oak tree in a forest. It looks like the others, except—a black bear uses this one as a scratching post. Every time she goes by, the bear sharpens her claws on the trunk.

You're walking in the woods. You see the tree and notice the scratch marks on the bark. Maybe you even catch a glimpse of the bear!

After a while the scratching chips some pieces of bark off the tree. A cut forms in the bark. A hole in the tree is beginning. ①

Next time you're walking there, you see that tiny bugs have found the cut. They're timber beetles, and they're about to set up housekeeping ② ③

412

413

Monitor Comprehension

PAGES 412–413 Have students look at the illustration. Have them read to find out how the bear is important.

① **CAUSE/EFFECT What happened as a result of the bear scratching her claws on the tree?** (Possible response: bark fell off the tree and made a hole.)

② **STORY EVENTS How do you think the timber beetles' moving into the hole is related to what will happen to the hole later in the story?** (Possible response: they will make the hole bigger; they will attract other animals to the hole.)

③ **AUTHOR'S PURPOSE What do you think the author's purpose was for writing this selection?** (to inform) **Why do you think that?** (The author tells about real things.)

Focus Skill

BELOW-LEVEL

Summarize Help students summarize what they have read so far:

- A bear sharpens her claws on a tree every time she walks by it.
- The scratches cause bark to fall off the tree.
- A cut in the bark begins the hole.
- Timber beetles make their home in the scratches on the tree.

Help students fill in their graphic organizer by writing what they have read to this point. Then help them set a purpose for reading, to find out why the beetles are important.

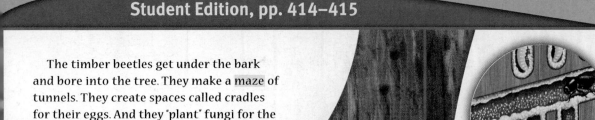

The timber beetles get under the bark and bore into the tree. They make a maze of tunnels. They create spaces called cradles for their eggs. And they "plant" fungi for the colony to feed on. Imagine that you can look inside. You see something like this. **1**

Soon the fungi spread and are growing all over the walls of the tunnels. The beetle eggs have hatched into grubs. The grubs are feeding on the fungi. **2** The fungi are feeding on the soft wood inside the tree.

The beetle grubs become full-grown timber beetles. They eat their way out of the chambers and make more holes in the tree. **3**

On your next visit you count more than ten holes. But the first one is the largest.

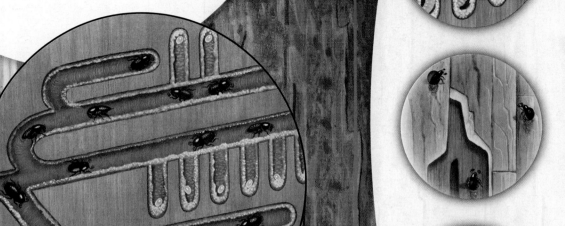

414
415

Monitor Comprehension

PAGES 414–415 Before reading, have students look at the illustrations. Ask what students think they show. Have students read to find out if they are correct.

1 **CONTEXT CLUES** On page 414 we read that the beetles "plant" fungi. Based on what you read, what do you think *fungi* are?
(Possible response: fungi must be something like a plant, since the beetles "plant" it.)

2 **CONTEXT CLUES** Based on the illustrations and what you read, what do you think *grubs* are? (Possible response: baby beetles hatch out of the eggs as grubs.)

3 **CAUSE/EFFECT** What effect do the beetles have on the tree?
(Possible response: They enlarge the first hole and make ten more.)

Connect Words and Pictures
Reread pages 414–415 aloud, and guide students to point to the illustrations as words are read in the text. Help students recognize beetles, fungi, bark, grubs, and chambers.

One time when you're near the tree, you actually hear the sound of the beetles chewing wood.

A red-bellied woodpecker hears it, too.

The bird flies to the tree holes. It spears the beetles with its sharp beak, or pulls them out with its long tongue.

Many woodpeckers visit the oak tree to eat. After a summer they've cleared the holes of beetles and beetle grubs. But they've made the big hole even bigger. **①**

Now disease strikes. Bacteria come in through the hole in the tree. You won't see the bacteria— they're too small. But you can see the damage they've done. The tree has heart rot. It's dying inside and out. **②**

Bark begins to loosen and fall off. The hole is now so large that you can actually see inside.

It has become a hollow place that looks as if it could be home for something. **③**

416

417

Monitor Comprehension

PAGES 416–417 Explain that the bird shown on page 416 is a woodpecker. Tell students to think about what this woodpecker might be doing and how it might affect the hole in the tree.

① **USE PRIOR KNOWLEDGE Why is the woodpecker trying to get the beetles and grubs?** (for food)

② **CAUSE/EFFECT What causes the tree to start dying?** (The woodpecker makes the hole larger and bacteria get in.)

③ **MAKE PREDICTIONS What do you think is going to happen to the hole next?** (Possible responses: it will keep getting bigger; animals will move into the hole.)

Use Multiple Strategies

Use Prior Knowledge Say: Using what I already know helps me better understand a story. This page says the woodpecker flies to the hole and spears the beetles, but it doesn't tell why the bird does this. I already know that woodpeckers eat bugs. This helps me understand why the bird is pecking at the tree and making the hole bigger. It is trying to get to the bugs so it can eat.

The first animal to use it is a flying squirrel. You find the squirrel "holed up" in there one winter day. You notice that it has stored some nuts under the loose bark around the hole.

When you come by in the spring, the flying squirrel is gone. The hole is empty, but not for long. A pair of bluebirds moves in. The hole is just right for blue birds—high enough off the ground for safety.

The bluebirds line the hole with weeds and grass. Soon there are six bluish eggs in the nest hole.

Next time you look inside, there are six bluebird chicks. The chicks stay safe in the nest until they're old enough to fly.

By this time the oak tree is no longer sending out leaves. Almost all of its bark is gone. But the hole-dwellers don't seem to care.

For the next three springs, the hole in the tree is a nest for the same pair of bluebirds.

For the next three winters, it's home to a family of white-footed mice. ❶ ❷

In all those three years, the tree hasn't grown at all. This oak tree is dead. But—the hole is full of life. ❸

418   419

Monitor Comprehension

PAGES 418–419 Have students read on.

❶ **IMPORTANT DETAILS What animals depend on the hole in the tree?** (a flying squirrel, bluebirds, and mice)

❷ **IMPORTANT DETAILS How do the animals use the hole?** (shelter, storing food, building nests, making a home)

❸ **MAKE PREDICTIONS What other animals do you think might be able to use the dead tree in some way?** (Possible answers: other small mammals, reptiles, bugs, or other birds)

SCIENCE

SUPPORTING STANDARDS

Interactions in Nature Discuss the animals that use the tree and the ways they depend on it. Explain that animals in an ecosystem, such as a forest, must share the limited resources and that living things depend on each other in many ways.

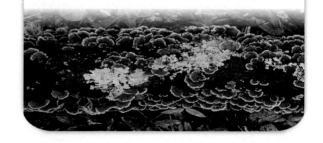

A hairy woodpecker sometimes comes to roost there.

A gray squirrel often uses the hole as a hiding place.

When the hole has water in it, you can sometimes see a tree frog there.

One day lightning, or a high wind, or heavy rain, or snow will bring this dead tree down. Many years later all that may be left will be a log with a hole in it. **1**

But the hole will still be a place for living things. A small garter snake may cool off in there.

A redback salamander may lay its eggs there.

Or maybe a hammock spider will make a web across the hole to catch swarming insects. **2** **3**

420

421

Monitor Comprehension

PAGES 420–421 Have students think about how animals have used the tree. Have them read to find out how other animals use it.

1 **CAUSE/EFFECT** **What can cause a tree to fall?** (Weather can cause a tree to fall.)

2 **IMPORTANT DETAILS** **In what ways are animals able to use a fallen tree?** (garter snake cools off in the log; Salamander lays eggs in the log; spider makes a web across the hole to catch insects)

3 **AUTHOR'S PURPOSE** **How can you tell that the author also wants to entertain the reader?** (Possible response: She tells the facts like a story.)

ANALYZE AUTHOR'S PURPOSE

Author's Purpose Remind students that authors have a purpose, or reason, for writing. After students have finished reading "One Small Place in a Tree," ask:

Why did the author write "One Small Place in a Tree"?

• to persuade readers to cut down trees

• to entertain readers with a story with animal characters

• to inform readers about the creatures who make their homes in a tree

Living trees are important. But so are dead and dying trees. A dead tree often has a hole—one small place that is usually home for something.

422

Think Critically

❶ What do you think was the author's purpose in writing "One Small Place in a Tree"?
   AUTHOR'S PURPOSE

❷ What important events happen after the bear scratches the tree? SEQUENCE

❸ What information surprised you most as you read the selection? EXPRESS PERSONAL OPINIONS

❹ How can you tell that the author thinks trees are useful, even when they are dead? DRAW CONCLUSIONS

❺ **WRITE** How is the tree helpful to other living things? Give examples from the story to support your answer. SHORT RESPONSE

423

Think Critically

Respond to the Literature

❶  The author's purpose was to inform readers in an entertaining way. **AUTHOR'S PURPOSE**

❷ The scratching chips some pieces of bark off. Then timber beetles move into the hole, followed by other animals. **SEQUENCE**

❸ Possible response: It surprised me that tiny bacteria could harm a huge tree. **EXPRESS PERSONAL OPINIONS**

❹ Possible response: She tells about the creatures that use the dead tree. **DRAW CONCLUSIONS**

❺ Possible response: The tree gives shelter to birds and animals. Some insects eat the wood of the tree and make their home there, too. **WRITING RESPONSE/PERSONAL EXPERIENCE**

ADVANCED

Classify Have students label three columns "Living," "Dead," and "Both." Have them list the creatures that used the tree when it was living, dead, or both. Tell students to think of and add other animals that depend on trees but are not mentioned in the selection.

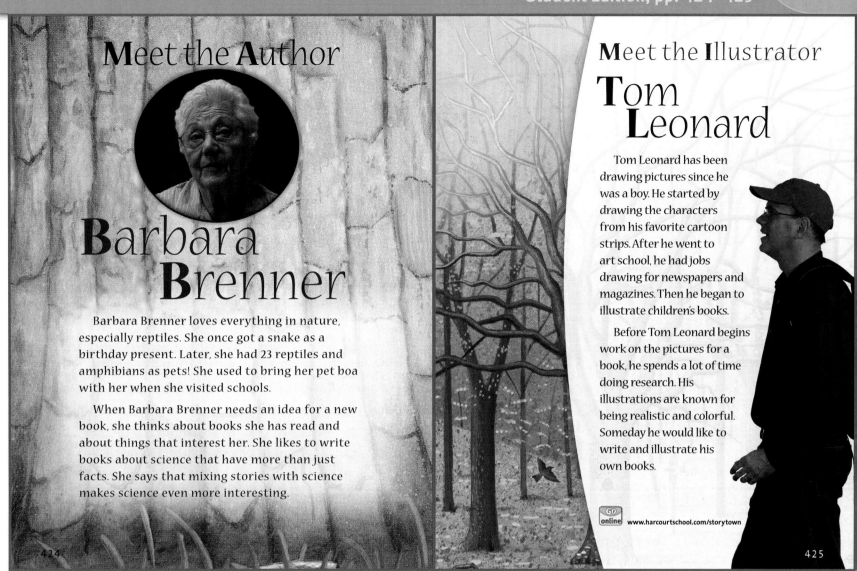

Meet the Author

Barbara Brenner

Barbara Brenner loves everything in nature, especially reptiles. She once got a snake as a birthday present. Later, she had 23 reptiles and amphibians as pets! She used to bring her pet boa with her when she visited schools.

When Barbara Brenner needs an idea for a new book, she thinks about books she has read and about things that interest her. She likes to write books about science that have more than just facts. She says that mixing stories with science makes science even more interesting.

424

Meet the Illustrator

Tom Leonard

Tom Leonard has been drawing pictures since he was a boy. He started by drawing the characters from his favorite cartoon strips. After he went to art school, he had jobs drawing for newspapers and magazines. Then he began to illustrate children's books.

Before Tom Leonard begins work on the pictures for a book, he spends a lot of time doing research. His illustrations are known for being realistic and colorful. Someday he would like to write and illustrate his own books.

GO online www.harcourtschool.com/storytown

425

Meet the Author and the Illustrator

PAGE 424 Tell students that the author, Barbara Brenner, has written more than 70 books for children. She writes both fiction and nonfiction, and five times she has received an award for writing an outstanding book on a science subject.

Page 425 Tell students that Tom Leonard has been illustrating books for more than 20 years, but that he did not start out drawing for children. In fact, he has drawn illustrations for a variety of things, from medical journals to football films. He admits that it surprises him to be drawing for children's books. However, he enjoys drawing subjects from nature, and he hopes one day to write and illustrate a children's book completely on his own.

Check Comprehension
Summarizing

Objectives

- *To summarize a selection*
- *To read with intonation*

SUMMARIZING RUBRIC

4	Uses details to clearly retell the story
3	Uses some details to retell the story
2	Retells story with some inaccuracies
1	Is unable to retell the story

Professional Development

Podcasting: Auditory Modeling

Name
▶ As you read "One Small Place in a Tree," fill in the first column of the graphic organizer with what you already know. In the middle column, write the information you read. Fill in the author's purpose after you finish the selection.

Reader's Guide
Lesson 14

What I Know	What I Read	Author's Purpose

1. What is the main reason the author wrote the selection?
to tell about the ways animals use living and dead trees

2. What is the author's purpose?
to inform

3. On a separate sheet of paper, summarize the selection. Use the graphic organizer to help you. Answers will vary.

117
Practice Book

▲ Practice Book, p. 117

Summarize

AUTHOR'S PURPOSE Remind students that an author's purpose usually is to entertain, inform, or persuade. Figuring out the main reason something was written can help readers better understand what they are reading.

Routine Card 6 **WRITE A SUMMARY** Have students recall the important information from "One Small Place in a Tree," reminding them that a summary contains the main idea and important details. Tell students that they can refer to the graphic organizer on *Practice Book* page 117. Then have them write a brief summary of the selection. Tell them to be especially careful to use the correct sequence of events, since several events lead to others.

Fluency
Intonation

Teach/Model

DIBELS Oral Reading Fluency ORF **READING WITH INTONATION** Explain that when good readers read aloud, they make their reading sound like normal speech by changing the pitch of their voices. Remind students that, when they speak, they use the pitch of their voice to emphasize certain words and to show whether sentences are questions or statements. Have students open to pages 412–413 of "One Small Place in a Tree." Read these pages aloud, using a natural rise and fall in your voice to indicate questions, anticipation, and excitement.

Practice/Apply

Routine Card 9 **PARTNER-READ** Have students use intonation to partner-read the next few pages of the text, trading roles after each sentence.

Build Robust Vocabulary
Words About the Selection

Teach/Model

Routine Card 3

INTRODUCE THE WORDS Use *Routine Card 3* to introduce the bottom two words.

❶ Put the word in **selection context.**
❷ Display **Transparency 94** and read the word and the **Student-Friendly Explanation**.
❸ Have students **say the word** with you.
❹ Use the word in other contexts and have students **interact with the word's meaning.**
❺ Remove the transparency. Say the Student-Friendly Explanation again, and ask students to **name the word** that goes with it.

❶ **Selection Context:** The **transformation** of the hole began when the bear scratched the bark.
❹ **Interact with Word Meaning:** What would be a bigger transformation—getting your bedroom tidied, or wearing a new outfit?
❶ **Selection Context:** Many of the animals lived in **harmony** with one another.
❹ **Interact with Word Meaning:** If family members lived in harmony, would they help each other, or would they quarrel?

Practice/Apply

GUIDED PRACTICE Ask students to do the following:

• Think about the different living things that go through transformations. Share your ideas and act out the transformations with a group.

• Work with a partner to list animals that live in harmony with each other.

Objective

• *To develop robust vocabulary through discussing a literature selection*

INTRODUCE **Tested** ✓

Vocabulary: Lesson 14

transformation

harmony

▼ **Student-Friendly Explanations**

Vocabulary	
1. sprout	When something sprouts, it begins to grow.
2. damp	If something is damp, it is a little bit wet.
3. transformation	If someone or something has gone through a transformation, it has been changed.
4. harmony	If two things are living in harmony, they are in agreement, living peacefully.

Grade 3, Lesson 14   **Rb**   Vocabulary

Transparency R94

Grammar
Pronoun-Antecedent Agreement

5-DAY GRAMMAR	
DAY 1	Define Antecedent
DAY 2	Agreement in Number
DAY 3	Agreement in Gender
DAY 4	Apply to Writing
DAY 5	Pronoun-Antecedent Agreement Review

Objectives

- *To use agreement between singular pronouns and antecedents*
- *To identify antecedents in sentences*

Daily Proofreading

1. The two boys ran to the play-
   grownd, and he went on the
   swings. (playground; they)

2. Kayla went on the slide. they
   had fun. (She)

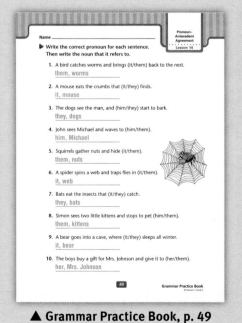

▲ **Grammar Practice Book, p. 49**

Teach/Model

DISCUSS SINGULAR AND PLURAL ANTECEDENTS Write these lines from "One Small Place in a Tree" on the board:

> **One small place in a tree. How does it get there?
> The bugs climb in, and they make a home.**

Ask students to identify the pronouns. (*it, they*) Remind students that an antecedent is the word referred to by a pronoun. Ask what the antecedent of *it* is. (*place*) Point out that *place* is singular, so the pronoun has to be singular. Ask what the antecedent of *they* is. (*bugs*) Explain that *bugs* is plural, so a plural pronoun has to be used.

Guided Practice

MATCH PRONOUNS AND ANTECEDENTS Say the following sentences and have students suggest the pronoun to complete each one. Have students say whether the antecedent is singular or plural.

> **The mice moved into the hole and made _____ home.** (*their*)
> **The frog liked the water. _____ could swim.** (*It, He,* or *She*)
> **When the tree was on the ground, the spider moved in so _____ could eat bugs.** (*it, he,* or *she*)
> **Some beetles eat tree bark for _____ meals.** (*their*)

Practice/Apply

USE ANTECEDENTS IN WRITING Have students write a sentence using one of the pronouns from the board. Tell them to make sure they leave a blank line in place of the antecedent. Instruct students to exchange sentences with a partner and fill in the blank with an appropriate antecedent. Invite students to share their sentences with the class.

Writing
Cause-and-Effect Paragraph

5-DAY WRITING
DAY 1	Introducte
DAY 2	Prewrite
DAY 3	Prewrite
DAY 4	Draft
DAY 5	Revise/Edit

Prewrite

DISCUSS AUDIENCE AND PURPOSE Remind students that the audience is whom they are writing for and their purpose is the reason they are writing. Suggest that students think about why they are writing their cause-and-effect paragraph.

MODEL PREWRITING Draw the following graphic organizer on the board:

Cause	Effect	Effect

Write *The bear scratched the tree bark* in the *Cause* box. Ask students to suggest the effect and write that in the *Effect box.* (Timber beetles move in under the bark.) Ask students what the effect of the timber beetles was, and write it in the second *Effect* box. (The timber beetles made more holes in the tree bark.)

 SENTENCE FLUENCY: ELABORATION Point out that cause-and-effect paragraphs explain why something happened. Remind students that they need to include enough details for readers to understand what happened and why it happened.

Practice/Apply

COMPLETE A CAUSE-AND-EFFECT CHART Direct students to draw a graphic organizer like the one on the board. Have them think of an event that they would like to write about. Have them write the cause and the effect in the chart. Explain that some events have more than one cause or more than one effect. Work with students to adjust their charts to reflect their ideas.

Objectives

- *To use graphic organizers to prepare for writing*
- *To choose a topic and generate ideas for a cause-and-effect paragraph*

Writing Prompt

List Have students work with a partner to list topics that they could write about in a cause-and-effect paragraph.

Prewriting Brainstorm two or three topics that students could use as the effect in the graphic organizer. Discuss topics that are common to most students, such as winning a game or being late to school. Have students complete their graphic organizers with partners.

Day at a Glance

Day 3

phonics and Spelling

- Review: V/CV and VC/V Syllable Patterns

Fluency

- Intonation
- "One Small Place in a Tree," *Student Edition*, pp. 408–425

Comprehension

- Review: Author's Purpose
- Introduce: Use Graphic Aids

Reading

- "Be a Birdwatcher," *Student Edition*, pp. 426–427

Robust Vocabulary

- Review: *sprout, damp, suppose, roost, spears, strikes, glimpse, maze, transformation, harmony*

Grammar

- Review: Pronoun-Antecedent Agreement

Writing

- Cause-and-Effect Paragraph

Warm-Up Routines

Oral Language

Objectives *To listen and respond to oral communication; to write several sentences related to a single topic or idea*

Question of the Day

How do other creatures help humans?

Remind students of the many kinds of living creatures around them. Discuss some of the ways these creatures affect human lives. On the board, start a list of creatures and the ways in which they improve our lives. (For example, birds eat insects that might bother us, insects devour fallen trees and turn them into soil, pets keep us company.)

After students have had a chance to share ideas, have them respond to the following prompt, writing several sentences in their notebooks:

Other creatures help us by _____.

Ask students to write one or two sentences responding to the prompt and telling how these creatures help us and one another. Encourage students to share their complete sentences with the group.

Read Aloud

Objectives *To listen and respond to poetry; to read poetry fluently*

REVIEW THE POEM Display **Transparency R95** from Day 2 or distribute photocopies to the students. Tell them you are going to reread the poem "Hey, Bug."

Set a purpose. Ask students why someone might want to read a poem again. (to enjoy; to listen for patterns, repetition, and rhyme; to gain meaning) Tell students to listen and follow along as you read the poem. Encourage them to listen for words that rhyme or have similar sounds.

Model fluent reading. Read the poem aloud, using a natural rise and fall in your voice to model intonation.

Echo-read. Tell students to echo as you read the poem again. Remind them to listen carefully to the rise and fall in your voice and to do the same as they read. Read the poem aloud again, pausing after each stanza so that students can repeat it. Track the words on the transparency to help students follow along.

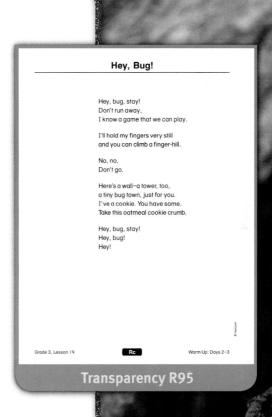

Hey, Bug!

Hey, bug, stay!
Don't run away,
I know a game that we can play.

I'll hold my fingers very still
and you can climb a finger-hill.

No, no,
Don't go.

Here's a wall—a tower, too,
a tiny bug town, just for you.
I've a cookie. You have some.
Take this oatmeal cookie crumb.

Hey, bug, stay!
Hey, bug!
Hey!

Grade 3, Lesson 14   Rc   Warm-Up: Days 2–3

Transparency R95

V/CV and VC/V Syllable Patterns

5-DAY PHONICS	
DAY 1	Introduce V/CV and VC/V Patterns
DAY 2	Words with V/CV Pattern
DAY 3	**Words with VC/V Pattern**
DAY 4	Identify Vowel Patterns in Words
DAY 5	Review V/VC and VC/V Patterns

Objectives

- *To recognize V/CV and VC/V syllable patterns in words*
- *To use V/CV and VC/V syllable patterns to decode multisyllabic words*

Skill Trace

 Tested ✔ **V/CV and VC/V Syllable Patterns**

Introduce	Grade 2
Reintroduce	T300
Reteach	**S38**
Review	T310–T311, T330, T346, T358, T420
Test	Theme 3

Words with V/CV and VC/V Syllable Patterns

tuba   habit

Part A

1. lo/mat

2. tra/tap

3. wap/ent

4. pu/dar

5. sil/ub

6. ri/nog

Part B

1. The baby tiger began to walk to the river.

2. We will go to a cozy cabin in the desert on Friday.

Grade 3, Lesson 14   **Rf**   Phonics: Day 3

Transparency R98

Teach/Model

REVIEW SYLLABLE PATTERNS Display **Transparency R98** and point out the V/CV and VC/V words *tuba* and *habit*. Ask students what kind of vowel sound, long or short, they hear in each word and with each syllable pattern. (V/CV: long-vowel sound with *tuba*, VC/V: short-vowel sound with *habit*) Remind students that the first vowel in V/CV words has a long sound. The first vowel in VC/V words has a short sound. Write *long* or *short* beside the sample words to show the vowel sounds. You may also refer to the Syllabication Cards on Teacher's Resource Book, p. 84.

Guided Practice

USE SYLLABLE PATTERNS TO DECODE NONSENSE WORDS Direct students to Part A and point to the nonsense words. Tell students that these are made-up words with no meaning. Have students use the syllable division to tell whether each word is V/CV or VC/V and whether the vowel sound is long or short. Then have students decode the nonsense word.

INDEPENDENT PRACTICE Direct students to Part B and ask them to copy the sentences. Have them underline the V/CV and VC/V words and then draw lines to divide them into syllables. Then tell students to write *long* or *short* under each underlined word to indicate whether each underlined word has a long or short vowel sound. Have students compare their answers with those of a partner.

V/CV and VC/V Syllable Patterns phonics and Spelling

5-DAY SPELLING

DAY 1 Pretest
DAY 2 State the Generalization
DAY 3 Spelling Practice/Handwriting
DAY 4 Use Spelling Strategies/Review
DAY 5 Posttest

Review Spelling Words

REVIEW THE GENERALIZATION Tell students to draw a line down the center of a sheet of paper to make two columns, as you do the same on the board. Label the column on the left *VC*, put a slash mark (/) over the line dividing the columns, and label the right column *V*. Have students do the same. Ask students to name one of the VC/V spelling words, reminding them that the first vowel sound in a VC/V word is a short vowel sound. On the board, write the first syllable in the left-hand column. Write the second syllable in the right-hand column. Ask students to complete the chart by writing all of the VC/V spelling words. Have students check their work by comparing their chart with that of a partner. (rob/in, pet/al, sev/en, sol/id, giv/en, col/or, wag/on, cab/in)

WRITE Remind students that writing is an excellent strategy for practicing spelling. Have students select two colors of crayons, pencils, or markers. Instruct students to write the spelling words in their notebooks, using one color for all of the vowels, and another color for all of the consonants. Then have students develop a list of words that rhyme with the VC/V spelling words. If the rhymes are spelled similarly (petal, metal), have students circle them.

Handwriting

CORRECT SPACING Remind students that when they write, they should space their letters

- far enough apart that they can be read clearly.
- close enough together to show that they are part of the same word.

ADVANCED

Word Riddles Have students select three spelling words and write a riddle for each. Invite students to share one of their riddles with the class and call on their classmates to guess which word they have selected.

Objective

- *To use knowledge of V/CV and VC/C syllable patterns to spell and write words*

Spelling Words

1.	robin	9.	wagon
2.	petal	10.	music
3.	seven	11.	total
4.	solid	12.	cabin
5.	final	13.	taken
6.	given	14.	pupil
7.	color*	15.	broken
8.	hotel		

Challenge Words

16.	recital	19.	colony*
17.	vanish	20.	visiting
18.	regret		

*Words from "One Small Place in a Tree"

▲ Spelling Practice Book, p. 45

 Fluency
Intonation

Objectives

- *To build fluency through reading a selection*
- *To read with proper intonation*
- *To read in a manner that sounds like natural speech*

Additional Related Reading

- ***The Secret Life of Trees*** by Chiara Chevalier. Dorling Kindersley, 1999. **EASY**
- ***The Life of a Tree*** by Clare Hibbert. Raintree, 2004. **AVERAGE**
- ***Shelterwood*** by Susan Hand Shetterly. Tilbury House, 2003. **CHALLENGE**

BELOW-LEVEL

Fluency Practice Have students reread for fluency, using Story 14 in the *Strategic Intervention Interactive Reader* or the appropriate *Leveled Readers*. (See pages T366–369) Guide students to select a small portion of a story and practice reading it several times.

Review

 DIBELS Oral Reading Fluency **ORF** **MODEL READING WITH INTONATION** Remind students that when good readers read aloud, they make their voices sound like normal speech. Tell students that good readers also:

- emphasize important words by making their voices higher or lower
- make their voices go higher or lower to show emotion or expression
- end questions with a slightly higher voice and end statements with a slightly lower voice

(Think Aloud) (Say the first sentence in a monotone and the remaining sentences in a regular voice.) **I'm going to read the first page of "One Small Place in a Tree." As I read, I'm going to make sure I do not read in a voice like a robot with every word said the same way. I'm going to let my voice go higher and lower, just as it does now as I speak to you.**

 Routine Card **8** **ECHO-READING** Read aloud page 411 of "One Small Place in a Tree," modeling good intonation and remembering to change your voice for the questions. Have students echo your reading.

Practice/Apply

GUIDED PRACTICE Read aloud page 412 using a monotone. Then reread the same page using effective intonation. Ask students to tell how the two readings were different. Point out the anticipation in your voice at the end of the last sentence on the page. Have students read the same page aloud.

INDEPENDENT PRACTICE Have partners take turns reading aloud pages 413–414 of "One Small Place in a Tree." Have students note especially effective intonation when they hear it.

Author's Purpose
Comprehension

Review the Skill

EXPLAIN AUTHOR'S PURPOSE Remind students that an author's purpose for writing usually is to inform, entertain, or persuade. The text and the illustrations give clues about the author's purpose for writing.

Practice/Apply

GUIDED PRACTICE Guide students to briefly revisit "One Small Place in a Tree" to find what information the author wanted to share and to determine why the author may have felt this information was important. Have students read the text and look at the illustrations on each page listed below before answering the questions.

- **PAGE 416 What information did the author give on this page?** (This page tells how the hole was made bigger and how animals immediately moved in.) **Why do you think the author felt that this information was important?** (Possible response: It helps readers understand the life of a tree and how animals use it.)

- **PAGE 419 SECOND AND THIRD PARAGRAPHS Why did the author include this information?** (Possible response: to show that different animals used the same hole during different times of the year)

INDEPENDENT PRACTICE Remind students that the author's purpose for writing "One Small Place in a Tree" was to inform, so students should be looking for information as they read. Draw the chart below on the board, and have students copy it in their notebooks. Have students fill in the chart, putting two pieces of information from page 418 in the left-hand column and in the right-hand column explaining why the author included them.

Information from the text	Why the author included it

Objectives

- *To determine the author's purpose in nonfiction text*
- *To extract appropriate information from text*

Skill Trace

Tested **Author's Purpose**

Introduce	T215
Reteach	S42
Review	T249, T255, T277, T302–T303, T333, T349, T361, T412, T433
Test	Theme 3
Maintain	Theme 4, T348

Use Graphic Aids
Comprehension

Objectives

- *To recognize that graphic aids provide information*
- *To use illustrations to clarify information*

Skill Trace

 Ask Questions

Introduce	T250–T251
Reteach	S44
Review	T334–T335, T434
Test	Theme 3

 **MONITOR PROGRESS**

Use Graphic Aids

IF students have trouble understanding the many types of animals that find food and shelter in the hole that was made in the tree,	**THEN** have them look at the pictures and tell about the different creatures that are using the hole.

Small-Group Instruction, p. S44:

- ● **BELOW-LEVEL:** Reteach
- ● **ON-LEVEL:** Reinforce
- ○ **ADVANCED:** Extend

Teach/Model

INTRODUCE USE GRAPHIC AIDS Tell students that good readers use more than just the main text to understand a selection and that illustrations and other graphic aids often can give important information. Tell students that the words under or near illustrations are called *captions* and that they tell about the illustration. Explain that charts, graphs, and maps also offer important information. Tell students to use the following steps when they read selections that include graphic aids:

- Look at the pictures or maps and determine what they have to do with the words on the page.
- Read charts, graphs, and captions with pictures.
- If you are unsure of what you are reading, check the graphic aids for clues or helpful information.

Guided Practice

PRACTICE USING GRAPHIC AIDS Direct students to the illustrations on the following pages. Read aloud each question about "One Small Place in a Tree," and guide students to use the illustrations to answer the questions.

1. **Look at page 412. How does the bear sharpen her claws?** (She scratches the trunk.)
2. **Look at the picture on page 414. What do grubs look like?** (Grubs look like tiny worms.)
3. **Look at the picture on page 416. Why does the word *spear* describe how the woodpecker gets the beetles?** (The woodpecker's beak is long and sharp. The beak could stab the beetles.)

Practice/Apply

LOCATE INFORMATION IN GRAPHIC AIDS Ask the following question and have students write their answer.

Look at the picture on page 421. If you did not know what a red-back salamander is, what could you tell about it by looking at the picture? (Possible responses: It must be small because its eggs are small; It lays several eggs at one time.)

Invite volunteers to share the illustration in "One Small Place in a Tree" that was most helpful in understanding the selection, explaining what information the illustration provides.

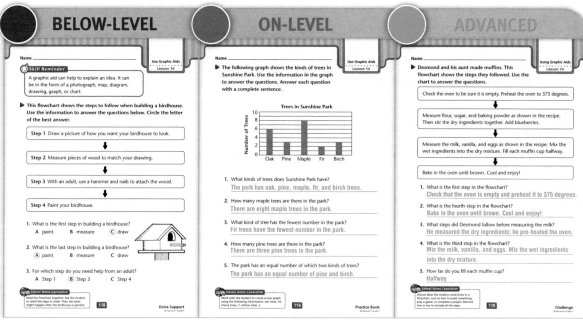

▲ Extra Support, p. 118   ▲ Practice Book, p. 118   ▲ Challenge, p. 118

E L L

- Group students according to academic levels and assign one of the pages on the left.

- Clarify any unfamiliar concepts as necessary. See *ELL Teacher Guide,* Lesson 14, for support in scaffolding instruction.

Reading
Student Edition: Paired Selection

Objective

- *To understand characteristics of nonfiction texts*

Genre Study

DISCUSS NONFICTION Tell students that "Be a Birdwatcher" is non-fiction because it presents information or ideas about real things.

TEXT FEATURES Remind students that nonfiction includes certain features that may include:

- facts about real things or events

- instructions on how to do or make something

- graphic aids, such as photographs, illustrations, or maps

USE PRIOR KNOWLEDGE/SET A PURPOSE Read aloud the title "Be a Birdwatcher" and point out the photographs. Direct students' attention to the binoculars the people are holding, asking how this helps them understand what the selection is about. (Possible response: It tells readers that it is about watching birds.)

Point out that much of the information in "Be a Birdwatcher" is in a list and that lists in nonfiction often have numbers or round bullet marks to separate items. This helps highlight the important information and make it stand out. Remind students that one purpose for reading nonfiction is to learn information. Discuss with students what they already know about the topic. Tell them they will read to find out how to be a good birdwatcher.

Respond to the Selection

MONITOR COMPREHENSION As students read, monitor comprehension by asking the following questions:

- **COMPARE AND CONTRAST What are some ways to tell different kinds of birds apart?** (Possible responses: color, size, beak, movement, song)

- **GENRE CHECK Does "Be a Birdwatcher" give facts or made-up information?** (facts) **How is this different from fiction?** (Nonfiction gives real information; fiction is made up.)

Writing Prompt

Reflect Have students write about whether they would like to be a birdwatcher. Direct them to include reasons to explain why or why not.

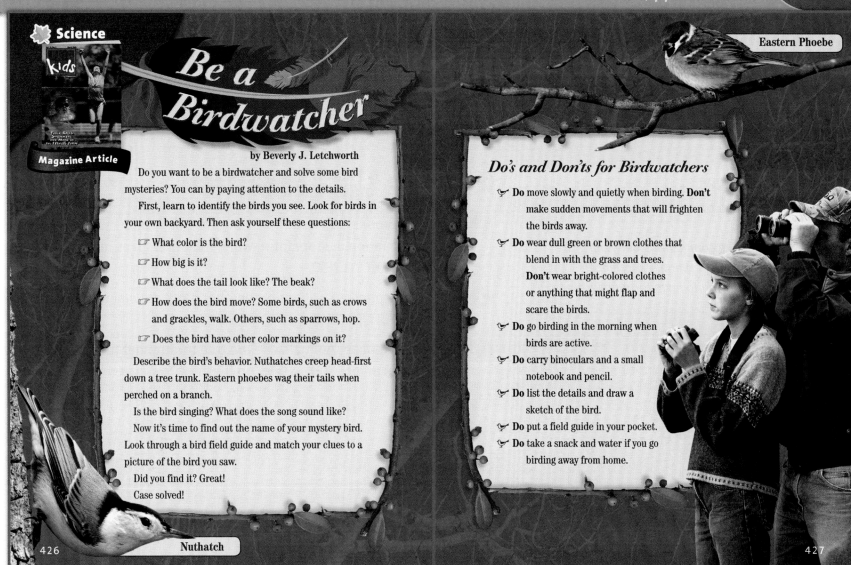

Science Kids

Magazine Article

Be a Birdwatcher

by Beverly J. Letchworth

Do you want to be a birdwatcher and solve some bird mysteries? You can by paying attention to the details.

First, learn to identify the birds you see. Look for birds in your own backyard. Then ask yourself these questions:

☞ What color is the bird?

☞ How big is it?

☞ What does the tail look like? The beak?

☞ How does the bird move? Some birds, such as crows and grackles, walk. Others, such as sparrows, hop.

☞ Does the bird have other color markings on it?

Describe the bird's behavior. Nuthatches creep head-first down a tree trunk. Eastern phoebes wag their tails when perched on a branch.

Is the bird singing? What does the song sound like?

Now it's time to find out the name of your mystery bird. Look through a bird field guide and match your clues to a picture of the bird you saw.

Did you find it? Great!

Case solved!

426   **Nuthatch**

Eastern Phoebe

Do's and Don'ts for Birdwatchers

🐦 **Do** move slowly and quietly when birding. **Don't** make sudden movements that will frighten the birds away.

🐦 **Do** wear dull green or brown clothes that blend in with the grass and trees. **Don't** wear bright-colored clothes or anything that might flap and scare the birds.

🐦 **Do** go birding in the morning when birds are active.

🐦 **Do** carry binoculars and a small notebook and pencil.

🐦 **Do** list the details and draw a sketch of the bird.

🐦 **Do** put a field guide in your pocket.

🐦 **Do** take a snack and water if you go birding away from home.

427

SCIENCE   SUPPORTING STANDARDS

Nuthatches Point out the bird in the photo on page 426 of the *Student Edition* and explain that it is a nuthatch. Nuthatches were named for the way they eat. They wedge their food, usually nuts or insects, into the bark of a tree. Then they use their beaks to hack open the food. These birds walk head first down tree trunks. They walk the same way underneath branches. They use their sharp claws to hang on to the bark of the tree. By walking upside down, with their backs facing the ground, they are able to see food hiding in the tree bark that other birds may not see. Ask students how this unusual feeding habit might help nuthatches survive.

E L L

Build Background Point out the binoculars the people are using in the picture on page 427 and point out the word *binoculars* in the text. Explain that binoculars are used to see things far away. Ask why these might be an important tool for watching birds.

Connections

Objectives

- *To make connections between texts*
- *To make connections between texts and personal experiences*
- *To respond to texts through writing*

Answers

1. Possible responses: The author's purpose in both is to inform; One gives information in story form, while the other gives information in a list form. **TEXT TO TEXT**

2. Possible response: I will notice whether birds are making a nest in the tree. **TEXT TO SELF**

3. Possible response: Animals use the tree throughout the tree's life and after its death. **TEXT TO WORLD**

Connections

Comparing Texts

1. How is the author's purpose in "One Small Place in a Tree" like the author's purpose in "Be a Birdwatcher?" How is it different?

2. What do you think you will notice about the next tree you see?

3. Why is a tree important to its environment?

Vocabulary Review

Word Webs

Work with a partner. Choose two Vocabulary Words and create a word web for each word. Put the Vocabulary Word in the center of your web. Then write words that are related to the Vocabulary Word in the web. Share your word web with your partner. Explain how each word in your web is related to the Vocabulary Word.

roost

suppose
roost
spears
strikes
glimpse
maze

Fluency Practice

Partner Reading

Choose a section from "One Small Place in a Tree." Meet with a partner. Take turns reading aloud. Let your voice rise and fall naturally. Have your partner give you feedback about your reading.

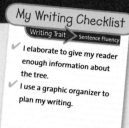

Writing

Write a Retelling

Write a paragraph that tells about the tree in "One Small Place in a Tree." Include events from the beginning, middle, and end of the selection. Share your paragraph with a partner.

My Writing Checklist

> Writing Trait ▸ Sentence Fluency

✓ I elaborate to give my reader enough information about the tree.

✓ I use a graphic organizer to plan my writing.

Beginning	Middle	End

428

429

VOCABULARY

Word Webs Assist students as they brainstorm words that go with the Vocabulary Words. Encourage students to use synonyms and antonyms in their word webs.

FLUENCY

Partner Reading Remind students that good readers make their reading voices sound like natural conversation. Encourage them to think about what is written in the text and how the sentences would sound if the student were telling someone the material rather than reading it. Encourage students to give each other positive feedback.

WRITING

Write a Retelling Have students complete the graphic organizer and use the information to write their paragraphs. Have students use their checklist to evaluate their writing. Students may choose to place their paragraphs in their portfolios.

 PORTFOLIO OPPORTUNITY

Build Robust Vocabulary

Objectives

- *To review rich vocabulary*
- *To demonstrate knowledge of word meaning*

REVIEW | Tested ✓

Vocabulary: Lesson 14

sprout	strikes
damp	glimpse
suppose	maze
roost	transformation
spears	harmony

Review Robust Vocabulary

USE VOCABULARY IN DIFFERENT CONTEXTS Remind students of the meanings of the Vocabulary Words introduced on Days 1 and 2. Then guide them to discuss each word in a new context.

sprout

- **Have you ever planted seeds and waited for them to sprout? If so, what type of seeds did you plant? How long did it take for them to sprout?**

damp

- **What do you think it is like to go out into cold, damp weather? How would it feel?**
- **What do you do with damp towels after swimming?**

transformation

- **What kind of transformation happens to a tadpole?**

harmony

- **How do people act when they are living in harmony with one another?**
- **What pets might not live in harmony with one another? Why?**

suppose

- **Which makes more sense: to ask what you suppose you will have for dinner tonight, or to ask what you suppose you had for dinner last night? Why?**

roost

- Does a hen roost, or does a hamster roost?

- Which would be roosting, a sitting bird or a flying bird?

strikes

- If an idea strikes you, does it come slowly or quickly?

- If a ball strikes you, does it hit you or miss you?

spears

- Do you need a long, sharp stick or a short, fat stick to spear something?

- If you wanted to spear a strawberry, would you use a toothpick or a spoon?

glimpse

- If you walked in the forest, what might you catch a glimpse of—a rabbit or a lot of trees?

- If you caught a glimpse of a person turning a corner, why might you not be certain who the person is?

maze

- If a building is like a maze, is it easy or difficult for you to find your way around?

- Do you think it would be fun to be in a maze? Why or why not?

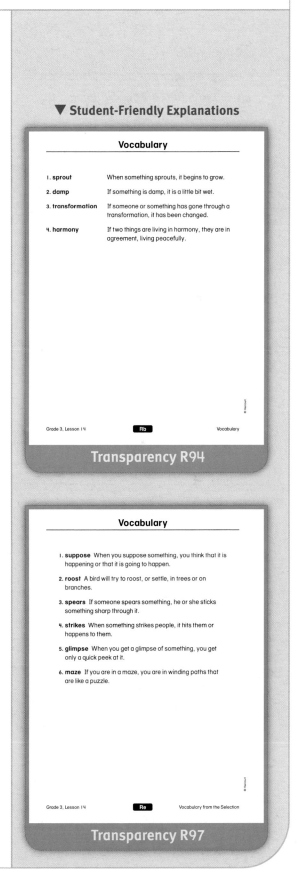

▼ **Student-Friendly Explanations**

Vocabulary

1. **sprout**   When something sprouts, it begins to grow.
2. **damp**   If something is damp, it is a little bit wet.
3. **transformation**   If someone or something has gone through a transformation, it has been changed.
4. **harmony**   If two things are living in harmony, they are in agreement, living peacefully.

Grade 3, Lesson 14   Rb   Vocabulary

Transparency R94

Vocabulary

1. **suppose**   When you suppose something, you think that it is happening or that it is going to happen.
2. **roost**   A bird will try to roost, or settle, in trees or on branches.
3. **spears**   If someone spears something, he or she sticks something sharp through it.
4. **strikes**   When something strikes people, it hits them or happens to them.
5. **glimpse**   When you get a glimpse of something, you get only a quick peek at it.
6. **maze**   If you are in a maze, you are in winding paths that are like a puzzle.

Grade 3, Lesson 14   Re   Vocabulary from the Selection

Transparency R97

Grammar
Pronoun-Antecedent Agreement

5-DAY GRAMMAR	
DAY 1	Define Antecedent
DAY 2	Agreement in Number
DAY 3	**Agreement in Gender**
DAY 4	Apply to Writing
DAY 5	Pronoun-Antecedent Agreement Review

Objectives

- *To use gender agreement between pronouns and antecedents*
- *To identify antecedents in sentences*

Daily Proofreading

1. Amy asked him, "Mom, can me have my allowance."
   (asked her; can I have my)
2. Jane told Mike her would help with him homework (she would; his homework.)

▲ Grammar Practice Book, p. 50

Teach/Model

DISCUSS GENDER AGREEMENT Write this sentence on the board:

> **Emma studies birds. He has learned a lot about bluebirds.**

Read aloud the sentences and have students identify the pronoun (He) and the antecedent. (Emma) Ask what is wrong with using the pronoun *He* in the second sentence. (*He* refers to a male, and Emma is a female.) Explain that the pronouns *he* and *him* should be used for males and *she* and *her* for females. Ask what pronoun would agree with the antecedent *Emma*. (She) Have a volunteer correct the sentence. Point out that if the antecedent is a thing, the pronoun *it* is used.

Guided Practice

MATCH PRONOUNS AND ANTECEDENTS Ask several students to name people they know. Write the names as a list on the board. In a second list, write the pronouns *he, him, she,* and *her*. Explain that any name can be an antecedent. Choose one of the male names on the list and underline it. Ask students which pronouns can be used in place of the name. (*he, him*) Do the same with one of the female names. (*she, her*) Continue with several more examples, sometimes beginning with one of the pronouns and asking students to select a name.

Practice/Apply

USE ANTECEDENTS IN WRITING Have students select a male and a female name from the list on the board or two other names of their choosing. Have them write sentences, using each name and one or more of the pronouns. Invite students to share their sentences with the class.

Writing
Cause-and-Effect Paragraph

5-DAY WRITING

DAY 1	Introduce
DAY 2	Prewrite
DAY 3	**Prewrite**
DAY 4	Draft
DAY 5	Revise/Edit

Prewrite

REVIEW A LITERATURE MODEL Draw the following graphic organizer on the board:

Cause: The tree fell down.	→	**Effect:** (a garden snake went into the log to cool off)
	→	**Effect:** (a red salamander laid its eggs in the log)
	→	**Effect:** (a spider made a web)

Have students read page 421 in "One Small Place in a Tree" to find three things that happened because the tree fell. Then work with them to fill in the graphic organizer. Point out the following:

> ### Cause-and-Effect Paragraphs
> - Include the cause or the effect in the first sentence
> - Use key words to show a relationship between the cause and the effect
> - May include several effects or several causes

PREWRITE A CAUSE-AND-EFFECT PARAGRAPH Tell students to draw a graphic organizer like the one on the board and to select a cause they might like to write about. Then instruct them to complete the graphic organizer. Remind students to use gender-appropriate pronouns.

DRAFT TOPIC SENTENCE Have students select one of their completed graphic organizers. Explain that the information in the single box on the left will be included in the topic sentence of the cause-and-effect paragraph. Have students write a topic sentence.

SENTENCE FLUENCY: ELABORATION Remind students that when they write their paragraphs, they will want to include details that explain the causes and effects.

CONFER WITH STUDENTS Meet with individual students, helping them as they write and offering encouragement.

Objectives
- *To recognize cause and effect in writing*
- *To use graphic organizers to prepare for writing*
- *To draft an effective topic sentence*

Writing Prompt

Reflect Have students write their thoughts about the ways in which living things are connected and depend on one another.

▲ Writer's Companion, Lesson 14

ADVANCED

Use Varied Sentence Structure
Encourage students to try using a question or an exclamation as their topic sentence. Ask students how they feel this will affect the readers' interest in their writing and the quality of the completed paragraph.

Warm-Up Routines

phonics and Spelling

- Review: V/CV and VC/V Syllable Patterns
- Review: Spelling Strategies

Fluency

- Intonation
- "One Small Place in a Tree," *Student Edition*, pp. 408–425

Read!

Comprehension

- Review: Author's Purpose
- Maintain: Main Idea and Details

Speaking/Listening

- Presentation of Writing

Robust Vocabulary

- Review: *sprout, damp, suppose, roost, spears, strikes, glimpse, maze, transformation, harmony*

Grammar

- Review: Pronoun-Antecedent Agreement

Writing

- Cause-and-Effect Paragraph

Oral Language

Objectives *To listen attentively and respond appropriately to oral communication; to express thoughts in an organized manner*

> **Question of the Day**
>
> What makes a good home for a person?
>
> What makes a good home for an animal?

Ask students to think about their homes and what makes it a good home for people. Then ask students what makes a good home for an animal. Then discuss how good animal and human homes are alike and different. Remind students to stay on the topic of homes as they speak. When several ideas have been shared, ask students to respond in their notebooks to the questions.

Students should write one or two sentences answering the prompt. Invite students to share their ideas with the class.

Read Aloud

Objectives *To listen attentively and respond appropriately to oral communications; to set a purpose for listening*

READ ALOUD A STORY Display **Transparency R99** or distribute photocopies to students. Tell them you are going to read the selection "The Perfect Pastime."

Set a purpose. Ask students what a *pastime* is (a hobby) and what the purpose might be for reading a selection called "The Perfect Pastime." (Possible response: to find out about a pastime, for enjoyment) Tell students to listen to find out about the pastime and to find the author's purpose.

Model fluent reading. Read the selection aloud, modeling good intonation as you read.

Discuss the selection. Talk with students about the selection using the following questions:

• Why does the author say birdwatching is the perfect hobby?

• What is the author's purpose for writing the selection?

• What information helped you determine the author's purpose?

The Perfect Pastime

Everyone needs a hobby, and birdwatching is by far the best hobby anyone could have. It offers a chance to be outdoors and breathe fresh air. It also is relaxing.

As you can imagine, it is exciting to walk in the woods and search for birds in their forest homes. It is thrilling to find a kind of bird that you might have only seen before in books. Another reason why birdwatching is great is that there is always something new to see. There are different kinds of birds to see at different times of the year. The forest changes, too, as the year goes on, and so do the other animals that live there.

If you have never been birdwatching, you should give it a try. You might even want to try a birdwatching club. In fact, that is the best way to take up the hobby. Look for one in the phone book or on the Internet. Join now. You'll be glad you did.

Grade 3, Lesson 14   **R9**   Warm-Up: Days 4–5

Transparency R99

V/CV and VC/V Syllable Patterns phonics

5-DAY PHONICS	
DAY 1	Introduce V/CV and VC/V Patterns
DAY 2	Words with V/CV Pattern
DAY 3	Words with VC/V Pattern
DAY 4	**Identify Vowel Patterns in Words**
DAY 5	Review V/CV and VC/V Syllable Patterns

Objectives

- *To identify V/CV and VC/V syllable patterns in words*
- *To use V/CV and VC/V patterns to decode multisyllabic words*

Skill Trace

 V/CV and VC/V Syllable Patterns

Introduce	Grade 2
Reintroduce	T300
Reteach	S38
Review	T310–T311, T330, T346, T358, T420
Test	Theme 3

Words with V/CV and VC/V Syllable Patterns

Part A

music color given broken

Part B

We have a cabin by the river. Our family has a habit of going there each Friday. We begin our trip at seven o'clock at night. It is great to get to that cozy house. Even if we never went outside, it would be a fun trip. But no day inside can equal a day on the open water. I will recall every detail of our weekends together for many years into the future.

Grade 3, Lesson 14   Rh   Phonics: Day 4

Transparency R100

Review

REVIEW V/CV AND VC/V SYLLABLE PATTERNS Remind students that words are made up of syllables and that each syllable has only one vowel sound. Explain that the first vowel in V/CV words is pronounced with a long vowel sound and that the first vowel in VC/V words is pronounced with a short vowel sound. Remind students that these syllable patterns are a good way to remember how to decode words. Write *final* and *habit* on the board, guiding volunteers to divide the words into syllables. Then help volunteers label the first vowels as long or short. (fi/nal, long; hab/it, short)

V/CV AND VC/V PATTERNS Display **Transparency R100** or distribute photocopies to students. Direct students to Part A and ask them to identify the words with the V/CV syllable pattern. (music, broken) Then have students identify the words with the VC/V syllable pattern. (color, given) Together, divide the words into syllables and mark the first vowel in each word to show the long or short sound. (mu/sic, long; col/or, short; giv/en, short; bro/ken, long)

Practice/Apply

GUIDED PRACTICE Direct students to Part B of **Transparency R100** and have them identify the VCV words in the first sentence. (cabin, river) Then have them read the paragraph aloud.

INDEPENDENT PRACTICE Have students list the VCV words from the paragraph. Instruct students to underline the VCV letters. Then have students divide the words into syllables and tell whether the sound of the first vowel is long or short. (cab/in, riv/er, hab/it, Fri/day, be/gin, sev/en, co/zy, e/ven, nev/er, e/qual, o/pen, wat/er, re/call, de/tail, man/y, fu/ture)

V/CV and VC/V Syllable Patterns phonics and Spelling

5-DAY SPELLING
DAY 1 Pretest
DAY 2 State the Generalization
DAY 3 Spelling Practice/Handwriting
DAY 4 Use Spelling Strategies/Review
DAY 5 Posttest

Use Spelling Strategies

SYLLABLE PATTERNS Make two columns on the board. Label the first column *V/CV* and the second *VC/V*. Explain that the word *robin* has the VCV spelling pattern. Ask whether the first vowel sound in *robin* is short or long. (short) Ask if the syllables in *robin* are divided after the first vowel or after the consonant that follows. (consonant) Write the word *robin* in the VC/V column on the board and divide it into syllables. Repeat with the remaining Spelling Words. (VC/V: pet/al, sev/en, sol/id, giv/en, col/or, wag/on, cab/in; V/CV: fi/nal, ho/tel, mu/sic, to/tal, ta/ken, pu/pil, bro/ken)

APPLY TO WRITING Explain to students that when they look for letter patterns, they should think about the way a word looks and sounds. Have students read through an unedited piece of their writing, paying close attention to the vowel sounds in the words. Have students look for words that they think might be misspelled. Direct students to underline some of these words and see if what they know about the V/CV and VC/V syllable patterns can help them determine the correct spellings of the words. Then have students use a dictionary to confirm the correct spellings of some of the words.

Objective
• *To use syllable patterns to spell multisyllabic words*

Spelling Words
1. robin
2. petal
3. seven
4. solid
5. final
6. given
7. color*
8. hotel
9. wagon
10. music
11. total
12. cabin
13. taken
14. pupil
15. broken

Challenge Words
16. recital
17. vanish
18. regret
19. colony*
20. visiting

*Words from "One Small Place in a Tree"

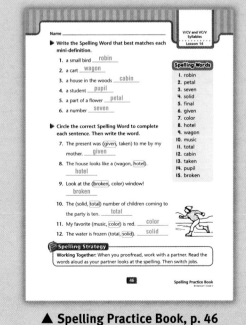

▲ Spelling Practice Book, p. 46

ADVANCED
Missing Letters Write the spelling words on the board in random order, using only the consonants. Have students determine which vowels are missing and write the words correctly.

p_t_l   m_s_c
f_n_l   c_b_n

Fluency
Intonation

Objectives

- *To build fluency through reading a selection*
- *To read with proper intonation*
- *To read in a manner that sounds like natural speech*

BELOW-LEVEL

Fluency Practice Ask students to think about how they would feel if they saw a bear in the woods. Have them imagine telling a friend about the sighting. Then read aloud page 412 twice, with and without effective intonation. Ask which sounds more believable and more interesting.

MONITOR PROGRESS

Fluency

IF students are having trouble using intonation to reflect ending punctuation,	**THEN** read aloud sentences from the selection that end in a period, a question mark, or an exclamation mark, and point out the differences in your voice.

Small-Group Instruction, p. S40:

- ● **BELOW-LEVEL:** Reteach
- ● **ON-LEVEL:** Reinforce
- ● **ADVANCED:** Extend

Review

 DIBELS Oral Reading Fluency **ORF**

MODEL READING WITH INTONATION Remind students that when good readers read aloud, their voices rise and fall as if they were telling a story or having a conversation. Tell them that as they read, they should:

▲ *Student Edition*, pp. 408–425

- think about the way the words would sound in normal conversation
- look ahead to be able to emphasize important words or phrases
- pay attention to punctuation

Think Aloud **As I read part of "One Small Place in a Tree," I am going to think about the words and punctuation as I read, so I can use my voice to emphasize important words.**

Read aloud page 419, modeling appropriate intonation. Direct students' attention to the last paragraph. Point out that most of the paragraph is talking about the tree being dead, so you made your voice lower as you read to indicate some sadness. Point out that a dash indicates a longer pause and often signals a contrast to the part of the sentence that comes before it. Remind students that you read the part of the sentence after the dash in a lively, higher voice.

Practice/Apply

 Routine Card 9

PARTNER-READING Have students partner-read pages 419–422 of "One Small Place in a Tree." Tell them to read each sentence silently before reading it aloud and to think about how their voices would sound if they were telling someone the words rather than reading them. Remind them to think about which words need emphasis and how to use intonation to show end punctuation.

Author's Purpose
Comprehension

Review

EXPLAIN AUTHOR'S PURPOSE Ask: **What are some of the reasons that authors write?** (to inform, to entertain, to persuade). **How can readers determine the author's purpose?** (by looking for clues such as whether the selection tells facts or is a story) Remind students that knowing why an author wrote a selection can help readers set their own purposes for reading. It can also help readers understand the text. Ask what the author's purpose would be for writing a textbook (to inform), a comic book (to entertain), and a commercial ad (to persuade).

Practice/Apply

GUIDED PRACTICE Display **Transparency R93.** Tell students to listen for clues about the author's purpose as you read the passage aloud. When you finish reading, ask:

- **What is the author of this selection telling you about?** (the importance of dead trees)

- **What was the author's purpose and why do you think that?** (to inform; the author gives information about how animals use the snags before and after they fall)

REREAD THE SELECTION Have students open the *Student Edition* to page 416 of "One Small Place in a Tree." Remind them that the author's purpose for this story was to inform, so they will be reading to find information. Have students read to find what information the author wanted to tell readers on this page. (Woodpeckers ate the beetles, which made the hole bigger. Bacteria got into the tree and caused disease, which eventually killed the tree.)

Objectives

- *To identify the author's purpose in nonfiction text*
- *To determine the author's message and extract important information from text*

Skill Trace
 Tested **Author's Purpose**

Introduce	T215
Reteach	S42
Review	T249, T265, T277, T302–T303, T333, T349, T361, T412, T433
Test	Theme 3
Maintain	Theme 4, T348

Full of Life

You might think that an old, dead tree standing in a forest is just an eyesore. Think again. Standing dead trees are called "snags," and snags are important to many kinds of wildlife. Wood ducks, woodpeckers, eagles, and owls build nests in snags. Hawks often use snags as perches. Many small animals such as raccoons, mice, and squirrels also call these hollowed out trees their home.

To us, some of the creatures living in snags are pests. Plenty of ants, beetles, spiders, and earthworms are found in wildlife trees. However, these tiny tenants are an important sources of food for many other species.

Snags may look ready to fall over any minute, but some large trees can stand for more than 150 years after they have died! So, when you see a dead tree, think of the life inside. What may look like an eyesore is actually home-sweet-home to many of our forest friends.

Grade 3, Lesson 14   R9   Warm-Up: Day 1

Transparency R93

Main Idea and Details

Objectives

- *To identify main idea and details in expository text*
- *To infer main idea*

Skill Trace

 Tested Main Idea and Details

Introduce	Theme 2, T217
Reteach	Theme 2, S30
Review	Theme 2, T247, T264, T273, T298–T299, T329, T345, T357, T410, T431
Test	Theme 2
Maintain	T350

Reinforce the Skill

REVIEW MAIN IDEA AND DETAILS Review with students that the main idea is the most important idea in a passage and that details support the main idea. Remind students that sometimes the author states the main idea in a sentence. Other times, the reader has to think about the details in the passage to decide the main idea. Invite students to open their *Student Edition* to page 416.

> **Think Aloud** As I read the last paragraph, I see that the first sentence is "Now disease strikes." Then I read the details. I ask myself, "What do these details have in common?" They are all about the bacteria in the tree. Then the last sentence says about the tree, "It's dying inside and out." So the main idea must be a combination of all of these parts: "Bacteria are killing the tree."

Practice/Apply

GUIDED PRACTICE Read aloud page 47 of the *Read-Aloud Anthology*. Reread the first sentence and elicit from students that this sentence starts the sequence of events described on the page. Ask students to name some important details from the passage. (Possible responses: The tall oak begins to topple; the wind tears the oak's roots; the tree crashes down.) Write them on the board. Then, with students, use the information in the first sentence and the details to determine the main idea. (The storm makes the tree fall.)

INDEPENDENT PRACTICE Have students read page 426 of "Be a Birdwatcher." Have them find the important details and then write the main idea in their notebooks. (Possible response: Paying attention to details can help you solve bird mysteries.)

Speaking and Listening
Presentation of Writing

Speaking

GIVE A PRESENTATION Have students publish their cause-and-effect paragraphs by reading them to the class. Encourage them to speak expressively in order to show their opinions about their topic. Share these **organizational tips** with students.

ORGANIZING CONTENT

- Read through your paragraph to become familiar with the words you have chosen.

- Underline each cause.

- Draw two lines under each effect.

Before students make their presentations before a small group, share the list of **speaking strategies** on the right with them. After each student's presentation, encourage audience members to ask questions. Encourage speakers to clarify their points, for example by providing insight into why things happened.

Listening

LISTEN FOR OPINIONS Before students listen to the presentations, share the list of **listening strategies** on the right with them. Invite them to listen for clues about how the speaker feels by listening to the speaker's words and tone of voice.

Invite volunteers to point out the cause or causes. Then have those volunteers try to identify the speaker's opinion about each of those causes. Remind students that listeners often can tell how speakers feel by how they present facts and information.

See rubrics for Speaking and Listening on page R5.

SPEAKING STRATEGIES

- Practice speaking in front of others. Ask for suggestions on how to improve your presentation.
- Make eye contact with the audience.
- Keep your voice steady and use expressive intonation.

LISTENING STRATEGIES

- Pay attention throughout the presentation.
- Listen for the speaker's tone of voice.
- Watch the speaker's movements and facial expressions.

Build Robust Vocabulary

Objectives

- *To review robust vocabulary*
- *To demonstrate knowledge of word meaning*

 **REVIEW** Tested ✓

Vocabulary: Lesson 14

sprout	**strikes**
damp	**glimpse**
suppose	**maze**
roost	**transformation**
spears	**harmony**

Extend Word Meanings

USE VOCABULARY IN DIFFERENT CONTEXTS Remind students of the meanings of the Vocabulary Words. Then discuss each word in a new context.

sprout Tell students that if you name something that might sprout, they should stand up and imitate a plant that is growing. If it will not sprout, they should remain in their seats.

a flower seed	**a rock**
a chair	**weeds**

damp Tell students if you name something that might be damp, students should pretend to dry themselves with a towel. If you name something that is not damp, they should shake their heads.

a cactus in the desert	**a towel in a bathroom**
a runner after a long race	**a swimmer**

transformation Read these changes. If they are transformations, students should nod their head "yes." If they are not, students should shake their head "no."

a tadpole becomes a frog

a child puts on a new shirt

a caterpillar becomes a butterfly

dough becomes bread

harmony Tell students that if you name something in harmony, they should purr like a happy kitten. If they are not in harmony, students should growl like a hungry lion.

brothers arguing over who is stronger

a family enjoying a meal

football teams battling in a game

musicians playing in an orchestra

Word Relationships

HOMOGRAPHS Have students find the word *watch* on page 411 of the *Student Edition*. Explain that *watch* has more than one meaning. Guide students to name the meanings. (to look at closely; to observe; something that shows time) Do the same with *chips* on page 413 (small pieces of bark; potato slices; to break off tiny pieces) and *bore* on page 414. (to make a hole; someone or something uninteresting)

Tell students that words with more than one meaning are called homographs. Write the following words on the board:

record   present   desert

Read the words aloud with each of their pronunciations. Tell students that some homographs have more than one pronunciation and that the only way to tell the correct pronunciation is to read the rest of the sentence. Then ask students to suggest a sentence for each meaning. Remind students that as they read, they should think about which meaning the author intends.

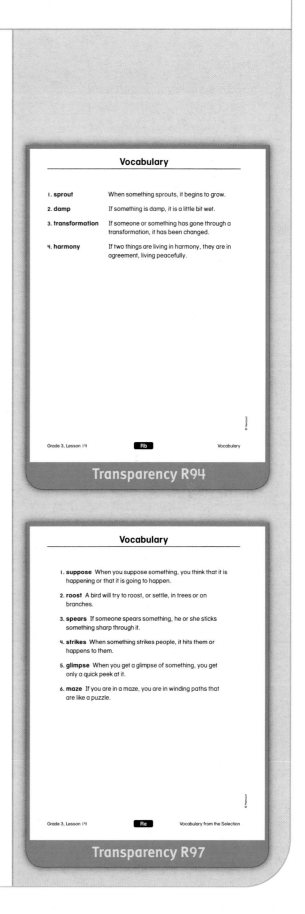

Vocabulary

1. **sprout** When something sprouts, it begins to grow.
2. **damp** If something is damp, it is a little bit wet.
3. **transformation** If someone or something has gone through a transformation, it has been changed.
4. **harmony** If two things are living in harmony, they are in agreement, living peacefully.

Grade 3, Lesson 14   **Rb**   Vocabulary

Transparency R94

Vocabulary

1. **suppose** When you suppose something, you think that it is happening or that it is going to happen.
2. **roost** A bird will try to roost, or settle, in trees or on branches.
3. **spears** If someone spears something, he or she sticks something sharp through it.
4. **strikes** When something strikes people, it hits them or happens to them.
5. **glimpse** When you get a glimpse of something, you get only a quick peek at it.
6. **maze** If you are in a maze, you are in winding paths that are like a puzzle.

Grade 3, Lesson 14   **Re**   Vocabulary from the Selection

Transparency R97

Grammar
Pronoun-Antecedent Agreement

5-DAY GRAMMAR

DAY 1	Define Antecedent
DAY 2	Agreement in Number
DAY 3	Agreement in Gender
DAY 4	**Apply to Writing**
DAY 5	Pronoun-Antecedent Agreement Review

Objectives

- *To use agreement between pronouns and antecedents*
- *To identify antecedents in sentences*

Daily Proofreading

1. Did Derrick ride him bike to school on Monday! (his bike; Monday?)
2. my room was a mess so i cleaned her. (My room; I cleaned it.)

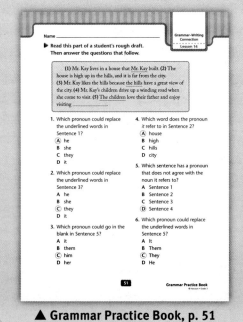

▲ Grammar Practice Book, p. 51

Review

DISCUSS PRONOUN-ANTECEDENT AGREEMENT Review that a pronoun takes the place of a noun and that the antecedent is the noun that is being replaced. Remind students that a singular antecedent needs a singular pronoun and that a plural antecedent needs a plural pronoun. Remind students that pronouns must have the same gender—male or female or none—as their antecedents.

Practice/Apply

GUIDED PRACTICE On the board, write the following sentences, leaving blank lines for the pronouns and antecedents:

> **Cindy says (she) loves Grandpa's house. (She/Cindy) always spends part of summer vacation there. Cindy says, "(He/Grandpa) has a pool and (he) lets (me) swim in (it) every day!"**

Have students tell what pronouns or antecedents could be written in the blanks to correctly complete each sentence and why. Fill in their answers on the board. Ask students to think of other statements with pronouns and antecedents that could be added to the end of the story.

INDEPENDENT PRACTICE Have students think of something that they like to do with their family or friends. Then have students write a paragraph telling about that activity. Explain that their writing should include at least four sets of pronouns and antecedents and that they should use both singular and plural pronouns. Have volunteers share their paragraphs with the class. Tell students to listen for pronoun-antecedent agreement as their classmates share their stories.

Writing
Cause-and-Effect Paragraph

Day 4

5-DAY WRITING	
DAY 1	Introduce
DAY 2	Prewrite
DAY 3	Prewrite
DAY 4	Draft
DAY 5	Revise/Edit

Draft

REVIEW A LITERATURE MODEL Have students read page 416 of their *Student Edition*. Call attention to the causes of the tree's death. Point out the following traits of a strong cause-and-effect paragraph.

Cause-and-Effect Paragraphs

- Include the cause or the effect in the first sentence
- Use key words to explain the relationship between the cause and the effect
- Include several effects or several causes to explain the effect

DRAFT A PARAGRAPH Have students use their topic sentences and their cause-and-effect graphic organizers to write a draft of a cause-and-effect paragraph. Point out that the remaining sentences in the paragraph should clearly support the cause or the effect that they stated in the first sentence. Remind students that they will be able to revise their writing later and that they should not worry at this point about making their writing perfect.

SENTENCE FLUENCY: ELABORATION Tell students that their sentences need to include enough details to explain why and how the event happened. If students are using pronouns to discuss the event, encourage them to check any pronouns they use for pronoun–antecedent agreement.

Objectives

- *To draft a cause-and-effect paragraph*
- *To include details in writing*

Writing Prompt

Analysis Have students choose a paragraph from "One Small Place in a Tree" that demonstrates good use of elaboration and write about how the details are used effectively.

BELOW-LEVEL

Elaboration If students are having trouble using elaboration in their sentences, have them read their work aloud to you or to a partner. At the end of each sentence, ask a question that could be answered by adding more details. Use question words such as *where*, *why*, or *how*.

Day at a Glance

Day 5

 **and Spelling**

- Review: V/CV and VC/V Syllable Patterns
- Posttest

Fluency

- Intonation
- "One Small Place in a Tree," *Student Edition*, pp. 408–425

 **Read!**

Comprehension

 Review: Author's Purpose

- Read-Aloud Anthology: "A Log's Life"

Robust Vocabulary

- Cumulative Review

Grammar

- Review: Pronoun-Antecedent Agreement

Writing

- Cause-and-Effect Paragraph

Warm-Up Routines

Oral Language

Objectives *To listen attentively and respond appropriately to oral communication; to write and speak in complete sentences*

Question of the Day

In what ways does a forest change over time?

Ask students to think about baby pictures of themselves, or to think about babies they know. Discuss how they have changed. Ask students to compare what they would see if they visited a forest in which all of the trees were very young, and a forest where the trees were very old. Encourage all students to participate in the conversation, but remind them to stay on topic.

After students have shared several ideas, ask them to complete the following writing prompt in their notebooks:

Over time, a forest _____.

Students should include several examples and write complete sentences. Invite students to share their writing with the class.

Read Aloud

Objectives *To listen and respond critically to oral communication; to set a purpose for listening*

REVIEW THE TEXT Display **Transparency R99** or distribute photocopies to the students. Tell students you are going to reread "The Perfect Pastime," and then they will read with a partner.

Set a purpose. Ask students why they might want to reread or listen to a story again. (to practice reading or listening; to get information; for enjoyment) Remind students that the selection is written to persuade, so readers must carefully judge the information by asking: What is fact and what is the author's opinion?

Model fluent reading. Read the selection aloud, making your voice rise and fall to model intonation.

Partner reading. Have students work with a partner to read the last paragraph aloud. Instruct one partner to read while the other listens and then offers feedback about the reading. Partners should then switch roles.

The Perfect Pastime

Everyone needs a hobby, and birdwatching is by far the best hobby anyone could have. It offers a chance to be outdoors and breathe fresh air. It also is relaxing.

As you can imagine, it is exciting to walk in the woods and search for birds in their forest homes. It is thrilling to find a kind of bird that you might have only seen before in books. Another reason why birdwatching is great is that there is always something new to see. There are different kinds of birds to see at different times of the year. The forest changes, too, as the year goes on, and so do the other animals that live there.

If you have never been birdwatching, you should give it a try. You might even want to try a birdwatching club. In fact, that is the best way to take up the hobby. Look for one in the phone book or on the Internet. Join now. You'll be glad you did.

Grade 3, Lesson 14   Rg   Warm-Up: Days 4–5

Transparency R99

V/CV and VC/V Syllable Patterns

5-DAY PHONICS	
DAY 1	Introduce V/CV and VC/V Patterns
DAY 2	Words with V/CV Pattern
DAY 3	Words with VC/V Pattern
DAY 4	Identifying Vowel Patterns in Words
DAY 5	Review V/CV and VC/V Syllable Patterns

Objectives

- *To identify V/CV and VC/V syllable patterns in words*
- *To use V/CV and VC/V patterns to decode multisyllabic words*

Skill Trace

 Tested ✓ **V/CV and VC/V Syllable Patterns**

Introduce	Grade 2
Reintroduce	T300
Reteach	S38
Review	**T310–T311, T330, T346, T358, T420**
Test	Theme 3

Review

V/CV SYLLABLE PATTERNS Write the following on the board: *broken, hotel, total, taken.* Have students read the words. Remind them that each syllable has only one vowel sound, and that in words with the V/CV syllable pattern, the first vowel is pronounced with a long sound. Invite volunteers to divide the words into syllables and to label the first vowels *long*. Then read the words aloud together. Ask students to think of other words with this syllable pattern and long-vowel sound.

VC/V SYLLABLE PATTERN On the board, write *robin, petal, wagon,* and *color*. Have students read the words. Remind them that in words with the VC/V syllable pattern, the first vowel is pronounced with a short sound. Invite volunteers to divide the syllables and to label the first vowel in each one *short*. Read the words aloud together. Ask students to think of other words with this syllable pattern and short-vowel sound.

broken
V/CV
hotel
V/CV
total
V/CV
taken
V/CV

BELOW-LEVEL   ON-LEVEL   ADVANCED

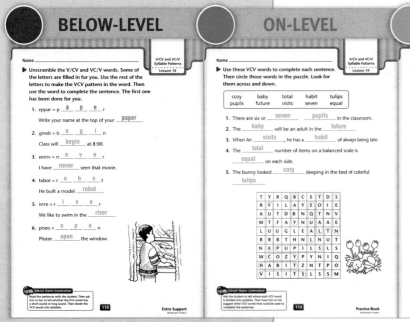

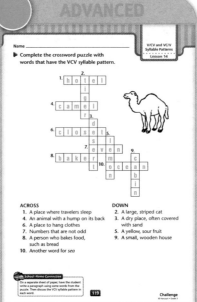

▲ **Extra Support, p. 119**   ▲ **Practice Book, p. 119**   ▲ **Challenge, p. 119**

E L L

- Group students according to academic levels and assign one of the pages on the left.

- Clarify any unfamiliar concepts as necessary. See *ELL Teacher Guide* Lesson 14 for support in scaffolding instruction.

V/CV and VC/V Syllable Patterns phonics *and Spelling*

5-DAY SPELLING
DAY 1 Pretest
DAY 2 State the Generalization
DAY 3 Spelling Practice/Handwriting
DAY 4 Use Spelling Strategies/Review
DAY 5 Posttest

Assess

POSTTEST Assess students' progress. Use the dictation sentences from Day 1.

Words with V/CV and VC/V Syllable Patterns:

1. robin — A **robin** built a nest in the oak tree.
2. petal — Each **petal** on the daisy is white.
3. seven — Marcus is **seven** years old.
4. solid — Water is a liquid, and ice is a **solid**.
5. final — What is the **final** word on the spelling list?
6. given — Have you **given** your permission slip to me?
7. color — Purple is my favorite **color**.
8. hotel — Emma's family stayed in a **hotel**.
9. wagon — Amar piled leaves in the **wagon**.
10. music — Ming danced to the **music** on the radio.
11. total — We have a **total** of nineteen students in our class.
12. cabin — Mr. Diaz built a **cabin** in the woods.
13. taken — Jada had her picture **taken** on her birthday.
14. pupil — Nick is a **pupil** in Miss Moore's class.
15. broken — My pencil is **broken**.

 WRITING APPLICATION Have students write a cause-and-effect paragraph that includes at least five spelling words. After they write, have students underline each spelling word in their paragraphs and make sure the words are spelled correctly.

Objective

• *To use syllable patterns to spell multisyllabic words*

Spelling Words

1.	**robin**	9.	**wagon**
2.	**petal**	10.	**music**
3.	**seven**	11.	**total**
4.	**solid**	12.	**cabin**
5.	**final**	13.	**taken**
6.	**given**	14.	**pupil**
7.	**color***	15.	**broken**
8.	**hotel**		

Challenge Words

16.	**recital**	19.	**colony***
17.	**vanish**	20.	**visiting**
18.	**regret**		

Words from "One Small Place in a Tree"

ADVANCED

Challenge Words Use these dictation sentences.

16. recital We went to Olivia's ballet **recital**.
17. vanish The dog seems to **vanish** at bath time.
18. regret Do you **regret** not going to the game?
19. colony I wonder how many ants live in that **colony**.
20. visiting Mario is **visiting** his uncle this weekend.

Fluency
Intonation

Objectives

- *To build fluency through rereading*
- *To read aloud fluently and with appropriate intonation*

ASSESSMENT

Monitoring Progress Periodically, take a timed sample of students' oral reading, measuring the number of words read correctly per minute. Students should be accurately reading approximately 92 words per minute in the middle of Grade 3.

Fluency Support Materials

Fluency Builders,
Grade 3, Lesson 14

Audiotext *Student Edition* selections are available on *Audiotext 3.*

**Strategic Intervention Teacher Guide,** Lesson 14

Readers' Theater

DIBELS Oral Reading Fluency **ORF**

PERFORM "ONE SMALL PLACE IN A TREE" Use the following steps:

▲ **Student Edition, pp. 408–425**

- Divide the class into groups of four and assign three to four pages of the selection to each group.

- Within each group, assign paragraphs or pages to each student.

- Have students follow along as you read aloud pages 411–412 of "One Small Place in a Tree," modeling fluent reading with intonation.

- Encourage students to discuss how they might use intonation to make the text sound as if it were natural conversation.

- Have groups practice reading their pages, using intonation as they read.

- Listen to each group read. Provide feedback and support.

- Invite groups to read their part of the selection to the class. Remind them to focus on reading with intonation.

E L L

Review Ending Punctuation Point out the question marks, colon, and exclamation point on pages 411 and 412 of "One Small Place in a Tree." Model how to read these sentences using intonation to show questioning, anticipation, and excitement. Then have students echo-read, using intonation to show the same emotions indicated by the punctuation.

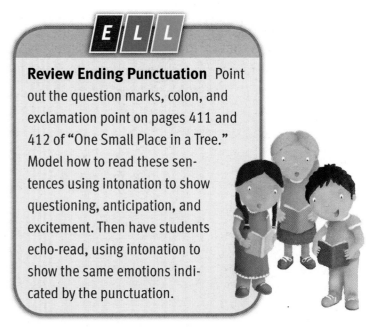

Author's Purpose
Comprehension

Review

REVIEW THE SKILL Have students restate the author's purpose for "A Log's Life." (to inform)

USE PRIOR KNOWLEDGE/SET A PURPOSE Tell students they will listen again as you reread "A Log's Life." Guide students to use prior knowledge and set a purpose for listening.

▲ **Read-Aloud Anthology** "A Log's Life," pp. 50

Practice/Apply

GUIDED PRACTICE Use the following questions to monitor students' listening comprehension:

- **What is the main reason the author wrote the selection?** (Possible response: to inform readers about the changes that happen to a tree during its life)

- **What information did the author want to share?** (Possible responses: A tree is used by different animals throughout its life; a tree is important when standing and also after it falls and becomes a log)

INDEPENDENT PRACTICE Draw the graphic organizer on the board. Have students complete it with information that helped them determine the author's purpose in writing the selection.

What I Know	What I Read	Author's Purpose

Objectives

- *To review author's purpose in a previous selection*
- *To listen for information in nonfiction text*

Skill Trace

 Tested **Author's Purpose**

Introduce	T215
Reteach	S42
Review	T249, T265, T277, T302–T303, T333, T349, T361, T412, T433
Test	Theme 3
Maintain	Theme 4, T348

Make Connections Remind students that the author is the person who wrote the selection and that it was written to inform, to entertain, or to persuade. Explain to students that when they tell their family members what happened at school each day, their purpose is to inform. When they tell a story or joke, their purpose is to entertain. When they try to talk their parents into taking them to a movie or the park, their purpose is to persuade.

Build Robust Vocabulary

Objectives

- *To review robust vocabulary*
- *To organize word meanings in order to understand word relationships*

REVIEW | Tested ✓

Vocabulary

Lesson 13	Lesson 14
tugged	sprout
paused	damp
columns	suppose
absorb	roost
protects	spears
rustling	strikes
dissolve	glimpse
particles	maze
scavenger	transformation
self-sufficient	harmony

Cumulative Review

REINFORCE MEANINGS Ask students the following questions:

- **Why might you want to protect a sprout?**

- **Suppose you are in a maze. Would a glimpse of the exit make you pause? Explain.**

MAKE WORD WEBS Guide students in completing word webs in order to enrich their understanding of *harmony* and *transformation*. Display **Transparency GO12** or draw a word web on the board, with *harmony* in the center oval. Have students share examples of things people would do in order to live in harmony with one another. Write their responses on the board and discuss. Some suggestions are shown.

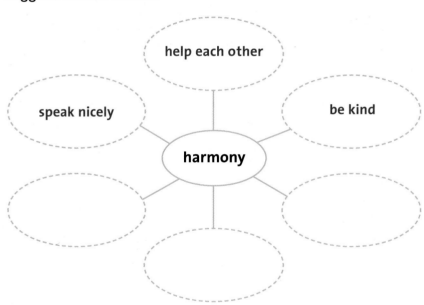

Have students create their own webs for *transformation*. After students write *transformation* in the center of their webs, ask them to add to their webs things that are or have been transformed.

REVIEW VOCABULARY Discuss students' answers to these questions.

1. **Suppose** you heard something **rustling** in the bushes outside your home. What might it be?
2. What would you expect a **scavenger** to do if it caught a **glimpse** of a garbage can?
3. When might an animal **roost** to **protect** something?
4. Would you expect something to **dissolve** if it were in a **damp** place or in a dry place? Explain.
5. If you **tugged** on a plant that was just beginning to **sprout**, what would probably happen?
6. Which would be more difficult to find your way through, a path that is like a **maze** or like a **column**? Explain.
7. Why might you **pause** before **striking** a drum?
8. Would it be easier to **spear** a large object or a small **particle**? Why?

MONITOR PROGRESS

Vocabulary

IF students are having difficulty understanding the meanings of the words, | **THEN** read one of the definitions, and ask students which word it describes. Offer two words from which the students can choose.

Small-Group Instruction, p. S46:

● **BELOW-LEVEL:** Reteach
● **ON-LEVEL:** Reinforce
● **ADVANCED:** Extend

Grammar
Pronoun-Antecedent Agreement

5-DAY GRAMMAR

DAY 1	Define Antecedent
DAY 2	Agreement in Number
DAY 3	Agreement in Gender
DAY 4	Apply to Writing
DAY 5	Pronoun/Antecedent Agreement Review

Objectives

- *To use agreement between pronouns and antecedents*
- *To identify antecedents in sentences*

Daily Proofreading

1. Tina says her likes to wear green dresses on monday. (she likes; Monday.)
2. lucy and Rita said she enjoyed their bike trip. (Lucy; they enjoyed)

 Language Arts Checkpoint

If students have difficulty with the concepts, see pages S48–S49 to reteach.

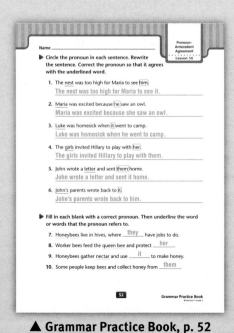

▲ **Grammar Practice Book, p. 52**

Review

REVIEW PRONOUN-ANTECEDENT AGREEMENT Review the rules for pronouns and antecedents:

- Singular antecedents need a singular pronoun.
- Plural antecedents need a plural pronoun.
- Male antecedents need a male pronoun.
- Female antecedents need a female pronoun.
- Antecedents that are things need a neutral pronoun.

Practice/Apply

GUIDED PRACTICE Write the following sentences on the board:

> **The students were told he had homework.**
> **Tomas said she liked the party.**
> **Ana asked if it could leave early today.**

Read the sentences together. Ask students to identify the antecedents and pronouns in each. (students/he, Tomas/she, Ana/it) Explain that the antecedents and pronouns in the sentences do not agree. Then have volunteers come to the board and change the pronouns to show agreement. (they, he, she)

Practice/Apply

INDEPENDENT PRACTICE Write the following pronouns on the board:

> she   they   us   it   him

Have students write sentences with each of the pronouns on the board. Remind students to use antecedents that agree with the pronouns. Invite students to share their sentences with a partner and check each other's work for pronoun-antecedent agreement.

5-DAY WRITING	
DAY 1	Introduce
DAY 2	Prewrite
DAY 3	Prewrite
DAY 4	Draft
DAY 5	Revise/Edit

Writing
Cause-and-Effect Paragraph

Revise/Edit

REVIEW CONVENTIONS Remind students that they should indent the first line of each paragraph. Each sentence must begin with a capital letter and have correct end punctuation. Remind students also that pronouns must match their antecedents. Additionally, have students look for places in their writing where elaboration would make their paragraphs more interesting and easier to understand.

Share

POLISH AND SHARE WRITING Have students exchange drafts with a partner. Have them use their checklists as they review each other's writing. Tell students to keep their writing in their portfolios.

Objectives

- *To revise and share a cause-and-effect paragraph*
- *To follow conventions of capitalization, punctuation, and agreement*

Writing Prompt

Self-Selected Writing Have students generate a list of ideas about a new topic for writing. Have them circle their best ideas.

WEEKLY LESSON TEST

▲ **Weekly Lesson Tests, Lesson 14**

- Selection Comprehension with Short Response
- **phonics** and Spelling
- Use Graphic Aids
- Focus Skill: Author's Purpose
- Robust Vocabulary
- Grammar
- Fluency Passage **FRESH READS**

GO online For prescriptions, see p. A5. Also available electronically on StoryTown Online Assessment and ExamView.

NOTE: A 4-point rubric appears on p. R8.

SCORING RUBRIC					
6	**5**	**4**	**3**	**2**	**I**
FOCUS Completely focused, purposeful.	Focused on topic and purpose.	Generally focused on topic and purpose.	Somewhat focused on topic and purpose.	Related to topic but does not maintain focus.	Lacks focus and purpose.
ORGANIZATION Ideas progress logically; paper conveys sense of completeness.	Organization mostly clear; paper gives sense of completeness.	Organization mostly clear, but some lapses occur; may seem unfinished.	Some sense of organization; seems unfinished.	Little sense of organization.	Little or no sense of organization.
SUPPORT Strong, specific details; clear, exact language; freshness of expression.	Strong, specific details; clear, exact language.	Adequate supporting details and word choice.	Limited supporting details; limited word choice.	Few supporting details; limited word choice.	Little development; limited or unclear word choice.
CONVENTIONS Varied sentences; few, if any, errors.	Varied sentences; few errors.	Some sentence variety; few errors.	Simple sentence structures; some errors.	Simple sentence structures; many errors.	Unclear sentence structures; many errors.

REPRODUCIBLE STUDENT RUBRICS for specific writing purposes and presentations are available on pages R5–R8.

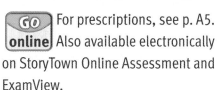

Podcasting: Assessing Fluency

Leveled Readers
Reinforcing Skills and Strategies

 BELOW-LEVEL

One Hickory Tree in a Forest

SUMMARY This story follows the life of a shagbark hickory tree from its beginning as a nut to its life as a full grown tree.

Genre: Expository Nonfiction

 Author's Purpose

 Ask Questions

• **ROBUST VOCABULARY:**
suppose, roost, spears, strikes, glimpse, maze

Before Reading

BUILD BACKGROUND/SET A PURPOSE Have students share what they know about how a tree grows. How long does it take for trees to reach their full size? How long do trees live? Guide students to set a purpose for reading.

Reading the Book

PAGE 5 IMPORTANT DETAILS What are two important uses of a hickory nut? (It is food for animals; it can grow into a new tree.)

PAGE 7 AUTHOR'S PURPOSE What dangers do hickory trees face? What is the author's purpose in giving you this information? (being cut down, fire, rot, insects, birds; to tell how it is difficult for a tree to live a long time)

REREAD FOR FLUENCY Have students reread a page to a partner. Encourage them to help each other find spots to raise and lower their voices for expression.

Think Critically *(See inside back cover for questions.)*

1 **IMPORTANT DETAILS** Possible response: The strong, hard wood has been a source of tools, fuel, and construction material.

2 **SPECULATE** Possible response: The nut is "lucky" because it rolled away and was not eaten. Now, it will grow into a mature tree.

3 **PERSONAL RESPONSE** Accept reasonable responses.

4 **SYNTHESIZE** Most hickory nuts are eaten; others fall where they can't grow; others do not grow well because other plants crowd them out.

5 **AUTHOR'S PURPOSE** Possible response: The author probably would like people to know about how things grow.

LEVELED READER TEACHER GUIDE

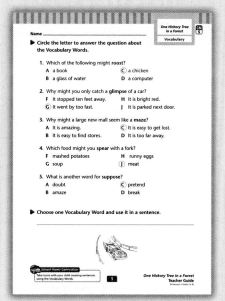

▲ Vocabulary, p. 5

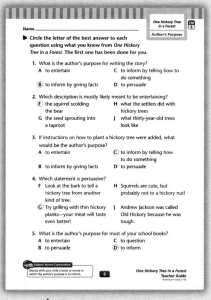

▲ Comprehension, p. 6

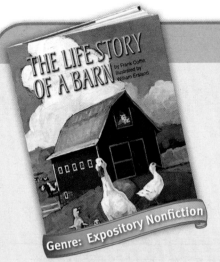

by Frank Coffin
illustrated by William Ersland

Genre: **Expository Nonfiction**

ON-LEVEL

The Life Story of a Barn

SUMMARY A farmer and his two sons build a small barn in the 1870s. The barn is useful for many years before it and the farm fall apart.

 Author's Purpose

 Ask Questions

• **ROBUST VOCABULARY:**
suppose, roost, spears, strikes, glimpse, maze

LEVELED READER TEACHER GUIDE

▲ **Vocabulary, p. 5**

Before Reading

BUILD BACKGROUND/SET A PURPOSE Have students discuss what barns are like and what they are used for. Then guide students to preview the story and set a purpose for reading.

Reading the Book

PAGE 5 DRAW CONCLUSIONS Why did the farmer need a barn for his animals and tools? (to protect them from the outdoors)

PAGE 8 AUTHOR'S PURPOSE What is the author's purpose in writing about the life of a barn? (Possible response: The author wants to show how the barn was an important part of the farm; the barn changed along with the farm.)

REREAD FOR FLUENCY Have students reread a page to a partner. They should help each other find spots to vary their voices for expression.

Think Critically

(See inside back cover for questions.)

1 **IMPORTANT DETAILS** Neighbors and friends came to help. They brought food so everyone could stay all day. They all worked together to raise the frame.

2 **AUTHOR'S PURPOSE** Possible response: The barn and equipment around it change through time.

3 **UNDERSTAND FIGURATIVE LANGUAGE** Possible response: Time destroys the barn because no one keeps it in good shape.

4 **SYNTHESIZE** Answers may vary, but an estimate of 110 to 130 years would be a good guess.

5 **AUTHOR'S PURPOSE** Possible response: The author probably feels sorry for the old barn and wants readers to remember it.

▲ **Comprehension, p. 6**

Leveled Readers
Reinforcing Skills and Strategies

Genre: Expository Nonfiction

ADVANCED

Livingston Hill

SUMMARY This selection describes how one neighborhood might have looked at different times in the past million years.

 Author's Purpose

 Ask Questions

- **ROBUST VOCABULARY:**
suppose, roost, spears, strikes, glimpse, maze

Before Reading

BUILD BACKGROUND/SET A PURPOSE Have students suggest how their neighborhood might have looked 100 years ago and discuss aspects of daily life. Guide students to preview the story and set a purpose for reading.

Reading the Book

PAGE 6 MAKE PREDICTIONS What kind of people might have lived on Livingston Hill a long time ago? (Possible responses: Native Americans; cave dwellers)

PAGES 11–12 AUTHOR'S PURPOSE What is the author's purpose in looking at Livingston Hill at different times in the past? (Possible response: to show how life and the land changed over millions of years)

REREAD FOR FLUENCY Have students reread a page to a partner. Have them help each other find passages in which to use their voices for expression.

Think Critically   *(See inside back cover for questions.)*

1. **EXPRESS PERSONAL OPINION** Answers will vary. Some students will be interested in the prehistoric eras, others in the human connections.

2. **AUTHOR'S PURPOSE** Possible response: to help me realize that changes have taken place.

3. **IMPORTANT DETAILS** It looked mostly like a swamp.

4. **SYNTHESIZE** Possible response: Land forms and usage, plants and animals, and climate may change in a given place over long periods of time.

5. **AUTHOR'S PURPOSE** Possible response: to have readers think about how ordinary places looked in the past.

LEVELED READER TEACHER GUIDE

▲ Vocabulary, p. 5

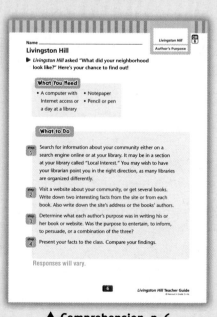

▲ Comprehension, p. 6

E L L

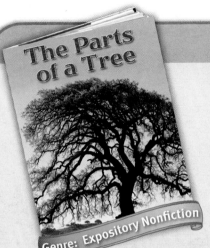

Genre: Expository Nonfiction

The Parts of a Tree

SUMMARY This story describes all the different parts of a tree and what each part does.

- **Build Background**
- **Concept Vocabulary**
- **Scaffolded Language Development**

Before Reading

BUILD BACKGROUND/SET A PURPOSE Have students name some of the different parts of a tree. Do they have a favorite tree to climb or sit beneath? What part of it do they like best? Why? Then guide students to preview the story and set a purpose for reading it.

Reading the Book

PAGE 6 DRAW CONCLUSIONS What is the job of the roots of a tree? (Possible responses: Roots hold the tree up; they take in food and water.)

🔵 **PAGE 14 AUTHOR'S PURPOSE** What is the author's purpose in calling trees an important part of our world? (Possible responses: The author wants to inform us about why trees are valuable; the author wants to encourage us to take care of trees.)

REREAD FOR FLUENCY Have students reread a page to a partner. Work with them to find a passage where they should use changes in their voices to express meanings and feelings.

Scaffolded Language Development

(See inside back cover for teacher-lead activity.)

Provide additional examples and explanation as needed.

LEVELED READER TEACHER GUIDE

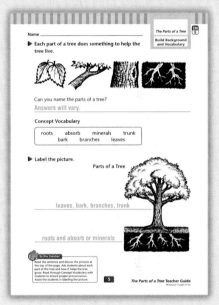

▲ Build Background, p. 5

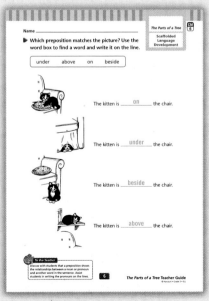

▲ Scaffolded Language Development, p. 6

Lesson 15

Theme Review and Vocabulary Builder

WEEK AT A GLANCE

✔ Phonics REVIEW
- C-*le* Syllable
- Consonant Digraphs /n/*kn, gn*; /r/*wr*; /f/*gh*
- Consonants /s/*c*; /j/*g, dge*
- V/CV and VC/V Syllable Patterns

✔ Spelling REVIEW

title, rattle, saddle, gnat, knight, wrench, rough, edge, police, giant, judge, hotel, seven, broken, taken

✔ Comprehension REVIEW

🌀 Plot

🌀 Author's Purpose

🌀 Use Story Structure

🌀 Ask Questions

✔ Robust Vocabulary

luscious, shudder, issue, advice, consult, recommend, sensible, devise, expertise, correspondence
REVIEW Lessons 11–14 Vocabulary

Reading

READERS' THEATER
"Ask the Experts" ADVICE COLUMN

COMPREHENSION STRATEGIES
"Iris and Walter, True Friends" REALISTIC FICTION

Fluency REVIEW
- Expression
- Intonation

✔ Grammar REVIEW
- Possessive Nouns
- Singular and Plural Pronouns
- Subject and Object Pronouns
- Pronoun-Antecedent Agreement

✔ Writing: Revise and Publish
Writing Trait: **REVIEW** Voice
Writing Trait: **REVIEW** Sentence Fluency

✔ Weekly Lesson Test

 = **Focus Skill**   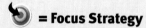 = **Focus Strategy**    = **Tested Skill**

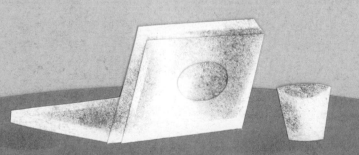

One stop

for all
your **Digital** *needs*

FOR THE TEACHER

Prepare  Professional Development

in the Online TE

 Videos for Podcasting

Plan & Organize Online TE & Planning Resource*

Teach  Transparencies

access from the Online TE

Assess Online Assessment*

with Student Tracking System and Prescriptions

FOR THE STUDENT

Read  Student eBook*

 Strategic Intervention Interactive Reader

 Leveled Readers

Practice & Apply Splash into Phonics CD-ROM

 Comprehension Expedition CD-ROM

 Also available on CD-ROM

GO online | eBook STUDENT EDITION

STUDENT EDITION

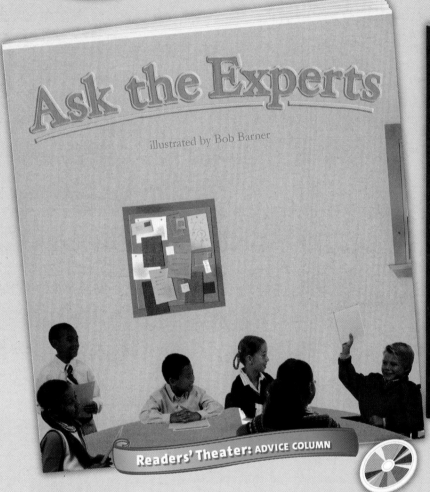

illustrated by Bob Barner

Readers' Theater: ADVICE COLUMN

Iris and Walter
True Friends

WRITTEN BY Elissa Haden Guest

ILLUSTRATED BY

Reading Fiction: REALISTIC FICTION

◀ **Audiotext** *Readers' Theater selections are available on Audiotext 3.*

THEME CONNECTION: AS WE GROW
Using Readers' Theater and Realistic Fiction

....

Paired Selections

READERS' THEATER | REVIEW

SOCIAL STUDIES | **Ask the Experts, pp. 432–439**

SUMMARY Student editors of *What Should I Do?* magazine answer readers' questions.

COMPREHENSION STRATEGIES | REVIEW

SOCIAL STUDIES | **Reading A Chapter Book: Iris and Walter, True Friends, pp. 440–445**

SUMMARY Walter teaches Iris how to make friends with a horse.

Support for Differentiated Instruction

LEVELED READERS

● **BELOW-LEVEL**   ● **ON-LEVEL**   ● **ADVANCED**   **E L L**

LEVELED PRACTICE

◀ **Strategic Intervention Resource Kit, Lesson 15**

◀ **Strategic Intervention Interactive Reader, Lesson 15**
Strategic Intervention Interactive Reader Online

◀ **ELL Extra Support Kit, Lesson 15**

◀ **Challenge Resource Kit, Lesson 15**

● **BELOW-LEVEL**
Extra Support Copying Masters, pp. 121, 123–124, 126–129, 131–132

● **ON-LEVEL**
Practice Book, pp. 121–132

● **ADVANCED LEVEL**
Challenge Copying Masters, pp. 121, 123–124, 126–129, 131–132

E L L
ELL Copying Masters, Lesson 15

ADDITIONAL RESOURCES

- Teacher Resource Book, pp. 48, 107, 121–124
- Spelling Practice Book, pp. 47–50
- Grammar Practice Book, pp. 53–54
- Reading Transparencies R71, R79, R95, R101–R102
- Test Prep System
- ◀ **Literacy Center Kit, Cards 71–75**
- Writer's Companion
- ◀ **Fluency Builders**
- ◀ **Picture Card Collection**

✓ ASSESSMENT

✔ **Weekly Lesson Test, Lesson 15**
 • Comprehension   • Robust Vocabulary
✔ **Rubrics, pp. R3–R8**

www.harcourtschool.com/storytown
• Online Assessment
• *Also available on CD-ROM—ExamView®*

Suggested Lesson Planner

90+ Minutes

Go online Online TE & Planning Resources

Step 1 Whole Group
90+ Minutes

Daily Routines
- *Oral Language*
- *Read Aloud*

Word Work
-  phonics
- *Spelling*

Skills and Strategies
- *Comprehension*
- *Build Robust Vocabulary*
- *Reading*
- *Fluency*

Step 2 Small Groups
45–60 Minutes

Step 3 Whole Group
45 Minutes

Language Arts
- *Grammar*
- *Writing*

Day 1

QUESTION OF THE DAY, p. T382
What is it like to work with others to solve a problem or complete a task?

READ ALOUD, p. T383
Transparency R71: "A Good Play"

✓ **phonics** p. T384
Review: Short Vowel and C-*le* Syllable

✓ **SPELLING,** p. T386
Pretest: *title, rattle, saddle, knat, knight, wrench, rough edge, police, giant, judge, hotel, seven, broken, taken*

COMPREHENSION, p. T387
Review: Plot

✓ **BUILD ROBUST VOCABULARY,** p. T388
Words from the Readers' Theater

READING READERS' THEATER
Read Aloud/Read Along:
"Ask the Experts," p. T391
FLUENCY, p. T391, Model Oral Fluency

✓ **BUILD ROBUST VOCABULARY,** p. T395
Words About the Readers' Theater

Day 2

QUESTION OF THE DAY, p. T398
When has someone or something surprised you?

READ ALOUD, p. T399
Transparency R79: "The Letter"

✓ **phonics** p. T400, Review: Consonant
Digraphs /n/*kn, gn*; /r/*wr*; /f/*gh*

✓ **SPELLING,** p. T400, Word Building

COMPREHENSION, p. T402
Review: Plot, Use Context Clues

READING READERS' THEATER
Read Together: "Ask the Experts," p. T404
Options for Reading

FLUENCY, p. T404
Expression and Intonation

✓ **BUILD ROBUST VOCABULARY,** p. T405
Words from the Read Aloud

▲ Student Edition

Suggestions for Differentiated Instruction (*See pp. T376–T377.*)

✓ **GRAMMAR,** p. T396
Review: Possessive Nouns

DAILY PROOFREADING

1. the boys bikes were in the garage (The boys'; garage.)
2. I can borrow one of Sandy pencils (Sandy's pencils.)

 WRITING, p. T397, Revise for Organization
Writing Trait: Voice

Writing Prompt *Write two or three sentences explaining which writing assignment you picked and why. Mention how you plan to improve the writing.*

✓ **GRAMMAR,** p. T406
Review: Singular and Plural Pronouns

DAILY PROOFREADING

1. james wore they coat (James; his coat.)
2. all the boys and girls need his books (All; their books.)

 WRITING, p. T407, Revise for Sentence Fluency and Voice
Writing Trait: Voice

Writing Prompt *Write about something that actually happened today. Include at least one sentence of dialogue.*

 = Focus Skill    = Focus Strategy    = Tested Skill

Review

Skills at a Glance

phonics Review	Comprehension Review	Fluency Review	Vocabulary
• C-*le* Syllable • Consonant Digraphs /n/*kn, gn*; /r/*wr*; /f/*gh* • Consonants /s/*c*; /j/*g, dge* • V/CV and VC/V Syllable Patterns	**Focus Skills** Plot, Author's Purpose **Focus Strategy** Use Story Structure, Ask Questions	• Expression • Intonation	**INTRODUCE:** *luscious, shudder, issue, advice, consult, recommend, sensible, devise, expertise, correspondence*

Day 3

QUESTION OF THE DAY, p. T408
What do you talk about with your friends?

READ ALOUD, p. T409
Transparency R79: "The Letter"

 **AND SPELLING,** p. T410
Review: Consonants /s/*c*; /j/*g, dge*

✔ **COMPREHENSION,** p. T412
 Review: Author's Purpose, Use Context Clues

FLUENCY:  READERS' THEATER
Choose Roles/Rehearse: "Ask the Experts," p. T414

✔ **BUILD ROBUST VOCABULARY,** p. T415
Review

▲ Student Edition

Day 4

QUESTION OF THE DAY, p. T418
What wild creatures have you seen in your neighborhood?

READ ALOUD, p. T419
Transparency R95: "Hey, Bug!"

 **AND SPELLING,** p. T420
Review: V/CV and VC/V Syllable Patterns

READING COMPREHENSION STRATEGIES
p. T422

FLUENCY: READERS' THEATER
Rehearse Roles: "Ask the Experts," p. T426

✔ **BUILD ROBUST VOCABULARY,** p. T427
Review

▲ Student Edition

Day 5

QUESTION OF THE DAY, p. T430
Why is it sometimes good to be patient about things?

READ ALOUD, p. T431
Transparency R87: "Autumn"

 **AND SPELLING,** p. T432
Posttest

✔ **COMPREHENSION,** p. T433–T434
 Review: Author's Purpose, Use Graphic Aids
Read-Aloud: "Thunder Cake"

FLUENCY: READERS' THEATER
Perform: "Ask the Experts," p. T435

▲ Student Edition

● **BELOW-LEVEL**   ● **ON-LEVEL**   ○ **ADVANCED**   E L L

✔ **GRAMMAR,** p. T416
Review: Subject and Object Pronouns

DAILY PROOFREADING

me gave the gift to he on tuesday. (I; him; Tuesday.)

 WRITING, p. T417
Introduce a Publishing Idea

Writing Prompt *Write to explain why good handwriting is important.*

✔ **GRAMMAR,** p. T428
Review: Pronoun-Antecedent Agreement

DAILY PROOFREADING

Mrs. Hall put they keys in his purse. (her keys; her purse.)

 WRITING, p. T429
Review: Publish

Writing Prompt *Write about how you feel about completing a piece of writing to the point of being published in a magazine.*

✔ **GRAMMAR,** p. T436
Review: Nouns and Pronouns

DAILY PROOFREADING

Mr. and Mrs. Diaz drove they car to me house. (their car; my house.)

WRITING, p. T437
Review: Present

Writing Prompt *Choose your own topic and write a short paragraph.*

Suggested Small-Group Planner

45–60 Minutes

	Day 1	**Day 2**

BELOW-LEVEL
15-20 Minutes

Day 1

Teacher-Directed
Leveled Reader:
"Ask *Pet Friends!*"
p. T438
Before Reading

▲ Leveled Reader

Independent
⭐ Listening/Speaking Center, p. T380
Extra Support Copying Masters, p. 121

Day 2

Teacher-Directed
Student Edition:
"Ask the Experts"
p. T391

▲ Student Edition

Independent
⭐ Reading Center,
p. T380
Extra Support Copying Masters,
pp. 123–124

ON-LEVEL
15-20 Minutes

Day 1

Teacher-Directed
Leveled Reader:
"Special Issue:
Brothers and Sisters!"
p. T439
Before Reading

▲ Leveled Reader

Independent
⭐ Reading Center, p. T380
Practice Book, p. 121

Day 2

Teacher-Directed
Student Edition:
"Ask the Experts,"
p. T391

▲ Student Edition

Independent
⭐ Technology
Center, p. T381
Practice Book, pp. 123–125

ADVANCED
15-20 Minutes

Day 1

Teacher-Directed
Leveled Reader:
"*Sport Kid* Answers
Back!" p. T440
Before Reading

▲ Leveled Reader

Independent
⭐ Word Work Center, p. T381
Challenge Copying Masters, p. 121

Day 2

Teacher-Directed
Leveled Reader:
"*Sport Kid* Answers
Back!" p. T440
Read the Book

▲ Leveled Reader

Independent
⭐ Word Work Center, p. T381
Challenge Copying Masters, pp. 123–124

ELL

English-Language Learners

• In addition to the small-group
instruction above, use the
ELL Extra Support Kit to promote
language development.

Day 1

LANGUAGE DEVELOPMENT SUPPORT
Teacher-Directed
ELL TG, Day 1

Independent
ELL Copying Masters, Lesson 15

Day 2

LANGUAGE DEVELOPMENT SUPPORT
Teacher-Directed
ELL TG, Day 2

▲ ELL Student Handbook

Intervention

▲ Strategic Intervention   ▲ Intervention Reader
Resource Kit

Day 1

Strategic Intervention TG,
Lesson 15
Strategic Intervention Practice
Book, Lesson 15

▲ Intervention Reader

Day 2

Strategic Intervention TG,
Lesson 15
Strategic Intervention Reader,
Lesson 15

▲ Intervention Reader

Day 3

Teacher-Directed
Leveled Reader:
"Ask *Pet Friends*!"
p. T438
Read the Book

Independent
 Word Work Center, p. T381
Extra Support Copying Masters,
pp. 126–128

▲ Leveled Reader

Teacher-Directed
Leveled Reader:
"Special Issue: Brothers and
Sisters!" p. T439
Read the Book

Independent
 Writing Center, p. T381
Practice Book, pp. 126–128

▲ Leveled Reader

Teacher-Directed
Leveled Reader:
"*Sport Kid* Answers Back!" p. T440
Think Critically

Independent
 Listening/Speaking Center,
p. T380
Challenge Copying Masters, pp. 126–128

▲ Leveled Reader

LANGUAGE DEVELOPMENT SUPPORT
Teacher-Directed
Leveled Reader: "Answer This!"
p. T441
Before Reading; Read the Book
ELL TG, Day 3

Independent
ELL Copying Masters, Lesson 15

▲ Leveled Reader

Strategic Intervention TG,
Lesson 15
Intervention Reader, Lesson 15
Strategic Intervention
Practice Book, Lesson 15

▲ Intervention Reader

Day 4

Teacher-Directed
Leveled Reader:
"Ask *Pet Friends*!"
p. T438
Reread for Fluency

Independent
 Technology Center, p. T381
Practice Book, pp. 129–130

▲ Leveled Reader

Teacher-Directed
Leveled Reader:
"Special Issue: Brothers and
Sisters!" p. T439
Reread for Fluency

Independent
 Word Work Center, p. T381
Practice Book, pp. 129–130

▲ Leveled Reader

Teacher-Directed
Leveled Reader:
"*Sport Kid* Answers Back!" p. T440
Reread for Fluency
Self-Selected Reading: Classroom
Library Collection

Independent
 Writing Center, p. T381
Practice Book, pp. 129–130

▲ Leveled Reader

LANGUAGE DEVELOPMENT SUPPORT
Teacher-Directed
Leveled Reader: "Answer This!"
p. T441
Reread for Fluency
ELL TG, Day 4

Independent
ELL Copying Masters, Lesson 15

▲ Leveled Reader

Strategic Intervention TG,
Lesson 15
Intervention Reader,
Lesson 15

▲ Intervention Reader

Day 5

Teacher-Directed
Leveled Reader:
"Ask *Pet Friends*!"
p. T438
Think Critically

Independent
 Writing Center, p. T381
Leveled Reader: Reread for Fluency
Extra Support Copying Masters, pp. T381

▲ Leveled Reader

Teacher-Directed
Leveled Reader:
"Special Issue: Brothers and
Sisters!" p. T439
Think Critically

Independent
 Listening/Speaking Center, p. T380
Leveled Reader: Reread for Fluency
Practice Book, pp. 131–132

▲ Leveled Reader

Teacher-Directed
Leveled Reader:
"*Sport Kid* Answers Back!" p. T440
Reread for Fluency
Self-Selected Reading: Classroom
Library Collection

Independent
 Reading Center, p. T380
Leveled Reader: Reread for Fluency
Challenge Copying Masters, pp. 131–132

▲ Leveled Reader

LANGUAGE DEVELOPMENT SUPPORT
Teacher-Directed
Leveled Reader: "Answer This!"
p. T441
Think Critically
ELL TG, Day 5

Independent
Leveled Reader: Reread for Fluency
ELL Copying Masters, Lesson 15

▲ Leveled Reader

Strategic Intervention TG,
Lesson 15
Intervention Reader, Lesson 15

▲ Intervention Reader

Leveled Readers & Leveled Practice
Reinforcing Skills and Strategies

LEVELED READER SYSTEM

- **Leveled Readers**
- **Leveled Readers, CD**
- **Leveled Reader Teacher Guides**
  - *Comprehension*
  - *Vocabulary*
  - *Oral Reading Fluency Assessment*
- **Response Activities**
- **Leveled Readers Assessment**

See pages T438–T441 for lesson plans.

For extended lesson plans, see *Leveled Reader Teacher Guides.*

BELOW-LEVEL

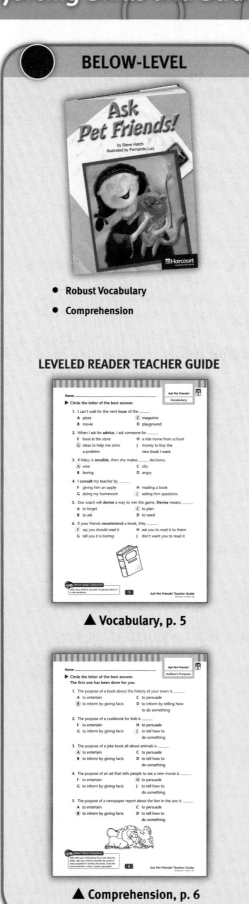

- Robust Vocabulary
- Comprehension

LEVELED READER TEACHER GUIDE

▲ Vocabulary, p. 5

▲ Comprehension, p. 6

ON-LEVEL

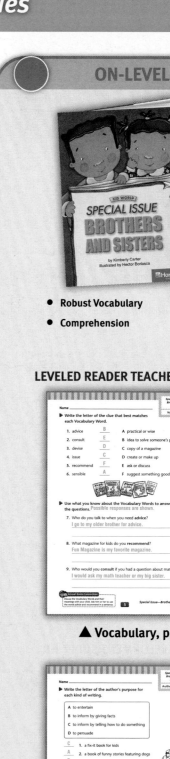

- Robust Vocabulary
- Comprehension

LEVELED READER TEACHER GUIDE

▲ Vocabulary, p. 5

▲ Comprehension, p. 6

www.harcourtschool.com/storytown

Go online

★ **Leveled Readers Online Database**
Searchable by Genre, Skill, Vocabulary, Level, or Title
★ **Student Activities and Teacher Resources,** *online*

ADVANCED

- Robust Vocabulary
- Comprehension

LEVELED READER TEACHER GUIDE

▲ Vocabulary, p. 5

▲ Comprehension, p. 6

E L L

- Build Background
- Concept Vocabulary
- Scaffolded Language Development

LEVELED READER TEACHER GUIDE

▲ Build Background, p. 5

▲ Scaffolded Language Development, p. 6

CLASSROOM LIBRARY

Self-Selected Reading

EASY

▲ *Officer Buckle and Gloria* by Peggy Rathmann, G. P. Putnam's Sons, 1995. FANTASY

AVERAGE

▲ *Day Light, Night Light* by Franklyn M. Branley, Harper Collins, 1998. EXPOSITORY NONFICTION

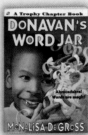

CHALLENGE

▲ *Donavan's Word Jar* by Monalisa DeGross, Harper Trophy, 1994. REALISTIC FICTION

▲ Classroom Library Teacher Guide, Lesson 13

Lesson 15   **T379**

Literacy Centers

15 Min. each

Management Support

While you provide direct instruction to individuals or small groups, other students can work on literacy center activities.

▲ **Literacy Centers Pocket Chart**

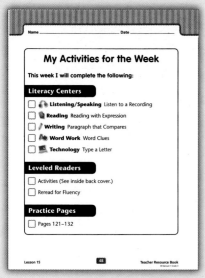

▲ **Teacher Resource Book, p. 48**

Homework for the Week

TEACHER RESOURCE BOOK, PAGE 18
The Homework Copying Master provides activities to complete for each day of the week.

LISTENING/SPEAKING

Listen to a Recording

Objective
To interact with peers and discuss a dramatic play

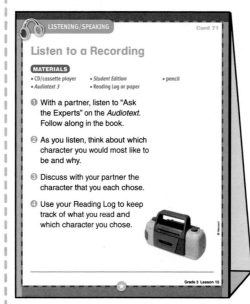

Literacy Center Kit • Card 71

READING

Reading with Expression

Objective
To practice reading with expression

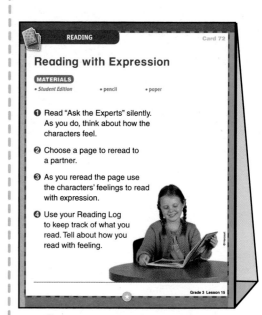

Literacy Center Kit • Card 72

I read the part of Healthy Heart with lots of energy, because the character talks about exercising.

WRITING

Paragraph That Compares

Objective
To write a paragraph that compares two stories

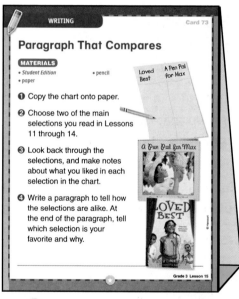

⭐ **Literacy Center Kit • Card 73**

WORD WORK

Word Clues

Objective
To use antonyms and synonyms to give clues to the Vocabulary Words

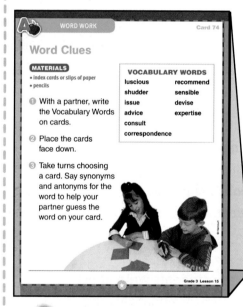

⭐ **Literacy Center Kit • Card 74**

TECHNOLOGY

Type a Letter

Objective
To compose a letter on a computer

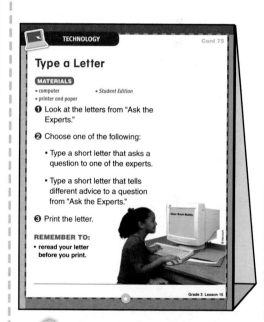

⭐ **Literacy Center Kit • Card 75**

Day at a Glance

Day 1

 **and Spelling**

- Review: C-*le* Syllable
- Pretest

Comprehension

 Review: Plot

- Monitor Comprehension

Robust Vocabulary

Words from the Readers' Theater

- Introduce: *issue, advice, consult, recommend, sensible, devise*

Fluency

READERS' THEATER

- Read Aloud/Read Along
  Model Fluent Reading
  "Ask the Experts," *Student Edition*,
  pp. 432–439

Robust Vocabulary

Words About the Readers' Theater

- Introduce: *expertise, correspondence*

Grammar

- Review: Possessive Nouns

Writing

- Select and Revise

Warm-Up Routines

Oral Language

Objectives *To listen attentively and respond appropriately to oral communication; to write and speak in complete sentences*

Question of the Day

What is it like to work with others to solve a problem or complete a task?

Remind students that people often work together to solve problems or do difficult tasks. Ask: **Were you ever part of a group that worked together to complete a task? What problem or task did you have? How did the people in the group divide the work? How did the group solve the problem or do the job?** Invite students to participate by sharing their ideas. Then have students complete the following writing prompt in their notebooks:

I worked with others to _____.

Have students write at least three sentences about why they worked in a group, what they did, and how things turned out.

Encourage students to share their writing with the class.

Read Aloud

Objective *To read for understanding and enjoyment*

READ ALOUD A POEM Display **Transparency R71** or distribute photocopies to students. Tell them that you are going to reread the poem "A Good Play."

Set a purpose. Ask students what the purpose might be for reading a poem again. (to enjoy or to learn) Tell students that while they are enjoying the poem they should listen for what the characters are doing.

Model fluent reading. Read the poem aloud, modeling how to read with feeling. Then reread, having students echo.

Discuss the poem. Ask students the following questions:

- What do the characters do together in the poem?

- Why do you think the author uses the word "a-sailing" rather than "sailing"?

- Do you think the writer continues playing? Why or why not?

A Good Play

by Robert Louis

We built a ship upon the stairs
All made of the back-bedroom chairs,
And filled it full of sofa pillows
To go a-sailing on the billows.

We took a saw and several nails,
And water in the nursery pails;
And Tom said, "Let us also take
An apple and a slice of cake;"—
Which was enough for Tom and me
To go a-sailing on, till tea.

We sailed along for days and days,
And had the very best of plays;
But Tom fell out and hurt his knee,
So there was no one left but me.

Grade 3, Lesson 11   Rc   Warm-Up: Days 2–3

Transparency R71

C-*le* Syllable

 phonics *and Spelling*

Objectives

- *To read words with /əl/le*
- *To determine which words with final* le *have short vowels and which have long vowels*

Skill Trace

Tested ✓ C-*le* Syllable

Introduce	T30
Reteach	S2
Review	T40–T41, T60, T76, T88, T384–T385
Test	Theme 3
Maintain	Theme 4, T76, T260

 phonics **Resources**

Phonics Practice Book, Intermediate, pp. 91–94

Review

SHORT VOWEL AND C-*le* SYLLABLE Write the following words on the board and read them aloud:

bundle   little   fiddle

Ask students what sounds they heard at the end of each word. (/əl/) Remind students that -*le* stands for /əl/ and that -*le* and the consonant before it form a syllable. Mark the syllable division in *bundle* (bun/dle). Have volunteers mark the syllable division in the remaining words. (lit/tle, fid/dle) Have students read the words and tell whether the vowel sound in the first syllable is long or short. (short) Remind students that whenever there are two consonants before -*le*, the vowel sound in the first syllable is short.

LONG VOWEL AND C-*le* SYLLABLE Write the following words on the board and read them aloud:

table   maple   beagle   needle

Remind students that -*le* stands for /əl/ and that *le* forms a syllable with the consonant that comes before it. Mark the syllable division in *table* (ta/ble). Have volunteers mark the syllable division in the remaining words. (ma/ple, bea/gle, nee/dle) Have students read the words and tell whether the vowel sound in the first syllable is long or short. (long) Remind students that whenever there is one consonant before -*le*, the vowel sound in the first syllable is long.

5-DAY PHONICS/SPELLING

DAY 1	Review C-*le* Syllable
DAY 2	Review Digraphs *kn, gn, wr,* and *gh*
DAY 3	Review Consonants /s/*c* and /j/*g, dge*
DAY 4	Review V/CV and VC/V Syllable Patterns
DAY 5	Combined Review

Practice/Apply

GUIDED PRACTICE Write the following words on the board:

apple	**eagle**	**staple**	**purple**

Ask students where the words should be divided into syllables and how they know. (ap/ple, ea/gle, sta/ple, pur/ple; *-le* and the consonant before it form a syllable) Have students tell whether the vowel sound in the first syllable of each word will be long or short. (*apple*—short; *eagle, staple*—long) Point out that *purple* does not follow this vowel rule because the vowel letter is followed by *r*. Have students read the words.

INDEPENDENT PRACTICE Write the following words on the board:

puzzle	beetle	sample
noodle	title	able

Have students write the words in their notebooks. Then have them divide the words into syllables, identify whether the vowel sound in the first syllable is long or short, and write *long* or *short* beside each word. Then have them check their words with a partner.

E L L

Build Words Point to the word *purple* on the board. Cover the letters *ple* and have students pronounce *pur*. Then cover the letters *pur* and have students pronounce *ple*. Then have them blend the sounds into one word.

ADVANCED

Identify C-*le* Words Have students look around the room for words with the VCC-*le*, VC-*le*, and VVC-*le* syllable patterns. Instruct students to list the words in their notebooks and use what they have learned about these patterns to divide the words into syllables and mark the vowels as long, short, or other.

E L L

- Group students according to academic levels, and assign one of the pages on the left.
- Clarify any unfamiliar concepts as necessary. See *ELL Teacher Guide,* Lesson 15, for support in scaffolding instruction.

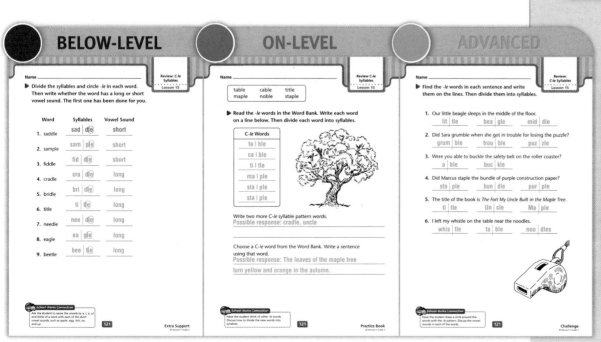

▲ Extra Support, p. 121   ▲ Practice Book, p. 121   ▲ Challenge, p. 121

Spelling
Review

5-DAY SPELLING	
DAY 1	Pretest
DAY 2	Review
DAY 3	Review/Handwriting
DAY 4	Review
DAY 5	Posttest

Objectives

- *To review spelling words from previous lessons*
- *To use a variety of spelling strategies*

Spelling Words

1.	**title**	9.	**police**
2.	**rattle**	10.	**giant**
3.	**saddle**	11.	**judge**
4.	**gnat**	12.	**hotel**
5.	**knight**	13.	**seven**
6.	**wrench**	14.	**broken**
7.	**rough**	15.	**taken**
8.	**edge**		

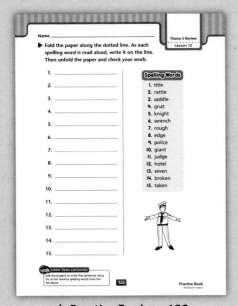

▲ Practice Book, p. 122

Reinforce the Skill

PRETEST Explain that this week's spelling words are review words from the previous four weeks. Say the first word and read the dictation sentence. Repeat the word as students write it. Write the word on the board and have students check their spelling. Tell them to circle the word if they spelled it correctly or write it correctly if they did not. Repeat for words 2–15.

Review Words

1.	title	The **title** of my favorite book is *Charlotte's Web*.
2.	rattle	Calvin's baby sister likes to play with a **rattle**.
3.	saddle	We put the **saddle** on the horse.
4.	gnat	A tiny **gnat** flew around our heads.
5.	knight	The heroic **knight** saved the princess.
6.	wrench	Dad asked me to bring his **wrench** to him.
7.	rough	Football can be a **rough** sport.
8.	edge	Do not set your glass on the **edge** of the table.
9.	police	We heard the siren on the **police** car.
10.	giant	Jack found a **giant** at the top of the beanstalk.
11.	judge	Our principal will **judge** the spelling bee.
12.	hotel	Did you enjoy swimming in the **hotel** pool?
13.	seven	Three plus four equals **seven**.
14.	broken	One of the eggs in the carton was **broken**.
15.	taken	Is this seat **taken**?

Plot
Comprehension: Review

Reinforce the Skill

DISCUSS PLOT Remind students that most stories have characters—the people or animals that the story is about. Remind them that a story has a setting—where and when the story takes place. Stories also have a plot, which is the sequence of events that happen. Most plots have a problem that the characters must solve. Have students think about the plot of "The Shepherd Boy and the Wolf." Model how to tell about a story's plot.

Think Aloud As I read, I think about what is happening in the story. I think about the important events. The boy cries "wolf" so people will come, but there is no wolf. Later in the story, he has a problem and cries "wolf," but nobody believes him.

Practice/Apply

GUIDED PRACTICE Work with students to select another story they have read recently. Then work together to identify the problem or goal, the important events, and the solution in the plot.

INDEPENDENT PRACTICE Have students select another story they have read recently. Then have them write a sentence telling the problem or goal and a sentence telling the solution. Have students share their work with a partner.

Objectives
- *To define plot*
- *To identify plot in a story*

Skill Trace
 Plot

Introduce	T32–T33
Reteach	S6
Review	T63, T79, T91, T128–T129, T161, T177, T189, T387, T402
Test	Theme 3
Maintain	Theme 4, T80

Build Robust Vocabulary
Words from the Readers' Theater

Objective

• *To build robust vocabulary*

INTRODUCE ✓ Tested

Vocabulary: Lesson 15

issue	**recommend**
advice	**sensible**
consult	**devise**

▼ **Student-Friendly Explanations**

Student-Friendly Explanations

issue *n.*	An issue is an edition of a newspaper or magazine. **Carlos was excited when the latest** *issue* **of his favorite magazine came in the mail.** *syn.* edition
advice *n.*	If you give someone advice, you tell what you think the person should do. **Lauren's** *advice* **was to choose the game that was the most fun to play.** *syn.* recommendation
consult *v.*	When you consult someone, you ask him or her for information. **Daniel wanted to** *consult* **his coach about how he could jump higher.** *syn.* Ask
recommend *v.*	When you recommend something, you tell someone that you think it is good. **Alexis asked her teacher to** *recommend* **a good book to read.** *syn.* suggest
sensible *adj.*	Someone who is sensible makes good decisions and judgments. **Jordan is a** *sensible* **eater who chooses fruits as treats.** *syn.* wise
devise *v.*	To devise is to figure out a way to do something. **Emma needed to** *devise* **a way to get her chores finished.** *syn.* invent, develop

Grade 3, Lesson 15   Ra   TK[Robust Vocabulary]?

Transparency R101

Teach/Model

INTRODUCE ROBUST VOCABULARY Introduce the words using the following steps:

❶ Display **Transparecy R101** and read the word and the **Student-Friendly Explanation.**
❷ Have students **say the word** with you.
❸ Have students **interact with the word's meaning** by asking them the appropriate question below.

• Would you want to read the latest **issue** of a magazine? Explain.

• Who might you ask for **advice** about a problem? Why?

• When did you **consult** with your teacher?

• If you disliked a movie, would you **recommend** it? Why or why not?

• Is it **sensible** to go for a walk during a thunderstorm? Explain.

• What might you do to **devise** a plan to save money?

Develop Deeper Meaning

EXPAND WORD MEANINGS Ask students the following questions about the Vocabulary Words. If students are unable to answer the questions correctly, refer them to the Student-Friendly Explanations on **Transparency R101.**

1. Where can you find the newest **issue** of your favorite magazine?

2. Where could you get **advice** about what kind of bike to buy?

3. Why might you **consult** a librarian?

4. What book would you **recommend** to a friend?

5. When is it **sensible** to fly a kite?

6. When might you need to **devise** a plan?

Managing Readers' Theater
"Ask the Experts"

Set the Stage

OVERVIEW Use the following suggestions to help students prepare a Readers' Theater presentation of "Ask the Experts."

Professional Development

Podcasting: Auditory Modeling

 Day 1

MODEL FLUENT READING Model fluent, expressive reading by reading aloud the script on *Student Edition* pages 432–439 (pp. T391–T394) as students follow along. Then read the script again using the Monitor Comprehension questions to assess students' understanding of the selection. Consider performance options for the end of the week. You may choose to invite parents or other guests.

 Day 2

READ TOGETHER Have students read the script on their own for the first time. Guide students to read with appropriate accuracy, reading rate, and expression. Encourage them to use the fluency tips to help them read more fluently.

 Day 3

CHOOSE ROLES AND REHEARSE Distribute copies of the script (*Teacher Resource Book*, pp. 121–124). Organize students in groups, and have them practice reading several roles. After students read, finalize roles by assigning them or having students choose their own. Encourage students to highlight their parts and practice reading at home.

 Day 4

REHEARSE Have students work in their groups to read the script as many times as possible. Informally observe the groups and give feedback on intonation and expression. You may want to have students rehearse using the backdrop for "Ask the Experts" (*Teacher Resource Book*, p. 107).

▲ Teacher Resource Book, p. 107

 Day 5

PERFORM Assign each group a scene to perform. Have students stand in a row at the front of the classroom and read the script aloud. Students who are not reading aloud become part of the audience. After the performance, encourage audience members to give feedback about each group's intonation and expression.

READERS' THEATER

Read Aloud/Read Along: "Ask the Experts"

5-DAY READERS' THEATER	
DAY 1	Read Aloud/Read Along
DAY 2	Read Together
DAY 3	Choose/Rehearse Roles
DAY 4	Rehearse Roles
DAY 5	Perform

Objective

- *To develop fluency by listening to a model read-aloud*

TECHNOLOGY

 eBook "Ask the Experts" is available in an eBook.

 Audiotext "Ask the Experts" is available on *Audiotext 3* for subsequent readings.

Humor and Meaning Be sure that students understand the humor in the names such as *Reid A. Lott* and *Friend Lee.* Explain unfamiliar vocabulary, such as *Web postings*, *dodging*, and *release*, during the second reading.

Build Background

DISCUSS GENRE Remind students that Readers' Theater is like a play that is read aloud rather than acted out. Tell students that the script "Ask the Experts" is about an advice column. Explain that people wanting advice write letters to a newspaper or magazine. The letters and the advice are printed in the newspaper or magazine for other people to read and learn from.

DISCUSS ADVICE Ask students to share what they know about giving and receiving advice. Talk with students about what might be involved in creating an advice column for children.

PREDICT Have students predict what kinds of things they will learn that children might want advice about.

REVIEW READERS' THEATER VOCABULARY WORDS: PAGE 432 Tell students that these words appear in the Readers' Theater selection. Have students read the words.

Reading for Fluency

DISCUSS FLUENCY TIPS: PAGE 432 Have students read the Reading for Fluency text. Remind them that they learned to use the two fluency strategies of expression and intonation in Lessons 11–14. Explain that throughout the Readers' Theater they will find fluency tips that will help them read with appropriate expression and intonation.

SET A PURPOSE Tell students to listen to hear how you read "Ask the Experts" with intonation and expression.

READ ALOUD/READ ALONG Remind students to follow along in their books as you read "Ask the Experts." Model how you use expression and intonation as you read.

> **Think Aloud** I read the script to find out what the characters say so I can read with expression to show their feelings.

Read the script aloud a second time. Tell students to listen carefully this time to what happens, because you will ask them questions.

Monitor Comprehension

PAGES 432–433 Ask students what questions they have about what is happening in this Readers' Theater. Have them read to find out.

①  PLOT **What problem or goal do the editors have? What do they need to do?** (The goal is to answer letters, e-mails, and Web postings with good advice.)

② IMPORTANT DETAILS **What are Taylor's and Corey's jobs?** (They are editors of *What Should I Do?* magazine.) **Who are the other characters?** (experts)

③ SEQUENCE **What have Taylor and Corey done? What will they do next?** (They have chosen the best letters; now they will talk to experts.)

HEALTH

SUPPORTING STANDARDS

Physical Activity Discuss physical activities students enjoy or might enjoy. Explain that regular physical activity will help keep their bodies healthy. Discuss other things they can do to stay healthy, such as eating fruits and vegetables and limiting sun exposure.

Corey: First, let's hear from Healthy Heart, our health expert.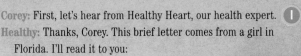

Healthy: Thanks, Corey. This brief letter comes from a girl in Florida. I'll read it to you:

> *Dear Healthy Heart,*
> *Are video games a good form of exercise?*
> *Sincerely,*
> *Video Girl*

Taylor: All right, Healthy. What is your answer?

Healthy: I wrote this reply.

> *Dear Video Girl,*
> *While video games can be fun to play, they are not a good form of exercise. You need to move your body and release a lot of energy. Activities that are safe and fun, such as jumping rope, playing soccer, or riding bikes with your friends, are great!*
> *Yours in health,*
> *Healthy Heart*

Taylor: That's good advice, Healthy.

Corey: The next letter is about friendship.

Taylor: Friend Lee is our friendship expert.

Friend Lee: This is an e-mail sent to us.

Fluency Tip
Make your voice rise and fall to show the letter writer's feelings.

> *Dear Friend Lee,*
> *Help! My father just got a new job on the other side of the United States. Now my family has to move. I'll miss my friends so much when I leave! Also, I'm afraid that I won't have any friends in our new town. What should I do?*
> *Your worried friend,*
> *Sad About Moving*

Corey: That's so sad!

Taylor: Moving to a new town is hard.

434

435

Monitor Comprehension

PAGES 434–435 Have students look at how the letters are organized. Tell them that they will read letters to and from the experts.

1 **FocusSkill** **AUTHOR'S PURPOSE** **How can you tell that the author might want people to have healthy habits?** (The author created the character Healthy Heart. Healthy Heart gives health advice to people.)

2 **DRAW CONCLUSIONS** **Do you think Healthy Heart gave Video Girl good advice?** (Yes. Healthy Heart told her to make sure she gets enough exercise. People need exercise to stay healthy, so that was good advice.)

3 **MAIN IDEA/DETAILS** **What was Sad About Moving worried about?** (Sad About Moving was worried that he or she wouldn't have any friends in his or her new town.)

Reading for Fluency

Fluency Tip **Intonation** Remind students that good readers make their voices go higher and lower to match the words they are reading.

Think Aloud I see that there are two sentences that end in exclamation marks. I'll read those sentences in a higher voice to show how badly Sad About Moving feels.

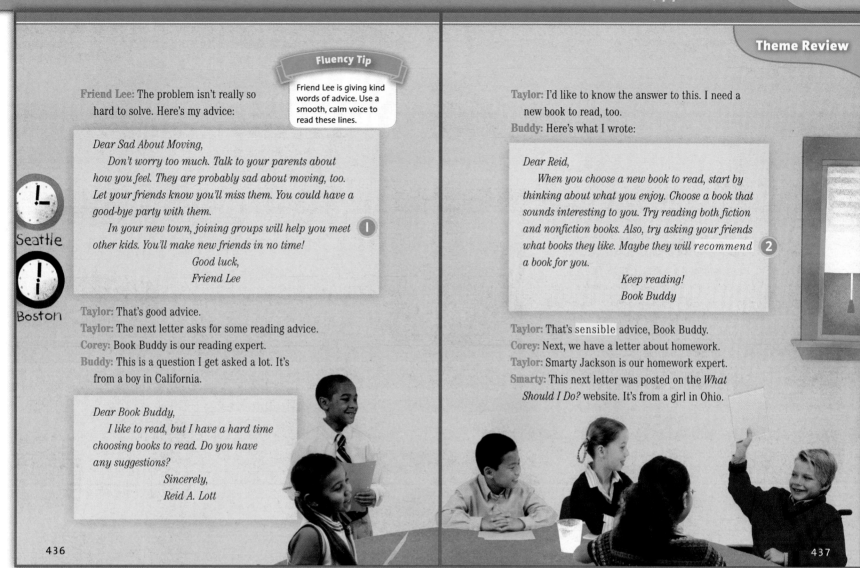

Fluency Tip

Friend Lee is giving kind words of advice. Use a smooth, calm voice to read these lines.

Friend Lee: The problem isn't really so hard to solve. Here's my advice:

Dear Sad About Moving,
Don't worry too much. Talk to your parents about how you feel. They are probably sad about moving, too. Let your friends know you'll miss them. You could have a good-bye party with them.
In your new town, joining groups will help you meet other kids. You'll make new friends in no time!
Good luck,
Friend Lee

Taylor: That's good advice.
Taylor: The next letter asks for some reading advice.
Corey: Book Buddy is our reading expert.
Buddy: This is a question I get asked a lot. It's from a boy in California.

Dear Book Buddy,
I like to read, but I have a hard time choosing books to read. Do you have any suggestions?
Sincerely,
Reid A. Lott

Seattle

Boston

436

Taylor: I'd like to know the answer to this. I need a new book to read, too.
Buddy: Here's what I wrote:

Dear Reid,
When you choose a new book to read, start by thinking about what you enjoy. Choose a book that sounds interesting to you. Try reading both fiction and nonfiction books. Also, try asking your friends what books they like. Maybe they will recommend a book for you.
Keep reading!
Book Buddy

Taylor: That's sensible advice, Book Buddy.
Corey: Next, we have a letter about homework.
Taylor: Smarty Jackson is our homework expert.
Smarty: This next letter was posted on the *What Should I Do?* website. It's from a girl in Ohio.

437

Monitor Comprehension

PAGES 436–437 Have students predict what Friend Lee might say to help Sad About Moving. Then have students read the page to find out.

1 CONFIRM PREDICTIONS Is Friend Lee's advice close to what you thought it would be? (Possible response: Yes, it is scary to think about finding new friends, but everyone can make them. You just have to find people who like the same things you like.)

2 EXPRESS PERSONAL OPINIONS Do you think Buddy's advice about picking out new books to read is good? Why or why not? (Possible responses: Yes, it is good advice because that's what I do. Also, I look for an interesting cover and I read the first page or the description on the back.)

Reading for Fluency

Fluency Tip **Expression** Remind students to read the words a character is saying and to think about how the words would be said in real life. Explain that if a character is saying something calmly like Friend Lee, he or she should not say the words in an angry or excited voice.

Dear Smarty,
What is the best time to do my homework? I usually wait until bedtime. Is that a good idea?
Sincerely,
Harriet

Corey: What should she do?
Smarty: Here is what I wrote.

Dear Harriet,
I think you might be dodging your work! You should start your homework earlier. Many students find that the best time to do homework is right after they get home from school. Other students find that they work best right after dinner. You need to devise a plan that will give you plenty of time to finish your assignments each night. Don't wait until bedtime!
Happy studying,
Smarty Jackson

Corey: Well, that's all the letters we have.
Taylor: Which ones should we put in the magazine?
All: Let's put them all in! They're all good questions.
Corey: That's what I was thinking.
Taylor: Me, too! I suppose our meeting is over.
Corey: Wait a second. I've found one last letter. It's from a student in Washington, D.C.

Dear What Should I Do? Editors,
What's your best advice about taking advice from other people?
Sincerely,
Need Some Advice

Taylor: What would you say, Corey?
Corey: I'd say that the best advice about taking advice is to be careful where you get it. Always make sure the person giving the advice knows what he or she is talking about.
Taylor: Good job, everyone. This issue of *What Should I Do?* will be our best one yet!

Fluency Tip
Think about how you would speak if you were giving advice to a friend.

438

439

Monitor Comprehension

PAGES 438–439 Have students think about some homework advice they might need. Then have them read the page to find out what advice Smarty gives.

1 **AUTHOR'S PURPOSE Why do you think the author included the letter about homework and Smarty Jackson's advice?** (Possible response: to give readers and listeners good advice about when to do homework)

2 **IMPORTANT DETAILS What advice does Corey give about getting advice?** (Possible response: He says to be careful about where you get your advice. Always make sure the person giving it knows what he or she is talking about.)

Reading for Fluency

Fluency Tip **Expression** Tell students to think about the conversation the magazine editors and the experts are having and how their words are spoken. Then tell them to think about how the letter writer might sound different.

Build Robust Vocabulary
Words About Readers' Theater

Teach/Model

Routine Card 3

INTRODUCE THE WORDS Use *Routine Card 3* to introduce the words.

❶ Put the word in **selection context**.
❷ Display **Transparency R102** and read the word and the **Student-Friendly Explanation**.
❸ Have students **say the word** with you.
❹ Use the word in other contexts, and have students **interact with the word's meaning**.
❺ Remove the transparency. Say the Student-Friendly Explanation again, and ask students to **name the word** that goes with it.

❶ **Selection Context:** Healthy Heart uses her **expertise** on healthy habits to answer the question about exercise.

❹ **Interact with Word Meaning:** Whose expertise do we depend on to make us healthy again when we are ill?

❶ **Selection Context:** The magazine staff read the **correspondence** sent in by the children.

❹ **Interact with Word Meaning:** Do you prefer to send correspondence by writing a letter or by using e-mail?

Practice/Apply

GUIDED PRACTICE Ask students to do the following:

- Brainstorm different means of correspondence.

- Think of your areas of expertise. What could you give advice about?

Objective

- *To use context clues to build robust vocabulary*

INTRODUCE

Vocabulary: Lesson 15

| expertise | correspondence |

▼ **Student-Friendly Explanations**

Student-Friendly Explanations

expertise	If someone has expertise, he or she knows a lot about a particular topic or skill.
correspondence	If you send correspondence, you are communicating in writing.
luscious	Something that is luscious appeals to your senses, such as your sense of taste.
shudder	If you shudder, you are trembling from fear or from being cold.

Grade 3, Lesson 15   Rb   TK[Robust Vocabulary]?

Transparency R102

Connect to Real Life Brainstorm a list of jobs and write it on the board. Beside each job, write the area of expertise associated with it. For example, doctor—medicine and health; teacher—education; chef—cooking.

Grammar
Review: Possessive Nouns

5-DAY GRAMMAR	
DAY 1	Possessive Nouns
DAY 2	Pronouns
DAY 3	Subject and Object Pronouns
DAY 4	Pronoun-Antecedent Agreement
DAY 5	Review Nouns and Pronouns

Objectives

- *To review possessive nouns*
- *To understand and identify possessive nouns*

Daily Proofreading

1. the boys bikes were in the garage (The boys'; garage.)
2. I can borrow one of Sandy pencils (Sandy's pencils.)

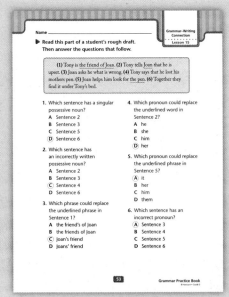

▲ Grammar Practice Book, p. 53

Reinforce the Skill

REVIEW POSSESSIVE NOUNS Remind students that possessive nouns tell who owns something. Write the following sentences on the board:

The writer's pencil is sharp.
The students' books were open.

Explain that the first sentence has a singular noun, or one writer. Ask what shows that the writer owns the pencil. (*'s*) Explain that the second sentence has a plural noun, or more than one student. Ask: **What is done to show that the books belong to the students?** (An apostrophe is added after the *s*.) Sum up with the following:

- To make a singular noun possessive, add an apostrophe (') and *s*.

- To make a plural noun possessive, add an apostrophe after the *s*.

Practice/Apply

GUIDED PRACTICE Write the following on the board:

girl/shirt   boys/hats

Invite students to suggest possessive sentences, using the first word as the possesive noun. Write some of the sentences on the board, inviting students to write *'s* or *s'* as appropriate. Have students tell whether the noun is singular or plural and explain how they made the nouns possessive. (Possible responses: *girl* is singular, so add *'s* at the end of the word; *boys* is plural, so add an apostrophe at the end of the word.)

INDEPENDENT PRACTICE Have students use the words *cat* and *teacher* plus the correct punctuation to write a singular possessive sentence in their notebooks. Then have them use *cats* and *teachers* to write a plural possessive sentence. Invite students to share their sentences with the class.

 # Writing
Select and Revise

5-DAY WRITING
DAY 1	Select a Piece and Revise
DAY 2	Revise
DAY 3	Proofread and Publish
DAY 4	Publish
DAY 5	Present

Revise

SELECT WRITING Ask students to think about which of this Theme's writing assignments they would like to revise and publish. Ask: **Which piece did you like best? Which would you like to give more time and attention to?** After they have chosen a piece of writing, students should think about how they want to improve it.

REVISE FOR ORGANIZATION Tell students that no matter what kind of writing they are working on, they should always pay attention to how they organize their ideas. Remind students that when they read a selection, knowing what kind of selection it is tells them what to expect. Readers of their writing will expect a story to have a plot and will expect a letter to have the parts of a letter. Have students check and revise their writing for organization.

CONFER WITH STUDENTS Meet with individual students or with groups of students revising the same writing type. Use questions such as the following to prompt students to look at the organization of their writing: **Is it clear what two items are being compared and how they are similar? Have the characters and problem been introduced at the beginning? Is the cause-and-effect relationship clear?**

 VOICE Explain that students use their words to express their thoughts and feelings about a topic. Their voices will be expressed in the words they choose. Have students look over their drafts and underline any words that show how they think and feel.

GRAMMAR-WRITING CONNECTION Have students look through their writing for possessive nouns. Remind students to use an apostrophe and the letter *s* to show singular possessive nouns. They should put an apostrophe after the *s* for plural possessive nouns.

girl's	girls'	Sam's

Objectives

- *To select a piece of writing for revision*
- *To revise for organization*
- *To revise for possessive nouns*

Writing Prompt

Write Sentences to Explain Have students write two or three sentences explaining which writing assignment they chose and why. They should mention how they plan to change or improve the writing.

Build Vocabulary Guide students to brainstorm a list of words that would show positive feelings about a topic and a list of words that would indicate negative feelings. Encourage students to refer to the lists to help them set a tone in their writing.

Day at a Glance

Day 2

 **and Spelling**

- Review: Consonant Digraphs /n/*kn*, *gn*; /r/*wr*; and /f/*gh*

Comprehension

 Review: Plot

- Review: Use Context Clues

Fluency

READERS' THEATER

- Read Together: "Ask the Experts," *Student Edition*, pp. 433–439

Read!

Robust Vocabulary

- *Read-Aloud Anthology*: "Thunder Cake"

Words from the Read-Aloud

- Introduce: *shudder, luscious*

Grammar

- Review: Singular and Plural Pronouns

Writing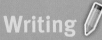

- Revise

Warm-Up Routines

 ## Oral Language

Objectives *To listen attentively and respond appropriately to oral communication; to respond using appropriate elaboration*

Question of the Day

When has someone or something surprised you?

Invite students to share what happened when they have surprised someone. Then ask students to tell about times when they have been surprised. (Possible responses: a surprise birthday party; someone jumping out from a hiding place; an unexpected visitor) Then have students answer the following writing prompt in their notebooks:

I was surprised when _____.

Instruct students to write one or two sentences telling what happened and why they were surprised. Remind students that exclamation marks are used to show excitement. Invite students to share their writing with the class.

Read Aloud

Objectives *To read poetry for understanding and enjoyment; to set a purpose for listening*

REREAD A POEM Reread the poem with students, using the following steps:

Introduce the text. Display **Transparency R79** or distribute photocopies to students. Tell them you are going to read the poem "The Letter" aloud.

Set a purpose. Ask students why they might read or listen to a poem more than once. (for enjoyment, to listen for rhyming words) Explain that students will enjoy the poem more if they compare it to their own experiences. Tell students that, as they listen to the poem, they should imagine how they would feel in this situation.

Model fluent reading. Read the poem aloud. Model reading aloud with expression to show the emotions in the poem.

Discuss the poem. Encourage students to discuss the girl's feelings about May and about receiving the letter. Ask students to use evidence from the poem and their own experiences to explain their points.

The Letter

I looked in the mailbox. What did I see?
A letter was sitting, addressed just to me.

I never received a letter before.
So I grabbed it and ran inside the front door.

I opened it, my head like a drum.
I looked at the end. Who was it from?

There at the bottom was the name "May"—
My very best friend who had just moved away.

She liked her new teacher, whose name was Miss Wu,
And she said that she missed me—"I want to see you."

I read my first letter again and again,
And answered it back, right there and then.

Grade 3, Lesson 12   R9   Warm-Up: Days 2–3

Transparency R79

Digraphs *kn, gn, wr,* and *gh*

 *and Spelling*

Objectives

- *To read words with consonant digraphs*
- *To explore words with the letter combinations* kn, gn, wr, *and* gh

Skill Trace

 Digraphs /n/ *kn, gn;* /r/ *wr;* and /f/ *gh*

Introduce	Grade 2
Reintroduce	T126–T127
Reteach	S14
Review	T136–T137, T158, T174, T186, T400–T401
Test	Theme 3
Maintain	Theme 4, T344

Spelling Words

1.	title	9.	police
2.	rattle	10.	giant
3.	saddle	11.	judge
4.	gnat	12.	hotel
5.	knight	13.	seven
6.	wrench	14.	broken
7.	rough	15.	taken
8.	edge		

Review

 DIGRAPHS Remind students that words often have groups of letters that stand for one sound. Write the following words on the board:

knee   gnaw   wrinkle   tough

Explain that each of these words has a letter combination that stands for one sound. Circle *kn, gn, wr,* and *gh* in the words. Ask students to identify the sounds made by each of these letter combinations. (*kn*—/n/; *gn*—/n/; *wr*—/r/; *gh*—/f/) Explain that *gh* can also stand for /g/. When it comes at the end of a word or syllable, though, it often stands for /f/. Have students read the words.

Practice/Apply

GUIDED PRACTICE Write the words *knit, sign, wrist,* and *cough* on the board. Have volunteers circle the *kn, gn, wr,* and *gh* letter combinations. Discuss the sound each letter combination stands for. Have students read the words.

INDEPENDENT PRACTICE Have students find the spelling words that contain *kn, gn, wr,* and *gh* and write them in their notebooks. (knight, gnat, wrench, rough)

BELOW-LEVEL

Identify Sounds Guide students to identify the digraphs in the spelling words. Then have them write lightly above each digraph a letter for the sound that is pronounced.

ADVANCED

Determine Phonics Rules Point out that *knight* contains two of the letter combinations discussed. However, *gh* in *knight* does not stand for /f/. Ask students what sound *igh* makes in *knight*. (long *i*) Have students think of other /ī/ *igh* words. (night, right, sigh, high)

5-DAY PHONICS/SPELLING

DAY 1	C-*le* Syllable
DAY 2	Digraphs *kn, gn, wr,* and *gh*
DAY 3	Consonant /s/*c* and /j/*g, dge*
DAY 4	V/CV and VC/V Syllable Patterns
DAY 5	Combined Review

Identify Sounds

APPLY PHONICS Tell students to look at the spelling words they wrote in their notebooks. Remind students that a single letter usually stands for the sounds represented by the letter combinations in these words. Point out that students will have to learn the spellings of words with these letter combinations.

WRITE Dictate the words *gnat, wrench, rough,* and *knight.* Have students write the words in their notebooks and circle the letter combinations *gn, wr, gh,* and *kn*. Then, have them write another word that has the same sound as each digraph but is spelled with a single letter. (Possible responses: gnat/nose; wrench/risk; rough/if; knight/nice)

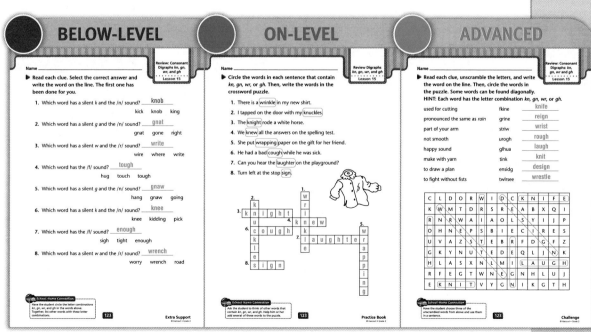

▲ Extra Support, p. 123   ▲ Practice Book, p. 123   ▲ Challenge, p. 123

ELL

- Group students according to academic levels, and assign one of the pages on the left.
- Clarify any unfamiliar concepts as necessary. See *ELL Teacher Guide* Lesson 15 for support in scaffolding instruction.

Plot
Comprehension: Review

Objectives

- To review that plot is the events in a story and often includes a problem and its solution
- To identify plot in a story

Skill Trace

 Plot

Introduce	T32–T33
Reteach	S6
Review	T63, T79, T91, T128–T129, T161, T177, T189, T387, T402
Test	Theme 3
Maintain	Theme 4, T80

▲ Test Prep System

Reinforce the Skill

DISCUSS PLOT Remind students that the plot is what happens in the story. The important events make up the plot. Explain that the plot often includes a problem that must be solved or a goal the characters must achieve. The characters try to solve the problem or reach the goal.

Practice/Apply

GUIDED PRACTICE Have students turn to *Student Edition* page 433. Ask what problem or goal the characters have. (They have to offer advice to the children who wrote to the magazine.) Discuss the important events. (receiving each letter and giving each piece of advice) Ask students whether the characters solve the problem or reach their goal and have students give reasons for their answers. (Yes, because the characters have advice for every letter they chose and they think the next issue of the magazine will be the best one yet.)

INDEPENDENT PRACTICE Have students complete a story map for "Ask the Experts."

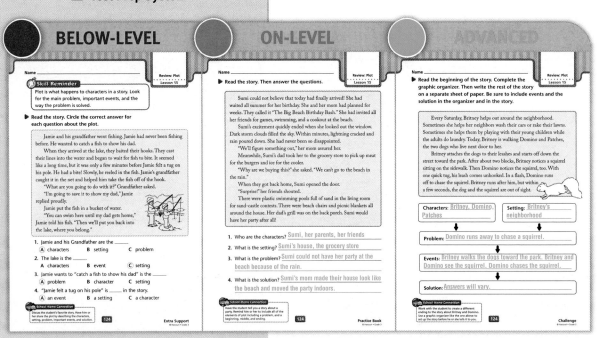

▲ Extra Support, p. 124   ▲ Practice Book, p. 124   ▲ Challenge, p. 124

ELL

- Group students according to academic levels and assign one of the pages on the left.

- Clarify any unfamiliar concepts as necessary. See *ELL Teacher Guide* Lesson 15 for support in scaffolding instruction.

Use Context Clues
Comprehension: Review

Reinforce the Skill

REVIEW USING CONTEXT CLUES Remind students that context clues can help readers figure out the meanings of unfamiliar words. To find the meaning of a new word, readers should look at the sentence in which that word appears. They may find a definition or a synonym for the word. They may also find clues that can help them figure out its meaning.

Practice/Apply

GUIDED PRACTICE Write the following sentence on the board: *On our way to school we got drenched by a heavy rainstorm.* Have students use the sentence to determine the meaning of *drenched*. (made soaking wet) Have a volunteer underline the sentence clue that was helpful. (heavy rainstorm)

INDEPENDENT PRACTICE Write the following sentence on the board: *I discuss problems with my mom because she is wise and solves them with sage advice.* Have students copy the sentence in their notebooks and write what they think *sage* means. (wise) Have them underline context clues that helped them figure out that meaning. (she is wise, solves them, advice)

Objective
- *To use context clues to find the meanings of unknown words*

Skill Trace
 Use Context Clues

Introduce	T70–T71
Reteach	S8
Review	T168–T169, T403, T413
Test	Theme 3
Maintain	Theme 4, T264

READERS' THEATER

Read Together: "Ask the Experts"

5-DAY READERS' THEATER

DAY 1	Read Aloud/Read Along
DAY 2	Read Together
DAY 3	Choose/Rehearse Roles
DAY 4	Rehearse Roles
DAY 5	Perform

Objective

• *To read with expression and intonation*

Fluency Support Materials

Fluency Builders, Grade 3, Lesson 15

Audiotext "Ask the Experts" is available on *Audiotext 3* for subsequent readings.

"RESEARCH SAYS"

Repeated Reading "Reading rate increased significantly from one to three readings, an occurrence that brought instructional-level readers to near mastery-level performance."

Rasinski, et al (1994), p. 224

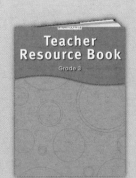

Teacher Resource Book
Grade 3

▲ Teacher Resource Book, pp. 121–124

Preview

GENRE Recall with students that "Ask the Experts" is a script about an advice column. An advice column takes questions from its readers and offers advice to answer them. Ask students if they have ever asked a friend or family member for advice or if they have read an advice column in a magazine. Discuss what kind of advice was offered and, if they know, whether that advice was followed.

Focus on Fluency

DISCUSS READING WITH EXPRESSION AND INTONATION Explain to students that, when they read aloud, good readers use their voices to show changes in action or characters' feelings. Remind students that one way to show action or feeling is the rise and fall of a reader's voice, also known as *intonation*.

Read Together

ORAL READING Post a list of roles. Place students in small groups. Have students take turns reading the different parts in the Readers' Theater script until each student has read several roles. Tell students that they will choose or you will assign parts on another day. Explain that, in this first reading, they should concentrate on reading with the appropriate intonation and expression in their voices. Tell students that when they make mistakes, they should first correct their errors and then continue reading.

Visit the different groups, listening to students read. Offer encouragement, and model fluent reading as students need it.

Think Aloud **I know that some children who write in for advice are really worried about their problems. I try to show that emotion in my voice.**

Build Robust Vocabulary
Words from the Read-Aloud

Teach/Model

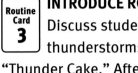

INTRODUCE ROBUST VOCABULARY
Discuss students' experiences with thunderstorms before reading aloud "Thunder Cake." After reading, discuss the plot of the story. Then use *Routine Card 3* to introduce the Vocabulary Words.

▲ Read-Aloud Anthology, "Thunder Cake", p.54

❶ Put the word in **selection context**.
❷ Display **Transparency R102** and read the word and the **Student-Friendly Explanation**.
❸ Have students **say the word** with you.
❹ Use the word in other contexts, and have students **interact with the word's meaning**.
❺ Remove the transparency. Say the Student-Friendly Explanation again, and ask students to **name the word** that goes with it.

❶ **Selection Context:** The low, rumbling sound of thunder makes the windows **shudder** in their panes.
❹ **Interact with Word Meaning:** Which sound is more likely to make you shudder—a loud crashing noise or the sound of a fountain?

❶ **Selection Context:** The boy picked three **luscious** tomatoes for dinner.
❹ **Interact with Word Meaning:** Would you think a slice of melon or a slice of onion is luscious?

Practice/Apply

GUIDED PRACTICE Ask students the following:

• **What might make a person shudder? Imagine one of those things has happened. How would you look?**

• **What do you think is the most luscious food? What would you do or say if you had just eaten some of that food?**

Objective
• *To develop rich vocabulary through discussing a literature selection*

INTRODUCE [Tested ✓]

Vocabulary: Lesson 15

luscious

shudder

▼ Student-Friendly Explanations

Student-Friendly Explanations	
expertise	If someone has expertise, he or she knows a lot about a particular topic or skill.
correspondence	If you send correspondence, you are communicating in writing.
luscious	Something that is luscious appeals to your senses, such as your sense of taste.
shudder	If you shudder, you are trembling from fear or from being cold.

Grade 3, Lesson 15　　Rb　　TK[Robust Vocabulary]?

Transparency R102

Grammar
Review: Singular and Plural Pronouns

5-DAY GRAMMAR
DAY 1 Possessive Nouns
DAY 2 Singular and Plural Pronouns
DAY 3 Subject and Object Pronouns
DAY 4 Pronoun-Antecedent Agreement
DAY 5 Review Nouns and Pronouns

Objectives
- *To review pronouns*
- *To recognize that pronouns replace nouns*

Daily Proofreading
1. james wore they coat. (James; his coat.)
2. all the boys and girls need his books? (All; their books.)

▲ Practice Book, p. 125

Reinforce the Skill

REVIEW PRONOUNS Remind students that a noun names a person, place, or thing and that pronouns take the place of a noun. Explain that a singular pronoun takes the place of a singular noun, and a plural pronoun takes the place of a plural noun. Write the following on the board:

I	we, us
you	you
he, him, she, her, it	they, them

Guide students to identify the pronouns that replace singular nouns (I, you, he, him, she, her, it) and plural nouns. (we, us, you, they, them) Point out that *you* can be singular or plural, depending on whether it replaces the name of one person or two or more people.

Practice/Apply

GUIDED PRACTICE Write the following sentences on the board:

The mail carrier gave Melissa's letter to _____. (her)

We told Raven and Darnell that _____ could join us. (they)

Have students read the sentences and think about what pronoun is missing in each sentence. Have volunteers come to the board and fill in the blanks.

INDEPENDENT PRACTICE Have students write two sentences that include pronouns, but have them leave blank lines for the pronouns. Tell students to exchange sentences with a partner and to use appropriate pronouns to complete each other's sentences. Have students discuss their answers. Invite volunteers to share their sentences with the class.

5-DAY WRITING	
DAY 1	Select a Piece and Revise
DAY 2	Revise
DAY 3	Proofread and Publish
DAY 4	Publish
DAY 5	Present

Writing
Revise

Revise

WRITING TRAIT **SENTENCE FLUENCY** Remind students that their sentences should be varied and flow easily from one to the next.

WRITING TRAIT **VOICE** Tell students that every writer has his or her own voice. Writers choose words to make their feelings clear and to make the reader feel the same way.

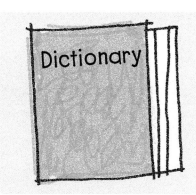

Dictionary

REVISE FOR SENTENCE FLUENCY AND VOICE Tell students to read their writing to see whether changing a statement to a question or an exclamation would make their writing more interesting. Explain that sentences of different lengths also make writing more interesting to read.

Remind students to check that their sentences flow from one to the next. If there is a connection between two ideas, perhaps they should add a transition word or phrase such as *however*, *but*, or *for instance*. Tell students to be sure that the reader knows whether a character is likeable or whether the topic is something the writer likes.

Think Aloud **As I reread my comparison, I see that I could begin with the question "What is similar about an apple and an orange?" Also, I wonder if I made it clear that I really like to eat apples and oranges? I'll add, "They are both luscious."**

CONFER WITH STUDENTS Meet with individual students to help them as they write. Point out positive aspects of students' writing as you make suggestions for improvement. "I like the way you began with a question. Can you vary some of the other sentences?"

GRAMMAR-WRITING CONNECTION Remind students that singular pronouns are used to replace singular nouns and that plural pronouns are used to replace plural nouns.

Objectives

- *To revise writing, in order to develop and refine ideas*
- *To achieve a sense of completeness in writing*

Writing Prompt

Use Dialogue in Realistic Writing
Have students write about something that has actually happened today. Tell them to include at least one sentence of dialogue in their writing.

Writer's Companion
Grade 3

▲ **Writer's Companion, Lesson 15**

Day at a Glance
Day
3

 phonics and Spelling

- Review: Consonants /s/*c* and /j/*g*, *dge*

Comprehension

Review: Author's Purpose

- Review: Use Context Clues

Fluency

READERS' THEATER

- Choose Roles/Rehearse "Ask the Experts," *Student Edition*, pp. 433–439

Read!

Robust Vocabulary

- Review: *luscious, shudder, issue, advice, consult, recommend, sensible, devise, expertise, correspondence*

Grammar

- Review: Subject and Object Pronouns

Writing

- Proofread and Publish

Warm-Up Routines

Oral Language

Objectives *To listen attentively and respond appropriately to oral communication; to respond using appropriate elaboration*

Question of the Day

What do you talk about with your friends?

Ask students what they enjoy most about talking with their friends. (Possible responses: It's fun; it's nice to have someone to share stories with or to discuss problems with.) Ask students how they communicate with their friends. (Possible responses: telephone, notes, letters, in person, e-mail) Then have students answer the following writing prompt by writing one or two sentences in their notebooks:

What do you and your friends like to talk about?

Encourage students to elaborate by including whether they like to talk on the phone, in person, or on the computer. Invite students to share their writing with the class.

Read Aloud

Objectives *To listen and respond to a poem; to read poetry fluently*

Share the poem with students using the following steps:

REVIEW THE POEM Display **Transparency R79.** Explain that you are going to reread the poem "The Letter" aloud.

Set a purpose. Have students tell what purpose they might have for reading or listening to a poem again. (for enjoyment, to practice reading aloud) Tell students they will follow along, listening carefully as you read the poem aloud. Then they will echo-read to practice reading fluently.

Model fluent reading. Read the poem aloud, using expression to match the emotion and content of the poem and to reflect punctuation.

Echo-read. Remind students to listen carefully as you read and to try to sound like you. Tell students to pay attention to punctuation as they read. They also should use their voices to show the excitement in the poem. Read the poem again, pausing at the end of each line for students to repeat the line.

The Letter

I looked in the mailbox. What did I see?
A letter was sitting, addressed just to me.

I never received a letter before.
So I grabbed it and ran inside the front door.

I opened it, my head like a drum.
I looked at the end. Who was it from?

There at the bottom was the name "May"—
My very best friend who had just moved away.

She liked her new teacher, whose name was Miss Wu,
And she said that she missed me—"I want to see you."

I read my first letter again and again,
And answered it back, right there and then.

Grade 3, Lesson 12   Rc.   Warm-Up: Days 2–3

Transparency R79

Consonants /s/ c and /j/ g, dge

 **phonics** *and Spelling*

Objectives

- *To use decoding strategies to clarify pronunciation*
- *To review common spelling patterns*
- *To use a variety of spelling strategies*

Skill Trace

 Tested /s/ c and /j/ g, dge

Introduce	Grade 2
Reintroduce	T212–T213
Reteach	S26
Review	T222, T246, T262, T274, T410–T411
Test	Theme 3
Maintain	Theme 4, T176

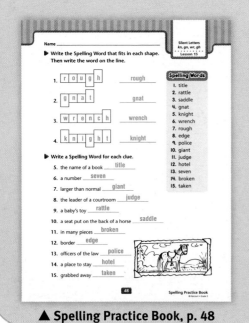

▲ **Spelling Practice Book, p. 48**

Review

REVIEW /s/ c AND /j/ g, dge Remind students that *c* usually stands for the sound /k/, but when it is followed by *e* or *i*, it usually stands for /s/. This sound is sometimes called the soft sound of *c*. The letter *g* usually stands for /g/, but when it is followed by *e* or *i*, it often stands for /j/. This is called the soft sound of *g*. Remind students that the spelling pattern *dge* also stands for /j/. Write the following words on the board: *circle, ridge, cereal, giant*. Have students identify the letter following *c* or *g* or the letter pattern *dge* and then read the words.

Read Words in Context

GUIDED PRACTICE Write the following sentences on the board:

> **Cindy gave celery to the rabbit.**
>
> **Margie wrote advice in the margin.**

Have students identify the words that have the soft sound of *g* or *c* and explain how they know. (Cindy, celery; Margie, advice, margin; *c* or *g* is followed by *e* or *i*)

INDEPENDENT PRACTICE Write the following sentences on the board:

> **The prince lived in a giant castle.**
>
> **I will give you my pencil so you can**
> **number your page.**

Have students copy the sentences in their notebooks and circle the words with soft *c* and soft *g* sounds. (prince, giant, pencil, page)

5-DAY PHONICS/SPELLING	
DAY 1	C-*le* Syllable
DAY 2	Digraphs *kn, gn, wr,* and *gh*
DAY 3	**Consonants /s/c and /j/g, dge**
DAY 4	V/CV and VC/V Syllable Patterns
DAY 5	Combined Review

Review Spelling Words

REVIEW SPELLING SKILLS Have students write the spelling words that have /s/c and /j/g, *dge*. (edge, police, giant, judge) Remind students that most words that have the /s/ sound are spelled with *s* and that most words with the /j/ sound are spelled with *j*. Remind students that the spelling *dge* comes at the end of a word or syllable.

WRITE Remind students that a good strategy for reviewing spelling words is to write them. Have students copy the spelling words into their notebooks.

Handwriting

LETTER SIZE Remind students that tall letters, such as *b, d, f, h, k, l,* and *t,* should reach up towards the line above. Letters with tails, such as *g, j, p, q,* and *y,* should reach approximately halfway down to the line below. Explain that this helps readers recognize the letters and read their work. Have students look over their work to be sure their letters are the appropriate size.

ADVANCED

Exceptions to Rules Remind students that words with the letters *ice* usually rhyme with *ice*. Ask students to identify a spelling word that is an exception. (police) Challenge students to think of other exceptions. (Possible responses: office, notice)

Spelling Words

1. **title**	6. **wrench**	11. **judge**
2. **rattle**	7. **rough**	12. **hotel**
3. **saddle**	8. **edge**	13. **seven**
4. **gnat**	9. **police**	14. **broken**
5. **knight**	10. **giant**	15. **taken**

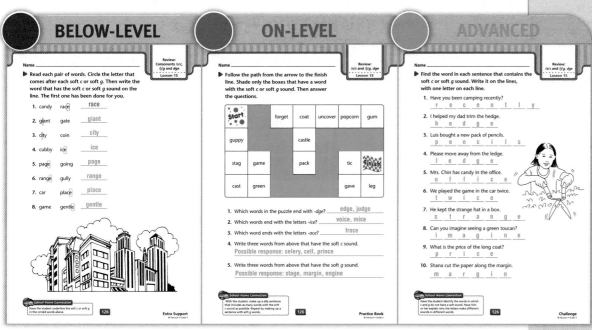

▲ Extra Support, p. 126   ▲ Practice Book, p. 126   ▲ Challenge, p. 126

E L L

- Group students according to academic levels, and assign one of the pages on the left.
- Clarify any unfamiliar concepts as necessary. See *ELL Teacher Guide* Lesson 15 for support in scaffolding instruction.

Author's Purpose
Comprehension: Review

Reinforce the Skill

DISCUSS AUTHOR'S PURPOSE Remind students that the author's purpose is the reason he or she wrote something. Talk with students about the most common purposes for writing. (to entertain, to inform, to persuade, to teach a lesson) Emphasize that understanding the author's purpose can help readers set a purpose for reading and better understand a selection.

Practice/Apply

GUIDED PRACTICE Tell students that you are going to describe several different writing situations and that students are to tell the author's purpose for each of them. Remind them that an author can have more than one purpose for writing.

- **Why might an author write a letter to the editor supporting someone who is running for mayor?** (to persuade, to inform)

- **Why might an author write a poem about the sea?** (to entertain)

- **Why might an author write a funny story that takes place on a farm?** (to entertain)

- **Why might an author write an article about his or her experience in a hot-air balloon?** (to inform, to entertain)

INDEPENDENT PRACTICE Have students work with a partner to discuss "Ask the Experts." Have partners determine the author's purpose or purposes and write three reasons for their conclusion. Have partners share their work with the group. (to inform and to entertain; Possible reasons: readers learn about an advice column; readers read advice for homework, making friends, and other problems; it's fun to read)

Use Context Clues
Comprehension: Review

Reinforce the Skill

REVIEW USING CONTEXT CLUES Remind students that good readers use context clues to figure out the meanings of unfamiliar words. Other words in the sentence can help them figure out what the word means.

Practice/Apply

GUIDED PRACTICE Write the following sentences on the board:

> Tamika <u>clutched</u> the coin and held it tight.
>
> The farmer made <u>furrows</u> in the ground and planted seeds in the cut lines.

Work with students to identify clues in each sentence for the underlined words. (clutched—held tight; furrows—cut lines)

INDEPENDENT PRACTICE Write the sentences below on the board. Have students write the clues for the underlined words.

> Tom likes to <u>roam</u> around the park.
>
> "I did NOT do that!" said Grace <u>indignantly</u>.

Objective

• *To use context clues to find the meanings of unknown words*

Skill Trace

Tested **Use Context Clues**

Introduce	T70–T71
Reteach	S8
Review	T168–T169, T403, T413
Test	Theme 3
Maintain	Theme 4, T264

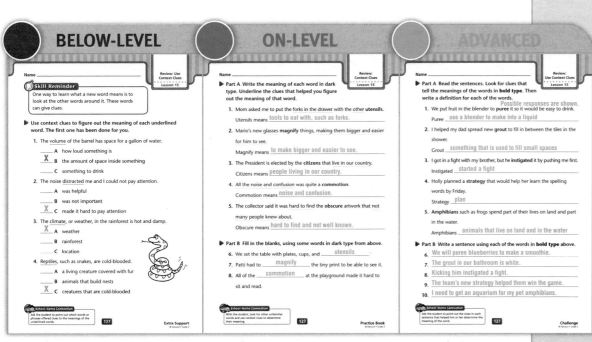

▲ Extra Support, p. 127 ▲ Practice Book, p. 127 ▲ Challenge, p.

E L L

• Group students according to academic levels, and assign one of the pages on the left.

• Clarify any unfamiliar concepts as necessary. See *ELL Teacher Guide* Lesson 15 for support in scaffolding instruction.

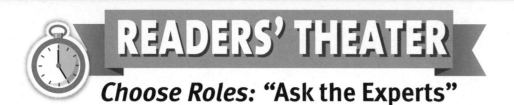

READERS' THEATER

Choose Roles: "Ask the Experts"

5-DAY READERS' THEATER

DAY 1 Read Aloud/Read Along
DAY 2 Read Together
DAY 3 Choose/Rehearse Roles
DAY 4 Rehearse Roles
DAY 5 Perform

Objective

- *To read fluently with appropriate expression and intonation*

Fluency Support Materials

Fluency Builders,
Grade 3, Lesson 15

 Audiotext "Ask the Experts" is available on *Audiotext 3* for subsequent readings.

ADVANCED

Leveled Parts Assign more challenging roles, such as Taylor, to advanced readers.

Leveled Parts Assign the parts of Corey and Friend Lee to students who need extra support.

Focus on Fluency

READ WITH EXPRESSION AND INTONATION Remind students that when they read aloud, they should read with accuracy. They also should read with appropriate expression and intonation. Tell them that, in plays, paying attention to the characters' feelings can help them know how to read specific parts.

Practice Reading

CHOOSE/ASSIGN ROLES Distribute copies of the script to the students if you have not already done so. Assign or have students choose roles. Then have students highlight their part. Also encourage them to make notes on their scripts to remind themselves of how and when to read with special expression. You may prefer to highlight and mark the scripts.

PRACTICE READING Remind students to follow along as others read. Some students may need to place a card or ruler under the lines to follow along, but others may be comfortable holding the pages farther from their bodies so they can look out.

As students read the script aloud, circulate, providing feedback to individuals and groups by modeling, encouraging, and praising students for their efforts and enthusiasm. If students make a mistake, encourage them to try again. Also encourage students to give positive feedback to each other as they read their parts.

Tell students to pay attention to how well they time their starting point, how smoothly they end, and how well they mimic natural speech.

Build Robust Vocabulary
Review

Reinforce Word Meanings

USE VOCABULARY IN DIFFERENT CONTEXTS Remind students of the meanings of the Vocabulary Words introduced on Days 1 and 2. Guide them to discuss each word in a new context.

- Would you rather receive an early **issue** of the newspaper or a late issue? Why?

- If you wanted to bake a cake, whom would you **consult**? What kind of cake would be **luscious**?

- What kind of foods would you **recommend** to a person visiting from a foreign country?

- Why would you ask a **sensible** person for **advice**?

- What kind of project might require you to **devise** a plan? What kind of **expertise** would you need?

Objectives
- *To review rich vocabulary*
- *To demonstrate knowledge of word meaning*

REVIEW | Tested

Vocabulary: Lesson 15

luscious	recommend
shudder	sensible
issue	devise
advice	expertise
consult	correspondence

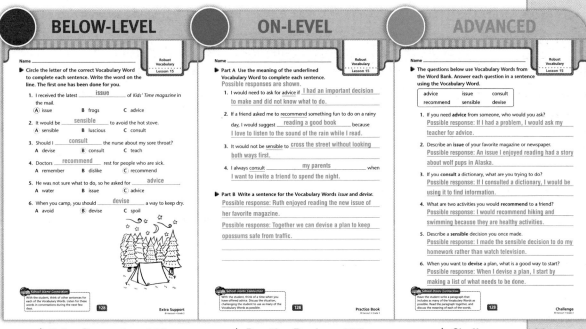

BELOW-LEVEL

▲ Extra Support, p. 128

ON-LEVEL

▲ Practice Book, p. 128

ADVANCED

▲ Challenge, p. 128

Grammar
Review: Subject and Object Pronouns

Objective

- *To correctly use subject and object pronouns*

Daily Proofreading

Me gave the gift to he on tuesday. (I; him; Tuesday.)

Reinforce the Skill

DISCUSS SUBJECT PRONOUNS Remind students that a pronoun takes the place of a noun. Explain that only subject pronouns can take the place of the subject of a sentence—whom or what the sentence is about. Write the following subject pronouns on the board and have students read them:

I   you   he   she   it   we   they

DISCUSS OBJECT PRONOUNS Remind students that an object in a sentence receives an action or has something done to it. Explain that object pronouns can take an place of an object. Write the following object pronouns on the board and have students read them:

me   you   him   her   it   us   them

Explain that object pronouns cannot be used to take the place of the subject. Point out that the words *it* and *you* are on both lists and that they can be used as the subject or an object in a sentence.

Practice/Apply

GUIDED PRACTICE Write the following sentence on the board:

_____ went to the park to watch _____.

Explain that the subject and object are missing from the sentence. Ask what kind of pronoun belongs in the first blank. (subject) Have students select a subject pronoun to fill in the blank. Ask what kind of pronoun belongs in the second blank. (object) Have students select an object pronoun to fill in the blank. Have students read the completed sentence.

INDEPENDENT PRACTICE Instruct students to copy the sentence frame above into their notebooks three times. Then have them use different subject and object pronouns on each blank line, to create three different sentences. Have students compare their sentences with a partner.

Writing
Proofread and Publish

5-DAY WRITING	
DAY 1	Select a Piece and Revise
DAY 2	Revise
DAY 3	**Proofread and Publish**
DAY 4	Publish
DAY 5	Present

Publish

INTRODUCE A PUBLISHING IDEA Tell students that they will be publishing their writing in a magazine. Tell them that after they have finished revising, proofreading, and making a clean copy of their writing, they will act as editors, just like Corey and Taylor, and decide how the magazine will be put together.

GRAMMAR-WRITING CONNECTION Tell students to check that they have correctly used subject and object pronouns.

PROOFREAD Allow time for students to finalize their writing. Then have them proofread for spelling, capitalization, and punctuation and make corrections.

PRESENTATION Explain that many people will have the opportunity to enjoy the works that the class publishes, so it is important that students' handwriting is neat and that all errors are corrected. You may wish to input, or have students input, their writing on a computer for publishing.

PREPARE FINAL WRITING Instruct students to begin working on the final copy of their story. Before students begin copying or inputting their writing, model leaving margins all around the page and indenting each new paragraph. Remind them to use their best handwriting.

Objectives

- *To develop drafts*
- *To follow the general conventions of capitalization, punctuation, and page format*

Day at a Glance

Day 4

 phonics and Spelling

- Review: V/CV and VC/V Syllable Patterns

COMPREHENSION STRATEGIES

Review: Use Story Structure and Ask Questions

Reading

- Reading a Chapter Book: "Iris and Walter, True Friends," *Student Edition*, pp. 432–439

Read!

Fluency

READERS' THEATER

- Choose Roles/Rehearse: "Ask the Experts," *Student Edition*, pp. 432–439

Robust Vocabulary

- Review: *expertise, correspondence, issue, advice, consult, recommend, sensible, devise, luscious, shudder*

Grammar

- Review: Pronoun-Antecedent Agreement

Writing

- Publish

Warm-Up Routines

Oral Language

Objectives *To listen attentively and respond appropriately to oral communication; to respond by using appropriate elaboration*

> ### Question of the Day
>
> **What wild creatures have you seen in your neighborhood?**

Remind students that there are wild creatures of all kinds just about everywhere. Ask students to share experiences observing wild creatures such as rabbits in a yard, ants on a sidewalk, birds on rooftops, or animals in a zoo or wildlife park. Lead a discussion on ways to observe wild animals without disturbing them. Then have students answer the following writing prompt in their notebooks:

I saw a _____. It was _____.

Tell students to complete the first sentence with the type of creature and the second sentence with what the creature was doing. Have students write one or two additional sentences about where they saw the creature and what they observed. Have students share their sentences with the group.

Read Aloud

Objectives *To listen and respond critically to oral communication; to set a purpose for listening*

READ ALOUD A POEM Display **Transparency R95** or distribute photocopies to students. Tell them that you are going to reread "Hey, Bug!"

Set a purpose. Ask what the purpose might be for reading or listening to a poem again. (to enjoy; to learn more about the author's thoughts) Tell students to listen and follow along to enjoy the poem.

Model fluent reading. Read the poem aloud, being careful to model appropriate intonation.

Discuss the poem. Talk with students about the poem. Then ask:

• **Why do you think the writer wants to play with the bug?**

• **What do you think the writer could do to make the bug want to stay?**

Hey, Bug!

Hey, bug, stay!
Don't run away,
I know a game that we can play.

I'll hold my fingers very still
and you can climb a finger-hill.

No, no,
Don't go.

Here's a wall—a tower, too,
a tiny bug town, just for you.
I've a cookie. You have some.
Take this oatmeal cookie crumb.

Hey, bug, stay!
Hey, bug!
Hey!

Grade 3, Lesson 14   Rc   Warm-Up: Days 2–3

Transparency R95

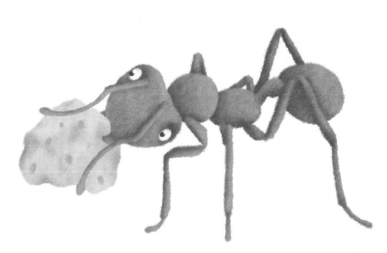

V/CV and VC/V Syllable Patterns

 and Spelling

Objectives

- *To identify V/CV and VC/V syllable patterns in words*
- *To use V/CV and VC/V patterns to decode multisyllabic words*

Skill Trace

 V/CV and VC/V Syllable Patterns

Introduce	Grade 2
Reintroduce	T300–T301
Reteach	S38
Review	T310–T311, T330, T346, T358, T420–T421
Test	Theme 3

 BELOW-LEVEL

Identifying Vowels Have students name the five vowel letters. Write *rapid*, *racing*, *favor*, and *sliver* on the board. Have students circle the vowels and draw squares around the consonants. Then have students look for the VCV pattern in the words by finding a circle-square-circle pattern.

 ADVANCED

Dividing Words Give student partners unfamiliar words such as *lava*, *prefer*, *record*, *vanish*, *cherish*, and *solar*. Have them divide the words and then use them in sentences. If students are unsure of the pronunciations or meanings, have them look up the words in a dictionary.

Review

V/CV AND VC/V SYLLABLE PATTERNS Write this sentence on the board:

The baby saw the shadow.

Point to the word *baby*. Tell students that this word has a consonant between two vowels. Remind students that when they see this pattern, they can try dividing the word after the first vowel and pronouncing the word with a long vowel sound. Mark the syllable and have students read the word. Ask if this sounds like a familiar word. (yes) Explain that if the word does not sound familiar, they can try dividing it after the second consonant and pronouncing a short vowel sound. Point to *shadow* and have students try dividing the word to pronounce a familiar word.

Practice/Apply

GUIDED PRACTICE Write the following words on the board:

final   habit   color   music

Have volunteers come to the board and guide them to divide the words into syllables. (fi/nal, hab/it, col/or, mu/sic) Discuss whether the first syllable of each word has a long or short vowel sound.

INDEPENDENT PRACTICE Have students draw two columns, labeling the first V/CV Long Vowel and the second VC/V Short Vowel. Instruct them to work with partners to write these words in the correct columns:

broken   given   Friday   begin   cabin   river

(V/CV: broken, Friday, begin; VC/V: given, cabin, river)

5-DAY PHONICS/SPELLING

DAY 1 C *-le* Syllables
DAY 2 Digraphs: *kn, gn, wr,* and *gh*
DAY 3 Consonants /s/c and /j/g, *dge*
DAY 4 V/CV and VC/V Syllable Patterns
DAY 5 Combined Review

Review Spelling Words

DIVIDE SYLLABLES Review the following syllable rules:

- Words with a consonant and *-le* at the end are divided so that one consonant and *-le* form a syllable. If the first syllable has a long vowel sound, there is only one consonant before *le*. If the first syllable has a short vowel sound, there are two consonants before *le,* and a syllable division is between them.

- VCV two-syllable words with a long vowel sound in the first syllable are divided after the first vowel.

- VCV two-syllable words with a short vowel sound in the first syllable are divided after the middle consonant.

Have students copy two-syllable spelling words into their notebooks. Then have them use these rules to divide the words into syllables. Point out that *giant* is divided between the two vowels because a syllable can only have one vowel sound. (ti/tle, po/lice, rat/tle, gi/ant, sad/dle, ho/tel, sev/en, bro/ken, ta/ken)

 WRITE Have students list the single-syllable spelling words in their notebooks.

Spelling Words

1. title	9. police
2. rattle	10. giant
3. saddle	11. judge
4. gnat	12. hotel
5. knight	13. seven
6. wrench	14. broken
7. rough	15. taken
8. edge	

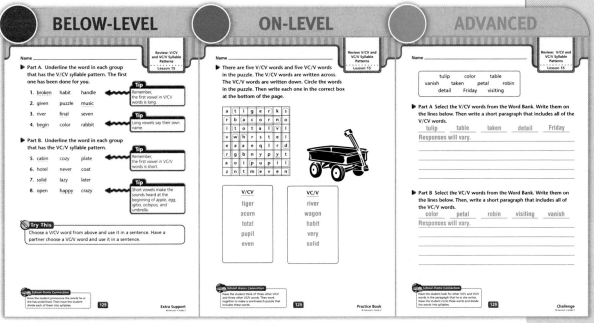

▲ Extra Support, p. 129   ▲ Practice Book, p. 129   ▲ Challenge, p. 129

ELL

- Group students according to academic levels, and assign one of the pages on the left.
- Clarify any unfamiliar concepts as necessary. See *ELL Teacher Guide* Lesson 15 for support in scaffolding instruction.

Comprehension Strategies
Review

Objectives

- *To review and use reading strategies*
- *To analyze genre features*

Reading Chapter Books

PREVIEW PAGES 440–441 Have students scan the pages. Tell them that these pages tell about the important parts of chapter books and how they can use those parts as they read.

SET A PURPOSE Tell students that their purpose for reading these two pages is to get information about chapter books.

DISCUSS TEXT FEATURES Have students read the information about reading a chapter book on page 440. Call students' attention to the first two pages of a chapter book, on page 441. Have students read aloud the explanatory boxes. Explain that

- The **title** often gives a clue to the plot of the book.

- Since chapter books are divided into parts called chapters, each chapter has a **chapter number and/or a title**.

- Chapter books have one long **plot** broken into chapters. The important events in the chapters lead to the big problem being solved, or the goal being reached, by the end of the book.

Review the Focus Strategies

DISCUSS COMPREHENSION STRATEGIES Have students read and discuss the information about using story structure and asking questions.

APPLY TO CHAPTER BOOKS Tell students that the main characters, setting, and problem are usually introduced in the first chapter. Explain that when students read a chapter book, they have to keep the big problem in mind and think about the important events. Remind them to ask themselves questions about what has happened, is happening, and will happen.

SET A PURPOSE AND READ THE SELECTION Tell students that "Iris and Walter, True Friends" is a chapter book about a boy, a girl, and a horse. Discuss what students know about horses. Then have them set a purpose for reading.

 BELOW-LEVEL

Use Story Structure Students may benefit from filling in a story map as they read "Iris and Walter, True Friends." Under **Plot** should be the subheadings *Problem* and *Solution*. Students can use the information on the story map to discuss with classmates what they read.

Theme Review

Lesson 15

COMPREHENSION STRATEGIES
Review

Reading a Chapter Book

Bridge to Reading Longer Fiction A chapter book is a long story divided into smaller sections called chapters. The notes on page 441 show some of the features of a chapter book. Before you read, scan a book for these features.

Review the Focus Strategies

You can also use the strategies you learned in this theme to help you read chapter books.

Use Story Structure
Use what you know about how stories are arranged to help you understand a chapter book. Think about the problem in each chapter. Think about the plot of the book as a whole and how it changes as you read each chapter.

Ask Questions
Ask yourself questions before, while, and after you read. What is happening in each chapter? How do the characters behave? What will happen next?

As you read two chapters from *Iris and Walter, True Friends* on pages 441-445, think about where and how to use the comprehension strategies.

440

TITLE
The title of the chapter book usually gives clues to what the book will be about.

CHAPTER NUMBER AND TITLE
Chapters may begin with a number, a title, or both.

PLOT
A chapter book has a plot that continues throughout the book. Look for smaller problems and solutions within chapters.

441

CHAPTER BOOK TEXT FEATURES

Point out the following additional information about chapter book features:
Book Title Sometimes the title is a clever way to get a reader interested in the book.
Chapter Number and Title A title might give a clue to what the chapter is about.
Plot Sometimes a chapter has a smaller plot of its own.

Apply the Strategies Read these two chapters from *Iris and Walter, True Friends*. As you read, stop and think about how you are using comprehension strategies.

Stop and Think

Think about the **story structure** in this chapter. What is the problem in this chapter?

1. DREAMING OF RAIN

Iris dreamed of riding Rain over green meadows, down a path of pines, straight into the sparkling stream.

"You can't ride Rain," said Walter.

"Why not?" asked Iris.

"Because," said Walter, "Rain is fast and wild."

But Iris *wanted* to ride Rain.

The next day, Iris put on her cowgirl boots. She put on her cowgirl hat. Then she and Walter went to see Rain. "Yoo-hoo, Rain. Come here!" shouted Iris. But Rain only snorted and stamped her hoof, then galloped away.

"Why doesn't she come?" asked Iris.

"Because," said Walter, "horses don't like shouting."

"Oh," said Iris.

The next day, Iris brought Rain a present. "Come here, Rain," said Iris. "I brought you Grandpa's special cookies."

But Rain did not come.

"Why doesn't she come?" asked Iris.

"Because," said Walter, "horses can be shy."

"Walter, what do horses like?" asked Iris.

"Horses like clucking and carrots and gentle hands," said Walter.

"Hmm," said Iris.

442

443

Monitor Comprehension

PAGES 442–443 Have students locate the book title and chapter title. To help students use comprehension strategies, have them read the Stop and Think box on page 443 before they read the chapter.

  AUTHOR'S PURPOSE **What do you think was the author's purpose in writing this chapter book?** (to entertain readers)

  PLOT **What is the problem in this chapter so far?** (The horse named Rain won't let Iris near her.)

Stop and Think

Apply Comprehension Strategies

 Use Story Structure, Ask Questions

Review with students how to use story structure and ask questions to comprehend the chapter.

Think Aloud I read that Iris, Walter, and the horse Rain are the characters in this story. I know that this is the beginning of the chapter, but already I see a problem with Rain and Iris. I'm asking why Rain is acting unfriendly or shy. Iris is thinking of a solution. I'll read on to find out what happens.

Stop and Think
What **questions** do you have so far? How does knowing about **story structure** help you keep track of the events?

(Text on pages 444-445:)

2. RIDING RAIN

The next day, Iris and Walter went to see Rain. They had carrots. They had hope. They had a plan.

Iris held out a carrot. "Come here, Rain," she said. But Rain did not come.

"Why doesn't she come?" asked Iris.

"Try clucking," said Walter.

So Iris clucked and clucked. Rain moved backwards. Rain moved sideways. But still, Rain did not come.

"Maybe Rain doesn't like me," said Iris.

"Maybe Rain is scared of you," said Walter.

"Don't be scared of me, Rain," said Iris.

Every day, Iris and Walter went to see Rain. Every day, Iris clucked and clucked—and held out a carrot.

Then one day, Rain walked slowly, slowly over to Iris. Iris felt Rain's hot breath on her hand. Rain stared at Iris. Then *chomp*—she ate the carrot!

"Oh," said Iris.

Day after day, Iris and Walter went to see Rain. They fed her carrots. They stroked her neck. They sang sweet songs in her ear.

Then one fine day, Iris climbed up on Rain's back. "Hold on, Iris. Hold on tight," said Walter. "Whatever you do, don't let go!"

And then Rain took off! Away Iris rode, over green meadows, down a path of pines, straight into the sparkling stream.

"Oh, Walter! Did you see me? Did you see me riding Rain?" asked Iris.

"Yes, you are very brave, Iris," said Walter.

"Thank you, Walter," said Iris.

"May I have a turn now?" asked Walter.

"You bet!" said Iris.

Monitor Comprehension

PAGES 444–445 Have students locate the chapter title and describe the clue that it gives about this chapter's events. Then tell students to read page 444. Have them stop and read the Stop and Think box at the top of page 445 before continuing reading.

1. **CHARACTERS' TRAITS What do you learn about Iris's character on these pages?** (She does not give up until she achieves her dream.)

2. **PLOT How is the plot's problem solved in this chapter? What do you think might happen in the next chapter?** (Rain learns to trust Iris over time. In the next chapter, Walter might get to ride Rain.)

Stop and Think
Apply Comprehension Strategies

Ask Questions

Review with students whether they noted the story structure in reading this next chapter. Ask them what questions they still have.

Think Aloud As I'm reading, I'm wondering whether Rain will ever go near Iris. Is Rain just scared? Why is she scared? As the story goes on, I see that Iris's problem is solved. It looks like there is perhaps another chapter to come, since Walter wants to try riding Rain, too.

READERS' THEATER
Rehearse Roles: "Ask the Experts"

5-DAY READERS' THEATER

DAY 1	Read Aloud/Read Along
DAY 2	Read Together
DAY 3	Choose/Rehearse Roles
DAY 4	**Rehearse Roles**
DAY 5	Perform

Objective

• *To read for automaticity and fluency*

Fluency Support Materials

Fluency Builders, Grade 3, Lesson 15

 Audiotext "Ask the Experts" is available on *Audiotext 3* for subsequent readings.

Focus on Fluency

READING WITH INTONATION AND EXPRESSION Have students rehearse in their groups, reading their parts aloud. Explain that since students are going to perform the Readers' Theater, they need to practice reading their lines with expression. Tell them that, as they rehearse, they should pretend that they have an audience in front of them.

> **Think Aloud** I practiced reading the role of Smarty Jackson several times. I realized that I want the other experts to take me seriously when I speak. I make my voice go higher and lower to sound natural when I read. This makes it easy for others to understand what I am saying.

Practice Reading

REHEARSE ROLES Have students reading the same roles assemble in groups so they can help one another with how the character speaks. Have students take turns reading the character's speech while group members listen and offer positive comments. For example, a student might say, "I like the way you changed your voice to sound sad."

Circulate and model reading particular lines if students are struggling. If you copied pages 121–124 in the *Teacher Resource Book* so students have individual scripts, they may want to draw two lines under sections that should be read with more emotion.

After students have read through the script in their character groups, have them reassemble in their complete cast groups to practice reading together. Tell them to stand or sit in the positions they will take on Day 5, when they read for their audience. Prepare the backdrop presented on page 107 of the *Teacher Resource Book*.

Build Robust Vocabulary
Review

Extend Word Meanings

USE VOCABULARY IN DIFFERENT CONTEXTS Use **Transparencies R101 and R102** to review the words. Remind students of the Student-Friendly Explanations of the Vocabulary Words introduced on Days 1 and 2. Guide them to discuss each word in a new context.

expertise

- If someone commented on your expertise in science, would that probably mean you were a scientist?

- In what areas do you feel that you have expertise?

correspondence

- How do you feel when you receive correspondence from someone?

- What type of correspondence do you like to receive?

luscious

- If you told your mom that something she fixed for dinner was luscious, does that mean you liked it?

- What type of dessert do you think is the most luscious?

shudder

- Does thunder make you shudder?

- What other things might make someone shudder?

Objective
- *To review robust vocabulary*

Vocabulary: Lesson 15

expertise	recommend
correspondence	sensible
issue	devise
advise	luscious
consult	shudder

Grammar
Review: Pronoun-Antecedent Agreement

5-DAY GRAMMAR

DAY 1	Possessive Nouns
DAY 2	Singular and Plural Pronouns
DAY 3	Subject and Object Pronouns
DAY 4	**Pronoun-Antecedent Agreement**
DAY 5	Review Nouns and Pronouns

Objectives

- *To identify antecedents in sentences*
- *To review agreement between pronouns and antecedents*

Daily Proofreading

1. Mrs. Hall put they keys in his purse. (her keys; her purse)

2. Michael notebook was in its backpack. (Michael's; his)

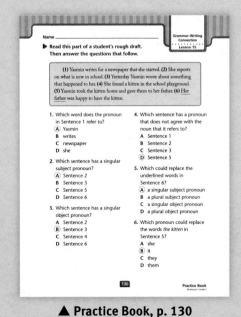

▲ **Practice Book, p. 130**

Reinforce the Skill

REVIEW PRONOUNS AND ANTECEDENTS Remind students that a pronoun takes the place of a noun. Ask students to suggest examples of pronouns. (Possible responses: *me, he, she, it, we, they*) Remind students that the antecedent is the noun that is referred to by a pronoun. Write the following sentences on the board:

> **Maria gave the puppies a bath. They were very wet.**

Ask students to identify the pronoun and antecedent. (they, puppies)

REVIEW PRONOUN-ANTECEDENT AGREEMENT Remind students that pronouns and antecedents must match, or agree. Singular pronouns are used to replace singular antecedents. Plural pronouns are used to replace plural antecedents. If an antecedent is male, the pronoun must be male. If an antecedent is female, the pronoun must also be female. If the noun is a thing or place, the pronoun must match.

Practice/Apply

GUIDED PRACTICE Write the following sentences on the board:

> **Amar and Sue went to the park. He played catch together.**
> **Mr. Green says she will teach math next year.**
> **Mother wore a new dress today. They likes it very much.**
> **The players felt good because he won the game.**

Read the sentences together. Have students tell how to make the pronouns agree with the nouns. (*Amar and Sue* needs a plural pronoun; *Mr. Green* needs a male pronoun; *Mother* needs a singular female pronoun; *players* needs a plural pronoun.)

INDEPENDENT PRACTICE Have students write the sentences correctly in their notebooks. Invite students to share their corrected sentences with the class.

Writing
Publish

5-DAY WRITING
DAY 1   Select a Piece and Revise
DAY 2   Revise
DAY 3   Proofread and Publish
DAY 4   **Publish**
DAY 5   Present

Publish

GRAMMAR-WRITING CONNECTION Have students read their writing and check that they have used the correct pronouns to refer to the antecedents.

COMPLETE FINAL WRITING Have students finish writing their final copy. Then have them proofread their writing one more time to be sure that they have copied everything correctly and that they have correctly capitalized and punctuated their sentences. Have students illustrate their writing, if they wish.

Taylor makes the Team

Handwriting

NEATNESS COUNTS Remind students that correct spacing between the letters in a word and between words will help make their writing easy to read. If they need to make a correction, they should do so neatly.

COMPILE A MAGAZINE Work with students as editors to determine how the pages of their magazine will be put together. They may want to put all of the same type of writing together in a section, or they may want to mix up the topics. Photocopy (or print from the computer) a magazine for each child or for each group. The original can be placed in the class library after sharing.

Objectives

- *To follow the general conventions of capitalization, punctuation, and page format*
- *To publish writing*

Writing Prompt

Reflect Remind students that they do not always need to follow a piece of writing through the publishing stage. Have students write in their notebooks how they feel about completing a piece of their writing to the point of having it published in a magazine.

Day at a Glance
Day
5

 **and Spelling**

- Posttest

Comprehension

 Review: Author's Purpose

- Review: Use Graphic Aids

Fluency

- Reading with Intonation and Expression
- "Ask the Experts," *Student Edition*, pp. 433–439

 Read!

Grammar

- Review: Nouns and Pronouns

Writing

- Present

Warm-Up Routines

 ## Oral Language

Objectives *To listen attentively and respond appropriately to oral communication; to respond by using appropriate elaboration*

> ### Question of the Day
>
> **Why is it sometimes good to be patient about things?**

Lead a discussion about patience. Remind students that some things, such as a flat tire, need to be fixed or changed quickly. In other situations, it is helpful to be patient and study a situation before trying to make changes. In some situations, in fact, things might even fix themselves in time. Have students respond to the following prompt in their notebooks:

When was it a good thing that you were patient about solving a problem?

Instruct students to write two or three sentences. Have them elaborate by including details such as what the situation was, how time and patience changed it, and how the problem was eventually solved. Have students share their writings and compare their thoughts.

Read Aloud

Objectives *To listen and respond critically to oral communication; to read orally with fluency*

REVIEW THE POEM Display **Transparency R87** or distribute photocopies to students. Tell them that you are going to reread "Autumn."

Set a purpose. Ask students what the purpose might be for reading or listening to a poem again. (for enjoyment, to practice reading) Tell students that as you read they will follow along to enjoy the poem. Then they will read the poem with a partner. Have them listen to see what the writer says about patience.

Model fluent reading. Read the poem aloud, using appropriate expression and intonation.

Partner-reading. Have students read the poem with a partner and then take turns listening as their partner reads. Remind them to offer positive feedback about each other's reading. Ask them to think about what is happening in the poem, especially how the writer has a different view of the falling leaves at the end of the poem.

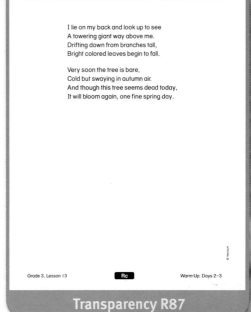

Autumn

I lie on my back and look up to see
A towering giant way above me.
Drifting down from branches tall,
Bright colored leaves begin to fall.

Very soon the tree is bare,
Cold but swaying in autumn air.
And though this tree seems dead today,
It will bloom again, one fine spring day.

Grade 3, Lesson 13   Rc   Warm-Up: Days 2–3

Transparency R87

Review Spelling Words

 **and Spelling**

5-DAY SPELLING

DAY 1	Pretest
DAY 2	Review
DAY 3	Review/Handwriting
DAY 4	Review
DAY 5	Posttest

Objectives

- *To review common spelling patterns*
- *To use a variety of spelling strategies*

Spelling Words

1.	**title**	9.	**police**
2.	**rattle**	10.	**giant**
3.	**saddle**	11.	**judge**
4.	**gnat**	12.	**hotel**
5.	**knight**	13.	**seven**
6.	**wrench**	14.	**broken**
7.	**rough**	15.	**taken**
8.	**edge**		

Review

SPELLING TEST Assess student's progress by using the dictation sentences.

Dictation Sentences: Review Words

1.	title	The **title** of my favorite book is *Charlotte's Web.*
2.	rattle	Calvin's baby sister likes to play with a **rattle.**
3.	saddle	We put the **saddle** on the horse.
4.	gnat	A tiny **gnat** flew around our heads.
5.	knight	The heroic **knight** saved the princess.
6.	wrench	Dad asked me to bring his **wrench** to him.
7.	rough	Football can be a **rough** sport.
8.	edge	Do not set your glass on the **edge** of the table.
9.	police	We heard the siren on the **police** car.
10.	giant	Jack found a **giant** at the top of the beanstalk.
11.	judge	Our principal will **judge** the spelling bee.
12.	hotel	Did you enjoy swimming in the **hotel** pool?
13.	seven	Three plus four equals **seven.**
14.	broken	One of the eggs in the carton was **broken.**
15.	taken	Is this seat **taken**?

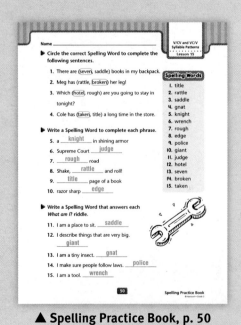

▲ **Spelling Practice Book, p. 50**

Author's Purpose
Comprehension: Review

Reinforce the Skill

REVIEW AUTHOR'S PURPOSE Review with students what they have learned about author's purpose. Discuss the most common reasons for writing. (to entertain, to inform, to persuade, to teach a lesson) Mention that knowing the author's purpose can help readers understand a selection.

Practice/Apply

GUIDED PRACTICE Recall with students the story "Thunder Cake," in the *Read-Aloud Anthology*, that they heard on Day 2. Discuss why the author wrote the story and what clues helped students decide. (to entertain, maybe to teach a lesson; made-up story; girl in the story overcomes fear of thunder, so readers can overcome their fears)

INDEPENDENT PRACTICE Have students reread "Iris and Walter, True Friends" on *Student Edition* pages 440–445 and find clues to determine the author's purpose. Have them discuss their findings with a partner.

Objectives

- *To identify the author's purpose in text*
- *To determine the author's message and extract important information from text*

Skill Trace

Tested **Author's Purpose**

Introduce	T215
Reteach	S30
Review	T249, T265, T277, T302–T303, T333, T349, T361, T412, T433
Test	Theme 3
Maintain	Theme 4, T348

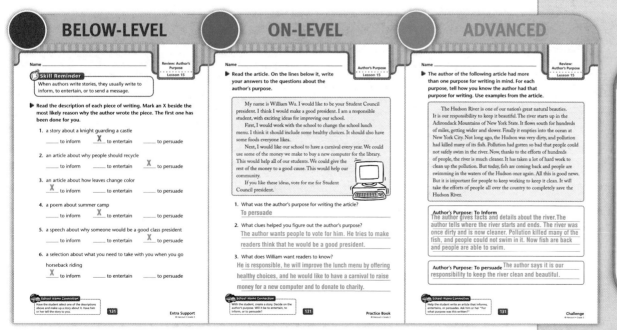

▲ **Extra Support, p. 131**   ▲ **Practice Book, p. 131**   ▲ **Challenge, p. 131**

ELL

- Group students according to academic levels, and assign one of the pages on the left.
- Clarify any unfamiliar concepts as necessary. See *ELL Teacher Guide* Lesson 15 for support in scaffolding instruction.

Use Graphic Aids
Comprehension: Review

Objectives

- *To identify how graphic aids help with comprehension*
- *To use graphic aids successfully*

Skill Trace

Tested **Use Graphic Aids**

Introduce	T250–T251
Reteach	S32
Review	T334–T335, T434
Test	Theme 3

Reinforce the Skill

REVIEW GRAPHIC AIDS Remind students that graphic aids such as photographs, illustrations, maps, charts, graphs, diagrams, and captions are often used to explain ideas, give additional information, and organize information. Paying attention to graphic aids will help readers understand what they are reading.

Practice/Apply

GUIDED PRACTICE Have students turn to *Student Edition* page 441. Explain that this page is an example of a graphic aid. Ask what it shows. (the first two pages of a chapter book) Call attention to the callouts pointing to various sections of the chapter book's pages. Explain that this is a type of diagram and that diagrams usually have information telling about the parts of something.

INDEPENDENT PRACTICE Have students create a diagram of an every-day object such as a book or a bicycle. Tell students to add callouts with lines pointing to the various parts.

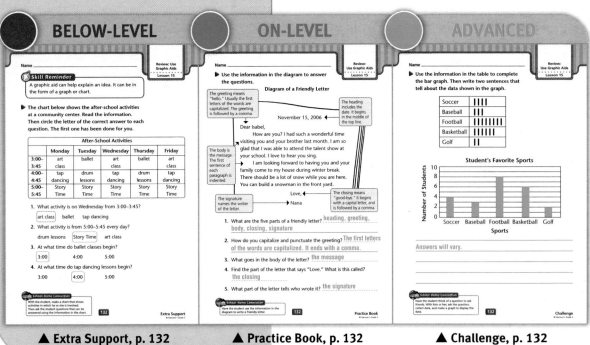

▲ **Extra Support, p. 132**   ▲ **Practice Book, p. 132**   ▲ **Challenge, p. 132**

ELL

- Group students according to academic levels, and assign one of the pages on the left.
- Clarify any unfamiliar concepts as necessary. See *ELL Teacher Guide* Lesson 15 for support in scaffolding instruction.

5-DAY READERS' THEATER

DAY 1	Read Aloud/Read Along
DAY 2	Read Together
DAY 3	Choose/Rehearse Roles
DAY 4	Rehearse Roles
DAY 5	Perform

READERS' THEATER

Perform: "Ask the Experts"

Objectives

- *To self-evaluate oral reading for fluency*
- *To speak in complete sentences*

Performance Ideas

PRESENTATION STRATEGIES Assure students that it is okay to be nervous, but it is important to keep going once a performance begins. Explain that after they finish performing, the cast will take a bow. You may want to project the backdrop for "Ask the Experts" against a board or screen.

Focus on Fluency

READING WITH EXPRESSION AND INTONATION Tell students that they will perform the Readers' Theater. Remind them of the following:

- Although you are reading aloud, look up at the audience occasionally.

- Read clearly and with emotion. Make your voice and words work together to make your part come to life.

Perform

SPEAKING AND LISTENING Explain that once they have completed their performance, readers will receive feedback. Provide a checklist.

Performance Checklist

- I read clearly and loudly.
- I read at a good rate and speed.
- I used expression and intonation.
- I listened quietly and politely as others read.

EVALUATE Invite students to give positive comments about the readings. Encourage them to speak in complete sentences and use the Vocabulary Words in their remarks. For example, "I liked the way you read Healthy Heart's sensible advice."

RUBRIC See rubric for Speaking and Listening on page R5.

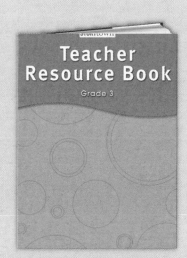

▲ Teacher Resource Book, pp. 121–124

Grammar
Review: Nouns and Pronouns

5-DAY GRAMMAR

DAY 1 Review: Possessive Nouns
DAY 2 Review: Pronouns
DAY 3 Review: Subject and Object Pronouns
DAY 4 Review: Pronoun-Antecedent Agreement
DAY 5 Review: Nouns and Pronouns

Objectives

- *To apply principles of agreement when using pronouns*
- *To identify nouns and pronouns*

Daily Proofreading

Mr. and Mrs. Diaz drove they car to me house. (their car; my house.)

Reinforce the Skill

DISCUSS NOUNS AND PRONOUNS Ask students to define *noun* (word for person, place, or thing), *pronoun* (word that takes the place of a noun), and *antecedent* (the noun that a pronoun replaces). Remind students that possessive nouns show ownership. Review the following with students:

- Add *'s* to make singular nouns possessive.
- Add *s'* to make plural nouns possessive.
- Some pronouns replace a subject.
- Some pronouns replace an object.
- Pronouns and antecedents must agree in number and gender.

Practice/Apply

GUIDED PRACTICE Write the incorrect sentences below on the board. Work with students to correct them, reminding students of the rules above.

Jon said they likes the boy green shirt. (Jon said he likes the boy's green shirt.)

The students desks are just right for it. (The students' desks are just right for them.)

INDEPENDENT PRACTICE Have students write a sentence that includes a possessive noun and two sentences that include pronouns. Invite students to share their sentences with the class. Ask students to identify nouns, pronouns, and antecedents in the sentences that are shared by their classmates.

Writing
Present

5-DAY WRITING	
DAY 1	Select Piece and Revise
DAY 2	Revise
DAY 3	Proofread and Publish
DAY 4	Publish
DAY 5	Present

Share

CELEBRATE WRITING Explain that students will share their contribution to the magazine by reading it to the class. Have students take turns reading their writing from the finished magazine. If you made copies of the magazine, encourage students to take their copies home to share with their families.

LISTENING AND SPEAKING SKILLS Remind students that they should demonstrate the skills used by good speakers and listeners during the presentations. Share the following tips.

Listening
- Listen attentively by facing the speaker and making eye contact.
- Give positive feedback.

Speaking
- Read and speak clearly, and use intonation and expression.
- Make eye contact with the audience.

NOTE: A 4-point rubric appears on p. R8.

SCORING RUBRIC

	6	5	4	3	2	1
FOCUS	Completely focused; purposeful.	Focused on topic and purpose.	Generally focused on topic and purpose.	Somewhat focused on topic and purpose.	Related to topic but does not maintain focus.	Lacks focus and purpose.
ORGANIZATION	Ideas progress logically; paper conveys sense of completeness.	Organization mostly clear; paper gives sense of completeness.	Organization mostly clear, but some lapses occur; may seem unfinished.	Some sense of organization; seems unfinished.	Little sense of organization.	Little or no sense of organization.
SUPPORT	Strong, specific details; clear, exact language; freshness of expression.	Strong, specific details; clear, exact language.	Adequate support and word choice.	Limited supporting details; limited word choice.	Few supporting details; limited word choice.	Little development; limited or unclear word choice.
CONVENTIONS	Varied sentences; few, if any, errors.	Varied sentences; few errors.	Some sentence variety; few errors.	Simple sentence structures; some errors.	Simple sentence structures; many errors.	Unclear sentence structures; many errors.

REPRODUCIBLE STUDENT RUBRICS for specific writing purposes and presentations are available on pages R5–R8.

Objectives
- *To publish and share writing with peers*
- *To listen attentively to oral presentations*
- *To speak clearly using appropriate intonation and expression*

WEEKLY LESSON TEST

▲ Weekly Lesson Tests, Lesson 15
- Selection Comprehension
- Robust Vocabulary

GO online For prescriptions, see p. A5. Also available electronically on *StoryTown Online Assessment* and *ExamView®*.

Podcasting:
Assessing Fluency

Leveled Readers
Reinforcing Skills and Strategies

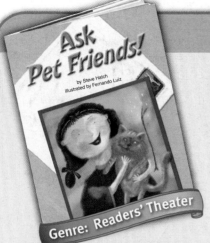

Genre: Readers' Theater

BELOW-LEVEL

Ask Pet Friends

SUMMARY A group of kids writes an advice column for *Pet Friends* magazine, answering other kids' questions about pets and pet care.

 Review: Plot, Author's Purpose

 Review: Use Story Structure, Ask Questions

• **ROBUST VOCABULARY:** *Review Theme Vocabulary*

Before Reading

BUILD BACKGROUND/SET PURPOSE Have students talk about any pets they have or the kinds of pets they would like to have one day. Next, ask if they have any pet questions they would like answered. Where could they find that advice? Then guide students to preview the story and set a purpose for reading.

Reading the Book

PAGE 3 PLOT What problem do the kids at *Pet Friends* face each month? (Possible responses: They have to put out the advice column; they also have to solve the problems of their readers.)

PAGE 8 AUTHOR'S PURPOSE What did you learn about pets? What is the author's purpose in giving you this information? (Possible responses: I learned that fish could remember things; to teach you how to care for pets.)

REREAD FOR FLUENCY Have small groups divide the characters' lines and read the script aloud, reading with expression and intonation.

Think Critically

(See inside back cover for questions.)

① **PLOT** Possible response: The kids at a *Pet Friends* magazine go through letters they will answer.

② **AUTHOR'S PURPOSE** Possible response: to share advice about pets

③ **MAKE PREDICTIONS** Possible response: Probably not. The advice should remind Flutter Fan that the bird wouldn't really enjoy the trip.

④ **DRAW CONCLUSIONS** Possible response: They are experts about certain pets so they choose questions about those pets.

⑤ **EXPRESS PERSONAL OPINIONS** Accept reasonable responses.

LEVELED READER TEACHER GUIDE

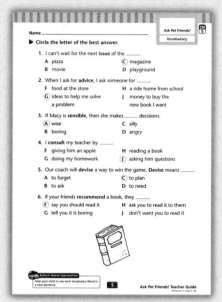

▲ Vocabulary, p. 5

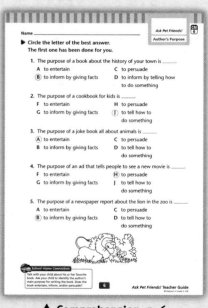

▲ Comprehension, p. 6

Genre: Readers' Theater

ON-LEVEL

Special Issue: Brothers and Sisters!

SUMMARY A group of kids answers questions about problems with brothers and sisters for *Kid World* magazine.

 Review: Plot, Author's Purpose

Review: Use Story Structure, Ask Questions

• **ROBUST VOCABULARY:** *Review Theme Vocabulary*

Before Reading

BUILD BACKGROUND/SET PURPOSE Have students discuss the kinds of problems they have had with a brother or sister. How did they solve the problem? Then guide students to preview the story and set a purpose for reading.

Reading the Book

PAGE 3 PLOT Where do the characters get the advice that they give to their readers? (Possible response: They think about the problems they have had to face and discuss how they solved them.)

PAGE 8 AUTHOR'S PURPOSE What is the author's purpose in writing about this advice column? (Possible response: to let us know that that many kids have the same problems with brothers and sisters.)

REREAD FOR FLUENCY Have small groups divide the characters' lines and perform the play aloud. Remind them to read with expression and intonation.

Think Critically   *(See inside back cover for questions.)*

1. **PLOT** Magazine editors discuss questions and answers for an advice column in a special issue about brothers and sisters.

2. **AUTHOR'S PURPOSE** to give readers advice about problems with brothers and sisters

3. **CHARACTERS' MOTIVES** Possible response: They want their readers to see that they have experience in dealing with siblings.

4. **DRAW CONCLUSIONS** Possible response: It has articles specifically about living with brothers and sisters.

5. **EXPRESS PERSONAL OPINIONS** Accept reasonable responses.

LEVELED READER TEACHER GUIDE

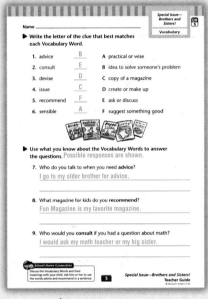

▲ Vocabulary, p. 5

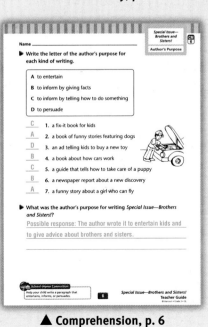

▲ Comprehension, p. 6

Leveled Readers
Reinforcing Skills and Strategies

 ADVANCED

SPORT KID ANSWERS BACK!

SUMMARY A group of kids writes an advice column for *Sport Kid* magazine. They answer questions from other kids about their sports problems.

 Review: Plot, Author's Purpose

 Review: Use Context Clues Use Graphic Aids

- **ROBUST VOCABULARY:** *Review Theme Vocabulary*

Before Reading

BUILD BACKGROUND/SET PURPOSE Have students discuss problems they have had playing a sport or being part of a team. Then guide students to pre-view the story and set a purpose for reading.

Reading the Book

PAGE 3 PLOT What problem does the staff of *Sport Kid* have? (Possible responses: They can't dodge their work; they have to pick a few letters to answer from many interesting ones.)

PAGE 3 AUTHOR'S PURPOSE What is the author's purpose in writing this column? (Possible response: to give readers advice about sports)

REREAD FOR FLUENCY Have small groups divide the characters' lines and perform the play aloud, reading with expression and intonation.

Think Critically   *(See inside back cover for questions.)*

1. **PLOT** Possible responses: the title; the first letter

2. **AUTHOR'S PURPOSE** to give readers information about playing sports

3. **IMPORTANT DETAILS** Possible response: Future Star wants to find out what kind of workout will help him improve at sports.

4. **SUMMARIZE** Possible response: He tells Last One to find out from the coach why she isn't playing more, and then to work on improving her game.

5. **EXPRESS PERSONAL OPINIONS** Accept reasonable responses.

LEVELED READER TEACHER GUIDE

▲ Vocabulary, p. 5

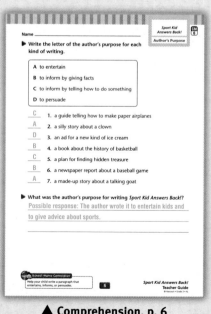

▲ Comprehension, p. 6

ELL

Genre: **Readers' Theater**

Answer This!

SUMMARY Four kids write an advice column for their school newspaper. They answer questions from other kids about problems with friends and school.

- **Build Background**
- **Concept Vocabulary**
- **Scaffolded Language Development**

Before Reading

BUILD BACKGROUND/SET PURPOSE Have students discuss how they could start an advice column for a school newspaper. What would they call it? What kinds of questions could they answer? How could they encourage other students to send in questions? Then guide students to preview the story and set a purpose for reading.

Reading the Book

PAGE 3 PLOT What happens in this script? (Possible response: The students who work on a school newspaper answer questions and provide advice to other people in the school.)

PAGE 14 AUTHOR'S PURPOSE Why do you think someone would want to write an advice column for kids? (Possible response: to help other people; to improve people's lives)

REREAD FOR FLUENCY Have small groups divide the characters' lines and perform the play aloud, reading with expression and intonation.

Scaffolded Language Development

(See inside back cover for teacher-led activity.)

Provide additional examples and explanation as needed.

LEVELED READER TEACHER GUIDE

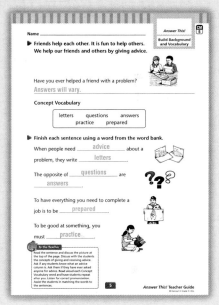

▲ **Build Background, p. 5**

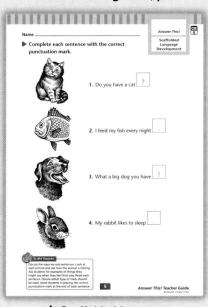

▲ **Scaffolded Language Development, p. 6**

Theme Wrap-Up and Review

Discuss the Literature

Use the following questions to help the students make connections across the texts in this theme.

- **What is the difference between the ways that the trees in the literature grow?** (Possible response: One tree grows bigger and stronger while the other grows weaker.)

- **Of the many changes that occurred in this theme, which changes were for the better?** (Possible response: Carolyn learned a good lesson.)

- **Which character from the theme grew the most?** (Responses will vary but should reflect personal growth.)

Return to the Theme Connections

Ask students to complete a chart like the one below to show what changes can happen as we grow.

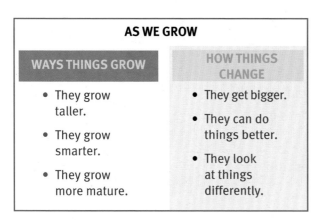

AS WE GROW	
WAYS THINGS GROW	**HOW THINGS CHANGE**
• They grow taller. • They grow smarter. • They grow more mature.	• They get bigger. • They can do things better. • They look at things differently.

Response Option

REFLECT   Have students reflect on and write about what they've learned about growth and change.

SELF-ASSESSMENT   Students can reflect on their own progress by reviewing their Reading Log blackline master on *Teacher Resource Book*, p. 64.

LITERATURE CRITIQUE CIRCLES   Have students meet in small groups to discuss the literature from this theme. Encourage students to share their likes and dislikes about the following:

- genres

- subjects/topics

- illustrations

Remind students to support their opinions with text-based reasons and details.

Students may also use this time to recommend to classmates any books they read and enjoyed during independent reading. Have them list titles to consider for future reading.

▲ **Teacher Resource Book, p. 64**

Interviews of School Staff Members

PRESENT INTERVIEW DISPLAYS Work groups that have completed their interview slide shows or posters can present their work to the class. Encourage them to share information from their interviews in a creative way.

Here is an idea you may suggest:

PRESENTATION IDEA You may suggest that students re-create their interviews in the form of a television talk show.

- Have one student in the group pretend to be the staff member. The other students in the group can take turns asking the questions, and the student pretending to be the staff member can give the actual responses gathered in the interview.

- Encourage students to dress appropriately. For example, if they interviewed the PE teacher, the student pretending to be the teacher might wear a ball cap and whistle. Have students talk as if the interview is going on at the moment.

- To evaluate students' work, you may wish to use the Rubric for Presentations on page R5.

School-Home Connection

Theme Project Presentations Consider having students invite parents and family members to watch the Theme Project Presentations. Have groups work together to write invitations. Discuss what information would be important to include, such as date, time, and location.

Meet
Coach
Washington

Monitor Progress
at the end of Theme 3

THEME 3 TEST After instruction for Theme 3, assess student progress in the following areas:

- Comprehension of grade-level text
- Comprehension Skills
- Robust Vocabulary
- Spelling
- Writing to a prompt
- Grammar
- Fluency*

*(*Note on Fluency: Assessment can be staggered to make sure all students can be individually assessed.)*

 Podcasting: Assessing Fluency

 ONLINE ASSESSMENT

✔ Theme 3 Test
✔ Weekly Lesson Tests
✔ Student Profile System to track student growth
✔ Prescriptions for Reteaching

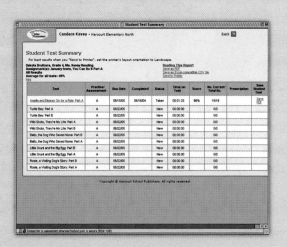

 www.harcourtschool.com/storytown

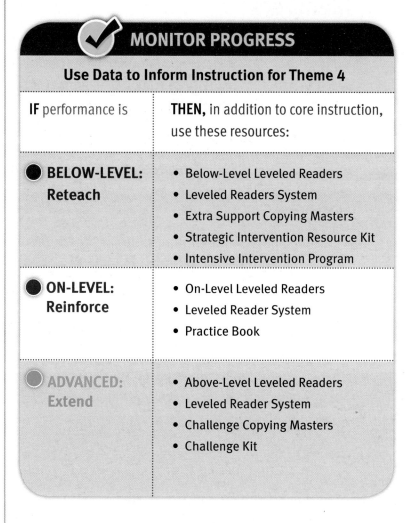

MONITOR PROGRESS

Use Data to Inform Instruction for Theme 4

IF performance is	THEN, in addition to core instruction, use these resources:
● **BELOW-LEVEL: Reteach**	• Below-Level Leveled Readers • Leveled Readers System • Extra Support Copying Masters • Strategic Intervention Resource Kit • Intensive Intervention Program
● **ON-LEVEL: Reinforce**	• On-Level Leveled Readers • Leveled Reader System • Practice Book
○ ADVANCED: Extend	• Above-Level Leveled Readers • Leveled Reader System • Challenge Copying Masters • Challenge Kit

BENCHMARK ASSESSMENT

Mid-Year Test

- Comprehension
- Robust Vocabulary
- Phonics/Spelling
- Writing
- Grammar
- Fluency

▲ Mid-Year Assessment

SMALL-GROUP INSTRUCTION

Phonics

Objective

To practice and apply knowledge of the Consonant + -le syllable pattern

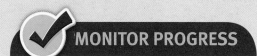

MONITOR PROGRESS

Phonics After small-group instruction, are students able to identify the Consonant + *-le* syllable pattern and determine whether the vowel before it is long or short?

If not, provide additional small-group practice with the Consonant + *-le* syllable pattern. See the *Strategic Intervention Resource Kit* for support.

**Strategic ►
Intervention
Resource Kit**

BELOW-LEVEL **RETEACH**

Review Consonant + *-le*

Routine Card 11 Reintroduce the Consonant + *-le* syllable pattern using *Routine Card 11*. Write the words *bottle, ramble, beetle,* and *able* on the board. Underline the *-le,* explaining that these letters often appear together at the end of a word and stand for the sound /əl/.

SHORT VOWELS Point out that *bottle* and *ramble* have two consonants before the final *-le.* Have volunteers circle those consonants in each word (tt, mb). Explain that, in words with this pattern, the vowel that comes before those consonants has a short vowel sound. Have students pronounce *bottle,* stressing the short /o/ sound. Then do the same with *ramble* stressing the short /a/ sound.

LONG VOWELS Point out that *beetle* and *able* have only one consonant before the final *-le.* Have volunteers circle that consonant in each word (t, b). Explain that, in words with this pattern, the vowel that comes before that consonant has a long vowel sound. Have students pronounce *beetle,* stressing the long /ē/ sound. Then do the same for *able* stressing the long /a/ sound.

ON-LEVEL REINFORCE

Word Building

Write the words *crumble, paddle, fable,* and *bridle* on the board. Ask students to copy the words into their notebooks and then underline the consonants that come before the final *-le*. Ask volunteers to describe the rules that help readers know whether a word ending with *-le* has a short or long vowel sound. (one consonant, long vowel; two consonants, short vowel)

Now have students read the words aloud, identifying which words have short vowels (crumble, paddle) and which have long vowels (fable, bridle).

ADVANCED EXTEND

Write Words with *-le*

Invite students to brainstorm words ending with the *-le* letter pattern and list them in two categories: long vowels and short vowels. Have them circle the consonant or consonant pair that comes before *-le* for each word. Encourage partners to read their words aloud, emphasizing the long or short vowel sound in each word.

Now have students write two sentences that each contain two words ending in the consonant + *-le* pattern.

E L L

Write the following words on the board:

table

apple

little

noble

Next to each word, write 1 or 2 for the number of consonants that come before *-le*. Then write *short vowel* next to the number 2 and *long vowel* next to the number 1. Remind students of the rule for long versus short vowels and help them pronounce the words.

Fluency

Objective
To use expression to read fluently

Use Expression Remind students that punctuation, such as question marks and exclamation points, helps show how a reader's voice should sound when reading. For example, an exclamation point is used to show excitement, so the reader might speak faster or more loudly.

Expression After small-group instruction, are students able to read their *Leveled Reader* with appropriate expression?

If not, provide additional modeling of fluent reading with small groups. See the *Strategic Intervention Resource Kit* for additional support.

Strategic ▶ Intervention Resource Kit

BELOW-LEVEL **RETEACH**

Model Fluent Reading

Remind students that good readers try to make their voices sound natural as they read, as if they are talking to someone. To do this, readers might change their speed, volume, or pitch.

 Routine Card 9 Distribute copies of "Felix's Turn" to students. Read the book aloud, modeling fluent reading with appropriate expression and having students track the print as you read. While reading, make sure to pause and explain how your voice changes to reflect what is happening in the story. Then have students take turns reading a page aloud to a partner. Guide students to use expression while reading.

ON-LEVEL REINFORCE

Echo-Reading

Routine Card 8

Remind students that good readers vary the tone and pitch of their voices to show expression and to give feeling to a story. Distribute copies of "The Battle for Aunt Jane" to students. Read a page aloud, emphasizing fluent expression and emotion. Then ask students to repeat the same reading, matching your expression and emotion. Continue echo-reading through the end of the story. Provide students with feedback to help improve their expression.

ADVANCED EXTEND

Partner Reading

Routine Card 10

Ask a volunteer to explain what it means to read with expression. Have students discuss several different ways they can read with expression and tell why expression is important to being a good reader. Then distribute copies of "Choosing Sides" to students and tell them they will read the book, practicing expression. Have partners take turns reading a page aloud, making sure to express how the characters act and feel. Tell the listener to give feedback to the reader about his or her use of expression while reading.

LEVELED READERS

● **BELOW-LEVEL**

▲ Felix's Turn

● **ON-LEVEL**

▲ The Battle for Aunt Jane

● **ADVANCED LEVEL**

▲ Choosing Sides

 **Comprehension**
Plot

Objective
To recognize the plot of a story

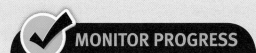

A Case of Nerves

Vonya woke up with her stomach doing flip flops. It felt like something was fluttering around inside her! "Mom!" she called. "I don't feel good."

Vonya's mother came to the bed, leaned down, and asked what was the matter.

"I don't know," said the girl. "I woke up thinking about the talent show. It's today, and I'm going to have to sing in front of a hundred people. All of a sudden my stomach feels AWFUL!"

With a smile, her mother patted Vonya's hand. "You're just nervous. Those are only butterflies in your stomach. It's a feeling some people have when they are nervous. Don't worry. Just practice your song while you get dressed. Keep practicing whenever you have a chance, even if it's only in your head. You'll be fine."

"Really?" Vonya asked. Before her feet were on the floor, the words of the song formed in her mind. Then, singing, she walked out of her room. She would be fine. The noise from her singing was sure to make those little butterflies go away!

Grade 3, Lesson 11   R69   Warm-Up: Day 1

Transparency R69

MONITOR PROGRESS

Plot After small-group instruction, are students able to identify and describe the plot of a story?

If not, provide additional small-group practice with the skill. See the *Strategic Intervention Resource Kit* for additional support.

Strategic ▶ Intervention Resource Kit

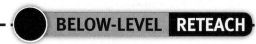

Identify Problem and Solution

Have students read page 302 in their *Student Edition* and review the concept of plot. Remind students that the characters and setting in a story are important parts of the plot.

Show students **Transparency R69** and reread the story "A Case of Nerves" aloud. Ask volunteers to identify an important event within the story and write it on the board. Continue until all the events within the passage have been identified. Review the events listed on the board and guide students in naming the problem in this story. (Vonya is nervous about singing in the talent show.) Then discuss how the problem was solved. (Vonya's mother soothed her and told her that practice would help.) Explain that this is how you determine the plot of a story.

Identify Plot

Remind students that the *plot* of a story is what happens to the characters and how they find a solution to a problem. Ask a volunteer to describe the problem in "Stone Soup," (*Student Edition*, pages 256–273) and tell students to write it in their notebook. (nobody in the town liked each other) Guide students to recall the events in the story aloud. Ask students which of these events led to the solution of the problem. (The little girl ran to ask her mother for a pot; all the people pitched in to make a feast.) Have students write the solution in their notebook.

Explore the Importance of Plot

Remind students that the events in a story are the plot. If one of those events happened in a different way, then the plot would be changed. Have students think about how "Loved Best" might be different by changing a major event from that story. Have students write in their notebook what might change in the story and how it would affect the problem and its solution.

Clarify Meaning The word *plot* can be confusing to students. Provide a simple question to get them started, such as "What happens in the story?" Then help them identify a problem and its solution within the story.

Vocabulary
Use Context Clues

Objective
To recognize and identify context clues to understand unknown words

Clarify Meaning Explain to students that context clues are hints in the text that can help a reader understand a difficult or unknown word. Tell students to reread the words surrounding an unknown word to see if they can figure out its meaning.

MONITOR PROGRESS

Use Context Clues After small-group instruction, are students able to recognize and identify context clues to understand unknown words?

If not, provide additional small-group practice with the skill. See the *Strategic Intervention Resource Kit* for additional support.

Strategic ▶ Intervention Resource Kit

BELOW-LEVEL RETEACH

Identifying Context Clues

Explain to students that context clues are hints that help readers figure out the meaning of a difficult or unknown word.

Have students open their *Student Edition* to page 307 and read aloud the second paragraph, which includes the word *praised*. Write *praised* on the board. Guide students in locating context clues that will help them understand the meaning of the word and write them on the board. (for reciting her poem perfectly) Say: **If someone recited a poem perfectly, I would think other people would be saying good things to him or her, because you cannot do something better than perfectly. So I think *to praise* means to say nice things, or give a compliment.** Have students copy the sentence into their notebooks, underlining the word *praised* and circling the context clue.

Finding Context Clues

Remind students that context clues are hints that can help readers understand difficult or unknown words. Write the following sentence on the board: **Art received two dollars as compensation for weeding his neighbor's garden.**

Circle *compensation* and identify it as the unknown word. Guide students to underline *two dollars* and *weeding his neighbor's garden*. Elicit from volunteers how the underlined words might be context clues. (Weeding is hard work, like a job; Art got money for doing it.) Then ask what *compensation* probably means. (getting paid for a job) Have students confirm the meaning in a dictionary.

Brainstorm Context Clues

Point out that context clues are important because they help readers learn new words and build vocabulary. Write the word *encouraging* on the board and tell students to brainstorm some context clues that would help readers understand its meaning. Once they have a list of four or five context clues, have them put the word and at least one context clue together in a sentence. Have students take turns reading their sentences aloud and ask volunteers to name the context clues.

Robust Vocabulary

Objective
To review robust vocabulary

REVIEW
Build Robust Vocabulary

swooned	soothing
astonished	sobbed
encouraging	praised
brief	envious
chuckling	rivalry

MONITOR PROGRESS

Vocabulary After small-group instruction, are children able to use and understand the Vocabulary Words?

If not, provide additional small-group practice with the words. See the *Strategic Intervention Resource Kit* for additional support.

Strategic ▶ Intervention Resource Kit

BELOW-LEVEL **RETEACH**

Reintroduce the Words

Routine Card 4 Use *Routine Card 4* to reintroduce all ten words to children. Display **Transparencies R70** and **R73** and review the **student-friendly explanations**. Then ask the following questions to check for understanding. Be sure students explain their answer each time.

swooned	When a person has swooned, are they lying down or standing up?
astonished	Would you be astonished if the lights went off in a storm?
encouraging	When would you want to be encouraging to a friend?
brief	Would you be more likely to spend a brief time washing your hands or washing the car?
chuckling	What is an example of something that left you chuckling?
soothing	What are you more likely to find soothing: getting a hug or getting a paper cut?
sobbed	How does a person look after he or she has sobbed?
praised	What was something you did for which you were praised?
envious	How would a baby communicate that he or she is envious of your toys?
rivalry	Is it agreeable to show rivalry in a baseball game?

Apply Word Knowledge

Display **Transparencies R70** and **R73** and review the **student-friendly explanations** for the Vocabulary Words. Then have students write sentences in their notebooks using each Vocabulary Word. Have volunteers share their sentences. Encourage students to rewrite each sentence using a synonym in place of the Vocabulary Word.

Word Clues

Write the ten Vocabulary Words on the board, reading each one aloud to students. Have them repeat the words, making sure they can pronounce them properly and recognize them by sight. Then review the **student-friendly explanation** for each word.

Write the following sentence on the board: *I began _____ when I saw the dancing dog.* Have students read the sentence and ask for volunteers to guess the missing Vocabulary Word. (chuckling) After giving this example, tell students to take turns making up sentences leaving out a Vocabulary Word, while a partner guesses the missing word.

E L L

Use Familiar Words Help students understand the meaning of the word *sobbed* by using the more familiar word "cried." Say, **My mother sobbed at the bad news.** Then say, **My mother cried at the bad news.** Repeat for other Vocabulary Words.

Vocabulary

1. **encouraging** An encouraging word from a friend make you feel that you can do something well.

2. **brief** If something is brief, it does not take much time.

3. **chuckling** If you are chuckling, you are laughing quietly to yourself.

4. **soothing** Something that is soothing makes you feel calm.

5. **sobbed** Someone who sobbed cried very hard.

6. **praised** If you praised someone, you told that person that he or she did something well.

Grade 3, Lesson 11   R73   Vocabulary: from the Selection

Transparency R73

Grammar and Writing
Language Arts Checkpoint

Objectives
- *To recognize possessive nouns*
- *To compose paragraphs that compare*

Student Model: Paragraph that Compares

Even though they are a year apart in age, the Melendez brothers are alike in so many ways that they could be twins. First of all, they look alike. Both boys have short, dark brown hair, big brown eyes, and are quite tall. Maybe their height is why they both are so good at basketball. They also like the same clothes and often dress alike. They even wear each other's shirts! Both boys are good students, but they are even better musicians. They play together in the school band. The brothers are the same way about food. Hamburgers are their number one choice, and pizza comes in a close second. These two brothers are so much alike that it is easy to understand why people get them confused!

Grade 3, Lesson 11   LA22   Writing: Paragraph that Compares

Transparency LA22

Possessive Nouns

1. The dog's ball rolled underneath the bushes.
dog's

2. We went to our cousin's basketball game.
cousin's

3. Josiah left his grandma's house on Tuesday.
grandma's

4. To get to the playground, walk past Eli's house.
Eli's

5. When the girl's package came, she was happy.
girl's

6. The zookeeper washed the elephant's trunk.
elephant's

7. I thought that character's actions were strange.
character's

8. My aunt's painting is beautiful.
aunt's

Grade 3, Lesson 11   LA21   Grammar: Possessive Nouns

Transparency LA21

Review Paragraphs that Compare

Display **Transparency LA22**, reminding students that they have seen it before. Explain that this paragraph compares two brothers; it shows how they are alike. Point out several sentences comparing the two brothers. Then invite a volunteer to give a sentence comparing him- or herself to a student in the group. Tell the student to write the sentence on the board. Invite the remaining students to suggest other sentences comparing the two students. Write them on the board. Then have partners think of comparative sentences about each other, writing them in their notebooks.

REVIEW POSSESSIVE NOUNS Display **Transparency LA21**, reminding students that they have seen it before. Point to the following sentence on **Transparency LA22**: *They even wear each other's shirts!* Explain that this sentence has a singular possessive noun in it and that a possessive noun shows ownership. Then do the following:

- Read the first sentence aloud.

- Guide students to identify the possessive noun in the sentence.

- Point out that the *'s* shows that the noun is possessive.

Guide students in repeating these steps for the remaining sentences. Point out that most plural nouns are made possessive by adding only an apostrophe.

Writing Comparisons

 Remind students that paragraphs that compare show how two or more people, places, or things are alike. Guide students to write two or three sentences comparing dogs and cats. Ask volunteers to read their sentences aloud to the group.

USING POSSESSIVE NOUNS Review with students that possessive nouns show ownership. Adding *'s* makes most singular nouns possessive. To make a plural noun possessive, you usually add only an apostrophe, but there are exceptions.

Ask a volunteer to dictate a sentence from his or her comparison paragraph that has a possessive noun. Write the sentence on the board, eliciting which word is the possessive noun and underlining that word. Continue, having volunteers suggest other sentences.

Make Connections Show students the meaning of possessive nouns by giving an example and then modeling it. For example, say: **This is the teacher's book,** picking up a book and showing possession of it. Make sure to emphasize the *'s* sound.

Apply the Skills

Invite students to come up with a topic for a paragraph that will compare two or more people, places, or things. Ask them to compose the paragraph using possessive nouns—for example, comparing Miguel's baseball mitt with Freddy's. Write the following characteristics on the board. Then have partners trade papers and use the list of characteristics to evaluate each other's work.

• Has a topic sentence that states which things are being compared

• Tells how two or more people, places, or things are alike

• Uses signal words such as *similar, like,* and *also* to show similarities

• Gives key details, using examples, of the things being compared

Phonics

Objective

To practice and apply knowledge of the consonant digraphs kn, gn, wr, gh

Identify Silent Letters

Routine Card 1 Reintroduce consonant digraphs *kn, gn, wr,* and *gh* using *Routine Card 1*. Remind students that letters can sometimes be silent, especially when they are paired with certain other letters. For example, when *k* comes before *n* at the beginning of a word, the *k* is silent and only the /n/ sound is pronounced.

REVIEW *KN, WR,* AND *GN* Write the words *knob, know, gnaw, sign, wrote,* and *wring* on the board. Have volunteers come up and circle the letter patterns *kn, gn,* and *wr* in each word. Guide students in sounding out each word, pointing out that *kn* and *gn* are pronounced /n/ and *wr* is pronounced /r/. Have students write each word in their notebooks, circling the consonant digraph and putting a line through the silent letter.

REVIEW *GH* Write the words *cough* and *tough* on the board. Explain that *gh* can stand for different sounds. In these words *gh* is pronounced /f/. Guide students to sound out each word, emphasizing the /f/ sound at the end. Have them write each word, circling the *gh* consonant digraph.

MONITOR PROGRESS

Phonics After small-group instruction, are students able to identify and sound out words with the consonant digraphs *kn, gn, wr,* and *gh*?

If not, provide additional small-group practice with the consonant digraphs *kn, gn, wr,* and *gh*. See the *Strategic Intervention Resource Kit* for additional support.

Strategic ▶ Intervention Resource Kit

ON-LEVEL REINFORCE

Sounding Out Words

Write the words *knee, gnat, wrong,* and *tough* on the board. Elicit the consonant digraphs that include silent letters or that have a sound different from what the letters normally stand for. (*kn, gn, wr, gh*) Underline those digraphs and ask students what sounds they stand for. (/n/, /n/, /r/, /f/)

After students have pronounced each word, ask them to write the words in their notebooks. Beside those words have them write another word that uses the target digraph.

 **ADVANCED EXTEND**

Write Sentences

Tell students that they will be creating sentences using words with the consonant digraphs *kn, gn, wr,* and *gh*. In their notebooks, have them make four columns with the headings *kn, gn, wr,* and *gh*. Instruct students to write four words for each digraph. Have them use a dictionary if they are having difficulty.

Once they have completed their lists, have partners write sentences using at least two of the words in each. Have students underline the words and circle the consonant digraphs.

 **E L L**

Remind students that sometimes letters in the English language are silent, or don't make a sound. Write the following words on the board:

gnat

knob

write

cough

Read aloud, circling each of the consonant digraphs *kn, gn, wr,* and *gh*. Cross out the silent letter in each of the words, and write beside it the letter sound the digraph makes. For *cough,* do not cross out any letter, and put an *f* next to it.

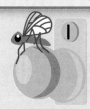

Fluency

Objective
To read fluently with appropriate expression

Read with Expression Remind students that reading with expression means reading with feeling. If they think a character is scared, they should make their voices sound scared. Guide students to use their voices to express fear, anger, surprise, excitement, and other emotions.

Expression After small-group instruction, are students able to read their *Leveled Reader* with appropriate expression?

If not, provide additional modeling of fluent reading with small groups. See the *Strategic Intervention Resource Kit* for additional support.

Strategic ▶ Intervention Resource Kit

Model Fluent Reading

Remind students that, when they read the speech a character says out loud or a letter a character writes, they should use expression in their voices to show the character's feelings and emotions.

Distribute copies of "Andrew's Boring Life" to students. Read the book aloud and ask students to listen to how your voice changes. They will notice that it changes with speech, especially as you go from one character to another. It will also change when sentences end with question marks or exclamation points. Have students echo-read the last three pages. Then, have partners take turns reading Sophie's and Andrew's letters aloud, guiding them to read with the same expression you used.

ON-LEVEL REINFORCE

Echo-Reading

 Routine Card 8 Remind students that reading with expression means that readers show the characters' feelings and can help explain the events in a story by changing the tone and pitch of their voices to sound like normal speaking.

Distribute copies of "An Ocean Away" to students. Read a page aloud, making sure to show emotion when reading the characters' letters. Have students listen to how your voice changes as you read. Then read the page again, with students echo-reading. Continue through the end of the book.

ADVANCED EXTEND

Practice Fluent Reading

Ask students what clues they look for in a story when they are reading with expression. (Possible responses: question marks, exclamation points, quotation marks, words that tell how a character feels) Then distribute copies of "Trading Places" to students, telling them to read the book and pay special attention to the characters' thoughts and feelings.

Routine Card 10 After reading, have students form small groups and choose a character (Ashwin, Emma, or the narrator; the narrator can also play the mother and father). Have listeners give feedback on whether the readers captured the characters' personalities and emotions in their reading.

LEVELED READERS

● **BELOW-LEVEL**

▲ Andrew's Boring Life

● **ON-LEVEL**

▲ An Ocean Away

● **ADVANCED**

▲ Trading Places

Comprehension
Plot

Objective
To recognize the plot of a story

Problem and Solution The plot of a story tells about a problem and its solution. To help students identify the plot, have them think about a small problem they have had. How did they solve it? Tell students that this could be the plot of a story.

MONITOR PROGRESS

Plot After small-group instruction, are students able to recognize and describe the plot of a story?

If not, provide additional small-group practice with the skill. See the *Strategic Intervention Resource Kit* for additional support.

Strategic ▶ Intervention Resource Kit

BELOW-LEVEL RETEACH

Identify Problem and Solution

Have students open their *Student Edition* to pages 334–335. Review the concept of plot with them. Explain that a story has a beginning, a middle, and an end. The main character's problem usually is found near the beginning, and the solution is found toward the end.

Have students think about the story "Loved Best," and ask for a volunteer to name the problem in that story. (Possible response: Carolyn feels like she's not loved best of her brothers and sisters and that she should be.) Write the problem on the board, asking students whether the problem occurred in the beginning, middle, or end of the story. (beginning) Guide students in a discussion of when the problem was fully explained in the story (middle) as well as when and how the problem was resolved (end). Explain that this is a good way to describe the plot of a story.

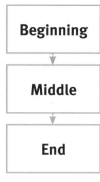
Beginning → Middle → End

Analyze Plot

Remind students that the plot of a story has a beginning, a middle, and an end. The author usually introduces the problem in the beginning of the story. Characters work on the problem in the middle and find a solution by the end.

Show students **Transparency R77** and reread the story aloud. Ask what sentence near the beginning describes the problem. (Ben spent his first day at school feeling lonely and afraid.) Next, ask students to identify the sentences in the middle of the story that show the events that lead to the solution.

Creating a Plot

Remind students that the plot of a story includes a main character's problem and the events that lead to the solution of this problem.

Tell students that they are going to create their own story plot by making up characters, a problem, and ways to solve that problem. Divide students into small groups. Each group should come up with two to three characters and give one of them a problem. The groups will then think of events that could happen that would lead to a solution. Encourage students to use a graphic organizer similar to the one on *Student Edition* page 334 to help them plan.

Ben's New School

Ben spent his first day at his new school feeling lonely and afraid. He did not know anyone through sixth grade. At his old school, the third-graders had been the oldest students. Nobody talked to him.

The next day, Ben went to gym class. His classmates all talked to one another and left him out. Mr. Smith quieted the class and said, "Today we have a special treat. Ms. Ramos is going to show us about archery. Who has tried archery?"

Ben's grandfather was a keen archer and he had been teaching Ben about archery since Ben could remember. Ben quickly raised his hand. Mr. Smith called on Ben to assist Ms. Ramos.

Ben helped set up the target and checked that the arrows and bow were in place. Then Ms. Ramos sent twelve arrows into the target. Next, she let Ben try. Ben hit the target, too. Other students also tried, but none of them could hit the target.

After class, all the students wanted to know how Ben had learned archery. Some of them said they wanted to learn. One boy, Chan, rode the same bus as Ben, so they sat together and talked about archery all the way home. He invited Ben to his house so he could learn more.

Grade 3, Lesson 12   R77   Warm-Up: Day 1

Transparency R77

Vocabulary
Use Context Clues

Objective
To recognize and identify context clues to understand unknown words

Make Connections Have students tell how they figure out the meaning of new words they hear in English. Elicit that when they use what they know about other words in the sentence, they are using **context clues.**

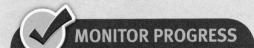

MONITOR PROGRESS

Vocabulary After small-group instruction, are students able to recognize and identify context clues to understand unknown words?

If not, provide additional small-group practice with the skill. See the *Strategic Intervention Resource Kit* for additional support.

Strategic ▶ Intervention Resource Kit

BELOW-LEVEL **RETEACH**

Identifying Context Clues

Remind students that there are two ways context clues help the reader to understand an unknown word. First, context clues may include familiar words that actually define the unknown word. Write this sentence on the board, underlining the unknown word:

The yellow bird was <u>massive</u>—so big that I was scared of it.

Guide students in locating the context clue for the word *massive*. Explain that the words *so big* help the readers understand *massive*.

Context clues also may be words that describe the unknown word. Write the following sentences on the board, underlining *repairs*:

After the <u>repairs</u> were made, the car worked well.

Then ask students what context clues there are for the word *repairs* in the second sentence. (worked well)

Learning Words with Context Clues

Remind students that they can figure out the meaning of a difficult word or an unknown word by looking at the words around it. These are called context clues, and they often define the unknown word or help describe it.

Have students open their *Student Editions* to page 346 of "A Pen Pal for Max." The first sentence of the last paragraph includes the word *din*. Guide students to find the context clues. (Don Manuel has to yell over the din, so a *din* must be a loud sound.) Have students write the sentence in their notebooks, asking them to underline *din* and its context clues. Tell them to underline context clues for *heaving* and write the meaning of the word.

Write Context Clues

Write the words *catastrophe* and *fortunate* on the board. Tell the students they will be writing sentences for both words. Each student should include context clues to help readers understand the words' meanings. Tell them that one sentence should use a context clue that defines the unknown word, while the other sentence should use a context clue that describes the unknown word.

Finally, have students take turns reading their sentences aloud. Ask volunteers to identify what clues in each sentence would help them figure out the word.

Robust Vocabulary

Objective
To review robust vocabulary

REVIEW ✓ Tested

Build Robust Vocabulary

deciphered	bothersome
mistaken	din
translate	dodging
repairs	catastrophe
heaving	fortunate

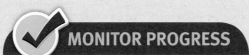

MONITOR PROGRESS

Robust Vocabulary After small-group instruction, are students able to use and understand the robust vocabulary words?

If not, provide additional small-group practice with the words. See the *Strategic Intervention Resource Kit* for additional support.

Strategic ▶
Intervention
Resource Kit

BELOW-LEVEL RETEACH

Reintroduce the Words

Routine Card 4 Use *Routine Card 4* to reintroduce all ten words to students. Review the **student-friendly explanations** before asking the following questions. Be sure students explain their answers each time.

translate — What does it mean to translate for a person who does not speak your language?

bothersome — Which would you be more likely to find bothersome, a long list of chores or going to a movie?

dodging — In what situation might you be dodging something?

din — Is a din something that is very loud or very quiet?

heaving — Would you be more likely to be heaving dirt with a shovel or with a spoon?

repairs — Which is more likely to need repairs, an old bike or a brand-new bike? Why?

deciphered — Would you be delighted if you deciphered a difficult math problem? Why?

mistaken — If you were mistaken about the spelling of a word, would you check a dictionary or a map?

catastrophe — Would a famine be a catastrophe? How?

fortunate — Which is more fortunate, a puppy in a good home or one in an animal shelter?

Find Similar Meanings

Use **Transparencies R78** and **R81** to review the **student-friendly explanations** for the Vocabulary Words. Draw an empty word web on the board or display **Transparency GO12**. Write the word *repairs* in the center and ask students to name words that go with re-pairs. *(fix, damage, mechanic)* List the words in the web. Have students choose another Vocabulary Word and create a web for this word in their notebooks.

Total Physical Response Help students understand the meanings of the words *dodging* and *heaving*. Have students dodge around their desk. Then ask them to pretend to *heave* something.

Vocabulary

1. **translate** If you translate something, you say or write it in another language.

2. **repairs** When something needs repairs, it needs to be fixed.

3. **heaving** Heaving is throwing something heavy with great effort.

4. **bothersome** When something is bothersome, it bothers you and causes problems.

5. **din** If there is a din, there is so much noise that it is hard to hear anything over it.

6. **dodging** When you are dodging something, you avoid something that is coming toward you.

Grade 3, Lesson 12   **R81**   Vocabulary: from the Selection

Transparency R81

Identify Synonyms and Antonyms

Use **Transparencies R78** and **R81** to review the Vocabulary Words. Ask volunteers to use the words in sentences.

Have students write questions that use the Vocabulary Words. Challenge students to think of questions that cannot be answered with *yes* or *no*. Then ask partners to take turns asking and answering the questions.

Grammar and Writing
Language Arts Checkpoint

Objectives
- *To recognize singular and plural pronouns*
- *To compose realistic stories*

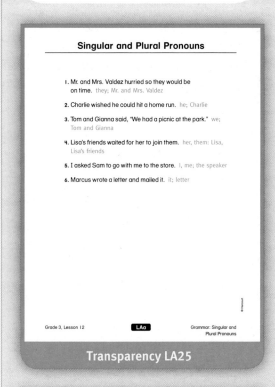

Transparency LA25

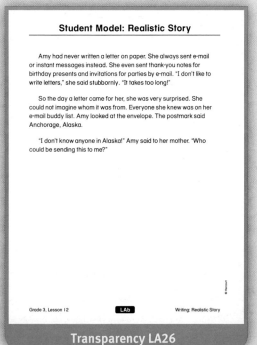

Transparency LA26

BELOW-LEVEL **RETEACH**

Review Singular and Plural Nouns

Display **Transparency LA25**, reminding students that they have seen it before. Explain that singular pronouns are words that take the place of a singular noun (*Max* can be *he*; *a letter* can be *it*) and plural pronouns take the place of plural nouns (*friends* can be *them* or *they*). Then do the following:

- Read the first sentence aloud.

- Guide students to identify the pronoun in each sentence and tell what noun it replaces.

- Then have students tell if it is a singular or plural pronoun.

Guide students in repeating these steps for the remaining sentences.

REVIEW WRITING REALISTIC STORIES Display **Transparency LA26**. Explain to students that a realistic story is one that includes characters, settings, and events that could be found in real life.

Then read "The Surprise Letter" aloud to students and invite volunteers to explain what makes this story realistic. (Kids really do write e-mails more often than letters; they are not used to receiving letters anymore.)

Using Singular and Plural Pronouns

Review with students that pronouns are words that replace nouns. A singular pronoun replaces a singular noun, and a plural pronoun takes the place of a plural noun or a group of nouns. Write the following sentences on the board:

John walked from the school to the store.

Mr. and Mrs. Harris left the party early.

Ask a volunteer to replace the underlined noun in the first sentence *(John)* with a pronoun. (he) Have students identify whether *he* is a singular or plural pronoun. Repeat with the second sentence.

WRITING A REALISTIC STORY Remind students that a realistic story is one that includes characters, settings, and events that could actually happen in real life. Have small groups brainstorm realistic story ideas and characters that could appear in those stories.

ADVANCED EXTEND

Apply the Skills

In their notebooks, ask students to write the first paragraph of a realistic story. They should create realistic characters with a real-life problem. Encourage students to use pronouns when appropriate. When students are done, have them trade their paragraphs with partners, who will check to see if the story beginnings include the following:

- Characters and settings that could exist in real life

- Events that could actually happen

- A problem that needs to be solved

- Correct use of singular and plural pronouns

E L L

Understanding Pronouns
Remind students that writers use pronouns to keep from using the same noun over and over again in a story. Use a boy and a girl to demonstrate the meanings of these pronouns: *I, me, he, she, you, they, them,* and *us.* Point out that in English the pronoun used to name things is *it* and is neither male nor female.

Phonics

Objective
To practice and apply knowledge of consonants /s/c; /j/g, dge

Review Words With /s/c and /j/g, dge

 Use *Routine Card 1* to reintroduce the sounds of soft *c* (/s/) and *g* (/j/). Explain that letters can sometimes stand for more than one sound, depending on what letters follow them in a word.

Write the words *mice, recipe, large,* and *page* on the board. Remind students that *c* can be pronounced /s/ and *g* can be pronounced /j/ when they are followed by the letters *e* or *i*. Guide students to sound out each word, making sure they pronounce the letters correctly. Have students write each word in their notebooks, circling the letters that make the soft *c* or soft *g* sound.

REVIEW WORDS WITH -*DGE* Use *Routine Card 1* to reintroduce letter pattern -*dge*. Remind students that the letter pattern -*dge* is pronounced /j/. Then write the words *judge* and *nudge* on the board. Guide students to sound out each word, emphasizing the /j/ sound at the end. Have them write each word in their notebooks, circling the letter pattern -*dge* in each word.

MONITOR PROGRESS

Phonics After small-group instruction, are students able to identify and sound out words with soft *c* and *g* sounds?

If not, provide additional small-group practice with the consonants /s/c and /j/g, dge. See the *Strategic Intervention Resource Kit* for additional support.

Strategic ▶ Intervention Resource Kit

ON-LEVEL REINFORCE

Identifying Sounds

Write the words *pencil, office, change,* and *fudge* on the board. Review with students that when the letter *c* and the letter *g* are followed by the vowels *e* or *i,* the *c* usually stands for the /s/ sound and the *g* often stands for /j/.

Have students pronounce *pencil* and *office.* Ask a volunteer to circle the letter *c* and underline the vowel that follows it in each of the words. Next, review that the letters *-dge* stand for the sound /j/. Write the words *hedge* and *fudge* on the board and have students pronounce them. Ask a volunteer to circle the letters *dge* in each word.

Explain that some letters have more than one sound. Write the following words on the board:

    ice

    age

    bridge

Read the first word aloud and circle the letters *ce* in *ice.* Make the /s/ sound. Explain that *c* stands for the sound /s/. Have students pronounce the word after you, emphasizing the /s/ sound. Repeat with *age* and *bridge,* explaining how *-ge* and *-dge* stand for the sound /j/.

ADVANCED EXTEND

Brainstorm Words

Remind students that they have learned different letter combinations that make the sounds /s/ and /j/. Point out that *c* can stand for the /s/ sound and that *g* and *-dge* can stand for the /j/ sound. Have partners brainstorm a list of example words. Then have partners write a poem in which they use those words to rhyme lines. When students are finished, they can share their poems.

Fluency

Objective
To read fluently, using intonation

Demonstrate Intonation Model how to speak with intonation. First, hum one note for several seconds and point out that it is a boring sound. Then hum a song. Point out that its notes go up and down, which makes it fun to hear. The same goes for speaking and reading.

Intonation After small-group instruction, are students able to read their *Leveled Reader* with appropriate intonation?

If not, provide additional modeling of fluent reading with small groups. See the *Strategic Intervention Resource Kit* for additional support.

Strategic ▶ Intervention Resource Kit

BELOW-LEVEL RETEACH

Model Fluent Reading

Remind students that good readers do not read every word in a sentence exactly the same way. Good readers change their tone of voice, making their voices go high or low to emphasize important words and to show punctuation. This is called *intonation*. Distribute copies of "Daffodil Spring" to students and read the book aloud, having students track the print as you read. Instruct them to listen carefully to how your voice changes as you read. Then read the first page, pausing after each sentence so students can echo-read. For the second page, have partners alternate reading the same paragraph with appropriate intonation.

Echo-Reading

Remind students that reading with intonation means that the volume and pitch of their voices change depending on what they are reading.

| Routine Card **10** | Distribute copies of "Wind in the Pines" to students, and explain that they will practice reading with intonation. Read a page aloud, demonstrating using your voice to emphasize important |

words. Point out how your voice rises and falls just as it does when speaking. Read the next page aloud, pausing at the end of each paragraph so that students can echo-read and imitate your intonation. Then have partners take turns reading the remaining pages to each other. Encourage them to give each other feedback on their use of intonation.

Partner Reading

 Ask a volunteer to explain intonation. Then distribute copies of "The Power of Corn" to students. Before having them partner-read, remind students to change the pitch of their voices for important words, punctuation, or feelings. Then have one partner read a page, after which the other will provide feedback. Students can then reverse roles.

LEVELED READERS

● **BELOW-LEVEL**

▲ Daffodil Spring

● **ON-LEVEL**

▲ Wind in the Pines

● **ADVANCED**

▲ The Power of Corn

Comprehension
Author's Purpose

Objective
To identify the author's pupose for writing a text

Sunflowers

Have you ever seen a sunflower seed? Actually, you might not know that you saw one because sunflower seeds are very small. Sunflower seeds are no larger than one of your fingernails. When a sunflower is fully grown, though, the plant can be more than six feet tall, and the flower may be larger than a dinner plate!

Once sunflower seeds are planted, it takes about a week for them to sprout. Then the flowers begin to grow. To reach their full size, sunflowers need a lot of sunshine. In fact, they need at least six hours of direct sunlight each day. Perhaps this is why sunflowers are so tall. They might be trying to reach the sun that they need so much!

Grade 3, Lesson 13   R85   Warm-Up: Day I

Transparency R85

MONITOR PROGRESS

Author's Purpose After small-group instruction, are students able to identify and describe the author's purpose?

If not, provide additional small-group practice with the skill. See the *Strategic Intervention Resource Kit* for additional support.

Strategic ▶ Intervention Resource Kit

BELOW-LEVEL RETEACH

Define Author's Purpose

Remind students that there are three main reasons why authors write: to entertain readers, to inform them, or to persuade them. Writers sometimes have one purpose in mind when they write, but often they have more than one reason for writing.

Display **Transparency R85**, reminding students that they have seen it before. Read the first paragraph. Ask students if they laughed at anything or if the writer asked them to do anything. Then ask students if they learned anything. Finally, ask students which of the three purposes the writer had in this piece. (to inform)

Analyze Author's Purpose

Remind students that an author's purpose is the reason he or she writes a story or article. Elicit three reasons authors write. (to inform, to entertain, to persuade) Point out that sometimes authors have more than one purpose for writing.

Have students open their *Student Editions* to page 370 and review "A Tree Is Growing." Ask what the purpose of the selection is. (to inform) Do the same for "A Pen Pal for Max" on page 338. (to entertain) Finally, review with students what happens in the *Read-Aloud Anthology* selection "The Money Tree." What might the story be trying to persuade you to think? (that people should not care so much about money)

ADVANCED EXTEND

Identifying Author's Purpose

Have students turn to "The Babe and I" on page 160 of their *Student Editions*. Tell them that sometimes an author can have more than one purpose in writing a story or an article. Have students review the story and discuss as a group how the story might entertain, inform, and persuade. Then, in their notebooks, have each student write a few sentences explaining the story's purposes.

Clarify Meaning Ask students to think about things they say to other people. Suggest that they may have a joke or funny story to tell. Maybe they want to let a friend know about a homework assignment. Or perhaps they want to try to get a parent to take them to a movie. Those are also the reasons to write: to entertain, to inform, and to persuade.

Research/Study Skill
Use Graphic Aids

Objective
To use graphic aids successfully

Clarify Meaning Use books from the classroom library to show students examples of graphic aids, including photographs, drawings, maps, charts, graphs, and diagrams.

Use Graphic Aids After small-group instruction, are students able to identify how graphic aids help with comprehension?

If not, provide additional small-group practice with the skill. See the *Strategic Intervention Resource Kit* for additional support.

Strategic ▶ Intervention Resource Kit

BELOW-LEVEL RETEACH

Look for Graphic Aids

Review with students that graphic aids are found in books, magazines, newspapers, and other reading materials. Graphic aids can help explain ideas, organize information, and make reading more enjoyable. Guide students as they look through classroom magazines and newspapers to identify different graphic aids. Explain how each graphic aid is used and how it helps the reader.

Have students locate one graphic aid and explain to a partner what information it gives.

Compare Graphic Aids

Remind students that graphic aids are used to help explain ideas, gather and organize information, and make reading more enjoyable. Students can find graphic aids in books, magazines, newspapers, and other types of reading materials.

Have small groups of students search the *Student Edition* for examples of the following graphic aids: photographs, drawings, charts, maps, graphs, and diagrams. In their notebooks, have students write the name of the graphic aid, the page on which they found it, and how it helps the reader.

Search for Graphic Aids

Have students review "How Animals Talk," beginning on *Student Edition* page 228. Have small groups think about what additional graphic aids they might want to see in the book. For example, they might add maps showing animal habitats. Have students write their answers in their notebooks.

Robust Vocabulary

Objective
To review robust vocabulary

REVIEW
Build Robust Vocabulary

tugged	rustling
paused	dissolve
columns	particles
absorb	scavenger
protects	self-sufficient

MONITOR PROGRESS

Robust Vocabulary After small-group instruction, are students able to use and understand the robust vocabulary words?

If not, provide additional small-group practice with the words. See the *Strategic Intervention Resource Kit* for additional support.

Strategic ▶ Intervention Resource Kit

BELOW-LEVEL RETEACH

Reintroduce the Words

Use **Transparencies R86** and **R89** to reintroduce all ten words to students. Review the **student-friendly explanations** until students are familiar with the words. Then ask the following questions to check for understanding. Be sure students explain their answers each time.

tugged	What could happen if you tugged on a dog's leash? Explain.
paused	Why is it important to pause before you cross the street?
columns	Describe some buildings you have seen that have columns.
absorb	What are you trying to do when you use a paper towel to absorb water on the floor?
protects	Would you be more likely to protect a favorite baseball card collection or a bag of dirt? Why?
rustling	What are some places where you have heard rustling noises? What made the noises?
dissolve	What things have you seen dissolve in water?
particles	Which is easier to break into particles, a cookie or a brick? Why?
scavenger	Which is a scavenger, a wild rabbit or a pet rabbit in a cage?
self-sufficient	Which person is more likely self-sufficient, a baby or an adult?

ON-LEVEL REINFORCE

Act It Out For Meaning

Display **Transparencies R86** and **R89**. Review the **student-friendly explanation** for each of the ten Vocabulary Words and have students repeat each word aloud. After writing the words on the board, ask volunteers to stand up, choose a word, and act out its meaning. For example, if the word chosen is *rustling*, the student might sway his or her arms slowly back and forth, like tree branches *rustling* in the breeze. Have the other students try to guess what word is being acted out. Continue until all students have had a chance.

Illustrate Write the words *columns* and *particles* on the board and then make drawings beneath them to illustrate the words. For example, draw a monument with *columns*. Next to large rocks, draw pebbles to show *particles* of rocks.

Charades

Write the ten Vocabulary Words on the board. Then cut out the words from a copy of p. 72 in the Teacher Resource Book and put them in a container or bowl. Tell students they will all take turns drawing a Vocabulary Word and acting out its meaning. The other students will try to guess the word. Once the word has been guessed, ask the student who acted out the word to put it in a sentence. Write the sentences on the board and continue until all students have had a chance or every word has been used.

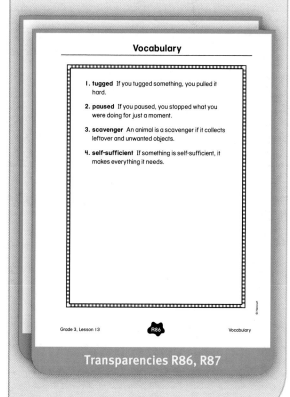

Vocabulary

1. **tugged** If you tugged something, you pulled it hard.

2. **paused** If you paused, you stopped what you were doing for just a moment.

3. **scavenger** An animal is a scavenger if it collects leftover and unwanted objects.

4. **self-sufficient** If something is self-sufficient, it makes everything it needs.

Grade 3, Lesson 13   R86   Vocabulary

Transparencies R86, R87

Grammar and Writing

Language Arts Checkpoint

Objectives

- *To recognize subject and object pronouns*
- *To compose a paragraph that explains*

Student Model: Explanation

It is easy to enjoy fresh vegetables from your own garden. First, you need a plot of ground. Clear the ground of weeds, dig the soil, and then rake it smooth. Choose the vegetables you would like to grow and buy seeds. Plant the seeds in a row and cover them with soil. Then water them gently. Keep the soil moist and hope the sun shines. In a few days, you will see tiny green shoots. Care for your plants by keeping them watered. Pull out some plants so the ones left are not crowded. In a few weeks, you will enjoy fresh vegetables picked from your own garden!

Grade 3, Lesson 13   **LAb**   Writing: Explanation

Transparency LA28

Subject Pronouns

1. Do you know Tami Rodriguez?
2. I read two books last month.
3. We all went to visit her.
4. He disagreed with Cami.
5. They always go to Miami for vacation.
6. "Yes, it is exciting," Matti answered.

Grade 3, Lesson 13   **LAa**   Grammar: Subject Pronouns

Transparency LA27

BELOW-LEVEL RETEACH

Review *What?, How?, Why?*

Display **Transparency LA28**. Tell students that this is a paragraph that explains, so it provides readers information by answering certain questions. Write the following words on the board: *What?, How?,* and *Why?*. Read the paragraph and then ask the following questions:

- What is the paragraph about? (growing vegetables in a garden)

- How do you care for a vegetable garden? (You plant seeds and care for the growing plants.)

- Why would someone plant vegetables? (to eat fresh food that he or she grew)

REVIEW SUBJECT AND OBJECT PRONOUNS Remind students that the subject of a sentence is who or what the sentence is about and that subject pronouns are used to replace subjects. Read the second sentence on **Transparency LA28**. Then display **Transparency LA27**. *You* is the subject pronoun in this sentence.

Explain that each sentence has either a subject pronoun or an object pronoun. Remind students that subject pronouns include *I, you, he, she, it, we,* and *they*; object pronouns include *me, you, him, her, it, us,* and *them*. Then do the following:

- Read the first sentence aloud.

- Guide students to identify either the subject pronoun or the object pronoun in the sentence.

- Ask students to see whether there is another noun in the sentence that can be replaced with a pronoun.

Guide students to repeat these steps for the remaining sentences.

Apply Skills

Have students write an explanation of school assemblies. Small groups should discuss these questions: What are school assemblies? Why does the school have assemblies? How should students act when they are in an assembly? Then each student should use the ideas that have been developed to write a paragraph of explanation in his or her notebook. Students should include subject and object pronouns.

As necessary, review the seven subject pronouns and write them on the board: *I, you, he, she, it, we,* and *they.* Remind students that these subject pronouns take the place of a noun that tells who or what a sentence is about. Object pronouns take the place of other nouns in a sentence and include *me, you, him, her, it, us,* and *them.*

ADVANCED EXTEND

Writing to Explain

Ask students to think of their favorite sport, hobby, or other activity. Then have them partner with a student who knows little about that activity. They will be writing a paragraph of explanation for that person. Remind them to use subject pronouns and object pronouns in their writing. When students are finished, have partners exchange paragraphs and have them check to see if the following points are included in each other's writing:

- Begins with a main idea contained in a topic sentence
- Gives facts and details about the activity
- Answers *What?, How?,* and *Why?*
- Gives examples related to the activity
- Follows a logical order
- Finishes by restating the main idea

E L L

Beginning or Not Explain that the pronouns *I, he, she, we,* and *they* are usually used at the beginning of a sentence. *Me, him, her, us,* and *them* are usually used in later parts of a sentence.

Phonics

Objective

To practice and apply knowledge of V/CV and VC/V syllable patterns

BELOW-LEVEL RETEACH

Review V/CV and VC/V Syllable Patterns

Reintroduce V/CV and VC/V syllable patterns. Remind students that words are made up of beats called *syllables*. Each syllable has only one vowel sound.

Write the words *open, even, camel,* and *model* on the board and read them aloud with students. Ask: **How many syllables are in each word?** (two) Ask: **Which two words have long vowel sounds?** (open, even) For long vowel words, the syllables break after the long vowel sound. This is the V/CV pattern. Invite volunteers to come up and make a slash mark between the two syllables in the words *open* and *even*. (o/pen, e/ven) Have students pronounce the words.

Point out that the remaining two words have short vowel sounds. (camel, model) Short vowel words break into syllables after the last consonant in the first syllable. This is the VC/V pattern. Invite volunteers to come up and make a slash mark between the two syllables in the words *camel* and *model*. (cam/el, mod/el) Have students pronounce the words.

Distribute copies of *Teacher Resource Book* p. 84. Have students keep a copy of Syllabication Cards 13 and 14 for their reference.

MONITOR PROGRESS

Phonics After small-group instruction, are students able to recognize and decode words with the V/CV and VC/V syllable patterns?

If not, provide additional small-group practice with the V/CV and VC/V syllable patterns. See the *Strategic Intervention Resource Kit* for additional support.

Strategic ▶ **Intervention Resource Kit**

Decoding Words

Remind students that words are made up of one or more syllables, with each syllable having only one vowel sound. Students can sound out words, trying both a long vowel and a short vowel sound, to see which sounds correct.

Distribute copies of *Teacher Resource Book* p. 84. Discuss the rules for V/CV and VC/V words with students. Write the following V/CV words on the board: *music, before, over.* Have students read each word aloud. Ask whether the first vowel is long or short in these words (long). After copying each word into their notebooks, students should use slash marks to show the syllable pattern. (mu/sic, be/fore, o/ver) Repeat the steps using these VC/V words: *river, seven,* and *robin.* (riv/er, sev/en, rob/in) Have students identify whether the first vowel is long or short (short).

Remind students that syllables are the beats in a word and each syllable contains only one vowel sound. Tell students that, in English, vowels have more than one sound. They might have to pronounce a word with both a short vowel sound and a long vowel sound to decide which is correct.

Write the following words on the board and have students pronounce them.

music	river
tiger	closet

Identifying Syllable Patterns

Remind students that there are syllable patterns that can help them decode words. Review the syllable patterns for long vowels—V/CV—and short vowels—VC/V. Write the following words on the board: *agent, legal, detail, civil, ever,* and *given.* Have students copy the words into their notebooks and make slash marks to show the syllable pattern. Next to each word, have them indicate whether the vowel in the first syllable is long or short and whether it follows the V/CV or VC/V syllable pattern.

Fluency

Objective
To read fluently using intonation

Using a Natural Voice Select a passage from "The Parts of a Tree" to read aloud. First read it with a monotone voice and no intonation. Then read the same passage again, this time using a natural voice and telling students you that you used intonation by saying important words loudly and paying attention to punctuation. Ask students which reading was more interesting to hear.

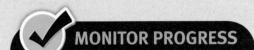

Intonation After small-group instruction, are students able to read their *Leveled Reader* with appropriate intonation?

If not, provide additional modeling of fluent reading with small groups. See the *Strategic Intervention Resource Kit* for additional support.

**Strategic ►
Intervention
Resource Kit**

BELOW-LEVEL RETEACH

Model Fluent Reading

Remind students that when good readers read aloud, they use a natural voice that sounds like they are having a conversation. The sound of their voice will change when they read important words or come to the end of a sentence or question.

Routine Card 8 Distribute copies of "One Hickory Tree in a Forest" to students and read one page in a monotone voice. Ask them whether they liked the reading and why. (Possible answers: No. It was boring to listen to. I lost interest.) Then read the page with natural intonation. Have students echo your reading. Finally, have students take turns reading pages aloud to partners, guiding them to use intonation and to make their reading voices more natural.

ON-LEVEL REINFORCE

Echo-Reading

 Routine Card 8 Distribute "The Life Story of a Barn" to students, and explain to them that they will practice reading the story fluently and with appropriate intonation. Read each page aloud to students, modeling appropriate intonation, and have them read it aloud after you, copying your intonation. After reading the story this way, have students practice reading the story with a partner. Listen to them read, and give them feedback about how well they adjusted the intonation of their voice.

ADVANCED EXTEND

Independent Reading

Routine Card 10 Ask students what they look for when reading and thinking about intonation. (Possible responses: important words, punctuation, words spoken out loud by characters) Distribute copies of "Livingston Hill," telling students that the book is nonfiction and does not include characters speaking. Add that good intonation also is important for nonfiction books. Have students read the book silently to look for punctuation and important words. Once they have read it through, have them read a page to a partner. The partner should provide feedback on intonation. Then have partners switch roles, continuing through the end of the book.

LEVELED READERS

● **BELOW-LEVEL**

▲ One Hickory Tree in a Forest

● **ON-LEVEL**

▲ The Life Story of a Barn

● **ADVANCED**

▲ Livingston Hill

Comprehension
Author's Purpose

Objective
To identify the author's purpose in text

Make Connections Students may not understand the terms *inform, entertain,* or *persuade.* Help students make connections with what they see on television. Elicit that a news program informs viewers; cartoons, stories, and game shows entertain viewers; and advertisements are intended to persuade.

MONITOR PROGRESS

Author's Purpose After small-group instruction, are students able to identify and describe the author's purpose?

If not, provide additional small-group practice with the skill. See the *Strategic Intervention Resource Kit* for additional support.

Strategic ▶ Intervention Resource Kit

BELOW-LEVEL **RETEACH**

Identify Author's Purpose

Remind students of the three main purposes for writing: to inform, to entertain, to persuade. Guide students to identify the author's purpose in the selection "A Tree Is Growing" and discuss how they decided on their answer. (Possible responses: to inform; because it gives a lot of information) Have students identify another selection in their *Student Edition* that was written to inform, and ask them to tell how they know. Then have students identify selections that entertain and persuade. Then have students share their favorite book or story and identify the author's purpose in writing it.

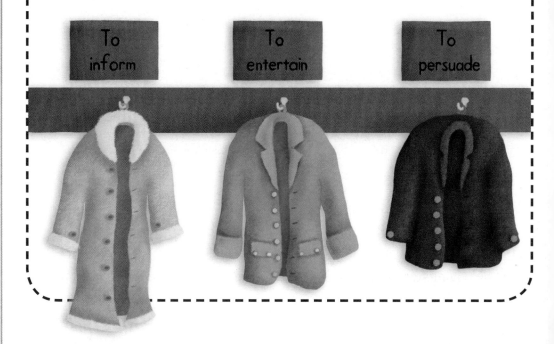

Reasons for Author's Purpose

Elicit from students the three different purposes for writing. (to inform, to entertain, to persuade) Remind students that they should look for clues about the author's purpose as soon as they start reading. Are there lots of facts? Does the author include his or her opinions? Does the author go out of his or her way to be entertaining?

Have students brainstorm different kinds of reading materials and categorize them by author's purpose. Some may fall into more than one category. For example, newspapers can inform and persuade. Create a chart with the three categories at the top and work with students to fill in materials that fall into each category.

Exploring Author's Purpose

Remind students that an author's purpose in writing is usually to inform, to persuade, or to entertain. Sometimes a writer can have more than one purpose.

Have small groups review all the selections covered in the *Student Edition*. Have them put each title into one of three categories: inform, entertain, persuade. Remind them that some selections might fit into more than one category.

Comprehension
Use Graphic Aids

Objective
To use graphic aids successfully

Use Photographs Explain to students that pictures are a great way to better understand what they are reading. Encourage students to think about what they see in a picture and how it relates to what is in the text. Display several Picture Cards and ask students to describe what they see in the pictures.

Use Graphic Aids After small-group instruction, are students able to identify how graphic aids help with comprehension?

If not, provide additional small-group practice with the skill. See the *Strategic Intervention Resource Kit* for additional support.

Strategic ► Intervention Resource Kit

BELOW-LEVEL **RETEACH**

Using Pictures and Captions

Review with students that good readers pay attention to graphic aids, such as photographs, illustrations, charts, maps, and graphs, because these help readers understand what they are reading. Remind students that the words that accompany and explain illustrations and photographs are called *captions*. Guide students as they search through classroom reading materials for examples of captions. Have students look at the picture and read the caption to predict what the passage is about.

ON-LEVEL REINFORCE

Use Graphic Aids

Remind students that graphic aids include charts, graphs, maps, diagrams, photographs, and illustrations. Graphic aids help the reader understand what they are reading.

Display **Transparency R93** and remind students that they have seen it before. Have students read the passage to themselves. Then ask small groups of students to discuss what kinds of graphic aids might help readers understand this passage. Have groups share their ideas.

ADVANCED EXTEND

Write From a Graphic Aid

Remind students that good readers use more than just the main text to understand what they are reading. Graphic aids are a good source of important information about a text. Have partners search the classroom's reading materials to find an example of a graphic aid. Then, using only the graphic aid, ask partners to write in their notebooks what they think the article or story is about. Then have students read the article or story to find out if their prediction was correct.

Full of Life

You might think that an old, dead tree standing in a forest is just an eyesore. Think again. Standing dead trees are called "snags," and snags are important to many kinds of wildlife. Wood ducks, woodpeckers, eagles, and owls build nests in snags. Hawks often use snags as perches. Many small animals such as raccoons, mice, and squirrels also call these hollowed out trees their home.

To us, some of the creatures living in snags are pests. Plenty of ants, beetles, spiders, and earthworms are found in wildlife trees. However, these tiny tenants are important sources of food for many other species.

Snags may look ready to fall over any minute, but some large trees can stand for more than 150 years after they have died! So, when you see a dead tree, think of the life inside. What may look like an eyesore is actually home-sweet-home to many of our forest friends.

Grade 3, Lesson 14   R93   Warm-Up: Day 1

Transparency R93

Robust Vocabulary

Objective
To review robust vocabulary

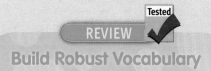

REVIEW
Tested ✓

Build Robust Vocabulary

sprout	strikes
damp	glimpse
suppose	maze
roost	transformation
spears	harmony

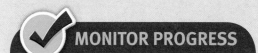

MONITOR PROGRESS

Vocabulary After small-group instruction, are students able to use and understand the vocabulary words?

If not, provide additional small-group practice with the words. See the *Strategic Intervention Resource Kit* for additional support.

Strategic ▶ Intervention Resource Kit

BELOW-LEVEL **RETEACH**

Reintroduce the Words

Routine Card 4 Use *Routine Card* 4 to reintroduce all ten words to students. Display **Transparency R97** and review the **student-friendly explanations**. Then ask the following questions to check for understanding. Be sure students explain their answers.

sprout — When do the buds on a tree usually sprout?

damp — If you left your socks outside overnight, would they be damp or dry in the morning?

suppose — Has there been a time when you supposed something might happen and it did not?

roost — Where are places you might see a bird roost?

spears — What does it mean to spear a fish?

strikes — What happens when lightning strikes?

glimpse — If you get a glimpse of something, would you be able to remember everything about it? Why or why not?

maze — How would you describe a maze to someone who did not know what it was?

transformation — Do you think the transformation in the weather from summer to winter is pleasant?

harmony — What are two animals that do not live in harmony?

Similar Meaning

Display **Transparency R97** and review the **student-friendly explanations**. Remind students that they can use context clues to define words. For example, read the word *glimpse* aloud and say: *I caught a glimpse of the new boy at school. I only got a quick look at him.* Point out that the word *glimpse* means a *quick look*. Have partners write two sentences for each of the remaining words. In the first sentence they should use the word. In the second they should include a context clue or synonym for the Vocabulary Word. Then ask volunteers to read their sentences aloud.

ADVANCED EXTEND

Cause and Effect

Display **Transparency R97** and review the **student-friendly explanations**. Write this example of a cause-and-effect relationship on the board: *Getting stuck in a maze would make you feel confused or lost.* Ask students to identify the cause (getting stuck in a maze) and the effect. (feeling confused or lost) Have small groups make a cause-and-effect sentence for each Vocabulary Word. When groups are finished with all the words, have them share their sentences.

E L L

Clarify Meaning Where would you most likely find a *maze*? A building with long hallways might feel like a maze. Sometimes fancy gardens have a maze of bushes.

Vocabulary

1. **suppose** When you suppose something, you think it is true.

2. **roost** Birds roost, or perch, when they sleep in trees at night.

3. **spears** If someone spears something, he or she sticks something sharp through it.

4. **strikes** If something strikes something else, it hits it.

5. **glimpse** When you get a glimpse of something, you get only a quick peek at it.

6. **maze** A maze is a winding set of paths that is like a puzzle.

Grade 3, Lesson 14   R97   Vocabulary from the Selection

Transparency R97

Grammar and Writing
Language Arts Checkpoint

Objectives
- *To identify antecedents in sentences*
- *To compose cause-and-effect paragraphs*

Cause and Effect Tell students they often can identify cause and effect by putting the word "because" in their sentences. For example, *I couldn't run during gym class because I twisted my ankle*. The *twisted ankle* is the cause and *not being able to run* is the effect.

BELOW-LEVEL **RETEACH**

Review Cause-and-Effect Relationships

Explain that cause-and-effect relationships tell why something happens or what happens as a result of something else. Write an example sentence on the board:

Ryan's parents got stuck in traffic so they missed the concert.

Read the sentence aloud and guide students to identify the cause (traffic) and the effect (missed concert). Have small groups write three cause-and-effect sentences using these events:

- woke up late
- got a good grade on my test
- played outside

Invite several students to share their sentences. Listen for sentences that contain pronouns and antecedents, and write several of them on the board.

REVIEW ANTECEDENTS Remind students that a pronoun takes the place of a noun. An antecedent is the noun that is replaced by the pronoun. Discuss the rules for singular, plural, male, and female antecedents and pronouns.

Return to the sentence about Ryan's parents. Explain that the sentence contains a pronoun and its antecedent. Then do the following:

- Read the first sentence aloud.
- Guide students to identify the pronoun and circle it on the board. Do the same for the antecedent, underlining it.
- Repeat with the remaining cause-and-effect sentences from the writing activity.

Identify Antecedents

Remind students that a pronoun takes the place of a noun. An antecedent is the noun to which a pronoun refers. Have students open to page 411 of the *Student Edition*. Ask: **In the first paragraph, to what antecedent does the word *it* refer?** (a tree hole) **On page 412, what is the antecedent for *she?*** (the bear) Have small groups search the rest of "One Small Place in a Tree" for antecedents.

WRITE Explain that cause-and-effect paragraphs tell why something happens or what happens as a result of something else. Have students continue to review "One Small Place in a Tree" and write sentences that summarize the causes and effects of things that happen to a tree. For example, *Cause—A bear needs to sharpen its claws on the bark. Effect—The bark chips away and a hole begins.*

Writing to Show Cause and Effect

Ask small groups to brainstorm a topic that would make a good cause-and-effect paragraph. Have students discuss the main idea and the supporting details before writing the paragraph in their notebooks. Encourage students to use at least two pronouns and two antecedents in their writing. Partners can trade paragraphs to make sure the following characteristics appear:

- The cause and effect appear in the first sentence.

- Key words explain the relationship between the cause and effect.

- Three effects support the cause or three causes support the effect.

Teacher's Notes

Assessment

Good assessments tell you what your students need to learn to meet grade-level standards.

It's not just about scoring the students—or the teacher, for that matter. It's about helping teachers **know what to teach and how much.**

Reading education is a **growing science.** We know more about how children learn to read than we did in the past. This **knowledge gives us the power** to use assessment to inform instruction. Assessment exposes the missing skills so that teachers can fill in the gaps.

Good assessment is part of instruction.

Think about it: if you are testing what you are teaching, then the test is another **practice and application** opportunity for children. In addition, when tests focus on the skills that are essential to better reading, testing informs teachers about which students need more instruction in those essential skills.

What is the best kind of assessment to use?

Using more than one kind of assessment will give you the clearest picture of your students' progress. **Multiple measures** are the key to a well-rounded view.

First, consider the assessments that are already **mandated** for you: your school, your district, and your state will, of course, tell you which tests you must use, and when. In addition to these, you should use **curriculum-based assessments** to monitor your students' progress in *StoryTown.*

The following curriculum-based assessments are built into *StoryTown.*

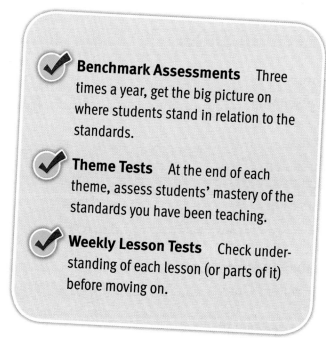

Benchmark Assessments Three times a year, get the big picture on where students stand in relation to the standards.

Theme Tests At the end of each theme, assess students' mastery of the standards you have been teaching.

Weekly Lesson Tests Check understanding of each lesson (or parts of it) before moving on.

On a daily basis, point-of-use **Monitor Progress** notes help you check understanding and reteach or extend instruction. Additional checklists and rubrics are provided to help you monitor students' comprehension, writing, listening, and speaking.

The *Benchmark Assessments,* the *Theme Tests,* and the *Weekly Lesson Tests* are all available online. Students can take the tests on the computer, or you can use pencil-and-paper and enter the scores into the database later. Either way, *StoryTown Online Assessment* will help you track students' progress and share their growth with administrators and families.

 StoryTown Online Assessment

Weekly Test

Using Assessment to Inform Instruction
Specific prescriptions based on Harcourt Reading Assessments.

✔ Tested Skills	Prescriptions

Phonics

C–*le* Syllable .... Reteach, pp. S2–S3

Fluency

Expression .... Reteach, pp. S4–S5

Focus Skill

Plot .... Reteach, pp. S6–S7

Vocabulary Strategies

Use Context Clues .... Reteach, pp. S8–S9

Robust Vocabulary

Lesson 11 .... Reteach, pp. S10–S11

Grammar and Writing

Possessive Nouns .... Reteach, pp. S12–S13

Weekly Test

✔ Tested Skills   Prescriptions

Phonics

Consonant Digraphs: /n/*kn, gn*; /r/*wr*; /f/*gh* ....Reteach, pp. S14–S15

Fluency

Expression...Reteach, pp. S16–S17

Focus Skill

Plot ....Reteach, pp. S18–S19

Vocabulary Strategies

Use Context Clues ....Reteach, pp. S20–S21

Robust Vocabulary

Lesson 12 ....Reteach, pp. S22–S23

Grammar and Writing

Singular and Plural Nouns ....Reteach, pp. S24–S25

Weekly Test

✔ **Tested Skills**	**Prescriptions**

Phonics
Consonants: /s/*c*; /j/*g, dge*................................Reteach, pp. S26–S27

Fluency
Intonation ....Reteach, pp. S28–S29

Focus Skill
Author's Purpose...Reteach, pp. S30–S31

Reference/Study Skill
Use Graphic Aids...Reteach, pp. S32–S33

Robust Vocabulary
Lesson 13..Reteach, pp. S34–S35

Grammar and Writing
Subject and Object Pronouns..........................Reteach, pp. S36–S37

Weekly Tests

✔ Lesson 14 Tested Skills   Prescriptions

Phonics
V/CV and VC/V Syllable Patterns ....Reteach, pp. S38–S39

Fluency
Intonation ....Reteach, pp. S40–S41

Focus Skill
Author's Purpose ....Reteach, pp. S42–S43

Reference Skill
Use Graphic Aids ....Reteach, pp. S44–S45

Robust Vocabulary
Lesson 14 ....Reteach, pp. S46–S47

Grammar and Writing
Pronoun–Antecedent Agreement ....Reteach, pp. S48–S49

✔ Lesson 15 Tested Skills

Selection Comprehension
"Ask the Experts" ....Monitor Comprehension, pp. T391–T394

Robust Vocabulary
Lesson 15 ....Build Robust Vocabulary, pp. T388,
T405, T415, T427

Theme 3 Test

✔ Tested Skills

Tested Skills	**Prescriptions**
Phonics..	Reteach, pp. S2–S3, S14–S15, S26–S27, S38–S39
Fluency	Reteach, pp. S4–S5, S16–S17, S28–S29, S40–S41
Focus Skill	Reteach, pp. S6–S7, S18–S19, S30–S31, S42–S43
Comprehension..	Reteach, pp. S8–S9, S20–S21, S32–S33, S44–S45
Robust Vocabulary	Reteach, pp. S10–S11, S22–S23, S34–S35, S46–S47
Grammar and Writing	Reteach, pp. S12–S13, S24–S25, S36–S37, S48–S49

BELOW-LEVEL **RETEACH**

- Below-Level Leveled Readers
- Leveled Reader System
- Extra Support Copying Masters
- Strategic Intervention Resource Kit
- Intensive Intervention Program

ON-LEVEL **REINFORCE**

- On-Level Leveled Readers
- Leveled Reader System
- Practice Book

ADVANCED **EXTEND**

- Advanced Leveled Readers
- Leveled Reader System
- Challenge Student Activities
- Challenge Resource Kit

To determine whether students need even more support, use your district-approved diagnostic and screening assessments.

ADDITIONAL RESOURCES

Using Rubrics

A rubric *is a tool a teacher can use to score a student's work.*

A rubric *lists the criteria for evaluating the work, and it describes different levels of success in meeting those criteria.*

Rubrics *are useful assessment tools for teachers, but they can be just as useful for students. They explain expectations, and can be powerful teaching tools.*

RUBRIC Rubrics for Retelling and Summarizing

- There is a separate rubric for fiction and nonfiction. Before students begin their retellings or summaries, ask them which rubric should be used. Then point out the criteria and discuss each one.

- Have students focus on the criteria for excellence listed on the rubric so that they have specific goals to aim for.

RUBRIC Rubrics for Presentations: Speaking and Listening

- Before students give a presentation, discuss the criteria listed on the rubric. Help them focus on the criteria for excellence listed on the rubric so that they have specific goals to aim for.

- Discuss the criteria for listening with students who will be in the audience. Point out the criteria for excellence listed on the rubric so that they have specific goals to aim for.

RUBRIC Rubrics for Short- and Extended-Response

- Before students begin a short- and extended-response, discuss the criteria for excellence listed on the rubrics so that they have specific goals to aim for.

- Tell students that the short-response task should take about five to ten minutes to complete, and the extended-response should take much longer to complete.

RUBRIC Rubric for Writing

- When you introduce students to a new kind of writing through a writing model, discuss the criteria listed on the rubric, and ask students to decide how well the model meets each criterion.

- Before students attempt a new kind of writing, have them focus on the criteria for excellence listed on the rubric so that they have specific goals to aim for.

- During both the drafting and revising stages, remind students to check their writing against the rubric to keep their focus and to determine if there are any aspects of their writing they can improve.

- Students can use the rubrics to score their own writing. They can keep the marked rubric in their portfolios with the piece of writing it refers to. The marked rubrics will help students see their progress through the school year. In conferences with students and family members, you can refer to the rubrics to point out both strengths and weaknesses.

Score of 4

The student:

- names and describes the main and supporting characters and tells their actions
- tells about the setting, including both time and place
- retells the plot in detail
- describes the problems and solutions in the story
- uses phrases, language, vocabulary, or sentence structure from the story
- accurately defines the theme or meaning of the story
- provides extensions of the story such as making connections to other texts, relating experiences, making inferences and/or making generalizations
- discriminates between reality and fantasy, fact and fiction
- requires little or no prompting

Score of 3

The student:

- names and describes the main characters
- tells about the setting
- retells most of the plot accurately with some details
- describes some of the problems and solutions in the story
- uses some phrases, language, or vocabulary from the story
- relates some aspects of the theme or meaning of the story
- provides some extensions of the story such as making connections to other texts or relating relevant experiences
- discriminates between reality and fantasy, fact and fiction
- may require some prompting

Score of 2

The student:

- tells some details about the story elements, including characters, setting, and plot, with some omissions or errors
- cannot correctly identify problems or corresponding solutions in the story
- uses very little language and vocabulary from story
- shows minimal understanding of the theme or meaning
- provides minimal extensions of the story
- confuses reality and fantasy, fact and fiction
- requires some prompting to retell the story

Score of 1

The student:

- tells few if any details about the story elements, possibly with errors
- has little or no awareness of the theme of the story
- provides no extensions of the story
- confuses reality and fantasy, and fact and fiction
- unable to retell the story without prompting

Scoring RUBRIC for Summarizing Nonfiction

Score of 4

The student:

- provides a summarizing statement
- relates the main idea and important supporting details
- creates a focused, coherent, logical, and organized structure; stays on topic; and relates important points to the text
- understands relationships in the text such as recognizing cause and effect relationships, chronological order, or comparing and contrasting information
- uses phrases, language, or vocabulary from the text
- clearly identifies the conclusion
- identifies the author's purpose for creating the text
- provides extensions of the text such as making connections to other texts, relating relevant experiences, making inferences and/or making generalizations
- requires little or no prompting

Score of 3

The student:

- tells the topic of the text
- relates the main idea and relevant details
- creates a coherent structure and stays on topic
- mostly understands relationships in the text such as recognizing cause and effect relationships, chronological order, or comparing and contrasting information
- uses some language, or vocabulary from the text
- tells the conclusion or point of the text
- identifies the author's purpose
- provides some extensions of the text such as making connections to other texts or relating relevant experiences
- may require some prompting

Score of 2

The student:

- minimally relates the topic of the text
- shows minimal understanding of main idea and omits many important details
- provides some structure; might stray from topic
- understands few, if any, relationships in the text or recognizes chronological order
- uses little or no language and vocabulary from the text
- does not fully understand conclusion or point of the text
- shows some awareness of author's purpose
- provides few, if any, extensions of the text
- requires some prompting to retell the story

Score of 1

The student:

- shows little or no understanding of main idea and omits important details
- provides a poorly organized or unclear structure
- does not understand relationships in or of the text
- does not understand conclusion of the text
- provides no extensions of the text
- unable to retell the story without prompting

Scoring RUBRIC for Presentations

	Score of 6	Score of 5	Score of 4	Score of 3	Score of 2	Score of 1
HANDWRITING	The slant of the letters is consistent throughout. The letters are clearly formed, spaced equally, and easy to read.	The slant of the letters is almost the same throughout. The letters are clearly formed. Spacing is nearly equal.	The slant and form of the letters is usually consistent. The spacing between words is usually equal.	The handwriting is readable. There are some inconsistencies in shape, form, slant, and spacing.	The handwriting is somewhat readable. There are many inconsistencies in shape, form, slant, and spacing.	The letters are not shaped, formed, slanted, or spaced correctly. The paper is very difficult to read.
WORD PROCESSING	Fonts and sizes are used very well, which helps the reader enjoy reading the text.	Fonts and sizes are used well.	Fonts and sizes are used fairly well, but could be improved upon.	Fonts and sizes are used well in some places, but make the paper look cluttered in others.	Fonts and sizes are not used well. The paper looks cluttered.	The writer has used too many different fonts and sizes. It is very distracting to the reader.
MARKERS	The title, side heads, page numbers, and bullets are used very well. They make it easy for the reader to find information in the text.	The title, side heads, page numbers, and bullets are used very well. They help the reader find most information.	The title, side heads, page numbers, and bullets are used fairly well. They usually help the reader find information.	The writer uses a title, or page numbers, or bullets. Improvement is needed.	The writer uses very few markers. This makes it hard for the reader to find and understand the information in the text.	There are no markers such as title, page numbers, bullets, or side heads.
VISUALS	The writer uses visuals such as illustrations and props. The text and visuals clearly relate.	The writer uses visuals well. The text and visuals relate to each other.	The writer uses visuals fairly well.	The writer uses visuals with the text, but the reader may not understand how they are related.	The writer tries to use visuals with the text, but the reader is confused by them.	The visuals do not make sense with the text.
SPEAKING	The speaker uses very effective pacing, volume, intonation, and expression.	The speaker uses effective pacing, volume, intonation, and expression.	The speaker uses effective pacing, volume, intonation, and expression.	The speaker uses effective pacing, volume, intonation, and expression.	The speaker needs to work on pacing, volume, intonation, and expression.	The speaker's techniques are unclear or distracting to the listener.

Scoring RUBRIC for Short- and Extended-Response

	Score of 4	Score of 3	Score of 2	Score of 1	Score of 0
EXTENDED-RESPONSE	The response indicates that the student has a thorough understanding of the reading concept embodied in the task. The student has provided a response that is accurate, complete, and fulfills all the requirements of the task. Necessary support and/or examples are included, and the information is clearly text-based.	The response indicates that the student has an understanding of the reading concept embodied in the task. The student has provided a response that is accurate and fulfills all the requirements of the task, but the required support and/or details are not complete or are not clearly text-based.	The response indicates that the student has a partial understanding of the reading concept embodied in the task. The student has provided a response that includes information that is essentially correct and text-based, but the information is too general or too simplistic. Some of the support and/or examples and requirements of the task may be incomplete or omitted.	The response indicates that the student has very limited understanding of the reading concept embodied in the task. The response is incomplete, may exhibit many flaws, and may not address all requirements of the task.	The response indicates that the student does not demonstrate an understanding of the reading concept embodied in the task. The student has provided a response that is inaccurate; the response has an insufficient amount of information to determine the student's understanding of the task; or the student has failed to respond to the task.
SHORT-RESPONSE			The response indicates that the student has a complete understanding of the reading concept embodied in the task. The student has provided a response that is accurate, complete, and fulfills all the requirements of the task. Necessary support and/or examples are included, and the information given is clearly text-based.	The response indicates that the student has a partial understanding of the reading concept embodied in the task. The student has provided a response that includes information that is essentially correct and text-based, but the information is too general or too simplistic. Some of the support and/or examples may be incomplete or omitted.	The response indicates that the student does not demonstrate an understanding of the reading concept embodied in the task. The student has provided a response that is inaccurate; the response has an insufficient amount of information to determine the student's understanding of the task; or the student has failed to respond to the task.

Scoring RUBRIC for Writing

	Score of 6	Score of 5	Score of 4	Score of 3	Score of 2	Score of 1
FOCUS	The writing is narrowly focused on the main topic and subtopics, and has a clearly defined purpose.	The writing is focused on the topic and purpose.	The writing is generally focused on the topic and purpose with occasional drifts.	The writing is somewhat focused on the topic and purpose with off-topic sentences common.	The writing is related to the topic but does not have a clear focus.	The writing is not focused on the topic and/or purpose.
ORGANIZATION	The ideas in the paper are well-organized and presented in logical order. The paper seems complete to the reader.	The organization of the paper is mostly clear. The paper seems complete.	The organization is mostly clear, but the paper may seem unfinished.	The paper is somewhat organized, but seems unfinished.	There is little organization to the paper.	There is no organization to the paper.
SUPPORT	The writing has strong, specific details. The word choices are clear and fresh.	The writing has strong, specific details and clear word choices.	The writing has supporting details and some variety in word choice.	The writing has few supporting details. It needs more variety in word choice.	The writing uses few supporting details and very little variety in word choice.	The writing uses few supporting details. The word choices are unclear, misused, or confusing.
CONVENTIONS	The writer uses a variety of sentences. There are few or no errors in grammar, spelling, punctuation, and capitalization.	The writer uses a variety of sentences. There are a few errors in grammar, spelling, punctuation, and capitalization.	The writer uses some variety in sentences. There are quite a few errors in grammar, spelling, punctuation, and capitalization.	The writer uses simple sentences. There are often errors in grammar, spelling, punctuation, and capitalization.	The writer uses unclear sentences. There are many errors in grammar, spelling, punctuation, and capitalization.	The writer uses awkward sentences. There are numerous errors in grammar, spelling, punctuation, and capitalization.

Scoring RUBRIC for Presentations

	Score of 4	Score of 3	Score of 2	Score of 1
IDEAS	The paper is clear and focused. It is engaging and includes enriching details.	The paper is generally clear and includes supporting details, with minor focusing problems.	The paper is somewhat clear but the writer does not effectively use supporting details.	The paper has no clear central theme. The details are either missing or sketchy.
ORGANIZATION	The ideas are well organized and in a logical order.	The paper is generally well organized and in a logical order.	The ideas are somewhat organized.	The ideas are not well organized and there is no logical order.
VOICE	The writer consistently uses creative ideas and expressions.	The writer's ideas and expressions are generally creative.	The writer's ideas and expressions are somewhat creative.	The writer lacks creativity in ideas and expressions.
WORD CHOICE	The writing uses vivid verbs, specific nouns, and colorful adjectives well. The writing is very detailed.	The writing may use some vivid verbs, specific nouns, and colorful adjectives. The writing is detailed.	The writing may use few interesting words. The writing is only somewhat detailed.	The writing lacks interesting word choice. The writing also lacks detail.
SENTENCE FLUENCY	The writing flows smoothly. The writer uses transitions, and a variety of sentences.	The writing flows generally well. The writer uses some variety in sentences.	The writing flows somewhat. The writer does not use much variety in his or her sentence structure.	The writing does not flow. The writer uses little or no variety in sentences, and some sentences are unclear.
CONVENTIONS	The writer uses standard writing conventions well, with few or no errors.	The writer uses most standard writing conventions well, but makes some errors.	The writer uses some writing conventions well, but makes distracting errors.	The writer makes continuous errors with most writing conventions, making text difficult to read.

Additional Reading

TWISTS AND TURNS This list is a compilation of the additional theme- and topic-related books cited in the lesson plans. You may wish to use this list to provide students with opportunities **to read at least thirty minutes a day** outside of class.

Theme 3 ▸ AS WE GROW

Ada, Alma Flor and Campoy, F. Isabel.
Smiles: Pablo Picasso, Gabriela Mistral, Benito Juárez. Santillana, 2000. Invites the reader to learn more about the creative lives of important personages of the Hispanic world. *Award-Winning Author.* **AVERAGE**

Brandon, Anthony G.
Moving Day. Harcourt, 2005. Annie Kim does not budge when her family tells her it is time to move to their new house, but then she notices the new puppy with them. **EASY**

Chevallier, Chiara.
The Secret Life of Trees. Dorling Kindersley, 1999. Details the parts and inner lives of trees and all the organisms that live within them. **EASY**

Ehlert, Lois.
Red Leaf, Yellow Leaf. Harcourt, 1998. A child describes the growth of a maple tree from seed to sapling. Boston Globe – Horn Book *Honor; Outstanding Science Trade Book; Notable Children's Book in the Language Arts.* **EASY**

Feeney, Kathy.
Get Moving: Tips on Exercise. Capstone, 2001. An introduction to the benefits of exercise, including warming up, drinking water, and eating right. **AVERAGE**

Garza, Carmen Lomas.
Family Pictures. Children's Book Press, 2005. The author describes, in bilingual text and illustrations, her experiences growing up in a Hispanic community in Texas. **CHALLENGE**

Greenfield, Eloise.
Under the Sunday Tree. HarperTrophy, 1991. A collection of poems and paintings that evoke life in the Bahamas. *ALA Notable Book; Coretta Scott King Illustrator Honor.* **AVERAGE**

Hibbert, Clare.
The Life of a Tree. Raintree, 2004. Explains how a maple tree develops from a seed into a tree, where these trees grow, and the dangers they can face. **AVERAGE**

James, Simon.
Dear Mr. Blueberry. Aladdin, 1996. Provides facts about whales through a series of letters between a student and her teacher. *Children's Choice; Outstanding Science Trade Book.* **EASY**

Keats, Ezra Jack.
A Letter to Amy. Puffin, 1998. Peter wants to invite Amy to his birthday party, but he wants it to be a surprise. *Award-Winning Author.* **AVERAGE**

Krull, Kathleen.
M Is for Music. Harcourt, 2003. An alphabet book introducing musical terms, from allegro to zarzuela. SLJ *Best Book.* **EASY**

Levete, Sarah.
How Do I Feel About: Making Friends. Millbrook, 1998. Discusses the importance of friendships, from making friends to resolving disagreements, and how to deal with feelings such as jealousy, shyness, and rejection. **CHALLENGE**

Locker, Thomas.
Sky Tree. HarperTrophy, 2001. Illustrates the changes of a tree during different times of the day and different seasons. Questions are interspersed throughout the book to encourage further thinking from readers. *Outstanding Science Trade Book.* **CHALLENGE**

Shetterly, Susan Hand.
Shelterwood. Tilbury House, 2003. While staying with her grandfather in his house in the woods, Sophie learns about the different kinds of trees and enjoys the beauties of the natural world. *Outstanding Science Trade Book.* **CHALLENGE**

Spengler, Kremena.
Chile: A Question and Answer Book. Capstone, 2005. Describes the geography, history, economy, and culture of Chile in a question-and-answer format. **CHALLENGE**

Lesson Vocabulary

Theme 3

The following words are introduced in Lessons 11–15.

Lesson 11	Lesson 12	Lesson 13	Lesson 14	Lesson 15
swooned*	deciphered*	tugged*	sprout*	expertise*
astonished*	mistaken*	paused*	damp*	correspondence*
encouraging	translate	columns	suppose	issue
brief	repairs	absorb	roost	advice
chuckling	heaving	protects	spears	consult
soothing	bothersome	rustling	strikes	recommend
sobbed	din	dissolve	glimpse	sensible
praised	dodging	particles	maze	devise
envious*	catastrophe*	scavenger*	transformation*	luscious*
rivalry*	fortunate*	self-sufficient*	harmony*	shudder*

* Listening and Speaking Vocabulary

Cumulative Vocabulary

abroad*
absence
absorb
accompany*
adamant*
advice
affordable*
agreeable
alert
aligned*
amazement
ambitious*
ample
amusing*
anticipation*
appears
apply
assembly
astonished*
attain*
autographed
awe*
babble*
banquet
beckoned
blanketed*
bleak*
boarding*
boasting
bothersome
brief
bristly*
brittle
burden
camaraderie*
camouflage
catastrophe*
certain
charging*
charming*
chatter
chores
chuckling
clutter
coincidence
collaborate*
collapses
columns
commendable*
communicate
compassion*

competent*
composed*
concealed
concentration*
confess
confidence*
confirm
conflict*
confused*
conquer*
conserved*
console
consult
contented*
contribution*
correspondence*
crept
criticize
culture
cunning
curiosity
damp*
dazed
decent
deciphered*
deliberately*
deliberation
delighted
demonstrate
dense*
detail
devise
dialogue
dilemma*
dim
din
disappointed
disgraceful
disguised
dismiss
dissolve
distinct*
diverse*
dodging
dominant*
donated
dozes
dreadful*
drifts
drowsy
dull*

eagerly*
effective*
effort
elaborate*
elevated
embarrass
embraced
emotion
encouraging
enormous
envious*
erupt
evidence
exclaimed
expand
expansive*
expedition*
expert
expertise*
famine
feature*
ferocious*
flawless*
flick
flustered
fluttering
fondness
fortunate*
frustrated*
functional
futuristic*
gaze
generates
generous
gimmick*
glancing
glimpse
glorious
grainy
gratitude*
grooms
gushed*
harmony*
harsh*
heaving
heritage*
heroic
hinder
humor*
image*
imitated*

immerse
independent
individually*
inevitable*
infinite*
ingenious*
ingredients*
inhabitants
inherit
initiative*
inquisitive*
invention
inventive*
inverted*
investigate
inviting*
issue
justice*
laboratory
limp*
literacy*
loyal
luscious*
magnify
mandatory
masterpiece*
maze
media*
memory
mentioned
midst
mistaken*
modeled
momentum*
murmured
nocturnal
nuisance
obey
oblige
observed
occur*
outwit*
overheard
particles
patchwork
patrol
paused*
permanently
perplexed*
persevere*
picturesque

pleasant
plenty
plummet*
ponder*
popular*
praised
preparation*
presentation*
prey
proper*
protects
racket*
reaction*
realistic*
recited
recommend
reels
reflects
rehearse
remark
repairs
required
research
resistance*
resources
responsibility
ridiculous
rivalry*
roost
rotates
ruined
rustling
safeguard
scarce
scavenger*
scent
scolding
sedentary
self-sufficient*
sensible
shabby
shallow
shelters
shifting*
shudder*
signal
skim*
slightly*
sobbed
social
soothing

span*
spears
spiral
sprinkled
sprout*
squirmed
steady
strands
streak
strict*
strikes
suggested
summoning
suppose
surface
surroundings*
survive
suspect
suspicious*
sway
swift
swooned*
swoops
talented
task*
tender
thorough
towers*
tragic*
transferred*
transformation*
translate
trudged*
tugged*
tutor
uncharted*
uniforms
vain
various
versions
viewers
visible
wanders
whined
yanked

* Listening and Speaking Vocabulary

Handwriting

Individual students have various levels of handwriting skills, but they all have the desire to communicate effectively. To write correctly, they must be familiar with concepts of

- **size (tall, short)**
- **open and closed**
- **capital and lowercase letters**
- **manuscript vs. cursive letters**
- **letter and word spacing**
- **punctuation**

To assess students' handwriting skills, review samples of their written work. Note whether they use correct letter formation and appropriate size and spacing. Note whether students follow the conventions of print such as correct capitalization and punctuation. Encourage students to edit and proofread their work and to use editing marks. When writing messages, notes, and letters, or when publishing their writing, students should leave adequate margins and indent new paragraphs to help make their work more readable for their audience.

Stroke and Letter Formation

Most manuscript letters are formed with a continuous stroke, so students do not often pick up their pencils when writing a single letter. When students begin to use cursive handwriting, they will have to lift their pencils from the paper less frequently and will be able to write more fluently. Models for Harcourt and D'Nealian handwriting are provided on pages R25–R28.

Position for Writing

Establishing the correct posture, pen or pencil grip, and paper position for writing will help prevent handwriting problems.

Posture Students should sit with both feet on the floor and with hips to the back of the chair. They can lean forward slightly but should not slouch. The writing surface should be smooth and flat and at a height that allows the upper arms to be perpendicular to the surface and the elbows to be under the shoulders.

Writing Instrument An adult-sized number-two lead pencil is a satisfactory writing tool for most students. As students become proficient in the use of cursive handwriting, have them use pens for writing final drafts. Use your judgment in determining what type of instrument is most suitable.

Paper Position and Pencil Grip The paper is slanted along the line of the student's writing arm, and the student uses his or her nonwriting hand to hold the paper in place. The student holds the pencil or pen slightly above the paint line—about one inch from the lead tip.

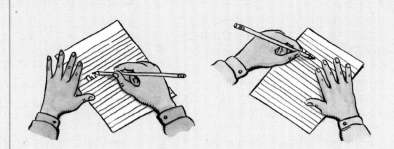

Meeting the Needs of All Learners

The best instruction builds on what students already now and can do. Given the wide range in students' handwriting abilities, a variety of approaches may be needed.

Extra Support For students who need more practice keeping their handwriting legible, one of the most important understandings is that legible writing is important for clear communication. Provide as many opportunities for classroom writing as possible. For example, students can

- **Make a class directory listing the names of their classmates.**
- **Draw and label graphic organizers, pictures, and maps.**
- **Contribute entries weekly to their vocabulary journals.**
- **Write and post messages about class assignments or group activities.**
- **Record observations during activities.**

ELL English-Language Learners can participate in meaningful print experiences. They can

- **Write signs, labels for centers, and other messages.**
- **Label graphic organizers and drawings.**
- **Contribute in group writing activities.**
- **Write independently in journals.**

You may also want to have student practice handwriting skills in their first language.

Challenge To ensure continued rapid advancement of students who come to third grade writing fluently, provide

- **A wide range of writing assignments.**
- **Opportunities for independent writing on self-selected and assigned topics.**

A B C D E F G H

I J K L M N O P

Q R S T U V W

X Y Z

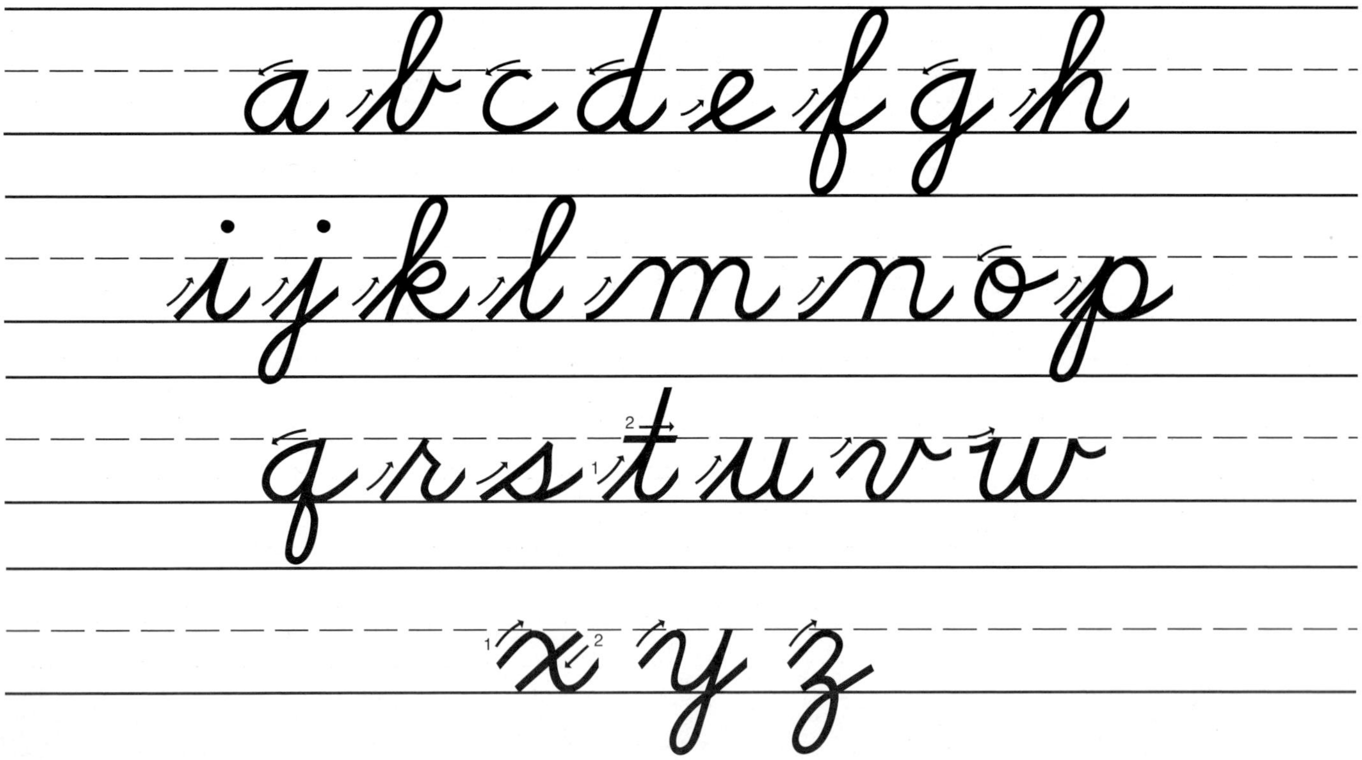

a b c d e f g h

i j k l m n o p

q r s t u v w

x y z

© Harcourt

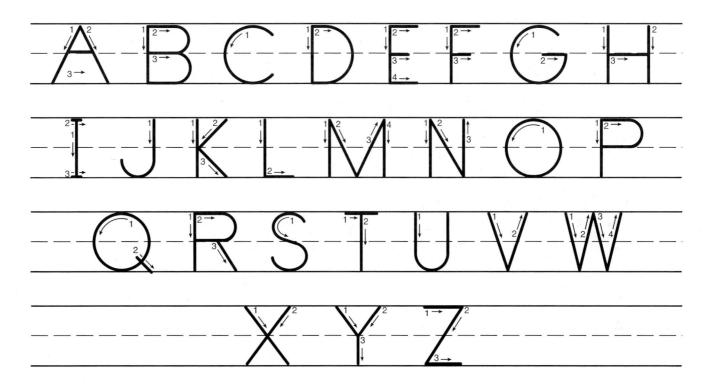

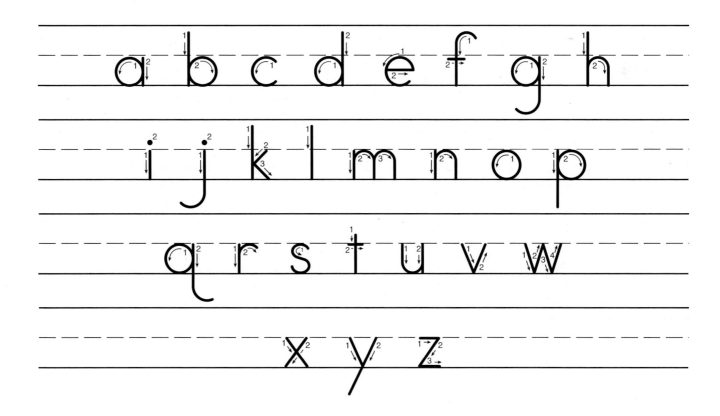

© Harcourt

D'Nealian Handwriting Cursive Alphabet

A B C D E F G H

I J K L M N O P

Q R S T U V W

X Y Z

a b c d e f g h

i j k l m n o p

q r s t u v w

x y z

D'Nealian Handwriting Manuscript Alphabet

A B C D E F G H

I J K L M N O P

Q R S T U V W

X Y Z

a b c d e f g h

i j k l m n o p

q r s t u v w

x y z

Introducing the Glossary

MODEL USING THE GLOSSARY Explain to students that a glossary often is included in a book so that readers can find the meanings of words used in the book.

- Read aloud the introductory pages.

- Model looking up one or more words.

- Point out how you rely on **alphabetical order** and the **guide words** at the top of the Glossary pages to locate the **entry word**.

- Demonstrate how to use the **pronunciation key** to confirm the correct pronunciation.

As students look over the Glossary, point out that illustrations accompany some of the Student-Friendly Explanations. Have students read a Word Origins or Academic Language note and discuss the type of information in each.

Encourage students to look up several words in the Glossary, identifying the correct page and the guide words. Then have them explain how using alphabetical order and the guide words at the top of each page helped them locate the words.

Tell students to use the Glossary to confirm the pronunciation of Vocabulary Words during reading and to help them better understand the meanings of unfamiliar words.

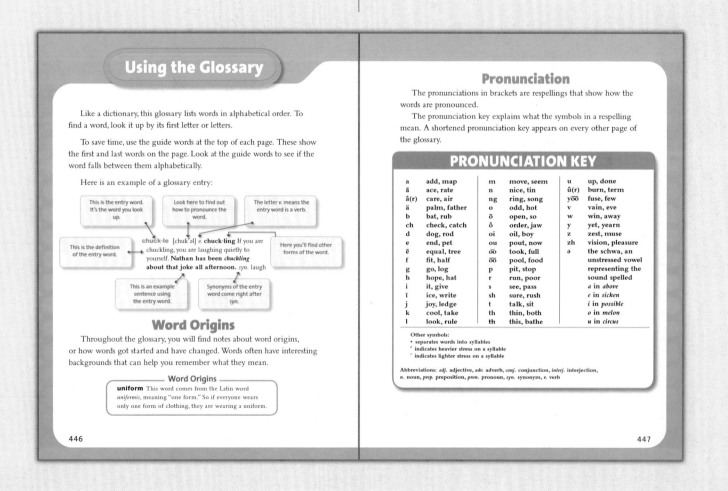

A

ab·sorb [əb·zôrb′] *v.* Something absorbs a liquid if it soaks up the liquid. **The towel will *absorb* the water.** *syn.* take in

ACADEMIC LANGUAGE
accuracy When you read with *accuracy*, you read without any mistakes.

ad·vice [ad·vīs′] *n.* If you give someone advice, you tell what you think the person should do. **Lauren's *advice* was to choose the game that was the most fun to play.** *syn.* recommendation

ACADEMIC LANGUAGE
advice column An *advice column* gives suggestions for how to solve a problem and is found in a newspaper or magazine.

a·gree·a·ble [ə·grē′ə·bəl] *adj.* Something that is agreeable is pleasing to the senses. **The smell of an apple pie baking was very *agreeable*.** *syn.* pleasant

a·lert [ə·lûrt′] *v.* If you alert people to something, you get their attention and let them know to be careful. **The smoke alarm will *alert* you to the fact that fire is present.** *syn.* notify

ap·ply [ə·plī′] *v.* When you apply for a job, you are asking for work. **Kiarra will call the company to *apply* for a job.** *syns.* request, ask

as·sem·bly [ə·sem′blē] *n.* An assembly is a group of people who have gathered for a reason. **The school will hold an *assembly* to honor the reading contest winners.** *syns.* meeting, gathering

au·to·graph [ô′tə·graf′] *v.* **au·to·graphed** If you autographed something, you signed your name on it. **Adam's friends *autographed* his yearbook.** *syn.* sign

autograph

B

ban·quet [bang′kwit] *n.* If you are going to a banquet, you are going to a special meal that will have a large amount of food. **There will be a lot of food at the *banquet*.** *syn.* feast

banquet

ACADEMIC LANGUAGE
biography A *biography* is the story of a person's life, written by another person.

both·er·some [both′ər·səm] *adj.* When something is bothersome, it bothers you and causes problems. **The broken zipper on my boot is *bothersome*!** *syn.* annoying

brief [brēf] *adj.* If something is brief, it does not take much time. **The class will take a *brief* break before continuing the test.** *syn.* short

C

cam·ou·flage [kam′ə·fläzh′] *n.* When something has camouflage, it blends into its surroundings. **An arctic hare has white fur in winter as *camouflage* against the snow.**

Word Origins
camouflage *Camouflage* comes from the Italian *camuffare*, which means "disguise or trick." This word got its start during World War I, when soldiers practiced hiding objects from the enemy.

cer·tain [sûr′tən] *adj.* A certain thing is one particular thing. **Cole wants a *certain* kind of candy.** *syn.* specific

chat·ter [chat′ər] *v.* When animals chatter, they repeat their sounds quickly. **I heard the squirrels *chatter* outside.** *syn.* talk

chore [chôr] *n.* **chores** Chores are small jobs that you need to do but may not enjoy. **Julia has to do her *chores* at home every day.** *syn.* duty

chuck·le [chuk′əl] *v.* **chuck·ling** If you are chuckling, you are laughing quietly to yourself. **Nathan has been *chuckling* about that joke all afternoon.** *syn.* laugh

co·in·ci·dence [kō·in′sə·dəns] *n.* A coincidence is when two things happen that seem to fit together but are not connected. **It was a *coincidence* that Sophia and Mackenzie wore identical shirts today.**

col·lapse [kə·laps′] *v.* **col·laps·es** When something collapses, it falls down because it is not well supported. **"Run out of the tent before it collapses!" I yelled.**

col·umn [kol′əm] *n.* **col·umns** A column is a tall, circular structure that holds up part of a building. **The roof of the porch is held up by *columns*.** *syn.* pole

column

com·mu·ni·cate [kə·myōō′nə·kāt′] *v.* When two people or animals communicate, they share information. **One way people *communicate* is by talking.**

Word Origins
communicate *Communicate* comes from the Latin *communicatus*, which means "share."

con·ceal [kən·sēl′] *v.* **con·cealed** Something that is concealed is covered up so it can't be seen. **Malik wanted to surprise his dad, so he *concealed* the gift under the couch.** *syn.* hide

a	add	e	end	o	odd	oo	pool	oi	oil	th	this		ə =	a in *above*
ā	ace	ē	equal	ō	open	u	up	ou	pout	zh	vision			e in *sicken*
â	care	i	it	ô	order	û	burn	ng	ring					i in *possible*
ä	palm	ī	ice	oo	took	yōō	fuse	th	thin					o in *melon*
														u in *circus*

con·fess [kən·fes′] *v.* When you confess, you tell the truth about something you did wrong. **It can be hard to *confess* that you have made a mistake, but it is best to tell the truth.** *syn.* admit

con·sult [kən·sult′] *v.* When you consult someone, you ask him or her for information. **Daniel wanted to *consult* his coach about how he could jump higher.**

cul·ture [kul′chər] *n.* A culture is made up of a group's customs and traditions. **In North American *culture*, people shake hands when they meet.**

cu·ri·os·i·ty [kyoor·ē·os′ə·tē] *n.* Something that is called a curiosity is something odd or unusual that interests people. **The flower's blooming in winter was a *curiosity*.** *syn.* oddity

D

dazed [dāzd] *adj.* If you are dazed, you are confused and cannot think properly. **The winner was *dazed* by the surprise announcement and didn't know what to say.**

dem·on·strate [dem′ən·strāt′] *v.* When you demonstrate something, you show how it works or how it is done. **Adrianne will *demonstrate* a basketball trick.** *syn.* show

demonstrate

de·vise [di·vīz′] *v.* To devise is to figure out a way to do something. **Emma needed to *devise* a way to get her chores finished.** *syn.* invent

din [din] *n.* If there is a din, there is so much noise that it is hard to hear anything over it. **The *din* of the crowd made it hard to hear my friend talk.** *syn.* racket

dis·ap·poin·ted [dis′ə·point′ed] *adj.* You are disappointed if you are unhappy about the way something turned out. **Elijah was *disappointed* that his team lost the game.** *syns.* saddened, upset

dis·miss [dis·mis′] *v.* To dismiss is to give permission to leave. **Savannah hopes the teacher will *dismiss* the class early for recess.**

dis·solve [di·zolv′] *v.* When something dissolves, it mixes completely with a liquid. **The powder will *dissolve* if you stir it into water.**

dodge [doj] *v.* **dodg·ing** When you are dodging something, you avoid something that is coming toward you. **Fast runners are usually good at *dodging* the ball.** *syn.* avoid

do·nate [dō′nāt′] *v.* **do·nat·ed** Something that has been donated has been given away for free. **Many parents *donated* flowers to be planted in front of the school.**

E

el·e·va·ted [el′ə·vā′ted] *adj.* Something that is elevated is lifted up. **The *elevated* walkway lets people cross the street by walking above it.** *syn.* raised

em·bar·rass [im·bar′əs] *v.* If you embarrass someone, you make that person feel uncomfortable or ashamed. **Courtney will *embarrass* herself if she forgets her lines in the play.**

en·cour·ag·ing [in·kûr′ij·ing] *adj.* Something that is encouraging gives someone hope or confidence. **The coach's speech before the championship game was *encouraging*.** *syn.* hopeful

ex·pert [ek′spûrt] *n.* An expert is someone who knows a lot about a certain subject. **The quarterback is an *expert* at throwing a football.**

ACADEMIC LANGUAGE
expository nonfiction *Expository nonfiction* explains information and ideas.
expression Reading aloud with *expression* means using your voice to match the action of the story and the character's feelings.

F

ACADEMIC LANGUAGE
fable A *fable* is a short story that teaches a lesson about life. A fable often uses animals that act like people.

fa·mine [fam′in] *n.* When there is famine, there is not enough food to feed everyone. **Hot, dry weather for a long period of time can cause *famine* in an area.**

flick [flik] *v.* When you flick something, you move it or snap it quickly. **The frog can *flick* its tongue to catch a bug.** *syn.* snap

flick

ACADEMIC LANGUAGE
folktale A *folktale* is a story that has been passed down through time.

G

gaze [gāz] *n.* A gaze is a long look at something. **Gabriella's *gaze* was directed at the sky.** *syn.* stare

gen·er·ous [jen′ər·əs] *adj.* People who are generous are happy to share with others. **Justin was *generous* when he shared his lunch after Desiree forgot hers.** *syn.* giving

ACADEMIC LANGUAGE
genre A *genre* is a kind of writing, such as fiction or nonfiction.

a	add	e	end	o	odd	oo	pool	oi	oil	th	this		ə =	a in *above*
ā	ace	ē	equal	ō	open	u	up	ou	pout	zh	vision			e in *sicken*
â	care	i	it	ô	order	û	burn	ng	ring					i in *possible*
ä	palm	ī	ice	oo	took	yōō	fuse	th	thin					o in *melon*
														u in *circus*

glimpse [glimps] *n.* When you get a glimpse of something, you get only a quick peek at it. **Anthony got a *glimpse* of his birthday cake in the box.** *syn.* peek

— Word Origins —
glimpse *Glimpse* comes from the German word *glim* which meant "to shine softly" or "to see a soft flash."

groom [groom] **1.** *v.* **grooms** When an animal grooms itself, it makes itself neat and clean. **Angelica's cat *grooms* itself by licking its fur.** *syn.* clean **2.** *n.* A groom is a man who is being married or was just married. **The *groom* stood quietly as the wedding music began.**

H

heave [hēv] *v.* **heav·ing** Heaving means throwing something heavy with great effort. **Davion needs help *heaving* this heavy bag onto the truck.** *syn.* throw

hin·der [hin′dər] *v.* When you hinder someone, you make it difficult or impossible for them to do something. **Tiana's sore ankle won't *hinder* her from finishing the race.** *syn.* stop

ACADEMIC LANGUAGE
historical fiction *Historical fiction* is a made-up story that is set in the past with people, places, and events that did happen or could have happened.

I

in·de·pen·dent [in′di·pen′dənt] *adj.* A person who is independent is someone who does things on his or her own. **Learning to tie his shoes made my little brother more *independent*.**

ACADEMIC LANGUAGE
intonation *Intonation* is the rise and fall of your voice as you read aloud.

in·ven·tion [in·ven′shən] *n.* An invention is something completely new that someone has made. **The scientist's *invention* will make life easier for everyone.**

in·ves·ti·gate [in·ves′tə·gāt′] *v.* When you investigate something, you try to find out the truth about it. **Tyler had to *investigate* the disappearance of his lunch box.**

is·sue [ish′ōō] *n.* An issue is an edition of a newspaper or magazine. **Carlos was excited when the latest *issue* of his favorite magazine came in the mail.**

J

ACADEMIC LANGUAGE
journal A *journal* is a personal record of daily events.

L

lab·o·ra·to·ry [lab′rə·tôr′ē] *n.* A place where experiments are done is a laboratory. **The scientist bought some brand-new equipment for his *laboratory*.**

ACADEMIC LANGUAGE
legend A *legend* is a story from the past that is often partly true.

loy·al [loi′əl] *adj.* Someone who is loyal stands by you in good times and bad. **Caleb's dog is *loyal* to him.** *syn.* faithful

M

ACADEMIC LANGUAGE
magazine article A *magazine article* is a short selection that appears in a magazine and gives information about a topic.

maze [māz] *n.* A maze is a winding set of paths that is like a puzzle. **Finding my way around town was like being lost in a *maze*.**

midst [midst] *n.* If you are in the midst of something, you are in the middle of it. **Andrew and Marissa were in the *midst* of discussing their project.**

mo·del [mod′əl] *v.* **mo·deled** If you modeled something, you showed it so that others could see it. **Francisco *modeled* his costume for the class.** *syn.* show, present

mur·mur [mûr′mûr] *v.* **mur·mured** When people murmur, they speak so softly that they can hardly be heard. **Trevor could not hear what Nia *murmured* to herself.** *syn.* mumble

ACADEMIC LANGUAGE
mystery In a *mystery*, something strange happens that is not explained until the end of the story.

N

ACADEMIC LANGUAGE
news feature A *news feature* gives information—about a person or topic—in a newspaper or magazine.

newsletter A *newsletter* presents information—about an organization—to a person or group of people.

news script A *news script* is a text that is read aloud and gives information about important events.

nonfiction *Nonfiction* gives facts and information about people, places, or things.

a add	e end	o odd	ōō pool	oi oil	th this		ə =	a in *above*
ā ace	ē equal	ō open	u up	ou pout	zh vision			e in *sicken*
â care	i it	ô order	û burn	ng ring				i in *possible*
ä palm	ī ice	ōō took	yōō fuse	th thin				o in *melon*
								u in *circus*

O

o·bey [ō·bā′] *v.* When you obey, you do what you are told to do. **Good citizens *obey* the law.**

ACADEMIC LANGUAGE
online information *Online information* is found on an Internet website.

P

ACADEMIC LANGUAGE
pace Reading at an appropriate *pace* means reading at the right speed.

par·ti·cle [pär′ti·kəl] *n.* **par·ti·cles** Tiny pieces of something are called particles. **Cody wiped the dust *particles* off the computer screen** *syn.* bit

patch·work [pach′wûrk] *n.* Patchwork is cloth made by sewing together small pieces of different fabrics. **The quilt Grandma made is a *patchwork* of pieces cut from the family's old clothing.**

patchwork

pa·trol [pə·trōl′] *v.* People patrol an area to watch over and guard it. **Police *patrol* a neighborhood to keep it safe.** *syns.* tour, watch, guard

ACADEMIC LANGUAGE
photo essay A *photo essay* presents information mostly with photographs and with some text.

phrasing *Phrasing* is the grouping of words into small "chunks," or phrases, when you read aloud.

pleas·ant [plez′ənt] *adj.* Something that is pleasant is enjoyable and makes you happy. **The weather is *pleasant* today.**

plen·ty [plen′tē] *n.* If you have plenty of something, you have more than enough. **There are *plenty* of toys for everyone.**

ACADEMIC LANGUAGE
poetry *Poetry* uses rhythm and imagination to express feelings and ideas.

postcards *Postcards* can be mailed without an envelope and usually have a picture on one side.

praise [prāz] *v.* **praised** If you have praised someone, you have told that person that he or she did something well. **The teacher *praised* the students for their fine drawings.**

pro·tect [prə·tekt′] *v.* **pro·tects** When you protect something, you keep it safe. **Amir *protects* his head by wearing a bicycle helmet.** *syns.* guard, defend

— Word Origins —
protect *Protect* comes from the Latin word *prōtegere*. The prefix *pro-* means "in front" and the root word *tegere* means "cover." So when you protect someone, you cover him or her from the front like a shield.

ACADEMIC LANGUAGE
punctuation Paying attention to *punctuation*, such as commas and periods, will help you read a text correctly.

R

ACADEMIC LANGUAGE
reading rate Your *reading rate* is how quickly you can read a text correctly and still understand what you are reading.

realistic fiction *Realistic fiction* is a story that could happen in real life.

re·cite [ri·sīt′] *v.* **re·cit·ed** If you recited something, you memorized it and then spoke it aloud. **Ali *recited* the names of all 50 states without looking at a map.**

rec·om·mend [rek′ə·mend′] *v.* When you recommend something, you tell someone that you think it is good. **Alexis asked her teacher to *recommend* a book to read.**

re·pair [ri·pâr′] *v.* **re·pairs** When something needs repairs, it needs to be fixed. **Cynthia needs to make *repairs* to her bike before the race.**

re·search [ri·sûrch′ or rē′sûrch′] *n.* Research involves getting information about a question or topic. **Isabel has done *research* on desert animals for her report.** *syn.* study

re·source [ri·sôrs′or rē′sôrs′] *n.* **re·sourc·es** Resources are materials, money, and other things that can be used. **Water *resources* are important to cities.** *syn.* supply

roost [rōōst] *v.* Birds roost, or perch, when they sleep in trees at night. **Many birds *roost* in the tree outside my window each night.**

rus·tle [rus′əl] *v.* **rust·ling** When objects are rustling, they are moving and making soft sounds. **Please stop *rustling* those papers.**

S

scent [sent] *n.* A scent is the smell of something. **Carol loves the *scent* of spring flowers.** *syns.* odor, smell

scent

sen·si·ble [sen′sə·bəl] *adj.* Someone who is sensible makes good decisions and judgments. **Jennifer is a *sensible* eater who chooses fruits as treats.** *syn.* wise

shab·by [shab′ē] *adj.* Shabby things look old and worn out. **This *shabby* coat will be fine for working in the garden.**

sig·nal [sig′nəl] *n.* A signal is a sound or an action that sends a message. **The green light is a *signal* to go.** *syn.* sign

a add	e end	o odd	ōō pool	oi oil	th this		ə =	a in *above*
ā ace	ē equal	ō open	u up	ou pout	zh vision			e in *sicken*
â care	i it	ô order	û burn	ng ring				i in *possible*
ä palm	ī ice	ōō took	yōō fuse	th thin				o in *melon*
								u in *circus*

sob [sob] *v.* **sobbed** Someone who sobbed cried very hard. **Brenda *sobbed* when she lost her favorite book.** *syn.* cry

sooth·ing [sŏŏth′ing] *adj.* Something that is soothing makes you feel calm. **Jazmine thinks the sound of rain is *soothing*.** *syn.* calming

spear [spir] *v.* **spears** If someone spears something, he or she sticks something sharp through it. **Steven *spears* the green beans with his fork.** *syn.* stab

squirm [skwûrm] *v.* **squirmed** If you squirmed in your seat, you kept wriggling around as if you were uncomfortable. **The puppy *squirmed* when Savion tried to pick it up.** *syn.* wriggle

strike [strīk] **1.** *v.* **strikes** If something strikes something else, it hits it. **Rod *strikes* a nail with his hammer.** *syn.* hit **2.** *n.* In baseball, a strike is a pitch that the batter misses. **After the third *strike*, Edward had to walk off the baseball field.**

strike

sup·pose [sə·pōz′] *v.* When you suppose something, you think it is true. **What do you *suppose* will happen tomorrow?** *syn.* believe

sur·vive [sər·vīv′] *v.* To survive is to remain alive, even after great difficulties. **Living things need food, water, air, and shelter to *survive*.** *syn.* live

sus·pect [sə·spekt′] *v.* When you suspect someone of doing something, you think that person has done it. **Knowing her brother made Emily *suspect* that he had eaten all the cookies.**

ACADEMIC LANGUAGE

syllable A *syllable* is the smallest part of a word that contains a single vowel sound.

T

tal·ent·ed [tal′ən·tid] *adj.* A talented person has the special ability to do something very well. **Serena is a very *talented* drummer.** *syns.* skilled, gifted

ACADEMIC LANGUAGE

textbook A *textbook* is a book that is used in schools to teach a subject.

time line A *time line* is a line that shows dates of past events in the order in which they happened.

trans·late [trans·lāt′] *v.* If you translate something, you say or write it in another language. **Can Kimberly *translate* this letter into English?** *syn.* interpret

---

tu·tor [tōō′tər] *n.* A tutor is someone who helps another person with schoolwork. **César has a math *tutor* to help him after school.** *syns.* teacher, instructor

U

u·ni·form [yōō′nə·fôrm′] *n.* **u·ni·forms** Uniforms are clothes that all the people in a group wear so that they are dressed alike. **Ian could tell his teammates by their *uniforms*.**

uniform

Word Origins

uniform This word comes from the Latin word *uniformis* meaning "one form." If everyone wears only one form of clothing, they are wearing a uniform.

V

var·i·ous [vâr′ē·əs] *adj.* When there are various objects, there are objects of different types. **The box was full of *various* items that students had lost.** *syn.* assorted

view·er [vyōō′ər] *n.* **view·ers** Viewers are people who watch something. **The host of the show told stories that were interesting to his *viewers*.**

W

wan·der [wän′dər] *v.* **wan·ders** A person who wanders travels without planning where he or she is going. **The tourist *wanders*, stopping at places of interest around town.**

whine [hwīn] *v.* **whined** If someone or something whined, it gave a long, high cry. **The toddler *whined* when his mother would not buy the toy.** *syn.* whimper

a	add	e	end	o	odd	ōō	pool	oi	oil	th	this		
ā	ace	ē	equal	ō	open	u	up	ou	pout	zh	vision	ə =	*a* in *above*
â	care	i	it	ô	order	û	burn	ng	ring				*e* in *sicken*
ä	palm	ī	ice	ōō	took	yōō	fuse	th	thin				*i* in *possible*
													o in *melon*
													u in *circus*

Index of Titles and Authors

Professional Bibliography

Armbruster, B.B., Anderson, T.H., & Ostertag, J.
(1987). Does text structure/summarization instruction facilitate learning from expository text? *Reading Research Quarterly,* 22 (3), 331–346.

Ball, E., & Blachman, B.
(1991). Does phoneme awareness training in kindergarten make a difference in early word recognition and developmental spelling? *Reading Research Quarterly,* 26 (1), 49–66.

Baumann, J.F. & Bergeron, B.S.
(1993). Story map instruction using children's literature: effects on first graders' comprehension of central narrative elements. *Journal of Reading Behavior,* 25 (4), 407–437.

Baumann, J.F., Seifert-Kessell, N., & Jones, L.A.
(1992). Effect of think-aloud instruction on elementary students' comprehension monitoring abilities. *Journal of Reading Behavior,* 24 (2), 143–172.

Beck, I.L., Perfetti, C.A., & McKeown, M.G.
(1982). Effects of long-term vocabulary instruction on lexical access and reading comprehension. *Journal of Educational Psychology,* 74 (4), 506–521.

Bereiter, C. & Bird, M.
(1985). Use of thinking aloud in identification and teaching of reading comprehension strategies. *Cognition and Instruction,* 2, 131–156.

Blachman, B.
(2000). Phonological awareness. In M. Kamil, P. Mosenthal, P.D. Pearson, & R. Barr (Eds.), *Handbook of reading research,* (Vol. 3). Mahwah, NJ: Erlbaum.

Blachman, B., Ball, E.W., Black, R.S., & Tangel, D.M.
(1994). Kindergarten teachers develop phoneme awareness in low-income, inner-city classrooms: Does it make a difference? *Reading and Writing: An Interdisciplinary Journal,* 6 (1), 1–18.

Brown, I.S. & Felton, R.H.
(1990). Effects of instruction on beginning reading skills in children at risk for reading disability. *Reading and Writing: An Interdisciplinary Journal,* 2 (3), 223–241.

Chall, J.
(1996). *Learning to read: The great debate (revised, with a new foreword).* New York: McGraw-Hill.

Dowhower, S.L.
(1987). Effects of repeated reading on second-grade transitional readers' fluency and comprehension. *Reading Research Quarterly,* 22 (4), 389–406.

Ehri, L., & Wilce, L.
(1987). Does learning to spell help beginners learn to read words? *Reading Research Quarterly,* 22 (1), 48–65.

Fletcher, J.M. & Lyon, G.R.
(1998) Reading: A research-based approach. In Evers, W.M. (Ed.) *What's gone wrong in America's classroom?*, Palo Alto, CA: Hoover Institution Press, Stanford University.

Foorman, B., Francis, D., Fletcher, J., Schatschneider, C., & Mehta, P.
(1998). The role of instruction in learning to read: Preventing reading failure in at-risk children. *Journal of Educational Psychology,* 90 (1), 37–55.

Fukkink, R.G. & de Glopper, K.
(1998). Effects of instruction in deriving word meaning from context: A meta-analysis. *Review of Educational Research,* 68 (4), 450–469.

Gipe, J.P. & Arnold, R.D.
(1979). Teaching vocabulary through familiar associations and contexts. *Journal of Reading Behavior,* 11 (3), 281–285.

Griffith, P.L., Klesius, J.P., & Kromrey, J.D.
(1992). The effect of phonemic awareness on the literacy development of first grade children in a traditional or a whole language classroom. *Journal of Research in Childhood Education,* 6 (2), 85–92.

Juel, C.
(1988). Learning to read and write: A longitudinal study of fifty-four children from first through fourth grades. *Journal of Educational Psychology,* 80, 437–447.

Lundberg, I., Frost, J., & Petersen O.
(1988). Effects of an extensive program for stimulating phonological awareness in preschool children. *Reading Research Quarterly,* 23 (3), 263–284.

McKeown, M.G., Beck, I.L., Omanson, R.C., & Pople, M.T.
(1985). Some effects of the nature and frequency of vocabulary instruction on the knowledge and use of words. *Reading Research Quarterly,* 20 (5), 522–535.

Nagy, W.E. & Scott, J.A.
(2000). Vocabulary processes. In M. Kamil, P. Mosenthal, P.D. Pearson, & R. Barr (Eds.), *Handbook of reading research,* (Vol. 3) Mahwah, NJ: Erlbaum.

National Reading Panel
(2000). *Teaching children to read.* National Institute of Child Health and Human Development, National Institutes of Health, Washington, D.C.

O'Connor, R., Jenkins, J.R., & Slocum, T.A.
(1995). Transfer among phonological tasks in kindergarten: Essential instructional content. *Journal of Educational Psychology,* 87 (2), 202–217.

O'Shea, L.J., Sindelar, P.T., & O'Shea, D.J.
(1985). The effects of repeated readings and attentional cues on reading fluency and comprehension. *Journal of Reading Behavior,* 17 (2), 129–142.

Paris, S.G., Cross, D.R., & Lipson, M.Y.
(1984). Informed strategies for learning: A program to improve children's reading awareness and comprehension. *Journal of Educational Psychology,* 76 (6), 1239–1252.

Payne, B.D., & Manning, B.H.
(1992). Basal reader instruction: Effects of comprehension monitoring training on reading comprehension, strategy use and attitude. *Reading Research and Instruction,* 32 (1), 29–38.

Rasinski, T.V., Padak, N., Linek, W., & Sturtevant, E.
(1994). Effects of fluency development on urban second-grade readers. *Journal of Educational Research,* 87 (3), 158–165.

Rinehart, S.D., Stahl, S.A., & Erickson, L.G.
(1986). Some effects of summarization training on reading and studying. *Reading Research Quarterly,* 21 (4), 422–438.

Robbins, C. & Ehri, L.C.
(1994). Reading storybooks to kindergartners helps them learn new vocabulary words. *Journal of Educational Psychology,* 86 (1), 54–64.

Rosenshine, B., & Meister, C.
(1994). Reciprocal teaching: A review of research. *Review of Educational Research,* 64 (4), 479–530.

Rosenshine, B., Meister, C., & Chapman, S.
(1996). Teaching students to generate questions: A review of the intervention studies. *Review of Educational Research,* 66 (2), 181–221.

Sénéchal, M.
(1997). The differential effect of storybook reading on preschoolers' acquisition of expressive and receptive vocabulary. *Journal of Child Language,* 24 (1), 123–138.

Shany, M.T. & Biemiller, A.
(1995) Assisted reading practice: Effects on performance for poor readers in grades 3 and 4. *Reading Research Quarterly,* 30 (3), 382–395.

Sindelar, P.T., Monda, L.E., & O'Shea, L.J.
(1990). Effects of repeated readings on instructional- and mastery-level readers. *Journal of Educational Research,* 83 (4), 220–226.

Snow, C.E., Burns, S.M., & Griffin, P.
(1998). *Preventing reading difficulties in young children.* Washington, D.C.: National Academy Press.

Stahl, S.A. & Fairbanks, M.M.
(1986). The effects of vocabulary instruction: A model-based meta-analysis. *Review of Educational Research,* 56 (1), 72–110.

Stanovich, K.E.
(1986) Matthew effects in reading: Some consequences of individual differences in the acquisition of literacy. *Reading Research Quarterly,* 21 (4), 360–406.

Torgesen, J., Morgan, S., & Davis, C.
(1992). Effects of two types of phonological awareness training on word learning in kindergarten children. *Journal of Educational Psychology,* 84 (3), 364–370.

Torgesen, J., Wagner, R., Rashotte, C., Rose, E., Lindamood, P., Conway, T., & Garvan, C.
(1999). Preventing reading failure in young children with phonological processing disabilities: Group and individual responses to instruction. *Journal of Educational Psychology,* 91(4), 579–593.

Vellutino, F.R., & Scanlon, D.M.
(1987). Phonological coding, phonological awareness, and reading ability: Evidence from a longitudinal and experimental study. *Merrill-Palmer Quarterly,* 33 (3), 321–363.

White, T.G., Graves, M.F., & Slater, W.H.
(1990). Growth of reading vocabulary in diverse elementary schools: Decoding and word meaning. *Journal of Educational Psychology,* 82 (2), 281–290.

Wixson, K.K.
(1986). Vocabulary instruction and children's comprehension of basal stories. *Reading Research Quarterly,* 21 (3), 317–329.

Program Reviewers

Elizabeth A. Adkins,
Teacher
Ford Middle School
Brook Park, Ohio

Jean Bell,
Principal
Littleton Elementary School
Avondale, Arizona

Emily Brown,
Teacher
Orange Center Elementary School
Orlando, Florida

Stephen Bundy,
Teacher
Ventura Elementary School
Kissimmee, Florida

Helen Comba,
Language Arts Supervisor K-5
Southern Boulevard School
Chatham, New Jersey

Marsha Creese,
Reading/Language Arts Consultant
Marlborough Elementary School
Marlborough, Connecticut

Wyndy M. Crozier,
Teacher
Mary Bryant Elementary School
Tampa, Florida

Shirley Eyler,
Principal
Martin Luther King School
Piscataway, New Jersey

Sandy Hoffman,
Teacher
Heights Elementary School
Fort Myers, Florida

Amy Martin,
Reading Coach
Kingswood Elementary School
Wickenburg, Arizona

Rachel A. Musser,
Reading Coach
Chumuckla Elementary School
Jay, Florida

Dr. Carol Newton,
Director of Elementary Curriculum
Millard Public Schools
Omaha, Nebraska

Alda P. Pill,
Teacher
Mandarin Oaks Elementary School
Jacksonville, Florida

Dr. Elizabeth V. Primas,
Director
Office of Curriculum and Instruction
Washington, District of Columbia

Candice Ross,
Staff Development Teacher
A. Mario Loiderman Middle School
Silver Spring, Maryland

Sharon Sailor,
Teacher
Conrad Fischer Elementary School
Elmhurst, Illinois

Lucia Schneck,
Supervisor/Language Arts, Literacy
Irvington Board of Education
Irvington, New Jersey

RuthAnn Shauf,
District Resource Teacher
Hillsborough County Public Schools
Tampa, Florida

Jolene Topping,
Teacher
Palmetto Ridge High School
Bonita Springs, Florida

Betty Tubon,
Bilingual Teacher
New Field Primary School
Chicago, Illinois

Janet White,
Assistant Principal
MacFarlane Park Elementary School
Tampa, Florida

KINDERGARTEN REVIEWERS

Denise Bir,
Teacher
Destin Elementary School
Destin, Florida

Linda H. Butler,
Reading First State Director
Office of Academic Services
Washington, District of Columbia

Julie Elvers,
Teacher
Aldrich Elementary School
Omaha, Nebraska

Rosalyn Glavin,
Principal
Walter White Elementary School
River Rouge, Michigan

Jo Anne M. Kershaw,
Language Arts Program Leader,
K-5
Longhill Administration Building
Trumbull, Connecticut

Beverly Kibbe,
Teacher
Cherry Brook Elementary School
Canton, Connecticut

Bonnie B. Macintosh,
Teacher
Glenallan Elementary School
Silver Spring, Maryland

Laurin MacLeish,
Teacher
Orange Center Elementary School
Orlando, Florida

Mindy Steighner,
Teacher
Randall Elementary School
Waukesha, Wisconsin

Paula Stutzman,
Teacher
Seven Springs Elementary School
New Port Richey, Florida

Martha Tully,
Teacher
Fleming Island Elementary School
Orange Park, Florida

Scope and Sequence

	Gr K	Gr 1	Gr 2	Gr 3	Gr 4	Gr 5	Gr 6
Reading							
Concepts About Print							
Understand that print provides information	▓						
Understand how print is organized and read	▓						
Know left-to-right and top-to-bottom directionality	▓						
Distinguish letters from words	▓						
Recognize name	▓						
Name and match all uppercase and lowercase letter forms	▓						
Understand the concept of word and construct meaning from shared text, illustrations, graphics, and charts	▓						
Identify letters, words, and sentences	▓						
Recognize that sentences in print are made up of words	▓						
Identify the front cover, back cover, title page, title, and author of a book	▓	▓					
Match oral words to printed words	▓	▓					
Phonemic Awareness							
Understand that spoken words and syllables are made up of sequence of sounds	▓						
Count and track sounds in a syllable, syllables in words, and words in sentences	▓						
Know the sounds of letters	▓						
Track and represent the number, sameness, difference, and order of two or more isolated phonemes	▓						
Match, identify, distinguish, and segment sounds in initial, final, and medial position in single-syllable spoken words	▓	▓	▓				
Blend sounds (phonemes) to make words or syllables	▓						
Track and represent changes in syllables and words as target sound is added, substituted, omitted, shifted, or repeated	▓						
Distinguish long- and short-vowel sounds in orally stated words	▓	▓	▓				
Identify and produce rhyming words	▓						
Decoding: Phonic Analysis							
Understand and apply the alphabetic principle	▓	▓					
Consonants; single, blends, digraphs in initial, final, medial positions	•	•	•	•			
Vowels: short, long, digraphs, r-controlled, variant, schwa		•	•	•			
Match all consonant and short-vowel sounds to appropriate letters	•	•					
Understand that as letters in words change, so do the sounds	•	•					
Blend vowel-consonant sounds orally to make words or syllables	•	•					
Blend sounds from letters and letter patterns into recognizable words	▓	▓					
Decoding: Structural Analysis							
Inflectional endings, with and without spelling changes: plurals, verb tenses, possessives, comparatives-superlatives		•	•	•			
Contractions, abbreviations, and compound words		•	•	•			
Prefixes, suffixes, derivations, and root words				•	•	•	•
Greek and Latin roots					•	•	•
Letter, spelling, and syllable patterns							
Phonograms/word families/onset-rimes							
Syllable rules and patterns							
Decoding: Strategies							
Visual cues: sound/symbol relationships, letter patterns, and spelling patterns		•					
Structural cues: compound words, contractions, inflectional endings, prefixes, suffixes, Greek and Latin roots, root words, spelling patterns, and word families		•					
Cross check visual and structural cues to confirm meaning							

Key:

Shaded area - Explicit Instruction/Modeling/Practice and Application

• *Tested—Assessment Resources: Weekly Lesson Tests, Theme Tests, Benchmark Assessments*

	Gr K	Gr 1	Gr 2	Gr 3	Gr 4	Gr 5	Gr 6
Word Recognition							
One-syllable and high-frequency words	•	•	•				
Common, irregular sight words	•	•	•				
Common abbreviations			•				
Lesson vocabulary		•	•	•	•	•	•
Fluency							
Read aloud in a manner that sounds like natural speech							
Read aloud accurately and with appropriate intonation and expression		•	•	•	•	•	•
Read aloud narrative and expository text with appropriate pacing, intonation, and expression			•	•	•	•	•
Read aloud prose and poetry with rhythm and pace, appropriate intonation, and vocal patterns			•	•	•	•	•
Vocabulary and Concept Development							
Academic language							
Classify-categorize		•					
Antonyms			•	•	•	•	
Synonyms			•	•	•	•	
Homographs				•			
Homophones				•			
Multiple-meaning words			•		•		•
Figurative and idiomatic language					•		•
Context/context clues			•	•	•	•	•
Content-area words							
Dictionary, glossary, thesaurus			•	•	•		
Foreign words							•
Connotation-denotation							
Word origins (acronyms, clipped and coined words, regional variations, etymologies, jargon, slang)							
Analogies							
Word structure clues to determine meaning			•	•	•		•
Inflected nouns and verbs, comparatives-superlatives, possessives, compound words, prefixes, suffixes, root words			•	•	•	•	•
Greek and Latin roots, prefixes, suffixes, derivations, and root words					•	•	•
Develop vocabulary							
Listen to and discuss text read aloud							
Read independently							
Use reference books							
Comprehension and Analysis of Text							
Ask/answer questions							
Author's purpose		•	•	•	•	•	
Author's perspective					•	•	
Propaganda/bias							
Background knowledge: prior knowledge and experiences							
Cause-effect		•	•	•			
Compare-contrast		•	•	•	•	•	•
Details		•	•	•			•
Directions: one-, two-, multi-step			•	•	•		
Draw conclusions		•			•	•	•
Fact-fiction				•	•	•	

Key:

Shaded area - Explicit Instruction/Modeling/Practice and Application

- *Tested—Assessment Resources: Weekly Lesson Tests, Theme Tests, Benchmark Assessments*

	Gr K	Gr 1	Gr 2	Gr 3	Gr 4	Gr 5	Gr 6
Fact-opinion					•	•	
Higher order thinking							
Analyze, critique and evaluate, synthesize, and visualize text and information							
Interpret information from graphic aids			•	•		•	
Locate information			•		•		
Book parts				•	•		
Text features				•	•		
Alphabetical order		•		•			
Main idea: stated/unstated		•			•	•	•
Main idea and supporting details		•	•	•	•	•	•
Make generalizations						•	
Make inferences		•	•	•		•	
Make judgments						•	•
Make predictions/predict outcomes		•	•	•	•		
Monitor comprehension							
Adjust reading rate, create mental images, reread, read ahead, set/adjust purpose, self-question, summarize/paraphrase, use graphic aids, text features, and text adjuncts					•		
Paraphrase/restate facts and details					•	•	
Preview							
Purpose for reading							
Organize information							
Alphabetical order							
Numerical systems/outlines							
Graphic organizers							
Referents							
Retell stories and ideas			•	•			
Sequence		•		•	•	•	•
Summarize				•	•	•	•
Text structure							
Narrative text			•	•	•	•	
Informational text (compare and contrast, cause and effect, sequence/chronological order, proposition and support, problem and solution)			•	•	•	•	•
Study Skills							
Follow and give directions			•	•	•		•
Apply plans and strategies: KWL, question-answer-relationships, skim and scan, note taking, outline, questioning the author, reciprocal teaching							•
Practice test-taking strategies							
Research and Information							
Use resources and references			•		•	•	•
Understand the purpose, structure, and organization of various reference materials							
Title page, table of contents, chapter titles, chapter headings, index, glossary, guide words, citations, end notes, bibliography			•	•	•		
Picture dictionary, software, dictionary, thesaurus, atlas, globe, encyclopedia, telephone directory, on-line information, card catalog, electronic search engines and data bases, almanac, newspaper, journals, periodicals			•	•	•	•	•
Charts, maps diagrams, timelines, schedules, calendar, graphs, photos			•		•	•	•
Choose reference materials appropriate to research purpose					•	•	•
Viewing/Media							
Interpret information from visuals (graphics, media, including illustrations, tables, maps, charts, graphs, diagrams, timelines)			•	•			•

Key:

Shaded area - Explicit Instruction/Modeling/Practice and Application

• *Tested—Assessment Resources: Weekly Lesson Tests, Theme Tests, Benchmark Assessments*

	Gr K	Gr 1	Gr 2	Gr 3	Gr 4	Gr 5	Gr 6
Analyze the ways visuals, graphics, and media represent, contribute to, and support meaning of text							•
Select, organize, and produce visuals to complement and extend meaning							
Use technology or appropriate media to communicate information and ideas							
Use technology or appropriate media to compare ideas, information, and viewpoints							
Compare, contrast, and evaluate print and broadcast media							
Distinguish between fact and opinion							
Evaluate the role of media							
Analyze media as sources for information, entertainment, persuasion, interpretation of events, and transmission of culture							
Identify persuasive and propaganda techniques used in television and identify false and misleading information							
Summarize main concept and list supporting details and identify biases, stereotypes, and persuasive techniques in a nonprint message							
Support opinions with detailed evidence and with visual or media displays that use appropriate technology							

Literary Response and Analysis

Genre Characteristics

	Gr K	Gr 1	Gr 2	Gr 3	Gr 4	Gr 5	Gr 6
Know a variety of literary genres and their basic characteristics			•	•			
Distinguish between fantasy and realistic text							
Distinguish between informational and persuasive texts							
Understand the distinguishing features of literary and nonfiction texts: everyday print materials, poetry, drama, fantasies, fables, myths, legends, and fairy tales			•	•			
Explain the appropriateness of the literary forms chosen by an author for a specific purpose							

Literary Elements

Plot/Plot Development

	Gr K	Gr 1	Gr 2	Gr 3	Gr 4	Gr 5	Gr 6
Important events		•	•	•			
Beginning, middle, end of story		•	•	•			
Problem/solution		•	•	•			•
Conflict					•	•	•
Conflict and resolution/causes and effects					•	•	•
Compare and contrast			•	•	•	•	

Character

	Gr K	Gr 1	Gr 2	Gr 3	Gr 4	Gr 5	Gr 6
Identify		•	•				
Identify, describe, compare and contrast			•	•	•		
Relate characters and events							•
Traits, actions, motives				•	•	•	•
Cause for character's actions					•	•	
Character's qualities and effect on plot					•	•	•

Setting

	Gr K	Gr 1	Gr 2	Gr 3	Gr 4	Gr 5	Gr 6
Identify and describe		•	•	•			
Compare and contrast			•	•			•
Relate to problem/resolution							•

Theme

	Gr K	Gr 1	Gr 2	Gr 3	Gr 4	Gr 5	Gr 6
Theme/essential message					•	•	•
Universal themes							•

Mood/Tone

	Gr K	Gr 1	Gr 2	Gr 3	Gr 4	Gr 5	Gr 6
Identify							•
Compare and contrast							

Key:

Shaded area - Explicit Instruction/Modeling/Practice and Application

- *Tested— Assessment Resources: Weekly Lesson Tests, Theme Tests, Benchmark Assessments*

	Gr K	Gr 1	Gr 2	Gr 3	Gr 4	Gr 5	Gr 6
Literary Devices/Author's Craft							
Rhythm, rhyme, pattern, and repetition							•
Alliteration, onomatopoeia, assonance, imagery						•	•
Figurative language (similes, metaphors, idioms, personification, hyperbole)				•	•	•	•
Characterization/character development				•	•	•	•
Dialogue							
Narrator/narration							
Point of view (first-person, third-person, omniscient)						•	•
Informal language (idioms, slang, jargon, dialect)							
Response to Text							
Relate characters and events to own life							
Read to perform a task or learn a new task							
Recollect, talk, and write about books read							
Describe the roles and contributions of authors and illustrators							
Generate alternative endings and identify the reason and impact of the alternatives							
Compare and contrast versions of the same stories that reflect different cultures							
Make connections between information in texts and stories and historical events							
Form ideas about what had been read and use specific information from the text to support these ideas							
Know that the attitudes and values that exist in a time period or culture affect stories and informational articles written during that time period							
Self-Selected Reading							
Select material to read for pleasure							
Read a variety of self-selected and assigned literary and informational texts							
Use knowledge of authors' styles, themes, and genres to choose own reading							
Read literature by authors from various cultural and historical backgrounds							
Cultural Awareness							
Connect information and events in texts to life and life to text experiences							
Compare language, oral traditions, and literature that reflect customs, regions, and cultures							
Identify how language reflects regions and cultures							
View concepts and issues from diverse perspectives							
Recognize the universality of literary themes across cultures and language							
Writing							
Writing Strategies							
Writing process: prewriting, drafting, revising, proofreading, publishing							
Collaborative, shared, timed writing, writing to prompts		•	•	•	•	•	•
Evaluate own and other's writing							
Proofread writing to correct convention errors in mechanics, usage, punctuation, using handbooks and references as appropriate				•	•	•	•
Organization and Focus							
Use models and traditional structures for writing							
Select a focus, structure, and viewpoint							
Address purpose, audience, length, and format requirements							
Write single- and multiple-paragraph compositions				•	•	•	•
Revision Skills							
Correct sentence fragments and run-ons							
Vary sentence structure, word order, and sentence length							
Combine sentences							

Key:

Shaded area - Explicit Instruction/Modeling/Practice and Application

- *Tested Assessment Resources: Weekly Lesson Tests, Theme Tests, Benchmark Assessments*

R30   Grade 3, Theme 3

	Gr K	Gr 1	Gr 2	Gr 3	Gr 4	Gr 5	Gr 6
Improve coherence, unity, consistency, and progression of ideas			▨	▨	▨	▨	▨
Add, delete, consolidate, clarify, rearrange text	▨	▨	▨	▨	▨	▨	▨
Choose appropriate and effective words: exact/precise words, vivid words, trite/overused words	▨	▨	▨	▨	▨	▨	▨
Elaborate: details, examples, dialogue, quotations	▨	▨	▨	▨	▨	▨	▨
Revise using a rubric		▨	▨	▨	▨	▨	▨

Penmanship/Handwriting

	Gr K	Gr 1	Gr 2	Gr 3	Gr 4	Gr 5	Gr 6
Write uppercase and lowercase letters	▨	▨	▨	▨			
Write legibly, using appropriate word and letter spacing	▨	▨	▨	▨			
Write legibly, using spacing, margins, and indention			▨	▨	▨	▨	▨

Writing Applications

	Gr K	Gr 1	Gr 2	Gr 3	Gr 4	Gr 5	Gr 6
Narrative writing (stories, paragraphs, personal narratives, journal, plays, poetry)	▨	•	•	•	•	•	•
Descriptive writing (titles, captions, ads, posters, paragraphs, stories, poems)	▨	•	•				
Expository writing (comparison-contrast, explanation, directions, speech, how-to article, friendly/business letter, news story, essay, report, invitation)			▨	▨	•	•	•
Persuasive writing (paragraph, essay, letter, ad, poster)					•	•	•
Cross-curricular writing (paragraph, report, poster, list, chart)	▨	▨	▨	▨	▨	▨	▨
Everyday writing (journal, message, forms, notes, summary, label, caption)	▨	▨	▨	▨	▨	▨	▨

Written and Oral English Language Conventions

Sentence Structure

	Gr K	Gr 1	Gr 2	Gr 3	Gr 4	Gr 5	Gr 6
Types (declarative, interrogative, exclamatory, imperative, interjection)		•	•	•	•	•	•
Structure (simple, compound, complex, compound-complex)		•	•	•	•	•	•
Parts (subjects/predicates: complete, simple, compound; clauses; independent, dependent, subordinate; phrase)		•	•	•	•	•	•
Direct/indirect object						•	•
Word order		•					

Grammar

	Gr K	Gr 1	Gr 2	Gr 3	Gr 4	Gr 5	Gr 6
Nouns (singular, plural, common, proper, possessive, collective, abstract, concrete, abbreviations, appositives)		•	•	•	•	•	•
Verbs (action, helping, linking, transitive, intransitive, regular, irregular; subject-verb agreement)		•	•	•	•	•	•
Verb tenses (present, past, future; present, past, and future perfect)		•	•	•	•	•	•
Participles; infinitives						•	•
Adjectives (common, proper; articles; comparative, superlative)		•	•	•	•	•	•
Adverbs (place, time, manner, degree)				•	•	•	•
Pronouns (subject, object, possessive, reflexive, demonstrative, antecedents)		•	•	•	•	•	•
Prepositions; prepositional phrases					•	•	•
Conjunctions					•	•	•
Abbreviations, contractions			•	•	•	•	•

Punctuation

	Gr K	Gr 1	Gr 2	Gr 3	Gr 4	Gr 5	Gr 6
Period, exclamation point, or question mark at end of sentences	▨	•	•	•	•	•	•
Comma							
Greeting and closure of a letter		▨	▨	▨	▨	•	•
Dates, locations, and addresses			▨	▨	▨	•	•
For items in a series		▨	▨	▨	•	•	•
Direct quotations					•	•	•
Link two clauses with a conjunction in compound sentences					•	•	•
Quotation Marks							
Dialogue, exact words of a speaker	▨				•	•	•
Titles of books, stories, poems, magazines					•	•	•

Key:

Shaded area - Explicit Instruction/Modeling/Practice and Application

   • *Tested—Assessment Resources: Weekly Lesson Tests, Theme Tests, Benchmark Assessments*

	Gr K	Gr 1	Gr 2	Gr 3	Gr 4	Gr 5	Gr 6
Parentheses/dash/hyphen						•	•
Apostrophes in possessive case of nouns and in contractions		•	•	•	•	•	•
Underlining or italics to identify title of documents					•	•	•
Colon							
Separate hours and minutes						•	•
Introduce a list						•	•
After the salutation in business letters						•	•
Semicolons to connect dependent clauses							

Capitalization

	Gr K	Gr 1	Gr 2	Gr 3	Gr 4	Gr 5	Gr 6
First word of a sentence, names of people, and the pronoun *I*		•	•	•	•	•	•
Proper nouns, words at the beginning of sentences and greetings, months and days of the week, and titles and initials of people		•	•	•	•	•	•
Geographical names, holidays, historical periods, and special events			•	•			•
Names of magazines, newspapers, works of art, musical compositions, organizations, and the first word in quotations when appropriate						•	•
Use conventions of punctuation and capitalization			•	•	•	•	•

Spelling

	Gr K	Gr 1	Gr 2	Gr 3	Gr 4	Gr 5	Gr 6
Spell independently by using pre-phonetic knowledge, sounds of the alphabet, and knowledge of letter names							
Use spelling approximations and some conventional spelling							
Common, phonetically regular words		•	•	•	•	•	•
Frequently used, irregular words		•	•	•	•	•	•
One-syllable words with consonant blends			•	•	•	•	•
Contractions, compounds, orthographic patterns, and common homophones				•	•	•	•
Greek and Latin roots, inflections, suffixes, prefixes, and syllable constructions				•	•	•	•
Use a variety of strategies and resources to spell words							

Listening and Speaking

Listening Skills and Strategies

	Gr K	Gr 1	Gr 2	Gr 3	Gr 4	Gr 5	Gr 6
Listen to a variety of oral presentations such as stories, poems, skits, songs, personal accounts, or informational speeches							
Listen attentively to the speaker (make eye contact and demonstrate appropriate body language)							
Listen for a purpose							
Follow oral directions (one-, two-, three-, and multi-step)							
For specific information							
For enjoyment							
To distinguish between the speaker's opinions and verifiable facts							
To actively participate in class discussions							
To expand and enhance personal interest and personal preferences							
To identify, analyze, and critique persuasive techniques							
To identify logical fallacies used in oral presentations and media messages							
To make inferences or draw conclusions							
To interpret a speaker's verbal and nonverbal messages, purposes, and perspectives							
To identify the tone, mood, and emotion							
To analyze the use of rhetorical devices for intent and effect							
To evaluate classroom presentations							
To respond to a variety of media and speakers							
To paraphrase/summarize directions and information							
For language reflecting regions and cultures							

Key:

Shaded area - Explicit Instruction/Modeling/Practice and Application

• *Tested—Assessment Resources: Weekly Lesson Tests, Theme Tests, Benchmark Assessments*

	Gr K	Gr 1	Gr 2	Gr 3	Gr 4	Gr 5	Gr 6
To recognize emotional and logical arguments					■	■	■
To identify the musical elements of language			■	■	■	■	■
Listen critically to relate the speaker's verbal communication to the nonverbal message			■		■	■	■

Speaking Skills and Strategies

	Gr K	Gr 1	Gr 2	Gr 3	Gr 4	Gr 5	Gr 6
Speak clearly and audibly and use appropriate volume and pace in different settings	■	■	■	■	■	■	■
Use formal and informal English appropriately	■	■	■	■	■	■	■
Follow rules of conversation	■	■	■	■	■	■	■
Stay on the topic when speaking		■	■	■	■	■	■
Use descriptive words		■	■	■	■	■	■
Recount experiences in a logical sequence			■	■	■	■	■
Clarify and support spoken ideas with evidence and examples		■	■	■	■	■	■
Use eye contact, appropriate gestures, and props to enhance oral presentations and engage the audience		■	■	■	■	■	■
Give and follow two-, three-, and four-step directions	■	■	■	■	■	■	■
Recite poems, rhymes, songs, stories, soliloquies, or dramatic dialogues	■	■	■	■	■	■	■
Plan and present dramatic interpretations with clear diction, pitch, tempo, and tone		■	■	■	■	■	■
Organize presentations to maintain a clear focus		■	■	■	■	■	■
Use language appropriate to situation, purpose, and audience		■	■	■	■	■	■
Make/deliver							
Oral narrative, descriptive, informational, and persuasive presentations			■	■	■	■	■
Oral summaries of articles and books			■	■	■	■	■
Oral responses to literature			■	■	■	■	■
Presentations on problems and solutions			■	■	■	■	■
Presentation or speech for specific occasions, audiences, and purposes			■		■	■	■
Vary language according to situation, audience, and purpose		■	■	■	■	■	■
Select a focus, organizational structure, and point of view for an oral presentation			■	■	■	■	■
Participate in classroom activities and discussions	■	■	■	■	■	■	■

Key:

Shaded area - Explicit Instruction/Modeling/Practice and Application

- *Tested— Assessment Resources: Weekly Lesson Tests, Theme Tests, Benchmark Assessments*

Index

A

Academic Vocabulary
See **Student Edition,** Glossary
Activity Cards
See **Literacy Centers**
Advanced Learners, Activities for, 3-3:
T31, T40, T61, T73, T77, T89, T127,
T136, T159, T171, T175, T187, T214,
T222, T247, T259, T263, T275, T301,
T310, T322, T331, T343, T347, T359,
T385, T400, T411, T420
See also **Differentiated Instruction**
Advanced Readers
See **Leveled Readers,** advanced
readers
Advertisements
See **Genre,** functional text,
advertisements
Alphabetical Order
See **Research/Study Skills,**
alphabetical order
Antonyms
See **Vocabulary,** antonyms
Art
See **Cross-Curricular Connections,**
art activities, fine art connections
Asking Questions
See **Focus Strategies,** ask questions
Assessment
benchmark assessments, **3-3:** T444
online assessment, **3-3:** T444
oral reading fluency assessment, **3-3:**
T90, T188, T276, T360
prescriptions, **3-3:** A2–A5
self-assessment, **3-3:** T109
spelling posttests, **3-3:** T89, T187,
T275, T359, T436
spelling pretests, **3-3:** T31, T127,
T214, T301
theme tests, **3-3:** T444, A6
weekly lesson tests, **3-3:** T95, T193,
T281, T365, T444

Assessment Prescriptions
See **Assessment,** prescriptions
Audiotext
See **Technology,** technology resources,
audiotexts
Author, Meet the
Brenner, Barbara, **3-3:** T323
Dorros, Arthur, **3-3:** T239
McKissack, Patricia C., **3-3:** T53
Rand, Gloria, **3-3:** T151
Author's Purpose
See **Focus Skills,** author's purpose

Background, Build, 3-3: T45, T96, T97,
T98, T99, T141, T194, T195,
T196, T197, T227, T282, T283,
T284, T285, T315, T366, T367,
T368, T369, T390
Below-Level Learners, Activities for,
3-3: T13, T40, T47, T51, T62, T78,
T85, T136, T144, T160, T176,
T183, T222, T229, T234, T238,
T248, T264, T310, T317, T332,
T348, T400, T420
See also **Differentiated Instruction**
Below-Level Readers
See **Leveled Readers,** below-level
readers
Books on Tape
See **Technology,** technology resources,
audiotexts
Brainstorming
See **Writing,** process, prewriting

Cause and Effect
See **Comprehension Skills,** cause/
effect

Centers
See **Literacy Centers**
Challenge Copying Masters
See **Differentiated Instruction,**
challenge copying masters
Chapter Books, 3-3: T422–T423
Charts
See **Graphic Organizers,** charts
Choral Reading
See **Fluency,** choral reading
Classroom Management
See **Literacy Centers**
Commas
See **Grammar,** punctuation
Comparing Texts
See **Student Edition,** connections
Comprehension Skills
See also **Focus Skills**
author's craft/imagery, **3-3:** T230
author's purpose, **3-3:** T162, T197,
T215, T216, T230, T239, T240,
T249, T265, T277, T282, T283,
T284, T285, T302–T303, T304,
T316, T322, T324, T333, T349,
T361, T366, T367, T368, T369,
T392, T394, T412, T424, T437,
S30–S31, S42–S43
author's viewpoint, **3-3:** T252
cause/effect, **3-3:** T47, T51, T149,
T194, T195, T231, T317, T319
characters' emotions, **3-3:** T47, T52,
T96, T97, T142, T144, T147,
T150, T194
characters' motivations, **3-3:** T50, T66,
T97
characters' traits, **3-3:** T44, T96, T98,
T128, T140, T147, T189, T196,
T387
classify, **3-3:** T232
compare and contrast, **3-3:** T49, T164,
T233, T283, T284, T336, T361
confirm predictions, **3-3:** T149, T238,
T318, T321, T393
conflict/resolution, **3-3:** T277

Prompts for Writing

See **Writing,** writing prompts

Pronouns

See **Grammar,** pronouns

Proofreading

See **Daily Proofreading; Grammar; Writing,** process, proofreading

Punctuation

See **Grammar,** punctuation

Purpose Setting

purposes for listening, **3-3:** T29, T39, T59, T66, T75, T87, T91, T135, T157, T185, T189, T211, T245, T261, T273, T277, T299, T309, T329, T345, T357, T361, T383, T399, T409, T419, T435

purposes for reading, **3-3:** T29, T39, T45, T59, T66, T75, T87, T96, T97, T98, T99, T125, T135, T141, T157, T164, T173, T185, T194, T195, T196, T197, T211, T221, T227, T245, T261, T273, T282, T283, T284, T285, T299, T309, T315, T329, T336, T345, T357, T361, T366, T367, T368, T369, T383, T390, T399, T409, T419, T422, T435

Read-Aloud Anthology

"Evie & Margie," **3-3:** T34, T91

"A Log's Life," **3-3:** T304, T361

"The Money Tree," **3-3:** T216, T277

"The Sunset in My Mailbox," **3-3:** T102, T189

Read-Alouds, 3-3: T29, T34, T39, T59, T75, T87, T125, T130, T135, T157, T173, T185, T211, T216, T221, T245, T261, T273, T299, T309, T329, T345, T357, T383, T399, T409, T419, T435

Readers' Theater, 3-3: T90, T188, T276, T360, T389–T394, T404, T414, T426, T439

Reading Centers

See **Literacy Centers,** reading centers

Reading for Information

See **Focus Strategies,** reading for information; **Purpose Setting,** purposes for reading

Reading-Writing Connection

friendly letters, **3-3:** T100–T109

project presentation, **3-3:** T81, T443

writing on demand, **3-3:** T110–T111

Realistic Fiction

See **Genre,** realistic fiction

Recognize Story Structure

See **Focus Strategies,** use story structure

Research/Study Skills

alphabetical order, **3-3:** T80

diagrams, use and interpretation, **3-3:** T267

reference sources, **3-3:** T12, T13, T266

Response to Literature

See **Student Edition,** think critically; **Writing,** forms, response to literature

Retelling Rubrics, 3-3: T54

Rhyme

See **Comprehension Skills,** understand figurative language

Robust Vocabulary

See **Vocabulary,** robust vocabulary

Routine Cards, 3-3: T45, T66, T141, T227, T252, T315, T336, T388, S2, S10, S14, S22, S26, S34, S38, S46, S50

Rubrics

4-point rubric, **3-3:** T95, T109, T111, T193, T281, T365, T441

retell and summarize fiction, **3-3:** T54, T152, T240, T324

Scaffolded Language Development, **3-3:** T99, T197, T285, T369

School-Home Connection

See **Teacher Resource Book,** school-home connection

Second-Language Support

See **English-Language Learners**

Sentence Fluency

See **Writing,** traits, sentence fluency

Sentence Structure

See **Grammar,** word order; **Writing,** forms, sentences

Sentence Variety

See **Writing,** traits, sentence fluency

Sequence

See **Comprehension Skills,** sequence

Setting

See **Comprehension Skills,** setting

Short Vowels

See **Decoding/Word Attack,** short vowels

Small-Group Instruction

See **Differentiated Instruction,** small-group instruction

Speaking and Listening

groups, working in, **3-3:** T13

oral language, **3-3:** T28, T38, T58, T74, T86, T124, T134, T156, T172, T184, T210, T220, T244, T260, T272, T298, T308, T328, T344, T356, T382, T398, T418, T434

organization, **3-3:** T81, T179, T267, T351

performances, **3-3:** T439

presentations, **3-3:** T81, T179, T267, T441

theme, discussion of, **3-3:** T15

Spelling

challenge words, **3-3:** T31, T40, T61, T77, T89, T127, T136, T159,

Acknowledgments

Teaching Transparencies

For permission to reprint copyrighted material, grateful acknowledgment is made to the following sources:

Laura Cecil Literary Agency on behalf of the James Reeves Estate: "The Wind" from *Complete Poems for Children* by James Reeves. Text © by James Reeves. Published by Heinemann.

HarperCollins Publishers: "Keziah" from *Bronzeville Boys and Girls* by Gwendolyn Brooks. Text copyright © 1956 by Gwendolyn Brooks Blakely.

Edite Kroll Literary Agency Inc.: "Tree House" from *Where the Sidewalk Ends* by Shel Silverstein. Text copyright © 1971, renewed 2002 by Evil Eye, LLC. Published by HarperCollins Publishers.

Harold Ober Associates: "Books" from *Poems for Children* by Eleanor Farjeon. Text copyright 1951 by Eleanor Farjeon.

Marian Reiner: "Hey, Bug!" from *I Feel the Same Way* by Lilian Moore. Text copyright © 1967 by Lilian Moore.

Adam Yarmolinsky: "A Pig Is Never Blamed" by Babette Deutsch.

Teacher's Notes

Teacher's Notes

Teacher's Notes